'A true magnum opus, *Macrocriminology and Freedom* is a thought provoking and generative book from one of criminology's intellectual giants. John Braithwaite reaches far and wide across societies, time, and disciplines to advance no less than a theory of how to build a society that simultaneously reduces both domination and crime. His ambitious ideas on cascades of non-dominating collective efficacy and crime prevention, for example, and their connections to social movements and political freedom, go well beyond usual criminological discourse. Chock full of theoretical propositions and bold insights, this a book that will keep criminologists busy for years. *Macrocriminology and Freedom* should not just be read, but better yet, savoured.'

– Robert J. Sampson, Henry Ford II Professor of the Social Sciences,
Harvard University

'In this majestic theorisation of the relationship between crime and freedom John Braithwaite isolates the unique power of macrocriminology as a lens through which to comprehend and challenge many of the fundamental crises facing our planet. Very few scholars have the breadth and overview to succeed in a mission of this order ... Braithwaite does. This extraordinary book is an object lesson for all who seek to understand and resist domination and the crimes of power that flow from it.'

– Penny Green, Professor of Law and Globalisation,
Queen Mary University of London

'For over 40 years, John Braithwaite has been a voice of wisdom, hope and humanity in criminology. This dazzling new book weaves together all the main themes of his influential work, reanimating many of the core concepts of the discipline, as well as incorporating interdisciplinary resources from south and north, east and west, to produce an elegant and ambitious explanatory and normative account of crime as freedom-threatening domination. Decentring criminal justice as the solution to crime, Braithwaite shows that, on a global scale, the aspiration to tackle crimes, ranging from interpersonal violence through corporate crimes to ecocide, lies in the development of freedom-enhancing, power-tempering institutions in the political, economic and social spheres.'

– Nicola Lacey, Professor of Law, Gender and Social Policy,
London School of Economics

'*Macrocriminology and Freedom* is a criminological epic, an expansive and erudite story that sweeps across history and contexts. The book is frightening in showing how cascading events can produce catastrophes from crime to environmental destruction. But in the end, its message is hopeful, identifying pathways—or "normative rivers"—for guiding freedom from domination and crime. Drawing on his distinguished career, John Braithwaite has bestowed an extraordinary gift—a book, like other masterpieces, that will yield special insights each time we take an excursion through its pages.'

– Francis T. Cullen, Distinguished Research Professor Emeritus, University of Cincinnati

'In this engaging book John Braithwaite reinvigorates discussions about crime and its control. While advocating a macro approach, the book is punctuated not only with insights and data from smaller-scale studies conducted in a range of jurisdictions, but also with auto-biographical vignettes. The effect creates a deeply personal account of the perils of state, non-state and market violence and authoritarianism and the potential and indeed duty, of criminologists to work towards their reduction, by refocusing their efforts on explaining and tackling crime in its myriad of forms.'

– Mary Bosworth, Professor of Criminology, University of Oxford and Monash University

'John Braithwaite has had a unique influence on criminology globally. In this encyclopaedic text he synthesises a wealth of criminological knowledge, particularly in the sphere of anomie theory, into broader debates about the nature of domination and freedom in contemporary society. He defends the relevance of criminological theory, while urging criminology to be activist rather than reactive and technocratic, counter-hegemonic rather than neutral. Not for the first time, John Braithwaite has challenged criminologists to construct theories that cut across micro and macro structures. This book will stir debate. It deserves a broad readership.'

– Harry Blagg, Professor of Criminology, University of Western Australia

MACROCRIMINOLOGY AND FREEDOM

MACROCRIMINOLOGY AND FREEDOM

JOHN BRAITHWAITE

Australian
National
University

ANU PRESS

For my beloved grandchildren, Emily, Joan and Jed, and for the next generation of criminologists as they confront huge challenges.

Australian
National
University

ANU PRESS

Published by ANU Press
The Australian National University
Canberra ACT 2600, Australia
Email: anupress@anu.edu.au

Available to download for free at press.anu.edu.au

ISBN (print): 9781760464806
ISBN (online): 9781760464813

WorldCat (print): 1293286464
WorldCat (online): 1293286482

DOI: 10.22459/MF.2021

Cover design and layout by ANU Press. Cover image: 'My Dress Hangs There', by Frida Kahlo.

This book is published under the aegis of the Law Editorial Board of ANU Press.

Contents

Abbreviations

2SLS	two-stage least squares
AA	Alcoholics Anonymous
ACCC	Australian Competition and Consumer Commission
AI	artificial intelligence
AMP	Awareness, Motivation and Pathways
ASIC	Australian Securities and Investment Commission
ATO	Australian Taxation Office
BCCI	Bank of Credit and Commerce International
BRA	Bougainville Revolutionary Army
CEO	chief executive officer
CFC	chlorofluorocarbon
CHIME	Connectedness, Hope, Identity, Meaning and Empowerment
CIA	Central Intelligence Agency
CSL	Commonwealth Serum Laboratories
DDR	Disarmament, Demobilisation and Reintegration
DRC	Democratic Republic of Congo
FBI	Federal Bureau of Investigation
GDP	gross domestic product
HOPE	Hawai`i/Honest Opportunity Probation with Enforcement
ICTY	International Criminal Tribunal for the former Yugoslavia
IED	improvised explosive device

IMF	International Monetary Fund
IRA	Irish Republican Army
NASA	National Aeronautics and Space Administration
NATO	North Atlantic Treaty Organization
NGO	nongovernmental organisation
NRA	National Rifle Association
OECD	Organisation for Economic Co-operation and Development
OLS	ordinary least squares
OSHA	US Occupational Safety and Health Administration
OTP	International Criminal Court's Office of the Prosecutor
PNG	Papua New Guinea
PTSD	post-traumatic stress disorder
SEC	US Securities and Exchange Commission
SGS	Société Générale de Surveillance
UK	United Kingdom
UN	United Nations
UNODC	United Nations Office on Drugs and Crime
US	United States
WTO	World Trade Organization

List of illustrations

Preface

The aim of this book is to inspire reflection by people who are intellectually serious about understanding crime. I love my criminology friends and what they do. Yet I have been cynical about criminology. This book represents a change of mind. Now that I perceive particular risks of the world stumbling into one environmental and economic crisis after another, ultimately into accidental nuclear war, perhaps followed by pandemics, I see renewed importance for criminology. That role is not just about preventing environmental and financial crime and the kind of cyberterrorism that can trigger accidental war. It is also about preventing catastrophes that cascade from the criminalisation of states, the criminalisation of markets and the cascading of violent imaginaries on social media. The book discusses the green shoots that have refreshed macrocriminology. They engender a politics of hope.

The book rethinks how different institutions can be designed to temper the excesses of other institutions. It argues that many societies have succeeded in growing freedom and reducing crime. There is no impossibilism about domination reduction and ecocide prevention. Progress is fragile. All societies are partial failures; all have strengths that can be expanded.

It is not new to emphasise the macro by injecting institutionalism into criminology. Emile Durkheim and Willem Bonger took this step around 1900. Then Robert K. Merton and Norbert Elias redeemed it in the 1930s in germinal ways. Their paths were renewed when Steven Messner and Richard Rosenfeld developed their institutional anomie theory. The contribution of this book is tiny compared with the foundations these scholars laid. It also builds on my love for Chicago and Chicago School foundations. This contribution is small, too, compared with others in that tradition, such as Robert Sampson today.

Even so, the book does more than theorise institutions more systematically, and with an eye to redeeming the neglect of crimes of the powerful in criminology. It integrates explanatory and normative theories into a theory of freedom and crime.

Reviewers might say this book does no more than build a bit on institutional anomie theory. I do not totally reject that way of seeing it. Or they might see it as just a distinctive twist on the theory of collective efficacy. Maybe that is right. Perhaps what is most distinctive is that it applies regulatory theory—particularly responsive regulatory theory and republican political theory—to crime. That is, its approach is to conceive the regulation of crime as a practice that can be enriched from what we know about the regulation of all manner of things, and therefore by regulatory theory.

It may be a theory of responsiveness, but it is more fundamentally a theory of freedom and crime. Chantal Mouffe's agonistic pluralism is an inspiration for institutional transformation, as is another feminist who was a republican thinker, Mary Wollstonecraft (1792). In terms of agonistic praxis, the life of Jane Addams (1860–1935) is one that inspired. Hers was a life of care for the poor and refugees and activism for a welfare state. She was a dangerous person in her influence as a peace activist and a leader of 'first wave' feminism that won women the vote. Addams understood the importance of trade unions and grassroots social movement politics across all these themes. She was also a co-founder of civil rights organisations, including the National Association for the Advancement of Colored People (NAACP), and of a discipline called social work that has to some degree veered away from her community-building vision and towards individualised casework. She is little recognised as a founding figure in sociology at her Hull House conversational circle in Chicago. Her Hull House group invented the restorative justice mantra of not doing *for*, nor doing *to*, but doing *with*. It was not a bad idea to found relational intellectual traditions that prioritised social support and agonistic contestation of macro-institutional questions of social justice. Today there are green shoots that renew Jane Addams's light on the hill in those jaded old disciplines. Burford et al. (2019) sought to nurture those shoots. This book is also an attempt to redeem macrosociology and political economy as they redeem macrocriminology.

I am inclined to think of this as a freedom theory of crime because free societies constitute conditions for low crime rates. Furthermore, freedom from fear of violence is constitutive of institutions of freedom. At its foundations, this is a civic republican way of thinking about crime, and about how to integrate explanatory and normative theories. I could not promote this book as 'A Republican Theory of Crime', because the subtitle of my book with Philip Pettit, *A Republican Theory of Criminal Justice*, was more Philip's invention than mine and manifested Philip's great influence on my thinking.

Crime is conceived as a form of domination in this book; crime control also poses a threat of domination. Freedom is conceived as nondomination; freedom from crime and from arbitrary and excessive punishment is theorised as constitutive of freedom. By paying more attention to freedom, we learn how to be more effective in preventing crime. So, my small contribution is to build on the larger foundations of the scholars mentioned so far, by rewriting normative order, institutions and collective efficacy as tools of freedom. Some of these tools are the master's tools that can be turned against the master; others are civil society tools. Both kinds of tools are imperative. So, the concluding chapter only partially supports Audre Lorde's (1984) subaltern mantra that 'the master's tools will never dismantle the master's house'.

Reducing domination and reducing crime are not the only worthy objectives of good governance. But I argue that one of the truths on which liberal, republican and social democratic traditions converge is that in a free society of citizens with self-efficacy and collective efficacy, the prospects of ensuring many other good things are greatly improved. For Pettit (2014: xix), freedom as nondomination is a 'gateway good' that unlocks a gate to other goods. Moreover, for Pettit (2014: xvii), 'justice is freedom, freedom justice': freedom as nondomination is the yardstick for deciding what is just.

This is a book that takes insight from quantitative social science seriously without seeing it as the most important knowledge. At the end of the journey, the book commends a suite of political and social ends and means for a society if it is to secure freedom and a low crime rate together. Yet these define no more than commendable directions for struggle towards the good society. The final chapter draws on Chantal Mouffe's writing on the political—in particular, on the politics of how to struggle to transform hegemonic institutional orders and how to struggle in ways that are democratic and have wide resonance.

Anomie is an important variable in the theory. It is prone to positive and negative feedback loops triggered by unpredictable historical events. We live in a world that is tightly coupled in ways that make it vulnerable to surprise by crises. The politics of strengthening freedom and reducing crime is as much an art of avoiding analysis paralysis in the face of recursive crises as it is a science. The art of politics and the social science of criminology are both vital to averting cascades of violence and authoritarianism.

This book embraces a quantitative social science that focuses on the character of institutions. Then there must be micro–meso–macro linkages to institutional transformation. I follow the footsteps of Sutherland to urge empirical criminology to take white-collar crime seriously as a larger source of domination than garden varieties of crime. In the study of organisational crime, there is an especially profound risk of the more measurable driving out the more important. Hence, the book valorises qualitative and historical work on the relationships among institutions, crime and freedom.

While anomie and freedom are the recurrent themes, those uninterested in anomie can read bits of the book to inform no more than a macrocriminology of global crises. The diversity of forms of social capital is another recurrent tradition. My work has always been about integrating and connecting these traditions to the study of organisational crime. Bits of the book can be read simply to grasp the relationships between inequality and crime, crime and freedom, crime and war, crime and justice, crime across human history and crime in specific institutions.

I wrote this throughout my 60s as a scholar-activist who for decades planned such an integrative macrocriminology that weaves together a line of works that have a coherence for me, but perhaps confuse everyone else. One purpose is to reveal the threads that weave my work together. Some are particularly acknowledged for specific chapters:

Braithwaite, John. 1979. *Inequality, Crime and Public Policy*. London: Routledge. [See especially its relevance to Chapters 4 and 5 of this book.]

Braithwaite, John and Philip Pettit. 1990. *Not Just Deserts: A Republican Theory of Criminal Justice*. Oxford: Oxford University Press. [Especially Chapter 2.]

Braithwaite, John. 1991. 'Poverty, power, white-collar crime and the paradoxes of criminological theory.' *Australian and New Zealand Journal of Criminology* 24(1): 40–58. [Especially Chapter 5.]

Ayres, Ian and John Braithwaite. 1992. *Responsive Regulation: Transcending the Deregulation Debate*. New York: Oxford University Press. [Especially Chapter 9.]

Braithwaite, John. 1993. 'Shame and modernity.' *The British Journal of Criminology* 33(1): 1–18. [Especially Chapter 3.]

Fisse, Brent and John Braithwaite. 1993. *Corporations, Crime and Accountability*. Cambridge, UK: Cambridge University Press. [Especially Chapter 5.]

Braithwaite, John. 1995. 'Inequality and republican criminology.' In John Hagan and Ruth D. Peterson (eds), *Crime and Inequality*. Palo Alto, CA: Stanford University Press, pp. 277–305. [Especially Chapters 5 and 12.]

Braithwaite, John. 1997. 'On speaking softly and carrying big sticks: Neglected dimensions of a republication separation of powers.' *University of Toronto Law Journal* 47: 305–61. [Especially Chapter 5].

Braithwaite, John. 1998. 'Institutionalizing distrust, enculturating trust.' In Valerie Braithwaite and Margaret Levi (eds), *Trust and Governance*. New York: Russel Sage, pp. 343–56. [Especially Chapters 6 and 7.]

Braithwaite, John and Philip Pettit. 2000. 'Republicanism and restorative justice: An explanatory and normative connection.' In Heather Strang and John Braithwaite (eds), *Restorative Justice: From Philosophy to Practice*. Burlington, VT: Ashgate, pp. 145–63. [Especially Chapter 2.]

Braithwaite, John and Peter Drahos. 2000. *Global Business Regulation*. Cambridge, UK: Cambridge University Press. [Especially Chapter 6.]

Ahmed, Eliza, Nathan Harris, John Braithwaite and Valerie Braithwaite. 2001. *Shame Management through Reintegration*. Cambridge, UK: Cambridge University Press. [Especially Chapter 9.]

Braithwaite, John. 2008. *Regulatory Capitalism: How it Works, Ideas for Making it Work Better*. Cheltenham, UK: Edward Elgar Publishing. [Especially Chapter 8.]

Braithwaite, John, Hilary Charlesworth and Adérito Soares. 2012. *Networked Governance of Freedom and Tyranny*. Canberra: ANU Press. doi.org/10.22459/NGFT.03.2012. [Especially Chapter 8.]

Braithwaite, John. 2018. 'Minimally sufficient deterrence.' *Crime and Justice* 47(1): 69–118. [Especially Chapter 9.]

Braithwaite, John and Bina D'Costa. 2018. *Cascades of Violence: War, Crime and Peacebuilding across South Asia*. Canberra: ANU Press. doi.org/10.22459/CV.02.2018. [Especially Chapters 4 and 11.]

Braithwaite, John. 2019. 'Tempered power, variegated capitalism, law and society.' *Buffalo Law Review* 67(3): 527–94. [Especially Chapter 8.]

Braithwaite, John. 2020a. 'Crime as a cascade phenomenon.' *International Journal of Comparative and Applied Criminal Justice* 44(3): 137–69. [Especially Chapter 11.]

Braithwaite, John. 2020b. 'Regulatory mix, collective efficacy, and crimes of the powerful.' *Journal of White Collar and Corporate Crime* 1(1): 62–71. [Especially Chapter 12.]

While I apologise for where these works are rehashed, readers will find most of the book completely new. In recent years, I have been excessive at self-citation. This book takes self-citation to even more pathological heights. To some degree, I excuse the vice because I have been drawing threads from one piece of a body of work to others as I built towards this work of integration. As you see sections of old Braithwaite stuff you already know, just skip it. Rehashed bits are for readers unfamiliar with them. The appeal of the book is in the ambition of its connecting tissue. Those uninterested in the crimes of coalmine safety, nuclear power plants or banks can skip over these sections and go to the discussion of street crime. Please keep your minds open as you do to the value of reflecting on crime in the corporate suites for opening imaginations to new ways of understanding crime in the streets.

As I draw together a history of these threads, occasionally, I indulge in autobiographical snippets of how my thinking backtracked as I was proved wrong. I squirm reading those passages, imagining young scholars thinking this is a self-indulgent old man. With a normative book, the biographical content does have the virtue of exposing political biases so readers can make their own judgements about how these colour analyses. My project is to take normative macrocriminology as seriously as explanatory theory after all. There are also citations explicitly to Valerie Braithwaite, so readers can better see some of the ways two people are writing this book who are tightly, lovingly, bound. Valerie and I founded RegNet (the School of Regulation and Global Governance) together at The Australian National University (ANU) from 1995 from building blocks that included the Centre for Restorative Justice and the Centre for Tax System Integrity. This book represents the ethos of our school and what I learned from its students and from students of law, sociology and the Reshaping Australian Institutions project of the old Research School of Social Sciences, where I was also privileged to serve. My intellectual interactions have been daily with Valerie since 1969, weekly with recidivist criminology co-authors since the 1970s, Brent Fisse and Peter Grabosky, amigos who enriched me, as have so many special co-authors whom I sadly see less often.

Two ANU students taught Val and me more than we can repay, our beautiful children, Sari and Ben. Yan Zhang helped so much as a research assistant. So did critics who kindly read drafts: especially Valerie Braithwaite and David Best, but also Manuel Eisner, Ross Homel, Susanne Karstedt, Shadd Maruna, Steven Messner, Christine Parker, Philip Pettit, Robert Reiner, Richard Rosenfeld, Clifford Shearing, Robert Sampson, David Weisburd and anonymous referees. There are citations of several dozen ANU colleagues and PhD students that represent how they nourished me. Without them, I would have been an even more flawed scholar and person. My admiration also goes to science colleagues who inspired with contributions to the technologies vital to extinction prevention, and social scientists of peace, even as my university at times succumbs to capture by markets in vice and national security states. Universities, particularly the leadership of their students, are freedom's greatest hope. My privilege is to be part of their conversations.

A particular privilege is to publish with ANU Press. Its open-access publishing model means all its books can be downloaded without charge by the poorest students in the poorest countries. We are proud of you for that, ANU Press and thankful for the leadership of Emily Tinker. Special thanks to the thoughtful process of reviewing by Law Series Chair, James Prest, and to my wonderful copyeditor, Jan Borrie.

Doubtless, I range across subjects for which my shallow reading produces howlers. This is not a text for the criminological positivists. It takes their contributions seriously, but if you want Braithwaite elucidating a tight set of propositions and then testing them quantitatively, you can find that at johnbraithwaite.com on topics herein. The value of this book is an attempt to integrate them. It might even motivate a better writer than me to write a more succinct and critical exegesis of macrocriminology and freedom. I ask traditional and critical criminologists alike to dip into it here and there in a spirit of openness to learning from an integrative project of wide sweep that may sit uncomfortably with their traditions. Thank you for giving that a try.

John Braithwaite
The Australian National University

1

From trickles to rivers of crime and freedom

The essence of crime and freedom

Chapter 12 argues that most of my propositions involve intertwined empirical claims and political claims that will always be resisted by those who hold power. Chapter 12 makes a pitch to young criminologists that they can lead satisfying intellectual lives by being politically serious. It is not really possible to be serious about reducing crime and expanding freedom without engaging with social movement struggles. Chantal Mouffe is an inspiration on being pluralist and agonistic rather than antagonistic. I hope this work stirs political passions in a Mouffe fashion.

Chapter 12 concludes that criminology has contributions to make to the survival of life on our planet. The combination of the criminalisation and militarisation of states and the rising cyber-sophistication of terrorism means that unintended nuclear war is a growing risk, not the fictional declining risk, post Cold War, of neoliberal triumphalism. This book shows that it is untrue that these risks are unknowable. They are known. Because they are complex nonlinear risks with feedback loops, however, we cannot estimate the probability of extinction events. For most people living comfortable lives in wealthy countries, climate change will not overwhelm them next year or even during this decade, though many poor people in Pacific Island states have already seen their homelands surrender to the tides. The risk of global famine and civilisational collapse from nuclear war may be small next year, quite small for the next decade, but multiplies to be high during the next century or two. Nuclear weapons are an acute danger in the hands of leaders like former president Donald Trump who countenance genocidal thought when they threaten to wipe Iran or North Korea from the face of the Earth. Former president Trump explicitly issued such thunderbolts. These are threats with tools of violence designed to be genocidal (Chapter 12).

Ecocide is at hand in the next century unless great powers like China, the United States and Europe learn to work together on better global and national regulatory institutions and green markets for a global Green New Deal (Tienhaara 2018; Drahos 2021; Braithwaite 2021d). Unfortunately, green markets are as prone to corruption as any other. As we have seen with the Covid-19 crisis, times of global crisis are particularly prone to criminalised markets. Fake Covid tests, untested vaccines and scientific fraud proliferated during 2020–21 in darknet markets. Chapter 12 also concludes that economic crises produced by criminalised markets, ecological crises and security crises conduce to crime–war–crime cascades. Hence, an immodest hope for this book is that it gifts our grandchildren glimmers of a politics and a social science of hope for surviving the next century. The United Nations has demonstrated that it can reduce the risks of ecocide through climate agreements (for example, closing the ozone hole). My empirical conclusion is that it has demonstrated that it can reduce war, reduce crime and support freedom through modest investments in peacekeeping. Therefore, the study of the impact of the United Nations and global social movements on crime and freedom is as central to macrocriminology as is the study of state policies. It is also pivotal to the kind of grassroots politics Jane Addams hoped we would continue. But as her Nobel Peace Prize citation warned: 'Those who set their sights on awakening and educating public opinion cannot expect swift victories of the kind that win popular acclaim' (Koht 1972).

The core argument of this book is that freedom is fundamental to building a low-crime society and crime prevention is fundamental to freedom. Sharp readers will detect this as partly tautologous. I define crime as conduct that threatens domination and then argue that crime increases domination and domination increases crime. Chapter 11 concludes that crime and domination are cascade phenomena. When crime and domination arise, they tend to reproduce instances of themselves. In the years of Covid, we all became that bit wiser about the science of contagion. Domination endogeneity and crime endogeneity (the topic of Chapter 11) are complemented by much exogenous explanation in this book and by domination–crime–domination explanations that reach beyond shared definitional features of crime and domination. For example, weak, distrusted states and weak, dysfunctional families allow both crime and domination to grow. Chapter 11 argues that criminology must become more comfortable with endogenous and exogenous explanation sitting side by side to explain recursivity in social change. Medicine also had that struggle. Too often it was insisting on external explanations in the air when the best explanation of disease was viruses reproducing themselves, even though an exogenous shock like the invention of a vaccine could reverse the dynamics.

Thin liberal freedom of choice—including the freedom to vote, choice in markets, freedom of movement and of religion—can contribute to crime prevention. Republican freedom as nondomination contributes much more. Republican freedom is a thicker freedom of the person, which Pettit (2012) juxtaposes with freedom of choice. It is freedom from being enslaved or dominated by arbitrary power. Narrowly conceived measures of inequality or poverty sometimes do not explain crime. The worst narrowing occurred in some of the thinking around US President Lyndon B. Johnson's 'War on Poverty'. It prioritised equality of opportunity to the neglect of the dominations of unequal outcomes. In recent decades, the inequality of outcomes has widened to pose deep dangers to the social fabric of societies and to global society. For most of human history, the richest societies were only twice as rich as the poorest and there were no wealthy business individuals who owned more than the richest kings, or more than many entire countries. These circumstances, I argue, are likely to drive further declines in trust in institutions and more authoritarian uprisings. A social democratic republican vision of simultaneously tempering all forms of domination, discrimination and inequality that drive domination can suppress crime and civilisational collapse. State-sanctioned discrimination (like slavery, Apartheid, inquisitions of religious heretics) has historically been the gravest threat to freedom, and the worst discrimination for driving crime and civil war. Nunn (2008) also found a robust negative relationship between the number of slaves exported from African countries and contemporary economic devastation. The domination of women in many societies is still infused with state-sanctioned discrimination. Hence, the thought of feminist republicans like Mary Wollstonecraft and Jane Addams is fundamental to free, low-crime societies that eschew war.

Domination is advanced as a more fertile concept than inequality for explaining crime and violence. Militarised domination and criminalised domination of governments and markets are particularly destructive. Yet struggles against domination and discrimination do best when they are responsive to those inequalities that are subjectively salient at particular times and places. Micro-dominations (for example, between landlords and peasants, white police and black suspects, at tiny locales) can be more critical than national inequalities to explaining violence. Because it is hard to predict which levels or kinds of domination will fuel raging fires of subjective oppression and violence, and which will not, I argue that societies do well to aim at tempering *all* kinds of domination. It is common for multicollinearity to produce results that inequality explains crime, *but poverty* or racial discrimination *does not*; or that poverty explains crime, but *inequality does not*; or that child mortality but none of these other measures explains crime (Chapter 4). Often what is true in individual or ecological data is not true in time-series studies, or at least not true with short lags. We do best to read such literature with a spirit of openness to the domination effects that are socially constructed as oppressive at different times and contexts in different ways with different lags. Chapter 4 advocates wariness of a selective positivism that, after failing to find a particular linear effect, empowers analysis paralysis over inequality and domination.

Not quite institutional balance

Mark Colvin (2000) laid an important foundation for the domination focus of this book with his theory that 'coercion causes crime and social support prevents crime' (Colvin et al. 2002: 19). There is special appeal for the responsive theoretical framework of this book in the specificity with which Colvin (2000: 26) defines social support as 'responsiveness to the needs and desires of others'. Gerald Patterson's (1982) *Coercive Family Process* showed that coercive discipline in families conduces to crime. This was an important insight for Colvin's work. Colvin is relational in how he thinks about social support. Coercive controls of diverse kinds produce an alienated bond between the controller and the controlled. Children who have been heavily coerced in families and schools carry their alienated relationality into workplaces, militaries and marriages. Tittle (1995) takes up a cognate approach to evidence that 'control balance' explains crime. Robert Agnew's (1992) empirical insight is that it is erratic coercion—

especially arbitrary and unjust treatment that is perceived as arbitrary and unjust—which produces extreme other-directed anger and high rates of crime. This is one motivation in explanatory theory for the move in this book from the concept of coercion to domination—defined as not just any kind of power over another, but power that is arbitrary and unjust.

Republican freedom requires richer separations of powers, both public and private, than we see in western societies. Sun Yat-sen's vision of pluralising the separation of powers more deeply than in Montesquieu's thinking is a light on my republican hill. It draws on ancient Chinese thought about institutions. Ancient thinking about anomie also originated in the East, travelling to the West through Persia, Babylon, Greece and Rome, with the most important modern thinking about anomie being French—that of Durkheim and Montesquieu. Ancient anomie arises when there is no agreement on norms about living together, and no agreement about which institutions should have the authority to set those norms. Anomie means want of a social fabric of shared understanding about which forms of power are arbitrary and intolerable. These are central themes of Confucian thought.

Anomie Américaine took splendid strides towards macrocriminology in the twentieth century. This flowed in a lineage from Merton to Cloward and Ohlin, Cohen, Messner and Rosenfeld, with help from many others. We have seen that *anomie ancienne* is also institutional. Yet *anomie Américaine* has come to be known as institutional anomie theory because it points to the need to strengthen many institutions, particularly to check and balance the burgeoning dominations of market power. This book radically expands the palette of institutions that must be strengthened by a strong state, strong civil society, strong markets and strong, agentic individuals. It also diverges somewhat from Messner and Rosenfeld's institutional anomie theory in conceiving of strengthening markets as fundamental to a freer, lower-crime society.

For example, the book argues that dominations of the financialisation of capitalism must be contested by new financial institutions that contest domination by big banks. This includes new ratings agencies that might be competitors to the likes of Moody's. Such market competitors might sometimes be publicly owned, with a charter of contesting extant market dominations. The dominations of tech giants must be contested by more market competition from competing platforms as well as tempered by more state regulation. People understand the model of how the BBC in

Britain or the ABC in Australia provide competition to the dominations of media barons like Rupert Murdoch as public broadcasters with a charter of political independence and investigative journalism. In some geopolitical contexts, the needed contestation of tech giants that suck the life out of professional journalism may be market competitors that are publicly owned platforms—an option raised with me by RegNet colleague Jensen Sass—or the kind of enforcement actions that have been signalled by the Australian Competition and Consumer Commission (ACCC) against monopolistic surveillance capitalism (Zuboff 2019). Contra institutional anomie theory when it is narrowly conceived, markets in crime-control strategies are important to crime and freedom, especially to corporate crime prevention. They are important to preventing bank robberies and car theft, too (Farrell et al. 2014; Weatherburn and Rahman 2021). A central idea of this book is that republicanism supplies a normative theory that distinguishes markets in virtue from markets in vice. Markets in vice increase the quantum of domination in the world; markets in virtue reduce domination.

Acemoglu and Robinson (2019) convincingly show that the reason the Dutch Republic and Britain evolved into freer, less-dominated societies than Spain and Portugal from the seventeenth century was that Spain's and Portugal's international trade were controlled by state monopolies. Spain and Portugal therefore sustained profound incentives for patrimonial state domination through elite networks. Private market entrepreneurs from Britain and the Netherlands, in contrast, were the actors who had seized the initiative to build national wealth through international trade. These were key actors behind England's Glorious Revolution of 1688 that took big early steps towards humbling the domination of kings through a parliament and a mixed constitution. This was also true of Switzerland as an example of a smaller, landlocked society with formidable state, business and civil society capacity (Acemoglu and Robinson 2019: 278–79; Adler 1983). Britain, the Netherlands and Switzerland became comparatively free, very wealthy, low-crime societies. Constantly emerging new elites were therefore always contesting the domination of old elites, demanding concessions towards balancing a mixed constitution. Acemoglu and Robinson draw a variety of other comparisons of this kind between societies that were similar in most other important respects apart from the growth of powerless little businesses into more potent private-sector actors who could check state domination. Another such contrast was the liberal republicanism of Costa Rica versus the despotism of Guatemala (Acemoglu and Robinson 2019: 193–302).

Then Acemoglu and Robinson (2019: 284) moved from state despotism contested by a bourgeoisie which emerged through markets, to contestation of despotism by the lowest classes. They argue that the Black Death so devastated peasants in fourteenth- and fifteenth-century Western Europe (less so Eastern Europe) that there was a critical shortage of manual labour (in Western but not Eastern Europe). Serfs felt empowered to challenge the feudal order by walking off the manor when their lord refused them a better share of the fruits of their labour. They moved to work for another master who offered less domination. In the long run of history, peasants became more organised as their demands evolved within markets into creation of the trade union movement. During the nineteenth century, incipient trade unions became powerful enough to demand that the vote should not be restricted to landowners. Ultimately, this empowered the working class to form social democratic and socialist political parties that won elections. The second great impetus towards this enhanced market power of manual workers was the Industrial Revolution that accelerated in the nineteenth century to empower peasants to walk off their estates to seek factory work. Factories and mines concentrated industrial workers, making political organisation more feasible to contest domination by the aristocracy and the bourgeoisie alike. In all these ways, markets enabled the contestation of domination at the same time as markets constituted new forms of domination that drove the depth and spread of inequality to levels never seen before.

Many of the poorest societies on the planet remain afflicted by exclusionary patrimonial domination because they are yet to have their power contested by the market power of either a rising middle class or a rising trade union movement. Uplift of these forms of market contestation of domination is fundamental to republican nondomination. These supranational dynamics of the contestation of feudal power are also a key to understanding why feudalism continued to dominate so many Eastern European societies until Napoleon's armies and France's legal code abolished feudalism. Feudalism outlasted Napoleon in many societies, however. Hence, during the centuries when democratic traditions became embedded in Western Europe, despotism became more deeply institutionalised in much of Eastern Europe and the Ottoman Empire. Acemoglu and Robinson (2012) even describe how the Habsburg and Russian empires sought to preserve their domination from the infrastructural impetus to trade that railways provided by resisting them and preventing the dissemination of other infrastructural industrial technologies. The Qing government in China purchased the first railway built in that country in 1870 by the British firm Jardine, Matheson & Co. and tore it up (Acemoglu and Robinson 2019: 226). This was of a piece with a long, intermittent history of Chinese dynasties banning international trade by ships, and other mercantile activities and technologies that Chinese regimes conjectured could destabilise the social order they dominated. Such anti-business politics was why states like the Netherlands and Britain that enabled business growth surpassed the previous geopolitical dominance and wealth of China for the first time during late modernity.

There is a difference between this book and Tittle's (1995) idea that there is an optimal control–balance ratio that produces low crime, and Messner and Rosenfeld's (2013) idea that institutional balance is associated with low crime. Messner and Rosenfeld believe that 'institutional imbalance[1] is positively associated with the level of crime' (Stephen Messner, personal communication commenting on this book). That can be true. At times there might be, as Rick Rosenfeld put it to me, a 'difference without a distinction' between my analysis of balance and theirs.

Yet I want to insist that the worst political errors achieve balance by weakening strong institutions. The worst socialist errors weakened markets; the worst Thatcherist errors weakened the state. My interpretation of balance goes to strengthening weak institutions. I argue that separated

---

1   Acemoglu and Robinson (2019) are even more explicit about favouring an equal-power view of the balance between the powers of different institutions. In contemplating that, readers may ask themselves, even if they understand what equal institutional power means, would they necessarily agree this is better than one institution having 10 or 30 per cent more power than some other institution in some circumstances? The equality formulation starts with Acemoglu and Robinson's (2019: 13–14) attraction to the ancient Sumerian intuition in the *Epic of Gilgamesh* found on 4,200-year-old tablets. They return to Gilgamesh throughout their book. Gilgamesh was the King of Uruk in what is today Iraq. Uruk was perhaps the world's first city. Gilgamesh was a despot. He created a wealthy city, but in time became so out of control that the citizens of Uruk appealed to their god: 'Create a double for Gilgamesh, his second self, a man who equals his strength and courage, a man who equals his stormy heart. Create a new hero, let them balance each other perfectly, so that Uruk has peace' (Acemoglu and Robinson 2019: 14). Acemoglu and Robinson articulate their ideal as a 'contained Leviathan', while I opt for Krygier's (2019) tweak of 'tempering' that makes states and markets stronger, as opposed to containing them in pursuit of balance. We certainly favour many of the same policies; nevertheless, as I pursue balancing to temper power, they pursue balance that contains power, 'controls' it, 'shackles' it. The perspective of Acemoglu and Robinson (2019: 16–17) that I endorse is when they say: 'When the state and its elites are too powerful and society is meek, why would leaders grant people rights and liberty? And if they did, could you trust them to stick to their word?'

institutional powers must be able to pursue power up to the point where the power of one institution cannot overwhelm the power of the others. Each separated power must be strong enough in its countervailing capacities to secure the exercise of its own power from being dominated by any other institutional power. I argue that more freedom and less crime can be accomplished by all institutions continuing to grow their capacities to deliver those outcomes, while they also check and balance all institutions from dominating others. This is one way I interpret Martin Krygier's (2019) concept of tempering power. The aim is for a free society in which all institutions continually grow stronger and continually grow their capacity to temper one another. It is not for a society with any optimal institutional balance. This also distinguishes Pettit and my normative framework from that of libertarians; libertarians want the state to be weaker so markets can be stronger. Conversely, socialists want markets to be weaker so the state can be stronger. Like Krygier, I argue that republican social democrats should want to grow both ever stronger and ever more tempered. What I share with Messner and Rosenfeld is the aim of many other institutions growing on that trajectory as well.

For all the richness of insight I find in Acemoglu and Robinson (2019), as with Messner and Rosenfeld, I conceive of them as advocating more institutional 'balance' in many circumstances when they would do better by freedom and crime control to strengthen weakened institutions rather than achieving 'balance' through weakening one kind of institution or another. We see this with Acemoglu and Robinson's (2019) persistent return to the importance to freedom of breaking down the 'cage of norms'. This book is very much about how to improve collective efficacy to make norms work better. When they do, they strengthen our wings and liberate rather than cage us. That is not to deny the many good points Acemoglu and Robinson make about domination caused by norms that form a cage. The fact is there are good and bad norms. This is true whatever your normative theory of the good and the bad is; for Pettit and me, good norms are those whose application reduces domination; bad norms increase domination. Chapter 3 argues that western justice took a wrong turn from the moment kings found it helpful to conceive of crimes as offences against the crown (which later morphed into crimes only against the state). Kings found the power to seize the lands of criminals politically attractive. By moving away from the idea that crimes are also against victims, who deserve compensation, kings crushed moot traditions with legal formalism. This error is being repaired today by restorative justice advocates who argue for legal formalism that empowers informal social control and informalism that empowers legal formalism. What we want is legal formalism that checks domination by the 'cage of norms', and informal restorative justice institutions that check domination by courts, police and presidents (when they pardon powerful state criminals). We will see that the latter are particularly critical with state denial of international crimes, where citizens' tribunals had to step in on matters like systematic rape by the Japanese military (of rape victims called 'comfort women').

Acemoglu and Robinson (2019) are right to point out that informal institutions like Germanic moots or *panchayats* (village councils) in ancient and modern India were ripe for domination by whoever were the local ruling class or the elite caste. It is hard to find examples of tribal informal justice that are not dominated by males and not biased in favour of male interests, excluding even the wisest female elders of the tribe. Ali Wardak, reflecting on male domination of *jirgas* (tribal assemblies) in Afghanistan, argues that the better path to freedom and justice for Afghanistan is to strengthen such male-dominated tribal justice institutions. Empirically, they enjoyed much more confidence from the people than corrupt state courts. At the same time, Wardak argues, it was possible during the 20 years after the 2001 western invasion of Afghanistan to strengthen countervailing women's *jirgas* that enjoin male *jirgas* in justice conversations and contestation. In addition, Wardak advocates contestation of the justice of *jirgas* by the Human Rights Commission, which happened to be a female-dominated institution in Afghanistan until 2021 (Wardak and Braithwaite 2013). Wardak's idea was to ensure the agents of women's rights who contest male agents of the *jirga* were female agents of the Human Rights Commission. What is missing from Acemoglu and Robinson's (2019) analysis here is an understanding that judiciaries and police forces, even in liberal western democracies, were also almost totally male institutions until the late twentieth century. In a country like India, it has proved easier to pass a national law that requires one-third of those who preside in the informal justice and informal village policymaking of *panchayats* to be female (the 1992 Panjayat Raj constitutional amendment) than it has to pass a law that requires one-third of judges to be female. Why? Because male judges can mobilise more national power to defend their privilege than can male *panchayat* members, who enjoy only village power with little national clout.

All that said, male agents of formal justice systems can be and are important to checking criminal abuses of male power. This is true with Ali Gohar's program on hybrid *jirgas* in Pakistan (Braithwaite and Gohar 2014), at which male police (who always attend) are trained to protest if it is proposed that a young woman be given as a bride to reconcile a blood feud. Police are trained to assert that this is against national law, against sharia law and against the policy of this restorative justice program. Those male police are a significant check and balance for women's rights, though much less important in the analysis of this book than feminist social movement politics. I argue that the most historically potent check against the cage of patriarchal norms has been feminist norms promoted by feminist politics.

Acemoglu and Robinson (2019) actually agree that strengthening rather than loosening certain informal norms is important to defending freedom. They also agree that checked and balanced state power—which Krygier (2019) would say is tempered—develops deeper state capacity. So, why use language that plays into the hands of legal formalists who seek to abolish informal justice; why use language that plays into the hands of libertarians who are opposed to deeper state capacity? I prefer the concepts of Acemoglu and Robinson (2019: 73) when what they value are 'capable states matched by capable societies'.

The bottom line here is that quite often I find myself thinking as I read the work of Acemoglu and Robinson (2019) and Messner and Rosenfeld, 'no, it is not more "balance" that is needed here but more checks' (in their elusive checks and balances formulae). A problem with Acemoglu and Robinson (2019), Messner and Rosenfeld and most thinkers about checks and balances (including me) is they do not have a clear enough view of how much balance is balance. It is better to be more cautious in usage of the balance concept. Better to advocate making all institutions that are useful to freedom stronger, including the 'cage of norms' (the particular bête noire for Acemoglu and Robinson) and markets (the bête noire of Messner and Rosenfeld). How much stronger? They should be as strong as they can be without dominating other institutions; as strong as they need to be to defend themselves from being dominated by other institutions (which involves a mix of balancing and checking); as strong as they must be to make the best contribution they are capable of making to reducing the amount of domination in the world. In the same manner as Chapter 9's conclusions about how to iterate towards reduced criminal punishment, any responsive journey towards continuously improved strengthening, checking and balancing of institutions involves endless iterative adjustment. This responsive adjustment fosters learning as global and local conditions change.

Recursive republican social science

'There is something deeply ironic' about the fact 'that from the life-changing experience of an entirely unexpected, non-linear event like the end of the Cold War', the West 'has derived a thoroughly linear expectation of the future'. (Thomas Bagger, quoted by Krastev and Holmes 2019: 90–91)

While this book conceives of stronger markets in virtue as vital to the control of markets in vice, its mission is to tweak and integrate *anomie ancienne* and *anomie Américaine* under a republican politics of hope. Republicanism has older roots than liberalism in America and Europe, the East and the West. It has more radically redistributive social democratic implications than modern liberalism. These wider social democratic implications have been richly developed by Philip Pettit (1997, 2012, 2014; Marti and Pettit 2010), building on our ordered set of propositions for a republican theory of criminal justice (Braithwaite and Pettit 1990). Subsequent publications cited herein elaborate this republican normative thinking to apply to regulatory questions with big implications for freedom. This is not a political philosophy book that labours those older foundations, but one that develops a list of 150 corollaries from a convergence of empirical propositions about crime and republican normative propositions elaborated from their initial explication in Braithwaite and Pettit (1990). The opening pages of Chapter 2 resume these themes.

Domination's deepest threats to freedom and crime occur when commanding-heights institutions—states and markets—are criminalised. These are not distant threats. Donald Trump's presidency was taking the United States well along a trajectory towards criminalisation of the state and criminalisation of markets. Similarly, long-cherished republican visions have been overthrown in diverse European states and by Turkish President Recep Tayyip Erdoğan's overturning of eastern leadership towards republicanism at the heart of what was the Ottoman Empire. This Turkish republican shift evolved erratically across the half-century following the government led by Kemal Atatürk from 1920 to 1938. This book argues that to contemplate the full violence of the criminalisation of states and markets, we might look hard at Democratic Republic of Congo or Jamaica. These were once flourishing democracies that were leaders of their regions in economic development, poverty reduction, modern culture from rumba to reggae and sporting excellence from sprinting to cricket. They have had their freedom ravaged this century by criminalisation of states and markets. Differences among societies across space and time are massive on these variables. These differences are at the centre of the theory of freedom and crime. Hence, the priority is clear for a more micro–macro criminology to repair criminologies that have denuded macro traditions since their zenith at the time of Edwin Sutherland in America and Willem Bonger in Europe.

Macrocriminology that is rich in insight is recursive and paradoxical in its explanatory approach. It resists linear conceptions of a civilising process, even as it admires Norbert Elias (1982) for grappling with ideas about societies becoming less violent as they craft institutions that temper the emotions, and institutionalised normative order. The evidence is strong that transitions to democracy and nondomination give rise to anomie, to high rates of crime and to heightened risks of civil war (for example, Zhao and Cao 2010). Crime, violence, substance abuse and self-harm are fundamental to understanding why, as in most of the Soviet Union and Eastern Europe, life expectancy in Russia plummeted from 70 years in 1989 to 64 in 1995 on the back of 1.3–1.7 million premature deaths (Krastev and Holmes 2019: 90–1). America's birth as a republic and its transition from slavery testify to the terrors of crime–war–crime cascades involved in transition to freedom through a revolutionary war, a frontier war against indigenous Americans and a civil war that scarred the society with criminogenic legacies.

Martin Luther King Jr and Mahatma Gandhi had the acute insight about how to be effective in struggles against domination—as did Angela Davis, who still shines as a contemporary light on the hill of the restorative justice movement. The evidence is now potent that when struggles against domination are advanced nonviolently, they are more likely to prevail politically and are more likely to leave a legacy of freedom in the aftermath of the struggle to destabilise the old order of domination. The paradox of 'destabilisation rights' and anomie is not the hard paradox of violence advanced by thinkers like Frantz Fanon in Algeria and Che Guevara in Argentina and Cuba. It is a paradox softened by the empirical discovery that patient, long-term, nonviolent social movement struggles against evils like slavery, ecocide and genocide—indeed, against war itself—are the struggles that advance freedom and subdue crime. This book has not theorised this as fully as it ought. A future book after data collection ends in 2030 will deploy the Peacebuilding Compared database to range in a more fine-grained way, case by case, across South Africa, India, Algeria, Sudan, Egypt, Iran, the Philippines, Timor-Leste, Indonesia, Korea, Myanmar, France, Russia, China, the United States and more, to study the history of violence and nonviolence in destabilisation rights. A key question is how social movements for nonviolent struggle against domination should negotiate with militaries to avert militarised societies in the washup, so violence does not cascade across the next century.

Learning from Sun Yat-sen

One political leader greatly influenced by Gandhi was Sun Yat-sen. He became the first president of the Republic of China after his republican movement overthrew the last dynasty, the Qing (Manchu), in 1911. Dr Sun wanted a China that was a force for peace in the world. He transacted his practical politics with grace and personal kindness to collaborators and adversaries. The peaceful aspect of his thought is not without influence in contemporary China, which, while its state increasingly throws its weight around, has had less of a penchant for invading other countries than the great western powers and Russia since 1911, indeed since 2001. Paradoxically, the social democratic aspects of Sun Yat-sen's philosophy were also not without influence in Chiang Kai-shek's despotic anticommunist regime in China, then Taiwan. Partly in homage to Sun and his following after death, partly from fear of the appeal of communism to Taiwan's peasants, from 1949, Taiwan enacted one of the most successfully redistributive land reform programs of any country (You 2014). It gave impoverished peasants a greatly increased stake in Taiwan's comparatively egalitarian market economy.

We can see from Sun Yat-sen's lectures on his 'livelihood' principle that he was a leading social democratic thinker a century ago (Wells 2001: 91–97). A priority was liberation from colonial yokes—many of them, in the case of China (Linebarger 1937). He was a pracademic who sought to build the society of his philosophy through republican social movement politics. Sun Yat-sen is uninfluential in western political philosophy not only because western philosophy is so closed to influence from eastern and southern thought, but also because after he fell ill with cancer in his 50s, he made time to systematise his scattered and sometimes inconsistent political philosophy. These manuscripts were destroyed in a 1922 bombardment of Sun's headquarters by an opponent with imperial ambitions, Chen Jiongming, and the Merchant Volunteer Corps funded by Hong Kong and Cantonese bankers whom Sun fought until his death in 1924. Sun ran out of time to rewrite these chapters, but did manage to present 16 of 18 of them as hastily prepared lectures with which he was dissatisfied because he could not access the books he needed to prepare them a second time (Wells 2001: 62). Given the way the financialisation of capitalism became such a threat to redistributive social democracy, there is poignancy in the burning of these manuscripts by forces backed by bankers. The sad fact of most western philosophers is that few bankers would find it worthwhile to bomb them and burn their manuscripts.

Sun's constitutional thought was more radically democratic than that of republicans like Philip Pettit (1997, 2012, 2014) (or me). His republican constitution for China conceived of the vote as just one of four forms of direct accountability to the people by election, recall, initiative and referendum (Linebarger 1937: 211). When he visited the United States more than a century ago, he was less than impressed by the populism of its elected politicians. He perceived many as stupid, others as corrupt, with the system putting too much emphasis on entertaining oratory (Wells 2001: 36, 81). His philosophy was Confucian in the belief that rulers must be learned, well educated, temperate, competent, as well as deeply accountable to ordinary people who will not be so educated, mostly peasants. This is why he continued to believe, when so few had higher education, in the Confucian institution of a (fourth) examinations branch of government to complement Montesquieu's tripartite separation of powers among a legislature, executive and judiciary. Chapters 3 and 8 discuss the greater import of Sun Yat-sen's fifth branch that became part of his constitution for the Republic of China (still partially implemented in Taiwan). This was an independent accountability and integrity branch that oversaw impeachment of the kind of venal and populist politicians who worried Sun in America, but also the impeachment of judges and senior members of the executive government. Its independence ideal (in Thailand as well, as discussed in Chapter 8) came to be secured by elected members of the accountability branch having no affiliation with political parties in the legislature and serving for only one term. This separated accountability branch also had the function of overseeing business regulatory institutions and regulators of the state itself such as the auditor-general, the human rights commission, the ombudsman, the electoral commission and the anticorruption commission.

It is easy to see, therefore, why Sun Yat-sen's innovations in pluralising the separation of powers are such an influence on how I think about Martin Krygier's (2019) tempering of power as central to crime prevention. His approach shows a better path for states to impeach the most criminalised members of their own state elites with decisiveness and political independence. Sun Yat-sen's redistributive social democratic politics was attractive for the purposes of this book, as was his commitment to maximally nonviolent means of pursuing power through republican social movement politics, his commitment to strong markets as vital for a strong China and his belief that a strong state (albeit a democratically accountable one) was necessary to subdue forces loyal to the Manchu Dynasty, to warlords and to triads who ravaged China for more than a century. His enemies in business characterised his commitment to a strong Chinese state as an intention to subdue liberty. Sun made many mistakes. His opposition to the Manchu Dynasty at times fuelled a Han Chinese nationalism that cascaded to violent racism against ethnic Manchurians (and Mongolians). This has legacies today in communist China's oppression of these minorities and is relevant to understanding the Han nationalist dimensions of the oppression of ethnic Uyghurs in Xinjiang.

Sun Yat-sen's greatest failing, however, was not understanding that his commitment to tempering power needed to be more total than it was. He allowed his movement to be seduced by one strand of Lenin's thought: the idea of a vanguard party (the Kuomintang for Sun Yat-sen) that would have to govern for a short period (until 1935, he suggested, though he flip-flopped awfully on this timing under Soviet pressure). The vanguard party would have limited accountability checks until it totally subdued the military power of the Manchu Dynasty and the warlords. Sadly, that Hobbesian transition to republicanism never blossomed beyond unaccountable Kuomintang and communist tyrannies. We do not know the inner workings of Sun Yat-sen's mind on this, but it could be that he was not actually seduced but tricked by Lenin's political guile in circumstances of Sun having few options. Sun wanted his republicans to rise to power with support from western democracies. The bankers who burned his manuscripts were among business interests who persuaded western leaders that his land-reforming, redistributive, anti-imperialist policies were dangerous. Without the western support Sun Yat-sen craved to keep his republican revolution afloat, he accepted the generous offers of material support volunteered by Lenin. Communists were also a radical flank of his republican movement in the way they were later in the century for Nelson Mandela in South Africa and Xanana Gusmão in Timor-Leste. So long as Sun's republicans allowed the communists a voice within the movement, republicans attracted increasing support from Lenin. Mao Zedong respected Sun Yat-sen, found great appeal in his redistributive land reform proposals for the liberation of peasants and joined his movement. The more the West spurned republicanism, the more Lenin's agents in China succeeded in targeting promising young republican leaders like Mao to flip them to communism. That is the background for a discussion of macrocriminology and freedom in contemporary China in the next chapter.

The tragedy of Sun Yat-sen is that after his premature death from cancer, two factions crystallised: the Nationalist Kuomintang under Chiang Kai-shek, who attracted western support by throwing the communists out of the republican movement; and the communists, who ultimately fell under the all-conquering Mao. One became a despotic regime of the right, the other a despotic party of left. Both tragically put Sun Yat-sen's transitional unaccountability of party rule to work for their opposing projects of dominating the people of China. It mattered little that Sun Yat-sen conceived of his transitional party hegemony not as a 'dictatorship of the proletariat', but as a period constrained by specified dates when the people would be educated in democratic norms as preparation for full constitutional democracy.[2] His political error remained the fatal one of creating a transitional structure of party domination sufficiently long for his despotic successors to secure enduring domination by regimes that supplanted the Manchus and warlords. A lifetime after Sun's death, both unaccountable parties continued to rule their regimes. Martial law was not replaced with democracy in Taiwan until 1987. One day mainland China may also more fully imbibe the liberation from despotism that was Sun Yat-sen's project.

---

2   Actually, Sun's writing conceived of three stages of transition from dynastic rule: 'Period of Military Operations; (b) Period of Political Tutelage; (c) Period of Constitutional Government … During the period of military operations the entire country should be subject to military rule. To hasten the unification of the country, the Government to be controlled by the Kuomintang should employ military force to conquer all opposition in the country and propagate the principles of the Party so that the people may be enlightened … The period of political tutelage in a province should begin and military rule should cease as soon as order within the province is completely restored … To enable the people to be competent in their knowledge of politics, the government should undertake to train and guide them so that they may know how to exercise their rights of election, recall, initiative, and referendum' (Sun Yat-sen, quoted in Linebarger 1937: 211).

Sun's project was about ending a century of anomie and terrible wars in China and ending the criminalisation of the state and of markets that came with defeat by the British in the Opium Wars. In reality, however, his republican revolution started another four decades of civil war that created the opportunity for Japan to start World War II in China in the 1930s. In the aftermath, two different kinds of criminalised states were created, under Chiang Kai-shek and Mao Zedong, which could launch a project with as large a criminal imagination as interring a million Uyghurs today just for being Uyghurs.

This book argues that Sun Yat-sen was right to want a strong state, strong markets and a strong republican movement. His folly was being too half-hearted about the separation of powers or, rather, too staged about transition to his more full-hearted commitment to separations of powers, compared with other republicans. Chapter 8 develops Timor-Leste as a twenty-first-century case of other great social democratic leaders making quite similar mistakes during periods of transition. The Timor-Leste story has a happier ending because UN peacekeepers came to its rescue when war and tyranny began to take off in Timor in 1999 and again in 2006. It is important to see that possibility for a low-crime republic to be brokered peacefully with UN support in Timor-Leste in the washup to a genocidal civil war. Had it been possible for UN peacekeepers to pacify the warlords, the Manchus and others with imperial ambitions such as the bankers, who were still ravaging China in the early twentieth century; if a UN transitional administration had supervised a free election at that time, Sun Yat-sen would have been elected president. If there had been the impossible dream of a UN-supervised constitutional convention, the constitution adopted would probably have been something like Sun Yat-sen's five-branch republican constitutional vision. There was no United Nations on which Sun Yat-sen could lean. That was an impossible dream. Timor-Leste illustrates in Chapter 8 that this is a possible dream for a republican social democracy today.

Hindsight is glib when political transitions are so fraught for leaders like Sun and Gusmão. They were militarily weak in confronting massive Chinese and Indonesian armies, respectively. Their only chance was to be diplomatically strong if they were to avert endlessly futile civil war. UN Security Council guarantees of peaceful transition with UN peacekeepers is a luxury Sun might have used to make transition work. Sun was a supporter of the League of Nations and initially optimistic about it, but he was disillusioned by the way colonised nations were marginalised and disrespected by western leaders at Versailles. Western thought has been too self-obsessed to look back on this as another historically devastating mistake born of Allied arrogance and will to domination at Versailles.

None of this is to say that UN peacekeeping is usually a midwife to an imperfect yet republican democracy, as it was in Timor-Leste. Usually, it is not. There are more experiences like that described by Broadhurst et al. (2015, 2018) for Cambodia (Chapter 3). We will see that UN peacekeeping did bring peace and a steeply lower crime rate in Cambodia. These are not accomplishments to sniff at. But the Cambodian low-violence society today is one in which the successor regime to the genocidal Khmer Rouge is only somewhat less despotic, led by a senior Khmer Rouge defector, Hun Sen. The regime honours rituals of democratic elections to placate the United Nations but delivers no democratic substance under its enduring one-party rule.

Do not despair, is my message to young, politically engaged criminologists. Yes, the despot Hun Sen inherits power, but his domination is somewhat less than that of the Khmer Rouge, and citizens there live in less fear of violent crime. The more redemptive path of Timor-Leste is also a low-crime and low-domination possibility (Chapter 8). Finally, Sun Yat-sen's life as a pracademic was far from wasted inside China. Democracy has finally arrived in Taiwan and it builds on a foundation of land reform that accomplished a society with a structurally low Gini index in land and wealth inequality. It is a democracy where remnants of Sun Yat-sen's five-branch constitution mean more leaders are impeached in Taiwan than in the United States, as was Sun's hope (Chapter 8). China may remain tyrannous and violent for Uyghurs. For Han Chinese, however, they live in less fear of warlords, drug lords, foreign armies and violent crime than they did before Sun Yat-sen's republicans confronted the structures of violence, even if they live under the domination of the Communist Party.

One Sun Yat-sen vision that was not totally burnt by bankers was reforesting northern and central China (Linebarger 1937: 251). A century on, it is finally being realised. The Green Great Wall plan is to plant 88 billion trees along a 4,800-kilometre frontier to hold back the expansion of the Gobi Desert. It is well under way, as is Chinese help for Africa to arrest desertification with Africa's Great Green Wall at the southern extremity of the Sahara. A *Nature* article reveals this afforestation is building a renewed Chinese carbon sink that in the past has been underestimated and now absorbs 45 per cent of estimated annual Chinese anthropogenic emissions (Wang et al. 2020).

While I have been able to find only one article in any philosophy journal about the political philosophy of Sun Yat-sen (Gregor 1981), there is hope in looking forward to a more intellectually plural academy that takes the thought of Sun Yat-sen seriously. Sun reveals ways to help all societies experience less crime with more freedom, as argued in Chapter 8. The next generation of young criminologists in China, Taiwan, Hong Kong, Thailand, Vietnam and Indonesia might renew the interest in the constitutional thought of Sun Yat-sen that has never been totally extinguished in those societies.

Reading this shortened narrative of the life and thought of Sun Yat-sen makes it easy to understand why many commentators write him off as a political opportunist who made a mess of things (Bergère and Lloyd 1998: 4–5). My narrative also makes it easy to understand why critics conclude his political philosophy is an incoherent hotchpotch of checks on the strong (allegedly illiberal) state he sought. Like Thomas Jefferson with his 600 slaves, it is true that Sun was no feminist; he was Confucian in valuing strong families much more than strong individuals who could stand up to families. Nevertheless, the 1890–1920 period of his republican revolution did permit a space of sufficient freedom for the blossoming of a Confucian vernacularisation of feminism (Li and Ackerly 2021) that I will argue in Chapters 2 and 3 created superior conditions for progress of the empowerment of women during most of the twentieth century in China than were seen in the West. I hope my narrative helps westerners understand why two Chinese universities bear the name of Sun Yat-sen—one of them among China's very best—and why another, in Moscow, is quaintly named The Sun Yat-sen Communist University of the Toilers of China. I hope we might see Sun Yat-sen as a kindly visionary who walked his republican talk, a social democrat who shone a faltering light of freedom from the hill of his Nanking republic where he rests, who remarkably managed to launch from social movement politics to become the first president of the Republic of China. He accomplished this without an army, through a revolution with little bloodshed.

Sun knew, however, that without control over a national military in a militarised society, and without international support in 1911, his republican government could not hold. After 45 days, he stood aside as president for one leader after another who could command more western support (but less Chinese legitimacy than Sun, and more Soviet opposition after the Russian Revolution). They failed. The warlords ran rampant, carving up local control of the country until Mao Zedong was able to unite China to defeat Japan and all internal enemies by 1949. The greatest failings were the avarice and bloodlust of the warlords internally, rapacious western powers and Japan, which also wanted to carve up China's wealth and territory for their imperial designs, and Soviet power that sponsored takeover by communist tyranny. I know my interpretation of the life, politics and constitutional thought of Sun Yat-sen will generate enthusiasm in neither the West nor China. The latter was clear from speaking in Beijing and having a Communist Party leader jump up to explain that Dr Sun was a great revolutionary, but Braithwaite's interpretation of his contribution was not the correct one! Even so, for the analysis of this book, it is the right provocation of the great powers to catalyse conversations between them about their responsibilities to prevent the extinction of both their civilisations.

One hundred and fifty propositions about crime and freedom

Each chapter that follows lists its key propositions. There are overlaps in the character of the propositions discussed in different chapters. A virtue within that vice is that we can induce from the list of specific propositions aggregated in Appendix I a shortlist of more general ones. Readers might choose to glance at bits of Appendix I that interest them before moving to Chapter 2. This will give you more of a feel for the complex of threads that weave together the fabric of the book. Without getting a feel for the holism of the set of 150 tributary propositions in Appendix I, and how they are sequenced, it is a challenge to grasp the significance of the six propositional rivers into which those tributaries run. Indeed, I worried that readers starting with the six abstract propositions rather than the 150 tributaries that constitute them might view the six as banal and overly abstract. It is in the 150 strands of the fabric that the analytic edginess found in the pages of this book is integrated into a normatively and empirically testable shape.

The parsimony of the six proposed rivers of transformation comes from them all being normative propositions. Normative propositions more readily lend themselves to overarching principles that cluster. The six rivers of my argument are:

1. Reduce all dimensions of domination.
2. Separate and temper powers.
3. Strengthen institutions of the market, state and civil society, and strengthen individuals.

4. Maintain a normative order that nurtures collective efficacy to resist domination.

5. Strengthen financial capital, human capital, social capital, recovery capital and restorative capital.

6. Prevent wars before they begin to cascade violence, anomie and domination.

The reason this is an explanatory and normative theory of crime and freedom is that these six rivers, with all their explanatory tributaries, then converge to power a light on the macrocriminologist's hill. This is one sentence that is actually a convergence of two explanatory and two normative hypotheses to contest in further normative and explanatory research:

- Strengthen freedom to prevent crime; prevent crime to strengthen freedom.

My hope is that this is a bright light because it motivates a wide fabric of more specific propositions that weave together prospects of preventing ecocide and genocide, plus many more minor dominations. They can balance and temper commodification, punitiveness and militarisation, while enriching the meaning of freedom.

A craft of institutional weaving is my political ambition. That weaving is accomplished by a politics of struggle from below that is recursively error prone. Republican social democrats like me spend a lifetime tugging at these 150 strands in ways that sometimes cause the fabric of social democracy to unravel rather than strengthen. While this final light on the hill is recursive (with feedback loops), it is not as complexly nonlinear as the 150 propositions. This is why the 150 tributaries are more important than the unifying light on the hill. A methodological proposition is that if many lives are spent at political work on many strands of freedom, the fabric can progressively become sufficiently resilient that freedom becomes that bit easier to strengthen through another strand. It becomes harder to unravel by pulling on the wrong strand at the wrong time. This is my upbeat reading of the flawed, yet inspiring political and intellectual lives of the social movements led by Sun Yat-sen and Xanana Gusmão.

Republican normative theory can be combined with explanatory theory about which institutions prevent crime and domination to power a light on the hill because it motivates the fabric of propositions in Appendix I.

Plan of the book

Chapter 2 argues that it is good to ask how we should treat individual victims and offenders to prevent further crime. Yet it is even better to ask how we should do so to maximise freedom and minimise domination. Then, we do well to inquire how the aggregated effect of many individual responses to crime will have structural effects. In turn, we can study how social structures enable and disable individual responsiveness of different kinds. In conditions of contemporary capitalism, the book argues that important macro questions are about how markets shape crime, how markets are criminalised and how markets criminalise other institutions such as states and, recursively, how institutions criminalise markets. By bringing to bear the multiple micro–macro lenses traversed in Chapter 2, we can think about doctrines such as deterrence, incapacitation, rehabilitation and situational crime prevention in transformed ways.

The first item of business in Chapter 3 is considering the normative order that makes criminality unthinkable for most individuals in most organisations at most times and places. It advances anomie as a central topic of macrocriminology. The proposed freedom theory of crime argues that a normative order that is legitimate because it guarantees freedom and minimises domination lays a pathway to low-crime societies.

Chapter 4 follows in the footsteps of Merton, Cloward and Ohlin and connects their writing to the theory of freedom and crime. Its hypothesis is that crime rates will be low when there are maximum legitimate opportunities to be free and minimum illegitimate opportunities to dominate the freedom of others. It reviews, reframes and reinterprets the literature on relationships between opportunity, inequality and crime. It sets up an analytical direction for building on the insights of Messner and Rosenfeld on the imperative to temper dominations of avarice with contributions from many institutions. Evidence is reviewed that places with extreme inequality tend to have a lot of crime. Inequality's criminals are freedom's termites.

Chapter 5 diagnoses how inequality empowers crimes of the powerful. Only some of the evidence that informs this analysis is quantitative. It is in the nature of crimes of the powerful that if we know about them at one point in history, they are unlikely at that point to be the most lucrative forms of such crime. With corporate crime, when a strategy of predation becomes well known, it becomes less lucrative. Hence, the counting of corporate crime tends to count what is least important.

Fortunately, however, at this stage in the development of the criminology of organisations, we can look back across several generations of ethnographic contributions to the study of past waves of organisational crime. These ethnographies cumulate to the theoretical insight that corporate crime and state crime are much more preventable than Edwin Sutherland used to think. The work of Farrall and Karstedt (2019) on middle-class crime suggests that unless we bring the 'crimes of the 1 per cent' to heel, anomic crimes of the middle 50 per cent—which are not counted in Uniform Crime Reports, Interpol or UN Office on Drugs and Crime (UNODC) counts of crime—might continue to take off. The chapter concludes from disparate qualitative sources that high levels of inequality in societies tend to increase crimes of those who dominate as well as crimes of the dominated. Good evidence now shows why and how. Chapter 5 proceeds to show that these insights inform how tempering the power of the most powerful officeholders in a society with power exerted by countervailing institutions can be effective in reducing crimes of the powerful. Hence, Chapter 5 nails down key institutional anomie themes. These are that separations of institutional power and reduced inequality of wealth and power can temper crimes of the powerful.

Chapter 6 considers how separated powers in the structure of a state and a society can prevent crime and defend freedom by closing off illegitimate opportunities.

Chapter 7 deals with how to temper anomic financial capital with checks and balances. In this sense, it picks up the institutional anomie tradition of criminological theory. Checks and balances come in the analysis of this chapter from other forms of capital that are critical to criminality. These checks on financial capital are human capital and social capital (and recovery capital and restorative capital as important variants of social capital). These different forms of capital are seen as checking and balancing one another in low-crime societies, low-crime markets and organisations, and low-crime times and spaces.

This is part of what we mean by tempering financial capital, making it accountable. The chapter then argues against libertarians who see a weak state as important to sustaining strong markets. It argues against socialists and institutional anomie theorists who see overly strong markets as a threat to an effective state. It argues for strong markets, strong states, strong civil society and strong individuals as all being important for crime prevention and domination prevention. These concepts are a challenge to define. Here is a definitional footnote that most readers can choose to skip because tweaking these starting definitions gets much attention in the body of the book.[3]

---

3   *Strong individuals*, from the perspective of republican political theory, are defined as individuals who can act independently of arbitrary power exercised over them. For example, if their family insists that every member of their family studies medicine, they are strong enough to choose to resist this and to say they will be a musician. *Strong markets* have robust competition between competing suppliers of the same products and services. This is even more difficult to operationalise. One reason is that it is fraught to define what is the same service. Do buses and trains provide the same service called transport, or do they provide somewhat different services? China and the United States have the most robust and competitive markets (even though one of them has a lot of socialism) because they are so big, with so many domestic competitors. Yet Australia has more efficient and competitive agricultural production than both these giants because there is virtually zero protection for farmers under Australia's open trade regime. But Australia has less competitive airlines and banks than the United States and China because the Australian economy is only big enough to support robust competitors in banking and airlines that can be counted on the fingers of one hand. It does not help the strength of banking markets for small economies to have dozens of banks that crash into bankruptcy on a regular basis (as most economies did during the nineteenth century). Import competition helps with international airline markets but not with domestic markets. With banking in Australia, import competition has not worked because foreign banks could not compete with the service infrastructure of local branches and mostly only served to weaken the integrity of markets. Chapter 5 discusses the Nugan Hand Bank and the Bank of Commerce and Credit International, which mostly only contributed dirty money services to the Australian economy and did not last many years before they collapsed. Hence, just counting the number of competitors, market by market, does not work to measure the strength of markets. It requires counts of the number of robust domestic competitors combined with the *effective* level of competition from import substitution. I will argue that it can be productive to measure the effects on crime and freedom of institutions designed to secure strong markets rather than the actual strength of markets. *State strength* confronts operationalisation problems with some similarities. The size of state budgets is useful, but misleading if much of those budgets is for subsidies to the private sector and/or corruption; likewise, with 'ghost employees' padding counts of public employees. This problem is not just about corruption. In some developing countries, large numbers of teachers are employed who infrequently turn up to teach children, especially in remote villages. More problematically still, measuring the size of the welfare state by the number of welfare bureaucrats can be misleading because states might improve the efficiency of getting welfare support to people by cutting the number of state officials so more of the cash goes into the pockets of the poor. The strength of civil society can be usefully measured by counts of the number of nongovernmental organisations (NGOs), but in most societies, it is not possible to know which NGOs have four members and which have 4,000 or 4 million. Peacebuilding Compared (available at: johnbraithwaite.com) aims to include such counts to operationalise *civil society strength*, but also codes dozens of other variables that include the Freedom House political pluralism and political participation indices, the number of journalists imprisoned, the capacity of civil society organisations, codes of Ackerman and Kruger's measures of organisational strength, access to critical resources, the strength of domestic networking and international networking in civil society with horizontal integration and vertical integration coded separately, various gender inequality and gender rights activism rankings, 'Were women's NGOs important peacebuilders?', 'Were religious leaders prominent in peacebuilding?', the frequency of a variety of civil society tactics of mobilisation including protests, strikes, boycotts, political engagement indices that measure inputs like the percentage of citizens voicing opinions to public officials, and diaspora support for marginalised ethnic minorities.

Tempering power implies a mutually constitutive approach to each of these arenas. When criminologists bring the state back in with a broader lens than simply the state as punisher, we see the importance of states in providing, redistributing and steering. States bake cakes, slice them and regulate processes of baking and slicing. This is a social democratic and republican vision of the low-crime, high-freedom state intended to unsettle neoliberal orthodoxies. When states become criminalised, many institutions can unravel; anomie cascades and so does the risk of catastrophic violence.

Following Martin Krygier (2017, 2019), Chapter 8 conceives of tempering capital as akin to tempering steel. It alloys steel with other elements that not only make the steel stronger, but also render the alloyed metals more resilient. The ideal for a low-crime society advanced in Chapter 8 is one that has strong financial markets, strong human capital, strong social capital, strong recovery capital and strong restorative capital, with each deploying its strengths to cover the weaknesses of the others. No form of capital is capable of totally dominating the society in this social democratic and republican vision. Chapter 8 moves on to put into this mix strong states checking the power of strong markets, strong civil societies and strong individuals constituted by strong human capital formation. States cultivate low-crime societies when they are strong on providing (for example, public housing), redistributing (for example, tax, minimum wage laws) and regulating (for example, antitrust, anticorruption and environmental law, regulation of the state by regulators inside the state itself).

Two centuries ago, when crime rates were much higher and economies much weaker, states had quite feeble capabilities. For today's advanced economies, the government share of national expenditure in 1870 was still only 11 per cent. This had almost doubled half a century later, and then doubled again in the half-century after that to hit 40 per cent by the 1970s. It has risen only moderately as a percentage during the most recent half-century, even if hugely in absolute spending capacity, but with high variation between government shares: 36 per cent in the United States in 2019 and even lower in some other liberal economies and 55–60 per cent in more social democratic economies like Sweden (Rodrik 2011: 17) and France in 2019 (OECD 2019). A combination of shifts from neoliberalism to authoritarian capitalism and the Covid-19 crisis saw the global average for government expenditure increase sharply in 2020—for example, to 44 per cent in the United States and 63 per cent in France and Belgium.

Chapter 9 discusses how to make punishment effective by checking it with other institutions to the point where it is rarely used, where it is minimally sufficient for crime prevention and domination prevention. Minimally sufficient punishment that is dynamic and buttressed by dynamically escalating social supports is the ideal. It is tempered punishment that speaks softly, firmly and fairly only after gentle persuasion has been attempted again and again. This minimally sufficient account of tempered punishment is also a restorative account of punishment (which many restorative justice theorists might not recognise or embrace).

Chapter 10 develops a different vision of incapacitation in criminology. Removing the capacity of the addicted surgeon or the recklessly administrated hospital to conduct surgery captures this alternative paradigm of incapacitation. It is quite different in institutional detail in the conceptual space it shares with imprisonment as incapacitation. The chapter argues that the most important forms of incapacitation precede yet anticipate punishment and are more fundamental to macrocriminology than punishment or deterrence.

Chapter 11 argues that crime is 100 times as bad in some police forces as in others, in some communities compared with others, some markets compared with others, some organisations, some whole societies and some periods of history compared with others, because crime is a cascade phenomenon—as are domination and anomie. Because violence cascades, war tends to cascade to crime, and vice versa. We cannot understand why some societies have such criminalised states and markets compared with others without understanding histories of warfare.

Chapter 12 concludes by discussing tempered violence and tempered domination. The freedom theory of crime argues that the pacification of all forms of violence (not just criminal violence) is critical for a low-crime society. State violence looms large here as does violence in childrearing in families, in sport and in education. The argument is that it is hard to secure a low-crime society if the state is recurrently a moral exemplar of violence, rushing into wars, assassinations, torture of 'terrorists', building brutally violent prisons and accepting capital punishment and excessive use of force by overly militarised domestic policing. It draws on Chantal Mouffe's theory of agonistic pluralism to reflect on how to struggle to transform institutions against resistance from those who benefit from the institutional order. It argues that macrocriminology must be politicised if it is to be relevant to the prevention of accelerated extinctions, and rebellion against extinction.

Sadly, the likelihood of failure in that political project of crime prevention is high. More than most criminologists, I see crime prevention and domination prevention frameworks of analysis as central to extinction prevention and extinction rebellion. Macrocriminology might surprise by making more constructive contributions towards preventing ecocide and genocide than we expect.

The research program ahead

The core conclusions of Chapter 2 are, first, that retrieving macrocriminology would improve the field so long as it does not lose the ambition of micro–meso–macro theoretical–empirical integration; second, that freedom and crime theory is a promising candidate for that project. The conclusion that a low-crime society is a marker of a good and free society can be critiqued as rosy utopianism of all good things going together. Actually, this book conceives of them as quite likely to fall apart to the point where extinction at the hands of genocidal weapons of mass destruction and ecocide will be our fate. The book does articulate an alternative politics of hope grounded in the histories of many societies that have fostered many good things to go together to create peace, low crime and freedom. Qualitative research is drawn on to reveal why and how the good things for which good political leaders have striven often have unravelled into violence and ecological catastrophe.

General theories such as the theory of freedom and crime can be valuable in explaining macro effects. They also pick out a light on the hill that defines a healthy direction for active citizens to struggle towards. Like all general theories in a complex world, it will be wrong most of the time, at least in some important respects, and in many local contexts of application where those locales confront unique historical events. Being evidence-based should not be a copout from the obligation to study local contextual variation and to listen to local voices. General theory improves when it relishes qualitative studies of the particularities it misses or distorts in interstices of specificity.

The concluding pages of Chapter 8 explain how the theory of freedom and crime might be tested against homicide rates, corruption levels and other crime variables cross-nationally. First, the hypothesis can be tested that thin liberal freedom, as captured by measures such as the Political Freedom Index, explains lower crime. Then we can add to the model measures of the legitimacy of the normative order (the variables of Chapter 3) and citizen acceptance of that order from sources such as World Bank Rule of Law indices and measures of legal cynicism. Testa et al. (2017) recently tested the effect of Rule of Law indices on cross-national homicide rates, finding that high scores significantly reduce homicide. The hypothesis here is that the addition of variables that measure the legitimacy, acceptance and understanding of the normative order should add to the explanatory power of the thin liberal model of freedom and crime. This first model and the 10 models that follow are all oriented to the measurement at the macrolevel of the institutionalisation of freedom and prevention, rather than to any measure of perceived individual freedom.

A third model adds Mertonian measures of legitimate opportunities being closed to many (Chapter 4). Chapter 8 makes a case for adding here a block of variables that includes overall inequality measured by the Gini coefficient, racial and gender inequality, state-sanctioned discrimination, poverty and infant mortality (because it is an unusually valid proxy for poverty in developing economies). This is rather than testing different forms of closed legitimate opportunities against one another to judge whether poverty is more important to explaining crime than inequality, for example.[4]

A fourth model adds Cloward and Ohlin's measures of illegitimate opportunities being open to many of the same people (Chapter 4). Measures of legitimate opportunities include the quality and inclusiveness of preschool, school, university and vocational education systems, including access to them for prisoners. Measures of illegitimate

---

4   Footnote 6 in Chapter 8 points out that some measures of inequality will have so much multicollinearity with others that it is best to form composite measures. But where correlations among different measures of domination are moderate, a preference is to enter them all as a block of variables. The deepest theoretical interest is in the coefficient for the whole block of variables. It is less in the correlations of individual measures of inequality with crime than it is with the multiple correlation of the block of inequality variables. This does not deny merit in replacing the block with each single variable, in one reanalysis after another, remaining open to some facets of inequality proving more empirically important than others. Extant research suggests these facets will be quite different for explaining crime than for explaining war, though some, like gender inequality, may be equally important to both.

opportunities include the comparative size of underground economies (such as drug markets and cash flows that cannot be accounted for in the legitimate economy). Chapter 8 argues that the size of dark markets may also be a measure of crime that feeds back to explain other types of crime that it does not measure.

To the measures of human capital in the previous model, a fifth model can add measures of the strength of social capital (including recovery capital and restorative capital) (Chapter 5). In other words, this fifth model adds a block of social capital variables.

A sixth model adds measures of the strength of the state, of markets (especially markets in crime prevention and domination prevention), of civil society and of individual autonomy (Chapter 7). Some institutions of civil society are more important than others according to the theory. For example, a strong women's movement is particularly important to crime reduction and domination reduction.

A seventh model adds measures of how strong more specific institutions are—such as families and the education, health and welfare systems that are identified by the insights of institutional anomie theory (Messner and Rosenfeld 2013) (Chapter 8). Social housing is an example of a particular facet of welfare institutions that is identified as particularly strategic for domination reduction and crime reduction in the freedom theory of this book.

An eighth model adds a block of variables that go to how richly separated are the separations of powers (Chapters 6 and 8). It seeks to rise to the difficult challenge of measuring contestation among different forms of capital and different kinds of institutions, picking up a variety of measures of checks and balances. While as basic an institution of freedom as the holding of elections is captured by the Political Freedom Index in Model 3, checks on this by institutionalising a politically independent electoral commission are a facet of Model 8. This is a test of the hypothesis that there will be less crime when all forms of power are tempered by other forms of power (Chapters 7 and 8). The strength of business regulatory institutions is an important addition in this eighth model.

A ninth model adds measures of the pacification of noncriminal forms of violence (frequency of participation in wars, physical punishment in schools, torture and corporal punishment in the criminal justice system itself and other forms of violent state crime, brutality of the prison system, the popularity of violent sports) (Chapters 7 and 11). Or it might consider these variables separately.

A tenth model would measure the strength of social movements for nonviolence in societies, the depth of sophistication of the institutionalisation of political strategies of nonviolence and the cascading of nonviolence—matters the Peacebuilding Compared project is particularly well designed to capture (Braithwaite and D'Costa 2018).

Each of the foregoing 10 models, according to the theory of freedom and crime, will explain more variance than the model that precedes it. They should explain according to the theory not only variation between societies in levels of homicide, robbery or burglary, but also levels of corruption, tax compliance and environmental stewardship cross-nationally. The challenge of measuring crimes of the powerful meaningfully remains daunting, but it must be tackled creatively where it can.

The theory hypothesises that an eleventh model will not add significant variance in explaining either crimes of the powerful or crimes of the powerless. This involves adding a composite measure of the punitiveness of the justice system for each country (the most important measures being the imprisonment rate and the frequency of executions) (Chapter 9). The theory of freedom and crime stipulates monitoring whether tougher deterrence is necessary for crime prevention. If the outcome is that societies with modest levels of punishment do not have higher crime rates then this is important validation of the hypothesis that freedom for offenders and their families can be enhanced by lower levels of punishment without jeopardising the freedoms of crime victims, present and future.

Of course, the real world of developing, elaborating and testing theory is more iteratively responsive to emergent pattens and clusters of variables in data than any predetermined sequence of 11 models. The hope is to complete the Peacebuilding Compared data collection by 2030. Data gathering has been under way since 2004 and includes the demands of fieldwork on the ground by me and others in each locale that has experienced a war. In 2030, the plan is to undertake the foregoing kind of stepwise analysis of Peacebuilding Compared. It will study war zones and war and crime recurrence, in preference to whole societies. Other datasets can grapple with similar kinds of analyses that would in some way be superior to a completed Peacebuilding Compared dataset, and in other ways inferior, especially on the war-related variables that are unusually important in this book.

The next few chapters turn away from the quantitative work Peacebuilding Compared will undertake to test these 11 models. Peacebuilding Compared and the macrocriminology of this book are both fundamentally dependent on qualitative work that connects events in very local spaces to global spaces, and historical work that is both fine-grained in its focus on critical junctures and of wide sweep across the entire history of the planet.

Chapter 12 draws on the scholarship of Chantal Mouffe to reflect on what kind of agonistic pluralist politics is required to struggle against existing hegemonic formations that would defend the status quo against the kind of transformations proposed to expand freedom and reduce crime. The conclusion describes the kind of society for which criminologists might struggle if further research supports the theory of freedom and crime. It would require minimally sufficient deterrence and maximum social support for relational prevention. It would require defence of a thick republican conception of freedom that takes domination more seriously than is the case in existing societies, while joining hands to a degree with those who would only go so far as to defend thin liberal freedom.

The theory of freedom and crime would require a global institutional imagination against the resistance of capital to build strong welfare states, strong labour rights, human rights and redistributive tax policies. It would give crimes of domination greater prominence in the normative order over crimes of the dominated, especially war crimes, environmental crimes and crimes of capitalism that risk the collapse of liberal forms of capitalism into the tentacles of authoritarian capitalism. The struggle for nonviolence, AMP (Awareness, Motivation and Pathways) away from cascades of violence, peacemaking and preventive diplomacy would be crime-prevention priorities (Honig et al. 2015). The theory of freedom and crime requires greater investment in building strong individuals and strong civil society through community development for collective efficacy, youth development circles and restorative justice that forms democratic citizens in families, schools and workplaces to ripple out social capital and CHIME (Connectedness, Hope, Identity, Meaning and Empowerment). According to the freedom theory of crime, relational restorative justice values that emphasise healing and love build more freedom and less crime than punitive thought about justice.

This is a lot for criminologists to be concerned about. It conceives of criminologists as having a heavy burden as stewards of their field. Criminologists are students and custodians of freedom and of the canary in capitalism's coalmine. Crime and punishment are that canary; compliance with legitimate, freedom-enhancing laws is a sign of that canary's health. Crimes of the dominated and crimes of domination—especially those that might trigger cascades from capitalism to despotism, from capitalism to ecological collapse, to accidental nuclear war, to intentional wars with killer robots and chemical weapons—are fates that macrocriminology might help our fragile planet to escape. By responding to that challenge, we might contribute to the survival of humankind. Let us be pessimistic and assume that the analysis in this book has but a few grains of truth. Even then, criminologists have redemptive responsibilities to attempt more meaningful macrocriminologies to add a few more grains. Then they might act on them towards a freer, safer humanity that struggles with fewer extinction threats.

2

Reframing criminology

Key propositions

- Crime control is fundamental to the constitution of freedom.
- Freedom strengthens crime control.
- Thin liberal freedom helps, but is brittle compared with thick republican freedom.
- It is freedom as nondomination that holds a key to crime control. Nondomination means the tempering of arbitrary power over others.
- Freedom from patriarchy, poverty and state and corporate tyrannies is central to nondomination.
- Freedom tempers power, making power less brittle and more responsive to justice in tackling challenges like crime.
- Macrocriminology demands a methodological pluralism of micro–meso–macro explanation that transcends methodological individualism.
- Macrocriminology reveals more when it integrates explanatory and normative theory.
- Macrocriminology reframes the referent beyond individual offenders to integrated explanation of criminalised markets, criminalised states, criminalised norms, criminal organisations, criminalised spaces–times–life-courses and macro-historical trajectories.
- The book argues for a macrocriminology that asks not only how to treat individuals, markets, states and civil society to prevent crime, but also how to be responsive to them to increase freedom and prevent domination.

- Therefore, the best solutions to crime problems are not found in the justice system. The most cost-effective solutions to crime are cost-effective partly because they help solve other deep problems like health disadvantage, suicide and environmental collapse.

Reframing crime and freedom

This chapter sets a conceptual framework for the book of broadening the relevance of criminology and mapping a bigger vision for future criminologists. It considers the above list of propositions in turn, starting with the proposition that crime control is fundamental to freedom and the wider ambition of the book to reveal something about how to realise freedom. The work can be described as a macrocriminology of freedom because it argues for a deeply structured compatibility between crime control and freedom, at least with respect to predatory crime. Societies structured and enculturated for the freedom of all citizens from domination by others tend to be low-crime societies. And societies with low levels of predatory crime are freer by virtue of that low crime rate. So, the book lays foundations for a freedom theory of crime and a criminological theory of freedom. It makes a normative case that decent crime-control policies increase freedom; bad criminal justice is a more fundamental threat to freedom than most citizens and political theorists realise. Tempering power is a key concept (Krygier 2017, 2019). Societies that temper power, it is argued, enjoy freedom, including freedom from the domination that is crime. This therefore is a book about how to weave webs to temper dangerous societies and enable liberation. Along the book's journey, it also weaves together a fresh interpretation of well-established findings about the character of crime.

The conceptualisation of freedom required for a macrocriminology that does heavy lifting is not the brittle freedom of neoliberalism. Rather, it is a thick version of civic republican freedom. It is freedom as nondomination (Pettit 1997), where citizens are freed from arbitrary impositions of power by the wise tempering of it. Nondomination also implies equality of prospects for liberty (Pettit 2012, 2014); it implies justice of a holistic kind that embraces restorative justice, procedural justice, distributive justice, justice as identity, racial justice and gender justice, among others. If all this seems difficult to grasp, think of the republican conception of thick freedom as incorporating, by definition, the ideals of *liberté, égalité* and feminist *fraternité*. Then you have the spirit of the basic idea.

Braithwaite and Pettit (2000) argue that a concept like domination that makes for a good normative theory of how to respond to crime has prospects of delivering a helpful explanatory theory of crime. That is, the methodological project of focusing on concepts that allow for the integration of explanatory and normative theory creates new insights about how to improve both explanatory and normative theory. If a normative ideal like nondomination is of sufficient importance and attraction to command wide allegiance, this may be because citizens can see ways that it is intimately related to concerns and capacities in their own actions and lives. If a normative ideal has a practical resonance of this kind, it might point us towards a way of explaining things that people do and the institutional patterns they create. It points us towards a useful explanatory category. If this thought is correct, any normative proposal should be subjected to the test of seeing whether it points us towards a plausible explanatory category. Indeed, if the thought is correct, equally, any explanatory category should be subjected to the corresponding test of seeing whether it directs us towards a plausible normative ideal—an ideal that people can be brought, on reflection, to find attractive.

If an ideal or category proves persuasive on both normative and explanatory fronts, it may be equipped to serve in both roles to support a political vision and transformed institutional arrangements. It will provide a basis on which to argue that such an arrangement is attractive, and it will serve at the same time to show us why the arrangement can work satisfactorily. This philosophy on integrating normative and explanatory theory is what led Braithwaite and Pettit (2000) to select domination as an explanation of crime and nondomination as a desideratum for a low-crime, low-punishment society. More modestly, their philosophy of method commends mutual adjustment between normative and explanatory categories of analysis. This proves in this book to be fertile for improving both explanatory and normative theory. To put the case negatively, any normative theory that works with an ideal category that lacks an explanatory resonance is likely to be utopian and will serve policymaking badly. Any explanatory theory that fails to connect with a normative concern risks being dangerously unguided. Chapter 9 argues that not all deterrence theory, but classical deterrence theory, is an example of a dangerous explanatory theory of this kind in its scientific, judicial and political enactments. Normative theory without explanatory theory can be empty; explanatory theory without normative theory can be blind— often dangerously so in criminology. This matters because criminology is of consequence. It is inherently a dangerous game.

The next section makes these abstractions concrete by taking crime and freedom tours to Cold War Moscow, Beijing and Washington. The following section considers why criminology must be a bird with two wings that takes the methods of both micro and macrocriminologies seriously, along with a large fuselage of meso-criminological tissue to connect them. While this sensibility is important, little depends on a clear definition of what distinguishes the micro, meso and macro. I conceive of microcriminology as being about individuals, their interactions and life-courses, or an even more micro-focus on genes or other facets of individual biology. I conceive macrocriminology as being about institutions, whole societies and international society. Meso-criminology is about a wide diversity of types of connecting tissue in between: the criminology of place and of organisational life are two kinds of meso-criminological connecting tissue that loom large in this book. The penultimate section of the chapter rejects abolitionism, finding virtue in crime as a social science topic and as a normative focus. Yet it dismisses the idea of criminology as a discipline. Finally, the chapter reframes macrocriminology's referent to see importance in the study of the criminalisation of organisations, markets, states, places, life-courses and historical eras.

Crime and freedom in Moscow, Beijing and Washington

Safe streets in Beijing and Moscow

During the Cold War, the Soviet and Chinese communist parties invited countless western leftists on study tours. They were not taken to see the ugly side of communist society. One virtue they would report back from China's communist utopia was the low crime rate. They returned to describe Chinese cities where people left their homes unlocked. This was a story that had validity for the China of the 1950s and 1960s. It was no longer true by the 1990s, when common property crime had become more widespread (Bakken 1993). The homicide rate had also gone up by the 1990s; however, it fell sharply again, according to UNODC figures, from 2.3 per 100,000 in 1996 to 0.6 in the three most recent years. There was more than a grain of truth to the low-crime narrative even in the Soviet Union in the immediate postwar decades.

China had a crime-control method based on a Communist Party–led system of enforced collective efficacy (Dutton 1992). Households were required to monitor the behaviour of households to their left, their right, the front and behind, so every household was monitored by four others. Citizens participated in local people's mediation committees. This allowed civil society to catch sight of itself and act with collective efficacy to solve the problems it saw. Reports of what was seen and mediated for a cluster of households also went to household inspectors, who were eyes for the state, allowing the state to act and 'see like a state' (Scott 1998). This had elements in common with Sampson et al.'s (1997) freely chosen collective efficacy that has been shown to reduce crime in western cities (Weisburd et al. 2021). But this was enforced collective efficacy that was entrenched authoritarianism. China has long had the most scaled-up—though hardly the best—collective efficacy programs for crime control. China has also long had the most scaled-up—but not the best—restorative justice programs in the world. People's mediation committees, police station mediation, prosecutor mediation and judicial mediation in China all embrace many central features of restorative justice, including relational victim empowerment, stakeholder empowerment, compensation, reconciliation, apology, forgiveness and reintegration. Often, however, this is also stigmatising and pursues agendas of state domination and 'harmony' infused with political quiescence, as opposed to freedom-enhancing restorative justice (Zhang 2021b; Pei 2016; Trevaskes 2009). Chinese restorative justice seems, however, to be helping to reduce imprisonment in China in a way it is not helping in the West (Zhang and Xia 2021).

Especially since the 2012 criminal reconciliation law reforms, China undoubtedly has the largest restorative justice program in the world (Braithwaite and Zhang 2017). Yet no national program of restorative justice is more disconnected from a social movement for restorative justice in civil society that can temper state domination—tempering that might have been advanced through a restorative movement and its collective efficacy. Contemporary Chinese evidence continues to indicate that voluntary individual gestures of collective efficacy, as captured by a standard western measure of collective efficacy, do not explain which Chinese communities have the lowest crime rates (Messner et al. 2017), but community solidarity does. Participation rates in *tiao-jie* (local people's mediation), *bang-jiao* (supportive community reintegration committees for offenders, when released from prison, for example) and neighbourhood watch organised by neighbourhood committees of citizens still explain lower crime rates (Messner et al. 2017). Hong Lu (1999) and Yan Zhang (2021a) conceive of *tiao-ji* and *bang-jiao* as Chinese forms of restorative justice that pre-dated the western invention of the concept.

How did the Washington commentariat react to this claim for the superiority of communism? During the Cold War, Americans worried about rising crime rates. America was filling overflowing prisons from Richard Nixon's law and order presidency and his hot War on Drugs. Americans looked across to a China that had its drug addiction problem largely under control. What a contrast with the early 1900s, when anomic China had levels of opiate addiction many times greater than any society had seen before or since. The communists were getting something right— or so it seemed in the eyes of their admirers. The Chinese communists even had an analysis that was fundamentally right about why it had such a massive drug problem in the first half of the twentieth century and such a small one in second half. Capitalist commercial exploitation through sophisticated marketing to addicts networked through opium dens orchestrated by the British East India Company delivered China's (and the world's) opiate pandemic. Communism ended this colonial legacy.

Social democracy and freedom

A widespread narrative of American Cold War commentators was that a high crime rate was the price of freedom. In a society in which people have wide freedoms to think and act however they like, many are bound to choose the lure of a life of crime. This had a ring of plausibility. Yet this book argues that the reverse was and is the case. It seeks to build a theory of freedom and crime. A core claim of the theory is that high levels of freedom are key ingredients for low-crime societies. This was not an armchair conclusion. Throughout the 1970s, I worked on the relationship between inequality and crime, which led to my 1979 book, *Inequality, Crime and Public Policy*. It made a more complex and variegated case than previous work for the proposition that reducing inequality and reducing domination can help reduce crime. It also found that being a disadvantaged person and living in a disadvantaged community had a multiplicative rather than an additive impact on crime.

Braithwaite and Braithwaite (1980) followed up with the impact on homicide rates cross-nationally of years of incumbency of social democratic parties in parliaments. It also tested the percentage of gross national product spent on social security. Yes, it turned out that when the kind of social democratic parties that existed before the 1980s had higher numbers of years in the corridors of power, homicide was lower in those polities. And homicide was lower when social security expenditure was higher. It was also true that the movement to Thatcherism from the social democracy of Harold Wilson, James Callaghan and Barbara Castle accelerated the rise of crime and punishment from the year our research was published (Farrall et al. 2020). This we interpreted in terms of the redistributive and welfare-state–building policies of social democratic parties of the postwar era. That interpretation may be less plausible today in the aftermath of the long incumbencies of post-Thatcher leaders of the likes of Tony Blair in the United Kingdom and Bill Clinton and Barack Obama in the United States, even though their years in power were periods of declining crime in both countries. Some might claim that these leaders were social democrats, yet they were more concerned with cultivating the interests of business elites than with building stronger, more redistributive welfare states.

Obama's 2007–08 presidential campaigning at first explicitly promised a Green New Deal, but in the end his presidency had more in common with Clinton and Blair than with Franklin D. Roosevelt or Clement Attlee. After a helpful embrace of Keynesian pump-priming during the 2008 Global Financial Crisis, western states quickly, excessively, retreated to austerity. Margaret Thatcher had succeeded in capturing the souls of social democrats with the catchcry to her acolytes that 'economics are the method: the object is to change the soul' (to acquisitive, commodified souls) (Reiner 2020: 2). The West returned in 2009 to what Robert Reiner (2020) describes as the poor-growth and poor-equality outcomes of the post–social democratic era of neoliberal ideology that followed the three decades of welfare state growth and economic growth. This growth during social democracy's heyday was twice as high from the end of World War II compared with the neoliberal decades that followed. It is hard to overstate the profundity of the shift from growth for the waged and welfare sectors to the decline in their share, and super-growth for the profit share, in the hands of the super-rich since 1975.

For the period 1901–98, however, it is not surprising that Page et al. (2002) also found an association between years of social democratic incumbency and lowered suicide rates, and between conservative governments being in power and elevated suicide rates. Female suicide rates were no less than 40 per cent higher in twentieth-century Australia when national and state governments were both conservative rather than social democratic. Shaw et al. (2002) produced remarkably similar results for England and Wales, concluding that if Labour had been in power during the 45 years of Tory government during the twentieth century, there would have been 35,000 fewer suicides that century. I do not contend that these crime and suicide effects are as important as physical health effects; I conjecture that more than 35,000 lives would have been saved in 2020 had a social democratic administration with a strong public health system been in power in the United States instead of Donald Trump, who was a hollower of the public health state. I do not suggest that crime and suicide reduction are the most important reason for being an old-fashioned social democrat who builds public housing and welfare states. They are good extra reasons for being one.

Forty years on, I am not certain why we did it, but Braithwaite and Braithwaite (1980) also put the Political Freedom Index into that regression. To our surprise, the correlation between freedom and homicide cross-nationally was –0.7. Perhaps our thinking was this would be a proxy for a competing liberal approach to politics to test against the social democracy effect. It turned out that social democracy, economic equality and political freedom were all associated with lower homicide rates. These empirical findings were the inductive seeds that began to grow this book in 1980. More recent analyses have supported an association between political freedom and lower homicide rates (Stringham and Levendis 2010; Stamatel 2016). Morris and LaFree (2016) report more mixed results on the relationship between political freedom and terrorism, with at least one study showing more politically free societies are more likely to be targeted by terrorist attacks (Kis-Katos et al. 2014). Others show that societies with high levels of political freedom have a lower incidence of terrorism (Kurrild-Klitgaard et al. 2006; Krueger and Malečková 2003; Dreher and Fischer 2011; Elbakidze and Jin 2012; Fleming et al. 2020). My theory is that the latter account may prevail as more data come in. But it argues that the important explanatory power of freedom, properly conceived, is more macro. This is that freedom can reduce the criminalisation of states and the criminalisation of markets.

A central argument of the theory of freedom and crime advanced here is that thin liberal freedom of the kind we measured in 1980 helps reduce crime, quite contrary to the claims of Cold War pundits that crime was a price of freedom. Furthermore, thicker, republican freedom conceived of as freedom from domination (Braithwaite and Pettit 1990; Pettit 1997) reduces crime even more strongly. Key elements of that thicker republican freedom are a legitimate normative order that is respected by citizens as securing them from domination; a strong welfare state, labour laws and redistributive tax policies that secure the poor against domination by the rich; and strong, plural, inclusive institutions that temper the power of other institutions in a robust separation of powers. It is argued that the good society is a low-crime society because it is a republic of strong individuals, strong families, strong civil society, strong communities, strong financial capital, strong human capital, strong social capital, strong recovery capital and strong restorative capital, where each of these forms of capital tempers the others. 'Tempered' here evokes the metaphor of tempered steel (Krygier 2017, 2019). Tempered steel is more supple, yet stronger and less brittle, for realising its purposes; it is resilient and responsive. The tempering of institutions means mutually checking other institutions against being brittle and corrosive, enabling them to be stronger at playing their part in the project of freedom in the republic. Tempering also means checking that they do not dominate citizens. And it means that they temper other institutions, enabling rather than crushing them.

Dark figures of communist crime

The reader will wonder where this leads us with reimagining the old communist parties? They did not pursue republican power. Soviet and Chinese communist parties opted for untrammelled power to crush all other institutions. The crime-control accomplishments on the surface of the old Communist Party regimes were not totally false, yet they were substantially an illusion. At the very least, the accomplishment was not resilient. If we force people to spy on their neighbours so they can be sent to prison-like re-education camps, as soon as we lift that tyranny, the people will have the opposite of collective efficacy. That is a neglected reason why China poses a profound risk to the world from a renewed surge of terrorism as a result of its current policies of interring and 're-educating' a million Muslim Uyghurs in Xinxiang Province. As soon as they escape across the border, they are more likely to become terrorists than harmoniously integrated Chinese citizens. Many have fought in Afghanistan and beyond. The biggest criminality is the initiation of this cycle by the mass enslavement and deprivation of the human rights of an entire ethnic group.

Social psychology experiments show that while laissez faire leads to disorder in classrooms, when order is enforced by authoritarian tyranny, as soon as the tyranny is lifted by the teacher leaving the room, disorder breaks out. An authoritative order that respectfully nurtures children, in which children choose to grant legitimacy to teachers or parents, delivers superior learning and more considerate behaviour than both laissez faire and authoritarian social control (Pinquart 2017). Reinterpreted in the theoretical frame of this book, the laissez-faire teacher exercises an order of thin liberalism; the authoritarian leader exercises a regime of untempered power; the authoritative teacher exercises tempered relational power that is nondomination.

The illusion of communist order was worse than an appearance of order that lacked resilience; it was disorder beneath the surface. The crushing of market institutions meant black markets were rife. Shadow economies and mafias thrived to protect these underground illicit markets (Karstedt 2003; Łoś 1990; Rose 1998). Such mafias could only survive because they enjoyed the protection of party apparatchiks who grew wealthy on their share of black-market profits. The daily thievery by communist workers from their own factories of things they had paid the mafia man or the party official to be allowed to steal actually created a society of thieves in the black markets tolerated by party bosses (Berliner 1957; Lampert 1984). None of this kind of thievery was recorded in the crime statistics. The mafias also had a licence to 'disappear' people who dared to encroach too successfully on party-sanctioned black markets. Paradoxically, in *Crime and the American Dream*, Messner and Rosenfeld (2013: 3) evocatively make this same point about how the hidden property crime of American black markets causes disputes to be resolved by violent means:

> The disputes arise from economic problems that are quite conventional in origin (faulty or fraudulent merchandise, payments overdue, bad debts, common thefts). However, none of these problems or the resulting disputes can be settled through conventional (i.e. legal) means, because they all involve illegal activities. Because access to conventional dispute-resolution mechanisms (lawyers, courts, legally imposed restitution, fines, etc) is blocked in these cases, their resolution requires the innovative use of unconventional means.

This is why there is a strong relationship between the size of shadow economies and high homicide rates (that occur in the shadows) (Tuttle 2019). Communist-era official homicide rates were comparatively low, until 1960 at least, but mafia disappearances and state murders were rarely counted in these official statistics. Party-tolerated mafia killings were unremarkable because they melted into the deeper reality that these regimes were murder machines, especially during the long reigns of Joseph Stalin (Rosefielde 1996) and Mao Zedong (Bianco 2016). The state itself disappeared millions of citizens of the Soviet and Chinese regimes; these millions of murders did not push up the official homicide rate. This must be combined with the state corruption and embezzlement that were rife in communist regimes. The theory of crime and freedom interprets this iceberg of crime below the surface as a result of unchecked party domination. Likewise, when capitalist societies are decimated by high rates of organised crime, this can be understood in terms of unchecked political machines on the take to protect mafias, shadow states (Reno 1995), deep states (Filiu 2015), crony capitalism (Haber 2013) or booty capitalism (Hutchcroft 1998). In sum, authoritarian control looks good because it can be potent in controlling crime that stands above the surface; but authoritative republican control is better at regulating crime by people with the power to keep their crime underground.

Communist domination; communist nondomination

The theory of crime and freedom is a general theory and a macro-theory. Yet erroneous narratives of Cold War commentators that high US crime rates were the price of freedom must also cause pause to caution that macro-theory of the national level is not everything. It is also important to diagnose particular societies, and particular bits of them, to learn particularistic lessons about the roots of crime. It has already been contended that there were grains of truth to the idea that communist societies were low-crime societies. We also must have the particularistic flexibility in our analyses to see the character of those grains of truth. Criminology during the Cold War was bad at recognising those truths and still is. Russians in Stalin's time, Yugoslavs in Josip Tito's, Cuba under Fidel Castro from the late 1950s to the late 1980s—all enjoyed full employment, for women as well as men. No-one needed to steal because of unemployment; everyone could get a job that paid at a rate comparable with the earnings of the majority of the population. Homelessness was abolished by government-guaranteed access to public housing. Women enjoyed more equality under Cold War communism than women in capitalist societies: more women were employed and more women were in senior political positions than in the West (Braithwaite 2017a). While inequality has widened hugely in contemporary China, the Communist

Party does remain highly committed to reducing extreme poverty, and no regime in human history has had more success at this; none has lifted larger numbers of people out of extreme poverty.

In addition, as mentioned above, there was an enforced collective efficacy that maintained a communist order on the streets. In China, people's mediation committees were often dominating agents of party tyranny, but they also had their crime-control strengths. *Bang-jiao* committees had a mandate to rehabilitate and reintegrate the wayward (Lu 1999; Messner et al. 2017; Zhang 2021a), so they did have capabilities in terms of the recovery capital and restorative capital that we discuss as being helpful to crime control in Chapter 7. Lu's (1999) research showed that citizens on local mediation committees often mobilised collective efficacy with kindness, care and reintegration. On the side of freedom, they played important roles in freeing communist societies from the tyrannies of local gangs of drug dealers. Against freedom, the tyranny of the majority in the people's courts in Cuba persecuted LGBTIQ people in the 1960s. Castro apologised for this long before he died (Crary 2014). In other words, as with western courts, to be balanced, we need to be able to see their effects in both increasing and suppressing freedom.

Women were empowered by the people's courts and by many other institutions in communist societies, especially in the Maoist people's courts of Nepal (Braithwaite and D'Costa 2018). In Cuba, 49 per cent of seats in the national legislature were held by women during the past decade—a higher proportion than for all western capitalist societies, according to the World Bank (2016). Between the two waves of the western narrative of feminism, both Soviet and Maoist communism were doing more to equalise educational, workplace, judicial and participatory rights for men and women than the West. After second-wave feminism, the West pulled ahead in certain ways. Yet that depends on where one looks. Communist women even came to break through capitalist glass ceilings more than women from the capitalist world: by 2011, half of the 14 billionaires on the *Forbes* list of the world's richest self-made women were from mainland China.[1] The theory of freedom and crime argues that

---

1   That remained the case in the 2016 ranking: the two richest women were mainland Chinese, with a big gap having opened between them and better-known western entries like Oprah Winfrey and Giuliana Benetton. This gap exists because the Chinese accomplishments were in core capitalist industries like information technology, as opposed to accomplishments in entertainment and fashion among some western entries (Forbes 2016). In 2020, however, Chinese women were driven down the list, with Alice Walton's Walmart holdings, Françoise Bettencourt Meyers' L'Oréal empire and MacKenzie Scott's Amazon Holdings taking the top three places. Only two Chinese women were in the top 10 for 2020—still exceeding China's share of the world economy.

gender equality is one of the forms of nondomination that helps build both freedom and low crime rates. The most fertile forms of micro–macro criminology manage to see particularities of strength among the structural weaknesses of communism, or any political system.

Communist societies, especially in Eastern Europe in the 1960s and 1970s, were ahead of the West in putting a price on carbon and other pollutants to protect the environment (Anderson et al. 1977: 40; Sand 1973; Johnson and Brown 1976: 151; Irwin and Liroff 1974: 113). Management and worker committees had responsibilities for monitoring, measuring and reporting levels of effluent from their factories' pipes and chimneys and, as they reduced them, the tax payments of the firm that paid them went down. Therefore, indirectly, employees' pay-packets went up when their plants polluted less. It would not be until this century that the West followed these environmental crime-control lessons from communist societies by putting taxes on carbon, albeit feeble ones. Communist societies did not do a good job of getting the detailed institutional design right for pricing the pollution that spewed out of control from late-socialist factories. Nor have capitalist societies yet done so. China today is at the same time the worst emitter of carbon and the biggest investor in renewable alternatives to carbon—and is still ahead of the United States in taxing carbon (Drahos 2021). Capitalist and socialist societies alike were slow to realise that freedom from gender domination and freedom from the collapse of ecosystems were important freedoms. Yet in some ways socialist thinkers were quicker with this realisation, as we see with Friedrich Engels (2010) on women's rights and Karl Marx on commodity fetishism and estranged labour as alienating human beings from nature (Ziegler 1990: 9–11).

Macrocriminologists can learn from the history of communism how to look more deeply to see the excesses of crime in a 'low-crime society' and the seeds of emergent understandings of freedom in an unfree society. As we learn to see a deeply structured relationship between unfreedom (domination) and crime, we must also learn to be more nuanced in seeing complex, paradoxical, societal particularities of crime and of freedom.

At the same time, we must see that communism was not a beautiful theory that when implemented corroded to ugly practices. Marxism was always an ugly theory because it did not take freedom seriously, nor did it empower individuals seriously or empower civil society to check the abuses of the party. It did not take seriously the separated powers and independent rule-of-law institutions that are at the heart of the theory of crime and freedom. All communisms came to realise that markets could do some things a lot better than the state, but because communism lacked the separated powers of vibrant market regulatory institutions, the dominations of markets in communist societies involved worse excesses than in neoliberal societies. Communist markets commodified and captured souls to acquisitiveness in societies like China to a level that did Margaret Thatcher proud—even more so than in Britain, according to data discussed in future chapters.

Criminologists from the rest of the planet like to demonise capitalist America and communist China as unfree and criminogenic, tolerant of abuses of the rights of the marginalised. Yet if we look at where their strengths have resided in expanding markets in virtue, in poverty reduction and the expansion of collective efficacy for freedom, various examples of those strengths are to be found as well, and in fact are huge. This book provides the tools to diagnose the contexts in which these societies destroy freedom and where they expand it. For readers who believe in America or believe in China, you can be sure that you will be defeated by the other great geopolitical adversary if you are unable to see their strengths, and if you are unable to cooperate with them on projects that expand those strengths to create a freer, less-criminalised world system (as Chapter 12 concludes). Influenced by the thinking of Ali Wardak since the time he was a PhD student, I have been arguing since 1989 that there is so much to learn from Afghanistan about domination and nondomination, and about how to prevent crime and war (as discussed in later chapters). I wish I had been clever enough in 1989 to say that if the West is unable to see Afghanistan's strengths and to learn how to cooperate to help expand those strengths, the combined military might of the North Atlantic Treaty Organization (NATO) is as capable of defeat as the Soviet Union in a protracted war in Afghanistan. By 2001, the western will to war in Afghanistan was too strong for that view to be given a good hearing even in good US universities. Worse, the West had learnt nothing from its failure to invest in Afghanistan after the fall of communism in the way it did invest after the collapse of European communism.

Macrocriminology tempers normal science

All fields of study benefit from a macro lens that is wider than its normal science. In history, it is the historiography of the *longue durée* complemented by archaeology that takes us to a wider imagination of ourselves. Macroeconomics is the study of aggregate economies in interaction with the political economy of world systems, as opposed to microeconomics, which is the study of bits of domestic economies (particular firms or markets), and behavioural economics, which is the study of individuals' economic behaviour. Macroeconomics comprehends whole economies and economic systems, aggregated economy-wide phenomena such as changes in employment, national income and inflation, not to mention crashes of global economies occasioned by the collapse of earth systems. Criminology has never really had a Keynesian moment. Keynes in his general theory positioned macroeconomics as central and concentrated the minds of policymakers on the institutions needed (the New Deal) to prevent another crisis like that of 1929 when a herd of 'animal spirits' cascaded off a cliff (Keynes 2018).

The usage of macrocriminology herein is similar in that it involves a shift to aggregated patterns of crime, putting particular emphasis on the shift away from simply understanding why some kinds of individuals are more likely to commit crime (microcriminology's preoccupation), or why particular neighbourhoods might have more crime, or why particular situational crime-prevention techniques might work (examples of meso-criminology). This conception of macrocriminology also has much in common with macrosociology, as the study of large-scale social systems, long-term patterns and societal processes.

In 2018, 15 of the most distinguished development economists wrote an open letter (Alkire et al. 2018). They included Nobel Laureates and chief economists from national development agencies. The letter argued that relying on randomised controlled trials to guide aid spending will lead to short-term, superficial and misplaced policies that miss the macro-imperatives. Their concern was that randomistas were shifting development economics excessively towards the micro-interventions of behavioural economics, and nudges in preference to structural shifts. Randomised controlled trials were expensive; the integrity of randomisation and measurement error runs deep in data collection in developing countries.

For example, when ethnic violence, civil war or gang violence breaks out in a village, the randomista abandons data collection partway through, compromising the randomisation, or moves on to collect data from the next peaceful village, compromising external validity. Systematically, researchers tend to collect data only from the villages they can access by car. The villages cut off from transport networks that are most vulnerable to violence and poverty are ignored. In contrast, for qualitative researchers of peacebuilding, such hotspot villages are not ignored; indeed, they are attractors for qualitative researchers with a macro-imagination.

A problem with randomised controlled trials is that they focus not only on evidence-based policy down to micro-phenomena, but also on outcomes that can be measured in the short term. In their open letter, the 15 development economists argued that the beguiling appeal of the randomistas channels development assistance away from challenges of macro and long-term importance. Testing the effects of performance bonuses to teachers is less important than reversing slashed education budgets caused by the need to pay down external debt. Testing the effects of distributing water purification tablets is too little, too micro, for the challenges of countries facing droughts induced by climate change; 'what is at stake is an emergency that demands coordinated public policy strategies' (Alkire et al. 2018: 2). With agriculture, genuine progress depends on ending the excessive subsidies paid by rich countries to large producers, regulating food commodity derivative markets and ending land grabs that 'dispossess the small-scale farmers who play vital roles in feeding the world' (Alkire et al. 2018: 2). Randomised controlled trials will not help developing countries wishing to claim a share of the tax revenue from the profits that transnational corporations make in their countries. It will not stop illegal shifting of those profits to developed economies or to tax havens to benefit wealthy western investors. Labour laws and their enforcement are required to assure a living wage to factory workers paid a pittance in poor countries when they work for western brands (Marshall 2019). So, a shift of focus is needed away from micro-projects and individualised interventions towards transformative shifts in public policy platforms.

At one level, this book argues this case for criminology. At another level, the 15 development economists got their contrast with medicine wrong. It is a false dichotomy to say that randomised controlled trials are good for medicine but a distraction from the main game of development economics. Both the micro and the macro are important and, in medicine, randomised experiments have been used to great effect to test the efficacy of treatments of individual patients. But medicine is similar to development economics in the sense that the biggest advances in human health have been about not individualised therapies but more macro-variables such as improved agricultural systems that secure communities against intermittent famine, structural reductions to tobacco consumption driven by regulation of that market, public health control of sanitation systems to guarantee clean water, sewers that separate whole human populations from their waste, regulation that keeps asbestos and multiple viruses away from our nostrils, ending wars that cut whole populations off from all medicines and all food and other macro-structural pathways to better health.

An argument of this book is that microcriminology should dispense with the claim that randomised controlled trials are the gold standard. That is a provocation to the rest of us who do bronze-medal research. Nevertheless, the work of randomistas is extremely important, even though it is hard to raise sufficient funds to do it well, because micro–macro synthesis is the foundation of the best macrocriminology. My competence has been primarily as a macrocriminologist and an ethnographic empirical researcher who deploys a pointillist ethnographic methodology to paint an ethnography of complex global systems (for example, Braithwaite and Drahos 2000; Braithwaite and D'Costa 2018). Yet at times I struggle against my comparative incompetence to do quantitative research. All macrocriminologists must take seriously the task of reviewing the evidence from quantitative criminology on everything they discuss. Yet macrocriminologists see that however hard they work at being quantitatively literate, on the broad canvas of macro-understanding there will be more holes than canvas. Methodological pluralism is imperative to painting the best canvas we can. Randomised controlled trials, historical criminology and diverse methodologies in between—all dab evocative paint on the canvas, and all have important strengths.

Crime as a research topic and an idea

Crime as a research topic is not beloved of some critical scholars. This book defends it. Many contemporary criminologists are more fundamentally interested in studying risk or punishment, for example. These are bound to be important in republican criminology. Yet one sense in which I am an old-fashioned criminologist is that I have a normatively grounded preference for crime as the central topic of our field. Some critical criminologists prefer abolitionism or replacing criminology with the study of harms. Some corporate law scholars advocate abolishing corporate criminal liability. I do advocate a preference for a domination-prevention lens over a crime-prevention lens, while still liking the crime concept and finding rich value in crime-prevention research. The short history of criminology that follows sees it as benefiting little from the contest of other social science disciplines to dominate it. In making a case for a macrocriminology that combines the micro and the meso into a fresh holistic understanding of patterns of crime, this book rejects the idea of criminology as a discipline with its own methodological orthodoxies. Rather, criminology is at its best when it is an interdisciplinary study by communities of scholars focused on a shared topic: crime and its patterns.

The attempts of the discipline of psychology to capture criminology for much of the twentieth century left the field with an excessive focus on why some individuals do and do not commit crime. While not rejecting that individualised referent, this chapter successively reframes criminology's referent to the study of the criminalisation of interactions (microsociology), organisations (sociology), markets (economics), states (political science), places (geography), times (history) and life-courses (developmental behavioural science).

Reframing criminology's referent

Mainstream criminology in the twenty-first century has ossified as a discipline focused heavily but not exclusively on explaining why some individuals become criminals, and in which most of the macro-work is on punishment rather than crime. The discipline was even narrower in its core focus in the mid-twentieth century—the heyday of Harvard University's Sheldon and Eleanor Glueck of psychologically oriented criminology: criminology as a study of criminal minds and pathological individuals. Sociologically oriented criminologists, in a charge led by Edwin Sutherland, then transformed criminology. From the 1980s, British Home Office leaders, Pat Mayhew, Ron Clarke and others were perhaps the most influential figures in taking criminology in a meso-direction towards regulatory strategies of crime prevention that decentred individuals (Freilich and Newman 2018). By the 1970s, psychologists had begun to become marginalised in criminology, after the rise of a sequence of alternative influences: Merton and Sutherland, risk paradigms inherited from the likes of Ulrich Beck (1992), situational crime prevention and the criminology of place, the new critical criminology of the 1970s (for example, Taylor et al. 1973), anti-psychiatry, constructivist early labelling theory, Foucauldian governmentality scholarship on diffused capillaries of power and neoliberal governmentalities, cultural studies and postmodernist thought. Though all these developments contributed to a retreat of the formerly dominant psychologists, they never went away. They fought back in the twenty-first century, rallying around themes that offered helpful new insights such as social cognitive psychology and feminist psychology; as did biologically oriented criminologists— sometimes in allegiance with neuropsychologists.

This battle of disciplines, methodologies and epistemologies to capture criminology has been at best a mixed blessing for the development of the study of crime as a topic. Many criminologists do not wish to see criminology captured by any dominant discipline or method. Most of us who attend criminology meetings find virtue in crime being a topic for interdisciplinary social science around which it is worthwhile to build theoretically and methodologically plural scholarly communities, rather than divisions into experimental criminologists, critical criminologists, life-course folk and ever more multiplications of silos. We should all bring a critical lens to work on crime; we should all grasp the important experimental research and life-course research on the topics on which we write. A reason for sharing this vision for criminology arises from the view that the current structure of the social sciences is a narrowly North Atlantic creation of late modernity that holds back all social science scholarship, especially in terms of its integrative capabilities and its ability to learn from relational holism in southern and eastern epistemologies (for example, Carrington et al. 2016).

I have repeatedly discussed that reasoning for an interdisciplinary social science of crime that is more open to the kind of revolutionary breakdowns of silos that the biological sciences have seen as they reorganised to marginalise disciplinary themes like zoology, botany and entomology that are about categories of phenomena. Research became more theoretically organised around macro-themes like evolutionary biology and ecology yet integrated with the theoretically micro of the molecular biology of DNA, for example. The social sciences need a revolution that sees the discipline of economics as a bad idea—a bad idea to privilege economic institutions (and rational choice models within them); a revolution that sees criminology as a bad idea when its focus is criminal justice institutions;

53

political science as a bad idea when it narrows our focus to the state; history as a bad idea when it narrows our interest to time; geography when it narrows our research to space; psychology when it narrows us to individual humans and how they interact, and so on. I have already argued that moral philosophy is a bad idea when it neglects explanatory theory. This book makes the case that the richest insights about crime and freedom are insights not about the criminal justice system, but about theorising disparate institutions with a curiosity that ranges across all these preferred disciplinary lenses.

A virtue of criminology is that it is a data-driven field. A received wisdom among criminologists, however, is that data on individuals are the easiest to collect. It is the simple way to generate a large n to aid statistical inference. That is much less true than criminologists believe it to be. For example, in the context of discussing criminalised markets as an alternative focus to criminal individuals, this book discusses a study by Choi et al. (2016) with two ns of more than 100,000 observations of Australian and New Zealand securities markets where each observation is averaged from the market judgements of many individual or corporate analysts. Because criminologists believe individuals are the primary source of data on crime and its correlates, the data-driven quality of the field drives its theoretical orientation too narrowly to the explanation of why some kinds of individuals commit more crime than others. That source of data must continue to be important, but to render criminology a more fertile field, the priority is to strengthen traditions that rely on more variegated data sources (Karstedt 2017).

The specific alternatives to the study of criminal individuals or criminal minds considered in this book for informing macrocriminology include criminalised markets, criminalised states, criminalised norms, criminal organisations and criminalised spaces, times, life-courses and macro-historical trajectories. All these lenses are alive in criminology, even if some are more marginalised than they should be. The contribution of this book is to argue for a new way of strengthening them and integrating them into a more holistic criminology. At the end of the analysis in this book, the advocacy is not of a purely macro-style of criminology, nor microcriminology, but of a micro–meso–macro criminology of which most criminologists approve in theory, but neglect in the practice of their craft. This embraces individual-level data. Yet the corrective needed for an intellectually fertile criminology is to discover how to more meaningfully 'bring the state back in', as Evans et al. (1985) influentially put it; how to bring organisations back in, bring markets back in and bring in space-time to reset the compass of an overly atomised social science.

It follows that this book is not the kind of critical criminology that would prefer to abandon the study of crime for harms (for example, Presser 2013). This is not to deny that harm-prevention projects will often perform better at crime prevention than crime-prevention projects (Berg and Shearing 2018). Nor is this to deny that criminologists might have some useful things to say about the prevention of harms that can be more important than crime, such as criminological insights on how to prevent climate change, war and economic crises. This book accepts that the concept of crime does useful normative work in all societies. Crime marks off certain kinds of wrongdoing as particularly harmful compared with other harms because they are acts of domination. At least that is how crime should be defined by republican lights of what should and should not be a crime (Braithwaite and Pettit 1990). For example, criminality marks a distinction between rape and distasteful forms of seduction; it marks a distinction between sharp business practices and fraud; it distinguishes wrongdoing committed intentionally or recklessly from merely negligent wrongdoing or accidental harm. Absent a law that distinguishes between rape and seduction, between war crime and legal armed conflict, between corporate homicide and accidents, the law will be less useful for preventing harms. These dangerous and devastating forms of domination will be less effectively checked by the rule of law if we fail to distinguish harms like lies or infidelity to our partners from crimes.

This book argues that if normative orders fail to secure moral clarity over these distinctions, societies will be riven with crimes of domination. Criminalisation is an evocative, culturally resonant and useful shorthand for intentional or reckless predation on people or the environment that is an act of domination. A normative justification is provided for this conception of what is crime in terms of republican criminal law jurisprudence by Braithwaite and Pettit (1990: 92–100). This is important, though perhaps less important than experience of the practical use of the crime concept in dealing with domination. With war, this goes to the potential for International Criminal Court prosecutors to write to a general to warn that a blockade that is causing mass civilian starvation, a planned bombardment or intent to fire a nuclear weapon at a civilian population would be not just an act of war, but a war crime (as discussed in Chapter 10). With business crime, those of us who do observational research on corporate crime enforcement report in the literature the power of regulators shocking businesspeople who think of themselves as reputable with the news that they are investigating their conduct as 'criminal' conduct. So, good business regulators and environmental and consumer advocates find it useful to be able to assert that what they discuss with business is more than just negligence that caused harm that could occasion a lawsuit. What they are discussing is an alleged crime that might warrant prosecution—likewise, to the general who shrugs his shoulders at shooting prisoners of war, saying 'that's war'. We should value the concept of crime, and therefore criminology, as a field of research and teaching focused on it. This is because the concept does useful work in delivering a world with less domination than would exist without the crime concept to do that work, and indeed without criminologists.

Asking the crime-prevention question

It also follows from this that there is nothing particularly wrong with a criminology that asks what can be done to prevent individuals from committing crime or to prevent victims from victimisation. The argument is, however, that criminology does better if it transcends methodological individualism. Hence, for a particular crime problem, we might ask not only micro-questions about prevention at the level of individuals or their individual interactions; we also ask macro-questions about whether some transformations of markets, of the state, of corporate power, communal life or family cultures and structures at the meso-level might expand horizons of understanding beyond individualist crime prevention.

To summarise this step in the argument, the contention of this book is that our analytical leverage will be greater if we integrate micro with macro and meso-criminologies. More than that, the macro is constitutive of the micro and vice versa. Here a micro–meso–macro–meso–micro criminology simply takes up Anthony Giddens' (1984) insight from the theory of structuration. Individual agency is constitutive of structures and structures shape and enable individual agency, which recursively constitute reconfigured structures. In Giddens, the interface between agency and structure becomes a central referent for social scientific inquiry.

Asking the domination question

A surprising thing about criminology is the way it plays only at the margins of the question of what should be a crime. The most influential example is Norval Morris and Gordon Hawkins' (1969) liberal tract, *The Honest Politician's Guide to Crime Control*, which so shaped the thinking of baby-boomer criminologists. Their book argued that phenomena like queer sexuality and vagrancy should not be crimes because the conduct does no harm to others. This said something important and liberal about what should not be a crime, but it did not say anything affirmative about what should be. Lying, shouting abuse at a person, infidelity in the context of a sworn commitment to monogamy—all cause harm. Should these be crimes? Braithwaite and Pettit (1990) attempted an answer to this question in *Not Just Deserts: A Republican Theory of Criminal Justice*. They argued that crime control is a dangerous game. At many points in space and time across human history, adultery, vagrancy and LGBTIQ identities have been criminalised. At these conjunctures, the criminal law has been a source of domination of the poor, of indigenous peoples, women and transgender people, among others. In Australia, for example, the criminal law and its policing are not just a small part of the domination of Indigenous people; they are absolutely central to it; arrest for criminal offences and the risk to legitimate life chances associated with this are something the majority of Indigenous Australians experience and the majority of non-Indigenous Australians do not. These facts exist against the background of colonial law that found the stealing of land from their ancestors not to be a crime. The genocidal decimation of their populations in frontier wars was not criminalised by courts as a war crime. Decolonising law and policing and enhancing Indigenous self-determination in matters of crime control therefore become central questions about freedom in such societies.

Hence, Braithwaite and Pettit identified domination as the harm done when criminal law is abused, even when it is abused in the unjust implementation of just laws, as when the alleged rapist is bashed by the police or imprisoned on fabricated evidence. Equally, we were attracted to specifying domination reduction as the benefit when criminal law serves the community with justice. Stealing property rightfully belonging to another, or physically assaulting the bodily integrity of another, should be a crime, we argued, because that is an act of domination against another person. One of the problems in the terms of our republican theory was that it advanced a humanistic theory, so it struggled to justify environmental crime as a crime of the unjust domination of nature, when nature has value that is more than just the value it delivers to humankind. The domination of rivers as flows of life rather than as objects is something indigenous jurisprudence helps westerners to begin to theorise more meaningfully.

The essence of the republican theory of criminal justice is that we should define conduct as criminal when doing so would reduce the amount of domination in the world. Then, in deciding whether to arrest, imprison, use restorative justice or to deploy this versus that rehabilitative or preventive remedy, we should choose the response that does best by reducing the amount of domination in the world. Under this test, it is an easy call for republican criminology to conclude that assault should be a crime. Yet it is a difficult judgement to balance any deterrent or incapacitation benefit from sentencing the assailant to prison with the fact that prison time might reduce future domination of future victims but increase the domination the offender experiences. This balancing is further complicated when there is structural domination of offenders from minorities who are oppressed by the racist way the law against assault is enforced. The domination poor children might suffer if both their mother and their father are thrust into prison under no-drop policies for domestic violence must also be given equal consideration by the republican in the balancing of all justice claims for domination reduction (Burford et al. 2019: 217–18). Braithwaite and Pettit argue that this should be a difficult and complex judgement—something societies should agonise over and deliberate on carefully in advance of any rush to action. They argue for a principle of parsimony in response to its complexity: if in doubt, do not imprison. Do not imprison if there is some less-dominating pathway available to prevent further domination. Restorative justice for this reason plays a large role in republican criminology. In Chapter 9, we explain how a massively expanded use of restorative justice might at the same time soften the domination of the criminal justice system while actually increasing the effectiveness of deterrence and incapacitation in crime prevention.

Alert readers by now will have detected a logical problem with this book. Because crime is conduct that threatens freedom, it is true by definition that a society with less crime will have more freedom. The list of propositions in Appendix I, however, delves into the intricacies of how crime is causally implicated in the onset of anomie, war, the collapse of the integrity of markets and states and indeed how crime cascades to more crime. These are among the bigger explanatory claims of the book concerning the impact of crime on freedom that are macrostructural. They reach up and beyond the definition of crime as individual acts of domination. To understand crime and domination, we must understand both as cascade phenomena that cascade into each other and into themselves in ways that can be theoretically specified.

So, what is domination? If policy judgements in the justice system should be made in terms of which policy choice will reduce the amount of domination in the world, how should domination be defined? Philip Pettit (1997) defines domination as the capacity to exercise arbitrary power over the choices of another person in ways that do not track the interests of that person. A just normative order (see Chapter 3), human rights and a rule of law that regulates arbitrary power are crucial. They hold institutional keys to taming domination and crime, and to freedom. This is not enough, however, because a person in circumstances of poverty whose voice about their interests is not taken seriously, who is not granted equal access to the rule of law and to legitimate opportunities, cannot enjoy freedom as nondomination. Hence, the republican theory of domination argues that continuous struggle for equality and elimination of poverty are crucial to republican freedom. This republican ideal of liberty as freedom from domination is distinguished from liberal freedom as non-interference in the choices of others. For the republican, the opposite of freedom is not interference, but slavery or arbitrary imposition of power. Braithwaite and Pettit (1990) called this republican freedom 'dominion'—a usage that Lode Walgrave (2013) has also influentially advanced.

One of the virtues of domination reduction as an objective of the justice system is that it is a 'satiable' objective. Braithwaite and Pettit argue that deterrence, crime prevention, just deserts, proportional punishment and harm reduction are all examples of insatiable objectives. They are politically dangerous objectives for that reason. In a policy context where deterrence is working in preventing crime or preventing harm, why not keep increasing it? If cutting off the hands of thieves actually works in reducing theft, why not sever the hands of as many thieves as can be apprehended? This is not so ridiculous a question. In the particular space-time context of the Taliban coming to power in Afghanistan in 1996, Wardak and Braithwaite (2013) and Braithwaite and Wardak (2013) concluded that cutting off the hands of some thieves may have played some part in ending the greatest extremes of anomie that society previously suffered in the years before it was pacified by the Taliban. The philosophical rationale for why we should not cut off hands, even if we do discover contexts where it may have worked, is open and shut in this easy case and in many harder cases. A republican should never cut off the hands of a thief even when it is working as a deterrent because to do so would create a world with greater rather than less domination (Braithwaite and Pettit 1990), as it certainly did with the rise of the Taliban (Braithwaite and D'Costa 2018: Ch. 9).

Just as any kind of harm prevention or crime prevention is a dangerously insatiable objective on its own, so is just deserts. If giving criminals their just deserts should be the goal of the criminal justice system, a way of realising that goal becomes building an ever-bigger police state that is capable of tracking down, prosecuting and punishing proportionately every single person who cheats on their tax, who makes a false claim on their company's expense account and every professor who funds the collection of their PhD student's data from a grant awarded for a somewhat different purpose. Why not pursue as best we can the imperative to give all of them their just deserts? Again, the answer is clear for the republican that such an insatiable police state would be a profound danger to freedom. It would be the dystopia, the unfreedom, the domination of George Orwell's 'Big Brother'. The dangers of such a dystopia are clear in the minds of voters in all democracies. What republican political theory does is render this political intuition philosophically coherent. Even the most liberal of democracies suffer much higher imprisonment rates than can be defended by republican political theory. All societies suffer criminal justice excess at the hands of devotees of deterrence, by enthusiasts for incapacitation, by defenders of just deserts. All democracies suffer criminal justice excess by the lights of republican theory in the hands of judges who sentence many to prison for no better reason than the doctrine that this is deserved or proportionate. For the republican, that is not a good enough reason to deprive anyone of their liberty.

Of course, there are many ways of tempering the excesses of these doctrines. Just deserts can do useful work in tempering the excesses of deterrence that are disproportionate to desert, and vice versa. Yet there remain countless cases where imprisonment would simultaneously fit the desert doctrine and enhance deterrence while *increasing* the amount of domination in the world. We see so many such tragedies in the prisons of the best democracies. We also see it as a result of the penal populism to which electoral democracy gives rise (Lacey 2008; Pratt 2007).

We saw the problem more graphically after the Rwandan genocide when 126,500 people were arrested, mostly on the principled liberal grounds that there was credible evidence they had participated in hacking other citizens to death during the genocide. Sadly, the Rwandan justice system could not resource 126,500 trials for crimes of this level of seriousness. The majority of the 126,500 languished in prison for more than a decade awaiting trials that, when they were conducted, were often presided over by a second or third-year law student. Many died in prison from AIDS while awaiting trial. According to republican lights, those deaths were morally wrong acts of domination by the justice system against those individuals and their families. Many who died in prison were children at the time of their arrest and were raped in prison. Some of those children did commit the *actus reus* of the genocide: hacking other humans to death. Yet had the allegations against them attracted a speedy trial, they would have been acquitted because they were children who had seen other children, including siblings, themselves hacked to death when they refused orders to join in the mass murder. Their prison deaths were acts of mass domination by a newly liberalised criminal justice system trying to do the right thing by deterrence of genocide, and by just deserts, by prosecuting all who deserved to be prosecuted. Sadly, the justice administrators who pursued insatiable justice by ordering the 126,500 genocide arrests perpetrated greater evil against humankind than many of those arrested, though not all of course. Fortunately, more than a decade on, many survivors among the 126,500 were released from prison to the sometimes more restorative form of traditional Rwandan justice of the *Gacaca* (Clark 2010, 2014).

For Braithwaite and Pettit (1990), asking the domination question was therefore a better path than asking the just deserts question or the crime-prevention question, or both. Philip Pettit went on to construct from a republican theory of criminal justice an influential general theory of republican governance, I am proud to say. Embarrassed though I am by a want of humility in saying this, it did illustrate some fertility of criminology for a more interdisciplinary and transformative social science and political philosophy. Pettit's republicanism has been explicitly acknowledged in statecraft as shaping the politics of national leaders and his republican work has become extremely influential in philosophy and political theory journals. I hope also that Chapter 11 illustrates the way macrocriminology can reinvigorate the discipline of international relations in ways that help it deliver better contributions to the prevention of war; that many chapters reveal ways the discipline of economics might be stimulated by insightful macrocriminology to better assist economies to flourish and that other chapters help political scientists see why there are few graver dangers to freedom and democracy than the criminalisation of states.

Integrating normative theory and explanatory theory

Lode Walgrave's (2013) work is one example of picking up the idea of a republican normative theory and applying it to the practical task of improving the explanation of crime and crime prevention. We have seen that Braithwaite and Pettit (2000) argued that integrating normative and explanatory theory can improve both. Explanatory theory is conceived of here as ordered sets of propositions about the way the world is; normative theory is ordered propositions about the way the world ought to be.[2] The virtues of a macrocriminology that is macro in the sense of embracing political philosophies of what makes for the good society partly goes to the dangers of narrow utilitarianism. Republicanism confronts an explanatory theory of crime that reveals some contexts of efficacy for tyranny; it confronts the risk of this being read as having the 'policy implication' that one should implement that tyranny. An example is an empirical finding in a particular society that a form of racial profiling helps the police fight crime. Requiring policy to pass the theoretical tests of normative–explanatory integration helps proof social science against such tyrannies.

---

2   I am not one for specifying how law-like, how certain or probabilistic sets of propositions must be to qualify as a theory, or to what degree ordered sets of propositions should be deductive and inductive. Theories are more than just a collection of propositions. The way a theory orders propositions and shuttles back and forth between induction and deduction gives those propositions meaning and helps explain them. A theory must say something about which variables are more important than others and something insightful about relations among them. I do like theory to have the ambition of constructing patterns that are not so visible to the naked eye. I like to hope my theoretical canvas imagines one useful reality that has value for making the world a better place. Theory guides the kind of data to seek. Deductive aspects of theory guide induction and induction informs better deductions in theories. While sometimes it is wise for theory to propose what might be unknowable and in what ways, it is good for the explanatory propositions in theories to be testable and be tested as broadly as possible. And it is good for the normative propositions in theories to be contested. All the theories I ever proposed seem to me wrong most of the time in some important respect. Nevertheless, they may have been useful and practical. I like to try to be useful by iterating between being parsimonious (in the case of this theory, reducing the story of the theory to one sentence) and giving the theory a rich texture of detail about how to put the theory to use in creating a better world (the 150 propositions in Appendix I). Ultimately, the proof of theoretical puddings is in the eating: this one will be sour to some, sweet to others, I hope, in helping their capacity to grasp the world and change it, and beside the point to others again.

This goes beyond normative–explanatory integration as a hygiene factor that protects justice as nondomination from the dangers of criminology. There is also the healthy motivation factor that concepts like freedom and domination that work in explaining the world are quite likely to come from normative theories that give an account of the good society that resonates with citizens. This motivates their deployment to do good things for crime prevention and freedom enhancement.

I had been writing since 1979 (Braithwaite 1979) on what I saw as a large body of evidence for an explanatory association between domination and crime when I took stock of that evidence to write:

> As a generalization, 'domination engenders crime' is not always true and when it is, it is often true in a complex rather than a direct way. For example, the direct relationship is that women tend both to be more dominated than men and to commit *less* crime than men do. Yet empirical criminology in the feminist tradition demonstrates a variety of ways in which the domination of women by men engenders crime. (Braithwaite 2003: 213)

This is also true of feminist peace studies (Braithwaite and D'Costa 2018). Jacqui True (2012: 136–39) has reviewed literature from 50 countries showing that the dominations of major wars drive increases in gender-based violence afterwards and we discuss later the work of Mary Caprioli (2000, 2003, 2005) and her colleagues on how gender inequality in turn increases the prospects of further war. No normative target, Philip Pettit and I argued, is likely to have appeal if it does not connect to things about which people care. In turn, things people care about become promising candidates for explaining other matters of concern to them. Normatively useful concepts are more likely to be useful as explanations, and vice versa. Hence, if we focus on some evidence for an association between inequality and crime, we might be able to improve on that association by reconceptualising inequality in terms that capture what people care more deeply about as matters of normative grievance. Domination is a dimension of normative grievance that people do tend to care about more than mere inequality. The inequality that women tend to live longer than men, for example, is a major inequality that has little edge as a grievance because it does not arise from domination of men by women, from arbitrary power of women over men. Braithwaite and Pettit (2000) discuss a range of reasons not rehearsed here for why people care so much about being dominated from an early age. There is value in Adler's (1964) theory that to be a child is to be a human who struggles towards release from domination by and dependence on one's parents. Struggle against domination motivates what all humans do and value. This is embedded in the biology of survival. Our struggle for independence as infants helps us to become capable of surviving on our own.

Braithwaite and Pettit (2000) argued in more detail that in doing social theory we should look for that adjustment between normative and explanatory categories of analysis. If we do so, we are likely to reach a higher level of insight on both fronts. The integration of explanatory and normative theory is no more a prerequisite for powerful theory than the integration of micro and macro theory. The claim in both cases is only that it is methodologically sound in theory-building to aim at both because there are reasons iterations between the two levels of theory drive mutual improvements in both.

Beyond criminalisation of individuals

Criminalisation of organisations

In addition to being the most important figure for moving criminology under the influence of sociology, Edwin Sutherland (1983) was the visionary scholar of criminal organisations. He invented the term 'white-collar crime', which now exists in many languages. He showed systematically the patterns of repeated criminality of America's largest corporations. This was one of the ways he challenged psychologism: were the responsible corporate executives emotionally unstable individuals, with a low IQ, a weak self-concept and lacking impulse control? The problem, he argued on the contrary, was they were very much in control of their impulses and their intelligence; they were smart, planful schemers of long-term enrichment. Schoepfer et al. (2014) found that desire for control explains white-collar criminality better than an absence of self-control. The motivational driver of crime in the suites is domination; the motivational driver of crime in the streets is being dominated. Their result captures brilliantly the fatal problem for criminological theory that is so preoccupied with crime in the streets that it sidelines crime in the suites.

As great a criminological opinion-leader as Sutherland was, he failed to attract massive movement in the academy to study white-collar crime. After Watergate, Lockheed and the other international corporate bribery scandals of the 1970s, there was a decade when many of the brightest and best criminologists of that generation prioritised the study of white-collar crime. That surge of interest gradually waned. It is not that criminologists have been unpersuaded by Sutherland and his followers that crime in the suites steals more of citizen's property than crime in the streets, and takes more lives. The evidence for Sutherland's conclusion has greatly strengthened. For example, Dukes et al. (2014: Ch. 7) conclude that corporate crime in just one industry, pharmaceuticals, in the United States costs many times more lives than violent street crime. Indeed, single offences by single 'Big Pharma' companies cost more lives than all violent street crimes. Moreover, Federal Bureau of Investigation (FBI) estimates of the ratio of the cost of healthcare fraud to the cost of burglary and robbery range from three to one to 11 to one. Pharmaceutical counterfeiting is not such a major killer in the United States, but in China and other Asian economies that domicile the major corporate counterfeiters, larger portions of the estimated 700,000 deaths a year that result from counterfeiting occur. The figure of 700,000 is more than all the deaths worldwide from homicide, terrorism and war during the twenty-first century up to the publication of Dukes et al. (2014: Ch. 7). Coffee (2020: 5, 43) points out that the most harmful recent corporate criminal offenders have continued to be Big Pharma. Coffee suggests pharmaceutical corporations—some now convicted—were responsible for the greatest part of 400,000 deaths in the United States alone from prescription opioid overdoses, for example. While there was controversy at the time, not many criminologists today would contest Fisse and Braithwaite's (1993) account of why it is coherent to hold organisations accountable for crime and at least the basics of their detailed account of how to accomplish this.

Criminologists all agree that corporate crime is a huge problem, but every discipline has its mainstream; for criminology, that is crime in the streets. Crime in the streets is easier to study quantitatively than crime in the suites, so the discipline's quantitative orthodoxy is a problem with these massive holes in the canvas painted by disciplinary research. The entrenched neglect of Sutherland's lessons is a concern to republican theorists because it means systematically less attention is given to the crimes of most devastating domination. The uncomfortable reality is that most of the teaching and research we criminologists do is oriented to the control of the poor. It is neglectful of the control of the rich, and the middle class as well (Farrall and Karstedt 2019).

Since the birth of criminology as a discipline, the nature of social action has changed dramatically. Corporatisation in the twentieth century changed the world to a place where most of the most important things done for good or ill were done by corporate rather than individual actors. The Anthropocene morphed into the Capitalocene (Haraway 2015). Even in New York, where this trajectory was most advanced, it was not until decades into the twentieth century that the majority of litigants in appellate courts were corporations rather than individual persons and the majority of actors described on the front page of *The New York Times* were corporate rather than individual actors (Coleman 1982: 11).

Of course, very small organisations like schools, and even smaller ones called families, can vary greatly in the frequency of criminality. When one member of a family sexually assaults another family member, individualised criminology sometimes errs in characterising one family member as an offender and the other as a victim. Family group decision-making processes sometimes discover these individuals to be embedded in family systems that transmit sexual abuse across generations to the point where many family members are perpetrators, many are victims and many are both perpetrators and victims (Braithwaite 2002). The challenge, then, is not so much to punish one person essentialised as a rapist, but to undertake a restorative process that structurally disentangles the family from all of its destructive and dominating relationships. The restorative aim is to build out responsively to the countervailing constructive relationships that are sources of strength for the family's future.

Criminalisation of the state

The rise of transitional justice after armed conflict as a field of study has meant that criminological interest in the criminalisation of states has grown. Growth of the global human rights movement as one driver of research on state crime has waned less than Ralph Nader and the consumer movement as a driver of corporate crime research. Genocide studies has been a particular impetus; historically recent genocides in Cambodia, Rwanda and with Myanmar's Rohingya increased the impetus. In the United States in the twenty-first century, the Black Lives Matter movement is a more recent uprising that contributed to motivating the study of state crime. Police forces in some democracies are more than a hundred times as murderous as others—occasionally a thousand times—with Brazil, El Salvador, Jamaica and the Philippines consistently extreme this century (as were many non-democracies, particularly Syria). The United States is exceptionally bad, with more than 1,000 people killed by police use of deadly force in many single years, while the United Kingdom always has fewer than 10 such deaths annually (three in 2019).[3] Even during the years of The Troubles in Northern Ireland, when the crimes of the Royal Ulster Constabulary were shocking, killings *directly* by police averaged fewer than 10. The United States has by far the highest number of recorded police killings among developed economies every year, with 1,146 in 2019 compared with Canada, which is second on the list, with 36 (2017 data). Not today, but for a long period around the turn of this century, one city in Australia, Melbourne, accounted for more police killings than the rest of the country combined. So, extreme variegation in this form of state crime has become a germinal puzzle for criminology.

Increasing numbers of states have established anticorruption commissions, which have revealed the devastating impact on societies of state corruption. Criminalisation of the state is a major cause and effect of the crime–war cascades discussed in Chapter 11. All this has meant that the criminalised state has increasingly grabbed some of criminology's attention away from the criminal individual, in quite a profound reframing of criminology's referent by some of our most intellectually serious criminologists (see Grabosky 1989; Tilly 1985; Green and Ward 2004; Ross and Barak 2000; Friedrichs 1998; Ross 2000; Kramer et al. 2002; Karstedt 2014b; Rothe and Kauzlarich 2014). For macrocriminologists, there is considerable appeal in Susanne Karstedt's (2012a) multifaceted measure of 'extremely violent societies' as a corrective to the tendency of murderous states not to count state homicides in their standard homicide statistics.

Like Tilly (1975), this book argues that crime made the state and the state makes crime. This reality is so structural that nothing is more fundamental to the criminalisation of markets, corporations and individuals than the criminalisation of the state. Colonialism, colonial states and postcolonial states are important parts of this (Blagg and Anthony 2019), but only part of it.

---

3   Various sources of data inform the numbers in this paragraph, but the evidence is fragmented into large numbers of studies of just one country or a comparison of two. Systematic cross-national comparativism of police killings has a long way to go. We cannot be confident of much beyond the claim that cross-national variation is huge and that the situation is particularly bad in the outliers mentioned above. For now, the most comprehensive set of sources can be accessed by searching data such as the 'Fatal Encounters Data Base' in the 78 footnotes of 'List of killings by law enforcement officers by country' on *Wikipedia* (available from: en.wikipedia.org/wiki/List_of_killings_by_law_enforcement_officers_by_country).

Criminalisation of markets

While the criminalisation of markets is intertwined with the criminalisation of states and corporations, it is conceptually different. The darknet is a criminalised market that allows internet trade in child pornography, drugs, contract killings, influencing elections, and more. The darknet criminalises in a way that is distinct from the actors who commit the crimes.

Banning legal slavery markets through the activism of the antislavery movement that grew in the eighteenth century gave rise to underground markets in human trafficking, just as the banning of the legal opium trade that the British East India Company once plied to China gave birth to illicit opiates markets that moved from control by Big Pharma to control by triads and the Mafia and then to control by fragmented street gangs. There are underground markets in gambling, smuggling, sex work, wildlife, money lending and laundering, and more.

This book argues that reframing criminology's referent to markets that can be criminalised, and to the challenge of humbling the power of capital in those markets, is a fundamental reframing of the referent for a new macrocriminology. Just as the world has changed from one in which most important social action is individual action to one in which it is mostly organisational action, the world has also changed so that more social action is embedded in networked markets, more than it is enacted by hierarchies (Williams 1998). Competition policy in societies with neoliberal ideologies can drive markets to the ever more efficient production of goods, yet doing so inevitably also induces the more efficient production of 'bads'. Not all markets in bads are illegal, yet all markets in what some citizens see as a vice, whether a legal or illegal vice, create demand for a countervailing market in virtue. For example, most of us see the market in sugar as a market in vice that induces obesity, heart disease and cancer. This creates a demand for markets in virtue to counter it: firms that market diets, health resorts, gyms and personal trainers. As markets in vice become more dangerous, citizen demands for the state to regulate them also grow. Stronger markets become associated with three major trends: more efficient production of goods, more efficient production of bads and stronger regulation of markets in response to the bads (Braithwaite 2005b, 2008).

Until a decade ago, tech giants were expanding the horizons of freedom through opening new gateways to knowledge access for the poor, and to collaboratively constituting knowledge in ways still well illustrated by a *Wikipedia* that can be read in minority languages. This so clearly was a market in virtue. Now the platforms of tech giants are more a market in vice sustained by monopolies in breach of antitrust laws that have the overarching objective of keeping us glued to the screen controlled by their platform so they can sell more advertising. The market in the vices of artificial intelligence (AI) has trained their platforms to understand that provocative lies are better than truths for eliciting clicks. Often the lies are unfiltered commercial fraud. Listening to the complexity of the political thought of our adversaries sells less advertising than spreading conspiracy theories about them and silencing them with reinforcement by our own dogmas. This market in vice promotes authoritarianism that threatens freedom as nondomination. Tweets by Donald Trump instantiate the kinds of clickbait that most attract revenue for tech giants, no less so when they stamped warnings on the truth value of claims that Trump won the 2020 election, for example. If we are Republicans, the tech giants track our screens to the most incendiary lies of Republicans; if we are Democrats, they track our screens to the most tantalising untruths of Democrats.

Most criminologists have little problem with the idea that organisations can act. If we say, 'The United States abides by its constitution', criminologists accept this as mostly true even though almost all the individual action in writing the Constitution and deciding court cases that demand compliance with it is the past action of dead individuals. Thinking of states as criminalised is therefore something criminologists can buy. Yet criminalised markets can be a step too far for them. Sociologically, the recursiveness of individual and collective action, of action and structure, involved in the constitution of criminalised states and criminalised markets is constitution by kindred ensembles of mechanisms. The concept of a sailor gathers meaning from the institutional infrastructure of the navy: ships, captains, rules of war at sea, other sailors (Fisse and Braithwaite 1993). Likewise, the concept of a stockbroker makes no sense without the constitution of this role by a market. For Giddens (1979: 5), this is the 'duality of structure' whereby the 'recursiveness of social life' is constituted in social practices such as market transactions: '[S]tructure is both medium and action in the reproduction of practices. Structure enters simultaneously into the constitution of the actor [the broker] and social practices [market transactions]' (see also Giddens 1984). Hence, many individual criminals constitute criminalised states and criminalised markets, while criminalised markets also constitute criminalised financial houses replete with criminal individual traders. Myopic methodological individualism delivers a criminology blinded to big structures in the character of variation in crime.

Asking questions about criminal markets

In the conditions of contemporary capitalism, the criminalisation of markets is central to macrocriminology. More facets of contemporary lives are ruled by markets than in any period of human history. Markets regulate aspects of our existence that were once regulated by the church, states, families, villages and their elders. Libertarians find this a controversial statement as they see the market as the antithesis of regulation. For libertarians, the market is a realm of choice where the individual citizen is sovereign. Markets, however, shape choices with profound potency, just as choices shape markets. This is the most important recursive process of structuration in the modern world. We see this rather dramatically when it is revealed how a firm like Cambridge Analytica can use Facebook and other technologies in the market for information services to skew democratic elections with alluring lies. Who could deny that Cambridge Analytica and Facebook were shown by these revelations in the US Congress and the UK Parliament to shape choices as marketers of unfreedom and of disrespect for privacy by defamatory means? Conversely, green economists seek to contrive markets that price carbon to steer the planet to survival.

In more routine ways, however, markets are harnessed with intent to steer the flow of events. This is how Braithwaite and Parker (2003) define the core of what regulation means: intentional action to steer the flow of events. In contemporary affluent societies, people die less from hunger than from excessive eating that is intentionally promoted by food marketing. People in affluent market economies die less from undermedication with drugs that save lives than from overmedication with pharmaceuticals, more from illicit and licit drugs of abuse, more from the search for a pick-me-up or a pill for every ill. Markets in the vice of excess pill-popping for conditions like depression can crowd out the market in virtue of exercise programs and relational social cognitive programs that are more effective for people with depression. We can understand all this as a glorious, liberated choice that free markets in food and drugs have delivered to the modern consumer. People can rationally choose to live happily by gorging sugar and drugging themselves into moments of pleasant torpor. Yet most young people who make those choices come to regret them as they age and struggle with their mental and physical health. They come to realise that those choices can cause great suffering for the people who love them. They become wise enough to reframe it as an untempered glorious consumer freedom of short-termism and self-indulgence to the neglect of those to whom we owe our love. This is a freedom shaped and nudged by markets, by marketing that causes us to crave factory food dripping with fat or sugar.

The criminology of markets in vice and markets in virtue

From the markets in vice perspective, the most important questions for criminology are which markets might be criminalised, decriminalised or regulated in some other way. Let us illustrate the nature of this choice with the fact that the United States and New Zealand are the only developed economies that have not criminalised mass media advertising of legal prescription drugs. American readers will have noticed that a huge difference in what is seen when they watch television in other countries is the absence of the overwhelming presence of advertisements touting pharmaceuticals. So which policy choice is right? Should the rest of the world enhance the consumer sovereignty of their citizens by deregulating the mass media advertising of drugs? Or should the United States criminalise that market? One argument for criminalising the US market is that marketing-driven overuse and inappropriate use of medicines are one answer to the puzzle of why the people of the United States live shorter lives than people from poorer countries with less technically sophisticated healthcare systems and with much lower levels of health expenditure as a percentage of gross domestic product (GDP) (Dukes et al. 2014). Poor people in the United States, in particular, live shorter, more brutish lives than the poorest people of many poorer countries.

I do not want to tarry arguing for that datum because the point here is a critique of extant criminology. Criminology as a field has shown little interest in the question of whether it would be good or bad to criminalise this market. How can it be that criminology is not interested in a macro-market question like this? How can this be when the study of drug markets is such a substantial subfield of criminology? Criminology could become a science that helps societies to reduce death and harms to their citizens and their property and reduce the domination of people's lives by addiction (Braithwaite and Pettit 1990). But it has risen to this challenge only in individualised ways. The accomplishments of criminology on that front, despite the funding thrown at drug researchers, have been modest. And, if the criminalisation of prescription drug mass marketing might reduce the domination of people by markets in vice, that could be a policy debate worth having. How can you have that debate if your crime and drug science is normatively unmoored? And drug science that is normatively unmoored will be captured and corrupted by drug money that captures state policy to legalise drug pushing. Sadly, criminology is caught up in that capture to a degree, just as pharmacology is captured by the corporate criminals of the drug trade (Dukes et al. 2014).

Liberal and libertarian criminologists have always been interested in advancing arguments for the decriminalisation of markets in illicit drugs and in sex work. These particular debates about markets in vice have been unusual in their intensity. Again, whichever side one takes on those debates, they are examples of a kind of debate we need more widely in criminology. We need that debate in respect of what many would argue are growing markets in vice that destroy lives: gambling, pornography that blurs towards child pornography on the internet, guns, nuclear technology, mercenary armies, killer robots and drones, the purchase of the votes of politicians, and many more. The warning signs are strong. In New South Wales this century, child pornography offences have risen almost twentyfold and child sexual assault by 83 per cent (Weatherburn and Rahman 2021: Ch. 1).

Criminalisation of space-time

It is now part of the shared language of criminology that at certain places and times hotspots of high criminality evolve. A corner where drug markets operate at night is a node of space-time that institutionalises the reproduction of crime through a normative order of the corner that might include norms about when it is justified to shoot people. Chapter 11 discusses how the violence of war and war crime also clusters in space and time and cascades from hotspot to hotspot. The criminology of place has old roots, particularly in Chicago School conclusions about areas of high social disorganisation and poverty, and high crime rates (Shaw and McKay 1942). In recent decades, reframing the referent to places rather than persons has generated important insights from many of this generation's finest on the criminology of place (for example, Weisburd et al. 2012; Sherman et al. 1989; Sampson et al. 1997; Bursik 1999). At a more macrolevel, there has been interest in why whole regions like Latin America have elevated rates of violence (Nivette 2011) and other regions, such as Western Europe and East Asia, have low rates, even though in previous periods of history Western Europe (Eisner 2001, 2003, 2014; Spierenburg 2008, 2013) and parts of Asia (Broadhurst et al. 2015) had rates of homicide 10 to 100 times as high as today. Space-time variance in crime rates is generally much higher than variance in crime among different types of individuals, as discussed in Chapter 11. This is one reason there is so much promise in reframing the referent to space-time clusters of crime.

Among the highest homicide rates recorded in the past century is that among the Gebusi in late colonial and early postcolonial Papua New Guinea (1940–89), particularly before 1975.[4] The literature described a society where 32.9 per cent of adult deaths were homicides (Knauft 1987, 2002, 2013), with updated evidence indicating a peak of 40 per cent (Knauft and Malbrancke 2017). That update also shows that for 28 years since 1989 there have been zero homicides—a shift from close to the highest recorded homicide rate worldwide for the twentieth century to the lowest in the twenty-first century. The Gebusi remain classified as an egalitarian, violent hunter-gatherer society by scholars such as Pinker (2011) and Acemoglu and Robinson (2019: 26). The reversal of homicide rates among the Gebusi is one of various reasons this book is not interested in 'hunter-gatherer societies' as an explanatory variable, if indeed that is what the Gebusi are. What have changed substantially are Gebusi institutions. What has changed is that mediation has greatly strengthened under the supervision of community elected councils of mediators for each ward. The councils have no enforcement powers. Decisions are upheld 'only by consensus', ritualised by all the parties snapping their fingers as confirmation that anger is over (Knauft and Malbrancke 2017: 6–7). A second change is improved health and nutrition. Murder occurred widely before 1989 as a result of people dying in the prime of life. When better health allowed longer life, an objective condition for sorcery allegations (the motive for 61 per cent of murders)

---

4   Steadman (1971: 215) reported a higher homicide rate, of 778 per 100,000, between 1959 and 1968 for the Hewa of Papua New Guinea.

was attenuated. A third factor was abolishing the institutions of public spirit séances to determine sorcery and public sorcery inquests, which had tended to stigmatisation, escalation of retribution, group anger and torture. A fourth was that no *inter*tribal warfare has afflicted the Gebusi since 1989. This book's arguments about the importance of a strong state had no explanatory relevance because the state is even more absent post 1989 than for the 1960–89 period. Gebusi have no access to police, and other state officials are no longer based in the district. But the embrace of Christianity by the Gebusi was institutionally important. The church has been active in supporting these other institutional changes: the rise of talking through and mediating conflicts; paying compensation in preference to retribution; the abolition of stigmatising public spirit séances and sorcery inquests; improved institutions of health and welfare; and absence of warfare. Knauft and Malbrancke (2017: 11) contend that in certain conditions of anomic violence, the church can better step into a Hobbesian vacuum than the state. In the words of one elected Gebusi councillor: 'If there are police but no Church, there *will* be killing. [But] if there is Church but no police, there *won't* be any killing.' Naing Ko Ko and Braithwaite (2019), writing on 'Baptist policing in Burma', also describe conditions for the relevance of this possibility. When a state that can regulate crime is absent, belief that a god or the ancestors can sanction crime and mediated settlements can substitute.

The criminalisation of markets and the space-time concentration of crime can intersect in revealing ways. Securities markets at hotspots called Wall Street and the City of London imploded into rapacious financial crime innovation at specific points in history: 1987 (Michael Milken's invention of the junk bond, 'Greed is Good'); 2001 (Enron, Arthur Andersen, tech wreck); and 2007 (crimes of the Global Financial Crisis). Earlier financial crises such as the savings and loans frauds in the 1980s (Pontell and Calavita 1992; Calavita et al. 1997) and the waves of corporate tax-shelter frauds in Australia in the mid-1970s and 2000s and in New York in the late 1990s (Braithwaite 2005b) were sometimes more diffused across space. Offshore financial centres (tax havens) were nodes of these waves of criminality, with disparate nodes being important at different points of history.

Reframing the referent to times of crime also intersects in analytically useful ways with the mainstream referent of individual criminality. Very young children and old people are minor problems as perpetrators of crime. Street crime begins to peak sharply during the second half of the second decade of human lives and then declines consistently across all decades after the third. Crime in the suites peaks considerably later, when corporate actors reach heights from which they can grasp the lure of corporate criminality. In recent decades, however, securities trading has become a sphere where people in their twenties confront the lure of 24-hour trading fraud to burn brightly as comets, masters of the universe who put their bonuses aside for a comfortable life after they crash and burn. Loss of normative order, of a moral compass, can be cultivated among such young traders by criminalised firms and markets.

Likewise, anomie that to some degree is inherent in the role transition of adolescents from child to adult can also be cultivated by street gang bosses who are keen to induce anomic adolescents to grasp the lure of drug markets or other forms of street crime. Life-course criminology can shift criminology's referent to a life sequence (Sampson and Laub 1995; Moffitt et al. 2002; Farrington 2003). For example, the research question might shift from how to prevent individuals from committing crime to how to shift the lifecycle of criminality so it always starts later and finishes earlier in this society (compared with another). Braithwaite (2001) discusses universal institutionalisation of youth development circles as a strategy to accomplish just that. It involves replacing school parent–teacher interviews with meetings of a community of care of family members and mostly retired outside volunteers with strong bridging capital that sticks with every high school child through their ups and downs until they are placed in a decent job or college. Life-course criminology can therefore benefit from bringing together many lenses: the individual lens, time and the criminology of place, of organisations and of markets. The essence of the mission of macrocriminology is the intersection of these lenses to create a more richly stereoscopic comprehension of the patterning of crime. Pathways to shifting those patterns cannot be seen without these multiple lenses. Life-course patterns are just one particularly important kind of pattern. Their path-dependencies can be laid down early by criminal subcultures in schools and families and by opportunity structures such as those on Wall Street.

Decentring punishment and criminal justice policy

The propensity for the policy lens of most criminologists to be focused on criminal justice institutions is misguided. It is not that criminology wastes its time when it addresses criminal justice solutions to crime problems. It is that criminology stunts its potential when that is what it mostly does. It has settled for strategies to shift high-crime societies into somewhat lower-crime societies, or to understand such shifts, eschewing the ambition of understanding how extremely low-crime societies are created in the *longue durée*. Chapter 11 argues that reconfigured hotspot policing can have a profound impact when it cascades macrosociological effects and when it pacifies dangerous spaces past a tipping point where citizens are able to return to the streets to cascade collective efficacy. Even so, it argues that the cascading of collective efficacy can be more profound from families, schools and workgroups than from places that are hotspots.

Places may or may not be the most fertile sites for planting roots of self-efficacy and collective efficacy that will spread. Places may be important, but thinner, sites for building thick freedom than institutions like families, schools, workgroups and indigenous tribes, which enjoy thicker institutional fabrics for relationality. Yet when cascades of collective efficacy enabled by hotspot policing complement more holistic, multidimensional strategies for cascading collective efficacy and tackling concentrated disadvantage, the micro-policing policy can connect to a macro-strategy that not only reduces crime, but also improves many outcomes constitutive of freedom, including health outcomes, homelessness, educational outcomes, employment outcomes, workforce productivity and an array of other forms of social wellbeing. For example, Chapter 11 argues that the effect sizes of strengthened collective efficacy in improving educational outcomes and reducing educational disadvantage in schools are higher than place-based collective efficacy impacts on crime. More counterintuitively, Chapter 12 concludes that multidimensional strategies for building collective efficacy are critical to the prevention of ecological catastrophe. If all this is true, narrowly micro criminal justice policies are never likely to be as attractive in cost–benefit terms as macrosocial strategies that are micro–meso–macro. These are ideas that are liberated from statist 'criminal justice' policy imaginations.

Many scholars agree with much of the previous two paragraphs but respond to this by becoming students of punishment—of the sociology of punishment if they are sociologists or philosophers of punishment if they are philosophers. If what one cares about normatively is domination, the implication of this book is that one would not make those choices. While punishment is hardly the central issue, according to this book, punishment does grow in importance when embedded in more encompassing theories of regulatory governance (Chapters 9 and 10). At least that is one lens of this book on how to productively shape social and political theory.

3

Macro-patterns of normative order

Key propositions

- Globally, crime is a much more deadly and destructive problem than war (so far) and suicide is much more deadly than war and crime combined (though less destructive of cities, civilisations and ecosystems). Yet a fertile path is to see war, crime and suicide as part of the same cascade of problems, all partially shaped by complex cycles of anomie that are difficult to steer, but that can be steered.

- Anomie is conceived of in ways more ancient than those popular in contemporary criminology. Anomie means widespread uncertainty about the normative order, about what are the rules of the game and uncertainty about whose authority is legitimate. Confusion about the arbitrary enforcement of arbitrary rules is domination by definition. Uncertainty about what the rules are also makes it harder for defenders of freedom to attack bad rules and bad rule and easier for despots to obfuscate, saying the rules are X to one group but not X to another.

- Legal cynicism about the rules of the game is a related concept and, like anomie, correlates with crime.

- Anomie is recurrently a factor in the onset of waves of crime and war.

- In a wide range of circumstances, anomie accelerates crime and, at times, other forms of dominating disorder, including civil war and terrorism.

- Anomie is one of the mechanisms that explains why crime risks cascades to more crime, and to war, and war risks cascades to more war and more crime.

- When an invading army or internal insurgency smashes a society apart, its normative order tends to shatter, cascading to further violence and anomie.

- Law enforcement that imprisons or kills the leaders of organised crime, terrorist or insurgency groups can also create an anomic fragmentation of those illegal groups that makes violence worse rather than better.

- However, when a social order that is not reeling from an invasion holds together during war, war can result in survivor societies rallying behind their normative order.

- Moreover, after wider spaces are pacified by a war than were pacified before the war, settled sovereignty over wider territories can diffuse peaceful coexistence.

- Vast empires of conquest have historically not only widened zones of pacification of violence; they have also quite often created spaces where the rule of law, human rights and the tempering of power could mature. So, war that transcends anomie with peaceful sovereignty can result in less crime, less domination and more freedom.

- Durkheim helps us see complex contingency and recursivity of anomie contributing to violence. At one historical juncture, anomie promotes violence. This then loops contingently to alternative cycles. One contingency is a cascade of anomie and violence in the next historical moment that shatters a society, creating cycles of more anomie and more violence. Then a communal revival from violence rises from the ashes to conquer anomie, even with nonviolence. If cascades of violence can be paused, prevented from becoming endless, the social order can hold under fire. During wars that are not too long or devastating, the social order often becomes more unified. This is more likely when the societies involved in wars are not invaded and occupied. Another loop can occur when violence establishes a monopoly of force and peaceful sovereignty over a swathe of territory that pacifies violence and anomie.

- A different loop arises when that monopoly of force dominates and excludes. When a monopoly of force is untempered, it risks unravelling that sovereignty in a return to cycles of anomie and violence (as Russia illustrates throughout its modern history to the present). All these are potential turning points that good governance can steer to the peaceful waters of freedom with low levels of crime. Most developed democracies have achieved these outcomes reasonably well since World War II, from small ones like Denmark, Norway and New Zealand to large ones like Germany, Japan and South Korea since it democratised. This is less true for the most militarised powers of this era, the United States and Russia. They have recurrently used their muscle in anomic and destabilising ways. At other times, the great powers have cooperated to support the United Nations and help it sustain the international normative order in the cause of peace and freedom.

- The complex ways in which the foregoing list of propositions interact give a helpful account of why violent crime has been in long-run decline in Europe for the past 800 years. At the same time, the propensity of anomie effects to pass tipping points can be understood to explain major reversals from that trajectory in and beyond Europe during those 800 years.

- More recently, the complex ways in which these propositions interact account for the short-term but steep reversal to increases in crime across most of the West from 1960 to 1992. They also give an account of why France is a major exception to that reversal to crime trending in this western way, why violence in Latin America, the Caribbean and Africa continued to increase during the post-1992 western crime drop and why the great East Asian crime drop preceded the western crime drop by more than four decades and continued to fall during the 1960–92 period when crime was rising in the West.

- The big-picture story of war, crime and normative order that this chapter tells demonstrates not a unidirectional civilising process, but human agency in making peace and making war, in making institutional choices that cascade crime and violence or that cascade nonviolence.

Modern and ancient normative order

Historians and international relations scholars tend not to discuss the conflict dynamics of this chapter as cascades of violence in which crime accounts for more deaths and destroyed lives than war. To be fair, not all historians of war are obsessed only with the deeds of great men and great armies to the neglect of little acts of violence that occur inside family homes, schools and on street corners. Yet there is a contribution for criminologists to make in studying waves of crime that bear relationships to waves of war.

Anomie is a central variable in macrocriminology. It is more than just one of those variables that can explain why these people have a 50 per cent higher crime rate than those people; it can be central to an account of why some places and times have 100 times as much violence as others. But anomie is a complex historical phenomenon that does not follow any simple linear path. Human history is punctuated by massive tipping points in anomie. Anomie recurrently accelerates cycles of crime, violence and further disorder to the point of the violent overthrow of states. In countries ravaged by fighting, anomie tends to get even worse. Peace settlements at the end of wars settle new sovereignties in ways that frequently become further tipping points. Anomie and violence can be pacified by the new sovereignty. Then I argue that a major variable in shaping whether pacification lasts is whether it is pacification with freedom, with tempered power, or pacification with unchecked powers for the secret police.

Consider, for example, how anomie gripped Germany following the collapse of the monarchy (the defeat of the Kaiser in World War I) and hyperinflation associated with the Great Depression from 1929. This normative disorder created a political opportunity for Adolf Hitler's Nazis, who actively schemed to accelerate anomie and violence. Ultimately, they seized power in Germany, criminalised the state and spread anomie and violence across Europe (and far beyond, with help from their allies). Less than 13 years after Hitler's election as chancellor, he was defeated militarily by a coalition led by the United States (which had become the western hegemon) and the Soviet Union (which thence became the eastern hegemon). China gradually began to re-emerge as an Asian hegemon after the communists won their long civil war in 1949. On both sides of the Iron Curtain that divided postwar Eurasia, these major powers pacified violence rather successfully. West Germany under American hegemony quickly became a low-crime society, as did East Germany under Soviet hegemony, but in a more limited and complex way. In the theoretical terms of this book, the hegemony of the United States bequeathed sovereignty to the successor West German state that was tempered by checks and balances on the abuse of power. The United States helped Japan to accomplish that as well. Japan and West Germany are no longer criminalised states, no longer anomic societies. They are low-crime societies that are no longer destabilisers or sowers of violence in other societies.

We saw in the previous chapter, however, that the formidably successful pacification of crime and violence by the successor communist states of Eastern Europe is a less solid and resilient accomplishment because these were criminalised states with massively criminalised black markets. This book will show that China is an even more complex case than the former Soviet bloc in this regard. China is rife with citizen protests at the local level. We saw in the previous chapter that local anomie is harnessed into a form of enforced self-efficacy steered by the Communist Party. China has grown capitalist markets that have competed more effectively than the black markets of its early decades of power. The Shanghai Stock Exchange is as different from the criminalised market that it was decades ago as it is different in its imperfections from western exchanges; it is governed today by a mix of 'more plural and hybrid forms of ownership, control, and regulatory governance' (Li et al. 2020). This chapter adds other complexities beyond these Chinese complexities in the role of anomie that rises, tips and falls to great declines in crime and violence.

The theory of freedom and crime developed in this book draws together older forms of macrocriminology. The approach weaves together webs of dialogue, support and control that temper dangerous societies. This chapter integrates conceptions of normative order heavily influenced by ancient Chinese, Mesopotamian, Persian and Greek philosophy and institutionalised in important ways in the empires their ideas shaped, particularly the ancient Roman Republic (Pettit 1997; Pocock 2016; Skinner 2012). While a foundational Greek version of anomie has a particular attraction for the theory of freedom and crime, this book also integrates newer interpretations of these ideas in Montesquieu, Durkheim and Merton. The framework in subsequent chapters integrates social capital theories of crime, particularly the theories of collective efficacy of Robert Sampson and his colleagues—integrated with the micro-theory of self-efficacy and social capital in Bandura (1986, 2000, 2016). In this chapter, even some empirically supported elements of control theory (Gottfredson and Hirschi 1990) and its Hobbesian foundations are integrated into the framework. This occurs even though my theoretical approach is one that in fundamental ways is at odds with control theory.

The next section is about the important ways in which normative order is different, particularly around questions of class structure, in the twenty-first century than in previous centuries. Subsequent chapters return to these themes of markets and late-modern institutional anomie, connecting the anomie insights of this chapter to market modernity. Before that, this chapter will discuss more ancient and early modern themes of war, sovereignty and anomie. First, in the section after next, the chapter makes the case for more ancient ways of thinking about normative order as being more useful than how anomie is deployed in contemporary criminology. Then the chapter considers the big-picture patterns of homicide across continents and centuries. How are they shaped by anomie, war and sovereignty? It is argued that war makes states and states make war (as do empires) when they are pursuing their sovereignty and repelling enemies. But states and empires also make peace when sovereignty is settled across pacified spaces. They become spaces where highwaymen, insurgents, terrorists and revolutionaries are likewise suppressed by sovereign domination of armed force, or rather are discouraged from so much as considering pursuit of their objectives at the point of a gun.

The class structure of normative order

Markets have been one of the great disrupters of normative orders in modern history. This is a theme in Farrall and Karstedt's (2019) book on the neglected importance of middle-class crime in criminology and the anomic forces implicated in it. Middle-class crime might be 'white-collar crime writ small', but it is writ far, wide and consequentially in Farrall and Karstedt's oeuvre. This is happening when Wilson and Dragusanu (2008: 1) find the middle class to be exploding in an unprecedented way as a 'world middle class' that is a globally 'expanding middle' that accounts for a growing proportion of the world's population and pollution in newly developed economies.

The theme of anomie and market structure is evocatively established in historiography—for example, in E.P. Thompson's (1963) *The Making of the English Working Class*. The transition to a market economy ruptured England's moral economy:

> Thompson argued that the riotous actions of peasants during the corn shortages of the 18th century could be understood as attempts to assert (and restore) a moral dimension to the market and to ensure traditional bonds and obligations against the emerging liberal economy. (Farrall and Karstedt 2019: 194)

Future chapters develop these themes as they consider institutional anomie theory. Farrall and Karstedt (2019: Ch. 8) found institutional anomie was a consistently strong explanation of middle-class crime in the

United Kingdom, West Germany and East Germany as it transitioned from communism. 'Legal cynicism' (Sampson and Bartusch 1998) contributed most to their quantitative explanation of institutional market anomie. Alongside fear of victimisation by the market, feelings of being treated unfairly in markets, motivation to 'retaliate' to get some of their share back through markets, celebrating risk-taking criminality as something discussed among friends, distrust in institutions, legal cynicism, perceptions of being overregulated by red tape, crime motivated by greed and lure (Shover and Hochstetler 2005) more than by need, and devaluation of informal rules of fair and ethical behaviour all became for Farrall and Karstedt patterns of a wider 'syndrome of institutional market anomie'.

I keep returning to their work in this book as a corrective to my own history as a Sutherlandesque criminologist dedicated to correcting criminology's theoretical errors arising from the neglect of crimes of the powerful. Farrall and Karstedt show that crimes of the middle class are distinctive because they are insufficiently alluring for the ruling class to be bothered with, and beyond the reach of the poor. They also bear a distinctively late-modern connection to anomie. One of the empirical gems in their results is that people who talk to their friends a lot about how to protect themselves from victimisation in the marketplace also talk to those friends about how to get away with being offenders in the marketplace. Most middle-class crime, Farrall and Karstedt (2019) find, is motivated by greed rather than need. Commodification, a marketised mentality, drives capitalism forward at the same time as it risks its destabilisation. Commodification becomes pathologised by the 'relentless promotion of self-interest' at the expense of citizenship values. When middle-class morality is maximally corroded, this is a danger for capitalism. Top-down corrosion of capitalism by crime in the business suites can cause markets to crash and is an important complement to corrosion by poverty and crime in the streets (and police violence in response). But crime in the lounge suites of middle-class citizens, laptops poised at their distrusting fingertips as they tap away at their petty frauds, is vital to rounding out the collapse of trust in major institutions—state institutions, private banks and private media—that worldwide is occurring top-down, bottom-up and middle-out from capitalism's middle-class heartland. Crime in business suites may help to motivate and neutralise both crime in the streets and crime in the middle-class lounge suites. All the forms of illegitimacy these classes inflict on one another may feed back in complex ways into anomie, into the crimes the members of each class impose on others.

This can make sense of the surveys of Valerie Braithwaite's Centre for Tax System Integrity that show that most Australians across all classes in most years commit some kind of fraud on their tax return (ctsi.org.au). Yet the research base from that project, particularly from estimates of the size of the underground economy (Schneider 2002, 2005; Schneider and Buehn 2018), also suggests that Australia is like the United Kingdom, the United States and Germany in being part of the high tax-compliance region of the world that is mostly concentrated in northern and Western Europe, North America and perhaps China. All southern European countries have lower tax compliance and a larger underground economy. Eastern Europe has much larger underground economies still (fluctuating at slightly below or above half the real economy in the worst cases of Russia, Ukraine, Georgia, Azerbaijan, Armenia, Moldova and Belarus). Many economies further east and south of Eastern Europe—such as Thailand, Cambodia, Myanmar, Afghanistan, Nigeria, Gabon, Tanzania, Zimbabwe, Bolivia, Peru, Guatemala, Haiti, Honduras, Panama and Uruguay—are so much lower that most of the real economy is outside the legitimate economy. In this latter list of economies, most of the real economy is consistently a black market of some kind. At their worst, large shadow economies in states with low legitimacy lead to high rates of murder in the shadows when disputes in criminal markets cannot be resolved in the courts because they relate to criminal transactions (Tuttle 2019).

Intergenerational conflict over the normative order is conceived of in this chapter as important in late modernity. Markets created adolescence as something important for the first time in western history only since 1950. Distinctive markets in fashion, music, social media and leisure for the young mean that teenagers are no longer junior versions of adults in their tastes and dress, but carriers of age-distinctive identities. In the West, the newest middle-class generation shows signs of resentment that their parents or grandparents, particularly the baby boomers, got a better deal than them on issues like free university education. In the course of the international collaborations of the Centre for Tax System Integrity, Valerie Braithwaite and I were privy to the in-house research of western tax authorities on tax morale, particularly in cases like Sweden, where the youngest generation of taxpayers was more willing to cheat than past generations for this reason. One vindication of this in Braithwaite and Ahmed's (2005) Australian research was that young university graduates who were carrying forward a debt on government loans to pay for university places that used to be free were more likely to cheat on their tax. They were more likely still to be tax cheats if they perceived the university education they paid for as a rip-off or shoddy in quality!

A different set of studies by Eliza Ahmed also resonates with Farrall and Karstedt's writing on middle-class victim–offender constellations— the middle class as victims of crimes that help neutralise their criminal offending. Ahmed and Braithwaite's (2006) research on bullying in schools and workplaces in Bangladesh and Australia showed that the world is not made up of bullies and victims. The larger group of bully-victims—people who both bully and suffer bullying—is more structurally important to the normative decay of nonviolent associational orders in schools and workplaces. One reason for this that Ahmed found is the bully-victims combined all the shame management and pride management (narcissism) pathologies of both the bullies and the victims. This resonance is valuable for seeing the richness of Farrall and Karstedt (2019) as connecting not only up to the high politics of anomie in capitalist societies, but also right down to more general insights of relevance to the low politics of anomie in school playgrounds.

Recursive anomie, cascades of violence

This section considers ancient thinking that lays a foundation for anomie theory, starting with Confucius, Cyrus the Great of Persia, the Greeks, Romans and Hobbes. It then considers its modern legacy, particularly from Emile Durkheim and Robert K. Merton. Durkheim (1952) helps us to see that crime is fostered by conditions of collapse of the normative order. In the process, the analysis begins to shape the case for a republican conception of freedom as nondomination in the footsteps of ancients of the Middle East like Cyrus (Ambler 2001; Briant 2002) and Romans like Cicero.[1]

In a Durkheimian way, the theory is advanced that anomie creates conditions for crime, for the violence of war and for the self-violence of suicide. Yet the existential threat of war and of crime waves also frequently

---

1   Cicero was a defender not only of a republican conception of the freedom of not being under the arbitrary power of a ruler (Pettit 1997), but also of the Roman Republic because he believed it pacified smaller states that constantly fought barbaric wars with each other—for example, Greece (Morris 2014: 34).

mobilises societies to rally around the normative order, bringing anomie under control. Recursivity is a term used in this book not just about the dynamics of anomie. Recursivity means here that the output of a macro process becomes an input of that process, generating a loop that unfolds sequences and structures that can be of unbounded length and complexity (Corballis 2014).

Complex Durkheimian recursivity of anomie and crime helps account for big patterns of criminality in human history. It does not submit neatly to linear models of positivist criminology. For example, in this chapter, it helps account for why a very long-run decline in violence was decisively reversed in Europe, North America, Australia and New Zealand between 1960 and 1992. Also involved in explaining this macro trend is an unprecedented surge in wars involving the West and East Asia between 1911 and 1953. We could possibly extend this wave of war later if the deadly wars in Indochina from the 1960s are included. The most recent data, however, locate the most decisive statistical turning point to reduced interstate battle deaths as 1950 (Cunen et al. 2020).

I argue that the huge waves of war up to the end of the Korean War, from 1911 to 1953, at first helped halt the long-run downward plunge of the homicide rate to form the bottom of a two-century-long U-distribution of crime in the West. These waves of northern and western wars then helped sharply increase western crime between 1960 and 1992. An argument is made for long lags in these cascades of violence because the impact of the violence of unprecedented killing in wars on the generation of veterans' children was often greater than the impact on the veterans themselves. This is because by the time the average veteran is discharged from the military their age already approaches or exceeds the end of the highest criminality phase of the life cycle. This is not so with their children. This macro-transgenerational impact was mediated by populist postwar glorification of the violence of war, by child abuse and gender-based violence in veterans' families. When cracks appeared in western normative orders from the 1960s, fuelled by the feeling that citizens were being squeezed between dishonest big business and big government, violence was seen by western protagonists of the left and the right as imperative for defending their ideologies.

This book identifies worrying structural risks in the global system without being pessimistic. Human actors have already grasped their agency in major ways to reject violence and build global movements for the nonviolent transformation of societies (see the trend in Figure 3.1). This book argues that cascades of criminalisation of markets and states have frequently been reversed in human history. We have a lot of experience as a species that has taught us much about how to reverse cascades of crime and violence. While criminalised markets and states are wicked challenges, we cannot tackle crime or climate change or prevent war without strong states and strong markets whose power is tempered by checks and balances. Tempered sovereignty is an important part of rising to the challenge.

Historical patterns of violence

This chapter deploys a macrocriminological lens to help see the big picture of global and local patterns of crime and violence across human history.

Unrecorded criminality associated with war—failure to count the crimes that hundreds of millions of combatants committed in other countries during the peak war years from 1911 to 1953—makes it problematic to claim that crime rates *actually* were at the bottom of a long U-curve between 1911 and 1953. We cannot be sure that criminality—especially murder, torture, other human rights abuses and black-market crimes by westerners—were not in fact increasing in the five decades before 1960. We can be more confident that crime was increasing in most western countries during the three decades after 1960.

It is likely that more rapes were committed in Germany in 1945 by Allied soldiers than have ever been reported in one year in any of the Allied countries. The rapes by Russian soldiers alone, but also by American soldiers alone, in that year were almost certainly greater than any number of rapes ever recorded officially in any western country in any year. Barbara Johr (1992: 58; Sander and Johr 2005) reported the highest estimates, that 1.4–1.9 million German women and girls were raped, particularly as the Red Army approached Berlin. She counted the deaths of 240,000 German women associated with war rapes. Most historians who are experts on this subject believe this estimate is too high, but that it is a large six-figure number. Kaiser et al. (2018) found that 6.8 per cent of a sample of children of the wartime occupation reported that they were born as a result of rape; while Gebhardt (2016) estimated 5 per cent from official records and estimated that for every rape that resulted in a pregnancy, there were 10 more that did not. Messerschmidt (2006) claims that 10 per cent of German rape victims committed suicide. Historian Geoffrey Roberts (2013) reported 70,000–100,000 war rapes by Soviet forces in Vienna. At the high end, German feminist historian Miriam Gebhardt (2016) estimated—partly from records of wartime and occupation rapes kept by local priests and partly from West German Federal Statistics Office records of children fathered by American soldiers—that 190,000 German women were raped by American soldiers during the occupation up to 1955 but most in 1945. The data exclude the rape of men and boys by American soldiers, which is certainly something that also happened in Germany (Williams 2016). American criminologist Robert Lilley (2007) estimated 11,000 rapes based on an analysis of US Army records for 1945–46. The West's 'Greatest Generation' (who grew up in the 1920s and 1930s and fought in World War II) is seen as a low-crime generation. Criminologically, this might be questioned as a myth, at least for its men. Rape was massively widespread in the Allied occupation of Japan as well (Takemae 2003). It is not part of Australia's history of World War II that women mopped up in the region devastated by the atomic war crime in Hiroshima could fear Australian soldiers most for the brutality of rape (Tanaka 2018).

In the broadest sense, this book concludes that Norbert Elias (1982) and Steven Pinker (2011) may be right that there has been a long-run trend towards reduced violence over the past millennium. Nevertheless, as Elias (1996) himself conceded in *The Germans*, there are big continental exceptions to this pattern. East Asia became more violent—indeed, the most violent part of the world—for many decades up to 1953; and Latin America (especially Central America) became much more violent after the crescendo of its waves of state crime and civil wars from the 1970s (many associated with the United States' War on Drugs), and then became the most violent region of the world (closely followed by Africa). We can also get clues to an explanation that might fit the macro-patterns by looking at country exceptions to the continental patterns of recent history, such as France, Cambodia and a cluster of South Asian countries (India, Pakistan, Afghanistan and Sri Lanka) that have experienced high violence in recent decades. We see that explanation as a long-run cascading of peace and nonviolence, complicated by the interruptions of cascades of war and cascades of crime, each reinforcing the other, at specific space-time hotspots (Braithwaite and D'Costa 2018).

In Pinker's long-run pacification, we see waves of war during the past millennium that badly disrupt that pacification of war and crime. This seems evident with the wave of war that culminated in the Hundred Years' War and the Thirty Years' War in Europe, and the 1911–53 wave of wars that encompassed the two most deadly wars of modernity. The wave of anticommunist and anti–drug-cartel wars of Latin America from the 1970s and 1980s was another important interruption to cascades of nonviolence. Latin American waves of state and anti-state violence from the 1970s also interrupted the consolidation of a normative order. In countries like Mexico, the wars against armed drug-trafficking organisations continued ferociously during the twenty-first century, accounting for more killings than the invasion, insurgency and drug wars in Afghanistan. Post-independence proxy wars between the Cold War powers from the 1960s right through the 1980s and beyond in Africa formed another wave of violence of profound historical importance. Another wave of prominence for global patterns of crime was the disruption of East Asian normative order from the time of the British attacks on China in the Opium Wars, if not earlier.

We can partially agree with Elias (1996) when he sees such reversals as decivilising movements against a long-run civilising trend. These cascade effects intersect with anomie effects on violence, and violence effects on anomie. Elias insightfully diagnoses Hitler as a masterful manipulator of anomie. He quotes Hitler as characterising the terrorists who destabilised the Weimar Republic as 'uprooted and [who] thus have lost all inner connection with a regulated human social order ... determined to take a stand against any kind of order, filled by hatred of every authority' (Elias 1996: 227). Elias concluded that '[t]he violence of the National Socialist movement, with the aid of privately organized defence associations ... brought about the almost complete dissolution of the monopoly of force ... destroy[ing] the Weimar Republic from within' and laying the foundation for Hitler to promise an end to anomie; 'this negative purpose was given a positive face' (Elias 1996: 228). For Elias, German fascism is also a 'paradigmatic' case of

> what the leaders of a civilized nation are capable of doing in their struggle for the restoration or preservation of their imperial role when a chronic feeling of decline, of being encircled by enemies and driven into a corner, awakens the conviction that only absolute ruthlessness can save their fading power and glory. (Elias 1996: 360)

Elias conceded to his critic Zygmunt Bauman (1989) that industrialised modernity concentrates power in ways that can be easy to capture and hard to control; this made incivilities like carpet bombing and the industrial slaughter of the Holocaust more possible (see also Balint 2011). The view of Bauman and Balint is what makes the tempering of power a critical issue for the twenty-first century.

Many are uncomfortable with Elias's usage of 'the civilising process' because the word civilisation has a western heritage meaning western civilisation as superior to 'backward' civilisations. As David Garland (1990: 245) points out, Elias's mission had no normative baggage of western superiority. His mission was to map specific transformations across time *within* the West in emotional life and behaviour that are linked to the expansion of social interdependencies; he does this by a close reading of historical sources such as etiquette manuals. For my project of integrating explanatory and normative theory, this book must reconcile a desire to make good use of Elias even though civility is not a theoretically central concept for the book. Pinker is right to see what Braithwaite and D'Costa (2018) describe as nonviolence as highly associated with Elias's civilising process. I have discovered and documented more learnings about nonviolence that could be read as a civilising process in Elias terms in Africa, Afghanistan, Kashmir and Bougainville than from the West, just as Broadhurst et al. (2015) learnt so much from the history of Cambodia by viewing it through Elias's lens. In practical terms, the way this book makes use of Elias is similar to how Pinker, Broadhurst and Bouhours or Eisner use Elias.

Pacified spaces and normative order

One paradoxical recursivity of classical anomie is that anomie can foster crime and violence (including wars) (Braithwaite et al. 2010a), and extremes of violence that are interpreted as existential threats to societies can mobilise commitments to, and the strengthening of, the normative order. This is complemented in human history by a paradoxical recursivity of sovereignty effects on violence. Bloody struggles to assert sovereignty over a territory—be it sovereignty over city-states, nation-states or great empires—cascade to waves of wars and cascades of crime (Braithwaite and D'Costa 2018). Yet something transformative happens once sovereignty is established with one armed force dominating all other armed groups across a territory. Max Weber called this the state monopoly of armed force that defines statehood. 'Monopoly' is slightly misleading for contemporary societies with so much privatised armed security, drug cartels, foreign proxy forces and UN peacekeeping. Nevertheless, once one armed force dominates all other armed forces across a territory, it eventually tends to accomplish pacification of violence. State and empire security forces over time pacify the warlords and highwaymen who once terrorised those travelling its roads. That sovereignty, when it is sufficient to sustain armed domination of the territory, subdues the ambitions of plotters of coups, revolutions, terror and other forms of armed insurrection. This Hobbesian conclusion lays a foundation for the analysis in future chapters of the recursive paradoxes of domination. On the one hand, military domination pacifies spaces under sovereign control; on the other hand, the persistence of militarisation and domination in a sovereign territory can sow the seeds of new wars.

The republican imperative is that the dominations of war that create state sovereignties must morph into a rule of law that underwrites nondomination. That rule of law can supplant the rule of the gun. Then a freedom is enabled that rejects domination by the arbitrary power of arms. A paradox for this chapter is that Charles Tilly (1975: 42) was insightful when he said 'war made the state and the state made war'. This means that 'extraction and struggle over the means of war created the central organizational structure of states' (Tilly 1992: 14). In particular, a heightened fear of war following the seventeenth-century 'military revolution' fuelled the creation of modern states with better infrastructure and more effective regimes for raising tax revenue to fund defence. Yet Morris (2014: 18) was also right when he showed that 'over the past ten thousand years war made the state and the state made peace'. Wars, Morris found, enabled more powerful states and empires to create wider zones of pacification than existed in earlier eras of smaller states such as city-states. That both Tilly and Morris are right is the paradoxical complexity of the recursivity highlighted in this chapter.

This is also true of empires. We will illustrate that truth in this chapter with the rule of the most brutal of empires such as the Roman Empire, the Persian Empire, the Chinese and Mongol empires and the British Empire. These empires pacified vast spaces by war and those pacified spaces then became places where freedom from violence could grow with guarantees of a rule a law. These empires then even gave birth to conceptions of human rights that guaranteed freedoms, abolished slavery and showed leadership towards tempering power through the separation of powers.

We see this paradoxical dynamic with the most murderous of empires, Genghis Khan's Mongol Empire (1206–1368). It was the Mongols rather than the Han Chinese who did most of the conquest that expanded to contemporary China. Genghis Khan's was the empire that conquered a larger territory than any in human history because it was more murderous than those it conquered. It defeated other great empires in China and Persia by laying siege to cities, making it clear that, unless there was total surrender without resistance, the entire population of the city would be slaughtered. After recurrent demonstration effects of such total slaughter, the next cities along Genghis Khan's ride to empire would surrender immediately and totally.

This was part of the paradox of pacification. In the end, Genghis Khan pacified all the societies along the Silk Road connecting East Asia to the Middle East and Europe so successfully that young women could travel safely along it without being robbed or assaulted. Other women could become rulers of the greatest of territories including the former Chinese and Persian empires that continued to be embryonic crucibles of progress towards good governance under their female Mongol rulers. These were feminist rekindlings of limited but significant empowerment of women (Weatherford 2010). The early kindling of freedom, feminism and competing conceptions of the rule of law as ideas were diffused by medieval intellectuals along the pacified Silk Road. Markets also flourished: China and India together continued to account for the majority of the global economy in purchasing power parity terms[2] until 1820 (until industrial capitalism) (Mahbubani 2020). The trade routes pacified along the Silk Road enabled the wealth of these two great trading empires.

The criminological literature at more meso levels shows comparable paradoxes of feedback loops in the relationship between violence and the control of territory. Street gangs in late-modern cities mobilised violence against competing gangs to secure domination of some small patch of urban territory. Police learnt that it was not always wise to deploy policing strategies that so disrupted the territorial control of gangs as to create new gang wars for control of territory. William Foot Whyte (1943) in *Street Corner Society* and Gerald Suttles (1968) in *The Social Order of the Slum* both showed ethnographically that older gang leaders calmed the violence of younger hotheads in the gang, and beyond the gang, in the domains

2   Mahbubani (2020) argues persuasively that purchasing power parity GDP is the most relevant measure of geopolitical sway and the extension of sovereignty.

they dominated. Putting those gang leaders in prison could therefore increase violence rather than reduce it. Systematic quantitative research has shown across the past two decades in Mexico that decapitation strategies that arrested or killed drug cartel leaders made violence much worse (Calderón et al. 2015; Dell 2015; Phillips 2015; Ríos 2013; Atuesta and Pérez-Dávila 2018; Lessing 2018). Spaces that were formerly zones with a certain degree of pacification under a gang leader became battle zones as successor leaders fought for the spoils of succession; larger gangs that oversaw wide zones of relative peace disintegrated into many smaller warring gangs. Papachristos and Kirk (2015: 530) also point to a gang-splintering dynamic of a more micro–meso kind in parts of Chicago that experienced steep rises in gun homicides during the past decade.

Comparably, when domination of the territory of an empire begins to disintegrate, war is more likely to break out, as we saw with the breakup of the Ottoman and then the Habsburg empires in the leadup to World War I. The Thirty Years' War, which we will see was associated with an earlier wave of war and crime, was also about a failed attempt to disintegrate the sovereignty of the Habsburg Empire. In 1918, the world looked back on the two most deadly wars of history both being about existential breakup threats to the Habsburg Empire. The evidence is generally strong for a long-run macro-association between the breakup of empires and waves of war and also of waves of criminal violence (Ferguson 2006; Braithwaite and D'Costa 2018).

Summary so far: Recursive anomie, recursive violence and sovereignty

In sum, the analysis of this chapter turns first on a paradoxical Durkheimian recursivity of anomie becoming destabilising crime and violence, resulting in more anomie. Second, however, once violence succeeds in establishing a monopoly of armed force in a space, the suppression of anomie can result. The Hobbesian paradox is that sovereignty is accomplished by terrible destabilising waves of violence and then it is sovereign power that pacifies violence. Braithwaite and D'Costa (2018) discussed the empirical evidence for all these dynamics. They found that cascades of nonviolence depend on peace agreements that generally cannot be secured only by rewarding armed groups that surrender their weapons. It is also necessary to create a successor state with a police and military that are sufficiently dominant in their control of armed force to suppress recurrent coups, terrorism, armed insurrections and criminal gangs. An interesting analysis of anthropological data from 32 societies from the Human Relations Area Files by Rosenfeld and Messner (1991) found that societies with a standing army or some other differentiated military organisation had lower levels of homicide and violence. Centralised specialists in social control, be they courts or armies, take the pressure off ordinary people and political leaders alike when trust and reconciliation fail. Future chapters describe this as the paradox of institutionalised distrust and enculturated trust. The distrustful militarised pacification of spaces enables civil societies to get on with the work of the enculturation of trust inside those spaces. These data also seem to affirm the importance of not forgetting Hobbes (1651) on the dangers of a war of all against all in the absence of centralised state authority to use legal coercion as a last resort to regulate violence.[3]

We will attempt to make sense of the big patterns of crime and violence in human history with a cascade analysis of the recursivity of anomie and violence combined with the complex recursivity of sovereignty and violence. Violence begets violence until a Hobbesian tipping point is reached, where a sovereign monopoly of violence entrenches pacification. This sense-making of macro-patterns of human history is part of what macrocriminology might seek. Yet the sense these recursivities make of long-run patterns of crime and war violence is not very decisive evidence for their explanatory power. This is because many other sets of complex explanations might account for these patterns. Indeed, for any place and time, more complexly attuned and fine-grained local explanations will almost always provide better accounts than a general macrocriminological theory. Braithwaite and D'Costa (2018) discussed less-macro evidence of associations between anomie and crime and between sovereignty (or its breakup) and crime. This evidence will be discussed in more summary ways in this chapter. These are the more important kinds of evidence

---

3   This goes to a grave error of early republican thinking about standing armies as a danger to freedom. This error was compounded by the constitution of the new US republic when it entrenched a constitutional right to bear arms to enable civilian militias as alternatives to standing armies. The gun culture that resulted was reinforced by high early homicide rates of 250 per 100,000 in Virginia, with rates reaching almost 500 in the seventeenth century (Roth 2012). Note that these English settlers came from England, where homicide rates had always been below 10 during these centuries (Eisner 2001, 2003, 2014). Hence, while US homicide rates may be much higher than those of Europe today, they have declined much more sharply than in Europe. There was much more for the progressive US regulation of gun carrying in public to accomplish than was needed in England, especially at the anomic southern and western frontiers of the United States as it spread genocide and land theft across a vast expanse.

for my hypotheses about recursive relationships among anomie, cascades of crime and war, and sovereignty that pacifies spaces and consolidates normative order in ways that ultimately allow freedom to flourish. The most important conclusion in the work of Braithwaite and D'Costa (2018) is that agency always rests in the hands of local and national actors like Gandhi or Mandela who can act to flip cascades of violence to cascades of nonviolence, healing and preventive diplomacy.

Ancient anomie

This chapter seeks to rehabilitate a classic interpretation of anomie. Anomie is interpreted to mean a disintegration of the normative order so that people do not know what the rules of the game are and do not know whose authority they should regard as legitimate. Anomie theorists in criminology pay little attention to whose authority citizens should regard as legitimate. This occurs even though Durkheim (1958: 79–89) wrote about the importance of democracy for granting legitimacy to rulers and to rules. In our Peacebuilding Compared project, it became clear how important this is to normative order and to violence when societies are at war with themselves, with one government in exile and another in the capital both claiming legitimacy, killing those who challenge that legitimacy. Normative disintegration produces normative vacuums that are dangerous for human societies. This is because normative vacuums attract the most tyrannous and violent forces (Dahrendorf 1985). At the same time, normative integration is also a dangerous game in the way it can induce violence by a majority community against those not embraced into that community (Karstedt 2011b). The Ku Klux Klan effected a white-supremacist normative integration of a certain kind in southern US communities that it dominated. The danger here, according to the analysis in this book, is the combination of a strong normative order and a politics of domination, stigmatisation and exclusion. We see both problems with the rise of the Taliban as an armed rule-of-law movement in Kandahar Province in 1994. The rise of the Taliban made women safe from rape and travellers safe from highwaymen in a society that had been disintegrating into a war of all against all (Braithwaite and D'Costa 2018; Kilcullen 2011). The rise of the Taliban to sovereignty, however, triggered a politics of domination, exclusion and stigmatisation across Afghanistan. From the space the Taliban pacified, terrorists it embraced ultimately contributed to a global cascade of violence that accelerated dramatically after 11 September 2001. The sequence here is anomic violence followed by pacification, sovereignty by a monopoly of force and violence reduction, followed by violent state domination and exclusion that cascaded another cycle of violence.

These ideas have a long history. Confucius was the most influential ancient thinker on normative order. He is the ancient whose influence most persists today. The Confucian perspective on normative order emphasises five norms and three bonds. The five key norms of the Confucian order are rather general principles that continue to resonate beyond East Asia. They are: *ren* (仁, 'benevolence'), *yi* (義, 'righteousness', which restorative justice theorists might want to reframe as 'just relationships'),[4] *li* (禮, 'respect'), *zhi* (智, 'wisdom') and *xin* (信, 'trust') (Liu et al. 2012; Liu and Palermo 2009). The three bonds, *sangang* (三綱), refer to appropriate vertical human relationships of authority and followership—namely, ruler–subject, father–son and husband–wife. Because dominating hierarchical relationships so often involve obligations of subjects to follow rulers, sons to fathers and wives to husbands, the three bonds are unattractive to liberals, republicans and feminists. For this reason, Dennis Wong and his colleagues[5] commend a contemporary freedom-enhancing interpretation of Confucianism that sidelines the three bonds and emphasises the five norms. Had Durkheim reflected on Confucianism, he might have advanced the alternative that the three bonds could also be transformed to respecting the fundamental humanity of others and reflecting on institutions of deliberation and democracy (Durkheim 1958: 79–89). Wong addresses this in a Confucian way by seeking to replace the valorising of *sangang* with Confucian *wuchang*. *Wuchang* valorises horizontal human relationships of the kind that are vital to deliberative democracy, relational justice and contemporary restorative justice in China, as opposed to the vertical relationships of the three bonds (Mok and Wong 2013; Wong 2014). Wong's idea is that a low-crime normative order is possible based more on the horizontal communal enforcement of relational justice and the basic principles of the five key norms and less on

---

4   In correspondence with Dennis Wong, he agreed that *yi* is hard to translate, but that 'just relationships' is a helpful way of doing so for western audiences. In one strand of the traditional Confucian literature, *yi* denotes appropriateness. It means interacting with others with appropriate attitudes, with a heavy emphasis on the Golden Rule and generous reciprocity. Wong continued in this correspondence: '[T]here is an old Chinese saying describing the spirit of *yi* by saying that "你敬我一尺 我敬你一丈" [If you respect me for an inch, I will respect you for one foot]'.
5   I am grateful to Dennis Wong from the City University of Hong Kong for a number of wonderful conversations on his reading of Confucianism during the past 20 years.

state and patriarchal enforcement of law. The role of law is relegated to a last resort in this contemporary Confucian vision. Western feminism also generally failed to notice that between the 1890s and 1920 (the era of Sun Yat-sen's republican revolution and first-wave western feminism), Chinese feminist political reformers, revolutionaries and cultural critics

> redeployed or reintegrated Confucian ideas, articulating their progressive ideas in Confucian vernacular. They addressed concerns about gender equality, education, and oppression by renovating Confucian terms. Reformers argued for a politics of embracing the contributions of all to humanity (*expansive ren*, 仁), of responding to lived experience (critical *dao, jian shu dao*, 谏恕道), and of co-cultivating self and healthy community (*xiushen da renhe, datong wei liren*, 修身达人和, 大同为立人). (Li and Ackerly 2021 [whose work bears the evocative title '(Ren)ovating feminism: Confucian feminism in times of political transformation in China'])

For similar reasons, Thomas Hobbes' (1651) offer of a choice between order through an absolute sovereign and chaos (the state of nature) is an unattractive one. It is seen as a false choice by advocates of liberty today. Hobbes was right that a strong state is necessary to restore order after civil wars. It was natural for Hobbes to value state normative ordering, living as he did in the war of all against all during and after the English Civil War. After periods of chaos, a despotic Leviathan is a less attractive way of mooring the normative order than state power tempered by countervailing sources of authority and contestation. This book shows why Hobbes was wrong to value state sovereignty that is absolute and indivisible. Hobbes was also important to criminology in laying the psychological foundations for control theory. Hobbes and control theory share the assumption that people will be knaves unless they are brought under control. Part of the motivation of restorative and responsive regulatory theory is the empirical insight that if you treat people as knaves, they are more likely to become knaves.

When the Romans left Britain a millennium and a half before Hobbes, Britons cheered their liberation from the Roman yoke. The country then quickly descended into such chaos and violence that terrified Britons wrote to Rome asking its legions to return to restore order (Collier 2009: 173). In the Monty Python film *The Life of Brian*, a group of disgruntled Jewish revolutionaries lament: 'What have the Romans ever done for us?' A fellow revolutionary answers, well, there are the aqueducts, then another mentions roads, another clean water, then bridges, education, medicine, sanitation, irrigation, peace and streets that are safe at night. Hobbes was not completely wrong in seeing British and Hebrew society as slow at learning the benefits of state sovereignty, but he was wrong in seeing domination as the key to successful state-building.

Thin modern freedom

After Confucius and the Roman republic and before Hobbes, thinking about what liberty means began to thin out according to a republican narrative of the history of freedom (Pettit 1997). Liberty increasingly came to mean non-interference rather than nondomination. As markets became institutionally more important, market mentalities of freedom took hold. The state continued to be granted a fundamental role in delivering the security and social order within which markets were free to flourish. But beyond that, liberty was valorised as non-interference in citizens' choices, particularly non-interference by the state. In the libertarian vision of the state's role in freedom that grew in popularity, the state should be but a 'nightwatchman'. A market mentality of freedom is what contemporary thinkers like to call neoliberalism. Scholars in the republican tradition contrast this with liberty before liberalism. Republican theorists conceive of this thinning of the ideal of freedom by market mentalities as being well under way by the time of Hobbes.

In the republican debates of the founding fathers of the American Revolution, and in the thinking of republican feminists of that era such as Mary Wollstonecraft (1792), the thicker republican conception of the freedom of not being a slave to dominant powers was still alive. We can see republican freedom as nondomination in the thinking of Thomas Jefferson, James Madison and other American founders and in Montesquieu, who so inspired them. To this day, that light on the republican hill has never been extinguished. Some capitalisms, especially Anglo-Saxon ones, became more determinedly neoliberal, while others— for example, in Scandinavia, Germany and other northern European societies—continued to sustain more social democratic sensibilities about social coordination to temper the excesses of domination by liberal markets (Hall and Soskice 2001). Other capitalisms still are more Hobbesian. Authoritarian capitalism is on the rise in post-communist Russia, Hungary and Poland and most notably in a China that, contra Dennis Wong, also leans heavily on hierarchical control by the 'three bonds'. Authoritarian capitalism also flourishes in Bangladesh, Saudi

3. MACRO-PATTERNS OF NORMATIVE ORDER

Arabia, Qatar, the United Arab Emirates and quite a number of other economies that have been growing faster than liberal market economies. Authoritarian capitalist ideology also gained impetus during its rise in formerly liberal capitalist societies such as Donald Trump's United States and in formerly social democratic capitalist societies such as India, Brazil, the Philippines, Turkey, Poland, Hungary and Austria.

While there are many differences in the way normative order is valued across these different contemporary versions of capitalism, let us return to Dennis Wong's project of a contemporarily relevant version of Confucianism as one option. In so doing, I do not advocate it, but simply point out that it is one of many visions of normative order that cleaves back to 'liberty before liberalism', while being aware of the dangers of domination and therefore rejecting hierarchical authoritarianism. Chapter 8 considers some of the strengths of Sun Yat-sen's republican constitution of China through Dennis Wong's lens.

Wong's adaptation of a rule of Confucian principles combined with a compassionate justice of horizontal relationships help us to see that normative order is about this to an important degree globally. One important principle in the writing of Confucius was the Golden Rule: do unto others as you would have them do unto you. The Golden Rule also later appears in the biblical teachings of Jesus and of the Prophet Mohammed and it probably exists earlier in the Egyptian and Persian empires (Hertzler 1934). For wars of conquest, the Golden Rule was always pushed aside, but during long periods of peace after recurrent wars, the Golden Rule played an important part in the normative order of the Silk Road along which traders could safely travel, as could ideas of freedom (Braithwaite 2017a, 2017b). The Golden Rule, by republican lights, is a helpful bedrock for forging a well-tempered intercommunal normative order. Because people do not want to be treated as slaves, doing unto others as you would have them do unto you prohibits slavery. We see this antislavery bedrock of freedom in the Old Testament liberation of the Hebrew slaves, in the Persian Empire of Cyrus the Great liberating various enslaved groups and carving in stone certain rights to freedom from domination (Ambler 2001; Briant 2002).[6]

---

6   Persia built the largest empire of the ancient world and a more enduring empire than other great empires like the Roman and British. A millennium and a half after Cyrus, one Persian prince told his son in 1080 to: 'Understand this truth. The kingdom can be held by the army, and the army by gold; and gold is acquired through agricultural development; and agricultural development through justice and equity. Therefore be just and equitable.' Morris (2014: 140) quotes this advice and then comments that 'conquerors who refused to learn this truth did not last long'.

That bedrock normative order against slavery is constantly under threat from rulers of powerful states and from capitalist markets. Powerful states resent attempts to constrain their will to enslave and torture others by warfare, or to push aside the Golden Rule in a war on terror, a war on drugs or a war on crime. Slavery might be 'abolished' at different historical moments, but resilient markets fight back with new modalities of human trafficking, new ways of enslaving factory workers in Bangladesh to the projects of western brands hell-bent on producing the cheapest possible clothing for western consumers. Entrepreneurs of the darknet defend their right to non-interference as they enable the enslavement of children by international paedophile networks. The persistent threats are clear. Those who control states defend their prerogatives of state domination. Rulers, fathers and husbands who control the prerogatives of the three bonds of Confucianism defend that patriarchal domination. Those who grow fat on market power defend non-interference in markets and neoliberalism; those who profit from cyber-commerce defend internet freedom and claim that cybercrime and cyberwar are the price we must pay for that freedom. Pluralist agonistic contestation of these hegemonies is no easy challenge (see Chapter 12).

This book explores hierarchical power and the power of markets as great criminogenic forces of human history. The deep bedrock of normative resonance in the Golden Rule and resistance to slavery and domination in 'liberty before liberalism' is hard to preserve against their sway, as is 'liberty before liberalism's' valorisation of relational justice under threat from monopoly control of justice by markets in legal professionalism. These interpretations of freedom have been constantly challenged at least since the time of Cyrus the Great by untempered state power and then by the rising power of markets untempered by concern to resist enslavement by markets.

Durkheim's anomie

Emile Durkheim (1952) is a foundational thinker in the history of seeing suicide and crime as fostered by conditions of collapse of normative order. This remains true even though there is more than a grain of insight in distinguishing Durkheim from Merton with the quip that 'for Merton, *anomie causes deviance*, while for Durkheim *deviance prevents anomie*' (Hilbert 1989: 242). Durkheim's writing reveals the importance of the way reactions to crime can consolidate a normative order,[7] so recursivity lurks in Durkheim's theory of the relationship between anomie and crime. Durkheim himself does not deploy the concept of recursivity. We can build on Durkheim by seeing the complex recursivity of anomie contributing to violence at one historical moment. This then loops contingently to a number of different kinds of cycles: violence in the next moment shatters a society, creating cycles of more anomie and more violence; then the communal response to violence reduces anomie when the society does not shatter (when the social order holds under fire); another loop occurs when violence establishes a monopoly of force and peaceful sovereignty over a swathe of territory; yet another loop arises when domination and exclusion unravel that sovereignty in a return to cycles of anomie and violence.

While it is a simple proposition that there is an imperative to secure sovereignty and to temper sovereign power, predicting when and how these recursive loops of normative order and disorder will feed one into another is complex. All we can hope for is an understanding that all of these are recurrent dynamics. Once we grasp their complex loops, we might seek to monitor and steer them wisely with a politics of checks and balances. Predicting crime along these recursive loops has challenges akin to those facing the world at the time of writing when the Covid-19 virus is spreading. Medical experts cannot predict the speed of spread for any country, when the pandemic will die out or when it will return for further waves. While the best medical brains cannot predict the trajectories of these cycles, they can understand the character of these dynamics to inform their monitoring of them and their agency to intervene aggressively or gently as required. And the evidence seems clear that some societies have saved lives by exercising this wisdom more adeptly and assiduously than others. Social scientists are not in such a wildly inferior position to this as they seek to monitor the recursivity of diverse loops of anomie, domination and crime.

---

7 'Crime brings together upright consciences and concentrates them. We have only to notice what happens, particularly in a small town, when some moral scandal has just been committed. They stop each other on the street, they visit each other, they seek to come together to talk of the event and to wax indignant in common ... If the offence is serious, the whole group attacked masses itself in the face of the danger and unites' (Durkheim 1933: 102–3). War would also seem to be the kind of 'great collective shock' that brings citizens together in rituals that concentrate relational life and give people meaning and a sense of identity. From relational work in 'moments of collective ferment' are born 'the great ideals upon which civilizations rest' (Durkheim 1965: 241; 1952: 91).

In the Greek, *anomia* has the broadest meaning, which remains fertile for understanding the crimes of contemporary capitalism. It means in the Greek, literally, a condition of being without norms. The Greek etymology of 'anomie' is from *a* ('without') and *nomos* ('law' or 'norms'). 'Norms' is a much wider concept than rules: it means customary expectations of behaviour that coordinate one's interactions with others. Biblical *anomia* was lawlessness that encompassed disregard of God's written and living word (Bible Hub 2004–21). *Anomia* encompassed a breakdown of principles as well as of rules in the original Greek meaning. Durkheim (1952) generally cleaves closer to the original Greek conception than contemporary criminologists, though Durkheim also gives anomie a range of more specific meanings that are used inconsistently between different works (DiCristina 2016). Durkheim's (1933, 1952) analysis of rising crime during the Industrial Revolution in France led him to propose that the breakdown of the traditional normative order fuelled crime as well as violence against the self. For Durkheim, priests, soldiers, lawyers and magistrates were little afflicted with anomie, but those involved in the occupations of trade and commerce were (Durkheim 1958: 29–30). Markets drive social disintegration and the disintegration of communal regulation and self-regulation. When there is 'abrupt growth of power and wealth … limits are unknown between the possible and the impossible, what is just and what is unjust, legitimate claims and hopes and those that are immoderate' (Durkheim 1952: 253). Durkheim mostly focused on rapid changes in the norms of a society (rather than normlessness) and the suicidal feelings of alienation, purposelessness and 'insatiable appetites' to which this gave rise.

This chapter focuses on those insights within the classical tradition, while the next chapter shifts focus to insight from *anomie Américaine* that starts with Robert K. Merton. A connection between the two is the recurrent tendency for the normative order to break down at the centres of power when power claws its way to domination and then contrives a polity that fails to temper power. 'Greed is good' normlessness on Wall Street recurrently threatens capitalism itself. It threatens the benefits that tempered capitalism can deliver (Chapters 6–8). The ethos of the untempered populist power of a Donald Trump or a Rodrigo Duterte in the Philippines is a threat to the separated powers of the republic. So, too, is an ideology of 'Make America Great Again' or 'Make China

Great Again'. Such ideology is a threat to the regulation of domination in international affairs by the normative order of a Golden Rule that can motivate the mutual benefits of international law.

Restorative inclusion and anomie

We will reveal from historical experience that the path to a low-violence society is normative integration combined with bridging capital to embrace society's outcasts within and its enemies without. Reconciliation institutions of multilevel governance hold some of the keys to that reintegration. These bridging institutions range from the high politics of the United Nations and its Security Council to interfaith dialogue between religious communities that have a history of stigmatising each other, down to community-level institutions that bridge reintegration between feuding families or fighting gangs in schools and on the street. In Jamaica, there have been two major waves of rising violence between organised crime gangs in recent history that were triggered by incidents of schoolyard bullying by the child of a gang leader that were responded to violently by children of members of a competing gang. Another such intergang 'war' started in a Dublin schoolyard.[8] Institutions to rebuild the relevant bridges, whether in the schoolyard or UN peace negotiations between war leaders, are more likely to succeed when they are infused with values of respect towards and dignity for the feared other (Braithwaite 2002: Ch. 6). A critical element of the normative order here is that it shames disintegrative shaming; it reintegratively shames stigmatisation as it values respect, human dignity and the inclusion of former outcasts (Ahmed et al. 2001).

This book argues that the macrocriminological evidence is formidable about the complex role of anomie in inducing violence. If we build a strong normative order without also eliminating stigmatisation and strengthening reintegration, we also risk a violent society in which the strength of the normative order stimulates crime (Karstedt 2011b). While the journey towards a low-violence society has made more than promising long-run progress in many societies, it has also planted the seeds of devastating reversal. The most worrying of these remain nuclear

---

8   The data that describe these incidents come from police interviews I conducted in Jamaica and Ireland for Peacebuilding Compared research in 2018.

weapons, which one day—more likely by accident[9] or perhaps by terrorist folly, rather than at the hand of a wilful great power—will cascade to a nuclear exchange. Those of us who survive it could suffer a return to a war of all against all. Nuclear war could cascade to an environmental catastrophe that in turn could return the West to something worse than the Hobbesian world left by the English Civil War or the Thirty Years' War of Catholic–Protestant religious conflict that wiped out so much of the population of Central Europe. Civility will not survive unless we do better at reinforcing the institutions that defend it. Unfortunately, the path from Hobbes to tempered modernity is littered with terrible reversals and errors of institutional design.

A great accomplishment for freedom was institutionalising a court system and a rule of law that have been remarkably successful in eliminating blood feuds. Indeed, we might say that one of the most undervalued benefits of the rule of law is that the rise of institutions like tort law allowed disputants to settle a conflict and move on without violence. Cooney's (1997) historical research developed this explanation of the long-run decline of English homicide rates. Eisner (2003: 126) also discussed sharply falling homicide rates between the sixteenth and seventeenth centuries across Europe, which was the period during which some European countries institutionalised courts to discipline violence. Pinker (2011) developed it further in terms of his interpretation of how the rule of law contributed to the rise of his version of a civilising process across Europe from at least the early seventeenth century and probably even

---

9   On risks of accident, miscalculation, misunderstanding or technical malfunction, see Morris's (2014: 3–5) account of the 26 September 1983 decision by Stanislav Petrov to defy a 'high reliability' launch order in response to an erroneous signal of a US missile launch directed at Russia. Later that year, the neurotic Soviet Premier Yuri Andropov, confined to bed with a failing kidney, convinced himself irrationally that NATO was mobilising for a first strike, causing another panic (Morris 2014: 286). Ellsberg (2017) and Beebe (2019) provide among the most sophisticated accounts of how and why near misses of nuclear war have occurred with such worrying frequency in the past on the US, Soviet and other sides. They show why cyberwar and cybercrime that are not aimed at disabling satellite communications vital for launching retaliatory nuclear strikes are increasingly likely to be nevertheless misinterpreted as preparation for war. They explain why the authority to launch must be decentralised away from the president to reduce the risks of presidential decapitation and why generals are at risk of seeing themselves as being too late to use nuclear weapons before they lose them to an enemy strike (see also National Security Archive 2020a, 2020b; Allison 2017).

earlier (Eisner 2003).[10] Yet this progress in the regulation of anomie came with the Enlightenment error of discarding the reconciliation institutions whose functions the courts took over. This is the restorative justice theory critique of Enlightenment criminal justice (Braithwaite 2002). Chapter 9 argues that state courts and state coercion are dangerous if they are not regulated by restorative justice, and restorative justice is dangerous if it is not regulated by state courts. The Hobbesian shift that occurred in the seventeenth century in Europe from the regulation of crimes up to murder by reconciliation meetings to regulation by state courts was a swing that was necessary and effective in reducing violence (Eisner 2001, 2003, 2008, 2014). But it was a pendulum that swung too far—leaving the courts insufficiently tempered by restorative justice and legal pluralism—according to this book. Valerie Braithwaite (2009b) would say it failed to find the sweet spot in the balance between Hobbesian security values and Gandhian or Confucian harmony values. The better path would have been to retain those older reconciliation institutions to operate in parallel with courts. It is possible to have a formalism that enables informalism in justice together with an informalism that enables formalism, creating constructive tension and mutual accountability, each to temper the other (Braithwaite 2002). This civic republican interpretation of the history of the effectiveness of justice institutions in preventing violence is just one special case of the more general theory of freedom achieved by tempering power.

One option is indeed to rebuild those pre-Enlightenment institutions in a contemporary way that reinvigorates restorative justice. This deserves consideration not because restorative justice is better than formal criminal law any more than the criminal law ideologues of the Enlightenment were right in believing that formal law is more civilised than reconciliation through medieval European moots. A key institutional challenge for building the low-crime, low-domination society is to bridge formal law to horizontal relational justice so people seeking justice shuttle back and

---

10   One of the underestimated strengths of a fair justice system is that it builds social capital, the crime-prevention strengths of which are discussed in Chapter 7. We want a society in which trust begets trust. As societies seek to enculturate trust, it is also imperative to institutionalise distrust (Braithwaite 1998). So, when we promise to work for an employer for pay, if the employer refuses to pay, we do not want to live in a society in which we have to personally threaten our employer, risking violence, to be paid. No, we want the institutionalised distrust of labour laws and labour inspectorates that force employers to obey the law. Through reliance on state regulators to institutionalise distrust with respect to the rights to protection from violence, from crooked bosses and from landlords who ignore fire safety, we create safe spaces for citizens to get on with the business of enculturating trust.

forth across those bridges, each enabling and strengthening the work of the other in protecting people from the ravages of anomie (Porter 2016, 2018). Hobbesian statism and criminology's statism have been compounded by market liberalism and New Public Management thinning out the 'relational state' (Muir and Parker 2014; Peake and Forsyth forthcoming). Punitive legalists in ancient China also worked for centuries at thinning out the relational aspects of state Confucianism that Sun Yat-sen so valued (Acemoglu and Robinson 2019: Ch. 7). This induced a wider failure of the Chinese state to keep pace with western development and western freedom in the eighteenth to twentieth centuries. That happened because its 'despotic Leviathan' was ultimately weakened by centralising bureaucratic and legal traditions that excluded societal mobilisation and political participation. It also spiralled East Asia into more widespread violence during these centuries than any continent may have suffered throughout recorded history. Acemoglu and Robinson (2019: 75) conceive of one weakness of the despotic Chinese state in competition with western states as being that it wants for state capacity driven by 'a robust society to push it, cooperate with it, or contest its power'. Paradoxically, when the Communist Party of China decided during the past decade to legislate for the biggest restorative justice program in the world with a law of the widest universality of sweep of any country, the reform failed to greatly transform because it was not backed by the restorative social movement politics that drove reform in other countries. As a result, restorative justice progress was widely trumped by the entrenched local professional interests of justice bureaucrats in legal formalism (Zhang 2021a, 2021b). This book argues that embedded autonomy (Evans 1995), the relational state, relational workplaces, relational families and relational communities form a social fabric that must be actively rebuilt.

This is a worry about modernity that we can also see in the late Durkheim (1933: 262): 'It is not enough that society take in a great many people, but they must be, in addition, intimately enough in contact to act and react on one another.' This means abandoning the way of thinking of legal scholars who conceive of Germanic moots as the justice of barbarians who destroyed Roman law when they destroyed Rome. Rather, we embrace Acemoglu and Robinson (2019: 47) when they conclude that domination was tempered through 'the marriage of the bottom-up, participatory institutions and norms of Germanic tribes and the centralizing bureaucratic and legal traditions of the Roman Empire' and the Christian church. This marriage allowed deliberative societal power to check state power, and state power to check the power of civil society deliberation. Rulers of empires as powerful as Charlemagne had to play by the rules of general assemblies. 'Very different types of states emerged in parts of Europe where either the Roman tradition or the bottom-up politics of the Germanic tribes were absent (such as Iceland or Byzantium)' (Acemoglu and Robinson 2019: 47). Intriguingly, this also goes to Acemoglu and Robinson's (2019: Ch. 13) diagnosis of what went wrong with German institutional balance in the first half of the twentieth century. They conclude that Weimar Germany descended into a vicious zero-sum battle between a state and a civil society that sought to destroy each other. German institutions lost their capacity to reconcile conflicts between the state and civil society; trust totally collapsed in a deadly winner-takes-all battle for survival in which the communists and the aristocracy were losers who rivalled the Nazis in their culpability. Acemoglu and Robinson diagnose the 1970 collapse of Chilean democracy in similar terms. The social democrats of the Weimar Republic were culpable, too. They were just learning how to be social democrats and how not to be communists in the 1920s and early 1930s. They were not social democratic enough, not Keynesian enough, resulting in worse mismanagement of the Great Depression than most societies suffered. Debt from World War I reparations rendered their challenges deeper than for other governments.

Now let us build this argument of the chapter step by step by first conceptualising anomie more clearly, then turning to whether Norbert Elias was right to discern a civilising process in the evolution of human affairs towards more effective self-regulation of excess in emotions like anger and revenge. My conclusion accords with Elias's (1996) that human societies suffer recurrent decivilising moments in their histories. If communal, national and international societies fail to build strong institutions to regulate cascades of violence, decivilising forces triumph over civilisational dynamics of peaceful order. The subsequent chapters of this book are about what is required to prevent the descent into a downward spiral of violence and domination, including balanced capital formation, regulation of markets in crony capitalism and policies to bridge inequalities between ingroups and outcasts, between the dominated and those who dominate.

Progress towards less violent and less criminal societies has been paradoxically advanced by the armies of tyrants. The Roman legions brought Roman law to some lawless lands. Before the Romans, the Persian Empire spread the idea of carving into stone laws that bound the king as well as his subjects across its vast empire. Genghis Khan's murderous Golden Horde re-pacified the Silk Road so bridges, interdependencies and civilisational ideas could travel it, such as the idea that the defeated Persian Empire and the defeated Chinese Empire could each be ruled by a woman. Napoleon's Grande Armée brought the French Civil Code into central and Eastern Europe to liberate serfs for the first time, ending feudalism and granting citizenship rights that applied to peasants. The Ottoman Empire successfully promoted religious tolerance among Muslims, Jews, Christians, Zoroastrians and others. All these empires had other moments when they brought tyranny and brutal militarisation and crushed freedom when freedom clashed with the empire's geopolitical objectives. When these empires disintegrated, anomie, violence and new tyrannies cascaded (Braithwaite and D'Costa 2018). It is hard to imagine any colonial tyranny worse than the slave society Belgian colonialism imposed on Congo. But when Belgium recklessly pulled out without a stabilising transition to local democratic rule, civil war cascaded again and again in ways that continue to make the Democratic Republic of Congo the society of the past 25 years in which the risks of being murdered or raped may have been higher than for any country (Braithwaite and D'Costa 2018: Pt I).

The age of empires ended before empires mastered the challenge of transitions that retain rule-of-law virtues left behind by the empire while building robust new guarantees of anomie prevention. Chapter 7 argues that a risk to the western world if China one day has an economic and political crisis so deep that it begins to disintegrate is that the West could suffer cascades of violence and its own collapse into depression or hyperinflation that will require vigilance against the risk of renewal of western authoritarianism. Reckless elements in western intelligence services who seek to destabilise the Chinese economy fail to understand that China played a major role in western recovery from the 2008 Global Financial Crisis and the 2020 Covid financial crisis; that the economic disintegration of China could be a bigger risk to the West than was Germany's economic disintegration after World War I. Unless we lift our imaginations to grapple with such macro-challenges that multilevel governance can and must conquer, criminology's micro-accomplishments in revealing techniques for reducing crime, in the narrowly circumscribed circumstances of today, will crumble along with the societal fabric that sustains such micro-accomplishments.

Anomie and social control

One of the four key hypotheses of control theory is that belief in the law contributes to compliance with it (Gottfredson and Hirschi 1990). This is the most self-evident part of control theory for many critics, as it is the most self-evident part of differential association theory (that definitions favourable to involvement in crime do encourage crime) (Sutherland 1947; Akers 1998). It need not necessarily be the case that because people have a strong belief in the law, they will be more likely to comply with it. Yet numerous empirical evaluations of control theory and learning theories of crime do support this hypothesis. Some evidence suggests that when moral belief in the law is strong, self-control does not explain crime; self-control explains crime when the normative order of strong belief in the law is absent (Schoepfer and A. Piquero 2006; Intravia et al. 2018). These data also lay a micro-foundation for the classical anomie claim that normlessness—normative breakdown—is associated with crime, as do other studies of anomie (Pridemore et al. 2007). We have seen that Karstedt and Farrall's (2006) survey data from three societies revealed a syndrome of market anomie was strongly associated with 'crimes of everyday life'. Anomic crimes of the twenty-first-century middle class, according to Farrall and Karstedt (2019), are associated with the fact that they feel squeezed between big government and big business exploitation. Farrall and Karstedt (2019) make a powerful case that it is the institutional anomie form of anomie theory discussed in the next chapter that may prove most important to explaining macro-patterns of crime. While some of their theorised coefficients are very small, in all cases, the institutional anomie path coefficients are high, as are the 'legal cynicism' coefficients.

At the meso-level, the Peacebuilding Compared research team found that in the periods and places where there was a breakdown of agreement on what were the rules of the game in Indonesia (and collapse of the consensus on who legitimately held the reins of the state), violence spiked dramatically in many hotspots across the society (Braithwaite et al. 2010a). Where anomie was less pronounced, however—which was in most places across this country—violence was stable and low. Moreover, these anomic spikes of violence occurred in the context of a diverse multicultural society of 270 million people with large cells of vibrant, violent subcultures of Islamic radicalism. Indonesia is a society that at the macrolevel has generally enjoyed a low level of violence, an imprisonment rate of less than 40 per 100,000 and a low level of anomie for most of its history, and particularly since 2002. From 1998 to 2004 was also the period when it experienced a more formidable increase in freedom and democratisation than any country since the end of the Cold War. While democracy and the thickening of fabrics of freedom conduce to the stabilisation of anomie and legal cynicism, transition to democracy recurrently disrupts the normative order (Braithwaite and D'Costa 2018). In future chapters, we will discuss the evidence for more specific versions of the anomie–crime relationship—most notably, institutional anomie theory.

A history of norms against violence since World War I

The church bells that chimed across Europe to rejoice in the 1918 armistice manifested cascade of a promising form of international social capital for a decade. This is referred to as Wilsonianism by Americans, after Woodrow Wilson, their president at the time of the armistice. It produced the League of Nations, which, while it collapsed under the weight of its failure to prevent the wars of the 1930s, laid the foundations for a second, more successful attempt with the creation of the United Nations after World War II.

Even more important were Gandhi's initial nonviolent struggles against oppression during these early decades of the twentieth century—first in South Africa, then in opposition to British colonialism in India. When Gandhi was assassinated in 1948 by a religious fanatic during the postcolonial partition of India, his project of nonviolence seemed in tatters. The most deadly war in human history had just happened in quick historical succession after World War I, and much of Asia was still in flames and would stay that way for years to come. The most violent and oppressive decades of the Apartheid regime in South Africa were still ahead of it. Gandhi's beloved India was tearing itself apart, with perhaps 2 million people murdered during the partition of Pakistan from India as Hindus murdered Muslims and Muslims killed Hindus, with many Christians and Sikhs also caught up in the slaughter. Yet Figure 3.1 shows that when Gandhi started his campaigns, nonviolent activism for maximalist political change (such as from colonialism, from dictatorship to democracy or some other regime change) barely existed on a planet plundered by violence. What Gandhi and his comrades laid was a platform for nonviolent struggle to overtake armed revolutionary struggle as the dominant strategy for regime change (as Figure 3.1 reveals). Gandhian nonviolence as an alternative to armed struggle became as influential among western activists (Scalmer 2011) as it was among eastern and southern revolutionaries.

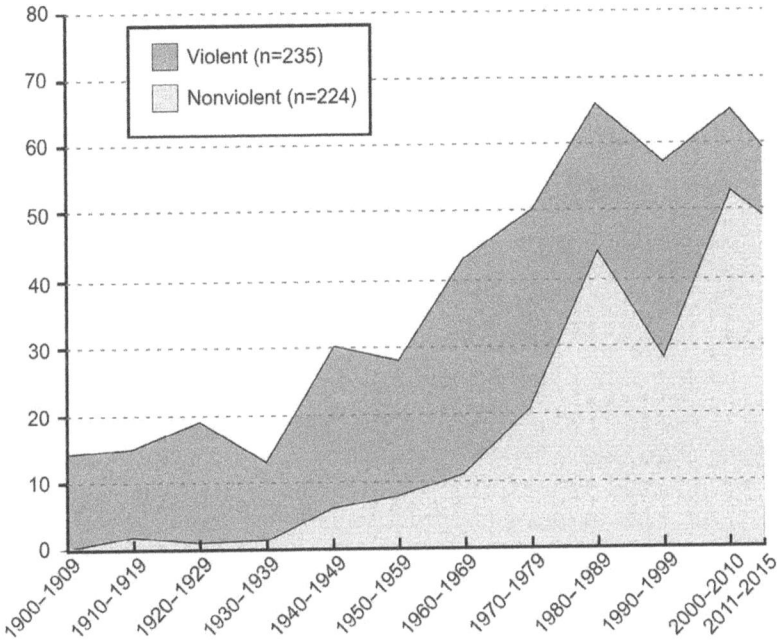

Figure 3.1 Nonviolent and violent uprisings
Sources: Author's graph, with thanks to Erica Chenoweth (2016a, 2016b: 2) for access to her Major Episodes of Contention dataset.

The chimes of the church bells of 1918 were silenced when hyperinflation, the Great Depression and the rise of fascism crushed the League of Nations along with the trust and hopes of peace-loving people everywhere. First, Japanese militarism started wars in Asia from 1928. Then, in 1936, the Spanish Civil War between fascists and republicans delivered four decades of fascist rule by General Francisco Franco, Benito Mussolini's Italian invasion of Ethiopia, Eritrea and Somaliland, and even fascists on the streets of Sydney. Finally, Nazis sought to conquer all of Europe. Yet good scholars of crime argue that before that great collapse of financial capital that cascaded to a deep crash of international social capital after 1929 there had been what Norbert Elias (1982) interpreted as a long-run civilising process (Eisner 2001, 2008, 2014; Pinker 2011; Broadhurst et al. 2018).

The crime statistics for western nations suggest the Great Depression was near the beginning of the bottom of a long U-curve in wealthy countries. The U plunged downwards for almost 100 years following a slight upturn in crime that ended around 1840. This slight upturn to 1840 ended after western societies began to work out how to manage the rapid urbanisation and urban crime that had accelerated alongside industrialisation (Braithwaite 1989: 111–18). Crime in most western countries stayed near the bottom of that U from the end of World War I, through the Great Depression, through the stagnant years of the 1930s when fascism grew, the World War II years and the postwar 1940s and 1950s, actually falling slightly at the bottom of the U across these decades right through to 1960 (Eisner 2008).

There were many books (including Braithwaite 1979) that tried to make sense of why crime did not spike during and after the 1930s depression by pointing out that inequality reduced as a result of the depression because, as great as the suffering of the poor was, the rich suffered an even greater decline in their income and wealth. The rich did most of the jumping from tall buildings, while the poor kept plugging away at what had always been bad circumstances. The great welfare state initiatives of the New Deal and its progressive tax policies were also game changers of domination reduction. While the Spanish Civil War and Italian, German and Japanese militarist expansionism were destroying freedom across a devastated planet, the 1939 outbreak of 'world war' was unifying for the combatant countries on both sides. Unity overcame anomie, promoting great national progress in building social capital among what some of the Allied powers called their Greatest Generation. The Greatest Generation trope is one of how a generation born amid the suffering of World War I endured the hardship of the Great Depression and World War II to steer western societies to the peaceful, reconstructive civility of the 1950s.

Yet we have seen that when that Greatest Generation of the western Allies occupied Germany, they raped massive numbers of German and Austrian women and that Australian occupying troops even did that around Hiroshima.[11] When the Greatest Generation returned from the war,

---

11 Yuri Tanaka (2018: 115–16) describes the precarious survival of one Japanese rape victim who was violated by no fewer than 20 Australian soldiers and abandoned in a wasteland. One of the Japanese sex workers from Kure (Hiroshima's port), most of whom had lost all their relatives in Hiroshima, said: 'Most of the people in Kure stayed inside their houses, and pretended they knew nothing about the rape by occupation forces. The Australian soldiers were the worst. They dragged young women into their jeeps, took them to the mountain, and then raped them. I heard them screaming for help nearly every night. A policeman from the Hiroshima police station came to me, and asked me to work as a prostitute for the Australians—he wanted me and other prostitutes to act as a sort of "firebreak" so that the young women wouldn't get raped. We agreed to do this, and contributed greatly' (Tanaka 2018: 115).

they threw their own generation of women who had kept the factories running during the war out of their jobs and put them back into domestic servitude just as surely as they put African-American and Aboriginal Australian war heroes back into servitude. President Roosevelt's World War II political leaders imprisoned a generation of Japanese-Americans for no crime beyond being Japanese. In Canada, great universities terminated the enrolments of Japanese-Canadian students for no better reason than the fact they were ethnically Japanese. My dear mother lost two husbands to the Sandakan Death Marches in North Borneo; her second husband (my father) was one of six who survived, compared with the 2,428 Australian and British soldiers and thousands of Asian slave labourers who perished at Sandakan. When Australian troops took North Borneo, they sent hundreds of Japanese prisoners-of-war to their deaths in a counter death march (R. Braithwaite 2016). When an Australian wing commander noticed that not all of the civilian housing of Dresden had been incinerated by the firebombing of 1945, he ordered his bombers to go around one more time to spread the conflagration fully across the remaining civilian housing (Taylor 2005: 326).

Australians from that Greatest Generation played important roles in developing the atomic bombs that decimated the innocents of Hiroshima and Nagasaki. One was a kind professor at my university whom I greatly admired. The Greatest Generation persuaded us that this war crime was not a war crime at all, but the only way fanatical Japanese could be persuaded to end the war. Our education did not invite us to question this, even though the evidence for it was thin. The Greatest Generation did not inform us that there had been advocacy by scientists for a demonstration explosion that would not be a mass atrocity, which they believed could have persuaded the Japanese to surrender. This was the Greatest Generation who continued to lead the alleged civilising process through the 1950s.

The 1960s saw the beginnings of political resistance to the politics of this generation by their children, particularly resistance to the ruthlessness of the politics of combating communism by promoting wars, coups and political assassinations in the Global South (Chomsky 1969). Crime and drug abuse also began to escalate steeply in the 1960s. They continued to do so through the 1970s and 1980s and into the 1990s in many western countries. LaFree and Drass (2002: 782) found that homicide rates for the period 1956–98 moved in a 'positive direction' for 88 per cent of industrialised and industrialising countries and showed 'rapid growth' for

65 per cent of them. The past 30 years have seen my rebellious, criminal baby-boomer generation all safely transitioned to the calm waters of their 60s and 70s. During this period when we baby boomers aged, crime rates fell across most of the western world (Aebi and Linde 2014). Lappi-Seppälä and Lehti (2014: 146) showed that western homicide rates increased from 1960 to the early 1990s and then declined. That decline from the 1990s until 2010 in the west was counterbalanced by an increase in Latin America. Latin America had become a crucial supply region for the widespread habits of drug abuse that took off during the youth of the baby boomers. Fajnzylber et al.'s (1998: 28) results show that the Latin American countries that had the highest drug production had the highest homicide rates:

> [A] rise in drug trafficking, as in Colombia in the 1970s, can raise the national crime rate. The econometric results suggest that the rise in the crime rate may be felt long after the initial shock—countries can be engulfed in a crime wave. (Fajnzylber et al. 1998: 31; see also Briceño-León et al. 2008)

Violence in Latin America also escalated when leftist political movements from the 1950s to the 1990s—many inspired by the triumph of Castro and Che Guevara in Cuba—were suppressed murderously by authoritarian regimes. So, Latin America in this period of history suffered a series of civil wars and drug wars that cascaded to street violence (Chapter 11).

American criminology created a new industry around explaining the great crime drop in the West from the 1990s (Blumstein and Wallman 2000). One reason so little of it was especially convincing was because it advanced so many contradictory explanations, including some to do with the brilliant work of the criminal justice system through the elevated imprisonment of felons or 'broken windows policing', for example. These were distinctively American explanations, when the same crime drop was evident right across the western world. Eisner's (2008, 2014) data show that these trends were synchronised to a remarkable degree across Western, central and southern Europe, the United States, Canada and Australia in the sense that in every one of his country cases the upturn started close to 1960. And in every country case the crime drop started close to 1992. The 'average year' across Europe for the start of the homicide rise is the same year as the start of the homicide rise in the United States, 1960. The average year of its end, 1992, is the same as the US date of the end of the crime rise. What varies is the magnitude of the rise and fall.

Hence, Eisner (2008) argues that US-centric explanations like broken-windows policing are unpersuasive. They leave unanswered why policing or deterrence policies could explain the phenomenon when deterrence and policing policies were moving every which way across these disparate countries (and indeed within different cities inside the United States). Another complication pointed out by Farrall and Karstedt (2019) is that 'crimes of the middle class', which have exceptionally low detection rates, seem to have increased sharply since 1992. This was partly driven by their finding that access to the internet doubled both middle-class victimisation and middle-class offending. Admittedly, these are mostly rather minor crimes. Farrall and Karstedt (2019: Ch. 8) point out that arrests for fraud and embezzlement have risen notably in the United States since 1988, as they have in other societies.

More fundamentally, the project of explaining the crime drop anywhere since 1992 aims at the wrong target. A better target is why crime increased so steeply across the West between 1960 and 1992. That is the period of exception, not the crime drop. Since 1992, the western world has been back on the same basic downward trajectory for violence that it had been on since at least the sixteenth century, though the US homicide rate turned back up in very recent years (Krajicek 2017), with one of the factors being what Chapter 11 interprets as a cascade effect with mass shootings, and perhaps with police shootings escalating anomie during the Trump presidency, even though police murders are almost never counted as homicides. Worldwide deaths from armed conflict have also reversed again to be up quite sharply since Pinker's (2011) book was published. The number of major civil wars tripled in the past decade, with battle deaths increasing even more steeply, after both declined throughout the 1990s and 2000s (von Einsiedel 2017). This is in spite of President Trump, who campaigned against the Bush–Obama wars, promised not to cascade any new ones and kept that promise as president. Communist China so far has been even less of a provocateur of wars than the United States, so we have seen a shift from great power rivalry as the great provoker of civil war to organised crime groups seeking wealth and power as the more important instigators of war (von Einsiedel 2017), thereby also blurring ever more profoundly the war versus crime distinction in armed killing. Most of the rise in civil war of the past decade was a cascading of recurrent wars rather than the start of new ones (von Einsiedel 2017: 3). Another decade of data has been sufficient to reach the conclusion that Pinker's (2011) civilising account was too simple and too linear.

Broadly, we would want to identify an explanation that accounts for something that changed in 1992 that was also going on until 1960, but not between 1960 and 1992. Eisner (2008) therefore questions the explanations for the crime drop related to shifts in the nature of capitalism that were occurring just as swiftly, if not more so, in the 32 crime-rise years before 1992. It would be tedious to track through all the US-centric explanations for the crime drop that fail to explain why this also occurs in so many countries that do not share the US-centric explanation, and that fail to also explain the preceding crime rise. Eisner (2008) has already done an excellent job of this explanation-by-explanation critique. I also do not argue that all this US-centric assessment of its crime drop gets it wrong in every way. Movements in crime rates are driven by complexes of multilevel micro and macro factors. It is just that for a book on macrocriminology, I agree with Eisner that the more exciting challenge is to search for macro explanations that might make more sense of the totality of the pattern in the data.

Eisner (2001, 2003, 2008) could be more self-critical of his own more cultural explanations that draw on Elias's civilising process, on similarities between Emile Durkheim's sociology and Elias and on Max Weber's (2002) *Protestant Ethic and the Spirit of Capitalism*. He does concede that culture is an 'elusive concept'; however, 'systems of values and ideas, when embedded in social institutions, do have the potential of changing everyday routines and interaction patterns' (Eisner 2003: 130). Exactly what these institutions are, however, is not developed in detail by Eisner. He finds a strong negative association between homicide and book production per capita across time and interprets this as being associated with institutions of self-discipline that diffused reading and writing skills—monasteries and schools (Eisner 2014: 107). Protestant institutions are clearly important candidates for Max Weber. Yet the preference of the analysis in this book will be to argue that the explosion of Protestantism into the Thirty Years' War initially decivilised Europe in a major way. After that, why were the institutions that Eisner believed did the embedding of the great civilising cultural changes: a) strengthening until 1960 (reflected in declining homicide rates between 1840 and World War I, though with an only slightly declining trend between World War I and 1960) (Eisner 2008: 296); b) weakening between 1960 and 1992 with the decivilising crime rise; and c) strengthening again after 1992, with homicide mostly falling again?

We could excuse ourselves, as Eisner does to a degree in his early work, from an obligation to explain the shifts since World War II by saying that they are small compared with the cumulative shifts of the six centuries before that. Yet we would expect a mostly unidirectional trend over many centuries to be large compared with trends that flatten (1920–60), reverse up (1960–92) and then reverse down (after 1992) in less than 100 years (Eisner 2008: 296). It would be wrong to say that the rise in crime between 1960 and 1992 of 179 per cent (averaged from the low to the high for 14 European countries) (Eisner 2008: 305) is a small trend across a short period. Under any normal social science interpretation, this trend is large, long and rather consistent, at least for the West. So, it will not do to dismiss it as small. Eisner (2008: 308) points out that a doubling of European homicide rates between 1960 and 1992 is small compared with differences that were more than 50 times as great for one period compared with another across the late Middle Ages and even perhaps for the United States between the seventeenth and the twenty-first centuries (see Footnote 3). However, Eisner notes that actually the rise in robbery rates in Europe after 1960 was of the same order (approaching a fiftyfold increase). Robbery was almost a nonexistent crime in 1950s Europe, and indeed in 1950s Russia and China perhaps even more so, as argued in Chapter 2. We must also bear in mind that the long-run rise in homicide between 1960 and 1992 was in fact kept artificially low by improvements in ambulance response times and medical care that increased the survival prospects of people stabbed or shot.

A suggestion for reinforcing the wonderful strengths of Eisner's analyses is to invoke militarisation (and how this connects to anomie) as a complementary institutional explanation of the trends since 1840. This is not a totalising explanation, but one to add into his mix of explanations towards building a comprehensive account of the macro patterns. It starts with what Eric Hobsbawm described as the comparatively peaceful 'long nineteenth century' ending with World War I, in comparison with warlike previous European history up to the defeat of Napoleon. Europe saw a comparatively peaceful take-off of capitalism for a century once the bloody Napoleonic Wars were settled. This was followed by the violence of *The Age of Extremes: The Short Twentieth Century, 1914–1991* (Hobsbawm 1994). Braithwaite and D'Costa (2018) concluded that, during the 107 years after 1911, cascades of militarisation drove cascades of violence. Chapter 11 takes up this evidence and also discusses the evidence of how war cascades to elevated postwar crime rates.

There is, furthermore, a great deal of evidence that wars or mass killings in one country cascade to heightened probabilities of further wars or mass killings in that country and in neighbouring countries (Braithwaite and D'Costa 2018; Sambanis 2001; Gleditsch 2002, 2007; Salehyan and Gleditsch 2006; Ward and Gleditsch 2002; A. Braithwaite 2016; Houweling and Siccama 1985, 1988; Chenoweth and Perkoski 2017). Alex Braithwaite and Li (2007), Braithwaite and Johnson (2012) and Braithwaite and Chu (2018) show quantitatively that terrorist incidents cascade from and cluster at geographical hotspots within and between societies. Chapter 11 argues that cascades of violence and militarisation are so powerful because: a) war cascades to more war; b) war cascades to crime; c) crime cascades to more crime; and d) crime cascades to war. Hence, a macro approach requires that we should not be overly criminological and should be open to explanations of violence as war–crime–war violence.

Eisner (2008: 311) makes the good point that culture is his 'favourite candidate' for explaining the trends because it is 'the only phenomenon that travels fast enough to affect such vast areas roughly simultaneously'. Braithwaite and D'Costa (2018) argue that war cascades rapidly and with wider effects than people notice through their historical reading. They cannot see it without examining the documented data on how widely the cascade effects of militarism run. Consider how historically rapidly so many countries joined World War I and World War II. Of the dozens of countries involved in Europe, the Middle East, Africa, Asia and North America, in both cases, the slowest cascade was to the United States, which was not so slow, taking just a few years for both World War I and World War II to unsettle its peace. Braithwaite and D'Costa (2018) argue that nonviolence is a cascade phenomenon as well, but sadly, while violence cascades fast, nonviolence cascades slowly.

Eisner (2014) invokes David Garland's (2001) *Culture of Control* and Gottfredson and Hirschi's (1990) control theory as pointing to cultural factors that might be effective in reducing homicide. The explanatory theory of reintegrative shaming (Braithwaite 1989; Ahmed et al. 2001) goes along with this to a degree because it explicitly integrates control theory into a more complex and macrostructural theory of interdependence, inequality, shame without stigma and reintegration. Yet there is not much explanatory power in explaining behaviour that is out of control, like most murder, with a want of self-control as the independent variable. Explaining hate speech with hatefulness might be accurate, but it does not get us as far as our explanatory ambition should take us. Moreover, Braithwaite and D'Costa's (2018) data support Gerlach's (2010) conclusion that extremely violent societies are not violent in some cultural or essential way. Rather, societies often rapidly transition in and out of extremely violent periods of their histories as a result of crises (as discussed further in Chapter 11).

When Eisner (2014) shows that, presumably because alcohol reduces self-control, historical levels of alcohol consumption move up and down in unison with homicide rates, here there are at least specific institutional policies we can consider to reduce alcohol consumption in order to reduce violent crime. These policy levers connect to alcohol regulatory institutions for markets in drug addiction and educational institutions, among others. The macrocriminologist is interested in explanations that connect to the macrosociology of institutions, including health regulatory institutions (as invoked by institutional anomie theory and as discussed in Chapter 8).

When war conquers anomie

This chapter has already argued that anomie quite often helps explain both military violence and crime. However, military violence that is an existential threat to a society can unify it in a Durkheimian way, conquering anomie, as we saw with the discussion around World War II's Greatest Generation. At least the martial conquest of anomie is possible when the war is not being fought on the streets of one's capital. This is what we mean by recursivity that can be built from Durkheim's approach to the relationship between anomie and violence. Violence can be reacted to by strengthened social cohesion; this explains violence control in Durkheim (including explanation of self-violence, suicide). We can understand broad patterns of violence and crime in terms of the crosscutting effects of militarisation on two key variables: anomie and the legitimisation of violence. Because war normalises violence, families can suffer much violence when veterans return home. Family violence is rarely reported and may not show up sharply in crime statistics. Especially when a soldier suffers post-traumatic stress disorder (PTSD) for their country, the family is inclined to forgive and the society is inclined to look away and even institutionalise reintegrative legal innovations like Veterans' Courts. But the criminality committed in public spaces by brutalised war veterans and their brutalised children (mainly as male-on-male violence) may show up more visibly. Recent Australian data show greatly elevated levels of drug abuse, alcoholism, PTSD, suicide risk and even rape among the children of Vietnam veterans (Commonwealth of Australia 2014; Chapter 11, this volume). Direct effects are also important, as evidenced by the datum (suppressed by the state and the media) that *at least* 36 per cent of US mass shooters were trained by the US military and by the datum that many mass shooters dress and act as if they are in the military during their crime (Swanson 2021).

Militarisation constitutes an institutional form that incubates a violent culture in which violence is legitimated rather than shameful. This is a way of adding an institutional layer of understanding to the institutional change already identified by Elias. Like Eisner (2008: 305), I read Elias's civilising process as 'reintegrative'. Elias articulates how violence becomes progressively more shameful during the civilising process (Braithwaite 1993). Hence, Braithwaite (1989) and Ahmed et al. (2001) long sought to understand historical trends in crime and other forms of violence in terms of patterns of reintegrative shaming, shame acknowledgement over violence and humble pride in nonviolence. In most cases, when someone wrongs a person, that person will not even contemplate solving this problem by murdering the person who committed the wrong. We refrain from murder because murder is unthinkable to us; it is right off our deliberative agenda. We do not decide against murdering the person who provokes us because we calculate the probabilities that we will be caught or the severity of the punishment (as discussed in Chapter 9).

A main game of criminology is therefore about understanding how this 'thinkable-ness' of murder *is* occasionally constituted. When soldiers return from war, their training and their battlefield experience have actively desensitised them to the unthinkable-ness of killing, and indeed rape. When the normalisation of violence they experienced in the military affects their childrearing, their male children, but also their female children, learn that one path to getting their way is violence and domination of the other. Violent male patriarchs may not have happy marriages; their children have little idea of what a happy marriage looks like. Yet those children can learn that violence is how to get one's way; threats and domination work in the practices of their male role model in getting what they want. Likewise, when children see that self-harm is thinkable when their veteran parents manage emotional problems through contemplating self-harm, violence against the self becomes an option their children are more open to consider. These are some of the war–crime cascade dynamics diagnosed in Braithwaite and D'Costa (2018), but only some of them.

Actually, militarisation as an explanation of violence is forcefully present in the writing of Eisner (2014)[12] and Elias. Yet the institutional layers of concern to Elias constitute a much wider canvas than militarisation. We turn now to that wider canvas.

Cascading nonviolent norms across the past millennium

Braithwaite's (1993) exegesis on Elias argued that Elias saw shame as being in the ascendent rather than declining during the past 700 years. Two related structural changes were important in the rise of social disapproval as the predominant form of social control: the growth of the state as a monopolist of physical force and the proliferation of a more elaborate division of labour. The process is illustrated by the transformation of the nobility from a class of knights into a class of courtiers as physical force was progressively monopolised by a monarch. The monopolisation of force created pacified social spaces. Prior to this pacification, with violence an unavoidable and everyday event, 'a strong and continuous moderation of drives and affects is neither necessary, possible nor useful' (Elias 1982: 236). A feudal era with a warrior upper class was a threat not only to the safety of warriors themselves, but also to all people.

The members of the warrior upper class enjoyed extraordinary freedom in living out their feelings and passions through uninhibited satisfaction of sexual pleasure and gratification of vengeful impulses through acts

---

12 Eisner (2014: 17), in discussing results from Ross's (1985) studies of 90 small-scale traditional societies, helpfully points out that: 'Violence was found to be high in societies with harsh socialization practices (.22) and lacking affectionate socialization practices (–.31). This would suggest that levels of violence are transmitted over generations through a socialization pattern that emphasizes the warrior abilities of young men and that promotes notions of masculine honour and toughness. Interestingly, though, the effects of both socialization variables became non-significant once the variable measuring external conflict (i.e. war) was added to the equation. This probably suggests, as Ember and Ember (1994) have argued, that external conflict promotes more martial and aggressive socialization practices, which in turn lead to higher levels of internal conflict.' Like Ross (1985), Ember and Ember (1994) found from a multivariate analysis of Murdoch and White's Standard Cross-Cultural Sample of 186 societies that the frequency of external wars and socialisation for aggression were important predictors of homicide.

of torture and dismemberment. This is consistent with the evidence we have on the extraordinarily high levels of homicide in the Middle Ages (Gurr 1980: 44). The evidence suggests a substantial downward trend in violent crime in England from the thirteenth century extending well into the twentieth century—a trend Gurr (1981) attributes in part to the strengthening of internal controls against violence (see also Garland 1990: 233–34). During the sixteenth century, according to Elias, unrestrained passion became less a source of power and more an impediment to it. The affective make-up of the nobility changed as warriors became courtiers (whence 'courtesy'), peddling influence at the court of a monarch who monopolised force (Braithwaite 1993: 3).

As La Bruyère wrote: 'Life at court is a serious melancholy game, which requires of us that we arrange our pieces and our batteries, have a plan, follow it, foil that of our adversary' (quoted in Elias 1982: 270). Gradually, the sword became less important than words and intrigue in competing for career success. This happened because the court of an absolute monarch was a social formation in which a great many people were continuously dependent on one another. Elias likened the court to a stock exchange, where the value of each individual was continually being formed and assessed. The most important determinants of this value were 'the favour he enjoys with the king, the influence he has with other mighty ones, his importance in the play of courtly cliques'. In this subtle game of building value in a diplomatic market, 'physical force and direct affective outbursts are prohibited and a threat to existence' (Elias 1982: 271). What was demanded of each participant was self-control and exact knowledge of every other player with whom they were interdependent. Loss of affective control could debase the currency of one's courtly reputation, threatening one's whole position at court:

> A man who knows the court is master of his gestures, of his eyes and his expression; he is deep, impenetrable. He dissimulates the bad turns he does, smiles at his enemies, suppresses his ill-temper, disguises his passions, disavows his heart, acts against his feelings. (Elias 1982: 272)

Elias illustrated how the affective structure of the warrior class was doomed through cases of bold and brave knights like the Duke of Montmorency being sidelined by consummate courtiers such as Cardinal Richelieu (Elias 1982: 279).

The role of the court and its associated institutions in dismantling the violent apparatus of feudalism remained influential for many centuries, even in England, where the court waned earlier than on the Continent as the preeminent site for politicking. The eighteenth-century reign of Beau Nash at the quasi-court of Bath civilised country squires by hastening the disappearance of the sword as the proper adornment of a gentleman's thigh; as a result, the settling of disagreements with cold steel became increasingly infrequent (Trevelyan 1985: 385). Similarly, among humbler males, stabbing was replaced with the 'civilised' rules of fair play of the boxing ring (Braithwaite 1993: 4).

In his comments on a draft of this book, Manuel Eisner commented that in his data from the *Interactive London Medieval Murder Map* (2018), goldsmiths were the most murderous actors, and much more murderous than the warrior class. Even the boxing ring came to be viewed as uncivilised in early Victorian times, and withered away, only to be revived in the twentieth century. Trevelyan (1973: 504) quaintly described it as a 'largely American' preoccupation, 'tempered with gloves'. State formation further aided Elias's civilising process by creating large zones of pacification that allowed the capitalism of transport, trade and money to circulate in ever greater safety. The rise of state security went hand in hand with the rise of markets that made trust-building and 'chains of interdependence' imperative for wealth creation. This interdependence and trust were the heart of financial capital and social capital formation (Chapter 7); unrestrained violence was a threat to social and financial capital formation.

Elias, like Nathan Harris (2001), does not distinguish guilt from shame because self-control is about the internalisation of macro-cultural imperatives of emergent modernity. The conflict expressed in shame–fear is not merely a conflict of the individual with prevalent social opinion; the individual's behaviour has brought them into conflict with the part of themselves that represents this social opinion (Elias 1982: 292). Elias illustrates with how shame works in the emotions required to manage travel on roads:

> One should think of the country roads of a simple warrior society with a barter economy. With a few exceptions, there is very little traffic; the main danger which man here represents for other men is an attack by soldiers or thieves. When people look around them, scanning the trees and hills or the road itself, they do so primarily because they must always be prepared for armed attack, and only

secondarily because they have to avoid collision. Life on the main roads of this society demands a constant readiness to fight, and free play of the emotions in defence of one's life or possessions from physical attack. Traffic on the main roads of a big city in the complex society of our time demands a quite different moulding of the psychological apparatus. Here the danger of physical attack is minimal. Cars are rushing in all directions; pedestrians and cyclists are trying to thread their way through the melee of cars; policemen stand at the main crossroads to regulate the traffic with varying success. But this external control is founded on the assumption that every individual is himself regulating his behaviour with the utmost exactitude in accordance with the necessities of this network. The chief danger that people here represent for others results from someone in this bustle losing his self-control. A constant and highly differentiated regulation of one's own behavior is needed for the individual to steer his way through the traffic. (Elias 1982: 233–34)

In summary, then, militarised relationships as paths to power, travel and security are progressively replaced in Elias with market relationships that require interdependence as paths to wealth and power. Interdependence, moreover, is vital for survival in urban life with its complex division of labour and multiplication of norms that regulate markets.

Thinking about decivilising exceptions

One clue as to where improved explanations of homicide trends since World War II might lie comes from Eisner's (2008: 307) text where he says: '[W]ith two exceptions (Finland and France, the latter because of the increased levels of homicide during the Algerian War) about 40–60 percent of the variation are represented by the joint trend' (all the European cases unified along the same homicide trend line).

Eisner's clue is to advance the extreme brutality of the Algerian civil war as a reason for the French exception to the general pattern of postwar homicide (with French homicides increasing from World War II and in the 1950s, when homicide was falling in the rest of the West, stabilising, then declining from 1994 to the 2018 UNODC homicide rate of 1.2). France mobilised 1.5 million troops to fight the Algerian war of independence between 1954 and 1962. During the peak years of fighting between 1956 and 1962, France averaged 470,000 troops fighting in Algeria;

25,600 never came home. Some 150,000 Algerian combatants perished and 350,000 to 1 million civilians were killed in a bloodbath close to France and vivid in the French imagination. From the 1950s, it also had troops fighting in other colonies, such as Indochina, as France resisted the decolonisation path agreed with President Roosevelt as World War II ended—a path the British and Dutch empires were taking at that time, and that the Spanish and Portuguese had mostly taken a century earlier.

Now I have five more clues that are also about war that have captured my imagination. This is not the same as saying they are necessarily clues with any generally evocative character. The second clue is the analysis of Broadhurst et al. (2015, 2018) that violence started to fall very sharply and more or less continuously in Cambodia within a couple of years of the UN Transitional Authority in Cambodia (UNTAC) finishing its work, and peace finally consolidating in the country. This sharp drop in crime and violence came after the long Indochina war, after genocide in Cambodia and then a Vietnamese invasion that started with border clashes in 1975, followed by a full invasion and regime change that removed the Khmer Rouge in 1977. According to UNODC, the homicide rate peaked in 1998 in Cambodia at 6.8—somewhat later than in the West—and did not come down to the level of most western countries until it settled at 1.8 for much of the past decade. The pattern is broadly the same, however, even though the rates of homicide and armed killing fell six years later and more steeply than in the West. The combination of this pattern of comparability with the West and the steepness of the decline in violence from large-scale genocide to below-average homicide (in global terms) holds the appeal of this clue. We will see that the decline in Rwanda to a below-average homicide rate after its genocide bears comparison with Cambodia.

A third clue is a much more major exception. It is the transcontinental exceptionalism of Latin America and the Caribbean. In Amy Nivette's (2011) meta-analysis of cross-national predictors of crime, the strongest mean effects were a Latin America and Caribbean regional dummy variable, with Latin American and Caribbean countries having much higher homicide rates than the rest of the world. A close second across the studies in Nivette's meta-analysis was income inequality. Latin American homicide rates, furthermore, *increased* formidably both before and after the great western crime decline from 1992 (LaFree and Drass 2002: 786–87), but especially strongly from 1990. As with France and Cambodia, in Latin America, we interpret the rise in interpersonal violence during the long-run crime drop in the West as a consequence of brutalisation by war and state violence. While the decline in state violence and war deaths in France and Cambodia saw recovery from that brutalisation after a notable lag, there has been no recovery yet in Latin America because state violence and war deaths are driven less by classic civil war than by a war on drugs that is ongoing. Likewise, we will now see clues of a brutalisation effect in Europe and long lags to recovery from the brutalisation of waves of wars in the early centuries of the second millennium. These waves included the Hundred Years' War and the Thirty Years' War (1618–48).

A fourth clue is particularly speculative, based as it is on much more limited data, with more vexing comparability issues, than we have on the first three clues. This is that England may have experienced a sharp rise in homicide rates starting in the mid-1200s and peaking in the mid-1300s, when the only homicide rate of 100 per 100,000 is recorded (Eisner 2014: 80). During the first half of the 1200s, before this crime rise, most of Eisner's (2001: 622) estimates are not far above 10 per 100,000 (though some are below 10, and two are below five). While homicide rates start to decline in the decades after 1350, these decades are still an exceptionally high homicide period. The decades after the 1350 peak are the last period in the dataset when all estimates are far above 10 per 100,000. Ninety per cent of datapoints after those decades that follow the 1350 peak are well below 10; *all* are below 10 after 1630. A steep rise in homicide appears to occur after those early decades of the 1200s, culminating around 1350 with estimates of more than 50 and as high as one hundred. While these data on rises in crime rates are from long ago, the English datapoints are much denser than for any other country in Eisner's (2001, 2003, 2014, 2017) data, which synthesises the research of many historians, and in any data that can currently be accessed by criminologists.

These are data that have been particularly influential in the big-sweep interpretations of Steven Pinker (2011). Note that this—the sharpest crime rise we can suspect in English history[13]—occurs during and after an exceptionally bloody and long warlike period, even for British history. It comes with large lags after unusually tumultuous invasions of England by the Vikings ending in 1066, by the Norman Conquest starting when the Viking invasions ended, followed by many Saxon revolts, the first three Crusades that started in 1096 and ended in 1192 and many and

---

13   For updated data on the sharpness of this rise for all of Europe, see Eisner (2014: 88).

varied revolts of barons. This was followed *during* the century and a half of homicide rises until 1350 and beyond by further Crusades and barons' wars, the bloody Wars of Scottish Independence that ran from 1296 to 1357 and then the Hundred Years' War, starting in 1337. Datapoints for England then disappeared during the latter part of the Hundred Years' War, which may have been the bloodiest period of European history since the defeat of the Roman Empire. Datapoints for England do not resume until the late 1500s, when all estimates are around or well below 10 per 100,000 (Eisner 2001: 622). While these early data are low in reliability, they are at least English data, and it may be the only place where criminologists can see anything like a 1,000 per cent increase in homicide rates in any 100-year period. This is a clue about the possible importance of periods of history that are militarised in a protracted and widespread way in the case of the Hundred Years' War and the Crusades, which affected and brutalised thinking across wide swathes of Christendom.

Apart from the steep decline in homicide from 1840 until World War I that is apparent for all of Europe (Eisner 2008: 296; see also Spierenburg 2008), the second period where a more complex pattern of sharp decline in homicide is evident in Eisner's (2003: 95) European data is in the 1600s. Homicide rates halved between the periods 1600–50 (the Thirty Years' War era) and 1650–1700 in Europe (Eisner 2014: 80–81). No other comparison of two adjacent 50-year periods approaches the steepness of this drop. This is followed by a period from the late 1600s to the late 1700s when there is no visible decline.[14] The sharpest decline in Eisner's (2001: 626; 2014: 80) data for this period comes at the end of the Thirty Years' War (1618–48) for Germany. Germany's average homicide rate for the period 1600–50 is 10; for 1650–1700, it is three (Eisner 2014: 80). This is our fifth clue. What we now call Germany was the part of Europe that suffered the most extreme horrors of the Thirty Years' War, which was even more deadly than the Hundred Years' War three centuries earlier, and the third most deadly war (after World Wars I and II in battlefield deaths as a percentage of the world population) (Ferguson 2006: xxxv). So, it is significant to note that the German homicide rate was more than three times as high between 1600–50 compared with 1650–1700. The Thirty Years' War may not have been as protracted as the Hundred Years'

---

14   Eisner's Table 2 (2003: 95) creates a misleading impression of average homicide rates falling sharply from the seventeenth century (average of 11) to the eighteenth century (average, 3.2) when the fall occurred from very high levels to very low levels inside the seventeenth century, then relative stability from the late 1600s to the late 1700s, then sharp decline again in the late 1700s.

War or the Crusades, but it was even more bloody and savage and so radically reshaped a macro-politics of inclusion, exclusion, stigmatisation and heresy across Christendom from which Northern Ireland has yet to recover.

We saw in Footnote 3 that English migrants who populated what became the United States after the American Revolution experienced homicide rates up to 50 times those of the England they left for a society seeking to expand its frontiers through force of arms and without settled institutions in those frontier zones. This was when a good number of them, such as the Quakers who went to Pennsylvania and other religious minorities who fled to North America, were pacifists! This early American exceptionalism is a sixth clue. William Penn worked sincerely at his pacifism and inclusion, but in the end, Pennsylvania was pacified by other men's guns, militarisation and indigenous genocide.

My six clues, it should be clear, are all about war and about long lags of the brutalisation effects of war on crime. Latin America and the Caribbean are such a macro-clue that cautions against thinking too narrowly about what counts as an armed conflict that cascades to crime. It vindicates Braithwaite and D'Costa's (2018: 309–10) choice to define an armed conflict broadly as one in which 'one armed group with a command structure is engaged in group attacks with weapons on another armed group with a command structure'. Mexican, Salvadorian and Colombian drug wars very much satisfy this definition. The Latin American clue also vindicates the possible importance of militarisation as 'control or shaping of other institutions by the military and imbuing other institutions with a military character' (Braithwaite and D'Costa 2018: 320).

These are only six clues towards inductive inference that might shape macrocriminological theory. They are not systematic quantitative analyses designed to refute the hypotheses they invoke. The final sections of Chapter 2 and Chapter 8 discuss what this would require. The six clues are just a journey making inductive theory-building transparent, as is the declaration that they are influenced by the macrocriminological induction in Braithwaite and D'Costa (2018) that war cascades to crime and crime cascades to further crime (Braithwaite 2020a), as crime and war cascade to further crime and war (Chapter 11). Next, I suggest that we can better understand why they might be evocative clues by considering the story of the unprecedented levels of war violence globally between 1911 and 1953.

Global decivilisation (1911–1953)?

The world can be interpreted as suffering a cataclysmic decivilising shift, in Elias's (1982) terms, across 42 years from 1911 to 1953. Or, at least, it suffered cascades of war at a scale of killing never seen before in human history (Braithwaite and D'Costa 2018). I mark its beginning with the 1911 Italian invasion of Libya, which may have caused half the population of that country to lose their lives. This continued through Balkan wars that further broke up the Ottoman Empire and finally brought us to World War I (1914–18). Japan sent troops to China to block the union of Manchuria with the Chinese Nationalist cause in 1928, commencing 17 years of Japanese militarism across many corners of Asia and the Pacific. Then, from the mid-1930s, fascist parties in Spain, Italy and Germany began to promote multiple wars that culminated 11 years later with the end of World War II. In the years immediately after World War II, many wars of nation-building and ethnic cleansing raged across Europe, especially the cleansing of Germans, and especially in Eastern Europe. But it was not only Eastern Europe that was affected and not only Germans who were being ethnically cleansed.[15] Meanwhile, a civil war that raged in China until 1949 finally brought Mao Zedong's communists to power. Postcolonial conflicts broke out in Greater India, Indonesia and other large and small emerging southern nations in the 1940s and 1950s. The Chinese Civil War was immediately followed by war between Chinese-backed communists in the north of Korea and American-backed anticommunists in the south. The Korean War finally ended with the loss of almost 5 million lives, mostly civilian, after a 1953 ceasefire.

This narrative reveals that neither World War I nor World War II was 'a war'; each was a cascade of many wars of varied kinds. The Chinese Civil War of the late 1940s (with approximately 10 million deaths) and the Korean War (almost 5 million deaths) of the early 1950s did not seem huge wars after the two cascades of world war. Yet these wars rank highly on the list of the most-deadly wars of modernity and contributed

---

15   For example, the 31 million people uprooted across Europe between 1944 and 1948 included Bulgarians driven out of eastern Macedonia and western Thrace, Greeks fleeing Macedonia and western Thrace, Greeks fleeing Turkey, Muslims fleeing Greece, Serbs ethnically cleansing Croats, Magyars expelled from southern Slovakia, Ukrainians driven from Poland, Ukrainian slaughter of Poles and Poles fleeing Russia. There was even a fully fledged pogrom against Jews in Kielce, Poland, in July 1946, among other cleansings (Ferguson 2006: 584; Lake and Rothchild 1998: 166–68). European states were greatly ethnically homogenised through this postwar bloodletting.

to the pattern of late-modern wars in which most of those slaughtered were civilians. Hence, the period from the disintegration of the Ottoman Empire from 1911 to the Korean War ceasefire can be conceived of as the most decivilising period of recorded human history in terms of warfare, and particularly warfare with civilian slaughter. This could possibly be qualified by saying this was true at least since the all-conquering, murderous lifetime of Genghis Khan and his Mongol successors eight centuries ago.[16] The big picture of violence can be seen this way even though the homicide rate recorded by domestic police in the West is at the long bottom plateau of the U during this period. That gently declining flatness of the crime rate in the records of western criminologists of the era means little during such an unprecedented tumult of human history, when so many countries saw prisoners-of-war shot and tortured, civilians raped, houses intentionally torched and property looted, and countless innocents intentionally imprisoned and starved for who they were rather than what they had done.

Could it be that the endless war crimes of the four decades ending in 1953 were motivated by such existential threats to states that war greatly unified them, defeating anomie, reinforcing the strong normative code of the western Allies' Greatest Generation, as they staved off their enemies? With US General Douglas MacArthur and other influential Republicans arguing for the deployment of nuclear weapons in Korea and fighting a total war against China to defeat it before it acquired nuclear weapons, the Korean War was certainly included among the wars seen in many corners of the planet as an existential threat. We will come to perceive what is going on here in the next chapter and beyond as existential threats strengthening both bonding and bridging social capital within one's national group yet severing bridging capital to enemies outside the nation. Societies suffering existential threats, such as the Blitz in London, for example, pull together; they become more reintegrative with one another inside, yet more stigmatising of outsiders. Public opinion data show that embattled political leaders often reunify normative commitment to their rule and to their political projects by starting or joining wars, especially when political elites are unified in support of the war (Berinsky 2007). When interventions go badly, however, elite and opinion poll support can disintegrate quickly.

---

16 Genghis Khan's wars did not kill anywhere near the numbers killed in war between 1911 and 1953, but possibly did kill tens of millions (Morris 2014: 145) and therefore possibly across many wars a larger proportion of the world's population of the time.

At the same time as there was a process that solidified national social capital during the world wars, it was also a decivilising movement in Elias's (1982) terms on the streets of the towns where the war was fought. Four decades of horrific wars normalised violence. While the wars since 1953 were much less terrible than those of the four decades preceding them, there were shocking tolls that started with the French colonial wars, particularly in Vietnam, Cambodia and a wider South-East Asian war, a shocking sequence of postcolonial civil wars and invasions by neighbours in Lebanon and Syria, the sequence of wars in Afghanistan, the Iran–Iraq war of the 1980s and the Congolese wars that started in the 1990s, among many other civil wars.

None of the last wars, however, was read by the baby-boomer generation in the West as a war that posed an existential threat to their societies, even as they were read that way by many Afghans or Iraqis. Most baby boomers wanted a generation of peace. In a sense, the barbarism their parents and grandparents suffered planted civilising seeds of pacifism in the baby boomers, especially in Germany and Japan, but also among the baby boomers of Paris, London, New York, Toronto, Sydney and Auckland. All wars plant both seeds of further barbarism and seeds of a politics of resistance to barbarism. The baby boomers mostly opposed military engagement in Asian, African, Latin American and Middle Eastern proxy wars against enemies of the West. This divided the baby boomers against their parents' generation, particularly on the desirability of fighting communists in proxy wars in the Global South 'so we would not have to fight them at home'. The Greatest Generation believed their struggles in the Depression and the world wars and the exit into the peaceful prosperity of the 1950s and 1960s vindicated the world order for which they had fought on the Allied side and surrendered to on the Axis side. It vindicated western capitalism led by the United States. A large proportion of the baby-boomer generation in the West simply did not buy this by 1968— not the virtues of western domination, particularly not the virtues of its dirty proxy wars, not even the virtues of its materialism and capitalism, and not the virtues of being a politically quiescent 'organisation man' (Whyte 1956). The most educated baby boomers particularly did not settle into being cogs in these machines as their fathers had, nor domestic servants to them as their mothers had.

Anomie grew in the face of contested wars, whereas it had declined inside western alliance societies during the wars to 1953. While the women of the baby-boomer generation were given far greater opportunities and suffered less domestic servitude than their mothers, female baby boomers unsettled the patriarchal normative order more forcefully than had their mothers in what came to be called second-wave feminism. They took up the cause of their grandmothers from the first feminist wave of the turn of the twentieth century. The Greatest Generation pushed back against the rebellion of the daughters, and against lesbianism with particular disgust. Gay, bisexual and transgender sons who came out in growing numbers were also met with revulsion by the Greatest Generation's 'fear of freedom' (Fromm 1942). By the 1990s, as the Greatest Generation began to die out, a new normative order had begun to settle, which accepted gendered and sexual diversity. Proxy wars against communists that had divided the Greatest Generation of the West against the baby boomers had largely ceased by the 1990s.

In recent years, terrorism has been widely seen as a serious threat, but it is not the case that one generation sees terrorism as an existential threat, while another is opposed to confronting it. The terrorist attacks of the twenty-first century perhaps did more to unify societies than to divide them anomically, though they did divide Muslim minorities against Christian majorities in many parts of the planet. Terrorism did not unify as broadly and deeply, however, as the existential threats nations confronted in World War II or in the massive confrontation with communism that risked nuclear war in Korea and beyond.

We can see the trajectory of this great normative fracture, and then healing, in the reaction of the young in Australia to Anzac Day marches (Australia and New Zealand's veterans' day). Many baby boomers vilified Anzac Day marches in their youth as glorifying war. My partner, Valerie, participated in the feminist marches against Rape in War that attempted to join Anzac Day marches, infuriating the Greatest Generation. Today, children of we baby boomers participate in Anzac Day commemorations with a homage to veterans that hugely exceeds that paid by their parents when they were young. At the same time, postwar and Cold War militarism have mellowed. Contemporary Anzac Day commemorations are less shrill and jingoistic; our former enemies attend to share in the sorrow of the tragic waste that is war. This is a normative order of the West both significantly repaired and significantly restored that has healed some of the wounds of past generational and international divides.

There are definitively short-term lagged effects on soldiers returning from wars and postwar increases in homicide and suicide rates. Archer and Gartner (1984) found that homicide rates rise after nations participate in wars at home or abroad and rise most after the wars in which the killing is greatest—a result replicated by Stamatel and Romans (2018). Ghobarah et al. (2003) confirmed this cross-nationally for suicide as well as homicide. Marks (2001: 89, 133) found in South Africa that former male combatants experienced anomie, powerlessness and emasculation that became a 'slippery slide into the underworld of crime'. We have learnt from Iraq (Boyle 2014: Ch. 8) that rates of violent death often go up after a war 'ends', perhaps more than fiftyfold (Otterman et al. 2010: 147), with only El Salvador—another post-conflict society—having a higher total violent death rate than Iraq between 2004 and 2009 (Geneva Declaration Secretariat 2011: Ch. 2). This result has also been discovered in a number of African and other conflicts in which killing (Duffield 2001: 188), and even more so sexual and gender-based violence, increases after a peace agreement is signed. Likewise, this occurred after some Latin American civil wars—most notably, the continent's biggest recent wars, in El Salvador and Guatemala, where a doubling of already extreme homicide rates at the end of the war delivered a higher death rate than during many of the peak years of civil war (Muggah and Krause 2011: 180; Richani 2007; Westendorf 2015: 8). El Salvador's peak homicide rate in 1995, three years after its war ended, was 142 per 100,000, according to UNODC's International Homicide Statistics database—a higher peak than any during the eight centuries in Eisner's (2014) European dataset and one of many considerable Latin American refutations of Pinker's (2011) claims that *The Better Angels of Our Nature* have triumphed. It is an even more considerable challenge when one takes account of the formidable evidence that 'the disappeared', if counted, would massively increase the homicide rate. Homicide rates have been massively contrived downwards by murderers both in state security forces and in drug gangs when they have an interest in claiming that the level of killing in El Salvador is not as bad as their critics allege (Carcach and Artola 2016). The widespread transformation of murders into disappearances that might be interpreted as a result of emigration continues to the present day in El Salvador. Ball et al. (1999) found in Guatemala between 1960 and 1996 that in years of low violence, 50 per cent of political killings were reported in the media, falling to 5 per cent in years of high violence.

In Ghobarah et al. (2003), the lags after war that showed significant effects on homicide and suicide were effects of war deaths on homicide over a five-year lag and suicide deaths two years after those five years. Ghobarah et al. (2003: fn. 8) seem to have also run 13-year lags, with this having positive but weaker effects. Yet we know that Australian children of Vietnam veterans had more elevated suicide risks than their veteran parents (Commonwealth of Australia 2014).[17] By the time veterans retire from the military, they may not have many of the peak years of crime and suicide risk left on their clocks, but their children are yet to enter their years of maximum risk. This suggests we should be studying a range of lagged effects longer than 20-year intergenerational lags in addition to the short-term lags in the extant literature. There should be both a short-term lag effect on the veteran generation and a 10–30-plus-year lag effect mediated through their children's generation that extends to children born a number of years after the war.

There has not been an empirically informed macrocriminology that has taken an interest in the possibility that the decivilising effects of unusually bloody wars may have cumulative and longer lags that are both short-term and longer-term because of their effects on two successive generations. The suffering of the children of Vietnam War combatants, however, is hugely less widespread in impact than the suffering of the children and then the grandchildren of the generations who waded through the blood of four decades of wars that finally ended in 1953. With the small states of the former Yugoslavia put in a separate category in the 1990s, across the rest of the West, the tens of thousands of westerners killed in all the wars of the past 68 years are a tiny number compared with the tens of millions of them killed in the wars of the previous 42 years to 1953.

Hence the hypothesis that those 42 years of fighting existential wars by the West left a postwar legacy of anomie when the children of the postwar generation grew up. An accumulation of lagged PTSD passed

---

17   Suicide attempts were found to occur among a remarkably high 62 per cent of Croatian male war veterans with PTSD (Maršanić et al. 2014). Hendin and Hass (1991) found that among Vietnam veterans, combat guilt—for example, memories of killing women and children—were associated with suicide attempts and contemplation of suicide. This also seems to be associated with transgenerational mental health problems for the children of Vietnam veterans (Rosenheck and Fontana 1998). Bremner et al. (1993) found Vietnam veterans who had suffered PTSD inflicted highly elevated levels of physical abuse on their children. Kaplan et al. (2007) found that veterans across all wars were twice as likely as the general population to die from suicide. The US Centers for Disease Control and Prevention, in statistics on suicide rates among Americans, long reported that Vietnam veterans experienced the highest suicide rates.

across successive generations of male warriors desensitised to violence and domination in the two world wars was transmitted to their children, who were often brutalised by the war veterans of the Greatest Generation. The baby-boomer generation was exposed constantly on the new medium of television to content that glorified these wars, legitimated killing and venerated the heroism of the Greatest Generation.

These cultural artefacts of the legitimation of violence are likely to have longer lag effects than suicide risks that themselves can be long: a veteran has a child 10 years after the war and his child suicides as a heroin addict 30 years after that—a 40-year lag that might contribute to explaining why the effect of the 42 years of war killing may not have extinguished even 39 years later in 1992 when the crime drop started. The cultural artefacts of the glorification of killing endure even longer than that lag. Films from the 1950s that legitimated war violence were rerun for the children of the 1960s and 1970s on their television sets. The evidence that television content that vindicates violence can engender violence in a generation is now clear enough (Paik and Comstock 1994; Anderson and Bushman 2002; but see Savage and Yancey 2008, who find more limited effects). The legitimation effect of the 42 years of war was instantiated in many other ways beyond television that were more than straightforwardly cultural. Some of the legitimation of war killing was widely politically structured. In Australia, most male high school students in elite schools and a large proportion in working-class schools participated in the cadet corps, in which they dressed in military uniforms, learnt drill, how to fire a rifle and a machine gun, how to patrol in a jungle environment and how to deploy and return fire. It taught elite high school students how to be 'officers' and 'sergeants' who led other boys into violent projects. These high school war games continued into university life in university army reserve regiments that trained in university drill halls. These were closed when the baby boomers became university leaders.

On the side of the generational opposition to militarism, the politics of violence was also deeply structural. There were cultural elements to it, such as the ubiquitous posters of Che Guevara in baby-boomer bedrooms. The radical student generation read Chairman Mao's *Little Red Book* on political power growing out of the barrel of a gun and Frantz Fanon's *The Wretched of the Earth* (1965), especially in 1968—the year the uprising in Paris was the spark for an amazing global cascade of student uprisings against the western politics of the Cold War. Fanon was a member of the Algerian National Liberation Front. His writing aggressively legitimated violence on the side of the oppressed. He characterised Europe as an incubus of decivilisation, as we see in this series of quotes from the concluding two pages of his book:

> When I search for Man in the technique and the style of Europe, I see only a succession of negations of man, and an avalanche of murders ...

> Two centuries ago, a former European colony decided to catch up with Europe. It succeeded so well that the United States of America became a monster, in which the taints, the sickness and the inhumanity of Europe have grown to appalling dimensions ...

> Comrades, have we not other work to do than to create a third Europe? The West saw itself as a spiritual adventure. It is in the name of the spirit of Europe, that Europe has made her encroachments, that she has justified her crimes and legitimized the slavery in which she holds four-fifths of humanity. (Fanon 1965)

What we see in the work of radical writers of the Global South in the 1960s like Fanon is the utter rejection of European institutions and the European normative order as civilising. This was because it preached peace internally from its pulpits but practised mass murder externally. Today, it is still hard to see the evidence that Africa has accepted embrace into the normative order of European 'civilisation'. Europe and North America are still seen in Africa as lands of violent racists and oppressors. If a genocide occurs in Rwanda or Congo, if a botched NATO regime-change operation unfolds to remove Muammar Gaddafi in Libya, the presidents of the United States and France can receive more of the blame in Africa than the local operatives who do the killing on the ground. With each mass atrocity, the normative divide between Africa and NATO widens that bit more. The interesting thing that happened from 1968 is that white western students started to identify with the advocacy of Fanon to fight fire with fire. A global anomic divide between the Global South and the West mapped on to a generational divide inside the West. Make no mistake, this mapping globalised the legitimation of violence. As a student advocate of nonviolence, I vividly remember the first university lecturer who approvingly quoted Fanon on the cleansing power of violence: 'Violence is a cleansing force. It frees the native from his inferiority complex and from his despair and inaction; it makes him fearless and restores his self-respect' (Fanon 1965).

Valerie Braithwaite and I remember being shocked when we participated in the Vietnam Moratorium marches from the late 1960s that the voices that took over the chanting were saying: 'One side right, one side wrong, victory to the Viet Cong.' We were part of the nonviolence wing of the student movement, but so many were not. Many advocated violence inside the West as well in a way that broke totally with the normative order. In the United States, Eldridge Cleaver and some other leaders of the Black Power Movement took this further to argue that for black men to rape white women was an insurrectional act against the colonisers of black humanity. The structure of the world system that drove this global pattern of violence was the West and the communist bloc fearing one another's nuclear weapons. They wanted to defeat the other militarily but feared doing so directly. This had to be done by a cold war in the Global North and a hot war in the Global South. They chose to fight each other through proxy fighters in the Global South. Che Guevara and Richard Nixon both believed in a domino theory whereby strategic violence would cause the dominoes of the Global South to fall either into the hands of communism or into the custody of the West. As Che put it: 'Create two, three, many Vietnams' (Guevara 2003).

So, I am suggesting a generational divide that absorbed violent ideologies from both sides of the North–South divide. In the West, it was a war-and-peace anomie effect that had short lags from proxy wars against communism in the Global South, especially once the Vietnam War started. And it was a PTSD and normalised violence effect of war that had long three-generational lags across veteran families decimated by domestic violence: from the World War I generation to World War II and to the violent baby-boomer generation.

This was vivid in my family biography. My beloved grandfather was a machine gunner of Germans at the Somme. Like Hitler, who was in the very trenches on the opposite side he sought to mow down, Grandad was gassed. Grandad threw my father out of his home as a young man when he threatened to hit Grandad after Grandad allegedly threatened Grandma with violence. Dad came back from the Sandakan Death Marches in World War II less traumatised than the other survivors, one of whom threatened to shoot his wife and children and then later turned the gun on himself. Yet still I remember the childhood visits to Dad in the 'nerve ward' of the veterans' hospital, the veterans with cigarettes in their shaking hands. Dad was such a fine, strong, principled man, but damaged. There were the screaming dreams at night in the years before his emotional recovery consolidated. Not that my dad thought Vietnam a wise war, but he thought it terrible disloyalty to our troops that his three children would protest in the streets against that war. One day, this kind of argument boiled over and my brother was thrown out of our house. Successive Braithwaite generations of veterans of the two world wars, both fathers ejecting their sons from the family home, never to return. Such sadness for the mothers. I inject this personal narrative for reasons of reflexivity, to allow the reader to judge that this author only thinks this way about the history of western violence because of an atypical family experience of the politics of violence. For this author, however, his family is a hologram that contains within its microcosm the deep structures of the whole historical pattern of violence, of all the macro images of the horrors of violence of the big wars that ran from the Somme of my grandfather Joe to Vietnam, which engorged my classmates. My generation is defined by those three terrible wars and so my generation must understand successive generations who are less defined by them. They think differently as a result.

One part of the anomie surge was a 'greed is good'[18] mentality among formidable fragments of the privileged populations of Wall Street and dominated fragments of deindustrialised cities formed into gangs to sell drugs. The fathers of the baby boomers, whether they frequented the streets of slums or Wall Street, could be greedy, but the Greatest Generation was less attracted to the creeds of the greed-is-good subcultures of criminality than their wayward children. The Greatest Generation also ruled in a more egalitarian world. We discussed earlier how the Great Depression and its Keynesian legacy pulled the rich back to the pack, as did World War II. The top marginal income tax rates on the rich remained more than 80 per cent in most western societies, including the United States, long into the 1950s as governments recovered fiscally from the burdens of fighting such huge wars over such long periods of history. After the 1950s, inequalities widened again and have continued to further widen since (Piketty 2014), which has not helped with sustaining low crime rates (as discussed in the middle chapters of this book).

Obviously, there is a great complex of other crosscutting variables to consider before we begin to fully understand why crime surged in the West from the early 1960s to the early 1990s and then settled back to lower rates. Nevertheless, there is another attraction of this macro interpretation

---

18   Words associated with Wall Street criminal offender Michael Milken and Michael Douglas's character in the film *Wall Street*.

of heightened western anomie between 1960 and 1992, and heightened trauma and desensitisation to violence and domination as a result of the four decades wading through blood: this is that it makes sense of the massive countertrend, which is Latin America. Remember Amy Nivette's (2011) meta-analysis of homicide showing the strongest mean effects were for a Latin America and Caribbean regional dummy variable, with Latin American and Caribbean countries having much higher homicide rates than the rest of the world. Recall that Latin American homicide rates increased formidably both during and after the great western crime decline (LaFree and Drass 2002: 786–87). One reason mentioned already for high and increasing Latin American homicide rates is the contribution made by gangs associated with the drug trade supplying the North American market. A second reason is that Latin America has the highest inequality of any region of the world; this inequality has been increasing, and income inequality had the second highest effect size after the Latin America and Caribbean regional dummy variable in increasing homicide in Nivette's (2011) meta-analysis. Schargrodsky and Freira (2021) confirmed not only the importance of the Gini coefficient in explaining why the countries of this region have higher levels of crime than the rest of the world, but also showed that within Latin America and the Caribbean, levels of inequality is the only variable showing a robust causal effect across national and sub-national levels to predict which are the hot spots of crime within the region, as measured by victimisation surveys as well as homicide rates.

A third factor is that Latin America's worst period of war and state violence was not World War I or II nor the Korean or Vietnam wars, none of which engaged Latin American armies. No, it was internal Latin American conflicts that started *after* the worst 42 years of conflict violence in the history of the West and progressively worsened in the 1960s, 1970s and 1980s. So, if there were enduring and long lags after the four decades up to 1953 of the West's wade through blood, we might expect long lags after the Latin American conflicts up to the 1980s. This would mean Latin American lagged violence still had some years to run if it lasted for four decades. Moreover, as already argued, drug wars were more deadly than civil wars in many countries and continue to be so this century, to the point that more people have been killed in Mexico's drug wars of this century than in Afghanistan's twenty-first-century wars (Marc 2016).[19]

---

19   The late twentieth-century war deaths were many times worse than the twenty-first-century war deaths in Afghanistan.

This book argues that the Latin American societies that have averted cascades of recurrent civil war and the worst excesses of the US-enforced War on Drugs, and the worst extremes of inequality, are the societies that have avoided the very highest homicide rates in recent decades. These countries include Chile (with a homicide rate of 3.6 per 100,000 at the time of writing) and Cuba (4.2) in the current UNODC statistics.

The regional problem is not limited to the former Spanish, Portuguese and French colonies. For a number of decades, the former British colony of Jamaica has ranked in the top few countries for homicide rates for the South American and the Caribbean regions (Harriott 2011). The major drivers are consistent with the regional pattern: armed violence waged between political factions with contesting views about how to respond to the postcolonial grievances of former slaves and peasants violently oppressed by a colonial landlord class. One Jamaican political party was armed by Cuba, the other by the US Central Intelligence Agency. Street gangs that mobilised violence to deliver votes and political loyalty to one side or the other morphed into organised crime groups that participate in the drug trade and diverse other forms of organised crime. While these organised crime groups perpetrate exceptionally high levels of killings that deliver the exceptional Jamaican homicide rate, the offshore wings of Jamaican drug traffickers murder more people overseas than in Jamaica, particularly in the United States, but also in Canada and the United Kingdom. This in turn has cascaded to Jamaica having among the highest rates of killings by police in the world. Of the 13 countries with the highest current rates of killings by police per capita, only three are not from the Americas (Syria, the Philippines and Afghanistan).

Asia

Military power plays a paradoxical role in the pacification of violence. We have already seen that before nation-states began to replace empires, the most murderous army in human history pacified the Silk Road. This was an instance of the trade-based interdependence that is central to Elias's civilising process. China had earlier pacified the Silk Road as well—for example, with the Tang Dynasty's seventh-century conquest of nomadic western powers, which allowed China to reassert control of, and expand, what were then long-degraded trading routes (Bowen 2017).

This is a profoundly important historical example of the paradox of military pacification being a stepping-stone to widened spaces of security and civility.

Between Genghis Khan's pacification of the Silk Road and Chinese President Xi Jinping's Belt and Road Initiative sit a number of periods when millions were killed in exceptional political violence in China. One was between the final disintegration of the Chinese Empire aided by western incursions and the Cultural Revolution near the end of Chairman Mao's rule. During this period, Asia was the most violent region of the planet. The last Chinese dynasty, the Qing, finally fell in 1911–12, but this was at the end of a long period of disintegration driven by western colonialism. As in Latin America, in China, drug wars contributed greatly to the disintegration of the empire and Asia's steep rise in violence, particularly the Opium Wars between the United Kingdom and China, which resulted in China losing Hong Kong to Britain and other territories to France and Japan. The Opium Wars of 1839–42 and 1856–60 were a result of the Qing (Manchu) Dynasty attempting to shut the British opium trade from India to China, which was hugely profitable for the British.

After the first Opium War came the Taiping Rebellion (1850–64). This civil war to overthrow the Qing Dynasty became one of the most deadly wars in human history, taking probably far more than 20 million lives, even possibly several times that number. The oppressive treaties Britain imposed on China after defeating it in the Opium Wars were a humiliation that showed its neighbours how feeble China had become. The Opium Wars thereby undermined Chinese regional power. This allowed France to colonise Indochina and Japan to seize Taiwan and effectively control Korea (both of which had been Chinese tributaries). The United Kingdom, France, Japan, Germany and Russia all established domains of influence inside China. Defeat by Japan in the Sino-Japanese War of 1895–96 further disintegrated the empire. In 1900, the Boxer Rebellion saw peasants rise up against the foreigners and the Qing Dynasty. The Qing eventually joined the uprising against the foreigners but was defeated and then replaced with Sun Yat-sen's revolutionary republican regime in 1911. This was the end of 2,000 years of empire in China. The democratic republic did not last. It disintegrated under pressure from the warlord era of 1916 to 1928 when different military factions fought to carve up control of the country.

Mao's communist army ultimately pacified the warlords and then the entire country into the comparatively low-crime society discussed in Chapter 2 after it took over (particularly during Chinese communism's early decades). The communist civil war raged from 1927 to 1949, taking probably 10 million lives. Then the Second Sino-Japanese War took more than twice as many lives as the civil war during the period from 1935 to 1945. After that, there was the Korean War. Asia then saw many wars against communism that took millions of lives in both Indochina and Afghanistan and large numbers of lives in more than a dozen other Asian societies. Drug wars in Burma (Myanmar) and Thailand started when the Kuomintang was pursued there by Mao's army and assisted by the CIA to set up drug empires in the Golden Triangle (McCoy 1972).

While Asia's most powerful societies—China, Japan, Korea and India—were pacified after the extremely bloody periods they all suffered up to 1953, they then became low-crime and falling-violence societies. This crime drop occurred during the period of the great crime rise in the West up to 1992. This began to disintegrate in India with the worst Muslim uprising in Kashmir commencing in 1947, threatening nuclear war between India and Pakistan, and continuing to the present (Braithwaite and D'Costa 2018). A proliferation of ethnic wars for autonomy and Maoist insurgencies continued in the twenty-first century in half of India's states. So, in fact, India (and Pakistan and Sri Lanka) was on a trajectory towards being counted among the most violent societies on Earth from the end of the 1980s (Karstedt 2012a, 2014b), just as the great crime drop was beginning in the West. The Asian Financial Crisis of 1997–98 was also followed by a brief, unusually violent period, especially in Indonesia (Braithwaite et al. 2010a). It only lasted a few years and we have seen that Indonesia quickly became a low-crime society again early this century. Like the southern regions of Asia—from Nepal to Bangladesh, Myanmar, Cambodia, India, Sri Lanka, Timor and Indonesia—even the fraught western periphery of Asia in Afghanistan and Iran has had far lower levels of war deaths in the twenty-first century than in the back half of the twentieth century.

It is much easier to summarise the macro crime picture for Europe than it is for Asia because Asia is such a big place, comprising half the world's population. Asia and the Pacific have many ongoing wars; the worst risks of nuclear war, across the borders between the two Koreas and between India and Pakistan; and many places where violence is still out of control, from Afghanistan to Myanmar to the Highlands of Papua New

Guinea (Braithwaite and D'Costa 2018). Even so, the macro picture is of a pacification of violence of the Elias and Pinker kind in Asia since the end of the Cold War or earlier, particularly in East Asia. Up to the end of the Cold War in the late 1980s, Asia was the most war-afflicted region of the planet, accounting for more wars and more war deaths than any other region, including Africa. After the Cold War ended, Asia (as long as we exclude the Middle East) became one of the most peaceful parts of the planet and the massive population of East Asia—from Siberia, Manchuria, Mongolia, China, Japan, Korea, Vietnam and Cambodia right down to Indonesia—had become the most peaceful on the planet. That has continued to the time of writing. Asia today has many countries with low homicide rates and lower imprisonment rates than the least-violent European countries. China continues to be a complicated case, however. It is very effectively pacified, with criminal gangs holding limited sway compared with past centuries and a UNODC recorded homicide rate that has reduced sharply this century to below 0.6 per 100,000 in the most recent three years. Yet market crime is booming and, in Xinjiang, we see genocide in this decade through a million Muslim Uyghurs forcibly interred in re-education camps, with Chinese Muslim terrorism cascading across the region—for example, to Pakistan, Afghanistan and other countries of Central Asia—as a reaction (Braithwaite and D'Costa 2018).

While the Latin American regional dummy had the largest positive coefficient in explaining where homicide is high in Nivette (2011), overall, the East Asian regional dummy had the strongest coefficient for low homicide rates.

Hence, the big picture for Asia is of more virulent twentieth-century militarisation than in Europe and war deaths from the mid-nineteenth century to the end of the Cold War many times greater than Europe's war deaths. For example, more people were killed in East Asia in World War II than in the rest of the world combined. Asia had declines in war deaths and crime, particularly in East Asia, that were more formidable, steeper and to much lower levels than the rest of the world. For all of Asia (including the Middle East in UNODC regions), the average homicide rate is slightly lower than Europe and less than half the world average. The picture is certainly more plural and woollier than it is for Europe, but it is of a massive civilising of war that comes first and then a civilising of violent crime, so that societies like Japan and Indonesia have the lowest homicide rates of any country with more than 100 million residents (indeed any society of more than 20 million), and Hong Kong, Macau and Singapore are countries with populations below 10 million with even lower homicide rates than Japan and Indonesia.

All the largest Asian countries also have comparatively low imprisonment rates. India, Pakistan, Indonesia and Japan have all fairly consistently maintained imprisonment rates of less than 40 per 100,000 this century, with Bangladesh mostly in the 40s (though 81 per cent of Bangladesh's prison population is on remand awaiting trial!). China is the outlier among large Asian countries, with an imprisonment rate of 118. China might still seem low given that 53 per cent of the world's countries have an imprisonment rate over 150 and the imprisoned Chinese include an unusually large number of political prisoners (Walmsley 2019). On the other hand, there is a great deal of unrecorded pre-trial detention in China.

Africa

Africa and the Middle East replaced Asia in the latter decades of the twentieth century as the regions accounting for the highest rates of war deaths, the largest number of wars and the longest wars. Africa's homicide rate (13), according to the UNODC (2019: 14), is only a little below that of the Americas (17.2; though half of Central America's 26 and South America's 24). Africa's rate is more than four times that of Europe (3) and five times Asia's including the Middle East (2.3). Southern Africa actually has a considerably higher average homicide rate than Central America, the Caribbean and South America (UNODC 2013: 23) and seems to be rising in recent years (UNODC 2019: 22). Even though the African data are the least satisfactory for all continents, Africa is interpreted as the most violent continent today because it simultaneously has homicide rates not far behind Latin America and the Caribbean and a substantially higher rate of war deaths. Africa and the Americas combined account for 73 per cent of the world's recorded homicide victims (UNODC 2019: 13) and undoubtedly far more than their share of unrecorded homicides. War deaths in Africa, nevertheless, are much lower this century than they were between 1980 and 2000 (Roser 2015). Many African wars were Cold War proxy wars. Furthermore, Africa's most murderous conflicts, in the Great Lakes region (the Congos, Rwanda, Burundi, Central African Republic, Uganda, Sudan, South Sudan), have been partially subdued. Such a downward movement is not apparent for homicide. South Africa is a clear exception, with homicide rates more than halved, falling from almost 80 per 100,000 to 65 in 1995 and to 31 in 2012 (UNODC 2013: 33)—still very high and it has edged back up somewhat in recent years. One is tempted to interpret this in terms of recovery from South Africa's armed conflicts of the 1970s and 1980s during which both sides aggressively legitimated violence until Nelson Mandela led the country to nonviolence in the peace process of the early 1990s.

Overall, more African countries have experienced upward than downward movement in homicide rates during the past 10 years. Long time-series data for Africa are simply not available. Where upward movement has occurred, UNODC (2013: 32–33) analysts note these are countries and regions that have suffered recent armed conflict. Hence, the best conclusion for Africa from limited data seems to be a decrease in war violence this century, but some new waves of disappearances (often uncounted as crimes because state security forces are the ones disappearing people), increased state crime and nonstate crime. Families have not recovered from the PTSD and the normalisation of violence that war continues to drive forward. Nor perhaps has Africa recovered from the violence of colonialism and the slave trade any more than African Americans have recovered from slavery. New waves of trade in slaves have arisen in war-torn countries such as Libya and Democratic Republic of Congo (as they have in Afghanistan).

Some African societies such as Rwanda have recovered remarkably well from total breakdown of the normative order, genocide and collapse of sovereignty, to build a strong renewed sovereignty and normative order, with a UNODC homicide rate down to 2.5 by 2015. Others such as Ghana have managed to build a civil society without cascading severe violence since independence, with a UNODC homicide rate of around 2 per 100,000 for most of the past decade.

Thinking in time about crime and freedom

Crime control is an art of freedom and freedom is an art of politics. Crime control requires a normative commitment to freedom that runs deeper than the desire to be politically popular. The art of thinking in time is imperative (Neustadt and May 1986). Peace diplomacy to prevent violence has not taken strides forward this century: the great powers are not working as well together to prevent conflict and promote disarmament as they did in the late twentieth century. Social science has value, too: if we know that a recurrent consequence of starting a war is cascades to diverse tyrannies, including to more wars, to homicide and suicide at home, and even to something as unexpected as elevated rates of rape among daughters of veterans 20 years later (O'Toole et al. 2018), we must eschew the politics of simply comparing the short-term costs of victory against the costs of inaction.

This chapter makes clear that thinking in time is the hard part. This is because anomie moves in recursive loops that have tipping points that can re-establish normative order through a new sovereignty or unravel and disintegrate an empire that had a peaceful settled sovereignty. If anomie's recursivity can have positive or negative feedback loops, this complexity allows no simple thinking from historical analogy. Thinking in time means creating lists of how this situation is similar *and different* to an analogy that appeals to us as a lesson of history. Thinking in time involves asking questions about whether each of the positive and negative feedback loops from anomie might tip into play. It involves asking what the story of this problem is in this moment of place-time, not just what science has to tell us about the problem. In the face of uncertainty about these judgements, monitoring of how the complex recursivity of normative order is playing out at any historical moment is central to the art of the politics of freedom. Finally, the art of freedom involves the courage to be decisive even when confronted with many unknowns and unknowables. It means rejecting analysis paralysis in favour of enacting one's theory of how to drive forward freedom's frontiers, but with humility. Humility means monitoring the recursivity of turning points to failure, continuously repairing the ship of politics at sea and adjusting its sails on the basis of feedback.

This book reveals no deadly simple mechanics of crime and freedom. It develops the beginnings of a theory to guide those who have a political commitment to less crime and more freedom. The book is grounded in a particular reading of the evidence. That reading, of course, must be contested. Surely, parts of it will be refuted in the years ahead. What I hope to have been persuasive about in this chapter is that loops of anomie might be repeatedly implicated in changes in the levels of crime and freedom that are massive compared with the changes in crime rates that even the most powerful crime science reveals as consequences of criminal justice policy changes. Positive criminology is therefore useful, but less important to comprehension of the low-crime society than anomie and the politics of freedom as nondomination.

Chapter 2 opined that Cold War commentators were wrong to see high crime rates in the United States between 1960 and 1992 as the price of freedom. This book will argue in the chapters to follow that they were a sign of unfreedom, of a society failing to deliver a fair share and failing to stick with its New Deal, creating a much less equal US society than existed before 1960. Compared with the market ethics of American capitalism in the 1950s, this century confronts us with a society of corrosive legal cynicism among the growing middle-class group that became victim-offenders of criminalised markets, in the terms described by Farrall and Karstedt (2019). The working class is shrinking; they have lost their jobs to deindustrialisation and, in a number of western societies, have turned towards authoritarian politics again, as they did in the 1930s. America, as in most of the West, became a society with low and falling levels of trust by citizens in its institutions—a society more willing to put its trust in demagoguery and social media clickbait. I have argued that generational divides have become more important to anomie, today dividing more between baby boomers and their children, who so often have less secure jobs and a welfare safety net with bigger holes than the net that protected their parents. Before that, I identified a massive normative divide between the baby boomers and their parents in countries like the United States and Australia.

The American normative order was comparatively unified during the New Deal era and during the existential struggles of World War II through to the end of the Korean War. The argument is that during the Vietnam War era considerable disintegration of the normative order occurred, however. Societies rot like fish from anomic breakdowns, from the head down, from the commanding heights of capitalism, from Wall Street down. Farrall and Karstedt's (2019) data suggest that in the United Kingdom and Germany, they also rot from the middle out. 'Greed is good' not only became a mantra on Wall Street and in the City of London; it also became relevant to middle-class people who became both victims of the scams of the internet era and perpetrators of middle-class crime. It is relevant in their conversations with middle-class friends about how to beat the system and its 'red tape'. For Indigenous minorities in Australia, or China or the United States for that matter, looking up to the contemporary greed of the business elite and the middle class whose ancestors stole Indigenous lands in genocidal frontier wars, stealing something back can even seem just.

It makes limited sense to view China as a very low-crime society today, even if it is hugely less violent than it was until 1950 and even though its UNODC homicide rate is very low. There are also cracks in China's normative order. Hundreds of thousands of riots by citizens about some grievance occur every year in China, often with violence. The Chinese Communist Party itself has estimated that there are more than 200 rural protests a day in the country, mostly about local corruption and inequality (Thornton and Thornton 2012: 84). China's citizens will have little trust in the state or its markets when its major economic crisis inevitably arrives. They see all too clearly that in the past, when the Shanghai Stock Exchange or the Chinese banks that are now the wealthiest corporations on the planet got the shakes in even little ways, the authoritarian state intervened to tilt the mirror, to create the impression that everything was rosy on the Shanghai bourse. Chinese investors hedge in western real estate markets because they know the trust in the smoke and mirrors their authoritarian leaders contrive into its markets could disintegrate into a massively distrustful run.

The victims of China's market crimes seem at least as greedy as their counterparts in the United Kingdom and Germany (Farrall and Karstedt 2019); Confucius's Golden Rule has lost its shine. Contrary to what might have been predicted by Robert Merton, Chinese respondents to the World Values Survey are less likely to agree that 'less emphasis on money and material possessions is good' than citizens from most countries, including the United States, England, Wales and Germany (Chamlin and Cochran 2007: 52). Not only are the market crimes of the commanding heights of Chinese capitalism, and of its massive middle class, out of control, but also common property crime has risen hugely since China's low-crime decades of the 1950s and 1960s. The chapters that follow, however, argue that more capitalism and more crime are no more inevitable than more freedom. Tempered capitalism can deliver more freedom and less crime than untempered socialism and untempered capitalism. The great historical discovery of the old social democratic politics was that some elements of socialism are among the ways to temper tyrannies of capitalism. A national health system that publicly guarantees health care to every citizen, however poor, is an example, as the United States should have learnt from its woeful response to the Covid-19 pandemic. The forthcoming chapters pursue these themes.

Continued recursivity of market crimes and anomie at these two brittle commanding heights of the world economy in the United States and China is a massive threat to the whole global system. We saw in 2008 how an epidemic of petty mortgage frauds in US housing markets could cause a crash in faraway countries that had no serious problems with the integrity of their mortgage markets. As we saw with the collapse of the German economy into hyperinflation in the 1920s and 1930s and the Yugoslavian economy in the 1980s and 1990s, a genuinely major economic crisis can cascade to extreme anomie and extreme authoritarianism and warmongering by leaders playing to outgroup narratives to secure their political survival (Braithwaite and D'Costa 2018).

Criminologists need not be mere spectators of such great events triggered by the recursivity of market crimes and anomie. Later chapters contend that a more competent American criminology could have helped, and a more competent FBI could have prevented, the Global Financial Crisis in 2004 or 2005 when the epidemic of housing loan frauds first became visible on FBI information systems. Just as a more responsive FBI and a more responsive criminology might have convened the right kinds of regulatory conversations to stop the rot of this financial market crime before it cascaded to crisis, so an FBI that was more oriented to prevention, and less obsessed with prosecution, might have prevented the 9/11 terrorist attacks (as the 9/11 Commission concluded) and the anomic adventurism of invading Afghanistan and Iraq to which this cascaded. Criminologists should have an important role to play when the drums of war beat as they did in 2001. Sadly, however, criminology was largely silent and social scientifically irrelevant.

This book argues that cascades of corruption and the capture of markets by a wealthy elite tend to cascade to criminalisation of the state. We see the worst examples of this in the contemporary states that have been most afflicted by post–Cold War violence—pre-eminently, the Democratic Republic of Congo. Yet we see the same phenomenon in the largely internally pacified United States and the number-two economy in the western alliance, Japan, where the Trump administration and various Liberal Democratic Party administrations (most famously, that of Kakuei Tanaka), respectively, criminalised the state in significant ways, though less catastrophically than we see in Congo.

Conclusion

Every local community at every point in human history has its own particularities of cascades of violence, cascades of nonviolence, pacifications by sovereignty and its breakup, cascades of normative order and breakdown into disorder when violence overwhelms society. Fine-grained intensive study of these particularities is the most revealing way to understand these worlds of war and crime, of sovereignty, normative order and pacification. Five previous books from the Peacebuilding Compared project have attempted to provide regional, national, provincial and hotspot case studies of violence and the rise and fall of normative orders (johnbraithwaite.com/peacebuilding/).

On that foundation, this chapter has begun to demonstrate that the macrocriminological lens contributes something distinctive. It can help us grasp bigger-picture understandings of the global and local patterning of crime and violence. The bigger picture is about crises that cascade anomie, anomie that cascades to crime, anomie that cascades market crises, criminalised markets that cascade other forms of criminalisation, including criminalisation of the state and authoritarian wars of aggression, but also corrosive crimes of greed by a disenchanted middle class and a collapse of tax system integrity that challenges the capacity of the state to be inclusive and to solve other large crises like climate change and Covid-19. We return to the theme of tax system integrity throughout the book.

If we build a strong normative order without also eliminating stigmatisation and without strengthening inclusion and reintegration, we risk a violent society in which the tyrannies of the majority prevail and the strength of the normative order promotes crime (Karstedt 2011b). The strength of the normative order of the Ku Klux Klan in some parts of the southern United States in the twentieth century illustrates this kind of reinforcement of violent crime. It is not just that a totalising Hobbesian sovereignty that is not tempered by rule of law, freedoms and the separation of powers will ultimately permit a resumption of cascades of violence of the disenfranchised. It is also that a Hobbesian politics of domination enables economic crimes of cronies, security crimes of the deep state, torture, disappearances, corruption, embezzlement and crimes of capitalists who capture state protection and patronage. In societies where dominations, inequalities and exclusionary, stigmatising practices reign unchecked, both crimes of domination and crimes of the dominated flourish. Crimes of exploitation cascade, and the crimes of those who are exploited also explode.[20]

Yet the paradox is that sovereignty, checked and balanced, is necessary to resolve anomic uncertainty over who will take responsibility to pacify spaces, to disarm highwaymen and roaming rapists, armed gangs and ambitious plotters of coups. Empires have, nevertheless, afflicted profound dominations in the process of claiming that sovereignty over the large swathes of territory that today we call the United States, China, Russia, Australia or Indonesia. When they do that dirty business of militarised domination, crime cascades for a generation after its worst excesses recede. This at least is a macrocriminological interpretation of some actual evidence from the history of violence that Chapter 8 ponders how to test more systematically.

International law is imperative to crime prevention in nailing down the stability of sovereignties so no state can in future get away with expanding its frontiers through war, nor with any other crime of aggression. Then we can hope for less violence of war that cascades to crime and new wars a generation later, as we have seen as a result of misguided military adventurism and war crimes in Iraq, Afghanistan, Libya and beyond this century (Braithwaite and D'Costa 2018). Military adventurism of the kind in which the United States indulged in Iraq and Vietnam and the Soviet Union in Afghanistan risks the undermining of state legitimacy. It is anomic. Genuine defence against existential threats, which is legitimated by international law and by the will of democracies, can unify, transcend anomie and disintegration, build the legitimacy of states and prevent future crime and future war. Yes, Tilly (1975: 42) was right that 'war made the state and the state made war'; yet, balanced and tempered state power, when legally stabilised, pacifies spaces and can help states prevent crime and make peace (Morris 2014: 18).

The big-picture story of the history of war and crime recounted in reaching these conclusions demonstrates no unidirectional civilising process, but a great deal of human agency in making peace and making war, in cascades

---

20   Criminologists who believe we must view political violence in a way that is disconnected from criminal violence might ponder LaFree et al.'s (2018) finding that violent extremists were distinguished from nonviolent radicals in the United States by violent political actors being less likely to have stable employment and more likely to have criminal records, a history of mental illness and violent peers.

of violence and cascades of nonviolence. Cascades of nonviolence and the institutions that enable them—the United Nations, the European Union, good peace mediation and trust-building practices, the laws of war and the kind of rejection of armed struggle to resist tyranny for which Nelson Mandela opted—can quell anomie in the global order and within states, reversing war–crime cascades.

The complex ways in which the propositions of the opening summary of this chapter interact give an account of why violent crime has been in long-run decline for the past 800 years. They can also give an account of major reversals from that trajectory during those centuries and why middle-class property crime trends differently. Emile Durkheim was right, as we discuss in more detail in chapters that follow, that crime and war can bring people together to consolidate normative order. But even when a society is unified by fighting a war, there are tipping points in anomie that throw it into reverse—for example, as intergenerational divides break up the postwar society. Macrocriminology can be no better at predicting when these tipping points of anomie and violence will occur than macroeconomics can be at predicting when market crashes will occur. Both, however, can get better at understanding how these recursivities work and how their tipping points tip. Most importantly, they can get better at putting in place checks and balances that prepare societies well for the inevitability of recursively complex anomie.

More recently, the complex ways the propositions opening the chapter interact help us to understand why there was a short-term but steep reversal to increases in crime across most of the West from 1960 to 1992. They also give an account of why France is a major exception to that reversal to crime trending up in the West, why violence in Latin America, the Caribbean and Africa continued to increase during the post-1992 western crime drop, and why the great East Asian crime drop preceded the Western crime drop by more than four decades, falling during the 1960–92 period when crime was rising in the West.

4

Opportunities for freedom and for domination

Key propositions

- *Anomie Américaine* is not a substitute for *anomie ancienne*; it complements it.
- Within *anomie Américaine*, Merton, Cloward, Ohlin, Cohen, Messner and Rosenfeld add decisively to an institutional anomie theory of a plurality of institutions that temper domination.
- The evidence grows increasingly suggestive that a rich plurality of institutions that temper the hegemony of economic institutions, that temper commodification, can reduce crime and increase freedom.
- When legitimate opportunities and opportunities for freedom are open, and when illegitimate opportunities and opportunities to dominate others are closed, crime is reduced and freedom is enhanced.
- Domination is the more fertile concept than inequality for explaining violence, with militarised domination and criminalised domination of governments and markets particularly critical. Yet struggles against domination and discrimination must be contextually attuned and responsive to what are subjectively salient inequalities.
- Local micro-dominations (for example, between landlords and peasants) can be more important in explaining violence than more macro or more national inequalities. Because it is hard to predict which levels of domination will fuel raging fires of subjective oppression and violence, and which will not, societies do well to aim at tempering all kinds of domination.

- It is common for multicollinearity to produce the result that inequality explains crime, but poverty or racial discrimination does not; or that poverty explains crime, but inequality does not; or that child mortality but none of these other measures explains crime. Often what is true in individual or ecological data is not true in time-series studies, or at least not true in time-series with short lags. We do best to read this literature with a spirit of openness to domination effects that are socially constructed as oppressive at different times, places and levels of analysis in different ways with different lags. We must be wary of a selective positivism that, after failing to find a particular linear effect, empowers analysis paralysis over inequality effects. Likewise, we must be wary of selectivity in attention to the data by social democrats like me on questions of inequality.

- Racial, gender, religious and caste discrimination and discrimination against children who perform poorly at school count among the recurrent contributors to domination and crime. Empirically, discrimination that is sanctioned by the state poses the gravest danger to societies.

- Reducing national inequality on its own is less likely to have an impact than an integrated struggle against local, national and global inequalities of the kinds that the oppressed perceive as most destructive and humiliating. This is because intersectional domination explains violence better than a thin conception of inequality measured by a national Gini coefficient. The integrated social justice strategy required involves making power accountable at all levels and tackling domination and humiliation at the level of the school, the local community, the refugee camp, the bank, at the national level and the level of global imaginaries and global institutions. Most importantly, these strands of a web of justice, peace and nondomination must be joined up. That is difficult work requiring patience for weavers of a fabric of peace and nondomination.

- Redemptive schooling can contribute to a less anomic society by assisting every citizen along the journey of discovering valuable ways they can excel.

- Societies and schools that institutionalise failure, and societies afflicted with a commodified and militarised vision of what success and failure mean, suffer high crime rates and domination.

- Inequality and poverty relate differently to crime and war and along different pathways. Because war tends to cascade to crime and crime to war, a helpful strategy for indirect prevention of crime–war cascades is to reduce extremes of poverty and inequality, particularly those most salient to the subjective sense of domination of a people in an incendiary situation of oppression.

- Explaining crime–war as a cascade can be attractive to the point of conceiving of violence and crime as variables that evolve together, collectively: from world wars to international wars, civil wars, 'small-town wars', drug cartel wars, street gang wars, tiny terrorist cells, and mass and individual shootings by individuals. There are also important distinctions among these types of violence. The criminalisation of states and markets is so responsive to organised criminality and militarisation that crime and war cannot and should not be completely separated in historiography and in violence research.

- Domination grows in radically unequal societies. The rich tend to enjoy unaccountable power, while the poor can be desperate in their powerlessness. A narrow elite can put in place extractive political institutions that concentrate power in their hands; they disable constraints on the exercise of that power. Therefore, no topic is more critical for criminology than understanding how states and markets become criminalised.

- The times and places where women are more dominated tend to suffer more war, more crime—particularly sexual assault and violence against women—and less freedom. This is not because feminised armies cascade wars that cascade to postwar sexual assault and violence by female veterans. Feminised armies are exceptionally rare; Nepal is the only case where female fighters approached a majority at the core of a post–Cold War conflict. There is no feminist Frantz Fanon espousing the cleansing power of violence against male oppressors. Understanding exceptions is important to macrocriminological method. It is notable that pacified postwar Nepal achieved more major feminist constitutional transformations than any other society, postwar or without war, and a female Maoist general who became president. Like Nepal, the genocide against Yazidis in Iraq was started by men but finished with women playing prominent roles in another instructive and liberating exception.

- It is important to understand in a Durkheimian way that industrialisation contributed to anomie and crime, as did *de*industrialisation (see also Chapter 11). This complements the understanding we gain from Mertonian anomie.

- Durkheim, Messner and Rosenfeld were astute to see that well-tempered institutions can temper appetites. They temper dangerous ambitions for narcissistic acquisitiveness. Plural institutions can shape aspirations for a humble pride that eschews vaunting pride.

- Commodification—market values that reduce all other values to their worth in markets—is a danger to freedom and to the tempering of crime.

- Militarisation—martial values that colonise other institutions, reducing other values to their worth for making the state great to dominate other peoples, or making the faith great to dominate other faiths—is a danger to freedom and to the tempering of crime.

American and North Atlantic anomie

The previous chapter was about anomie of an ancient and more Durkheimian kind. This chapter goes to *anomie Américaine*, following a trajectory that reads the most critical contributions as coming from Robert K. Merton, Richard Cloward and Lloyd Ohlin, Albert Cohen, and Steven Messner and Richard Rosenfeld. The decisive turning point was Merton, who came first along the journey towards what has come to be called institutional anomie theory. I cling to my attraction to *anomie ancienne* because of the possibilities revealed in the previous chapter for opening up the widest historical vistas of massive movements of crime and freedom improving or collapsing together. Yet this chapter hopes to give a flavour for why Merton and his American successors are equally important to the French building blocks of Durkheim and Montesquieu on the foundations of ancient anomie.

Chapter 3 showed that historians of crime made an important empirical contribution in showing that there is a semblance of something linear about the big picture of crime and violence in human history. Norbert Elias showed how humans faced increasingly complex institutions after the Middle Ages along the journey of modernity. Durkheim was also on that wavelength in the way he saw the importance of emergent complexity in the division of labour created by industrialisation. That institutional complexity required emotional self-regulation in the eyes of Elias. This also meant self-regulation of violence and institutional regulation of violence in institutions like schools (even Sunday schools later in this trajectory during the nineteenth century) (Wilson and Herrnstein 1985: 113). Such institutionalisations of the self-regulation of conduct were useful for ambitious parents who wanted to help their children be successful in navigating the emergent institutional complexity that Elias diagnosed.

Yet Elias (1996) himself saw in *The Germans* that his civilising process of the *longue durée* would be punctured by decivilising loops. That complexity utterly deflated the intellectual impact of Elias in an academy that prefers simple linear thinking that delivers clear predictions. Social science still struggles to cope with the complex, the nonlinear, a world of more unknowables than knowables and more unknown knowables than knowns. Chapter 3 argued that it is often unknowable how long the lags are in the cascade effects of violence. Some effects might have short lags while other effects simultaneously have longer lags. Some of the bigger violence lags might be intergenerational, as we saw with unusually high rape victimisation of daughters of Australian Vietnam War veterans (O'Toole et al. 2018). This chapter adds to our understanding of why it is the macro picture that matters most to understanding why some times and some places have less crime and more freedom than others. It concludes that analysis paralysis is the wrong response to complex and substantially unknowable macro loops of anomic institutional forces.

If human beings cannot grasp the capability to respond to mixes of linear and recursive explanations that head in contradictory trajectories at different moments of history, sadly, they may ultimately all fall victim to one big crime called ecocide. When ecocide might happen, when the next pandemic will shut whole societies across the planet, can no more be predicted with accuracy before the event than when the Roman Empire would fall. Yet this book concludes that criminologists cannot afford to fiddle only at micro projects when Rome might be burning. So, let us not be excessively pessimistic in spirit as we confront the macrocriminological project, even as we understand that as Elias was writing he was unable to predict that he was soon to lose his family to genocide.

Merton is a good place to start because, by the 1970s, criminologists had become as pessimistic about the capacity of Merton to make policy predictions as they might have been of Elias, had they heard of him. While we cannot predict the next ecocide, the next mass extinction of species, the next genocide or the next pandemic, we can know enough about history to grasp that they are likely to arrive again and again. And we can be prepared with useful tools to monitor and steer the outbreaks of disease or violence or extinctions of species as they begin to cascade. We can think in time and game scenarios for countervailing nonlinear dynamics. To steer a better macro future, we can be armed with good questions to ask about the trajectory of crime, inequality, freedom and anomie—the topics of this chapter—even if we are not armed with decisively predictive algorithms.

Robert K. Merton

Robert K. Merton won no Nobel Prize for work that had profound implications for the social structure of freedom and domination, while his son, Robert C. Merton, was a Nobel Laureate for what might be perceived as technocratic commodification work on derivatives. Merton the son also won the Inaugural Financial Engineer of the Year Award from the International Association of Financial Engineers. It was research on how to game markets. This genre of research was significant in its contribution to domination in the leadup to the Global Financial Crisis. Robert K. Merton's 1938 essay 'Social structure and anomie' in the *American Sociological Review* was for decades the most cited article in his field (DeFlem 2018). Today, his book that encompasses this work, *Social Theory and Social Structure*, has five times as many Google Scholar citations as the article (Merton 1968).

Merton's contribution to the study of deviance was motivated in part by his belief that criminology was excessively influenced by the behavioural and biological sciences and insufficiently interested in bigger questions that arise in 'theories of the middle range' about social structure. Merton was very much the sociologist of his day in being more theoretically interested in deviant behaviour than crime, and in fact the place of deviance in a theory of American social structure. In my correspondence with him 40 years ago, he was generous and relaxed with the work of a young scholar who was little interested in theories of deviance in America, who preferred to use his work as an aid to the development of cosmopolitan criminological theory. He would be not only relaxed but also pleased with the internationalisation of his thinking by many other scholars today.

Merton put a distinctive spin on Durkheim's ideas about the breakdown of the normative order. Merton's anomie was the breakdown of pathways between cultural goals that were a framework of aspirational reference in the normative order and legitimate means for achieving those goals. The rupture between widely shared cultural goals and institutionalised means to achieve them is the crux of Mertonian anomie. For Merton, this is what is fundamental to 'strain toward the breakdown of norms, toward normlessness' (Merton 1968: 217). This quote reveals Merton as closer to ancient anomie and Durkheim than he is often read to be. Like Durkheim, and doubtless like me, Merton is not always consistent in the way he uses anomie. Merton was open to the view that rupture of the normative order might come from other sources beyond the breakdown between cultural norms and the institutionalised means to achieve them. Scholars who chide *The Flight from Ambiguity* in social science (Levine 1988) might commend the ancients for implanting an ambiguity into anomie that has helped its fertility as an idea!

Merton's theory was applied to his homeland, where a central, widely shared cultural goal was material individual success. Legitimate means to that success was blocked to the poor and to those who performed poorly in school. One result of concern to Merton was a lot of poor people resorting to crime. Merton interpreted the criminological import of his theory to be fundamentally about 'the theory of anomie-and-opportunity-structures' (Merton 1997: 519). The legitimate means for achieving the cultural goal of material success include a good education, a good job and investment. This Mertonian question from late in his career is how to open opportunities when these legitimate means are systematically blocked to the disadvantaged. Merton suggests that American society is characterised by an obsession with the overriding goal of material success, without an equal emphasis on the proper way to achieve it. 'The morality of such a society is summed up by the expression, "it's winning that matters, not how you play the game"' (Box 1971: 104). This establishes the relevance of Merton beyond the crimes of the needy to crimes of the greedy. Andrea Schoepfer and Nicole Piquero's (2006) empirical study of the association between embezzlement and institutional anomie illustrates this relevance. By crimes of the greedy, I mean crime committed by those who have rich access to legitimate opportunities, but who have an insatiable desire to be not just a winner, but also an endlessly bigger winner, even to be number one. Corruption of all institutions arises when those with the vaunting pride to want to be extreme winners care not how they win or how they play the game. This is not a modern observation that begins with Sutherland (1983) or Willem Bonger (1916), insightful though they were. Aristotle said: 'The greatest crimes are caused by excess and not by necessity' (1932: Book II, p. 65). It took powerful military institutions to go to the excess of murderously exposing their own soldiers to fallout from nuclear explosions in the 1940s and 1950s.

While history has not researched this systematically, it is perhaps plausible that Merton is right that the goal of material success has been held out as important across most sections of American society for most periods of its history. Conversely, in some societies in Europe and Asia that experienced lower levels of crime than the United States, we can perceive many historical periods when peasants might be deeply disadvantaged but did not perceive it as their lot to aspire to the material success of the nobility or the bourgeoisie. Then, we frequently observe other periods in those societies when the aspirations of underclasses *are* stirred and rebellion cascades into violence (Braithwaite and D'Costa 2018). This is what Merton was driving at when he said: '[C]rude (and not necessarily reliable) crime statistics suggest that poverty is less highly correlated with crime in Southeastern Europe than in the United States' (1968: 201). As an arrogant young criminologist in my 20s, I argued in correspondence with Merton about this, as well as in a conversation with Merton's mentor Talcott Parsons. They liked to quote Pitirim Sorokin (1928: 560–61) on his (correct) observation that many poorer countries had less crime than rich countries like the United States. Sorokin, Parsons and Merton did not think very clearly about the distinctions between the poverty of a country, the poverty of persons and inequality within rich and poor countries. The evidence warrants some cynicism about how exceptional is Americans' obsession with their 'dream'. I excoriated systematic reviews of the class–crime relationship of that time conducted in the North Atlantic for the way they excluded data and insights from the East and the South. I included a lot of Antipodean data in my literature reviews, as well as data from Nigeria, Uganda, South Africa, Argentina, Japan, India, Sri Lanka, Mexico, Puerto Rico and various more 'obscure' European locales such as Sardinia and Yugoslavia. After traversing this literature, I would chide the American sociologists:

> Where are these societies which, lacking differential class symbols of success, show no class differences in criminal involvement? It is reasonable to reject Merton's qualifications and assert that all twentieth century nations for which we have data tend to

evidence patterns of crime where the poor commit traditional criminal offences at a higher rate than the rich. This seems to be true irrespective of the extent to which differential class symbols of success are present in the society. (Braithwaite 1979–80: 91)

The next page will illustrate with more nuanced recent data from Nepal why my perception of this universal was crude. Young Braithwaite was right, I think, to see Parsons as a genuine conservative who wanted to wilfully misread the systematic evidence on poverty and crime so Americans could take comfort in the belief that sprinkles of equality of opportunity in forms such as scholarships for black students to study at Harvard were the kind of thing needed, while improved equality of outcomes was irrelevant to accomplishing a less criminal society.

While I felt it was Merton who was on the right track, he pandered and conceded too much to the views of Parsons and Sorokin on the limited relevance of structural inequality to crime. Today, I think that in seeing them as myopic specimens of American sociology, I also was myopic. Moreover, our eyes must be open to the importance of Parsons in the way he laid a foundation for institutional anomie theory. Parsons did this by conceiving of what institutions are in an elegant way (Parsons 1990), thereby laying foundations for the 'new institutionalism' across social sciences of which it could later be said that 'we are all new institutionalists now'.

Merton was insightful with his understanding that the common impact of poverty in explaining crime was conditioned by the degree of legitimation in the society of poverty's inevitability, and the degree of acceptance by the poor that their poverty was the natural order of things—something they could not aspire to escape. This chapter diagnoses why there are many reasons for the consistent inconsistency in relationships between poverty and inequality and crime, but it was Merton who in this way put his finger on such an important source of indeterminacy in the inequality–crime relationship.

Hence, in a society like Nepal (Braithwaite and D'Costa 2018: Ch. 9), the caste system can be settled and well accepted by most sections of society for long periods of history. Then, grievances at particular locales are exploited politically to mobilise lower-caste resentment by Dalits (formerly called Untouchables) and other oppressed castes, and to stir feminist resentment among oppressed women as well. Where inequality for centuries was not particularly associated with violence, a Maoist uprising in Nepal became the last successful communist uprising of world history, with the fall of Nepal's monarchy in 2006. In that surge of killing of rulers, inequality between the landlord caste and the peasants at the local level suddenly became highly predictive of which districts had the highest rates of killings by Maoists (Nepal et al. 2011). At a more qualitative level, locales where there was widespread rape of Maoist women by state security forces were where women surged to fight for the Maoist army (Braithwaite 2015). Nepal today has returned to being a high-inequality but low-violence society. While Nepal has not become a Maoist society, Maoists have been able to win, then lose and then win again elections since 2006. Democracy is more consolidated and feminist reforms have been quite impressive from the most politically and militarily feminised insurgency the world has seen (Braithwaite 2015; Braithwaite and D'Costa 2018: Ch. 9). Today, the President of Nepal is a woman who was formerly a Maoist general. Among other feminist reforms, today, Nepal's constitution requires a minimum of one-third of judges to be women, one-third of Members of Parliament and senior civil servants and even one-third of the military and the police. The Maoist uprising was associated with a particularly remarkable improvement in gender equity in health, even as many other inequalities remain or returned to being deep, and implementation of transformation has been fraught (Braithwaite 2015). A peace agreement and law reform to abolish the caste system and legislate for gender and ethnic equality, however, have not hugely diminished the underlying structural and cultural realities of caste, gender and ethnicity in Nepal.

Caste is structurally central for understanding not only violence from ancient times in 'Greater India', but also for understanding freedom. Acemoglu and Robinson (2019: Ch. 8) conclude that even though ancient *panchayat* traditions energised the popular participation and accountability that Gandhi sought to harness as 'village republicanism', its caste system was a 'cage of norms' and a cage of oppression that stultified freedom as nondomination. For Acemoglu and Robinson (2019), the Greater India that was much wealthier and more powerful than Western Europe during ancient, medieval and early modern times fell behind western economic development during late modernity because it was unable to transcend this deeply structured inequality and normative domination through the caste system, while the West managed to almost completely unburden itself of feudalism.

There are many of these high-inequality and low-violence societies at the time of writing, such as Rwanda (which, like Nepal, in 1995 shifted to high inequality and high violence). Rwanda's conflict was a cataclysmic upsurge of genocidal violence by the majority ethnic group (the Hutu), which had been economically and politically marginalised from colonial times, against the privileged Tutsi minority. Other societies with very high inequality and low homicide rates include Ghana, Malaysia, Brunei, Hong Kong, Iran, Saudi Arabia, Qatar and the United Arab Emirates. Again, systematic research needs to be done, but studying these societies in a Mertonian frame might have appeal. By this I mean that the poor and women in these societies may suffer levels of inequality and discrimination possibly considerably worse than in the United States, but the aspirations of the poor are more contained than in the United States. This might explain why the United States has experienced many periods of far higher crime rates than these societies. When Merton (1938) first published 'Social structure and anomie', he was more preoccupied with serious adult criminals like Al Capone during a period of escalated US violence (Prohibition). He was more concerned with this than with the juvenile delinquents whose self-reported petty offences became the research mainstay of his scholarly successors of the anomie tradition in the 1960s and 1970s. Likewise, Merton perhaps has his most powerful relevance to the kind of adult genocidal criminality seen in Rwanda, or indeed to how a comparatively low-violence but unequal society like Syria could explode into street violence, terrorism, state violence, ethnic cleansing and war after the Arab Spring of 2011.

As important as Merton is, my mission here is not exegesis on the further dimensions of Merton's contributions, as others have already done that admirably (for example, Passas and Agnew 1997; Messner and Rosenfeld 2013; DeFlem 2018). It is more important to move on to building the idea of opportunities for freedom and opportunities for others to dominate the freedom of fellow citizens, through the work of fine scholars in the American anomie theory tradition, starting with Cloward and Ohlin.

Cloward and Ohlin and illegitimate opportunities

Cloward and Ohlin (1960) maintain that if delinquency is to result from the desire to achieve a cultural goal, two things are necessary. First, like Merton, they say legitimate means for achieving the goal must be blocked; but second, illegitimate means for achieving the goal must be open. Within any given community there may or may not be a system of illegitimate opportunities (for example, a criminal subculture that values a subcultural goal of success in drug dealing). Subcultures are important in constituting illegitimate opportunities. They expose neophytes to criminal role models who enjoy success in achieving a generally valued goal like material success by an illegitimate means such as selling drugs. Criminal gangs can also help to constitute such criminal opportunities by supplying protection and on-the-job training in how to make money through illegitimate means. Gangs and subcultures are among the vehicles for Cloward and Ohlin to link Merton's anomie to Sutherland's (1947) and Cressey's differential association theory. A meta-analysis of 179 studies shows that gang membership is a quite strong predictor of criminality (Pyrooz et al. 2016). An important way to explain the extraordinary levels of crime in societies like Democratic Republic of Congo or in Central America are the hybrid forms of criminal organisations in those societies that are more than just drug gangs; they are also organisations that dominate large spaces militarily, fragmenting state monopolies of pacification, trafficking enslaved individuals and putting them to work in criminalised markets to create different versions of corrupted capitalism where markets in vice dominate markets in virtue.

The criminological evidence that illegitimate opportunities are important to explaining crime is large and convincing. At the level of micro opportunities, the literature on situational crime prevention has shown that strategies for regulating opportunities for crime before the event tend to be more effective interventions than strategies for punishing crime after the event. A special issue of *The ANNALS of the American Academy of Political and Social Science* edited by Joshua Freilich and Graham Newman (2018) is persuasive on this. At the more macrolevel of insight, the work of Shover and Hochstetler (2005) and others shows the importance of lure to understanding patterns of white-collar crime.

Ecological theories of crime are helpful for understanding the dynamic quality of opportunities. Bank robbery no longer has the importance as a crime problem that it had in the era of Bonnie and Clyde. One reason is that modern security has hardened banks as targets. A more fundamental answer is that the opportunity structure has moved on. It was but is no longer an insight for Willie Sutton to say he robs banks 'because that's where the money is'. Such money as is there may come with dye packs that stain both the money and the robber. Banks are no longer where the money is in the sense of it being found behind tellers' desks. As soon as cash arrives in the bank, it moves to cyberspace, where it can be sliced and diced into securities that are globally mobile. Early this century, the best criminal opportunities then came to reside in fraudulent ways of doing that slicing, dicing and onselling of securities. Cybercrime is where contemporary criminals who lack the capital to trade securities found the money to be—a new frontier of criminal opportunity that supplanted old ones such as bank branches and bundles of cash. Farrall and Karstedt's (2019) data from early this century in the era of the transition to cybermarkets showed that middle-class people who had access to the internet were more than twice as likely to be in the victim-offender group who experienced both high levels of criminal victimisation and high levels of participation in middle-class crime. The growth of the internet this century has driven new market structures of lure and predation across issues as diverse as paedophilia, financial scams and electoral disruption to constitute the modern anomic election. The internet is fundamental to Shover and Hochstetler's (2005) analysis of the 'cornucopia' of new opportunities available to sophisticated criminals. Criminology that continues to evaluate crime-prevention strategies and theories for explaining crime overwhelmingly in terms of theft and violent crime becomes more out of touch with each passing decade. As contended in Chapter 3, analyses of such old-criminology sources of data to show that there was a crime drop since 1992 fail to account for the fact that this was when there was the great rise of new crimes in cyberspace, as testified by the rise in fraud and embezzlement convictions in the United States during this period (Farrall and Karstedt 2019).

Chapter 5 uses the scamming industry in Jamaica to show that even in a poor, high-crime society today, more people make a criminal living from electronic scamming than from theft or robbery and this scamming generates much higher levels of violence than nineteenth and twentieth-century outlaws with guns blazing breaking into wealthy western banks crammed with cash. That Jamaican scamming industry is both about the lure of Cloward and Ohlin's illegitimate opportunities and about blocked Mertonian legitimate opportunities for many impoverished foot soldiers for whom scamming is one of the few jobs they can get (Marsavelski and Braithwaite 2018).

Cloward and Ohlin's contribution is important because, in extremis, the lure of the criminal opportunity can be so large that it is a more important explanatory factor than the blockage of legitimate opportunities. As discussed in the previous chapter, most Australians are occasionally lured to cheat a little on their tax return when presented with an illegitimate opportunity they can get away with. This is so even when they have a good job, a fine education and live in a wealthy country that provides legitimate opportunities for most of them.

This book (like the discussion of earlier evidence in Braithwaite 1979) concludes that the explanatory power of both blocked legitimate opportunities and open illegitimate opportunities enjoys moderately strong empirical support in criminology. A large number of excellent studies using various levels of awareness of limited opportunity measures soon followed Cloward and Ohlin in finding that delinquents perceived their opportunities as more limited than nondelinquents (starting with Elliott 1962; Landis 1962; Short 1964). Short and Strodtbeck's (1965: 268–69) pathbreaking research of this era found that members of delinquent gangs both perceived their legitimate opportunities to be lower than did a sample of non–gang members and perceived their illegitimate opportunities to be greater compared with the non-gang boys.

While Messner and Rosenfeld (2013) back away from the redistributive progressivism of the prescriptions Cloward and Ohlin drew from their work, they make an incisive Cloward and Ohlin point about the great crime drop in the United States from 1992:

> As the crack epidemic crested and declined, the illegitimate opportunities for 'making it' through drug selling also diminished. Fortunately, opportunities within the legitimate economy began to grow at the same time, as the United States entered a period of record economic expansion in the 1990s. (Messner and Rosenfeld 2013: 97)

But what of the problem with this American story that almost all western societies had a great crime rise until 1992 and a great crime drop afterwards? And there is the further qualification that, for the poor, the boom of the 1990s was only in low-pay 'go-nowhere' jobs (which required regulated increases in the minimum wage). Mandated buttressing of such jobs with vocational training was often needed if they were to instead become 'step up the ladder jobs'. Average incomes for working-class families fell between 1960 and 1992 to the point where only with two jobs in the family could people afford to buy a house. As argued in Chapter 3, the key analytical move is to focus not on the crime drop from 1992, but on the great crime rise from 1960 to 1992 because that is the period of exception from the longer-run western historical trajectory, which has been downward or 'civilising', as Elias and Pinker put it.

European societies did not have the crack cocaine epidemic fuelling the extremes of gang gun violence suffered in US cities, which likely was important to the severity of the great American crime rise. On the other hand, the United States mobilised its hegemony to globalise its War on Drugs during this period, which Chapter 3 argues helps explain why, across the northern two-thirds of Latin America and the Caribbean, there was no general drop in crime between 1992 and 2020, but rather, a rise in crime. European police forces might have taken to the war on drugs with less tyranny and more moderation than US police, and more infrequent shootouts with street gangs selling crack. Yet they suffered some of the criminogenic consequences of the War on Drugs up to 1992, after which that war became even more moderated in Europe. But the more fundamental similarity among the United States, Europe, Canada, Australia and New Zealand between 1960 and 1992 is that this period encompasses nearly all of the economic catastrophes of deindustrialisation, which for most of these societies peaked in the 1970s and were mostly slowing by the mid-1980s, though there was one final shock with the 1990 western recession that was driven by overly restrictive monetary policies and an oil price shock. That general deindustrialisation of 1960–92 did not occur in Asia, particularly East Asia, where there was rather a modest consolidation of industrialisation and of impressive job creation of diverse kinds in new tourist industries, the information economy and the service sector; and there was a general drop in violence and crime in Asia during the western crime rise of 1960–92, as Chapter 3 also concluded.

Rapid deindustrialisation was anomie coming full circle. Durkheim popularised anomie to make sense of the dislocation of the transition to industrialisation and the 'idolisation of wealth' in nineteenth-century France. Japan was the major early exception to this; it continued to industrialise in the 1960s, 1970s and 1980s, producing a higher percentage of the world's automobiles and steel than it had in the 1940s and 1950s. Japan was also the big exception among the wealthiest countries in experiencing a steep, continuous decline in crime rates before 1960, between 1960 and 1992 and beyond 1992. The great crime drop in Japan until 1992 was a drop to exceptionally low crime rates—a longer and bigger trend than in the West in a society with excellent crime statistics. It was so parochial and unscientific for most (but not all) western criminologists to take so little interest in the crime drop in the world's second largest economy while they were so absorbed with the US drop. Hence, like Messner and Rosenfeld for the United States in the above quote, we can make good sense of the macro patterns of crime across all developed economies since World War II with the rise and fall of industrialisation (and the opportunities it provided for working-class people) and the rise of the information and services economy of the 1990s that created new opportunities.

These patterns do not apply to Latin America, Africa and the rest of Asia, which were not yet industrialised societies in the 1960s. Their poor did not suffer the shocks of deindustrialisation at the level that changed working-class landscapes in the West during this period.

Combining old insights from Cloward and Ohlin with new ones from Farrall and Karstedt (2019), we might say that when the working class shrinks and gets poorer, we see greater closure of legitimate opportunities for the working class and greater creation of markets in illegitimate opportunities; when the middle class expands, their greater wealth attracts growth in crimes that target them as victims and also a proliferation of opportunities for petty middle-class crime. The middle-class pattern is complex, however, because the middle class has too much to lose, too much of a stake in conformity, to shoot people while committing serious street crime, and too little capital to rob banks while owning them.

One tweak to Cloward and Ohlin that is attractive for the integration project of explanatory and normative theories in this book is to substitute legitimate opportunities with opportunities for freedom, and illegitimate opportunities with opportunities to dominate others. A limitation of this, however, is that not all legitimate opportunities are opportunities for freedom, even if the most critical ones might be. Moreover, many will disagree that illegitimate opportunities should not be viewed as crimes if they involve no domination. Normatively, this tweak is a response to the problem that where prostitution has been legalised, sex work is a legitimate opportunity; where it has not, it is an illegitimate opportunity. This will be a normatively unacceptable response to some; elegant to others. Both formulations have their virtues. My main argument is simply that criminologists should not duck normative choice through spurious claims to be 'value free' about what is legitimate and illegitimate.

It is the domain of crimes of the powerful where this choice is most troubling for scholars of criminal justice. To be one of the Soviet citizens who worked in Stalin's gulag under Cloward and Ohlin's normative frame was to have a job that was a legitimate opportunity. To work in China today disciplining Uyghurs in detention is likewise an opportunity for domination; it is not a legitimate opportunity under a nondomination normative frame. Likewise, it was work of domination to be an interrogator at Guantanamo Bay, Abu Ghraib or Camp Bucca, where Islamic State leader Abu Bakr al-Baghdadi was imprisoned during his radicalisation and recruited so many followers among fellow prisoners. Likewise, it was work of domination to be a private intelligence contractor like Lockheed Martin that trained and supplied the interrogators (King and Cooper 2004; Stockman 2004; Chatterjee 2005). It was a dominating 'legitimate opportunity' to be highly paid for work in western 'extraordinary rendition' of political prisoners to be tortured in Gaddafi's Libya. The latter was worse than work that was legal under US law; it was work that reduced rather than increased the quantum of freedom in the world. A republican rule of law must absolutely forbid oppressive imprisonment for 20 years without trial at sites of tyranny like Guantanamo. Great-power dominations married mercilessly at these gulags when the CIA locked up innocent Uyghurs at the behest of Chinese intelligence operatives. A democracy is required to make a legally defensible call as to whether such individuals are prisoners of war, who are therefore accorded the rights of prisoners of war, or criminal defendants, who are thereby accorded the rights of criminal defendants. Many of those thrust into Guantanamo Bay were as innocent of any crime as many in the gulags of the other great powers. Many were thrust there on the tainted testimony of their political enemies in Afghanistan. Many 'Taliban' were handed to the United States by bounty hunters paid wads of cash to fabricate allegations; often they handed over their Afghan political opponents (Braithwaite and D'Costa 2018: particularly Ch. 9).

Doubtless many Chinese, Russian and American criminologists do not see these as fundamental questions for the integrity of their science in the way I do. We return to these normative questions for the field throughout this book, particularly in the concluding chapters. The terrorism industry in the United States, Chinese and Australian criminologies and perhaps others may be the best funded and the most fraught parts of our field. A starting point for excising the excesses of dominations from the field might be to be clear that the definitions of legitimate and illegitimate opportunity must be profoundly normative and political; they must not be 'value free'.

Cohen and the micro–macro

Albert Cohen (1955) followed Merton by prefacing his theory of male delinquency with the assumption that boys from all social classes begin their school careers with a commitment to traditional success goals. But because boys brought up in poverty are ill equipped to compete at school, more of them become failures in the status system of the school. This failure arising from blocked legitimate opportunities initially engenders shame, resentment and bitterness. Loss of a sense of personal worth can be intensified by teachers who withhold privileges and opportunities from unsuccessful boys, by other students who label poor performers 'dumb' and by the realisation that future job prospects are dimmed by school failure.

Having failed in the status system of the school, the student has a status problem and is in the market for a solution. He solves it collectively with other students who have been similarly rejected by the school. The outcasts band together to set up their own status system with values the exact inverse of those of the school: contempt for property and authority instead of respect for property and authority, immediate impulse gratification instead of impulse control, apathy instead of ambition, toughness instead of control of aggression. The delinquent's conduct is right by the standards of his subculture precisely because it is wrong by the standards of the school. By participating in this subculture, the poor academic performer can enhance his self-image by rejecting his rejectors. The boy's status problem is solved by the collective creation of a new status system in which he is guaranteed some success. This can be taken further when the oppositional subculture of a school that can deliver only symbolic rewards is coopted for recruitment by an adult street gang or drug distribution organisation that can deliver the material rewards of a criminal career. The dynamics of rejecting your rejectors by joining a violent subcultural group continues to resonate today as an explanation for the recruitment of stigmatised young people to terrorist cells.

The first proposition of Cohen's theory—that disadvantaged boys are more likely to fail at school than middle-class boys—was strongly confirmed by a wealth of evidence such as Deutsch's (1967) *The Disadvantaged Child*. It is also beyond doubt that those who fail at school are more likely to engage in delinquent behaviour (Braithwaite 1989). Moreover, Toby and Toby (1957) soon established that poor academic performance precedes delinquency, more than vice versa. This was important because it was plausible that the reverse direction of causality to that posited by Cohen applied: poor performance might result from participation in a delinquent subculture. Although the most fundamental propositions survived the confrontation with empirical evidence, Cohen's theory was vulnerable at a number of points. For example, Downes (1966: 236–39) concluded from his study of young offenders in Stepney and Poplar in the United Kingdom that the typical response to failure was not Cohen's 'reaction formation' but 'dissociation'. Rather than rebelliously turning the values of the school upside down, it was more typical for the British delinquent to simply withdraw interest from the work world of the school. Box (1971: 107–8) also suggested that there was no 'reaction formation' because boys born into poverty, at least in the British context Box studied, did not 'internalise' the status criteria of the school in the first place; they simply could not 'be indifferent to' the status criteria of the school. For Matza (1964), the intervening variable between failure in a status system and delinquency was 'drift'. This was such an elegant synthesis of these dilemmas:

> The delinquent belongs to a subculture characterized by values which allow delinquency but do not demand it. The delinquent is neither compelled nor committed to deeds nor freely choosing them; neither different in any simple or fundamental sense from the law abiding, nor the same … He is committed to neither delinquent nor conventional enterprise … The delinquent transiently exists in a limbo between convention and crime,

responding in turn to demands of each, flirting now with one, now the other, but postponing commitment, evading decision. Thus he drifts between criminal and conventional action. (Matza 1964: 28)

Drift may still be equally elegant in its application to Farrall and Karstedt's (2019) middle-class criminals. Drift, nevertheless, had special appeal for the disengaged drug offender in comparison with materially ambitious property offenders. Irrespective of whether disadvantaged children 'internalise' or 'can't be indifferent to' the status criteria of the school; irrespective of whether the response to failure is shame or rebellion; irrespective of whether there is 'drift', 'reaction formation' or 'dissociation'; regardless of whether differential association with delinquent peers following rejection by the school is critical or not—the fact that school failure and domination at school ultimately encourage delinquency is the big Mertonian point. That remains the big picture of blocked legitimate opportunity and anomie. Being unfree has the sense of domination across many of these formulations: 'Being pushed around puts the delinquent in a mood of fatalism. He experiences himself as effect. In that condition he is rendered irresponsible' (Matza 1964: 89). Domination is particularly critical when people are 'pushed around' in ways they perceive as unjust or oppressive, because a sense of injustice can abrogate the moral bind of law. 'The subculture of delinquency is, among other things, a memory file that collects injustices' (Matza 1964: 102). Again, Farrall and Karstedt (2019) say the same thing about petty middle-class offences on their padded insurance claims and their tax returns. The same might be said of business subcultures of resistance to regulatory or tax laws that share narratives about the excessive taxation of free enterprise and regulation that cripples the economy with red tape (Passas 1990). Business subcultures that encourage corporate crime are now well documented in the criminological literature (Simpson 2002). Mexican and Colombian drug 'cartels', street gangs in US cities, Japanese *yakuza*, Chinese triads, Russian organised crime—all clearly exist. On both sides of the long war in Afghanistan, murderous Taliban and Islamic State units and murderous special forces units of western militaries—such as those currently facing war crime prosecutions in Australia in respect of 55 alleged crimes against humanity—existed as criminal subcultures. Operatives on both sides believed they were doing God's work to eliminate evil as they committed uncounted war crimes.

Much of the stuff of illegitimate opportunities in an increasingly complex society is in the nature of knowledge about how to do it; this knowledge is largely preserved and transmitted by subcultures. Granted, most of the groups that transmit these subcultures are not highly organised. Typically, they are loosely structured, even brittle, social organisations. Most crime is not perpetrated in organised gangs; the majority of juvenile offences are deeds done in groups of two or three (Zimring 1981). Victim surveys suggest that much adult crime is a more solitary affair. This is less true of state crime, which tends to be highly organised under formations like secret police units that educate inductees in how to disappear targets and how to waterboard or extract fingernails from them first to get intelligence. In this sense, counterterrorism units can be schools for terror. Even solitary crime of all types is often made possible by a learning process that occurs within loosely coordinated groups that provide support for solitary crime in the form of social approval, neutralisation or transmission of knowledge of how to do it.

It is of course unnecessary for schools to dominate. They do not need to be the mouse race that prepares children for the adult rat race. Redemptive schooling can allow all children to succeed against their own past performance. Those who are not good at sport can be helped to find a form of physical activity at which they improve and which they enjoy. All children can be found to be outstanding at something and can be helped to improve against their own past performance in education outcomes. Groß et al. (2018) showed with multilevel data from 4,150 students in 69 German schools that schools with a 'competitive/egoistic school culture' experienced higher levels of youth offending.

If we value education, if we are open to learning lessons from Albert Cohen, students can be free to opt out of schooling. They can be provided liberated alternative pathways in educational institutions that give them the right to choose to learn the kind of things they value learning. Even if these are not the best choices about what to learn, in that they exclude mathematics, for example, it is best for students together with their parents to be free to make the choices that will at least allow them to receive guidance in the art of learning how to learn. In such a world of freer education, most children will continue to opt for conventional schools, though perhaps only if these schools learn to be sufficiently redemptive to hold the students who are most at risk of educational anomie. This is what their parents will want to do and this is what most will choose. Those who do opt out will often be students who have disruptive impacts that we now know substantially reduce the learning of all the other students in conventional schools. The founders of the International Institute of Restorative Practices, Susan and Ted Wachtel, have devoted lives well spent to arguing for the right of children to opt out of school and into self-directed education (www.buildinganewreality.com/learning-is-natural-school-is-optional/). They have built schools that accept children who have been thrown out of so many schools for crime and behavioural problems that no school will now accept them. Paul McCold's (2008) study of 1,636 children with behavioural problems sent to the Wachtels' restorative schools found a 58 per cent reduction of reoffending for those who completed the program. This impact reduced after two years, though the percentage reduction in offending was greatest for children with the highest risk factors for offending.

Anomie theory in its Mertonian form is not a theory of why some individuals offend and others do not. It is a macro theory about how institutions like schools are run, about how poverty and inequality are constituted by economic institutions to block legitimate opportunities and open illegitimate opportunities. In this book, the kind of blocked legitimate opportunities that matter most are opportunities to be free, to be liberated from domination by others and by institutions. And the kind of illegitimate opportunities of concern are opportunities to dominate others. This, of course, is a narrowing of Merton to an even more circumscribed middle-range theory. A large tradition of American criminology dubbed 'strain theory' has translated Merton to the microlevel of predicting which kinds of individuals will offend. This tradition of anomie theory fosters microlevel testing of anomie theory that supports its credibility (Agnew 2016), often without testing it at the macrolevel of the institutions at which Merton pitched his theory. That is not to say that work in this tradition has limited value. A good example of movement from the micro to the macro is Kaufman et al.'s (2008) analysis that African Americans experience more strain through justice system discrimination and criminal victimisation and more economic, educational, familial and community strains and that this explains higher rates of African-American offending (Unnever and Gabbidon 2011: 17–18).

Pluralising by Messner and Rosenfeld

Mertonian seeds were falling on stony ground in late twentieth-century criminology because his work was read in those decades as a theory meant to explain why some kinds of individuals commit crime and others do not, when in fact it was a theory of how some institutional configurations are conducive to rule-breaking. An influential example of this kind of empirical critique of anomie theory was Ruth Kornhauser (1978) questioning the association between delinquency and the gap between American *individuals'* life aspirations and their opportunities. Up to the present, studies have found associations of this kind, but inconsistent ones, and sometimes weak ones, between self-reported delinquency and measures of rupture between the aspirations of individuals and blocked opportunities (Agnew 2016).

At the same time, the data continue to show that very poor young people are more likely to break the law, especially with very serious offences (Agnew 2016). For example, African Americans (an overwhelmingly poor minority) accounted for 52.5 per cent of all homicide offenders in the United States between 1980 and 2008 (Cooper 2012). The truly disadvantaged in all societies are especially likely to go so deep into the justice system as to fill prisons. The evidence continues to show that individual poverty in combination with poverty in the area in which one lives remain strongly associated with crime (Braithwaite 1979; Agnew 2016). Indeed, the relationship between the two is multiplicative rather than additive (Braithwaite 1979). At the macrolevel, poverty, racial disadvantage and inequality continue to bear strong relationships to crime, as do what came to be known as institutional anomie theory variables (Pratt and Cullen 2005). Patterns do vary, but I will argue that recurrent inequality and poverty associations are similar in pattern and just as strong for international comparisons of crime rates and comparisons among societies, cities and neighbourhoods today as when Braithwaite (1979) traversed this literature.

Perhaps it takes an old-fashioned, white, male criminologist today to admire the work of Merton, Cloward, Ohlin and Cohen, not to mention Durkheim. I relished conversations with three of them and about them with Ian Taylor, which included laughs about a *British Journal of Criminology* review in which Ian found my *Inequality, Crime and Public Policy* a 'curiously anachronistic text' with the 'character of a treatise from the 1950s' particularly because of my 'faith in the effects of social democratic state intervention in the class structure' and 'disingenuous faith' in the 'development of public housing policies' (Taylor 1980: 184–85). Not only was this research that those on the right would hate, according to Ian, it was of 'no interest to the Left'. This was all pretty correct.[1]

In a way, Merton, Cloward, Ohlin, Cohen and Cressey suffered the same fate in the United States in a more visible way because the War on Poverty, Mobilization for Youth and the President's Commission on Law Enforcement and Administration of Justice in the 1960s were significantly influenced by their ideas. Richard Cloward personally worked on Mobilization for Youth in Manhattan. Such War on Poverty programs generally did not succeed in transforming America. As Ronald Reagan's putdown of attempts at social democracy beamed, the 'government declared war on poverty and poverty won'. The programs spectacularly failed to prevent three more decades of rising crime and six decades of rising inequality.

Feeling the criminological fossil as I did then and now because of this circle I admired, I was grateful for the impact of the work of the institutional anomie revivalists Steven Messner and Richard Rosenfeld (2013). Their work in this tradition since its initial publication in 1994 has had not

---

1   Still, I take a strange comfort in the fact that another emeritus, Robert Reiner (2020), could have been publishing such a soulmate of a book to this one, with the title *Social Democratic Criminology*, at the same time as I finished the fourth draft of this one, and that the book of such a fellow fossil could even be published in a series called *New Directions in Critical Criminology*! I loved Reiner's book. When it was insisted that I say something about the concrete contributions I had made to social democratic politics on the occasion of being made a life member of the Australian Labor Party, I genuinely was at a loss to think of anything credible. I mention this partly because social democratic politics continues to play an important role in the normative and explanatory frameworks of my criminology and life. When I won a scholarship from my dad's trade union to support my education, in presenting the certificate, the head of the union graciously opined that he was not sure these scholarships were a good idea because they helped kids to grow up to become Tory voters. I promised him I would never become a Tory voter! Readers should know what kind of politically active person I am so they can make their own judgements about how this colours my work. I have doubts whether Ian Taylor was even right that my work might have found favour among social democrats of the 1950s. I remain content to choose to make the case that criminology is politically dangerous if it lacks normative moorings to prevent threats to freedom. Then there is satisfaction in laying out a theoretical viewpoint on what kind of criminology, moored to what kinds of norms and what kinds of politics, might be associated with better or worse outcomes for crime and freedom. That is a project of contesting with criminological colleagues what sort of theory of crime and freedom is useful to humankind and other species. This can be agonistic (Chapter 12) and need not appeal to any political leader of any state. It still might resonate with enough people to have some prospect of being viewed as worthy at some future time. The test is whether it adds something to an improved conversation about crime and freedom.

only much more impact than my own on inequality and anomie; it has also fuelled a suite of encouraging research findings, especially in the past decade. Their contributions renewed hope that perhaps fossils can return to life to add a little to the enthusiasm for Merton, Cloward and Ohlin and Cohen that Messner and Rosenfeld renewed.

Messner and Rosenfeld viewed the most conspicuous limitation of Merton on anomie as being its exclusive focus on a single facet of social structure: unequal access to legitimate means to success. This has now been shown empirically to be the key theoretical move contributed by Messner and Rosenfeld. Messner and Rosenfeld insightfully diagnosed problems of American society that go beyond its economic institutions. Indeed, it is a diagnosis about economic institutions being overly dominant over all other institutions. For Messner and Rosenfeld, crime levels can be explained by the degree of countervailing power of non-economic institutions—specifically those of the family, the education system, the welfare state and the polity—against economic institutions.

Like Merton, unfortunately, Messner and Rosenfeld initially framed their story parochially as being one about the American Dream. Here the data are not encouraging that there is anything exceptionally American about the 'American Dream' (Chamlin and Cochran 2007). Let us consider that limitation first before revealing the virtues of a more cosmopolitan reading of the power of the theoretical insights of institutional anomie theory. The next section argues that the American Dream as something distinctively American is, like America as the 'land of the free', part of an American myth-scape that is wanting in comparativist empirical foundation.

Keeping American exceptionalism in perspective

Criminology has been obsessed with American exceptionalism to the neglect of more strategic and multiplex comparisons. Perhaps this is because so many leading criminologists are American. Nevertheless, criminologists across the globe embraced the specificities of institutional anomie theory for application to their own societies for the good reason that helpful insights were on offer. Merton's anomie theory and Messner and Rosenfeld's (2013) that built on it are theories of something distinctively American. If we look at homicide data—which is imperfect but the most meaningful crime category for international comparisons—it is true that the United States has a higher crime rate than European societies or other developed economies (adding other non-European comparator developed economies like Canada, Australia, New Zealand, Japan and South Korea). But in the wider sweep of comparisons across all societies, while the United States might have had a comparatively high crime rate during and after the peak of the crack cocaine epidemic in the 1980s, and perhaps during the internationally unusual increase in gang killings at the height of the prohibition of alcohol during the 1920s when Merton was finishing his education, the extent to which the United States was ever an outlier of extreme violence has always been modest since the wars of its western frontiers receded. Today, after the great crime drop since 1992 (discussed in Chapter 3), the US homicide rate, at 5.3 per 100,000, is actually below the global officially recorded homicide rate of 6.2.

US exceptionalism is more about the punitiveness of its culture of control (Garland 2001), for which its only competitors in imprisonment rates have been Russia and South Africa. The United States has been exceptional among developed economies in retaining capital punishment, though use of this has historically moderated substantially in the United States, as it has in the other countries that are most genuinely exceptional in the heavy use of capital punishment, China and Iran. The United States is like many societies that have a large number of neighbourhoods with exceptionally high crime rates that are responded to very punitively, and a much larger number of neighbourhoods with exceptionally low crime rates.

So, the balanced way to view the United States is as, on average, only a high crime rate society compared with other developed economies, and only high at its hotspots. Chapter 3 concluded that the exceptionally high-homicide societies are overwhelmingly to be found in Latin America, the Caribbean and Africa. My temptation is to see whether what is distinctive about these highest-homicide societies is the same as what is distinctive about the United States compared with the lower homicide rates of other developed economies. It is that these high-homicide societies, whether in Latin America, the Caribbean or Africa, are societies still recovering from the Atlantic slave trade, still recovering from other forms of intergenerational trauma associated with other kinds of great waves of violence (drug wars, civil wars, Apartheid), and societies still with high inequality and with a major armed gang problem among the excluded. On the African side of the Atlantic, so many societies have never fully recovered from colonialism and from the internal conflicts associated with capturing outgroups and selling them to the Americas as slaves on a massive scale. It has long been established that export of the largest numbers of slaves from Africa to the Americas is a predictor of the worst national economic outcomes. New data for 2SLS instrumental regressions from Schargrodsky and Freira (2021: 48) shows that cross-nationally 'African slaves received' and being an ex-colony are also predictors of homicide rates. South Africa is a distinctive case of a society with some of the highest-homicide cities on the planet outside the Americas. It is a society in which the sins of enslaving indigenous black peoples were compounded by Apartheid as a distinctive post-slavery form of violent racial domination that bore a functional equivalence to slavery. Most societies on the opposite side of the Atlantic are still recovering from the domination, the deprivation of freedom, the flogging and the torture that were slavery. In many parts of Latin America, indigenous peoples were also flogged into slavery and submission to work in plantation economies. These were the survivors of a transcontinental genocide from which First Nations Americans have never recovered.

As an outsider looking at the United States, it seems that the greatness of Abraham Lincoln in US history is not that he was a war leader who selected great generals to defeat the southern enemy who actually should have been easier to tame than these northern generals found. No, the greatness of Lincoln was as the leader who was able in his best speeches, such as the Gettysburg Address, to re-story what it is to be an American (Meister 1999). To be an American—North or South, black or white, slave or free—is to be a person who is recovering intergenerationally from a deeply structured institution called slavery. Likewise for South Africa, Nelson Mandela was the historic leader who could re-narrate what it was to be a South African. Black or white, European, Boer, African or coloured, to be a South African is to be a citizen in recovery from an institution of unfreedom called Apartheid. Sun Yat-sen could re-narrate being Chinese as being a survivor of colonial domination, dynastic domination and warlord domination.

In a similar way for my own country, to be an Australian—Aboriginal, Torres Strait Islander, white or Asian—is to be a victim of the genocide of the frontier wars, of the nineteenth-century anti-Chinese pogroms, of the vilification of Asian boatpeople and their stigmatisation by anti-Asian political parties of the far right. The overrepresentation of Indigenous Australians in Australian prisons is worse than the overrepresentation of

African Americans in US prisons. The difference is just that this does not drive up imprisonment rates or affect homicide rates in Australia to the degree that racial domination does in the United States because Indigenous Australians are a much lower percentage of the population. In fact, First Nations Americans are also greatly overrepresented in homicide arrests in the United States and in imprisonment rates. It is just that Indigenous Americans are not the statistical drivers of homicide and imprisonment statistics that African Americans and Hispanic Americans are. This is because, in Australia and the United States alike, genocide was so totalising in frontier wars and ethnic cleansing combined with European diseases. They wiped out indigenous populations within remarkably short periods. The same history of rapid depopulation of indigenous peoples from the plains and their rapid filling of prisons is true of other major white settler societies such as Canada and New Zealand. This is in contrast to the white enclave colonies where small white populations came and went, such as India and China.

The indigenous genocide was a more massive bloodbath in Latin America than in the English settler continents of North America and Australia. Latin America was much more densely populated by indigenous peoples. Tens of millions of them were slaughtered in genocides by the Spanish and Portuguese invaders. Again, one must ask oneself whether scars of the scale of this indigenous slaughter are still relevant to understanding the extreme violence of both civil war and homicide in societies like Colombia, El Salvador and Guatemala in recent times. The historical cascades of intergenerational trauma and crime–war violence in my theoretical work contend that it could be relevant (Braithwaite 2020a).

Empirically, the American Dream is not so exceptionally American (Chamlin and Cochran 2007). Comparing the world's two most powerful economies, it is common for China specialists to argue, partly based on public opinion data, that aspirations for material success might actually be stronger and wider in China than in the United States. Cao's (2004) data on Mertonian anomie, however, find little difference on the measure between US and Chinese samples, with the United States slightly higher. Cao (2004) systematically failed to find that Mertonian anomie is uniquely strong in the United States. Levels of anomie in the United States are comparable with those in other English-speaking societies and lower than in continental European and Latin American societies. It is noteworthy in this study that the society with by far the highest Mertonian anomie score was the society with the second-highest homicide rate in the study, Mexico. The only country with a higher homicide rate than Mexico in the study, Brazil, also had a notably higher anomie score than the United States.

Hence, a weakness of *anomie Américaine* in the writing of Merton (1995) and Messner and Rosenfeld (2001) is that it is parochially American, failing to examine critically with a cosmopolitan theoretical imagination whether the American Dream is American. This criticism might also apply to the meta-analysis of Pratt and Cullen (2005), which, in showing that the evidence does support the propositions of institutional anomie theory, includes some non-US data, yet seems to bias the meta-analysis in favour of studies published in US journals (Pratt and Cullen 2005: 388, footnote 3). That does not mean that the fundamentals of the conclusions of Merton, Messner, Rosenfeld, Pratt and Cullen are wrong; this book concludes that, in the fundamentals, they are right.

In spite of the failure to demonstrate that the American Dream is a distinctively American driver of unusually high crime in America, the contributions of *anomie Américaine* remain richly attractive. Mine is just another contribution by an old white male who has not been as distinguished a contributor to anomie theory as these Americans. I will argue, however, that feminist criminology, corporate criminology, postcolonial criminology and international criminology, among others, are deepening the insights of institutional anomie theory. Another ambition is to reboot *anomie Américaine* by connecting it back more strongly to *anomie ancienne*. This means connecting the concept back to rapid, destabilising social change, as opposed to anomie being a stable characteristic of American social structure. It also means reframing anomie as a globally cosmopolitan theory in a way Messner and Rosenfeld themselves have now done in an admirable fashion through their cross-national empirical work.

Tempering institutions

While we should be ambivalent about the American Dream aspect of the Mertonian anomie tradition, what is particularly valuable about the way Messner and Rosenfeld contribute to it is the imperative to temper the influence of economic institutions with influence in the social structure from balancing institutions. In this fundamental way, there is a cosmopolitan influence in the theory that delivers its greatest strength.

Messner in particular has followed through on this with a huge volume of quality cosmopolitan empirical work. At one point in their book, Messner and Rosenfeld discuss the risks from the economy taking precedence over social institutions and colonising other institutions in conditions of neoliberalism—for example, with the 'fetishism of money' (Taylor et al. 1973: 94). Messner and Rosenfeld even use the word 'tempering' to refer to that balancing by the institutions of education, family and the polity. This is Elliott Currie's (1991: 255) Mertonian point about the pathologies of contagion from a market economy to a 'market society' in which the pursuit of market values is not regulated to be limited to accomplishing certain circumscribed ends. Rather, commodification infects all areas of social life.

Freda Adler's research on low-crime societies was also an influence. Adler (1983: 131) emphasised low crime rates in societies as different as Saudi Arabia, Bulgaria, Japan and Switzerland through strong commitments to familial institutions providing a mooring during times of instability for the wider normative order. For Messner and Rosenfeld (2013), schools are also important for inculcating tempering beliefs, values and commitments that are different from those of the marketplace—less so, this book argues, when schooling is commodified as a mouse race. A stabilising and balancing strength of Confucian societies against market hegemony—such as in Taiwan, South Korea, Japan and Singapore—is that teachers and professors widely enjoy lifetime reverence from their students. In East Asia, it is such a touching experience to go for a drink with a Chinese police chief in his sixties and a junior female academic who taught him in his master's course and to see the older man show the young woman so much deference, respect and honour. The problem with market institutions is that, by design, they have the least self-restraint and are the most laissez faire of all major institutions. This is the danger that lurks behind capitalist commodification that must be tempered by other institutions. Confucian reverence for the teacher above reverence for the dollar is simply an example of this.

While the United States might have the best universities, we must look beyond its shores to find the societies in which schools are the best funded and the most innovative, the teachers are most revered and the outcomes on internationally standardised reading, mathematics and other capabilities are most impressive. This is Messner and Rosenfeld's point about the weakness of the United States at balancing the dangers of its economic institutions with the strengths of its educational institutions.

The familial and educational institution weaknesses are intertwined in Messner and Rosenfeld's analysis because US parents simply do not spend enough time with their children to nurture and support their learning and social maturation outside school hours. Chapter 7 further develops this theme of how fundamental are mutual interdependence and support between institutions of human capital, social capital, recovery capital and restorative capital formation.

Messner and Rosenfeld point out that the United States is an exceptionally laggard society in terms of paid parental leave and corporate openness to job-sharing by husbands and wives during peak childcare years, flexible family-friendly working hours, employer-provided child care and other pro-family labour market regulation and economic policies. As a result, Messner and Rosenfeld lament that American families sit down to fewer meals together than they did in the decades after World War II. Such pro-family ensembles of policies and labour market institutions are hypothesised by Rosenfeld and Messner to be fundamental to forging a low-crime society. One might add that children in other developed economies do not need to forgo visits to the doctor, other health professionals or the purchase of medicines because their parents cannot afford them, in the way this is sadly common under comparatively weak US welfare-state institutions.

Institutions of gender equality are also relevant here. Because the evidence is that women's prioritisation of an ethic of care in families is more healthily in balance with materialist and careerist values, institutions of gender equality can be helpful in resisting the commodification of everything, just as they can be useful in resisting the unfreedom of patriarchal domination discussed later in this chapter (see Applin and Messner 2015). Halpern (2001) showed that self-interested values are much higher in men and that self-interested values in combination with high inequality and low social capital explain national crime rates as measured by the International Crime Victims Survey.

Institutions that are fundamental to freedom and the low-crime society depend on the effective functioning of other institutions. These other institutions must be enabled to deliver on their distinctive institutional functions. The interdependence among institutions of education, family, the labour market and health and welfare (particularly for children with the gravest developmental deficits) is perhaps the most profound example of this crux of social capital formation. It is the failure of these institutional interdependencies that explains why prisons have become the most important mental health institutions for children who grow into young adults with mental health or intellectual challenges. The problem of prisons as the new institutions for the mentally ill exists in all western societies, but in some more than in others.

The lack of support for and supervision of children also have adverse implications for crime control through weakened guardianship in neighbourhoods and denuded capabilities for the cascading of collective efficacy, which are theorised to be fundamental to crime control in Chapter 11.

Chapter 7 argues that public provision is the essence of universalised excellence in education and health. Markets in education and health leave too many gaps to be able to deliver this. Marketised education and health care are prone to gamed outcomes at times when they should professionally commit to the intrinsic importance of education and health outcomes. Markets have a place in delivering innovation to education and health care, yet these are benefits that must be checked and balanced by institutions of public provision and regulation of private markets in public virtue.

Messner and Rosenfeld (2013: 76) are on the same track as this book when they chide Merton for walking away from one particular strength of Durkheim's thinking on anomie. This is that Durkheim was attentive to the issue of how societies regulate appetites to keep them realistic and indeed how normative orders regulate themselves to repair the ship of normative order at sea. This book argues that plural institutions can shape aspirations for humble pride that eschew vaunting pride—narcissistic pride, in Eliza Ahmed et al.'s (2001) theoretical and empirical work. The humbling of appetites becomes imperative when order and civility begin to crumble in societies at times of crisis (from war, the breakup of empire, pandemic, hyperinflation, famine or environmental collapse).

The stasis of Merton in comparison with the dynamism of Durkheim makes Durkheim more relevant to the sociology and politics of regulating crises. An example is the literature on anomie and rapid crime increases in Russia and other countries behind the Iron Curtain after the collapse of the Soviet Union (Kim and Pridemore 2005; Pridemore 2005; Zhao and Cao 2010).

Messner and Rosenfeld's (2013) institutional anomie theory took Merton's American brand of thinking about anomie out to a much broader conception. In a rather Mertonian way, Messner and Rosenfeld see all societal institutions as being shaped by structural and cultural imbalances between economic and other institutions—notably, the family, the polity, religion and education. Markets, they argue, must be embedded in and intertwined with the institutions that balance them. This, I will argue, is right, while I also argue that we must temper markets to make them stronger if our objective is to reduce domination. Institutional anomie occurs when the economic sphere is dis-embedded and shakes off the balancing, the countervailing power, of other institutions. 'Commodification'—market values that reduce all other values to their worth in economic markets—comes to dominate other institutions in conditions of Messner and Rosenfeld's institutional anomie.

In this sense, institutional anomie takes us close to what political economy writers call neoliberalism—a state of affairs where markets and market values are ascendant on all fronts. The remedy is embedded autonomy for the multiple institutions that build developmental states (Evans 1995). Untempered markets and unbounded commodification are conducive to crime (both violent crime and property crime). This is because unbounded tyrannies of markets sharpen perceptions of injustice and create legal cynicism (Sampson and Bartusch 1998) and cynicism towards the wider normative order. Karstedt and Farrall (2006) call this 'market anomie', in which the profit motive is not balanced by other concerns such as protection of the weak, fair play and the rule of law. Moreover, markets that are cut off from countervailing accountabilities to other institutions are at risk of becoming criminalised. It should be added that the commodification of politics captured by markets also conduces to the criminalisation of the state.

For Messner and Rosenfeld, it is important that the institutions that balance markets sustain their ability to regulate naked pursuit of interests. They see a loss of institutional integrity when balancing institutions are captured hegemonically by the quest for material success. For example, Messner and Rosenfeld (2013: 78) argue that 'education is regarded largely as a means to occupational attainment' in pursuit of economic success. Institutions captured in this way fail to deliver to citizens what we discuss in Chapter 7 as CHIME (Connectedness, Hope, Identity, Meaning and Empowerment). CHIME is a countervailing bulwark against anomie.

Domination by markets weakens the capability of other institutions to enhance human wellbeing, check the abuse of power and therefore weave the web of controls that prevent crime.

Evidence and institutional anomie theory

Operationalising the institutional anomie theory idea of the strength of non-economic institutions as a balance to criminogenic market anomie has been attempted in various indirect ways, mainly by testing relationships between crime and structural antecedents in the form of the strength of countervailing institutions. In Pratt and Cullen's (2005: 399) meta-analysis of macrolevel predictors of crime, by a good margin, the strongest of 31 predictors was the 'strength of non-economic predictors' that operationalised institutional anomie theory. This result was based on a small number of studies, though further studies have continued to be encouraging since 2005, without being totally consistent. Messner and Rosenfeld (1997) and Savolainen (2000) deployed a 'decommodification index' that combined several measures of the strength of welfare-state policies. Both studies confirmed institutional anomie theory predictions. Savolainen found from two cross-national comparisons that countries that protected their citizens from the vicissitudes of market forces through strong welfare states were protected from the homicidal effects of economic inequality. Within one US city, Cancino et al. (2007), in a kindred way, supported institutional anomie theory, finding that the criminogenic effect of areas of concentrated disadvantage was ameliorated by welfare generosity. Hughes et al. (2015: 100) found only mixed support for institutional anomie theory in a cross-national study of 50 countries, but they did find that 'homicide occurs most often in countries where free-market principles and practices drive the economy and where core cultural commitments are oriented toward achievement, individualism, fetishism of money, and universalism'. Rudolph and Starke (2020) found cross-nationally that a strong welfare state suppresses crime, mainly through social support and generous unemployment benefits, but did not support a decommodification explanation. In Rudolph and Starke's (2020) review of 41 published studies, only nine reported negative, mixed or disconfirming results, while the other studies showed that a stronger welfare state was associated with less crime in cross-sectional or time-series studies.

Chamlin and Cochran (1995) tested a combination of the strengths of three non-economic institutions: families (measured by divorce to marriage ratios), religious institutions (measured by the rather Christian index of church membership) and engagement with political institutions (measured by voter turnout). They found that strong non-economic institutions ameliorate the criminogenic effect of high levels of poverty in a comparison among US states. Piquero and Piquero (1998) likewise measured the strength of familial, political and educational institutions and found some evidence for institutional anomie theory. Bjerregaard and Cochran (2008) also revealed that the strength of these institutions was important to explaining homicide and theft cross-nationally, though it was more important in moderating the relationship between inequality and crime than in mediating it. Weld and Roche (2017) tested cross-nationally the effect of time-use surveys to compare the time spent working in economic and non-economic institutions and did not find statistically significant effects on homicide rates. The time spent by individuals in different institutions does not seem to be a strong measure of the sway of such institutions.

Chamlin and Cochran (1997) found that property and violent crime were lower in US cities where altruistic commitment to civil society institutions was stronger as measured by charitable donations. They found that, at least among developed economies, homicide and robbery were worse where more people believed work was about making money and more disagreed that 'Less emphasis on money and material possessions is good'.

Since Pratt and Cullen's (2005) meta-analysis, further research has been overwhelmingly encouraging and consistent with its fundamental findings. Nivette's (2011) meta-analysis found that, consistent with various aspects of the institutional anomie discussion above, the predictors of homicide with the strongest mean effects were a Latin America and Caribbean regional dummy variable, income inequality indicators and the 'Decommodification Index'. The Decommodification Index is based on Esping-Anderson's concept of decommodification and has been widely deployed, including by Messner and Rosenfeld themselves, to operationalise institutional anomie theory. It measures protection from the severity of the market by combining measures of social welfare as a percentage of GDP, average annual benefits per capita and sometimes other welfare measures. Nivette's (2011) results are also strongly consistent with Pratt and Cullen's (2005) results from their systematic review at other levels of analysis.

Some more recent international comparative studies have supported institutional anomie theory for both property crime and violent crime cross-nationally (Cochran and Bjerregaard 2012) or have supported institutional anomie theory for differential violent crime rates between countries but not for property crime (Bjerregaard and Cochran 2008). Using the World Values Survey, Chen et al. (2021) found strong support for an institutional anomie effect measured as countries having high levels of pecuniary materialism among managers in supervisory roles reporting a willingness to engage in ethically suspect behaviours. Tuliao and Chen (2019) also supported institutional anomie theory in this way, using World Values Survey data to discover an economic inequality effect and the effects of the strength of non-economic institutions of family, education, polity and religion. Likewise, Hövermann and Messner (2019) were able to show on a sample of 84,398 individuals from 58 countries both the individual effects of a 'marketised mentality' and the societal effects of institutional imbalance. This study again showed that enfeebled religious institutions enabled justification of instrumental offences. It built on an earlier study of the willingness to excuse behaviours such as bribery, tax cheating and fraud by Cullen et al. (2004), which provided more mixed support for institutional anomie theory. Chamlin and Sanders (2013) explored levels of drug trafficking among 43 European states using aggregated measures from the European Values Survey of the acceptance of material success goals, absolute and relative deprivation, and interaction terms between material success goals, absolute poverty and relative inequality (Gini). All these predicted drug trafficking in accordance with institutional anomie theory.

Other studies after Pratt and Cullen's (2005) review have been supportive of institutional anomie theory at subnational levels of analysis for property and violent crime. Baumer and Gustafson (2007) used US General Social Survey data measures of commitment to monetary success goals to predict place-based rates of robbery, burglary, larceny and auto theft. Crime was higher in areas where commitment to monetary success was strong and commitment to legitimate means was weak. The tendency for this goals/ means rupture to translate into higher rates of crime was reduced by higher levels of welfare support and more frequent family socialising— consistent with Messner and Rosenfeld (2013). Stults and Baumer (2008) elaborated on these effects, also showing that they arise in areas with high property crime, drug market activity and an unbalanced pecuniary value system, and that property crime more often leads to homicide when structural disadvantage is high.

Low educational and economic attainment and high inequality in this now considerable literature tend to enhance institutional anomie effects. This resonates with Albert Cohen's contribution to the tradition from the perspective of schools as institutional generators or suppressors of anomie and delinquency. As some institutional anomie researchers have put it, the results are consistently inconsistent on how or whether the effects of the strength of non-economic institutions moderate or mediate the effects of economic institutions on crime. More is unsettled than settled in this literature, yet I have shown that there are some core effects that are increasingly settled and strong.

Steven Messner has begun through his empirical work to adapt the theory to cover more institutional checks on market hegemony—first, for religion, which was neglected in his original formulation with Rosenberg. While churches no longer temper economic institutions to the degree that African-American churches did in the United States in previous centuries, churches continue to do that in a huge way in many societies— for example, Pacific Island nations. Likewise, in some Muslim societies, mosques do extremely important work in regulating crime and regulating markets (indeed, they do important work in regulating Muslim crime inside western societies as well) (Wardak 2018), as do monasteries in many Buddhist communities.

Messner co-authored a study that showed that the progressiveness of tax systems was another empirically relevant institutional tempering of neoliberal economic institutions that was neglected in earlier writing. It helps explain why some jurisdictions have lower crime rates (Piatkowska et al. 2020). Messner and Rosenfeld have shown a healthy humility about whether they got their list of institutions that are important to temper economic institutions right. We all do well to share in that humility as we join hands with them on their theoretical construction site.

Religious institutions and tax system integrity can temper the abuse of power. At some historical moments, abuse of the power of tax systems can drive domination, as we saw with the Boston Tea Party at the onset of the American Revolution and with Britain's colonial domination and destruction of India's flourishing precolonial economy by extractive tax policies alongside extractive environmental policies (tax Britannia and axe Britannia) (Braithwaite and D'Costa 2018: Ch. 5). At so many critical junctures, religious fundamentalism connects to militarism and business power to share in the domination of a society. In the trajectory of many wars, religious leaders have important roles as cheerleaders for aggression. For 23 of the 67 armed conflicts studied by Braithwaite and D'Costa (2018), religious leaders were both prominent in advocacy of violence at the early stages of the cascade to war and prominent in the advocacy of nonviolence at later stages, leading cascades to peace.[2]

Hence, theoretical humility also means that positivist projects of testing linear institutional effects cannot do all the work. Quantitative research must be complemented with a historical method that thinks in time about tipping points like those we revealed with religious leaders tipping from being major pro-violence to anti-violence actors. Institutions that once contributed to domination, violence, militarism and commodification frequently pass tipping points to a politics of nonviolence and nondomination. Nelson Mandela's biography manifests a shift from the leader who persuaded the African National Congress (ANC) to be a party of violent revolution in alliance with the Communist Party, to leading the ANC to be a party of peace and democracy that included whites. The most important things we must gradually learn to comprehend are tipping points from domination to freedom and how agonistic pluralism can be mobilised to the politics of tipping domination (Chapter 12, this volume; Mouffe 2013).

The next chapters argue that beyond institutions of taxation and religion, many more supplementary institutional checks and balances are needed for a low-crime, high-freedom society. In this respect, Messner and Rosenfeld and the empirical research they have stimulated have put us on the right path towards a pluralisation of the range of institutions for freedom. What the next chapter seeks to theorise is how to develop a strategy for taking their institutional pluralisation further and for thinking in time about that pluralisation. We should learn so much from the accomplishment of Messner and Rosenfeld in their first widenings of the scope of institutions considered in anomie theory and from the quantitative comparativists who followed in their footsteps.

---

2   This number is an update that includes some extra armed conflicts coded since Braithwaite and D'Costa (2018).

Evidence on inequality, crime and violence

Evidence of the relationship between inequality, poverty and crime is important to the analysis in this book and to figuring the normative implications of institutional anomie theory. I deal with this evidence somewhat briefly because my review of evidence on institutional anomie theory incorporates so many studies of the inequality–crime, poverty–crime, unemployment–crime, welfare–crime and even tax equality–crime relationships, particularly in Pratt and Cullen's (2005) and Nivette's (2011) meta-analyses, but also in so many studies since. The data on the relationship between inequality and crime discussed in this section measure overwhelmingly what are crimes of the powerless, such as individual homicides. To understand how inequality might also contribute to crimes of the powerful that are more effectively covered up (and almost impossible to count with reliability and validity), we will mainly rely on more ethnographic forms of data in the next chapter.

Braithwaite and D'Costa (2018: 519–33) juxtaposed some differences between the evidence of the relationship between inequality and crime and that between inequality and war. This is of note for the macro-frame of this book, which posits an important relationship between cascades of war and cascades of crime (Chapter 11). Braithwaite and D'Costa used their South Asian data as well to make new sense of the confusing state of the evidence on the relationships between poverty, inequality and different kinds of violence. They argued that continuous struggle to halve global poverty and inequality again and then again is important for a less violent world. Even though low GDP predicts war but not crime, and national inequality predicts crime but not war (in a lot of studies), Braithwaite and D'Costa's research shows why tackling poverty and inequality in a complex way at multiple levels might reduce both crime and war. Part of the integrated social justice strategy required involves making power accountable at many levels. These are the topics of the next few chapters, as are tackling domination and humiliation at the local and national levels and the level of global imaginaries and global institutions. Most importantly, policymakers can aim to join up these strands of a web of global and domestic pacification to form a progressively more resilient fabric of peace and prevention.

Indonesia is a good example of a society that has performed quite well at the structural level in reducing poverty and in progressively becoming freer, democratising and delivering good outcomes in countering terrorism and violence. Only a small handful of developing economies have less inequality than Indonesia as measured by the Gini coefficient. Yet, the Peacebuilding Compared data (Braithwaite et al. 2010a) show that when a local ethnic or religious minority felt dominated by being excluded from a fair hearing over a land dispute, with political and legal institutions controlled by another group, 'small-town wars' resulted at the turn of the century (van Klinken 2007), and small-town wars cascaded from local domination to nationally militarised violence. Likewise, in Indonesia and Timor-Leste, abuse of power by tiny cabals of cronies with military connections is a form of domination at the very top that has recurrently ignited violence, notwithstanding Indonesia's creditable macro-equality (Braithwaite et al. 2010a, 2012). The Indonesian case study shows it is hard to temper the commodification of societies without tempering militarisation. Peacebuilding Compared data from Indonesia and Timor-Leste show why we specify domination reduction more than inequality reduction, as a more insightful way of seeing what is required to tame violence. We conclude that brute structural remedies to inequality can only address some of the interactions among local, national and international imaginaries of domination and injustice.

Braithwaite and D'Costa (2018) argue that structurally more equal parts of the world enjoy less-criminalised states, less-criminalised militaries and local institutions and suffer less violence from both war and crime. Gender discrimination is a particularly important structural factor in explaining violence. Gendered domination generates violence, which engenders more gendered domination. Also important are inequalities between destitute landless people and their often-criminal landlords, between homeless Indigenous Australians and the European criminals who stole their land at the point of a gun, between poor people who pay tax and crony capitalists with western bankers who do not, and contextually endless other modalities of inequality. These structural inequalities demand structural remedies that grapple with the diverse character of such dominations, the most important of which are separations of powers to render governance more accountable to the disenfranchised—governance that can be criminalised by money politics or tyrannies of the majority (discussed in Chapter 8 of this book). Hence, Braithwaite and D'Costa's conclusion is that domination is the more fertile concept for explaining violence than inequality, with militarised domination and criminalised domination of governance particularly critical modalities of domination. Yet struggles against domination and discrimination must be contextually attuned and responsive to what are subjectively salient inequalities. Perceived racial discrimination explains crime. Being yelled at with racial slurs or insults is subjectively important in explaining crime (Unnever and Gabbidon 2011: 78–79). Discrimination tends to be perceived as highly salient and dominating when it is state sanctioned, which particularly strongly predicts civil war when it is extreme (Goldstone 2008: 5; Gurr 2000). Conversely, Saiya (2018) demonstrates empirically the capacity of what he calls 'religious liberty' to shut down state-sanctioned discrimination and thereby extinguish religious terrorism and religious violence. Fleming et al. (2020) found that where ethnic economic inequality is low, terrorism deaths are low.

Twenty years ago, few in the West would have seen humiliation and discrimination against Muslims as a major risk factor for violence that required a concerted antidiscrimination politics of inclusion, nationally and globally. The Allied powers were much quicker to learn from the geopolitical humiliation of Versailles that the right prescription for Germany, Austria, Italy and Japan in 1945 was a politics of inclusion (the Marshall Plan and the European Union).

Many heavily militarised societies that were infused with a politics of domination, corruption and extreme inequality in the twentieth century have become more egalitarian, less-dominating low-violence societies in recent decades, including Japan, Germany, Italy, Spain, South Korea and Taiwan. It is harder for highly militarised societies such as Russia, Pakistan or the United States, where violence and domination are less tempered (Krygier 2017) and less shameful (Braithwaite and D'Costa 2018), to deliver low levels of violence to their citizens. In societies like Congo, where men with guns can also monopolise money power, inequality became hard to conquer.

An inference from Braithwaite and D'Costa's (2018) data was that domination more richly and consistently explained violence than a thin conception of inequality measured by a national Gini coefficient. One way domination as unfreedom is thicker than inequality is that it better enables the integration of explanatory theory and normative theory (see Chapters 1 and 2 and Braithwaite and Pettit 2000). Yet thin inequality is an important constituent of thick domination. Hence, it remains valuable to consider the vast quantitative literature on the relationships between economic inequality, poverty, crime and war.

These bodies of literature are contradictory and confusing. At the individual level, people who are poor are much more likely to commit direct crimes of interpersonal violence such as assault, murder and rape, and common property crimes such as robbery, burglary and serious theft—an issue long debated between Braithwaite (1979) and Tittle et al. (1982). In that debate, my argument was that individual class effects on more serious crime were stronger than class effects on less serious forms of self-reported crime. I argued there was a danger of the variance in self-reported measures being dominated by the higher frequency of petty delinquency (such as stealing things worth less than $5) and drug use. Petty delinquency and drug use were independent of general delinquency in Braithwaite and Law's (1978) factor analytic work on the structure of self-reported delinquency. Moreover, we found middle-class children were more concerned to conceal minor delinquency.

I had so much respect for Charles Tittle and his colleagues. The tensions over our contestation of the class and crime data remain a general tension over how we should read the literature, as we will see again in the paragraphs that follow for the literature on unemployment and crime. At the ecological level, different results are often found at neighbourhood, city, provincial, national and international levels. For those with a more positivist mindset, the tendency is to want to scan separately at each level of analysis and focus on the effect size in systematic reviews at that level. Usually there are inconsistent results. These are especially driven by the fact that domination-relevant variables can be and are measured in different ways that are positively correlated—the percentage poor, inequality, black–white inequality, unemployment, long-term unemployment, infant mortality, and more. We can and should respect the legitimate point of view of those who finger inconsistent results at each level of analysis to sow a criminology of doubt. At the same time, my argument is that we must stand back from that approach with a broader vision to see that just because sometimes there is no black–white inequality effect after controlling for general inequality, and sometimes there is no general inequality effect after controlling for black–white inequality, we do well to be reluctant to conclude that black–white inequality and general inequality have questionably inconsistent effects. Rather, we can read these data with a wider theoretical vision about how the kinds of inequality that are most dominating in different space-time contexts vary greatly. What is less invariable is that, when and where people are in the crosshairs of many intersecting forms of inequality, one or another of them risks becoming subjectively salient in ways that increase crime. Both the straight-counting positivist perspective and the open-textured macro-theory reading are valuable ways of seeing. Our job as criminologists is to be transparent about the ideology of data that leads us to favour one set of data over the other, and then leave it to the reader to make their judgement as to which synthesis is most insightful for them.

Consider again Nivette's (2011) systematic review of cross-national studies. One of her models finds inequality measured by the Gini coefficient is the strongest predictor of homicide across all studies. When a dummy variable for countries from Latin America and the Caribbean is added to the model, this becomes the strongest predictor and inequality becomes the second most important. Does this mean that inequality is not the most theoretically important predictor? Perhaps; perhaps not. We can take the view that the theoretically general thing in these data is inequality, and a central reason why Latin American countries have high homicide rates is that they have high inequality. This is also a central reason why the United States has a higher homicide rate than all other countries of high GDP per capita. Inequality is deeply structured in the Americas by histories of slavery, conflict over slavery and conflict over violent dispossession of the lands of indigenous peoples in unusually recent history. These dominations have also fed into highly racially politicised drug wars right across the Americas, which I have argued have criminogenic consequences. On this reading, inequality is seen as a measure of criminogenic domination, which remains the variable of greatest theoretical import. But there is another reading that says that the peoples of South and North America are culturally different in ways that make them more violent. There is a culture of violence that explains the patterns, which are stronger in some parts of the Americas than others—for example, stronger in the southern states of the United States (Thomas et al. 2018). A third theoretical reading is that the peoples of the Americas are to varying degrees genetically different from those on the rest of the planet. There is more than a bit of politics in how people choose among these three possible readings of this evidence. That is why I like to be so explicit about my social democratic politics of freedom in attempting interpretative work.

Unemployment may have a stronger impact on increasing the criminality of individuals with prior criminal records or with a propensity to crime than individuals who lack such predispositions (Aaltonen et al. 2013: 587). Short-term unemployment occurs for many reasons and does not have the impact of long-term unemployment on individuals' criminality (as found by Carlson and Michalowski 1997). Long-term unemployment has unusually strong explanatory power for violent crime (Nordin and Almén 2017). Much short-term unemployment reduces domination because it can mean that people quit oppressive, precarious jobs to find more satisfying work in empowering jobs that provide a long-term future. In some studies, a rise in short-term unemployment is associated with a reduction in crime; this may also occur for routine activity reasons such as improved guardianship of homes and children when adults are not at work (Pratt and Cullen 2005: 59). Bell et al. (2018) found evidence of long-term scarring and resultant crime for young people entering job markets during recessions; some are forced into employment in unrewarding jobs that are a poor match to their skills; for others, the experience of long-term unemployment at the beginning of their adulthood leaves long-term scars. Chapman et al. (2002) found that long-term unemployment for young men is the kind that has the largest impact on crime rates, as did Pratt and Cullen (2005) in their meta-analysis. The long-term impact that matters is whole generations who are truly disadvantaged, year after year from a young age, left without hope, giving up on their own future and that of their children.

Time-series studies of the impact of unemployment on crime continue to have the somewhat inconsistent results identified in my earlier work, though the inconsistencies are being clarified (Braithwaite 1979; Kapuscinski et al. 1998; Carmichael and Ward 2001; Edmark 2005; Alves et al. 2018; Costantini et al. 2018; Hazra and Cui 2018; Jawadi et al. 2021; Mittal et al. 2019). The effects of unemployment on property crime are often stronger (Aaltonen et al. 2013). Using US time-series data, Lin (2008) concluded that ordinary least squares (OLS) analyses have underestimated the impact of unemployment on crime because of endogeneity effects. He finds OLS to estimate that a 1 percentage point increase in the unemployment rate increases the crime rate only by 1.8 per cent; but the increase is 4 per cent with a two-stage least squares (2SLS) method. Of strategic importance was Lin's (2008) finding that during the decade when the great US crime rise flipped to the great US crime drop (the 1990s), after accounting for endogeneity, unemployment rates explained 30 per cent of changes in property crime rates in this era.

Some of the best recent economic modelling of the complexity of endogeneity concludes that because crime increases unemployment as well as unemployment increasing crime and inequality, different neighbourhoods end up with radically different unemployment–crime–inequality equilibriums from identical starting points (Burdett et al. 2003). Falk et al.'s (2011) result that high unemployment contexts specifically increase right-wing extremist crime is an important one for the contemporary politics of domination. Chapman et al. (2002) found that the intersections between long-term youth unemployment and high school completion are critical to the explanation of high crime rates. Like the effect of participation in war on subsequent crime, deciding what is the right lag is difficult when most people who lose jobs are beyond the age of maximum crime risk while their children may be in that age group or about to enter it. The interaction between unemployment and welfare institutions is also critical to how lags work because crime does spike with a delay that kicks in after unemployment benefits expire following layoffs (Bennett and Ouazad 2020).

Most studies that compare census tracts of cities, whole cities, counties, states or standard metropolitan statistical areas find that districts and cities with higher levels of poverty or income inequality have higher crime rates (Braithwaite 1979; Chamberlain and Hipp 2015; Cheong and Wu 2015; Hsieh and Pugh 1993; Pratt and Cullen 2005; Scorzafave and Soares 2009). The effects of poverty were somewhat more consistent than the inequality effects on homicide in 47 studies analysed by Pridemore (2011: 752–53), while Nivette (2011) found that inequality was a strong predictor (see also Lappi-Seppälä and Lehti 2014). Time-series results on the impact on crime of changes in the level of inequality, poverty or unemployment have always been more inconsistent than data on individual poverty or ecological inequality cross-sectionally (see Brush 2007).

With property crime, class-related opportunity structures again complicate the picture as studies move from the individual level of analysis to ecological analysis. The richer opportunities in wealthy areas for crimes such as burglary and car theft have some effect in driving up rates in wealthy areas. Poor people who live close to rich areas commit more property crime than other poor people. Poor areas adjacent to rich areas have higher property crime rates than poor areas far from wealthy census tracts (Boggs 1965; Chamberlain and Hipp 2015; more generally on the spatial mobility of offenders, see Eck and Weisburd 2015: 17). When we aggregate to the societal level, statistical comparisons of national property crime rates have limited meaning because some police forces are more efficient than others at recording petty property crimes (and the more common petty crimes drive the numbers, not serious crime that is more infrequent). Also, in different legal systems, 'burglary', 'break and enter', 'break without entering' and 'entering without breaking in' can mean different things.[3]

With homicide rates, reasonably meaningful comparisons are possible, however, because it is hard for police forces to fail to record a body that turns up with a knife in its back. Homicide is also measured imperfectly but it has reasonably similar meanings cross-nationally. On the other hand, officially measured homicide rates tend to undercount homicide in the countries where it is worst and most militarised, as Braithwaite and D'Costa (2018) discussed in relation to the Peacebuilding Compared data failure for El Salvador to count disappearances as homicides. The society that had the highest homicide rate in the world at the time of writing was massively undercounting disappearances as something other than homicide. With homicide, high income inequality is consistently associated with high homicide rates (Braithwaite and Braithwaite 1980; Fajnzylber et al. 2000; Hsieh and Pugh 1993; Nivette 2011; but see Pare and Felson 2014;[4] Pridemore 2011).[5] Evidence of low-income countries having more crime than others has historically been inconsistent, although in recent decades it has become quite a consistent pattern that the high-income societies of Western Europe and East Asia have extremely low homicide rates (Chapter 3). Countries with a wide gap between the rich and the poor (or countries with a high Gini coefficient for income inequality) very consistently have higher homicide rates. While poverty is the better predictor of crime than inequality in subnational ecological analyses, and inequality is a better predictor than poverty in international

---

3   When survey data are collected consistently across a large number of countries, as in Elgar et al.'s (2009) finding of a correlation of 0.62 between income inequality and rates of bullying in 37 countries, we can take an interest in the possibility that inequality is conducive to societal cultures of bullying. We should also be cautious, however, that the bullying measure might mean rather different things in translation among different tongues and societal contexts. In most, however, bullying has a meaning close to our conception of domination.

4   Pare and Felson (2014) found both strong inequality and strong poverty effects in increasing crime at the cross-national level. However, inequality effects disappeared after controlling for poverty.

5   Pridemore (2011) compares 47 studies to show that income inequality is consistently associated with higher homicide rates cross-nationally, but not as consistently as poverty. His analyses further show that such relationships always remain if GDP per capita is included in the model. Most interestingly, he finds in a number of studies that, when child mortality is included in the model, the income inequality effect disappears.

comparisons (but see Pridemore 2011), both massive literatures have many crossover studies that show the reverse, more that show that both are important and a few studies that show that no measures of poverty or inequality matter. Generally, one or more of these effects persists even after significant impacts of racial inequality on crime are controlled for.

The next chapter argues that at the societal level the complication caused by the organisational crimes of the rich might be elegantly resolved. In radically unequal societies, the rich tend to enjoy unaccountable power, while the poor are desperately powerless. A narrow elite puts in place extractive political institutions that concentrate power in their hands; they disable constraints on the exercise of that power. This in turn allows the elite to put in place extractive economic institutions that exploit the rest of society (Acemoglu and Robinson 2012). Put another way, the institutional economics of Acemoglu and Robinson's *Why Nations Fail*, and the now considerable empirical support it enjoys, means that the criminalisation of states by elites creates the conditions for institutional anomie explanations to be true. When inclusive institutions are rejected in favour of extractive institutionalism, institutional anomie and high crime rates follow. Inclusive institutions on Acemoglu and Robinson's account are the key to lifting failing nations to prosperity. Being lifted out of the 'bottom billion' is a protective factor against civil war and the crime that cascades because of war (Braithwaite and D'Costa 2018; Chapter 11 of this book).

Political institutions that concentrate power for the few and exclude the many do not prioritise quality public education, health and welfare systems for the many, particularly not for excluded groups who are disfavoured by the rulers. Macro-institutional mechanisms that conduce to the criminal society and the criminalised state are therefore shared between institutional anomie and the economic institutionalism of Acemoglu and Robinson. The extractive institutions of a criminalised state by definition allow the elite to exploit all those excluded from elite networks. This plays into the analysis of future chapters that crimes of the powerful are expropriative and exploitative, while crimes of the powerless are crimes of the exploited. The exploited make the best of a bad job while the exploiters take advantage of a good job enabled by the lure of extractive institutions.

More broadly, the work of many of the most influential scholars of the politics of development connects in a non-criminological way to Cloward and Ohlin's criminological insights on the lure of illegitimate opportunities and Messner and Rosenfeld's on the preventive power of plural and inclusive institutions. I do not assert that the political economy scholars discussed above accept my interpretation of their common ground with institutional anomie theorists. Nor do I suggest that either group accepts my interpretation of the intersections between their theories and what they imply for the politics of inequality. I do hope, however, that finer-grained delineation of the separation of powers needed to temper concentrated power makes that interpretation more credible in the next two chapters.

Commanders of criminalised states strip away the institutions that might limit their opportunities by, for example, arresting or firing anticorruption commissioners or judges. Samuel Huntington's (1991, 2006) work is fundamentally about how the corrosion or absence of institutions explains instability and violence (likewise Francis Fukuyama's 2014 research). Criminalisation of the state conduces to what Michael Mann (1986, 1993) calls despotic power: the capacity to suppress dissent, rights, the media and opposition parties. Despotic power gives states the appearance of strength. More effective state strength comes from what Mann calls infrastructural power: the power to secure public safety by legitimately making and enforcing laws, and the power to deliver peaceful growth through infrastructures of education, health and other public goods. For Acemoglu and Robinson (2012), criminalised states crush peaceful development because they are extractive, pushing aside the inclusive institutions that enable peaceful development. In Douglass North et al.'s (2009) *Violence and Social Orders*, mafias and other organised criminal groups that strip state assets are examples of 'limited-access orders' wherein a coalition of rent-seeking elites deploys political power to prevent both political and economic competition. For North et al. (2009), violence and poverty are endemic in criminalised states because institutionally they are limited-access orders. Merton might approve of this interpretation of their comparative data.

The powerful are also able to buy their way out of trouble with the law, while the poor are denied access to justice in radically unequal societies. Hegemony and the purchase of impunity create profound opportunities for crimes of the powerful; the degradation, hopelessness, loss of identity and meaning of the poor foster crimes of the powerless. Hence, unequal societies have both more crimes of the powerless, because the powerless are exploited, and more crimes of the powerful, because the powerful exploit. This argument is developed with institutional detail in the chapters that follow.

Poverty versus inequality; war versus crime

The quantitative literature on civil war, GDP per capita and income inequality seems at first glance to paint a somewhat opposite picture to that for crime. It is poverty conceived as national GDP per capita that predicts war, not inequality between rich and poor—the top explanation of homicide rates in Nivette's (2011) meta-analysis after controlling for the Latin American dummy (as confirmed by Schargrodsky amd Freira 2021). 'The bottom billion' in GDP per capita are at profoundly greater risk of civil war. Moreover, Collier (2007: 19–20) summarises the literature as clearly showing that poverty contributes to war, and war (or the anticipation of war) contributes to disinvestment and poverty. Wars also last longer in low-income countries (Collier 2007: 26). Fearon and Laitin (2003), furthermore, found that low GDP per capita and weak institutions were associated with the onset of civil war, but they argued that GDP may be a proxy for weak institutions.[6] This insight might be reinterpreted in institutional anomie terms. In most studies, countries with high income inequality do not have higher risks of war, although Collier et al. (2004) found that conflicts in unequal societies lasted longer than elsewhere.

When we move down to the village level, as in Nepal et al.'s (2011) study of 3,857 Nepalese villages, villages/districts with a wide gap between landlords and the landless do have higher rates of war deaths. Systematic qualitative comparisons of dozens of rural Indian districts that have and have not experienced Maoist uprisings likewise conclude that locally unequal development is the key variable (for example, Chakrabarty and Kujur 2009), as opposed to national inequalities. Local dominations are critical to decisions to join civil wars in village societies. Rome is far away, and most poor people do not know or care much about the politics of

---

6   The frequency with which infant mortality emerges as a considerably stronger predictor than GDP per capita of the probability of civil war recurrence (for example, Quinn et al. 2007: 187) might mean that infant mortality is an even better proxy for weak governance institutions.

the capital. Most critically, mobilisation is local rather than national in terms of putting together armed units that are motivated to take and hold a district. Armed gangs cannot recruit and mobilise if grievances are only national and do not cut through as local grievances. As illustrated by the rise of the Nepalese Maoists and the Taliban from very local injustices, as diagnosed by Braithwaite and D'Costa (2018), once a local armed group pacifies a remote niche, this can become a base for building bigger ambitions and wider imaginaries, as victories expand the opportunities for power and plunder, and alliances are forged with other armed groups in control of other districts. Grievances over national inequalities are not as critical to this process as the aggregation of grievances over disparate, distinctive, local inequalities.

This perspective helps account for why Philip Verwimp (2005) found that poor and tenant farmers were overrepresented among *génocidaires*, while landlords were disproportionately victims. Poverty and promises of wealth were associated with recruitment to rebel armies in Sierra Leone (Humphreys and Weinstein 2008). Catherine Riordan points to this research and other data to suggest a conclusion for the inequality–war relationship similar to Braithwaite's (1979) about the inequality–crime relationship:

> Recent findings indicate that in societies characterized by greater levels of inequality, members of both wealthy and poor ethnic groups are more likely to be involved than those whose income is near the national average (Cederman, Weidmann and Gleditsch 2011). This could be explained by the engagement of the wealthy in conflict to defend their property, and the engagement of the poor in order to increase their wealth; or as a synergistic product of inequality: poor people increasingly participate in conflict as they become poorer, and wealthy people have more to contribute financially to conflict as they become wealthier, meaning that greater inequality drives greater participation into conflict (Esteban and Ray 2011). (Riordan 2013: 35)

Riordan's interpretation of the data goes to the often-heard rebuttal of the claim that terrorists are disproportionately poor by reference to the wealth of the likes of Osama bin Laden. Yes, top terror leaders may be disproportionately wealthy exploiters. The suicide bombers and foot soldiers, however, are disproportionately poor, manipulated and exploited. The inequality–war relationship is complicated by the fact that fighting an uprising requires the organisational capacity to mobilise many fighters and to buy credible weaponry. In this business, the rich have more organisational capacity (to enrol and coopt foot soldiers) than the poor, and greater buying power for weapons and wages. Poverty and injustice do not cause war unless poor people with a grievance can connect with wealthy benefactors who fund the logistics of feeding and arming troops. Barrington Moore (1966) reached the conclusion that landless peasants are unlikely to rise against their domination unless some external power takes their side against the power that oppresses them. Insurgencies of the disenfranchised do not scale up to winning wars without external sponsors. Indigenous defenders of the Australian continent did not inflict major defeats on white land thieves because no external power, wealthy benefactor or diaspora was supplying them with arms. For the comparatively poor Taliban fighters of Kandahar in 1994, these financial backers initially were the Quetta trucking mafia who were fed up with being shaken down in this lawless zone; later, Pakistan's intelligence services funded the Taliban. Later still, the destitute Taliban fighters of Peshawar's refugee camps were supported by the wealth of Persian Gulf funders like Osama bin Laden, and later still many overcame their resistance to the opium trade and used opium sales to fund their war (Braithwaite and D'Costa 2018: Chs 6 and 9).

Riordan (2013) contends that as a long-deprived group in a society becomes better off, it has better means to engage in conflict (Besançon 2005). Consistent with Nepal et al. (2011), Riordan (2013: 35) then contrasts local with national inequality effects:

> When examined at the micro-level, however, areas of countries which had more absolute poverty were more prone to outbreaks of conflict, suggesting that inequality increased the risk of conflict (Buhaug et al. 2011; see also Buhaug and Rød 2006). It seems that not only does inequality play a role in the incidence of conflict, conflict itself further exacerbates economic inequality, although this effect diminishes over time and inequality typically returns to pre-war levels within five years after conflict ends. (Bircan, Brück and Vothknecht 2010)

The capacity and opportunity to mobilise against governments and to have complaints listened to reduce armed violence, as does the absence of state-led discrimination (Braithwaite et al. 2010a; Cederman et al. 2011; Fearon and Laitin 2000, 2003; Goldstone 2008: 5; Gurr 1993, 2000; Linder and Bächtiger 2005; Rørbæk and Knudsen 2015; Wimmer et al. 2009). The power of these state-led discrimination effects is one reason state-sanctioned slavery might be fundamental to understanding both long-run global patterns of violence and even contemporary patterns. The *World Development Report* (World Bank 2017: 8–9, 119) has taken up this theme, showing that societies with more even internal balances of power have better national security with less violence. We can interpret this considerable body of studies in different ways as measuring the positive impact of inequality of political power on armed violence, as opposed to inequality of wealth, although these different forms of inequality are themselves correlated.

Cramer and Richards (2011) have made a fine contribution on the risks of being seduced by surface appearances created by quantitative studies of the relationship between inequality and civil war. They explain how the terrible levels of rape, murder and amputations in Sierra Leone's civil war have been advanced by quantitative scholars as being more about greed than grievance and inequality. Specifically, greed for conflict diamonds was important in that war, and in the quantitative literature. Cramer and Richards (2011: 278) conclude that this 'poster child for "greed not grievance" theories' was a 'product of systematic exploitation of the countryside' and 'fed off rural impoverishment and despair'. It was a peasant revolt with agrarian roots against the way urban produce and marketing boards, currency speculators and cronies of the state made peasant land tenure insecure, collapsed state welfare in rural areas and redistributed wealth from peasants to urban powerholders to the point of driving deep resentments over rural–urban inequalities. Researchers cannot grasp the texture of such case-specific inequalities without getting their boots wet. Gender inequality was also tragically in play, as the subsequent rape conviction of President Charles Taylor at the International Criminal Court demonstrated in 2012. The conviction was based on a rich mix of qualitative and quantitative data on patterns of rape. If researchers just pore over the tables of quantitative studies, valuable as that is, their work can miss the mark, as in the Sierra Leone case.

Evidence on gender inequality and violence

Positive associations of different kinds of domination are the core of the theory of intersectionality in feminist theory (Crenshaw 2017; Cooper 2015; Henne and Troshynski 2013). The theory of intersectionality is about the idea that while different forms of domination—for example, domination based on race and gender—are distinctive, diverse dominations intersect to reinforce one dimension of domination with another. Societies in which gender-based violence is normal in families are more likely to engage in militarism and war than societies with lower levels of gender-based violence (Cockburn 2001; Erchak 1994; Erchak and Rosenfeld 1994; Levinson 1989; see also Caprioli 2005; Hudson et al. 2009, 2012). One interpretation of this is that boys and young men learn in families that they can get their way through violence. This lived reinforcement of violence then generalises to how they conduct themselves as men in the community and in international affairs (Patterson 2008). Quantitatively, societies with high gender inequality are more likely to experience deployment of military power in conflicts (Caprioli 2000, 2003; Caprioli and Boyer 2001; Caprioli and Trumbore 2006; Hudson et al. 2009, 2012; Melander 2005; Sobek et al. 2006). In a variety of ways, Hudson et al. (2009, 2012: Ch. 4) have shown that states are more likely to enjoy security when the women who live in them enjoy security from domination. The evidence is consistent with the interpretation that gender inequality in a society grows sexual and gender-based violence and this increases the prospects of violence in the national and international politics of that society. Moreover, Braithwaite and D'Costa (2018) showed that across South Asia, war has increased sexual and gender-based violence during and after conflict. There is a recursivity that reinforces cycles of gender inequality, violence against women and war, and then further increases in violence against women. The macro-shift in the history of civilisations here may have been the proliferation of the professionalisation of militaries that came with the blades of the Bronze Age. Feminised elites were more common until gender partnership was displaced by militarised domination in the Bronze Age (Eisler 1987; Min 1995). Men were not kept close to home by childbearing in the years of their peak physical powers, so men were the ones who roamed far in murderous cavalry units and navies. The militarisation of societies structurally mediates the recursiveness of violence engendering inequality and inequality engendering violence (Braithwaite and D'Costa 2018).

Intrasocietal violence against women is driven by an unequal politics of domination and humiliation in a way that helps us understand how violent patriarchy at home might promote armed violence against women abroad. The next chapter discusses how humiliation can motivate violence among those humiliated and enables violence among those who humiliate.

Heirigs and Moore (2018) confirm that, after controlling for the Gini coefficient (and other variables), higher gender inequality is associated with higher homicide rates cross-nationally. Narvey et al. (2021) also found that women's economic equality, economic empowerment and legal rights were associated with lower homicide rates cross-nationally.

One reason exploited poor people find it hard to organise nationally for the violent overthrow of the state is that a society's poorest people are often a minority. Consider the invasions of the continents of North America and Australia by comparatively rich people from Europe. The invaders quickly became organised in states such as Massachusetts and Virginia and then in federal states—the United States of America, Canada and Australia—militarised with the most modern technologies for killing. Aboriginal Australians and Native Americans could give the first settlers a tough time in pushing back their invasion but, as soon as European numbers grew and mounted troops followed, genocide diffused and resistance collapsed. Aboriginal Australians did not have the resources or the national organisational capabilities to unify sufficiently to fight a credible war against the white state. Local grievances often triggered local uprisings, which created opportunities to 'teach blacks a lesson'. But once Indigenous Australians were stripped of the land that was the source of their wealth, once their population fell to less than 3 per cent of the population of their colonised country—an impoverished, dispersed 3 per cent without the resources to buy the guns to take on the superior firepower of the colonisers—civil war became unthinkable for them.

Hence, the deepest structural inequalities in the world, such as those that Aboriginal and Torres Strait Islander Australians continue to suffer, rarely lead to civil war. That is one important reason the statistical association between national inequalities and war is inconsistent. Inequality drives high crime rates in a different way, however. Aboriginal Australians committed murder and were victims of murder at seven to eight times the rate of the general population between 1989 and 2000 (Mouzos 2001). Their overrepresentation in the prison system is twice as bad again. Indigenous Australians continue to this day to be disproportionately victims of state crime such as police violence. They are impoverished peoples whose identity and sense of meaning have been decimated, who have often lost hope for themselves and who struggle to pass on hope to their children, who therefore enjoy few legitimate opportunities.

Women are not a minority. Nevertheless, wars are rarely fought to reverse the domination of women. An ethnic, religious or political minority of just 20 per cent of a national population can, ironically, more readily concentrate its 20 per cent in particular regions where it controls local political parties and local resources for war fighting in that locale if, for example, it is 80 per cent of the population in that locale. Women may be 51 per cent of the population, but they will also be around 51 per cent in enemy territory. Concentration is more difficult. Freeing up women from obligations tied to childbirth in the peak years of kill-before-being-killed war-fighting capability (18–30 years of age) is difficult. Fighting for equality through civil war is not something women can easily concentrate womanpower to do, even if they want to transact their politics violently, which most do not. A feminist leader with the ideology of Frantz Fanon (1965) on the cleansing power of violence against male oppressors seems implausible and unthinkable to women who lead. Gendered inequality is the deeply structured inequality that most consistently fails to cause war. It also fails to then cascade from war to postwar domestic violence by women.

That is not to diminish some remarkable pacifications and transformations that have been accomplished by female fighters in local contexts such as in Rolpa at the heart of Nepal's Maoist insurgency. In that case, however, the transformation of domination was accomplished by transforming the conflict, Mandela-style, from an armed struggle to a people-power nonviolent uprising on the streets of the capital in 2006 (Braithwaite 2015; Braithwaite and D'Costa 2018).

The ending of the Yazidi genocide in Sinjar, Iraq, on the other hand, was totally accomplished by armed force. Brave Kurdish and Yazidi women interviewed in Iraq and Iran during Peacebuilding Compared fieldwork surged to the frontline of the fight to stop the rape and genocide. Most of the Kurdish female fighters were from Syria and Turkey, but many were also from Iraq and Iran. Their commander showed me their horrific training video for how female fighters must kill themselves quickly because 'girls must not allow themselves to be captured by Islamic State'. I wept tears of shame at the thought that western fighters, including from my country, had started this cascade of violence in Iraq that became a genocide in Sinjar. Now we were asking these young female fighters to do what we were unwilling to ask Australian fighters to do at the frontline, though Australian flyers did fight Islamic State from the air. The Australian people would not have tolerated sending our female fighters into house-to-house combat with Islamic State with instructions on killing themselves rather than surrendering as a prisoner of war. And so I wept again with a complex kind of shame at the circle of Kurdish and Yazidi women singing a song of courage in the dark around the fire before joining the frontline combat.

For me, this was partly shame in complicity in what later became a more total betrayal of Kurdish allies by President Trump. These Kurdish fighters, perhaps as many as 25,000 of whom were women (Khezri 2019), had done most of the house-to-house combat against Islamic State in Syria. More than 10,000 Kurdish fighters lost their lives, perhaps 1,000 of them women, as 30 per cent of the Kurds who fought Islamic State in Syria were women (Lemmon 2021). Certainly, many times more Kurdish women lost their lives fighting Islamic State (and Al-Qaeda) than the less than 100 Western warriors who gave their lives in these battles from 2014.

Around the fire, these brave young women encouraged one another to taunt the Islamic State fighters that there would be no virgins in heaven for men killed by women. Many Islamic State fighters did indeed believe this was a path to shame rather than martyrdom. That was one reason women were wanted by commanders at the very frontline in the hope of causing desertions, shattering Islamic State morale. These women's sacrifices contributed greatly to ending a genocide. The West does not even speak of the Yazidi genocide in the way it speaks of other admittedly larger genocides. Coming to terms with shame for those we fail to save from the worst dominations of violence is something the West must get better at. It is a crucial step towards learning how to prevent cascades of crime and war before they accelerate to genocide. That is a central focus of *Cascades of Violence* (Braithwaite and D'Costa 2018).

Like Nepal's feminist Maoists, the Kurdish feminists insisted on inspiring the institutionalisation of grassroots political empowerment of women in the areas liberated from Islamic State through the Charter of the Social Contract, the constitutional law for the local councils of northeastern Syria. It guaranteed 40 per cent women's representation in legislative and 'all governing bodies, institutions and committees' (Lemmon 2021: 61). This empowerment was disrupted when the Turkish military advanced against those Kurds who liberated us all from Islamic State (Khezri 2019).

Domination as a specification

Domination and inequality are highly correlated phenomena. The inductive theoretical conclusion of Braithwaite and D'Costa (2018) is that domination is a better specification than inequality to explain civil war. We can focus on domination within Kalyvas's (2003) model of local cleavages that interact with supralocal structural inequalities. As in Nepal et al.'s (2011) data, because mobilisation against grievances is local, village dominations can give rise to the mobilisation of local armed groups, especially if supralocal linkages enable local access to the organisational and financial capacities for army formation. Chairman Mao understood this. It is why Maoist strategy was about building rural armed groups around the local grievances of the most immiserated peasants, who were most dominated by their landlords. Then Maoists spread this strategy from hotspot to hotspot until, ultimately, these village struggles connected up. An armed countryside ultimately surrounds the capital. Braithwaite and D'Costa's (2018) empirical conclusion is that dozens of Maoist struggles, mostly in quite remote regions of South Asia, continue today to successfully exploit local grievances and cause local killing. They are not so successful at connecting up across a whole country today (except in Nepal until 2006) and not so successful today in spreading a Maoist imaginary.

Braithwaite and D'Costa (2018) also explored the rise of very different kinds of grievances over local dominations, typified by the rise of the Taliban. Local jihadist groups might derive their sense of domination from the militarised oppression and exclusionary practices they experience in their corner of the Kashmir Valley, the Swat Valley, Iraq or Libya. But, as with Maoism, their sense of local grievance is connected to a global imaginary (about jihad and against oppression by western infidels and their eastern dupes). Peacebuilding Compared found that refugee camps and the *madrassas* near them funded by jihadists are critical local sites for allying resentment over the local experience of domination with global cleavages, with a global domination imaginary and with global crowdsourcing from rich sponsors.

This is another sense in which national inequality is not the best specification with which to approach domination. Why is national inequality not the best way to see the effects of domination that explain terrorism? Why is domination at the local level (which intersects with more global imaginaries of domination) the more pressing imperative for the prevention of civil war and terrorism? The domination of being a Palestinian refugee in Lebanon or Syria with no job, no home, no right to return home, no country, no access to education and subject to targeting and systematic murder by foreign armies illustrates why. In Peshawar, Al-Qaeda proved more adept at fixing those dominations than the UN High Commissioner for Refugees and western humanitarian NGOs (see Braithwaite and D'Costa 2018: Box 9.2). In addition, the *global* domination of Muslims must be addressed. It is just as hard to reverse the colonial occupation of Arab lands by the West from World War I or the humiliation of the Mughal Empire by the British army in the previous century, as it is to reverse the European decimation of Aboriginal Australia or the indigenous nations of South Africa. Yet Apartheid can be dismantled and discrimination against Aboriginal Australians and Aboriginal land rights can be tackled—for example, through achieving Australia's initial 'closing the gap' targets and then empowering Indigenous people to choose how to broaden and tweak those targets. Likewise, discrimination against Arabs in Israel can be confronted, Palestinian land rights can be addressed with justice, Palestinian refugees can be given the right to return to their homeland, the bombing of Gaza's economic infrastructure can end and cutting off its economy from global markets (which delivers Gaza a 43 per cent unemployment rate) can end. In South Asia, Muslim Kashmiris can be given an active voice in shaping a permanent peace settlement for Kashmir that they view as fair in all the circumstances, against the background of the complex of geopolitical realities that confronts their valley.

An important recursive relationship here is, first, that state-based discrimination, particularly as measured in the Polity dataset, is associated with higher armed conflict (Akbaba and Taydas 2011; Cederman et al. 2011; Gurr 1993, 2000; Regan and Norton 2005; Wimmer et al. 2009; but see Jakobsen and De Soysa 2009). Vadlamannati (2011) has confirmed Gurr's (1970) *Why Men Rebel* conclusion on quantitative data across nine north-eastern Indian states. Vadlamannati found that poverty (compared with the rest of India) and economic and political discrimination explained outbreaks of violent conflict after controlling for income, population pressures, state capacity, ethnic affiliations, the amount of forest area, years of peace, neighbouring conflict incidence and distance to New Delhi. Furthermore, Rodrik (2000: 25), using the Polity dataset, showed that the ability of non-elites to access political institutions increases national economic growth. In other words, while national income equality might not consistently predict reduced armed conflict directly, poverty reduction might, and the nondiscriminatory access of non-elites to political institutions predicts poverty reduction.

An important conclusion about the tendency for different kinds of inequality or discrimination to be inconsistently important to freedom and crime in different contexts is to be wary of selective positivism. After failing to find a particular linear effect at a particular place and time, selective positivism should not drive a renunciation of domination effects. Because it is hard to predict when particular dominations will fuel raging fires of subjective oppression and violence, and when they will not, societies do well to aim at tempering all kinds of domination.

Domination, humiliation and reconciling violence

The exploitation of Muslim societies by western oil magnates backed by colonial gunboat diplomacy has already receded. However, Muslims still experience so many other forms of humiliation and stigma in and by the West. Some westerners consider insulting the prophet Mohammed a show of pride in the exercise of their freedom of speech. Some politicians can see the humiliation of Muslims as paving a path to power. Some westerners view 'banning the burqa' as a secular security policy that applies equally to all, as a measure to liberate women and not as a policy of religious discrimination. Global dominations must be connected to the observation that most of the dominations local Muslims feel have a local character. In Sydney, resentment over racism towards 'Lebs' (Lebanese) had been palpable in restorative justice conferences over incidents of racial and religious abuse in local high schools years in advance of the 2005 Cronulla riots between 'Aussies' and 'Lebs'. Local restorative justice over local dominations in high schools, refugee detention centres, prisons, workplaces and rural towns is a way that countries such as Australia can struggle against these dominations that can lead some young Muslims beyond rioting with rocks to suicide attacks and to Islamic State.

That is also a reason restorative reconciliation committee work in the areas of Pakistan bordering Afghanistan is important. As Braithwaite and Gohar (2014) argue, the reconciliation committees matter because they help prevent the cascading of civil war by resolving local dominations and humiliations and restoring order to areas where a collapse of the capacity to regulate violence gives the Taliban a foothold. My fieldwork experience of these reconciliation committees sees them as rituals of anomie reduction, humiliation reduction and revenge reduction. For children who have been dealt a wretched hand in a refugee camp, as a survivor of a family wiped out by a drone attack, reconciliation rituals must also do better at offering placement into a high-quality education, excellent vocational training and job placement into an economy that pays decent wages to people from impoverished backgrounds. The integration of economic justice and restorative justice is difficult but achievable. For the rape victims of Rolpa (Nepal), the integration of restorative forms of justice and economic justice in the people's courts was critical (Braithwaite 2015). Halving national gender inequality or the national Gini coefficient on its own is unlikely to have much effect on the probability of further civil wars. The powerful linkage is to harness national equality policies to local reconciliation that heals local hurts, restores local dignity, repairs local harms and reverses local discrimination against the poor and excluded. This can reduce local crime, as well as local armed conflict, and the way they cascade one into the other. On this analysis, the healing of cleavages with an integrated local–national strategy might make a difference. Micro–macro methods lead us to see the interaction between local, national and international imaginaries of domination and injustice as needing a reparative policy yeast for the bread of positive peace to rise. That is why brute structural remedies to national injustice cannot do the job in isolation.

Let me, then, be more specific about the hypotheses Braithwaite and D'Costa (2018) induced from these various data. National inequality reduction on its own bears a weak relationship to reduced prospects of war. National inequality reduction coupled with local inequality reduction, however, contributes to effectiveness in peacebuilding that reduces the prospects of war. Combining global reductions in inequality with addressing global imaginaries of domination and with national and local reduction of inequality can, even more strongly, reduce the incidence of war and crime on the planet. Reducing gender inequality at all levels seems particularly strategic, as does reducing racial inequality and religious discrimination. These seem to be the conclusions most consistent with the current state of the diverse kinds of evidence on inequality, crime and war. Because high crime rates, criminalised states and criminalised markets are forms of disorder that often spark wars, and because inequality increases the risks of crime, inequality reduction can also reduce the risks of war through this indirect path.

National income inequalities between Muslims and non-Muslims therefore matter, even if local and global dominations and humiliations seem in Braithwaite and D'Costa's (2018) data to matter more. Having individual young Muslims being economically marginalised, unemployed or treated unjustly by the police renders them more vulnerable to terrorism (Fleming et al. 2020), just as it leaves them more vulnerable to all other forms of violent crime. Muslims who experience these things are more susceptible to recruitment to violence in the same way as non-Muslim young people who experience them are susceptible to crime. Reducing poverty helps—and that is certainly a challenge of national policies. Yet very few young Muslims who experience the extreme poverty of refugee camps become suicide bombers. Even so, a society that lifts its young people out of poverty can have less crime and chaos on its streets and fewer people who are susceptible to recruitment to violent jihad in prison, in refugee camps or in front of their internet screens. Jihadist strategists learned the lesson that poor children who need an education, or bereft refugees, are good targets. They learned that rural anomie enables the seizure of local power. So why cannot those who work against their violence give priority to fixing these same dominations?

Changing tack, one critical reason that states with low GDP per capita have recurrent civil wars is that poor states cannot afford good state institutions, especially the accountability and welfare institutions discussed in the next few chapters. Extremely poor societies have not even learnt how to build them. As a result, the state often falls prey to criminalisation. Ultimately, ambitious alternative leaders seize opportunities to use armed force to overthrow the criminals who strip state assets. Sadly, the successors are often warlords who have the ruthlessness and resources to organise armies. Usually, their ambition is a renewed criminalisation of the state to their benefit. Hence, a fundamental way to prevent war is to help states grow out of poverty and grow their institutions. This is also Collier's (2007) empirically grounded prescription about 'the bottom billion'.

In sum, even though low GDP predicts war but less so crime, and national inequality predicts crime but less so war, both crime and war can be reduced in the long run by consistent application to tackling poverty and inequality in an integrated way at all levels. Braithwaite and

D'Costa (2018) showed, for Nepal and Indonesia, for example, that it is hard to predict whether it will be inequality at a very local level, a regional level, a national level or global inequalities between Muslims and Judaeo-Christians, caste inequalities, racial inequalities or some other identity politics that will mobilise grievance or violence. Albert Cohen alerted us to the possibility that inequality at the level of the school can mobilise grievance, subculture formation and violence. Any one study that compares high with low inequality at just one of these levels of analysis neglects the possible sources of crime and violence at all the other levels of analysis.

In Mertonian terms, at most levels of analysis, at most historical moments, the inequality at that level may not tap into a salient frame of aspirational reference. Most Christians may not care or even know whether Muslims are richer or poorer than them; Nepalese peasants may not aspire to be as wealthy as landlords and may accept their poverty without grievance or anger; the Colombian underclass may be reconciled to their poverty. Yet we know that at critical historical junctures Christians can become crusaders who slaughter geopolitically dominant Muslims, Nepalese peasants can become bloodthirsty Maoists who murder landlords and underclass Colombians can form cocaine cartels that cascade violence across two continents. In all these histories, inequalities are bound up with other grievances. If we have democratic and legal institutions that genuinely listen to grievances of all kinds, and institutions of redistribution that strive to reduce inequalities of all kinds, crime and armed violence can be kept within moderate bounds. This can occur even though grievances can never be fully resolved, and even though inequalities and the power that feeds on them are so resilient that they can never be fully dissolved. What seems clear enough and evidence-based enough for those who care about domination, crime and violence is that grievance responsiveness, institutional inclusiveness and inequality reduction are the right directions for political struggle. The complexity and historical contingency of the multiplicity of grievances and levels of inequality make the struggle towards this light on the hill difficult. That is no excuse for political paralysis.

Part of the integrated social justice strategy required also involves making power accountable at all levels and tackling domination and humiliation at the level of the school, the local community, the refugee camp, the bank and at the national level and the level of global imaginaries and global institutions. Most importantly, these strands of a web of peace with justice must be joined up. Expressed another way, reducing inequality at the national level is part of an integrated crime-prevention and peacebuilding design that can help create an enabling environment for crime and war prevention at the local level. Quality schools and jobs near refugee camps might be more important to crime–war–suicide prevention than macro-national equality; yet, without national institutions for creating good schools, good jobs and good state services for placing disadvantaged people into them, local restorative justice or peace committees cannot pull in the state welfare capabilities to realise their potential for crime–war–suicide prevention. Wherever poverty remains at the local level, wherever desperate refugees congregate, local domination will drive crime and will drive war when it connects to a more global imaginary of armed struggle against injustice.

Restorative justice that is also locally redistributive can therefore help. Peace committees that listen to stories of dominations and humiliations at all these levels and follow up on plans to ensure that domination and humiliation end can assist. Reconciliation with social justice is required at higher levels for more aggregated dominations. Reconciliation with social justice at the local level must be put in the context of local dominations and humiliations. That is why reconciliation committees in rural Pakistan, Afghanistan, Libya, Iraq and Congo are important as both peacebuilding and crime-prevention initiatives (Braithwaite and D'Costa 2018). For groups who have suffered national degradation, this aggregates to the importance of national reconciliation, reintegration and 'justice as a better future' (Froestad and Shearing 2012). Or, as Vesna Pesic's thinking about the former Yugoslavia put it, 'fear of the future, lived through the past' can motivate 'terrible evils in the present that can only be transcended by a politics of justice as a better future' (quoted in Lake and Rothchild 1998: 7). Former German Chancellor Willy Brandt illustrated the connection of justice as a better future to what criminologists call collective efficacy in projects of his political life such as his agonistic resistance to the Nazis and then apologising on his knees at the Warsaw ghetto after the event.

> The best way to see the future is to influence it … Peace like freedom is no original state which existed from the start; we shall have to make it. (Brandt 1971: 1)

Gender, domination and culturally shared values

Applin and Messner (2015) have applied institutional anomie theory to gender and institutions. They point out that 'the economic domain is constructed as a "masculinized" space' (Applin and Messner 2015: 46). Women's values are less criminogenic because they are more institutionally tempered than those of men, who tend to be more ruthlessly committed to their individual career success. In the value framing of institutional balance, women accord a more balanced priority to the flourishing of all family members from the very young to the very old, and of all being cared for within the bosom of the family. Empirically, women give more time and priority to maintaining family infrastructure, including to ensuring that all family members flourish to their full potential through wise use of educational opportunities. Men are the ones who must change to become more like women in this regard. In many societies, women also accord more priority to community-level social capital formation and therefore contribute more to the impact of collective efficacy for crime reduction in communities, schools and families (as discussed in Chapters 7 and 11). This book has already argued that in the balance between achieving good and bad objectives by peaceful and warlike means, male values and political practices are more warlike.

Messner and Rosenfeld (2013: 91–92) summarise evidence that in the United States the American Dream is less about competitive individualism and materialism for women than it is for men. Across 84,398 individuals in 58 countries, Hövermann and Messner (2019: 17) show that men do have a more marketised mentality than women. They also point out that this observation about American society is not new, quoting Tocqueville on women's values as 'the counterweight to the pursuit of selfish interests in the marketplace' (Hövermann and Messner 2019: 423). One of the interesting contributions of Messner and Rosenfeld (2013) is their reflection on how to shift shared cultural values to make them less criminogenic. One path is to seek to feminise the values of men, to foster a culture of reflection and self-criticism among men concerning their materialism and competitive individualism. Family-level restorative justice can play a role here in asking adult men to return to listening and learning from the wisdom of elderly mothers and aunties so their families might flourish more holistically, and of course listening to their own partners and their own children on that same issue.

An inspiring development in many Australian First Nations communities is grandmothers becoming politically organised for civil society transformation. These groups often call themselves 'the G'mars'. They insist the males of their community—as well as male political leaders of the country—listen to them in 'yarning circles'. Larissa Behrendt's award-winning film, *After the Apology*, shows the political and communal leadership of the G'mars and aunties in confronting the problem of a new 'Stolen Generation' of children recklessly removed from struggling Indigenous families.

Of course, there are dangers in saying to women that you are more virtuous than men in sacrificing your individual interests for the public good and the good of your family. Nondomination requires that women have as much access to individual career opportunities as men, not that women suppress their ambition. Here, institutional anomie theory needs a sharper normative grounding than it currently has. In Applin and Messner's (2015) and Messner and Rosenfeld's (2013) approach to gender politics and shared cultural values there is an incipient brilliance of insight about what is needed for the low-crime society that also has less domination. But my argument is that this promise cannot be fully realised without being clear about the value commitment to a society that maximises freedom as nondomination.[7] Without clarity of normative commitment, the danger of falling into the trap of patting women on the back for making sacrifices is something for the institutional anomie theorist to explicitly resolve— likewise with the oppressed Dalit peasants in Nepal discussed above. How profound is the danger of UN peacebuilding that it might have the effect of saying to Nepalese peasants: 'For the sake of stopping the violence, please go back to not caring about the fact that the landlord class has stolen your land, deprived your children of educational opportunities, raped Dalit women and kept you in circumstances of servitude.' In some ways, UN peacebuilding, as strongly as we must support it, can say something even worse than that. All kinds of peacemaking frequently work by doing deals in which peace negotiators offer commanders of armed groups positions and perks in postwar power-sharing. The proposition is put to them that they can later use their power in the power-sharing arrangements of the new government to develop new land reforms and laws that can secure the objectives of their political movement to return to peasants land that

7   Steven Messner replied to a draft of this section that a normative vision of the good society is clear in his work with Richard Rosenfeld, which it is. This is that the good society 'facilitates the development of everyone's talents and capacities to the fullest extent possible'.

has been stolen from them. In the event, what so often happens is that male insurgency commanders get a lot of land, but their foot soldiers from the peasantry do not (Braithwaite et al. 2012; Braithwaite and D'Costa 2018).

Whether for women, or for landless peasants, the politics of the oppressed returning to historical moderation of their aspirations risks a slippery slope to domination. For peacebuilding, there must be checks and balances that ensure independent reviews by the United Nations of whether there has been full implementation of peace agreement provisions on land rights and gender rights, or at least substantial progress. Sanctions such as UN member states holding back some foreign aid for successor states may be needed if they are not, and shifting that aid to civil society. In advance of all those implementation nuts and bolts, we must be clear about our values.

An implication of institutional anomie theory is that shared cultural values must be tempered. Cultural change is needed to temper financial objectives with the human and social capital objectives discussed in Chapter 7. The conclusion to that chapter argues that financial objectives must be tempered with environmental objectives if we are to maximise freedom as nondomination. Nondomination requires that in a rebalancing of burden-sharing towards a Green New Deal, a feminist New Deal for women and children and a better deal for the poor who miss out on material values are imperative. Sacrifice is not the right word for men who would be better off with a more feminised value-balance partly because their children and their partners will love them more, and they will enjoy being more rounded and decent. What is going on there is that making an extra million is less intrinsically rewarding than raising a beautiful child because the relationality of love for a child is more intrinsically human. Yet sacrifice is the right word when men do all the careerism and women the housework, child care and aged care. So, the feminist politics of what is required for the low-crime and low-domination society here seems very clear. It is relentless social movement and political party activism for the modulation of materialism as a cultural value. It means equality of sacrifice in the required rebalancing of culturally shared aspirations and commitments.

This political implication is more than slightly implicit in the service Applin, Messner and Rosenfeld have done in moving beyond the War on Poverty implications of opportunity theory to add that emphasis on reframing the American Dream in a feminist way. Politically and pragmatically, the civic republicanism of the Federalist Papers and of the next generation of constitutional debates after the Civil War (Richards 1993) seems to this outsider an inspiring font of value framing for any country. To further fuel this optimism with a more contemporary political point, there is one thing in common between the post-1968 rebelliousness of my ageing baby-boomer population against the Greatest Generation (Chapter 3) and the rebellion of the newest generation of Greta Thunberg's Generation Z activists. It is the spurning of materialism as the measure of success. This can be a foundation for intergenerational renewal to temper the hegemony of ruling generations by rippling social capital outwards from families and schools into economic and political institutions. This feminist take on 'extractive institutionalism' and 'limited-access orders' (that drills down to feminised family extraction, women's domination and limited access) is a strength of contemporary institutional anomie theorists more than for so many leading institutional economists and political economy thinkers. The flaws in political economy arise from the disciplinary myopia of a political science that analytically privileges state institutions and an economics that privileges market institutions to the exclusion of family institutions. Here is one site of intellectual struggle where criminology can contribute to a more institutionally plural interdisciplinarity with thanks to feminist criminology.

While this normative framing of institutional anomie theory seems clear enough, the empirics of what has happened in response to the consciousness-raising of different waves of feminism are more difficult to assess. There has been some feminist progress, with the first wave of feminism winning the vote for women, with more women in politics after the second wave, more women on corporate boards and in professional jobs than in the past. Whether these have been counterbalanced by the 'feminisation of poverty' and declining relative pay for 'feminised' professions like nursing, teaching and aged care; whether there has been little feminisation of men's values or whether there has been much masculinisation of powerful women's values—all these shifts of the historical short term may continue to be hard to assess (Applin and Messner 2015).

Patriarchy as an ideology entails men feeling humiliation at the suggestion that their partner could be equal or superior to them on as critical a dimension of male dominance as breadwinning. This is why criminologists can get Gartner and McCarthy's (1991) result that employed women married to an unemployed husband had six times the homicide victimisation one would expect given the proportion of the population in this group. Just as such facts complicate the direct employment–crime nexus and the patriarchy–crime nexus, they affirm the more general underlying proposition that domination engenders crime. They provoke an underlying normative vision that sets nondomination as the light on the hill for men and women.

My argument has been that a steadfast feminist politics and an intersectoral politics that embraces concern for all dominations are implications of normative–explanatory theoretical integration amid the many contingencies in the empirical effects of diverse inequalities. Hopefully, feminists would not stop being feminists if it happened to turn out that feminist politics increased crime or prolonged wars. As it happens, the empirical evidence reviewed is that feminist politics has made big contributions to crime reduction and even bigger contributions to political struggles against war (from the early days of the first wave of feminism) and to building societies that are freer. This dovetails with the feminist analysis of Chapter 3 and future chapters that concludes that in the *longue durée*, violence against intimate partners and rape have reduced and for the past century and a half feminist politics has been the most important contributor to this. We see the contribution from New Zealand, where women first won the national vote and where Prime Minister Jacinda Ardern today helps us see what social democratic nondomination looks like, to Nepal, where female Maoist fighters won the most feminist constitutional transformation seen so far (Braithwaite 2015).

Opening blocked opportunities: Equality of freedom versus equality of opportunity

Cloward and Ohlin wanted to see an America with less poverty and more equality of results. Their writing, however, can be criticised for playing into the diagnoses of the 'middle of the road' politics of those who believed that the only kind of War on Poverty America needed was a war on inequality of opportunity. Social democrats and socialists across the world looked upon America's War on Poverty of the 1960s as involving no semblance of a transition of the United States to social democracy, only another version of the thin liberalism of equality of opportunity. There would be no systematic egalitarian reparations for the crimes of slavery; there would be some more points of entry for slightly expanded numbers of descendants of slaves into Ivy League universities, but nothing profoundly structural.

It would continue to be the case that the money spent on each of the hundreds of black students at Harvard University would be less than the spending on each of a million non-white citizens still enslaved in prisons, police lockups or jails. Even Messner and Rosenfeld (2013) slightly shocked me when they approvingly cited James Q. Wilson's (1975) claim in President Gerald Ford's favourite book of the 1970s that poverty did decline in the 1960s and early 1970s, yet crime went up. What is true is that the unemployment rate almost halved between 1960 and 1969 but then, from 1969 to 1992, it almost tripled (with deindustrialisation) (Chegg Inc. 2003–21). Moreover, under the Republican administrations that were in power for most of these years, there were some significant retrenchments of the welfare state and, as Piketty (2014) showed, the tax system became much less progressive, with a top marginal income tax rate that had hit 91 per cent in the 1950s falling step by step throughout that period. Then, most fundamentally, as Piketty (2014) found, those dependent on income to pay their bills became poorer and poorer in comparison with those who lived off shares or other financial assets for some or all of their spending. It was thus not only deindustrialisation that widened the gulf between the rich and the poor, between black and white Americans, during the great crime rise from 1960 to 1992. Piketty showed it was also the financialisation of capitalism and the capture of tax policies by the wealthy. And remember, Messner and his co-authors have shown that the regressive nature of tax systems cross-nationally is associated with higher crime rates (Piatkowska et al. 2020).

Let us concede to conservatives of the James Q. Wilson ilk who say that the War on Poverty failed. Let us concede that the not inconsiderable influence of institutional anomie theory on the War on Poverty strategy also failed. But let us be reflective on the reasons for this. The War on Poverty put only the slightest dent in the rise in poverty and inequality in the United States during deindustrialisation. Before and after the War on Poverty, the United States continued to be disengaged from the imperative for universal access to health care for all citizens, continued to have a weaker welfare state than other developed economies with lower crime rates and continued to have a more inegalitarian tax system and a more inegalitarian financialisation of capitalism than most of them. To their credit, Messner and Rosenfeld (2013: 112) do approvingly quote Ruth Sidel on why it was facile for any commentator to expect that the War on Poverty might have turned back the wave of rising American crime up to 1992:

The War on Poverty was woefully inadequate to reverse the damage that was done, particularly to blacks, in our society: and no sooner did it get started than Vietnam, inflation, and the Nixon administration had begun to subvert it.

One misstep by Cloward and Ohlin played into the hands of conservatives like James Q. Wilson and his Republican Party fan club of the era who wilfully promoted these analytical errors. It arose from the exaggerated emphasis Cloward and Ohlin (1960: 111) placed on the observation that delinquency is more likely when there is 'attribution of the cause of failure to the social order rather than oneself'. Cloward and Ohlin conjectured that the belief that failure is a result of one's personal deficiencies results in pressures to improve oneself. This leaves the legitimacy of the social order intact. One thing they saw as important in shaping whether attributions of blame were internal or external was whether they perceived systematic prejudices in conferring success, such as racial prejudice. For this reason, Cloward and Ohlin saw equality of opportunity as fundamental to reducing system-blame and therefore delinquency. Equality of opportunity could give the poor hope that they can lift themselves out of poverty, if not in this generation, then in the next. This aspect of Cloward and Ohlin's work was widely read to imply an imperative for the War on Poverty to prioritise equality of opportunity over equality of results. Braithwaite (1979–80: 92) reviewed the considerable evidence that blaming the system was *not* more associated with delinquency than blaming the self and the evidence that many serious offenders simultaneously blamed both the system and themselves. Subsequent work reveals even more complex intersections, such as external attribution sometimes resulting in a sense of powerlessness and learned helplessness that is then internalised (Davies and Best 1996; Davies 1997). 'Contrary to Cloward and Ohlin, it is reasonable to hypothesise that if one fails in a system, one will withdraw attributions of legitimacy to that system, irrespective of the reasons for failure' (Braithwaite 1979–80: 92). Considering all the complexity, this still seems to have correctly concluded that Cloward and Ohlin in this respect were contributing to sending the War on Poverty towards a rationale for the neglect of equality of outcomes—and that was the most important feature of its failure. Equality of opportunity is definitely important, but it is not as important for a free society as continuous struggle for more equal outcomes. Liberal interpretations of the irrelevance of the War on Poverty to solving America's problems opened the door to neoliberal excess in decentring the welfare state in crime-prevention discourse.

Conclusion

This chapter has concluded that societies and schools that institutionalise failure and societies afflicted with a commodified and militarised vision of what success and failure mean suffer high crime rates. Messner and Rosenfeld have set criminology on a productive path towards also grappling with the role that a plurality of institutions plays in tempering the corrosive effects on crime of market institutions. The next chapter seeks to systematise what kind of pluralisation of institutional checks and balances is needed. To contemplate why this is imperative, consider Messner and Rosenfeld's thin discussion of the importance of political institutions as checks and balances on economic institutions. Operationalisation in the empirical testing of institutional anomie discussed above is even thinner. The strength of political institutions is operationalised in most studies by the percentage of voters who turn out in national elections. This is a particularly poor measure when a number of societies have compulsory voting.

Before rising to that challenge, the next chapter rises to a related challenge. In arguing that the War on Poverty in the heyday of Merton, Cloward and Ohlin and Cohen mostly failed, Messner and Rosenfeld (2013: 125–26) further opined:

> We may question the effectiveness of the progressive approach to crime control for additional reasons. First, it is difficult to see how the proffered explanation of crime and the policies based on it would apply to the crimes committed by persons at the top of the opportunity structure, crimes that are far from rare and that are very costly to society.

This understates the challenge because, in Chapter 2, we have already established that crimes of the powerful cause greater property loss and greater loss of life than all other crimes combined. The next chapter seeks to rise to this challenge of elaborating institutional anomie theory to explain why societies with high inequality of wealth and power have elevated rates of crimes of the powerless and crimes of the powerful. Then it argues that if we broaden criminology's concerns from crime in the streets to crime in the suites, an even more pluralised tempering of market institutions by a rich plurality of countervailing institutions is needed.

5

Tempering the inequality that empowers crimes of the powerful

Key propositions

- Middle-class crime is stupendous in volume, increasing, but mostly minor in seriousness compared with crimes of the powerful and crimes of the powerless.
- The middle class often appears more criminal than they are because of systematic patterns of passing organisational accountability downwards in the class structure.
- Middle-class complicity in crimes of the powerful and how to prevent this are major issues, however.
- A less anomic, less legally cynical middle class is one key to civilising capitalism and tempering the domination of national security states.
- Crimes of the powerful are the biggest crime problems. While they are enabled by concentrations of wealth and power, they cannot be fixed by killing off wealth and power. A challenge of this book is to show how greater equality in the distribution of wealth and power can strengthen capital accumulation. It is to show how tempering of state and market power can make states and markets more powerful builders of social and financial capital for distribution to the poor.
- Economists are generating growing evidence suggesting that income inequality can explain proxies for environmental crime and corruption cross-nationally and by province. Corruption induced by higher levels

of inequality is in turn associated with terrorism and organised crime. Corruption and organised crime criminalise states and markets, rendering both extractive, rather than inclusive and enabling.

- Chapter 4 concluded that redemptive schooling is important to anomie prevention; this chapter concludes that schooling is a foundational institution for creating a society in which all citizens find how they can work at things at which they excel.

- There can be no freedom in societies that send some citizens to the scrap heap as children or as elderly citizens, or in between because they are a person with disabilities. There is a feasible politics for delivering every citizen a responsive education, freedom from hunger, decent housing supported by constant contestation for greater redistribution of wealth and power in favour of the marginalised.

- Extreme inequality and the politics of domination are structurally humiliating and stigmatising for the dominated. This domination and stigma drive crime.

- More wealth *for use* in the hands of the poor increases wealth creation overall even as it takes wealth away from the rich *for exchange*. More extreme concentrations of wealth for exchange in the hands of the rich also worsen the most dominating forms of illegitimate opportunities.

- By heightening domination, more inequality means more crimes of the exploited and more crime by those who exploit.

- Crimes of exploitation require tempering of wealth and power for exchange by the rich through pluralising separations of powers.

Sutherland's wrong turn

In contemplating the fate of an unemployed, landless Aboriginal person heading for prison, most of us wonder whether poverty may have something to do with their plight. If we ponder a rich person setting up a complex of shell companies in a tax haven to commit fraud, we might think that wealth has something to do with their crime. Many criminologists do not think this way.

> If it can be shown that white-collar crimes are frequent, a general theory that crime is due to poverty and its related pathologies is shown to be invalid. (Sutherland 1983: 7)

Messner and Rosenfeld (2013: 125–26) embraced Sutherland's point. This book takes the different tack of diagnosing how inequality empowers crimes of the powerful and induces crimes of the powerless through domination. It then moves on to consider what kinds of institutional separations of powers would be more responsive to how inequality empowers crimes of the powerful. Responsiveness to the organisational crime part of the crime problem leads to a much more ambitious institutional agenda. It requires an even more pluralised checking and balancing of institutions than that commended in Messner and Rosenfeld's pluralisation of institutional balances to check anomie. Chapters 8 and 9 conclude that corporate crime and state crime cannot be deterred effectively by prosecutions alone. They are reasonably well deterred in some countries by a regulatory mix that includes prosecutorial deterrence alongside pluralised separations of powers. This is discussed in detail in the next chapter. Along the way, this chapter contends that institutional separations of powers designed to combat crimes of the powerful can also assist in reducing crimes of the powerless and the complicity of the middle class in criminalised markets and states.

Most of the evidence that informs this analysis of the effect of inequality on crimes of the powerful is not quantitative. Some quantitative studies suggest that income inequality does increase environmental offending as measured by cross-national measures of emissions and kindred pollution indices (Ridzuan 2019). Quantitatively, regional levels of organised crime violence before elections in Italy shift electoral success away from parties opposed to the Mafia, away from the left and towards corrupt politicians (Pinotti 2015b). Cross-national evidence suggests that such political impacts of entrenched organised crime cripple economies (Pinotti 2015a). Tuliao and Chen (2019) used data from 20,025 supervisors from 52 countries responding to the World Values Survey to show that a country's economic inequality (Gini) predicted the propensity of its managers to justify unethical and illegal acts.

You and Khagram's (2005) comparative analysis of 129 countries using 2SLS methods with a variety of instrumental variables and World Values Survey data on how inequality affects corruption and norms supported the following explanation with formidable explanatory power:

> The wealthy have both greater motivation and more opportunity to engage in corruption, whereas the poor are more vulnerable to extortion and less able to monitor and hold the rich and powerful

> accountable as inequality increases. Inequality also adversely affects social norms about corruption and people's beliefs about the legitimacy of rules and institutions, thereby making it easier for them to tolerate corruption as acceptable behaviour. (You and Khagram 2005: 136)

Economic research repeatedly reports an association between inequality and corruption measured by corruption perceptions cross-nationally (Gupta et al. 2002; Gyimah-Brempong 2002; Fakir et al. 2017) and by counts of US corruption convictions explained by inequality (Dincer and Gunalp 2008). Across Chinese provinces, Yan and Wen (2019) found that high income inequality was associated with high corruption, which in turn reduced citizens' subjective wellbeing. The economic research increasingly suggests a recursive relationship whereby inequality engenders corruption and then corruption further increases inequality. We see this in a comparison of US states (Apergis et al. 2010) and cross-nationally (Uslaner 2008; Policardo and Sánchez Carrera 2018; Policardo et al. 2019; Urbina 2020). Krieger and Meirrieks (2019) found for 113 countries that income inequality was associated with domestic terrorism and this was partly mediated through corruption levels. Moreover, Krieger and Meirrieks (2019: 125) found that 'countries that redistribute more' through progressive tax policies or transfer payments 'see less domestic terrorism, in part because redistribution improves institutional conditions'.

If we know about crimes of the powerful, they are not likely to be the most remunerative forms of organisational crime at the time of that knowing. With corporate crime, when a strategy of predation becomes well known, it becomes less lucrative. Hence, the counting of corporate crime tends to count what is least important. Fortunately, however, at this stage in the development of the criminology of organisations, we can look back across several past generations of ethnographic contributions to the study of past waves of organisational crime. These ethnographies cumulate to the theoretical insight that corporate crime and state crime are much more preventable than Edwin Sutherland thought, and much more related to inequality than he thought. Several synoptic works have traversed these insights across many corporate crime waves. These waves include the nineteenth-century era of robber barons that led to the invention of antitrust laws, the crimes that were regulated in the Progressive Era and the New Deal in the United States, the war crimes from the wave of wars from 1911 to the Vietnam War, the Watergate era, the foreign bribery scandals of the late 1970s, the Greed is Good era of the 1980s on Wall Street that included the US Savings and Loans scandal and European bank collapses, the rise of the Russian mafia in the aftermath of privatisations in post-communist societies, the tax shelter stampedes of the 1970s and 1990s in many countries, the tech-wreck era of crimes at the turn of the century from Enron in the United States to HIH in Australia, and the financial engineering crimes of the 2008 Global Financial Crisis. There is as much to learn from the ethnographies of earlier waves of crimes of the powerful, but most to learn from detecting an evolution across many waves. That evolution reveals enduring principles about how to temper the abuse of power. Many recent synoptic works traverse ethnographic studies of these waves of organisational crime, each with their own interpretations of them (Simpson 2002; Rosoff et al. 2002; Gobert and Punch 2003; Shover and Hochstetler 2005; Clinard and Yeager 2006; Friedrichs 2010; Rothe and Friedrichs 2014; Bittle et al. 2018; Rorie 2020).

Chapters 2 and 3 discussed how the work of Farrall and Karstedt (2019) on middle-class crime might imply that, unless we bring the 'crimes of the 1 per cent' to heel, the anomic crimes of the middle 50 per cent (most of which are not counted in official crime statistics) might continue to take off. This chapter argues that it is difficult to tame the legal cynicism that fuels crimes of the middle class without moderating crimes of the powerful. It also shows that ruling classes are adept at exploiting organisational complexity to pass responsibility for their crimes down to middle-class fall guys. Legal cynicism takes off in societies if the buck stops not at the top, but with sacrificial middle-manager scapegoats.

The conclusion from disparate sources of qualitative evidence is that high levels of inequality in societies tend to increase crimes of those who dominate as well as crimes of the dominated. This chapter shows why and how. It then explains that these insights inform how tempering of the power of the most powerful officeholders in a society with power exerted by countervailing institutions can be effective in reducing crimes of the powerful. Hence, this chapter begins to nail down the institutional anomie themes that separations of institutional power and reduced inequality of wealth and power can temper crimes of the powerful.

There is an important criminological literature about why powerlessness over one's own life promotes crime, and why extreme levels of unchecked power over the lives of others enables a different kind of crime. There are particularly rich debates around this theme in the exegesis and testing of Charles Tittle's (1995) control-balance theory (for example, Piquero and Hickman 1999; Karstedt 2014b; Karstedt et al. 2021). Tittle views crime in an evocative and elegant way. He sees crime as more likely when people are much more controlled than controlling, or much more controlling than controlled. Tittle clicks into a cognate intuition to those that shape this book. Tittle's insights are grounded in an understanding of relevant evidence. It is harder, however, to attune Tittle's theory to the normative theory of tempering controls and the separation of powers in this work. Tittle said his was an explanatory criminological theory and not a normative theory. My freedom theory of crime searches not for quantification of an optimum control-balance ratio, but for specification of separations of powers that empower all with tempered power. The approach of this book may be more fertile than Tittle's *Control Balance* because its normative theory sharpens the explanatory theory to a focus on more practical policy specificities than the ratio of how much a person is controlled to controlling. My tweak of institutional anomie as an explanatory theory also transforms the abstract normative theory of Montesquieu's separation of powers to lists of institutional specifics that must be reformed.

'Domination engenders crime' is a generalisation with force from the most micro to the most macro of contexts. Domination in families breeds family violence and socialises children with the idea that violence is not shameful. At the micro end, relationships based on domination in the schoolyard engender the violence we call bullying. It turns out empirically that schoolyard bullies do become corporate bullies and physically violent adults (Homel 2013) or criminal offenders as adults (Farrington et al. 2012). This is another sense in which the school is a mouse race that prepares corporate criminals for the rat race. Micro-institutional domination constitutes macro-patterns of domination. More unequal societies have more bullying. Elgar et al.'s (2009) survey data from 37 countries found a strong association between income inequality and societal rates of bullying. At the macro end, the structures of national economies that dominate or exclude fractions of the population are criminogenic. Inequality of wealth and power not only fosters crime by creating an underclass that is dominated; it also creates an upper class that dominates. This chapter is about domination and crime; it is about how greed as well as need are implicated in different kinds of crime.

Theoretically, I conceive of greed as an untempered market value. Greed is unbridled commodified avarice in communal life. Some economies bring about greater extremes of need and greed than others. Greed motivates unaccountable and rapid accumulation: fast money. Empirically, much white-collar crime is motivated by what Gottschalk (2020) calls 'convenience'—wanting to speed up the business of making money or getting things done. At the same time, Gottschalk's phenomenological approach based on interviews with 408 convicted white-collar criminals reveals that they do not perceive themselves as greedy but rather as pursuing a 'convenient' way of getting something done. Offenders perceive their crimes as being more about timesaving, effort-reduction and pain-avoidance than about avarice or even corner-cutting. Gottschalk (2020: 73) finds they use techniques of neutralisation (Sykes and Matza 1957) similar to those of powerless offenders. Finding the relevance of techniques of neutralisation is recurrent across the ethnographic work on crimes of the powerful.

Greed militates against the kinds of investments that might alleviate need—investment that creates decent jobs for those in need. This will be illustrated by Congo's President Joseph Kabila extracting wealth from his country for personal use to purchase an extravagant chateau in France rather than investing in businesses that create Congolese jobs. The other reciprocal relationship here is that when large, segregated sections of a population are in need, they are easy prey for the greed of the fast-money set. They are prey both as consumers and as street-corner sellers of goods like opium in the opium dens of nineteenth-century China. Populations in need are also vulnerable to becoming prey as consumers to enforcers of services like loan-sharking, and to becoming suppliers of sex work at the hands of human traffickers. Sutherland failed to theorise both need and greed as criminogenic, to ponder that the political economy of need is causally dependent on the political economy of greed. Conversely, Sutherland failed to see that the political economy of greed preys on the economy of need. The economy of need—for example, for housing—creates market niches for criminogenic greed.

A second proposition is that domination engenders humiliation that motivates crimes of humiliating the humiliator or some other target. This involves an attempt to move the humiliated actor from being the oppressed to the oppressor. The proposition that domination engenders crime continues to have explanatory power at the supranational level. Consider crimes of genocide such as in Rwanda. Much persuasive historiography goes to the domination of the Allied powers at Versailles being used to humiliate Germany. Thomas Scheff (1994) argued how the appeal of *Mein Kampf* was an appeal to a humiliated people. Hitler's rhetorical calculation was to foster a shame–rage spiral. Similarly, US and British hegemony in Asia and the Pacific between the two world wars, and the way it was used to crush Japanese expansion through trade, was actively read by Japanese ultranationalists as western humiliation of Japan. Some of the extraordinary crimes of Japan during World War II can be understood in part as rage against what it saw as western oppressors. Consider my father as a survivor of the Sandakan Death Marches (Chapter 3). Why do I interpret this crime as a shame–rage spiral? Well, there were various circumstantial aspects of it. These were degradation rituals of public display to local Asian peoples of the literal collapse of white masters. There were specific incidents along the way such as Asian sex slaves ('comfort women') being encouraged by guards to pour the contents of their chamber pots on to the emaciated bodies of our fathers from the balconies of the buildings in which they were enslaved. There was the fact that when the commandant of my father's camp was executed, he bit the hangman's hand. There was such anger in playing out an evil that one might have thought could have induced remorse; the righteous anger, I surmise from his statements, of a man engulfed by the humiliation of his people, determined to resist to the end the idea of white men being masters over Asians. My father recalled him saying near the end: 'We may lose this war. But if it takes 100 years, one day we will be your masters.'

Crimes of greed and need

Braithwaite (1979) sought to respond to the challenge in Sutherland's quote that opens this chapter. The response was a tweak of Lord Acton's dictum: power corrupts; absolute power corrupts absolutely. With too little power and wealth, a great variety of problems of living that are conducive to crime of one type are endured. Excessive power and wealth corrupt, and this cascades crime of another type. The contention was that greater equality of wealth and power can be a pathway to reduce both types of crime. Yet there are obstacles along this path. Underclass or lower-caste crime arises from the fact that the poor are exploited. White-collar crime starts from the wealthy deploying their capital to exploit. Since powerlessness and an excess of power contribute to crime, this book argues against the assertion that crime associated with inequality ceases if the poor accept their fate as deserved. The assertion ignores the fact that the poor in this situation remain powerless and the rich powerful.

My 1970s analysis was insufficiently nuanced. Since then, we have seen so many inconsistent results on the impact of inequality on crime—inconsistencies that can be explained by the effects of inequality on crime being tempered by the poor and the rich valuing things other than acquisition. Excesses of power tempered by regulatory checks and balances on domination also help account for some of the mixed empirical results. This is where one important potency of Messner and Rosenfeld's contribution plays a part.

Braithwaite's (1991, 1995) analysis was that where needs are satisfied, further power and wealth enable crime motivated by greed. New types of criminal opportunities and new paths to immunity from accountability are constituted by concentrations of wealth and power. Inequality thus worsens both crimes of poverty motivated by the need for goods for use and crimes of wealth motivated by the greed enabled by goods for exchange. The accumulation of goods for exchange enables the constitution of illegitimate opportunities for the rich that cannot be constituted for the poor.

More precisely, this argument is that inequality encourages crime by: 1) decreasing the goods available for use by the poor to satisfy their socially constructed needs; and 2) increasing the goods available to rich people (and organisations) who have their needs satisfied, but whose accumulation of goods for exchange constitutes criminal opportunities. These are often opportunities to indulge greed (often socially constructed as 'aspirations' or 'convenience').

However relativist needs are in their social construction, one claim about them is of general import. As we become wealthier, it becomes more likely that any and all conceptions of need will be better satisfied. If my income doubles—irrespective of whether my needs are framed in terms of subsistence, the average standard of living, unrealistic expectations or aspirations, or downright greedy ones—it is likely I will view those needs as better met than they were before. This hypothesis is consistent with the standard welfare economics point that marginal gains from satisfying needs decline as need satisfaction increases. This parallel to welfare economics insights is drawn without narrowing the analysis to a welfare economics framework.

In sum, inequality at the same time induces:

Crimes of *poverty*:
- motivated by *need*
- for goods for *use*

Crimes of *wealth*:
- motivated by *greed*
- enabled by goods for *exchange* (that are surplus to those required for use)

Diane Vaughan (1983: 59) concluded that a cultural emphasis on economic success motivates the setting of a new goal whenever the old one is attained. While needs are socially constructed as wants that can be satisfied, I distinguish greed as a want that can never be satisfied: success is ever-receding; having more motivates wanting more again.

> While it is meaningless to accumulate certain sensual use-values indefinitely, since their worth is limited by their usefulness, the accretion of exchange-value, being merely quantitative, suffers no such constraints. (Haug 1986: 18)

A great thing about greed in the hands of the ruthless is that it accumulates surpluses that fund the constitution of new worlds of criminal opportunity. The ideology that sustains accumulation is commodity fetishism, which Messner and Rosenfeld (2013) argue is a driver of institutional anomie and crime. Greed fetishises money for its value for exchange, as opposed to value for use. For some rich people, accumulation is also a game of winning by moving up the rich list and conspicuous consumption.

This said, the theory of greed and crime is not bound by commodification. If we consider Hitler or any other political leader responsible for genocide, what we find in their political thought and emotional rhetoric is an insatiable lust to dominate. A surplus of control (Tittle 1995) fuels that insatiable drive for even more domination, doing deals to exchange power in pursuit of that insatiable lust for power. This is the part of the empirical grounding of Tittle's control-balance theory that I find very persuasive.

Stan Wheeler (1990) discovered the motivational importance of fear of falling as a complement to the lure of greed for gain in white-collar crime. There is no problem in accommodating this within the foregoing theoretical framework. Crime can be motivated by: a) the desire for goods (or power) for use; b) the fear of losing goods (or power) for use; c) the desire for goods (or power) for exchange; or d) the fear of losing goods (or power) for exchange. My hypotheses are that (a) and (b) are more relevant to motivating the crimes of the poor; (c) and (d) are more relevant to the crimes of wealthy people, the crimes of capital and the crimes of powerful organisations. These distributional tendencies can hold even though (a) to (d) might all be involved in the mixed motives driving a single corporate crime. Some individuals who play a part in the crime may be motivated by (a), others by (b), others by (c) and others by (d). Indeed, within some individuals, there may be mixed motives that range across these four categories, and beyond. So, we cannot easily segregate and essentialise criminal action in these terms, even as they are diagnostically useful.

This does not change the distributional hypothesis that use-motivations will more often be involved in the criminal choices of the poor, and exchange-motivations more often involved in the criminal choices of the rich. I now argue that just as the poverty of the poor in unequal societies contributes to crime, so does the wealth of the wealthy. We have established that it cannot be that the wealth of the wealthy increases crime because of a purely Mertonian analysis of legitimate opportunities to satisfy needs. This is because the rich have more of their needs satisfied by ready access to legitimate means of need satisfaction.

One line of argument is that conspicuous concentrations of wealth increase the illegitimate opportunities available to the poor (and indeed the non-poor). Being a car thief is more remunerative when there are many $100,000 cars available to be stolen than when $10,000 cars are the best one can find. Evidence that wealthy neighbourhoods located near slums are especially likely to be victimised by property offenders supports this line of analysis (Boggs 1965; Chamberlain and Hipp 2015). But it is not a theoretical path I wish to pursue here.

The theoretically important criminogenic effect of increasing concentrations of wealth is in enabling the constitution of new forms of illegitimate opportunity that are not available to the poor or the middle class. Wealth and power constitute opportunities that can be extremely lucrative. It is important to understand here that increasing wealth for the poor or the average income-earner does not constitute new illegitimate opportunities through wealth for exchange. Obviously, I have found Marx's distinction of value-for-use and value-for-exchange helpful here. In his *Economic and Philosophic Manuscripts*, use is associated with need:

'[E]very real and possible need is a weakness which will tempt the fly to the gluepot' (Marx 1973: 148). Also, every product that can be used 'is a bait with which to seduce away the other's very being, his money'. Up to the point where legitimate work generates only value-for-use for the worker (in meeting needs), the worker has no surplus. Up to this point, extra income is used, instead of invested in the constitution of illegitimate opportunities. But when surplus is accumulated (value-for-exchange rather than for use), it can be invested in the constitution of illegitimate opportunities.

A limitation of Cloward and Ohlin's (1960) analysis is that it tends to view illegitimate opportunities as a fact of society independent of the agency of the criminal actor—ready and waiting for the criminal actor to seize. This conception forgets the point that, if criminal actors are powerful enough, they can actively constitute illegitimate opportunities. This power is not totally explained by the control of surplus value; a youth offender can constitute a gang as a vehicle for collective criminal enterprises that would be beyond their grasp as an individual. But surplus value can be used to constitute criminal opportunities of an order that is not available to a poor young person. As Weisburd et al. (1991: 79) found in their systematic study of white-collar criminals in New York:

> The most consequential white-collar crimes—in terms of their scope, impact and cost in dollars—appear to require for their commission, that their perpetrators operate in an environment that provides access to both money and the organisation through which money moves.

Those with some spare capital can start up a company; the company can be used as a vehicle to defraud consumers and investors; the principal can siphon off funds into a personal account, bankrupting the company and leaving creditors stranded. They can set up bank accounts and shell companies in tax havens. But to launder dirty money, to employ the lawyers and accountants to evade taxes, they must have surplus to start with. And the more they have, the grander are the illegitimate opportunities they can constitute. When they become big enough, shares in their company can be traded publicly. They can then indulge in some unusually lucrative forms of insider trading and share ramping. If they become billionaires like Nelson Bunker Hunt and William Herbert Hunt, they can even try to manipulate the entire market for a commodity like silver (Abolafia 1985). On becoming oligopolists in a market, they can work with the other oligopolists to fix prices and breach other antitrust laws. If they become a monopolist, financial or political, a wide array of illegal predatory practices becomes available. The proposition is that capital can be used to constitute illegitimate opportunities; the more capital, the bigger are the opportunities. Obverse to my analysis of need, an egalitarian redistribution of wealth away from surplus for the rich in favour of increased wealth for the poor will not correspondingly expand illegitimate opportunities for the poor. This is because, in the hands of the poor, income is for use; it is not available as surplus for constituting illegitimate opportunities.

Other things being equal, the rich will prefer to stay out of trouble by investing in legitimate rather than illegitimate opportunities. But when goals are set with the expectation that they will be secured legitimately, environmental contingencies frequently intervene to block legitimate goal attainment. Powerful actors regularly have the opportunity in these circumstances to achieve the goal illegitimately. The production target cannot be achieved because the effluent treatment plant has broken down, so it is achieved by allowing untreated effluent to flow into the river late at night. Most capital investment simultaneously constitutes a range of both legitimate and illegitimate means of further increasing the wealth of the capitalist. The wealth that creates legal opportunities at the same time brings into existence illegal opportunities for achieving the same result. In this additional sense, investment creates criminal opportunities in a way that use does not. It is just that there is a difference in the way we evaluate illegitimate opportunities that are inherent in any legitimate investment compared with illegitimate opportunities that are created intentionally. Legitimate investments that bring about illegitimate opportunities are unfortunate side-effects of the mostly desirable processes of creating wealth. Intentionally created illegitimate opportunities are the main and intended effects of a mostly undesirable process of criminal exploitation. They are particularly undesirable when the illegitimate opportunities enable domination, because then freedom is reduced and crime is increased. Whatever the mix of desirable and undesirable effects of wealth shifted from the poor to the rich, the effects of theoretical interest here are expanded illegitimate opportunities for the rich. My main point is that surplus can be used intentionally to constitute illegitimate opportunities and to constitute domination—whether by setting up illegal traffic in arms or drugs or by setting up a tax-evasion scheme—in a way that income for use cannot when people depend on the use value of that income to survive.

The evolutionary ecology of expropriative crime

Cohen and Machalek's (1988) evolutionary ecology approach to expropriative crime has profound implications for crimes of the powerful. The first point in their analysis is that the returns from an expropriative strategy vary inversely with the number of others who engage in the same strategy. In nature, a behavioural strategy of predation is more likely to persist if it is different from that used by other predators. There is no 'best' strategy that will be adopted by every predator because it is the best; for a predator to opt for a strategy, it must be one that is not crowded out by others using a similar strategy. Minority strategies can flourish.

Extreme wealth fosters extraordinarily lucrative minority strategies. The wealthy and powerful can pursue illegitimate strategies that are novel and that excel because they cannot be contemplated by those who are not wealthy. Where there is no limit on what can be spent on an expropriative strategy, it can be designed to beat all alternative, less adequately funded strategies against which it must compete. This is why the most damaging and lucrative expropriative strategies are crimes of the powerful. Those who have no inhibitions against duck-shooting out of season, who need spare no expense on their artillery, for whom no strategy is too novel (even shooting other hunters), are likely to get the best haul of ducks.

Anyone can stage a bank robbery. These days bank robbery has detection risks, however, that make it an irrational form of illegitimate work. Sutherland (1983) explained that it is better to rob a bank at the point of a pen than at the point of a gun. The US Savings and Loans scandal of the 1980s suggested 'the best way to rob a bank is to own one'. Lure constituted by the anomie of warfare and transition to capitalism in the former Yugoslavia revealed that the best way to rob a bank is to control the banking system rather than individual banks—that is, to control the regulatory system of the central bank. This made possible an ingenious theft by the president of all the people's money held in all the banks, all the businesses and all the wallets of an entire society. The criminological imagination must attune to anomie created by capitalism, and to the evolutionary ecology of lure that continually invents new and bigger ways to rob a bank (Marsavelski and

Braithwaite 2018).[1] In this evolution, while many could try their hand at becoming a Bonnie or Clyde, few could buy a bank, few could order a bank to lend to their son at near-zero interest and insist later that the bank forgive the loan, and fewer still could criminalise a central bank and order it to print money for their personal use.

Cohen and Machalek (1988) theorise this in terms of the 'resource holding potential' (RHP) of the poor, meaning that they commit crimes that amount to 'making the best of a bad job'. The RHP of the rich, in contrast, allows them to 'take advantage of a good job'. The rich and powerful rarely resort to the illegitimate means that are criminal staples among the poor because they can secure much higher returns by pursuing legitimate means or illegitimate means to which the poor have no access. There is only limited direct competition between the powerful and the powerless criminal. Instead, they develop different minority strategies that reflect their different RHPs. Where there is direct competition, it is fragile. The small drug dealer can be crushed by the powerful organised criminal unless she finds a way of complementing him, picking up his crumbs or operating outside his area, instead of competing with him.

The other peculiar advantage powerful criminals have is in the domain that evolutionary ecologists call counterstrategy dynamics. Fast predators activate a selective force favouring faster prey and vice versa (Cohen and Machalek 1988). The expropriative strategy of conning consumers into buying dangerous or ineffective patent medicines was countered by the strategy of regulatory agencies seizing drugs that had not been through

---

1 This invention of a better way to rob a bank worked like this: 'After taking over a state, a political party announces an impending change to the currency. Citizens and businesses are urged to hand in their old currency for credits in their bank accounts in the new money. The banks gather up all the old currency for destruction. Instead of destroying it, the political leadership sends truckloads of old currency to other countries that are still trading it—to exchange it for hard currency. This allows all the cash from all the wallets and purses of all citizens, from every business in the country, from the vaults of all its banks, to go into the pockets of ruling party leaders and cronies. This is not an imaginary crime strategy. It was executed by the leaders of Slovenia, then Croatia, in 1991 at the outset of the Yugoslav Wars through the conversion of Yugoslav dinars (that were supposedly all destroyed). As an innovative strategy of predation through the banking system, this created the initial fortunes of some of the wealthiest businessmen in post-war Yugoslavia. A theoretical insight that follows from seeing this innovation in bank crime is the need to connect anomie theory to the ecological theory of crime. Durkheim (1952 [1897]) helps us to see that crime is fostered by conditions of collapse of normative order: anomie. When it is no longer clear what the rules of the game are, nor even who should enforce those rules, new levels of criminal innovation become possible that were impossible before the onset of anomie. War enables that perfect storm of anomie, as we see in the former Yugoslavia of the 1990s. One senior journalist who had researched the Yugoslav dinar scandal said Yugoslavia at that time was an "El Dorado of anarchy"' (Marsavelski and Braithwaite 2018: 124).

a pre-marketing clearance. The most ruthless participants in the industry used their considerable resources to short-circuit such counterstrategies, however. They bribed those responsible for pre-marketing clearance decisions; they paid unethical researchers to produce fraudulent evidence that their products were safe and efficacious (Braithwaite 1984; Dukes et al. 2014). To indulge in this kind of thwarting of the counterstrategy process requires abundant resources of a sort unavailable to indigent criminals. Box (1983: 59) diagnosed how the greatest comparative advantage of corporate criminals 'lies in their ability to prevent their actions from becoming subject to criminal sanctions in the first place'. Pontell and Calavita's (1992) case study of the Savings and Loans crisis is illustrative: the counterstrategy relevant there was deregulatory reform of the financial sector extracted from the state in the early 1980s, thus rendering banker power less accountable. This was how it became true that the best way to rob a bank in that era was to own one (Black 2005).

Braithwaite (1979) developed in some detail the proposition that unaccountable power that has accrued to the most wealthy is what explains how to get away with crimes of extreme seriousness. Power corrupts and unaccountable power corrupts with impunity. Sorokin and Lunden (1959: 37) made a similar point:

> The greater, more absolute, and coercive the power of rulers, political leaders, and big executives of business, labor and other organisations, and the less freely this power is approved by the ruled population, the more corrupt and criminal such ruling groups and executives tend to be ... With a progressive limitation of their power, criminality of rulers and executives tends to decrease qualitatively (by becoming less grave and murderous) and quantitatively (by decreasing the rate of criminal actions).

The financial masters of our universe use their resources to ensure that their power is unaccountable. They benefit from a hegemony that renders their power corrupting. At its most basic level, only people in positions of power have the opportunity to commit crimes that involve the abuse of power. The more power they have, political and financial, the more abusive those crimes can be.

In this analysis, power and money are assets that can be exchanged, invested to generate more power. Hence, the crimes of someone like J. Edgar Hoover (Geis and Goff 1990) can be interpreted as motivated by an insatiable desire to accumulate more power for exchange. In contrast to the insatiable demands of a totalitarian ruler to control more totally or to rule more people and territory, the criminogenic powerlessness of the poor is bounded—mostly to control over the life of just one person: themselves.

My work with Aleksandar Marsavelski on the best way to rob a bank found that in this hierarchy of more lucrative illegitimate opportunities, the best opportunities require a combination of wealth and sufficient political capital to dominate the financial system.

Marsavelski and Braithwaite's (2018: 125–26) hierarchy of reinvention of lucrative ways to rob a bank includes:

1. Rob a bank at the point of a gun (Bonnie and Clyde).
2. Rob a bank at the point of a pen (Sutherland's insight).
3. Build a Ponzi banking structure that forces all depositors to pass on a higher liability to another until collapse when new depositors cannot be found (Charles Ponzi).
4. Use your power over the CEO of a bank to order payment of a large loan to your relative or crony at a ridiculously low interest rate (Republika Srpska's President Milorad Dodik).
5. Own a bank, then loot deposits (Charles Keating; US Savings and Loans).
6. Rob a bank at the point of a keystroke (Soviet scam over the Bank of Spain's gold bullion; robbing a bank in cyberspace).
7. Pull out money from the central bank by abusing your political power (Democratic Republic of Congo's Mobutu Sese Seko; Yugoslavia's Slobodan Milošević; Iraq's Saddam Hussein).
8. Mortgage the future wealth of a country you control to foreign powers; send offshore the proceeds from the loans for mortgaging that future (Democratic Republic of Congo's Kabila).[2]

---

2 'After a president like DRC's Mobutu has lost power because he looted foreign aid and loans, then looted the currency by printing bank notes, what does the next president do? Confidence in his country as a recipient of aid or loans was shot. His currency was worthless. What Mobutu's successors did to stay rich and stay in power was to promise military commanders' sovereignty over a section of the country and the enslavement of its people, or a sector of its natural resources, in return for using their soldiers to keep Mobutu's successors in power. This deal also involved giving the military commanders a personal share up-front of the future resources that would be looted in this mortgage of sovereignty. In this way, generals from the Rwandan and Ugandan army were given control of regions of DRC rich with diamonds, coltan and other resources, as were factions of the DRC's own national army and ethnic militias. As the armies that replaced Mobutu with the first President Kabila moved across the country conquering new territory, Laurent Kabila paid them' (Marsavelski and Braithwaite 2018: 128–29).

9. Create a bank that serves the dirty-money needs of the intelligence services of major powers; use the superpower protection to become the bank of choice for the world's leading corporate and organised criminals; then loot that bank (Nugan Hand; Bank of Credit and Commerce International [BCCI]).[3]

10. Structure derivatives to conceal the true state of the national debt of an entire country; use this opportunity to corruptly skim off wealth as you drive the country to bankruptcy (Goldman Sachs' scam for Greece's leaders).

11. Manipulate derivatives—for example, slice and dice the bad loans of banks in a sophisticated economy; misrepresent and sell the securitised bad loans to banks in less-sophisticated economies and other naive investors (longstanding scams that became visible after the 2008 Global Financial Crisis).

12. Change the currency; keep the new and sell all the old cash (Croatian Democratic Union's political leadership).

In 2020, we saw the culmination of a new, 13th strategy that I first observed during my 2019 fieldwork for Peacebuilding Compared in Lebanon. It is what the World Bank (2020) described as creating a 'deliberate depression' for an entire country. Elites in control of Lebanon's financial system moved their own assets into US dollars, then crashed the Lebanese currency, locked ordinary people's savings and small business assets into bankrupt banks and proceeded to buy the best real estate and the best business assets in the country extremely cheaply with their scarce US dollars. The Lebanese 1 per cent was able to make itself very rich by making the 99 per cent very poor. The Hezbollah leadership is one elite beneficiary of this strategy of criminalising the state and the financial system to intentionally cause a depression. Hezbollah is the most militarily powerful, and ultimately the politically decisive, minority actor in the country. Because Hezbollah does not depend on Lebanese banks for its income, it can use Iranian-sourced income to buy national assets cheaply in devalued Lebanese currency.

Braithwaite (1979) argued that if crime in the suites arises when privileged people have great wealth and power, and crime in the streets arises from others having little wealth or power, policies to redistribute wealth and power may simultaneously suppress both types of crime. If wealth

---

3   These cases are discussed in detail in Chapter 10.

and power are what enable a range of extremely harmful expropriative strategies that are distinctive to those at the top of the power structure, redistribution of wealth and power in favour of the ruling class will increase that which enables their crimes. This is the kind of redistribution that political leaders with a neoliberal ideology do and leaders of criminalised states also do. Redistribution of wealth and power away from the poor will worsen the 'bad lot' of which the best they might make is crime. It will further exacerbate the blockage of legitimate means, thereby increasing the attraction of illegitimate means for satisfying needs. And it will increase the alienation, the hopelessness, the live-for-the-moment desperation of those who feel they have no power over their own future.

Moreover, extremes of wealth and power increase the attraction for the rich to justify their exploitative position with exploitative and criminogenic ideologies not so unlike the caricature 'greed is good'. Historically, this has also been true of empires and land-grabbing states. White colonial elites in Australia and North America in the nineteenth century justified the greed of land-grabbing from indigenous owners, as one peace agreement after another was breached by the westward march of frontier wars. The justification was the myth that land theft and genocide would civilise the continent and its indigenous owners. This is Sorokin and Lunden's (1959: 44) belief induced by intoxicating power that those with power are 'chosen and anointed' to be above the ruled and above the rules. They are chosen to pick the fruits of anomie.

It may be that just as the criminality of the rich can be explained by the fact that they exploit, the criminality of the poor is accounted for by the fact that they are exploited. While the forms of crime that predominate at the two ends of the spectrum are sharply distinguishable minority strategies, they may be different sides of the same coin. This is the coin of inequality and domination. The inequality engenders the exploitation perceived by those who are exploited. And that same inequality engenders the exploiting legitimated for those who exploit. Exploitation and domination are what destroy the freedom of the poor and make the rich free to expropriate.

At both ends, criminal subcultures develop to communicate symbolic reassurance to those who decide to prey on others, to sustain techniques for neutralising the evil of predatory crime (Sykes and Matza 1957) and to communicate knowledge about how to do it. Underclass criminal subcultures in America collect, dramatise and transmit the injustices of a society dominated by whites and ruled by their oppressive criminal justice system. The subcultures of Wall Street rationalise exploitative behaviour as that which made America great, in the words of one iconic president born of those subcultures. Sorokin and Lunden (1959) pointed out that there can be an intergenerational aspect to these criminal subcultures. They quoted John D. Rockefeller's statement on the education of his sons: 'I cheat my boys every chance I get; I want them sharp. I trade with the boys and skin them and just beat them every time I can. I want to make them sharp' (Braithwaite 1979: 191). Sorokin and Lunden emphasised social selection. The chances of people getting into positions of power are greater if they are 'callous, unsympathetic, aggressively selfish, hypocritical, dishonest, and cynical manipulators of human relations' (Sorokin and Lunden 1959: 46). Geis (1967) discovered that in the General Electric Corporation, the selecting out of people with moral scruples against price-fixing from senior positions where price-fixing was demanded was one factor that made possible the heavy electrical equipment conspiracy that sent senior vice-presidents to prison.

Business subcultures of tax evasion are memory files that collect the injustices of the Internal Revenue Service (cf. Matza 1964: 102) and communicate resentment over the disproportionate tax burden shouldered by the rich. An oligopolistic price-fixing subculture under the auspices of an industry association communicates the social benefits of 'orderly marketing'; it constitutes and reproduces an illegitimate opportunity structure.

The focus of the discussion so far has been excessively on property crime. It need not have been. A business subculture of resistance to an occupational health and safety agency can foster methods of legal defiance, circumvention and counterattack that kill. The unaccountable power of a Stalin or Mao can be deployed to kill millions. A wealthy person can use their capital to establish a toxic waste disposal company that cascades the violence of cancer from illegally dumped chemicals. The resentment of a black person who feels powerless and exploited because of their race can be manifested by violent as well as acquisitive crimes. There are, however, some arguments about inequality that may have some special force in the domain of violent crime. To these we now turn.

The social structure of humiliation

Much crime, particularly violent crime, is motivated by the humiliation of the offender and the offender's perceived right to humiliate the victim. Inegalitarian and dominating societies—for example, patriarchal societies—are the most structurally humiliating.

Jack Katz (1988: 10) is a sociologist who stood with Sutherland in saying:

> Because of its insistence on attributing causation to material conditions in personal and social backgrounds, modern social thought has been unable either to acknowledge the embrace of evil by common or street criminals, or, and for the same reason, develop empirical bite and intellectual depth in the study of criminality by the wealthy and powerful.

Katz's insights reside in his analysis of violence or rage as 'livid with the awareness of humiliation' (1988: 23). Rage both recalls and transforms the experience of humiliation. The experience of a sense of righteousness is the stepping-stone from humiliation to rage; the embrace of righteous violence resolves humiliation 'through the overwhelming sensuality of rage' (Katz 1988: 24; see also Marongiu and Newman 1987). For Katz, it is not coincidental that intimate partner violence is often associated with taunting about sexual performance or innuendo of sexual infidelity. For patriarchal men, domestic homicide, according to Katz, can transform such sexual degradation 'in a last violent stand in defence of his basic worth' (1988: 26). Rage transcends the offender's humiliation by taking him to dominance over the situation and over his partner.

Katz's analysis of righteous slaughter is a useful complement to my rather instrumental analysis of opportunity and strategy in the past few pages. This is precisely because Katz has such a non-instrumental take on violence. He notes the frequency with which murderers cease an attack long before death and indeed in the midst of evidence of persistent life such as screams and pleas for mercy (Katz 1988: 32).

Violence transcends humiliation by casting the person perceived to have degraded the offender into an ontologically lower status. Mounted in a flurry of curses, the attack 'will be against some morally lower, polluted, corrupted, profanized form of life, and hence in honor of a morally higher, more sacred, and—this bears special emphasis—an eternally respectable realm of being' (Katz 1988: 36). Far from being a self-interested instrumental evildoer, the attacker is immersed in a frenzy of upholding the decent and respectable. Just as humiliation of the offender is implicated in the onset of his rage, so the need to humiliate the victim enables her victimisation.

Katz reached these conclusions from an analysis of several hundred criminal acts quite independently of similar conclusions reached by scholars of psychiatry. Kohut (1972) identified 'narcissistic rage' as a compound of shame and rage. Lewis's (1971) cases led her to conclude that unacknowledged shame and anger cause a feeling trap—an alternation between shame and anger that can produce explosive violence she calls humiliated fury. The work of Lansky (1984, 1987) and Scheff et al. (1989) similarly emphasises the importance of humiliation that is unacknowledged. Innuendo and underhanded disrespect more than overt insult open up a cycle of humiliation, revenge, counter-revenge and, ultimately, violence. Scheff (1987) identified two ways of reacting to scorn: shame or anger. But sometimes humiliated actors alternate between the two in what Scheff calls a shame–rage spiral.

Katz denies that material circumstances have anything to do with his conclusions about humiliation and rage. He is wrong here. Some societies and institutions are structurally more humiliating than others. For a black person, living in Apartheid South Africa was structurally more humiliating than living in Tanzania. Living in a prison is structurally more humiliating than living in an aged care home and the latter is more humiliating than dwelling in a luxury villa. Slavery is structurally more humiliating than freedom.

There was structural humiliation in the school systems I experienced as a child, where children were ordered linearly in the classroom according to their rank, with 'dunces' sitting at the front where the teacher could hit them. The seating arrangements and the blows were structurally humiliating for those who failed. Often the children subject to this humiliation at the front of my childhood classroom were Aboriginal boys. These were school systems where the truly disadvantaged were regularly afflicted with degradation ceremonies. There are structural alternatives— notably, Knight's (1985: 266) conception of redemptive schooling:

> A redemptive schooling practice would aim to integrate students into all aspects of school learning and not build fences around students through bureaucratic rituals or prior assumptions concerning student ability. A clear expectation from teachers must be that all students can be taught, and in turn an expectation

on the part of students that they can learn. A school succeeds democratically when everyone's competence is valued and is put to use in a variety of socially desirable projects. Indeed, the same may be said to hold for a good society.

More broadly, inegalitarian societies are structurally humiliating. It is structurally humiliating for the poor when parents cannot supply the most basic needs of their children, while at the same time they are assailed by the ostentatious consumption of the affluent. Where inequality is great, the rich humiliate the poor through conspicuous consumption and the poor are humiliated as failures for being poor and inconspicuous in their consumption. Both sides of this equation matter. Crime is enabled by both the propensity to feel powerless and exploited among the poor and the propensity of the rich to see exploitation as legitimate. Intersectionality in injustice is structurally humiliating.

Racist societies are structurally humiliating: In these societies, the despised racial group is viewed as unworthy of respect, the superordinate group humiliates the subordinate group and the subordinate group feels daily degradation. Such racist oppression is criminogenic.

Patriarchy is structurally humiliating: In patriarchal societies, women are dominated, men do not respect dominated women and women are humiliated by men. However, it is common in patriarchal societies for women to not feel humiliated. Similarly, it is not uncommon for oppressed racial minorities and for the poor to not feel humiliated in racist and inegalitarian societies. That can be about the dignity of agonistic resistance by women or racial minorities (Mouffe 2013). Or humiliation can be bypassed by undignified submission to hegemony. Gramsci's (1971) concept of hegemony does useful work here. It often happens that part of the success of domination by the superordinate group is in persuading many in the subordinate group that they should accept the ideology of superordination; they identify their own interests with those of their rulers. Their subordination is regarded as something natural rather than something to resent and resist (see also Scheff 1990).

One path to understanding why women commit less crime than men in the face of oppression is understanding why it is that women sometimes feel less humiliation or rage, and more shame and guilt, than many men. Braithwaite (1989) and this book attempt to address this. Shame and guilt are more likely when hegemony is present; humiliation and anger, when it is not (see further Scheff 1990).

The fact that patriarchy does not engender feelings of humiliation and rage among many women does not absolve patriarchy of criminogenesis. Remember, there are two sides to our story. The hypothesis is that humiliation both motivates violence among those humiliated and enables violence among those who humiliate. Hence, the degradation of women countenanced by men who do not grant women dominion enables rape and violence against women on a massive scale in patriarchal societies, not to mention commercial exploitation of the bodies of sex workers by actors who might ambiguously be labelled white-collar criminals. Empirical work on homicides by men against women confirms that homicide can be viewed as an attempt by the male to assert 'their power and control over their wives' (Wallace 1986: 126; Polk and Ranson 1991). In passing, it is important to note that willingness to humiliate women should, according to the theory, be more profound among men who see themselves as having been humiliated—as a black person humiliated by whites, as a war veteran humiliated by protesters against the war back home and by an authoritarian military.

Ageist societies are structurally humiliating: Where the very young or the very old (or the disabled) are not worthy of respect, where they do not enjoy the dominion accorded humans at the peak of their powers, the young and the old (or people with disabilities) will be abused, including physically—both in the home and in institutions specialising in their care (schools and care homes). While the very old rarely have the physical power to transcend their humiliation with violent rage, the young do, especially as they become older, stronger young males. The physical powerlessness of the very old makes their abuse the most invisible and insidious in complex societies. As Joel Handler (1989) said, even prisoners can riot, but the frail aged have neither muscle nor voice. The evidence indicates that the very young, and particularly the very old (Fattah and Sacco 1989: 174–77), are also vulnerable and attractive targets for consumer fraud.

Ageist and gendered exploitation interact in important ways. We see this in studies of elder abuse, which report that more than 70 per cent and sometimes more than 80 per cent of the victims of elder abuse are women (Hudson 1986). Historically, we see it in the victimisation of older women labelled as witches in the sixteenth and seventeenth centuries (Stearns 1986: 7) and still today (Atata 2019).

This is why aged care regulatory institutions are particularly critical to a less-dominated society, as was evident in the reckless loss of millions of residents of aged care homes during the 2020–21 Covid crisis. Care home residents accounted for 80 per cent of Australia's 2020 Covid-19 deaths, but preventability was palpable in the fact that 97 per cent of aged care facilities had excellent infection control and zero Covid deaths at the time of writing. Aged care regulation has helped create a freer society in which fewer old people are physically tied up or chemically restrained every day of their lives (Braithwaite et al. 2007).

Despotic societies are structurally humiliating: Despotic societies are, by definition, disrespectful of the dominion of ordinary citizens. They are societies that trample on the dominion of individual citizens to serve the interests of the ruling party. Atrocities by the state are enabled by disrespect for its citizens. The disrespect that degraded citizens in turn accord to the laws of despotic states is also criminogenic. This is an ancient anomie effect. Institutions for regulating political accountability are keys to tempering despotism, which will be discussed in the next few chapters.

Retributive societies are structurally humiliating:[4] These are societies in which wrongdoers are viewed as unworthy of respect, as enjoying no right to have their dominion protected, as worthy of humiliation. The degraded status of prisoners and arrestees in retributive societies frees those responsible for their daily degradation from restraints to respect their dominion. The result can be deaths in custody and systematic violence directed against 'black lives that do not matter'. We can see this in Stotland's (1976: 88) interpretation of the slaughter of prisoners at Attica: 'For both troopers and guards, [a] sense of competence, violence and self-esteem … are linked.' 'A person's self-esteem can be threatened by failure [and] insults' (Stotland 1976: 86; see also Scheff et al. 1989: 187; New York State Special Commission on Attica 1972). In another study, of the 1970 killings by National Guardsmen at Kent State University, Stotland and Martinez (1976: 12) reached the same conclusion:

> Events … leading up to the killings were a series of inept, ineffectual, almost humiliating moves by the Guardsmen against the 'enemy' … The answer to these threats to their self-esteem, to their sense of competence, was violence … Another aspect … which added to

---

4   Retributivism may not seem to be a dimension of inequality, but Braithwaite and Pettit (1990) argued that under retributive policies, 'just deserts' tends to be imposed successfully on the poor and unsuccessfully on the rich.

> the threat to the self-esteem of the Guardsmen [was that] during their presence on ... campus ... the students insulted Guardsmen ... [and the Guardsmen] were not in a position to answer back. Their relative silence was another humiliation for them.

Scheff et al. (1989) discussed cases of collective violence like Attica as illustrating the 'humiliation of the inmates' (such as forcing prisoners to crawl through mud) documented in the report of the New York State Special Commission on Attica (1972). But the prison officers were also humiliated by the assertion of inmate power and the recognition their superiors in the prison administration gave to prisoners' demands (treating them 'as if they were equals'). Prison and police inspectorates, independent ombudsmen, independent anticorruption commissions and human rights commissions are particularly critical institutions for regulating the dominations of retributivism we will discuss.

When two parties each stigmatise the other, on both sides, stigmatisation can enable one's own violence and provoke the violence of the other. Braithwaite (1989) and Ahmed et al. (2001) developed the criminogenic consequences of stigmatisation. Humiliation means disrespectful disapproval. Stigmatisation is humiliation that is sustained over an indefinite period. Stigmatisation fosters crime by increasing the attraction of criminal subcultures to the stigmatised; I have also concluded that humiliation directly provokes violence. Here, I have sought to suggest that stigmatisation not only encourages crime by those stigmatised; it also enables crime to be targeted against those stigmatised. For example, carers for the aged who have stigmatised images of the elderly are more likely to be found among those who abuse their old folk (Phillips 1983).

Summarising the empirical hypotheses

Nations risk more crime and less freedom the more they are unequal in wealth and power, racist, patriarchal, ageist, despotic and retributive. To the extent that hegemony works to convince subordinated fractions of the population that their oppression is natural rather than humiliating, these effects may be attenuated; we see evidence of feeling ashamed rather than feeling humiliated, of quiescence rather than resistance, perhaps more inwardly directed rather than other-directed violence, self-harm more than assault. The prediction of the theory, nevertheless, is that even where hegemony is strong, inequality may still have negative effects on crime because: a) hegemony will never be total, and b) hegemony undermines feelings of being exploited without undermining the ideology of exploitation that enables the victimisation of the exploited. These hypotheses are not banal; they cut against the grain of influential accounts of crime—for example, the accounts of Sutherland, Katz and others that materialist explanation does not work, the account that a high crime rate is a price we pay for freedom, the account that retributive crime-control policies will have crime-reducing deterrent effects.

It may be that when humiliation is deeply structured into a social system, it is not only the subordinated who suffer frequent humiliation. In a class system dripping with motivation to conspicuously flaunt wealth, or a school system driven by ranking in the class and between schools, dropping from number one to number two can be humiliating. Merton (1968: 190) saw this point, quoting a well-to-do Hollywood resident of the 1930s: 'In this town, I'm snubbed socially because I only get a thousand a week. That hurts.' We also saw this with the Attica riot: in a social system that totally subordinates prisoners, the very willingness of the administration to negotiate with them was humiliating to prison officers.

This two-way street is perhaps most vivid in the domain of gender and sexuality. Patriarchy is often manifested as measuring the worth of women against a yardstick of youthful physical beauty, while machismo is about male domination of women through the sexual conquest of large numbers of beautiful women by alpha males. Needless to say, societies in which success is so measured are structurally humiliating for women, who inevitably lose their youth and who resent being used as a score. But when resentment and humiliation are structured into sexuality, the male is also at risk. Katz's (1988) work shows how women can taunt men for their poor sexual performance, for being a loser economically and how violence can be unleashed when they do so.

One key to a feminist criminology of some explanatory power is to understand the relationship between gender and contrasting types of shaming. The sexually stratified structure of shame is one reason women kill less than men (Braithwaite 1989; but see recent evidence on the contestation of such hypotheses in Scheuerman and Keith (2022)). The sexually stratified structure of humiliation is why when women do kill, it is rarely other women (Zahn 1980: 125; Katz 1988; Polk and Ranson 1991).

Katz (1988: 312–13) makes much of the 'badass' who takes pride in a defiant reputation as bad:

> The badass, with searing purposiveness, tries to scare humiliation off; as one ex-punk explained to me, after years of adolescent anxiety about the ugliness of his complexion and the stupidness of his every word, he found a wonderful calm in making 'them' anxious about his perceptions and understandings.

For a badass, pride that transcends humiliation might just as well be the badness of vandalism, theft or insider trading as the badness of violence. This has been a repeated theme in street-corner criminological research. We have seen its articulation in Albert Cohen's (1955) reaction formation. Humiliation at school brings about a status problem for the children who fail in a competitive school system. This problem is solved collectively with other students who have been similarly humiliated through a status system with values that are the exact inverse of those of the school. This inverted status system is one in which the delinquent is guaranteed some success.

Tittle connects to property crime the idea of being humiliated and dominated and wanting to dominate. He draws quotes from ethnographies of burglars such as the following: 'As I rifled through those people's most private possessions, I felt a peculiar power over them, even though we'd never met' (Tittle 1995: 193). Benson (1990) has shown the importance of humiliation and rage among convicted white-collar property offenders. The adjudication of their cases engendered anger and rage as well as shame and embarrassment. The way humiliation unfolded meant that anger usually won out over shame as a way of dealing with the situation. The likely result of feeling unfairly stigmatised, according to Benson, is reduced commitment to the legitimacy of the law. In this sense, Benson concludes, a justice system based on reintegrative shaming is less likely to be counterproductive than one based on stigmatisation.

This chapter has argued that it would be perverse indeed to interpret its humiliation analysis as only a story about the explanation of common violence in the streets. In the same year that Sutherland introduced white-collar crime into our lexicon, the most organised criminal of the century set the world alight. His name was Adolf Hitler. Scheff (1987: 147) points out: 'Every page of Hitler's *Mein Kampf* bristles with shame and rage.' Indeed, Hitler's appeal was of humiliated fury—an appeal that struck a responsive chord with many German people who felt they had been tricked and humiliated at Versailles, defeated by those whom Hitler called 'traitors, communists and Jews'. War crimes are partly about blocked legitimate opportunities to achieve national economic objectives. But they are also about being humiliated, wanting to humiliate and fear of being humiliated on both sides of international conflicts.

> There is fear of defeat and fear of humiliation. There is the great fear of being seen as a loser. It could be argued that the reason the British war fleet was sent to the Falklands in 1982 was really the fear of humiliation. The preservation of a self-image on a personal or national level is extremely important and fear of losing that image is a strong motivator. Indeed, Enoch Powell goaded Mrs Thatcher from her right flank in the House of Commons with exactly this reproach: how could she, of all people, stand for this Argentine insult? (de Bono 1985: 145)

When Saddam Hussein broadcast his appeal of 10 August 1990 to all Arabs, humiliation was a repetitive element of his text:

> Rise up, so that the voice of right can be heard in the Arab nation. Rebel against all attempts to humiliate Mecca. Make it clear to your rulers, the emirs of oil, as they serve the foreigner; tell them, the traitors, there is no place for them on Arab soil after they have humiliated Arab honour and dignity. (Braithwaite 1991: 54)

The macrocriminology of this section can be seen to integrate four ideas theoretically:

1. the reasoning individual (the strategist) and the reasoning collectivity (the corporate strategist)
2. the somatic, the body, emotions (humiliation, rage, shame, forgiveness, love, respect)
3. the micro-interaction (the degradation ceremony, the assault, the proffering of forgiveness, apology, the ceremony to decertify deviance)
4. the macro, the structural (relations of production, patriarchy).

Each of these four levels actively shapes, enables and constrains each of the others.

Katz failed to go beyond the interface between the compelling force of emotions and individual reasoning in the micro encounter. It is the failure for which an earlier generation of microsociologists was so eloquently condemned by Taylor et al. (1973). Why can we not put these elements together with the legacy of Sutherland to make criminology one of the best exemplars we have in the social sciences of how to do social theory and praxis? It is within our grasp to constructively bring together normative and explanatory theory. It is possible to have an explanatory theory that illuminates the mutual shaping that occurs among reason, emotion, microprocess and macro-structure.

Bringing the middle manager and the middle class back in

The results of Farrall and Karstedt's (2019) pathbreaking study of middle-class crime do not fit comfortably with this analysis of crimes of the powerful and crimes of the powerless. Across 25 European countries, they found that crimes of the middle class were a bigger problem in more equal societies. Societies with the more social democratic welfare-state legacies advocated in this book (such as the Nordic countries, Germany, Austria and the Netherlands) had the more virulent middle-class crime. Crimes of the middle class were fewer in more unequal societies such as Turkey, Portugal and Poland. These data pose a challenge to the politics of equality in pursuit of a low-crime society. Farrall and Karstedt also make the point that less equal societies such as Turkey, Portugal and Poland have a smaller middle class that proffers less lure to criminal entrepreneurs such as scammers. Farrall and Karstedt use their data to diagnose middle-class 'market anomie' as being significantly driven by those middle-class targets who are victimised a lot and perpetrate a lot of their own little scams against insurance companies, padding claims against tax authorities and more, in a world about which they are legally cynical.

Hence, comparatively equal societies like Germany or the Nordic countries that appear to be quite low-crime societies are actually societies that have a growing pool of middle-class criminal perpetrator-victims. Farrall and Karstedt's (2019: 238) insight is that the middle class has access to a number of illegitimate means that are blocked for the poor but that are not sufficiently alluring to tempt upper-class criminals. At the time of Farrall and Karstedt's twentieth-century data collection, most poor people did not have access to the internet to commit petty crimes that use or involve victimisation via the internet. Internet crime was only beginning to become widespread during their research. Access to the internet, however, almost doubled for those in the high-victimisation and high-offending group (Farrall and Karstedt 2019: 124). A large problem with middle-class targeting was non-internet scamming by telephone. This has also become more complex in inequality terms as telephone scamming radically internationalised this century.

Chapter 3 discussed Jamaica as a country with one of the highest homicide rates. We saw this was driven by unusual rates of gang killings perpetrated in Jamaica and in the United States, Canada and the United Kingdom by mobile Jamaican gang members expanding their drug and other illicit markets offshore and internationalising their reach in ordering murders. Jamaica is also a society with a high rate of property crime, but by far the largest part of it targets middle-class Americans and Canadians. In the late twentieth century, many call centres were established in what was then the low-violence area of Jamaica on the opposite side of the island from Kingston—for example, the tourist safe havens around Montego Bay where English-language skills were well honed for speaking to American tourists. Entrepreneurial local supervisors of call centres who gave out lists to their callers to ring in the United States had the bright idea of setting up their own scamming. They would steal the Walmart list, for example, and direct their scam callers to suitable targets. They would say the US target had won a Mercedes Benz in the national Walmart draw for good customers based on their sales dockets. If a target was on the west coast, the caller would say it had to be collected on the east coast. When a financially comfortable elderly target said that would be hard for them, they were offered the service of Walmart organising delivery by a person driving it across the country for some hundreds of dollars. Paying that money was the scam. For those triaged as suitably plump, soft targets, there was another scam when a call would come back to the target saying that the Walmart Mercedes was a scam; the new caller was a private investigator who could get their money back if they paid them! So, the class dynamic here had some complexity. Middle-class Americans were scammed by poor Jamaican callers working for rich criminal call centre entrepreneurs.

I draft this chapter at the time of the Covid-19 pandemic when the darknet scams *du jour* are products to save the planet's middle classes from Covid touted on markets like White House, Empire, DarkMarket and DarkBay. This ranges from facemasks pilfered from national health system stocks to antivirals, repurposed medicines and vaccines allegedly diverted— perhaps some actually diverted—from clinical trials for experimental vaccines promising Covid prevention (Broadhurst et al. 2020a). Vaccine dose offers were priced as high as US$16,000 during mid-2020. This kind of victimisation of the global middle class, which Farrall and Karstedt (2019) document, is perhaps a far more dangerous crime problem than the petty financial rip-offs they count by middle-class perpetrators who have limited capabilities for mobilising the organisational imperatives for high-value modern crime. As with child pornography or the trafficking of children on the darknet, darknet crime is more dangerous crime because it endangers lives globally.

Perhaps the greatest emerging contemporary crime risk to human life is not Covid fraud but aggressive marketing on the darknet of fentanyl—the unusually potent, cheap, compact opioid—as part of a 'revolution in the distribution of illicit drugs' (Broadhurst et al. 2020b). The names of the biggest darknet fentanyl markets Broadhurst et al. found dripped with the commodified domination of market anomie: Dream, Berlusconi, Wall Street, Empire, Valhalla. Terrorism promoted on the darknet that empowers cybercrime to trigger an accidental nuclear war—say, between India and Pakistan—or more directly deadly terrorist tools of mass destruction that go beyond hacking kits, are perhaps even bigger long-run threats, as discussed later in this book. The masterminds of the darknet are so dangerous because they orchestrate 'a cornucopia of new criminal opportunities' enabled by technological innovation (Shover et al. 2003: 490). Let us illustrate further with the Jamaican case on the violent side of why middle-class victimisation may be the bigger crime problem than Farrall and Karstedt's (2019) middle-class fightback financial crimes.

Sadly, the Jamaican property crimes against the global middle class contributed greatly to the violence of Jamaica and the criminalisation of the Jamaican state. Montego Bay's regional scammers made so much money that they found it difficult to launder. When they used gang contacts for help with money-laundering, the gangs would find it more profitable to raid the premises where scammers had millions of dollars hidden under the floorboards of their own or their relatives' homes. The scammers responded by hiring large numbers of their own gunmen. Gang wars were fought between them and the old gangs, to the point where areas around Montego Bay became the parts of Jamaica with the highest homicide rates. Corrupt police were also attracted to the scammers' cash; they would also raid their premises, threatening to steal their cash and shut them down unless they paid large protection payments to the police commander. They would also sometimes imply a police assassination threat, as police assassinations of gang leaders in Jamaica have been common. I was told in 2019 by a very senior Jamaican police commander of a call he received from an 'underworld informant' late on a Friday after the banks had closed. The call named a police superintendent who had abused an undertaking of police protection to a scammer. The superintendent raided and stole drugs from the scammer (who had diversified into drug trafficking). The police superintendent had been informed that he 'would be killed by the end of the weekend if he did not hand over US$50 million'. My fieldwork notes continue:

> [The senior police leader] said who can find $50 million over the weekend when the banks are closed? Well, if he can't he will be dead was the reply, full stop. Late on Sunday [the senior police leader] got another call from this underworld figure to say that the $50 million had been paid and the superintendent would be free to show up at work on Monday. Apparently, [the superintendent] called around various criminals with stacks of hidden cash and together they lent him the $50 million. It is also presumed he would be able to pay it off reasonably quickly after selling the drugs he had seized, perhaps combined with other assets and future illegal income streams. [The senior police leader] called [this superintendent] and said there is a rumour that a certain [unnamed] superintendent had paid this $50 million. [The superintendent] said he had heard the rumour, too, but he did not think it was true! (Peacebuilding Compared Jamaica interview 091903)

This example from high-crime Jamaica is laboured to make the point for the class dynamics analysis that much crime in the contemporary global system comes from little places where very rich crime bosses hire poor people to be criminal foot soldiers and criminalise powerful or murderous state officials to be their minders in their business of scamming the world's middle class. This consolidates Jamaica as a criminalised state rife with criminalised markets that diversify. Jamaica's class dynamics are complex and international but are fundamentally driven by wealthy people who exchange accumulated wealth for contract murder and state corruption and who are attracted by the lure of the American middle class as plump targets. Today, the lure is less bank vaults than personal middle-class bank accounts subject to weak internet guardianship—a lure that can be harvested with systematic criminal organisation by those with the capital and ruthlessness for a startup.

The accumulation of wealth, power and gunmen for exchange is still at the heartland of this macrocriminogenesis. We cannot understand these dynamics from the quantitative analysis of national crime numbers. So let us turn to the lessons from international multisite ethnography on how the organisational class dynamics of inequality and crime work down the class structure to the middle class. At the macrolevel, my analysis must be troubled by Farrall and Karstedt's (2019) results, but at the same time, it remains motivated to explore the macro-dynamics of how inequality in markets is implicated in the targeting of the large and growing pool of middle-class victim-perpetrators of market anomie.

My ethnographic research has shown that one of the many ways that inequality drives criminality down the class structure is by a more dominant person or organisation enrolling a less dominant person or organisation to do their dirty work. The research for *Corporate Crime in the Pharmaceutical Industry* (Braithwaite 1984; Dukes et al. 2014) showed this at the level of just one step down from the commanding heights. That fieldwork discovered three American Big Pharma corporations that had vice-presidents with strange job titles. When I inquired of their colleagues what these titles meant, I was told they were the 'Vice-President Responsible for Going to Jail'. This meant their job was to protect the CEO and board from the taint of knowledge of criminality. The buck was designed to stop with them rather than with the CEO. Lines of accountability were drawn so the finger of responsibility would point to them. After a period of loyal service as the vice-president responsible for going to jail, they would be promoted sideways to a safe vice-presidency.

Insider exposés of the power politics of various US administrations since President Richard Nixon have shown that plausible deniability also works in the White House for crimes like assassinations, torture or ordering illegal covert operations against political adversaries. White House staff likewise accept responsibility in return for political rewards that might come later. They protect the president from the taint of knowledge after being told to 'do what you have to do to fix this'. This is very much what Lord Acton meant when he said that power corrupts, and absolute power corrupts absolutely.

Braithwaite's (1984) research showed that Big Pharma would routinely hire contract laboratories to do some of their more fraudulent tests of the safety and efficacy of drugs. They would hire both reputable and disreputable university professors to test their products. If the most reputable professors came up with encouraging results, theirs were the data they would highlight. If these reputable professors generated discouraging results, their corporate sponsors would often suppress these results or fund the researchers to go away and collect a bigger sample. Meanwhile, they would highlight results from disreputable professors who in many cases got rich by fabricating results to please their benefactor. We have seen the same dynamic of domination driving criminality down the power hierarchy in the financial sector, with bankers paying huge bonuses to traders for getting results without wanting to know the lies or the dirty deeds done to get those results.

My work showed that this runs right down the organisational hierarchy of capitalism, from high finance and the White House to low-level used-car frauds or tiny trucking companies that dispose of waste. A reputable chemical corporation contracts out disposal of toxic materials to a waste disposal company that, being controlled by organised crime, is not particularly fussy about environmental protection laws (Raab 1980). Leonard and Weber (1970) showed how oligopolistic control over the supply of new cars by the US 'Big Three' manufacturers in the 1960s allowed them to impose sales quotas on their franchised dealers, who were then forced to turn to consumer fraud to move their cars in sufficient volume to stay afloat. General Motors did not perpetuate the frauds, which included 'accessories not ordered but "forced" on buyers, used cars sold for new, engines switched in cars, excessive finance charges, automotive repair overcharges, [and] "fake" repair diagnoses' (Leonard and Weber 1970: 415–16). However, General Motors was, in Taft's (1966) terms, a 'dangerous person' setting economic conditions that had the effect of driving subordinates into crime. Farberman (1975: 456), in a participant-observation study of automotive dealers, confirmed Leonard and Weber's conclusion. These are crimes of very middling people in the car industry who are often on the edge of bankruptcy. The criminality nevertheless pushes from the top down to middling organisational power. These are criminalised markets that do much more damage than the individual middle-class crimes measured in Farrall and Karstedt's (2019) data.

A limited number of oligopolistic manufacturers who sit at the pinnacle of an economically concentrated industry can shape economic policy to create a market structure that drives lower-level dependent industry participants to engage in patterns of illegal activity. Denzin (1977) found similar criminogenic market pressures at work in the liquor industry (see also Needleman and Needleman 1979). These pressures on responsibility for illegality percolate downwards within organisations as well as between them. While used-car sales managers are put under enormous pressure by quotas imposed on them by the distributor, these pressures are passed on to salespeople who, in turn, are set their quotas by the sales managers. If the salespeople do not meet the quota, they are dismissed. Hence, within used-car firms, it is often the salesperson who comes to the manager pleading for approval (or a blind eye) for the turning back of odometers (Braithwaite 1978). If you set up a cutthroat system, throats will get cut. The classic illustration of the passing of blame downwards in the class structure is with ethnographies of mine safety. A common strategy of mine owners was to put workers on piece rates based on the amount of coal or asbestos extracted in a day. Such a strategy often produced the situation of miners wanting to go into workings that were unsafe, or even doing so against the counsel of management (Scott 1974: 220; Braithwaite 1985).

Structured communication blockages occurred early in the study of corporate crime in the heavy electrical price-fixing conspiracy of the 1950s that saw vice-presidents of firms like General Electric and Westinghouse imprisoned, and the foreign bribery scandals of the 1970s that implicated firms like Lockheed and Exxon:

> One almost Kafkaesque ploy utilized to prevent an appeal by a subordinate was to have a person substantially above the level of his immediate superior ask him to engage in the questionable practice. The immediate superior would then be told not to supervise the activities of the subordinate in the given area. Thus, both the subordinate and the supervisor would be left in the dark regarding the level of authority from which the order had come, to whom an appeal might lie, and whether they would violate company policy by even discussing the matter between themselves. By in effect removing the subject employee from his normal organizational terrain, this stratagem effectively structured an information blockage into the corporate communication system. Interestingly, there are striking similarities between such an organizational pattern [for price-fixing] and the manner in which control over corporate slush funds deliberately was given [in the 1970s] to low-level employees, whose activities then were carefully exempted from the supervision of their immediate superiors. (Coffee 1977: 1133)

This may be the reason for the neglected result in the work of Cressey and Moore (1980: 48) that only 25 per cent of senior executives would say one had to compromise personal ethical standards to achieve company goals, while 59 per cent of more junior executives said this. The increasingly transnational nature of business means that the possibilities for those at the top of the organisation to distance themselves from the dirty work has become ever more profound.

> Headquarters may insist that their subsidiaries meet certain profit (or other) goals, while at the same time making it clear that headquarters can hardly be intimately acquainted with the laws of foreign countries. Hence, under the guise of local autonomy (which may be hailed by local enthusiasts as throwing off the shackles of colonialism), the subsidiary may be forced to engage in crime for which they will be held responsible by their government. Meanwhile, headquarters (in New York, Tokyo or Rotterdam), while hardly pleased with the result (loss of income), nevertheless escapes criminal prosecution. (Gross 1978: 209)

On the other hand, Braithwaite and Fisse (1985) found that this was not the pattern during fieldwork at Japanese companies like Mitsui, Toyota, Nippon Steel, Sumitomo and Idemitsu Kosan (Japan's largest oil company at that time). Japanese top managers often took responsibility for something that was collectively decided at levels of the organisation below them.

Criminogenic tendencies for top managers to keep their own hands and consciences clean while contriving pressures that give those in more middle-class roles dirty hands are complemented by burgeoning legal cynicism bubbling up in the opposite direction from the middle class (Farrall and Karstedt 2019). Main Street did not like what it saw on Wall Street in 2008. It saw bankers who used to be risk managers who had become risk shifters—slicing and dicing loans they knew were bad, selling them off in chopped-up securities on the other side of the country or the other side of the Atlantic.

The middle class preferred the older world where bankers took responsibility for managing their risks. They reviled the ethics of playing pass-the-parcel banking until the music stops. One reason for the revulsion is that unsophisticated middle-class investors were so often the ones left holding the parcel. They longed for an era when bankers were respected people whom they might have trusted to keep the financial world of the middle class safe from shocks that might cost them their job and their home. A degree of middle-class and working-class loathing converged toward the ruling 1 per cent.

Farrall and Karstedt's (2019) data resonate with this middle-class resentment and humiliation. After Farrall and Karstedt's data collection, we saw so many middle-class citizens participating in the Occupy Wall Street movement. The 99 per cent—taken as fools by the 1 per cent, Wall Street, the bankers—for a brief historical moment had had enough. Not rich versus poor, but 99 per cent of us taken for fools, humiliated by the 1 per cent. This same wave of convergence that initially could be ridden by the left, later could be harnessed by forces of authoritarianism.

Universities are such important institutions for building a world with low levels of crime and domination. At the same time, nuclear and biological weapons and dangerously destabilising new technologies for cyberwar and for future space wars, and AI for racially biased facial recognition, have been invented by professors of my university and perhaps yours. This makes it vital for all of us who work in contemporary universities to view self-critically our complicity in grave crimes against humanity that our universities sometimes help Big Pharma, the military-industrial complex, states and others to execute. University academics count as just one kind of a wide category of middle-class professionals who manage to live dual lives as caring liberal professionals in how we do our part of our jobs on the one hand, and on the other as quiescent professionals in the face of deeply structured entanglements between our university and deep states or criminalised markets. Lifton's (1986) research on doctors in Nazi Germany documented how two-faced professional lives could be. Some doctors did do good things to cure the sick, but inside hospitals where terrible experiments were being done for the Nazi regime. Or kind doctors worked in institutions where some of the patients were headed for gas chambers or were starved of adequate nutrition. Lifton's doctors had an old self that was a caring and ethical professional self and an 'Auschwitz self' that was Nazi. They learnt techniques of 'numbing' themselves to victims' suffering. We find it easy to dismiss their pleas that they only did things to make lives that bit better for people, as we denounce them simply for working in a health facility associated with a gas chamber. Middle-class people might have little power or capability to prevent horrors; that does not excuse us from being self-critical of failures for not doing enough. Academics like me have been complicit in the face of suspicions that my university is unethically entangled with the military-industrial complex in ways that destabilise the planet and threaten the future of my grandchildren. We, too, like so many middle-class actors, complicitly succumb to numbing.

Contesting hegemony: An interim conclusion

The big-picture concern about middle-class complicity is that when it really matters it connects to larger patterns of state and market domination; likewise for the modestly paid middle manager of a Montego Bay call centre whose peccadillo is to look the other way when a list of phone contacts of well-heeled Americans is passed to someone not authorised to get it. Complicity with a criminalised market that corrupts the Jamaican police at the top and results in contract killings across three continents is the middle-manager complicity issue here.

With war crimes, corporate crimes and criminalised states, we have seen that crimes of commission rather than sins of complicity are the important issue and that these are enabled by concentrations of power and capital. One of the things concentrations of power and capital are recurrently deployed to deliver is moving accountability down the class structure to vice-presidents responsible for going to jail and more junior middle managers. Institutional tempering of that power is the central political challenge. We move on to consider it more deeply and widely in the next chapter.

It is an illusion that simply redistributing wealth or power away from the rich can fix corporate crime. It can help a little to limit it as the redistribution helps more markedly to reduce the crimes of the poor. Where inequality reduction can help a lot in crime reduction is with very extreme historical contexts of domination; leaders like Hitler, Mobutu or Kabila, who saw themselves becoming 'presidents for life', tend to criminalise the state—as do one-party states. Robber barons who monopolise markets tend to criminalise markets. Low levels of organised crime are problems most societies have and can manage. However, in those historical contexts when an organised crime group becomes so powerful that it can buy or terrorise any police officer or prosecutor, both markets and the state tend to become criminalised. Braithwaite and D'Costa (2018) found that crime–war–crime cascades have recurrently occurred throughout the modern history of South Asia, Africa and beyond when there is a criminalisation of the state and a criminalisation of whole economies through crony capitalism, 'deep states' (Filiu 2015) in which intelligence and security operatives hold the key, or 'shadow states' (Reno 1995, 1999) in which business tycoons who buy the state are more crucial. That danger is ever-present for any economy. Even the world's most successful economy has been at risk of falling under the control of robber barons during the very decades when it became the number-one economy (until antitrust and other Progressive Era reforms clipped their wings). Half a century later, in the middle decades of the twentieth century, the Mafia could shape the fortunes of the Democratic Party and even the Republican Party in some major US cities where it rather than the police was untouchable (until fear in the US establishment that maybe the Mafia did have something to do with the Kennedy assassinations became such a concern that the Mafia was brought to heal even in New York from the 1990s). The Kennedys, the most respected civil society leader in American history (Martin Luther King Jr) and the glitterati of Hollywood had a great deal to fear from the deep state during J. Edgar Hoover's long and criminal reign over the FBI. Even Edwin Sutherland's (1983) uncut exposé of elite criminality only appeared after he and Hoover were dead (Geis and Goff 1990, 1992). Once a figure like Hoover, the Mafia or robber barons are in charge of large chunks of the state or economy, it is too late. Monopolists of money power or state power must have their wings clipped before they become monopolists, even before they become oligopolists (in the way Mafia families and their 'commission' became American and Cuban oligopolists in the decades after World War II).

The saddest thing about the power of business cronies, shadow states or deep states is that they usually choose to back political leaders who will criminalise democracy. Braithwaite and D'Costa (2018) concluded that in 23 of their 39 case studies of Peacebuilding Compared armed conflicts, a root cause of war was democracy as a driver of domination. Our initial hypothesis had been quite the opposite—a democratic peace hypothesis— because it is true that democracies infrequently go to war with each other. Most of the innovations in how to criminalise democracy are historically recent. The corruption in the Global South that festered under Cold War proxy conflicts was one key incubus of innovation. Aspiring coup leaders did not need much encouragement to grasp the benefits of the innovations in how to corrupt a democracy devised by brilliant minds in the deep states of Moscow, Paris and Washington. Later entrepreneurship was stimulated by private strategists who could be hired by international business interests to destroy democracies, such as the criminal work of Cambridge Analytica (Berghel 2018; Wylie 2019).

This continues today. Paris decided that the peaceful exit of Gaddafi from power in Libya that African Union leaders were negotiating in response to an initially peaceful Arab Spring in 2011 was not what it wanted. France wanted a violent decapitation of the entire family regime, with Gaddafi killed rather than tried, allegedly because Gaddafi had made huge secret political contributions to French President Nicolas Sarkozy's election campaigns. US President Barack Obama reluctantly went along with the militarised French approach, against the advice of the Pentagon (Braithwaite and D'Costa 2018). As I first drafted this chapter in August 2020, the resultant destabilisation of the entire region around Libya, which the wise heads in the African Union had feared from a Libyan civil war, was producing a military coup in Mali and militants were planning for an invasion of the capital of Chad. Evidence of Russian masterminding of the Mali coup to cash in on Obama's stupidity and Sarkozy's cupidity is already compelling. Two colonels were in Moscow for a training course for months before a coup they launched with masterful step-by-step execution as soon as they returned to Mali (Obaji 2020) followed by deployment of the Russian private military corporation, the Wagner Group, in Mali.

Paul Collier (2009) has systematically advanced the empirically grounded thesis that, in many societies, politicians win elections by methods that require them to misgovern. In particular, to survive, they are required to dismantle the separation of powers. Collier's research concludes that a democracy without checks and balances conduces to corruption and state criminality—and that prevents societies from lifting themselves out of 'the bottom billion'. Misgovernance driven by criminalisation of the state is also a problem for more economically successful societies that are still reasonably democratic, including India, where 34 per cent of the winners of the 2014 elections had criminal indictments pending against them (Fukuyama 2014: 547).

Separations of power help democracies prevent civil wars (see also Hegre and Nygård 2015). Unfortunately, however, 'it has proved much easier to introduce elections than checks and balances' (Collier 2009: 44). Moreover, 'taken together, the results on elections and democratisation are consistent: if democracy means little more than elections, it is damaging to the [good government] reform process' (Collier 2009: 45). The reason is that good government is not the most cost-effective way of benefiting from power. If you can get away with it, it is better (more economically rational) to buy elections, corrupt an electoral commission, intimidate or kill opponents, scapegoat a minority to cultivate majoritarian support, jail strong opponents for corruption and run against weaker ones, or simply miscount the votes. Once in government, you can reimburse these costs by pillaging the state. Incumbents do this by strategies that include embezzling billions from state coffers, favouring cronies and family members with government contracts and welcoming foreign investors when they make huge political contributions. If politicians try to win elections with good government, their capacity to benefit from power is much reduced. This is because good government means the rule of law and checks and balances on abuse of power that place limits on political opportunities to pillage the state.

The best way to accumulate power and money is to win elections by methods that require the winner to misgovern. We have seen that the best way to rob a bank is to misgovern banking institutions. Once in place—with the rule of law and checks and balances in place—good government may become a good way to win elections. Checks and balances create a healthy path dependency in this way. Being cursed with lootable natural resources does increase a country's susceptibility to corruption, corporate crimes of cronies and civil war. Yet, for countries with democratic institutions that include strong checks on the executive, the lure of resource rents does not predict corruption (Bhattacharyya and Hodler 2009). Comparatively free Botswana, which is developing and democratic with its diamond riches and its checks and balances of corporate and state power, is often advanced to illustrate the alternative path.[5]

The question of the wealth of the wealthy side of this equation is complex and paradoxical. More redistributive social democratic policies actually help economies to grow faster than societies with vast gaps between the rich and the poor (Quiggin 2019), as we discuss in the final chapter. We need an economy that restores more hope to the poor so they become stronger economic contributors, and an economy that better steers the high motivation of the wealthy to make their contributions in ethical, inclusive and productive rather than extractive ways (North et al. 2009). We do not achieve that by continuing to hand the rich the ever-larger slice of the cake their lobbyists demand. Likewise, the checks and balances of good anticorruption, antifraud and antimonopoly policies discussed

---

5   While Botswana's affliction with armed conflict is low, its homicide rate is not low, but average for Africa, even if considerably lower than the rest of southern Africa (UNODC figures).

in the following chapters also help economies to grow. Tempered power is more effective power for constituting flourishing economies and flourishing freedom.

Effective countering of corruption does clip the wings of those who accumulate the most power and most endanger the criminalising of states and markets. By clipping the wings of power to corrupt markets, we strengthen the capability of the market to award contracts to the most efficient rather than the most corrupt and the most ruthless. Averting the criminalisation of states and markets is the most important thing to prevent both the rich and the poor from becoming poorer and less free. It is the essence of preventing regress to a Hobbesian world of extreme violence. Constant political and civil society pressure for the redistribution and tempering of power is imperative to avert the criminalisation of states and markets. That is necessary because whenever the powerful have one of their privileges curtailed, they struggle and normally succeed in buying power with their surplus money to get privilege restored. This is the agonistic contestation story of the final chapter.

At the bottom, for the powerless, the central issues are closed opportunities, poverty and inequality of outcomes. Extremes of unchecked power engender crimes of exploitation enabled by the power of those who dominate. Such extremes also engender crime among those who so suffer from this domination that they feel they have little to lose and much to resent. Pursuit of less domination, more freedom and less crime of the powerless invites us to pursue an endless politics of agonistic contestation of hegemony and extremes of inequality.

6

Closing illegitimate opportunities by separating powers

Key propositions

- The way to control the abuse of power is not to destroy power but to share it and temper it.
- A separation of powers into the legislature, the executive and the judiciary is insufficiently complex for the contemporary division of labour.
- In the world of contemporary capitalism, the separation of private powers is as important as the separation of public powers.
- Corruption is controlled by continual reinvention of new ways of sharing separated organisational powers so that domination is always being put off balance.
- Separated institutional powers must be able to pursue power up to the point where the power of one is not so strong as to overcome the power of the others. Each separated power must be strong enough, however, to secure the exercise of its own power from being dominated by any other institutional power.
- Workplace democracy has an important niche in a separation of powers.
- The deterrence trap means that sanctioning of an organisation sufficient to deter it may risk crippling it and crippling innocent citizens who depend on it.

- One escape from the deterrence trap is to replace narrow, formal and strongly punitive responsibility (the 'find the crook' strategy) with broad, informal, weak sanctions.

- A second escape from the deterrence trap is to separate enforcement targeting from identification of the actor who benefits from the abuse of power. Together, this escape and the one above constitute a strength of weak sanctions.

- A third escape from the deterrence trap is to rely heavily on street-level bureaucrats who mobilise the 'relational state' and a wide mix of preventive strategies, each of which is weak as a standalone strategy, but strong when woven into a fabric of relational prevention. These street-level relational regulators can be police, state, self-regulatory or NGO inspectors, state or NGO welfare supporters or citizens who mobilise collective efficacy at street level.

- Separations of private power can be crafted to prevent corporate domination by a variety of well-tried techniques developed in this chapter (and summarised in Appendix I).

- Most fundamentally, crime prevention must shift its focus from hard targets who are committed to criminal subcultures to indirectly leveraging change through caring and prosocial actors who surround them—such as daughters, accountants or the priests of Mafia bosses or Wall Street predators alike.

Old insights on checks and balances on white-collar crime

If limiting the power of the powerful will reduce white-collar crime, how might this be achieved? The purpose of this chapter is to discuss some of the options that can be deployed to achieve a redistribution or tempering of power relevant to regulating the dynamics discussed in the preceding chapter. The strategies considered in this chapter and the next are not about destroying that power to get things done, but about sharing power to do so, and tempering power with checks and balances that make power less arbitrary and therefore less dominating. Then it is argued that tempered power can be more capable of getting good things done. All of that depends on contextual wisdom in the design of a rich plurality of separations of powers.

After diagnosing secrecy and unaccountable power in the executive branch of government, Lieberman's (1973) study of state illegality concluded that open government, making all government reports open to the public, freedom of information legislation that works, unlimited freedom of the press, ombudsmen, welfare-rights officers, limitations on police power and the right for citizens and interest groups to challenge government decisions in court were all important. As a check on the arbitrary exercise of power, he perhaps idealistically argued for a convention whereby reasons accompany all official decisions. This is idealistic perhaps, but political institutions like US congressional oversight committees and daily question time that ministers and the prime minister cannot avoid in Westminster systems are institutional examples of practical paths to demanding this result. In this chapter, these are all theorised as suggestions for more variegated and complex separations of powers (drawing heavily on Braithwaite 1997).

The suggestions for limiting white-collar crime put forward by people with wide experience investigating business crime involve limiting the power of those in positions with great illegitimate opportunities. A former president of the US Fidelity & Guaranty Co. made these suggestions long ago about limiting crime against companies by senior employees:

> It is generally good practice not to put one employee in complete charge of any one phase of administration where accounts receivable or payable are involved; for example, a credit manager should not be permitted to receive money and at the same time be in charge of posting and deposits and the preparation, mailing and distribution of monthly statements to clients. Cashiers or accountants should prepare the reports of receipts, which should be verified by someone else who would be responsible in turn for deposits and the posting of ledgers. Shipping and receiving, whenever possible, should be two completely separate operations and the responsibility of at least two individuals, each having to submit individual returns to the accounting office. Collection receipts and bank deposits should be verified as to their individual entries and not as to totals only. And this should be done by someone other than the person preparing the statement. Also, the monthly itemized statement should be verified with the bank. Spot-checks, audits, and inventories should be made at frequent intervals, and on a surprise basis, and the results compared with other results that will corroborate them or prove them in error. (Jeffery 1970: 19)

These are simple, practical examples of what I mean by sharing power to get things done rather than destroying it and sharing power in ways that enhance accountability. Jaspan and Black (1960) also drew on wide practical experience investigating white-collar crime during those early years of white-collar crime prevention. They made the following suggestions about how the limitation of the power of senior employees is central to a system of preventive management against white-collar crime:

> Protection from fraud demands that work be subdivided so that no employee has complete control over any record or transaction. Responsibility is allocated so that, without duplicate effort, an employee verifies the work of others in the normal course of his duties. This check and review which is inherent in any good system of control, greatly reduces the possibility that errors or fraud remain undetected for inordinate periods. The following are examples of how dual responsibility is maintained over typical work functions: 1. The preparation of the payroll and the payment of employees is handled by two different groups of employees, especially if employees are paid in cash. 2. Persons who maintain inventory records are not allowed to participate in the actual physical counting of inventory. 3. Persons approving payments on invoices or customers' bills are not allowed to participate in the actual receiving of supplies or merchandise. 4. Shipping records are matched against billings to customers by employees in two different departments. 5. Wrappers in stores compare items and prices on sales checks made out by sales clerks with the items to be wrapped. 6. Employees in sensitive positions are rotated from one job to another. For example, branch managers should be periodically shifted to different stores, warehouses, sales offices. Truck drivers' routes can be changed. Factory foremen and supervisors should be rotated. Payroll and accounts receivable clerks who handle alphabetical listings should be shifted from say a, b listings to e, f listings. (Jaspan and Black 1960: 248)

The next chapter describes contemporary markets in crime-prevention software; these have assisted such separations greatly. For example, in customs authorities, if one official records the value of a traded item for the calculation of customs duty, it is only possible for designated officials to change this, and for any official who does change it, this can only be done by an electronic signature being left behind identifying the person who made the change. Most of these measures are geared to catching people at middle levels of management who offend against the organisation itself. There always was clear evidence that the amounts of money involved in these kinds of offences increase dramatically as we move up the hierarchy of the firm (Jaspan and Black 1960: 51–52). This reality can be combined with a prosecution strategy of threatening the small fish responsible for small takings with prison unless they give up a bigger fish, then the bigger fish is offered the opportunity to give up an even bigger fish, until the sharks responsible for massive takings are netted. This was the strategy that enabled New York prosecutors to move up to potent penalties for the massive crimes of Michael Milken and other senior figures of the 'greed is good' frauds of late 1980s Wall Street.

Writers such as Sharpston (1970) suggested the solution to corruption was to change radically the situation in which power was concentrated in a few hands. Industrial democracy could help structurally to temper opportunities for crime enjoyed by managers. It could increase scrutiny of the behaviour of managers where opportunities for illegitimate discretion remained. If the accounts of a firm can be scrutinised under workplace democracy, the more democratic workplace poses a more constant risk that cheating will be unmasked by employees checking the books against the facts of workers' daily organisational experience, sometimes with professional accounting or union advice. A union grapevine can provide an intelligence network—gratis—that no government regulator could hope to rival. This may be why the unusual level of industrial democracy in the old underground coalmining industry in the United States and other western democracies resulted in unionised mines with elected union safety inspectors recording far lower rates of miners killed and injured (Braithwaite 1985). It is hard to escape the conclusion that this was because the institutionalisation of old-fashioned industrial democracy meant that miners, and especially their elected safety representatives, were looking over the shoulders of company safety and production executives. Workplace democracy is less fashionable today. If we want a society free from dominations that kill, making it fashionable again merits consideration as an evidence-based corporate crime-control strategy.

Employee and union empowerment to regulate corporate crime is just one variant of civil society empowerment to check regulatory capture and corruption by state regulators (Ayres and Braithwaite 1992: Ch. 3). Ayres and Braithwaite argue that it might not be so critical whether the third party that checks police corruption in the regulation of sex work is a sex workers' union, a feminist group or a religious group. If any or all of these have sight into regulatory encounters, shady deals and the re-emergence of modern slavery are at risk of being exposed. Obviously, environmental groups play a critical role here in tempering the abuse of environmental laws, as do consumer groups with consumer laws and shareholders' associations with securities laws. Ayres and Braithwaite (1992) said that secrecy and indirect victimisation made it hard for civil society scrutiny to work for the capture of tax authorities by the big end of town. Yet today Citizens for Tax Justice and Oxfam, among other organisations concerned with tax equity, do just this. And there is little doubt that some of their highest-profile targets, like Google and Facebook, are paying much more tax in many countries as a result of their campaigns and scrutiny (Dyreng et al. 2016; van der Walt forthcoming).

What old and new analyses—from microcorporate practices of separated corporate roles of receiving and paying accounts, separated roles of unions and management to separated roles of civil society and state regulators—have in common is an understanding of the principle of variegation in separations of powers. We can conceptually ratchet this up a notch to the institutionalisation of separations of powers. Unfortunately, we see a wide gap between what we learn inductively from waves of white-collar crime and institutional abstractions about the separation of powers in legal theory. These legal theory insights are derived from the thought of Montesquieu. The separations of powers described above for the prevention of white-collar crime must be continually adapting to counterstrategy dynamics (Cohen and Machalek 1988). Astute readers will have guessed what I am driving at here: stronger families, schools, welfare and religious institutions, as discussed by Messner and Rosenfeld, will hardly be enough to institutionalise the tempering of criminal power on Wall Street. That is not to say that some virtues instilled by good mothers and fathers, good schools and ethical religious leaders might not help to civilise markets. They really might. What is also needed is separations of political and legal powers that cut with rather deep specificity into structures of avarice. This is missing, or at best out of balance, in the writing of Messner and Rosenfeld (2013).

At a higher level of abstraction, the next chapter addresses the need for strong financial capital to be checked by strong human capital, social capital, recovery capital and restorative capital. This, in turn, is taken up another notch in abstraction in Chapter 8 to an ideology and an institutionalisation of strong markets, strong states, strong civil society and strong individuals each tempering the power of the other. Finally, the book seeks to retheorise institutional anomie theory as requiring state and nonstate institutions that are strong on provision (the welfare state, the infrastructure state), strong on redistribution (tax policy, multilateral aid policies that create opportunities for poor people in poor countries) and strong on regulation. Both nonstate and state institutions bake cakes, slice them and regulate the processes of baking and slicing. None of these roles of institutions should be neglected in the politics of institutional design. These are abstractions that assist rethinking towards a more ambitious version of institutional anomie theory in this book.

Neglect of concentrations of private power

The separation of powers may be the most central idea in the theory of institutional design, yet this is only true of thinking about public institutions. This chapter extends the relevance of the doctrine into thinking about checking the power of private institutions. The practice of separating powers dates at least from the ancient Babylonian Code of Hammurabi, when laws were carved in literal stone that would constrain the actions not only of subjects but also of the king. There follows a more or less cumulative history of the separation of powers sedimented in the institutions of contemporary democracies as commanding-heights institutions became larger with more complex divisions of labour.

Among the important moments in this history were the mixed Spartan Constitution, the Roman Senate and Justinian's Code, Magna Carta, the jury, the rise of judicial independence, bicameral parliaments, professional journalism as a fourth estate and the growth of universities as accumulators and communicators of knowledge. These decisively important institutions of ideas called universities became progressively more independent of church and state until national security states and corporate power came to see it as important to deeply penetrate universities.

Notwithstanding the important contributions of John Locke (1960) and other Enlightenment scholars, the practice of the separation of powers was ahead of the theory until Montesquieu published *The Spirit of the Laws*. The richest development of these ideas flowed from the debates between the federalists (Hamilton et al. 1963) and antifederalists (Ketcham 1986) in the drafting of the US Constitution. The political philosophies of both the federalists and the antifederalists were republican. Philip Pettit has been the primary inspiration in a program of work at The Australian

National University and Princeton University to excavate the foundations of the republican approach to the tempering of power as a commitment to freedom as nondomination (Braithwaite and Pettit 1990; Pettit 1997, 2012, 2014). In that work, checking power under a rule of law designed to minimise the capacity of others to exercise arbitrary power over us is seen as the keystone of the freedom republicans cherish. While the republican theorising and constitution-writing of the late eighteenth century clarified thinking about the separation of powers, their legacy was also to constrict vigilance to narrow checking of state power.

State despotism and autocracy were seen as threats to our freedom. As a result, when we think of the separation of powers today, we think of the separation of these branches of the state: the legislature, the executive and the judiciary. Yet equally important in the history of the separation of powers has been the separation of church and state. More important in terms of contemporary structures of domination is the separation of business and the state. For many decades now, the 50 largest global corporations all have had greater resources, stronger global political connections and more practical coercive capabilities than most of the world's states (Barnet and Cavanagh 1994).

The technology that monitors all our financial transactions, the tracing of our movements about a city, the things we do in the most private spaces of the metropolis—all are captured digitally not by the state tyrant that George Orwell (1949) feared, but by private platforms and nodes of power. This is not just about platforms like Facebook and its Chinese equivalents. It is also about privatised intelligence organisations like Lockheed Martin (the largest of them) that are asked to do some of the street-level intelligence work that states find too sensitive to do. The legacy of the republican tradition is an obsession with the powers of state police in societies with twice as many private as public police (Shearing and Stenning 1987). For societies like Australia, Rupert Murdoch has more influence over the Prime Minister and Cabinet than any member of the judiciary. Moreover, that is only a tiny part of Murdoch's power compared with the influence he has in the United States and beyond. Through influence in several states, such private actors sometimes shape global regulatory regimes in ways that make the citizens of all states subservient to them.

Today, therefore, the separation of business and state has an importance that the separation of church and state and the separation of powers within the state once had. Even more neglected in the scholarly literature, however, is the separation of powers within business. The major exception is the vast literature on national antitrust and the breakup of global cartels. If the reason we take the separation of powers seriously is the republican concern to protect liberty from domination by concentrations of arbitrary power, the separation of private powers must be of equal importance today to that of state power. One objective of this chapter is to help redress this imbalance in the separation of powers literature by focusing primarily on separations of private powers. This book shows that the different perspective developed on separations of private powers is relevant to public power as well.

The way the need for separations of powers is reconceptualised in this chapter is in terms of certain deep practical difficulties in monitoring and deterring the abuse of power. This book will show why attempts to deter the abuse of power often rebound, making things worse for citizens who suffer abuse. It then shows how innovative separations of powers can ameliorate this. Using research on corporate regulation and self-regulation, the book suggests that the most innovative practice is decades ahead of theory.

One aspiration is to make a minor contribution to republican political theory. Two ideals under that theory are the separation of powers and dialogic democracy—'deliberation in governance in order to shape as well as balance interests (as opposed to deal making between prepolitical interests)' (Sunstein 1988: 1539). Hitherto, these have been regarded as separate desiderata, albeit ones that can be justified in terms of the promotion of freedom as nondomination. A contribution will be to show how the separation of powers nurtures the possibility of deliberative decision-making.

The next section clarifies the reconceptualisation of the separation of powers advanced for consideration and the method by which societies might seek it. Following is a review of an increasingly coherent body of criminological and regulatory theory and data on why attempts to deter the abuse of power with countervailing power evoke defiance and counter-control. The chapter then shows why weak sanctions, especially dialogic ones, generally do better than strong sanctions directed against those who abuse power. Chapter 9 more fully develops the idea that wider use of restorative justice can strengthen the power of deterrence when it is deployed. The book argues that weak sanctions are least likely to work when directed against those who benefit from the abuse of power; they are more likely to work when directed against nonbeneficiaries of the abuse who have preventive capabilities.

Then this chapter contends that plural separations of powers both within and between the public and private sectors create the conditions in which deliberative mechanisms to control the abuse of power can flourish. It explains in a little more detail what separations of powers mean within the private sector and sketches some implications of the analysis for the economic efficiency of separations of powers. Tempered power strengthens the power of all branches of governance to perform their functions decisively. The next chapter argues more fully that tempered private and public powers also strengthen the power of markets to function effectively. The conclusion of the chapter is that a plural republican separation of powers is a midwife of deliberative democracy wherein webs of dialogue are more important than webs of coercion to control the abuse of power (Braithwaite and Drahos 2000). Dialogic responsibility among powers with richly pluralised separations means the abuse of power is checked through the process of soft targets simply being persuaded by discussion into accepting accountability for putting things right. Republican dialogue itself is also concluded to be the best guarantee we can hope for to protect us against economically inefficient ways of transacting the separation of powers.

The method in this chapter is not to analyse the history of the idea of the separation of powers. Rather, it is to move inductively towards a reconceptualisation of the idea from: 1) an understanding of contemporary practices of separating private and public powers, and 2) the revelations of empirical social science about the difficulties of deterring the abuse of power with countervailing power. At the same time, the method is to move deductively from a republican political theory to a proposed reshaping of the doctrine of the separation of powers.

An analysis of the history of the idea of the separation of powers is of less use to making such a contribution to the theory of institutional design than the abductive[1] analysis of practices employed here. This is because of

---

1   Abduction means shuttling backwards and forwards between induction and deduction (see Scheff 1990).

the limited theoretical coherence of the distinctions that have been made in the great historical contests between the competing, yet related, ideas of the separation of powers, mixed government, balanced government, and checks and balances. A mixing or balancing of powers logically entails a separation of powers,[2] yet these labels in history are attached to competing concrete programs of institutional reform, and indeed to disparate reform programs in different societies. Moreover, as Vile (1963) showed, the competing reform programs of the separation of powers, mixed and balanced government, and checks and balances have all left their traces. These traces survive in the complex constitutional theories that are the contemporary inheritance of these contests over the nature of good government.

From Sparta to Madisonian separations of private powers

Mixed government is the oldest idea, figuring in the writing of Aristotle and Plato and justified in terms of securing moderation rather than excess in government and avoiding arbitrary rule (Plato 1892). The mix in Sparta was between the powers of dual kings (replicated in recent times by transnational corporations such as Philips, which have had dual CEOs) and the Council of Elders and Ephors elected by lot (Vile 1963: 35). During the transition from feudalism to capitalism, the reform program of mixed government involved the king or queen, the lords and the male bourgeoisie sharing power so that no single power would predominate. 'The importance of the ancient theory of mixed government … is its insistence upon the necessity for a number of separate branches of government if arbitrary rule is to be avoided' (Vile 1963: 36). It was not based on a separation of the functions proper to each branch, as each branch was expected to check the arbitrary power of other branches by getting involved in all aspects of government. The mid-seventeenth-century theory of the balanced constitution was a hybrid of mixed government between king, lords and commoners, and some division of functions among them.[3] Then, in the late seventeenth century, the

---

2   One cannot 'mix' or 'balance' powers that are unified; they must first be separated.
3   James Harrington and John Milton were important thinkers on these hybrids, as discussed in Vile (1963: 29–30, 39–40, 98–101).

American antifederalists embraced a purist conception of the separation of powers that mapped on to a strict division of the functions of executive, legislative and judicial branches (Manin 1994).

The contemporary republican reconceptualisation of the separation of powers suggests the ancients were wise to see the objective of mixed government as the checking of arbitrary power. Historically contingent judgements are then needed about whether arbitrary power will be better checked by associating more or less clearly separated functions with the powers that different branches of governance exercise. Neither a purist commitment to dividing power as strictly as possible among branches that do not interfere in each other's functions nor a purist commitment to empowering all branches to be equally involved in all functions of government will prove attractive if one has the republican objective of checking arbitrary power. Sometimes we will need a strong state to exercise countervailing power against strong private interests, or vice versa. Sometimes we will want to constrain one branch from a kind of interference in the governance of another branch that would completely compromise the latter's capacity for independent action.

International relations theorists of the balance of power have provided useful formulations for republicans who must reject such purisms. Hans Morgenthau (1973: 169) conceptualises the 'balance of power' as

> allowing the different elements to pursue their opposing tendencies
> up to the point where the tendency of one is not so strong as to
> overcome the tendency of the others, but strong enough to prevent
> the others from overcoming its own.

While this is useful, Morgenthau is even more myopic than Montesquieu in the powers he sees as contesting the balance. They are unitary nation-states, while for Montesquieu they are limited to the legislative, executive and judicial branches of states. Closer to the position reached here is James Madison's in 'Federalist No. 10' that more rather than fewer factions in a republic provide better protection against domination of our liberty by one faction because of 'the greater security afforded by a greater variety of parties, against the event of any one party being able to outnumber and oppress the rest' (Hamilton et al. 1963: 321). Madison also made passing reference to the importance of separating private powers, 'where the constant aim is to divide and arrange the several offices in such a way that each may be a check on the other' (Hamilton et al. 1963: 320).

Contrary to Montesquieu, my conclusion will be that it is better to have many less-clear separations of public and private power than a few very clear ones. This is better for freedom, better for crime prevention and better for preventing the criminalisation of states and the criminalisation of markets. The republican canvas Madison sought to paint was more a Jackson Pollock than a Mondrian. The splashed canvas will be one on which private powers will need to be granted some autonomy from state powers and vice versa, yet where private power is able to check public power and vice versa. It will be a canvas on which powers are separated between the private and the public, within the public and within the private spheres, where separations are many and transcend private–public divisions. The ideal is enough independence for one branch of private, public or hybrid governance for it to be able to make its best contribution to advancing republican freedom without being prevented from doing so by the domination of some other branch. The ideal is also enough interdependence for many branches in combination to be able to check the power of one branch from dominating others. I will argue for the ideal of many semi-autonomous powers (Moore 1978) recursively checking one another rather than a few autonomous branches of governance. More richly plural separations into semi-autonomous powers better advance freedom, crime control and flourishing of the economy. Sufficiently plural separations mean that the dependence of each power on many other guardians of power will secure their independence from domination by any one power. In a relational state (Peake and Forsyth forthcoming), there is space for Hannah Arendt's insight that widely enmeshed relationships freely grant power to powerholders who are responsive and nondominating. The embedded autonomy of developmental states in the writing of Evans (1995) is on a similar track here in terms of how to prevent states from becoming predatory.

Just as this conception of separations of powers in the modern world is pluralist about the variety of branches of private and public power that should be involved in pursuing and checking power, so we should be pluralist about what we mean by the nature of the power that is separated. Madison was loose in the way he switched between talking about the power of factions, of parties, of 'the multiplicity of interests', 'the multiplicity of sects', of branches of governance and of guardians. Many kinds of power can be exercised by many kinds of individual and collective actors. I perhaps get looser still in arguing for strong markets, strong states, strong civil society and strong individuals that each temper the power of the other.

The character of the powers that are separated will be variable. Sometimes the separated power will be the power of one actor to impose their will on others (Dahl 1957). In other cases, the separated power will be the power to *write* rules that the writer has no power to *enforce* (Clegg 1975: 67–75). Some powers will be Lukes' (1974) 'second face' of power: a capacity to keep items off or on the agenda without a need for any imposition of will. Other powers will be Latour's (1986) capacity to enrol others to one's projects without directly imposing one's will on the object of control. Others might be Foucauldian (Foucault 1977) disciplinary networks partially advanced through the practices of agents rather than intended or willed as acts of power. Or they could be Foucauldian shepherds governing, caring for and steering flocks (Garland 1990; Hindess 1996). Separated powers could amount to a Gramscian (1971) hegemony that constitutes individuals who cannot recognise that they are being steered and shaped. The last entry is analytically strategic because the final chapter joins arms with Chantal Mouffe (2013, 2018) on agonistic pluralism for renegotiating a reshaping of hegemony. Normatively, what republicans of my stripe want preserved is freedom as nondomination; in different contexts, different types of power exercised by plural agents of power will do that job best. So, one wants such plural separations of disparate modalities of private and public power as will maximise freedom as nondomination. None of this is particularly novel; it is simply a somewhat radicalising extension of tendencies that can be found in the writing of James Madison. Indeed, the idea of inequality and domination as the great drivers of corruption that must be contested by the citizens and institutions of the republic can also be found in Machiavelli's *Florentine Histories* (Maher 2016).

There are a few reasons Madison and other advocates of the separation of powers found the doctrine attractive. There is the desire to limit the damage that one all-powerful bad ruler can do, to expand the diversity of perspectives that have influence in politics, to foster deliberative democracy by requiring one branch of governance to persuade another that it has exercised its power wisely, to constrain the arbitrariness of power by constraining the rule of men by the rule of law and to empower those who might otherwise be powerless. This book adds to Madison's list the importance of separated powers to the prevention of the criminalisation of the state and the criminalisation of corporations and markets. This chapter will not systematically evaluate the desirability or feasibility of all these rationales for the separation of powers. The analysis will focus on a fresh perspective on just one rationale for the separation of powers, albeit one that republicans should regard as the most fundamental: tempering the abuse of power, especially domination and crime by powerful actors.

Before we can reach the point of understanding why pluralities of checks are the reconceptualisation of the separation of powers needed for the contemporary world, we must begin with an understanding of the empirical literature on why efforts to check the abuse of power so often backfire.

Deterrence failure

The starting point for reaching the conclusions promised is to abstract from what we have learned empirically about the way the regulation of private power works, or rather why it so regularly fails to work. The republican idea of checking power with countervailing power is often read as a deterrence model for controlling the abuse of power. Indeed, deterrence will have an important place in the conclusion ultimately reached in Chapter 9 on tempered deterrence.

This section will first briefly explain why deterrence often does not work well with the crimes of the powerful. Deterrence often backfires and organisational deterrence has a capacity to defeat its own objectives because, for example, of the way powerful corporations can snatch victory from the jaws of defeat by counter-publicity to combat adverse publicity (Fisse and Braithwaite 1983). My argument will be that if we understand these problems properly, separations of powers will prove relevant to their amelioration.

Criminology is the field that has grappled most systematically with why deterrence does not work well. People almost universally value their lives, so it is surprising that introducing capital punishment is not shown to significantly reduce the rate of any kind of crime, and nor does abolishing the death penalty increase it (Bailey and Peterson 1994). It is surprising that building more prisons and locking up more people in them for longer periods do not have predictable effects in substantially reducing the crime rate. We discuss the evidence for this in Chapter 9. It is surprising that people who perceive the expected severity of punishment for committing a crime to be high are not more likely to refrain from crime than people who expect the severity of punishment from committing a crime to be low. The evidence for the expected certainty of detection reducing crime is much stronger, as discussed in Chapter 9. The United States, with a death penalty in some states that other developed nations do not have, with more private and public police than they, with imprisonment rates many times higher than the average for wealthy countries, has not the lowest crime rates, but the highest of any of the wealthy nations. How can this be?

One reason discussed in Chapter 9 is that the protection we get from many of the worst crimes is not bound up with calculative deliberation. Rather, the prevention that matters is delivered by institutions that constitute the unthinkableness of murder or burglary for most people. This is a core message of *Crime, Shame and Reintegration* (Braithwaite 1989; Ahmed et al. 2001). Another reason for corporate deterrence failure is the defiance effect of punishment that can increase crime rather than reduce it. Human emotions turn out to be complex in ways that make people less than rational in their calculations about compliance with laws (Makkai and Braithwaite 1994a). Braithwaite (1997) argued that the limitations of deterrence for organisational crimes are even more profound than for the crimes of individuals. Among the reasons for this are that powerful corporations have well-documented capacities to organise their affairs so no-one can be called to account (Fisse and Braithwaite 1993).

The larger and more powerful the organisation, the more inherently complex and hard to prove are their abuses of power. More than that, complexity is something powerful actors can contrive into their affairs. This includes organisational complexity as to who is responsible for what, jurisdictional complexity as to which state was the site where each element of the offence occurred, the complexity of the accounts and the complexity that 'repeat corporate players' have been able to contrive into the law on previous occasions when they have 'played for rules' as much as played for outcomes. The more punitive a regulatory regime is, the more worthwhile it is for powerful corporations to have 'vice-presidents responsible for going to jail' (Braithwaite 1984). The more powerful the corporate or state actor, the greater is the capability for putting countermeasures in place; the more credible the corporate deterrence, the more reason tyrants have for counter-deterrence.

This connects to the ideas of a retribution trap and a deterrence trap. The retribution trap is that there is no punishment proportionate to the harm banks do when they cause a financial crisis and a recession, and if there were it might cause another recession; the retribution trap is the risk that the only sanction a people will judge as proportionate to a genocide is a counter-genocide.

Coffee's (1981) 'deterrence trap' is that precisely when the stakes are highest with an abuse of power, the regulator is likely to fall into a deterrence trap because the inherent and contrived complexity associated with the biggest abuses of organisational power mean the probabilities of both detection and conviction fall. Imagine, for example, that the risks of conviction for insider trading are only one in 100 for a corporate stock market player who can afford quality legal advice. Imagine that the average returns to insider trading are $10 million. Under a crude expected utility model, it will then be rational for the average insider trader to continue unless the penalty exceeds $1 billion. Assume this would be a large enough penalty to bankrupt many medium-sized companies, leaving innocent workers unemployed, creditors unpaid and communities deprived of their financial base. This is what is required to deter the average insider trader under these crude assumptions. But the criminal law cannot be designed to deal simply with the average case. It should be designed so it can deter the worst cases, which, with sophisticated corporate crime, involve not millions, but billions. Here, the deterrence trap seems inescapably deep. These problems are further compounded with public-sector abuse of power.

This chapter advances two counterintuitive strategies for beating the low detection risks, the defiance, the rational countermeasures and the deterrence traps that make legal checks on the abuse of power difficult at best, and counterproductive at worst:

1. Replace narrow, formal and strongly punitive responsibility (the 'find the crook' strategy) with broad, informal, weak sanctions.
2. Separate enforcement targeting from identification of the actor who benefits from the abuse of power.

It argues that at the macrolevel of the polity, these strategies depend on plural separations of powers both within and between the public and private sectors.

The strength of weak sanctions

The above two strategies for beating defiance, and counter-publicity, scapegoating, contrived complexity and other counterstrategies enabled by corporate power rely on an obvious fact about the abuse of power: the more serious the abuse, the more likely it is that many people will be involved. The most egregious abuses of power arise when whole armies, police forces, bureaucracies or global corporations can be mobilised to execute exploitative conduct. Fisse and Braithwaite (1993) concluded from their various empirical studies that a feature of corporate crime is that it is overdetermined, as the philosophers say, by the acts and omissions of many individuals, organisations and subunits of organisations. While only a small number of people may be involved in committing a corporate crime, our empirical work shows that a much larger number usually have the power to prevent it. These people vary in the degree they care about the conduct being regulated and, therefore, in their susceptibility to defiance and deterrence.

This also means their susceptibility to what Christine Parker (2006) calls the compliance trap: deterrence failure because of failure to address perceptions inside organisations of the morality of regulated behaviour. The compliance trap is a defiance trap in that a regulator's messages induce defiance, undercut intrinsic motivation for compliance and ultimately threaten political support for the regulatory institution.

One fresh approach in the literature for responding to the compliance trap is to marry responsive regulation to Tversky and Kahneman's (1981) framing effects for perceptions inside organisations. Netta Barak-Corren (2021) found that reframing regulatory mandates as *affirming* organisational subcultures, leaving organisational cultures unchallenged (but actually adding some value to them), substantially increased compliance, most strongly so among the most conservative opponents of regulatory values. Whether this is a good approach normatively will depend on how much of organisational subcultures can be affirmed as opening doors to non-domination. The most macro approach to tempering the form of power manifest in the compliance trap throughout this book is radical redesign of democracy to temper anomie and dampen legal cynicism. The I for Identity in CHIME is an important part of the freedom theory of crime prevention for Barak-Corren's identity threat analysis of the compliance trap. Part of this that is particularly important to responsiveness to the compliance trap is outside-in regulatory design that involves active deliberation with business and civil society, rather than inside-out regulatory design dominated by the state. This in turn is enabled by the enculturation of trust combined with the instiutionalisation of distrust. Restorative justice deliberation at the base of regulatory pyramids combined with escalation of deliberative supports alongside punitive escalations up the pyramid is, I will argue, another remedy to the compliance trap. One reason is that the responsive regulatory strategy thereby nurtures intrinsic motivation to comply by being circumspect about extrinsic approaches that crowd out intrinsic motivation to comply. The evidence has grown that motivational interviewing is a helpful micro competence in soft skills that can be trained for persuading personal and organisational reform. It is particularly helpful for getting agreement, I will argue, that prosecution for a future offence would be fair after prosecution is deferred for a current offence. Finally, the book argues that widening restorative justice circles when every participant in a first circle is defiant can escape the compliance trap by widening the circle until an organisational actor is found with the will and the power to prevent reoffending.

It may be that rational actors need a billion-dollar fine if they are to be deterred from insider trading from which they benefit. But they, the beneficiary(ies) of the crime, are not the only potential deterrence targets. They may have a boss; their boss may have a boss who is able to stop the misconduct. They may have a variety of subordinates who can prevent the wrongdoing by exposing the crime or failing to execute some critical component of it. A secretary or executive assistant, for example, who is privy to information, frequently does the 'whistleblowing' that lands their employer in jail for major fraud. Then there are auditors, law firms, consultants, investment bankers, suppliers and buyers upstream and downstream who know what is going on in the criminal organisation. Most of these actors may spurn the morality of those who seek to regulate them, but some may share the morality of the regulators or of the community that is protected by the regulation. Hence, Fisse and Braithwaite (1993: 220) concluded:

> In a complex corporate offence there can be three types of actors who bear some level of responsibility for the wrongdoing or capacity to prevent the wrongdoing:

1. hard targets who cannot be deterred by maximum penalties provided in the law;

2. vulnerable targets who can be deterred by maximum penalties; and

3. soft targets who can be deterred by a sense of responsibility, by shame, by the mere exposure of the fact that they have failed to meet some responsibility they bear, even if that is not a matter of criminal responsibility.

The organisational crime literature has revealed several ways of exploiting the possibility that there are many enforcement targets beyond the primary perpetrators and primary beneficiaries of the crime. One is the strategy mentioned earlier. You grab a minor member of the major perpetrator's team and accuse them of some much more minor illegality around which secrecy is not so tightly guarded. This charge may then be dropped after the defendant gives up a more senior member of the team for matters more serious. These gotcha moments move up a hierarchy of seriousness to the major corporate crime. Along the journey of the regulator and the prosecutor kicking the corporate tyres initially on more minor regulatory offences, and long before reaching billion-dollar criminals, experience with corporate crime investigations shows that the board of directors becomes concerned and tends to start finding its own perpetrators, firing them, demoting them and introducing compliance reforms. Waldman (1978) was the first to show systematically that with corporate crime most deterrence and prevention precede rather than follow conviction. The overdetermined organisational form of corporate crime makes the dynamics of deterrence totally different from that with individual crime in this respect.

Compliance remediation to pre-empt sanctions is well-documented in empirical studies of enforcement cases en route to court. Of Fisse and Braithwaite's (1983) case studies of corporations that had been through major adverse publicity scandals over corporate offences, only five suffered criminal prosecutions and few suffered significant financial impacts from the adverse publicity. Yet every one of them implemented some worthwhile reform in response to the crisis, and some implemented major reforms. Waldman's (1978) neglected study of the impact of antitrust prosecutions found that some of the most positive changes in the competitiveness of markets came in cases that prosecutors lost. Waldman, like Fisse and Braithwaite, found systematic pre-emptive deterrence and reform effects in their empirical work. While an antitrust prosecution is incubating (often for years), defendant companies find that one of the best ways to defend themselves in court, or to get the case dropped, is to improve the competitiveness of their behaviour. As it awaits trial, the firm sometimes pulls down barriers to entry to the industry that it had erected. It may cease retaliating against weaker competitors (as in predatory pricing). It sometimes even eschews monopoly by actively inviting a competitor into the industry and in other cases breaks up monopoly by divesting itself of part of its business in advance of a trial. And it very commonly improved antitrust compliance policies and fired executives responsible for past misconduct, all in the cause of winning or dealing with its big case (Waldman 1978). Karpoff et al. (2008a) found in 585 US Securities and Exchange Commission (SEC) cases that 92 per cent of managers identified by the SEC as responsible for financial misrepresentation lost their job—81 per cent of them *before* the SEC imposed any formal sanctions.

Put another way, most specific deterrence effects precede corporate sentencing, precede trial and, as our nursing home inspection data demonstrate (Braithwaite et al. 2007), can even precede the arrival of the inspector at the front door. As Fisse and Braithwaite (1983: 243) concluded from their empirical study: 'When a company is struck by publicity concerning an alleged crime, it typically implements reform measures to persuade the government against following the publicity with a prosecution.' This book reinforces Marsavelski and Braithwaite's (2018) findings that complex war crimes trials define another domain where prosecutors have been shown to use the 'gotcha' strategy of moving from small fish to ever-larger sharks. It is hard to exterminate a large number of people by shooting without many people being involved in the killing, in the transmission of the orders to shoot, in transport and logistics and in simply standing by watching it happen. The risk that someone hiding behind a tree is filming the killing on their phone has also grown in a world of most citizens having a movie camera in their pocket. This multiplies the opportunities to mobilise this strategy.

A second strategy that worked by putting regulatory pressure on targets who were not the primary beneficiaries of the corporate crime was Stanley Sporkin's innovations as Director of Enforcement for the SEC in the 1970s when he lifted the lid on the foreign bribery scandals. Fisse and Braithwaite (1983) interviewed Sporkin and very senior executives in the companies involved like Lockheed, Exxon, McDonnell-Douglas, General Dynamics, IT&T, General Motors, Ford and most US Big Pharma corporations. The huge early case was Lockheed, which was paying bribes to top officials in many countries to sell aircraft. Among them were Prime Minister Tanaka of Japan and Netherlands Defence Minister Prince Bernhard. Sporkin asked all companies to make fulsome and systematic voluntary disclosures of their questionable foreign payments if they wanted to avoid criminal prosecution. So, who cracked at Lockheed to open this can of worms? It was their external auditor, the firm Arthur Young (Boulton 1978: 276). Arthur Young was a targeted gatekeeper rather than a perpetrator (Kraakman 1984). By refusing to let Lockheed's annual report through the gate it guarded, Arthur Young brought Lockheed's bribery of defence ministers and heads of state to an end, not to mention the careers of the company's chairman and president. Large corporations have many kinds of gatekeepers, such as the general counsel, environmental auditors, insurers, board audit or ethics committees, and occupational health and safety committees. Each has the power to open and close gates that give the organisation access to things it wants.

A gatekeeper like Arthur Young surely had an interest in doing Lockheed's bidding so it could keep the Lockheed account. Yet Arthur Young was much more deterrable than Lockheed itself, which benefited so directly from the bribery (as did Lockheed's top management). Arthur Young, as a nonbeneficiary of the bribes, had less to lose from stopping them; as a gatekeeper that was not responsible for paying bribes, but only for failing to detect them, it also had less to lose from the truth than did those who were handing over the cash. Yet it had much to lose in reputational capital as a gatekeeper of hundreds of other corporate clients if someone else revealed the truth. In this case, they were the comparatively soft target which felt compelled to sound an alarm that led to the demise of some of the hardest targets one could find in the world at that time, such as Prime Minister Tanaka.

Economists', lawyers' and criminologists' intuitions alike tend to be that the state should design enforcement systems to target the beneficiaries of wrongdoing. They are the actors who make the criminal choice based on the benefits of lawbreaking exceeding its costs. From a simple rational choice perspective, we should target the increased costs of lawbreaking on them, those choosing criminals, not on their guardians. The flipping of Arthur Young triggered an enormously consequential cascade. Hundreds of companies rushed to beat their accountants to the SEC to disclose bribes that the SEC allowed them to describe as 'questionable payments'. Thousands of executives were fired or disciplined by boards concerned to pre-empt external criminal enforcement. Prime Minister Tanaka, leader of the second-most powerful country at the time, resigned before he was dismissed; Prince Bernard, from one of the remaining influential royal families in Europe, resigned as defence minister before he was pushed. This led in turn to a cascade of resignations of many top government officials in many countries who had taken bribes from major US corporations. The United States then legislated for the *Foreign Corrupt Practices Act*. The US elite was concerned that the Act would make its firms less competitive against foreign competitors that were still wantonly paying bribes.

US diplomats successfully lobbied for a globalisation of the prohibitions and enforcement strategies in the *Foreign Corrupt Practices Act*. A law reform cascade as well as a global enforcement cascade and a resignation and reform cascade were triggered past a tipping point by an American accounting firm that was a soft target that had done nothing worse than being a careless gatekeeper.

Another empirical demonstration of the power of targeting gatekeepers rather than beneficiaries of the wrongdoing came from the most global of regulatory problems: pollution from ships at sea. Ronald Mitchell (1994a, 1994b) demonstrated how the International Convention for the Prevention of Pollution from Ships was an utter failure. Signatories were required under the convention to impose penalties for intentional oil spills. The most important targets, petroleum-exporting nations, were committed to not enforcing these laws. Most states simply did not care to invest in proving offences that were difficult to detect. Only a few petroleum-importing nations took the requirement seriously. This meant ships had simply to be a little careful to discharge pollution outside the territorial waters of these few countries. Noncompliance with the regime was the norm.

Then in 1980 the oil spill regime was reformed in a way that Mitchell (1994a: 270–71) estimates generated 98 per cent compliance. This was a remarkable accomplishment given the costs of compliance with the new regime were high for ship owners, and given that predictions grounded in the economic analysis of regulation were for minimal compliance. The key change was a move away from the imposition of penalties on ships responsible for spills to an equipment sub-regime that enforced the installation of segregated ballast tanks and crude oil washing. One reason for the improvement was transparency; it was easy to check whether a tanker had segregated ballast tanks, but hard to catch it discharging at sea. The other critical factor was the role of third-party enforcers: a) on whom ship operators are dependent, and b) who have no economic interest in avoiding the considerable costs of the regulation. These third-party enforcers were shipbuilders, classification societies and insurance companies. Shipbuilders had no interest in building cheaper ships that would not get certification by international classification societies nominated by national governments. Classification societies had no interest in corrupting the standards they enforced, which were the whole reason for the generation of their income. Finally, insurers would not insure ships that had not been passed by a classification society acceptable to them because they had an interest in reducing the liabilities that might arise from oil spills.

The revised regime therefore achieved 98 per cent compliance in large part because the effective targets of enforcement shifted from the ship operators that benefited from the pollution to shipbuilders, classification societies and insurance companies which did not benefit. However, because the ship operators (and builders) were totally dependent on classification societies and insurers, operators had no choice but to insist on regime-compliant ships, which the classification societies had an interest in ensuring were the only ones that got through their gatekeeper's gate.

The best-known examples of separating enforcement targeting from the actor who benefits from the abuse is requiring employers to withhold tax from the taxable income of their employees, or banks withholding and/or reporting tax payments on the interest earned by their customers. Little enforcement is needed against the employers and banks that withhold and report because they do not benefit from any underreporting of income. Tax cheating is only a major problem in those domains where it is impossible to harness such disinterested gatekeepers. These withholding policies have possibly counted among the most successful crime-control policies of our time.

Peter Grabosky (1990a, 1990b, 1992, 1994a, 1994b, 1995a, 1995b, 2017) pursued a program of work that continuously discovered new species of third-party enforcers of regulatory regimes—from volunteer divers who check compliance with South Australia's historical shipwrecks legislation to elected worker health and safety representatives. Note the good governance efficiency in the fact that divers and workers have natural, frequent lines of sight to locales of criminality as they do what they normally do. Grabosky's work showed just how disparate are the possibilities for shifting enforcement targeting—from actors who benefit from the cheating to actors who do not but on whom the cheat depends for something critical to their welfare. This simple shift can make headway with some of our seemingly most intractable law enforcement challenges.

Grabosky's *Smart Regulation* (Gunningham and Grabosky 1998) co-author, Neil Gunningham, long despaired about the way hazardous chemicals regulation succeeded in changing the practices of the top-20 global chemical corporations, but barely touched thousands of little chemical companies which were too numerous, too unsophisticated and too dispersed to be effectively supervised by state inspectors. Worse, the major chemical companies often spin off their most hazardous activities upstream or downstream to fungible contractors. Eventually, Gunningham realised that most of these small chemical companies are dependent on global chemical firms as suppliers, distributors, customers or all three. This led Gunningham (1995) to the insight that a private or public regulatory regime that requires major companies to ensure not only that their own employees comply with the regulations, but also that the upstream and downstream users and suppliers of their products comply may massively increase its effectiveness. The reason is that a global firm that supplies a little chemical company has much more regular contact with them than any government inspector, more intimate and technically sophisticated knowledge of where their bodies are buried, greater technical capacity to help them fix the problems and more leverage over them than the state. Often, they get to know what is going on because of explicit auditing practices that put them in a better position to regulate malpractice than any government regulator. For example, in analysing the implications of the chemical industry's 'Responsible Care' program, Gunningham explained:

> Dow insists on conducting an audit before it agrees to supply a new customer with hazardous material, and routinely audits its distributors. The audit involves a team visiting the distributor's operations to examine handling, transportation, storage and terminating techniques and prescribing improvements aimed at achieving environmental standards far in advance of current regulatory requirements. Many large chemical manufacturers go further. (Gunningham 1996)

Building a thousand gates to the power of corrupt officials

Privatising public gatekeeping can be one way of separating powers so that enforcement can be targeted on an actor who does not benefit from the abuse of public power. Many national customs services have a lot of corruption. Both senior managers and street-level bureaucrats benefit from bribes paid for turning a blind eye to the under or over-invoicing of goods. The fact that public customs services have an organisational interest in continuing to sell favours creates a market opportunity for a private organisation set up to 'sell trust'. This is just what the Swiss company Société Générale de Surveillance (SGS) set out to do when it took over the customs services of Indonesia and other developing countries. It persuaded nations to contract large parts of their customs work to SGS through its reputation for incorruptibility, which enabled it to deliver huge savings to governments. The Indonesian Government claimed SGS saved it tens of billions of dollars. Because testimonials of this kind from major states bring SGS business, SGS has a financial incentive to catch cheats and weed out corruption in its own ranks. A major corruption scandal that would strike everyone as quite normal in the customs service of a developing country might cause financial ruin for SGS. SGS set up its inspection gates in the country of export (where superior intelligence on over-invoicing or under-invoicing was available) rather than in the importing country. It accomplished this by having more than 1,000 scrupulously audited offices at all the world's key exporting sites. The company constrained itself from engaging in any manufacturing or in any trading or financial interests that would threaten its independence.

'Selling trust' is profitable, so operatives are well paid. As the company's Senior Vice President, J. Friedrich Sauerlander, confessed to me in the 1990s, in an organisation of 27,000 people (which had grown to 94,000 in 2020), his internal security organisation had uncovered 'some slip-ups'. But, in the ways that mattered most, it had been possible to sustain an organisation with an incentive structure that rewarded trust. The beneficiaries of the old breaches of trust were left where they were, but through building 1,000 gates to their power on the other side of the world and guarding those gates with SGS units that flourished in proportion to how much abuse of trust they stopped, targeting enforcement on the bad guys inside the gates became mostly redundant.

From Lockheed to polluters from ships, from employers and banks withholding tax to chemical companies and outside (instead of inside) directors targeted by public interest groups over corporate abuse of power,[4] we can see some promise in shifting enforcement targeting from actors who benefit from their abuse to actors who do not benefit but on whom the abuser depends for something critical to their welfare.

A third strategy for enforcement that works by hitting soft rather than hard targets is restorative justice. Fisse and Braithwaite (1993) and Parker (2004) described the early restorative justice innovations of the Australian Competition and Consumer Commission (ACCC). This was a strategy of sitting responsible managers down in a restorative circle—preferably one involving victims of the corporate crime—in which the responsible executives were given the opportunity to admit responsibility, apologise to victims, offer compensation and responsive corporate reform and leadership in industry-wide campaigns, even for global self-regulatory reforms. Frequently in ACCC restorative enforcement practice, this did not happen in the first circle. The reason was simple. The commission asked for a meeting with the managers who they believed were criminally responsible for the offence. These managers had the strongest interest in denial within the organisation. Their lawyer who sat beside them also had some interest in failure of the restorative circle and escalation to a criminal prosecution that they might fight and win for the company, thereby earning more fees. After the first circle failed, instead of saying we will see you in court, the ACCC would say it was disappointed the managers did not want to put the injustice right, so let us adjourn this meeting and go away to reflect on our positions. Then the commission would call the boss of those responsible executives to say how disappointed it was that the firm did not want to put the injustice right in the restorative circle and ask the boss to attend a reconvened meeting. Often when that circle was convened the boss turned out to be a tougher nut in resisting formal admissions of responsibility than the directly responsible executives. The ACCC then moved up to another circle with the boss of the boss, then the CEO and in one case even the chair of the board. In that case, the chair was shocked that his CEO should resist a reasonable approach from a respected government regulator to put a serious fraud right voluntarily

---

4   A germinal example here was the 'Corporate Campaign' against the J.P. Stevens corporation over its abusive labour practices. The top management team were very hard nuts, but the campaign was able to so embarrass external directors that they resigned from the board—a consequence that really did concern top management (see Fisse and Braithwaite 1983: Ch. 2).

rather than contest the wrongdoing in court. He fired the CEO (not very restorative perhaps), voluntarily paid millions of dollars in compensation to victims of the fraud for a case for which the commission believed, had it won, the fine would be less than $1 million. The chair also undertook to lead an industry-wide monitoring campaign to detect future frauds of this kind, not only by his own company, but also by all major competitors in this industry.

This third strategy is to widen the circle of targeted harder targets who are rational actors until a softer target is found in the restorative circle who is motivated by a concern to be ethical, who can be touched by shame over fraudulent conduct.

Summarising mixed relational prevention through softer targets

Hence, this aspect of past work on corporate crime really exposes six strategies that enable the discovery and mobilisation of the preventive power of ethical soft targets inside culpable organisations, be they public or private. One is the 'gotcha' strategy, which we will see is also fundamental to success in prosecutions against powerful war criminals, with smaller fish who give up bigger fish until the law enforcer nets the sharks. The second is Sporkin's strategy of triggering a cascade of self-disclosure, self-enforcement and reform by inviting the hard targets to beat the soft targets to be first in a race to the regulator's door with voluntary disclosure of wrongdoing. The third is a restorative strategy of widening the circle of hard targets until a more senior soft target enters the circle and cascades responsible reform right down the organisation and right across an industry. The fourth is relevant to all the first three strategies: it is to exploit the fact that firms will do better in court if they repair harm and discipline responsible executives in advance of a trial. A consequential fifth strategy is *qui tam* that encourages those without personal responsibility with a bounty payment to beat those with responsibility to the prosecutor's door to disclose the crime (Dukes et al. 2014: Ch. 10). Evidence for the effectiveness of whistleblower bounties is particularly strong with cartel enforcement (Coffee 2020: 81). The healthcare industry is where *False Claims Act* payouts are most common and highest. Dyck et al. (2010) concluded that the probability of fraud detection in healthcare became three times as high compared with other industries in which large *False Claims Act* bounty payouts were not offered to whistleblowers. It has also worked well with tax enforcement in the United States (Ventry 2014; Wilde 2017; Johannesen and Stolper 2017; Amir et al. 2018; Masclet et al. 2019). This fifth *qui tam* strategy exploits the reality that many insiders are likely to know about complex organisational crimes, while few or no outsiders do. So, the essence of this strategy is to change the incentive structure to one where those who blow the whistle with their insider knowledge get large financial bounties. This is needed because without it, whistleblowers are punished by ending their careers and ruining their lives. This whistleblower bounty strategy also connects back to Sporkin's second strategy because it motivates a race among whistleblowers to get the reward by being the first to report the crime to the regulator, and it motivates management to beat the whistleblowers to the regulator with a voluntary disclosure.

Coffee (2020) has advocated further development of some incipient privatisation of corporate crime prosecutions by public prosecutors contracting top private law firms with a contingency fee for two to five–year campaigns to take on massively complex corporate crimes. This may be another privatisation that would reduce domination and increase freedom. Coffee (2020) probably rightly believes that to make this work corporate financial penalties need to be hiked in ways that will not bankrupt firms. The solution is equity fines, so that up to 20 per cent of shares in a criminalised corporation would be issued as new shares to a crime victim compensation fund. A reason Coffee may be right is that, structurally, the problem of modern corporate crime is one of criminalised markets. Extreme levels of executive compensation are on offer for managers who are encouraged to take extreme risks with the criminal law (Coffee 2020: x).

A sixth strategy that is relevant to all five foregoing strategies is to rely on the preventive work of street-level regulatory bureaucrats (Lipsky 2010) more than on the courts. This strategy also applies to policing individual street crimes. We know that if police are deployed to hotspots of individual crime, even if they make no moves towards arresting anyone, they can deter or prevent crime, and potently so (Sherman et al. 1989; Sherman 1995; Ariel et al. 2016). Likewise, the seemingly passive deployment of peacekeepers at hotspots can protect civilians, prevent war crimes and prevent war (Braithwaite and D'Costa 2018).[5] We say passive deployment of peacekeepers, but we really know little empirically about what these peacekeepers do and say on the ground when they have these passive

---

5   War recidivism is high: of 108 countries that experienced civil war between 1946 and 2017, only 27 per cent avoided a return to war (Walter et al. 2020: 7). While peacekeeping is well known to have failed catastrophically to prevent war crimes in various cases like Rwanda, the statistical impact across all cases is of effectiveness. Collier's (2009: 96) program of empirical research concluded that US$100 million spent on UN peacekeepers reduced the cumulative 10-year risk of reversion to conflict from 38 per cent to 17 per cent. That risk falls further, to 13 per cent, if the investment in peacekeeping is scaled up to US$200 million. Collier's team presented his conclusions on the benefits and costs for the world economy of investment in peacekeeping to a panel of Nobel Laureate economists for the Copenhagen Consensus. This involved 10 rival research teams making a case for international public money to be spent on something. The Copenhagen Consensus panel's verdict selected peacekeeping as one of their endorsed public expenditures. Doyle and Sambanis (2006: 336) found that the greater effectiveness of a combination of treaties and transformational UN peacebuilding is particularly dramatic when local peacebuilding resources and capacities are low. In a follow-up of these data, Sambanis (2008: 23) found that UN peace operations reduce the risk of peace failure in the longer run by about 50 per cent, as did Fortna (2008). Quinn et al. (2007: 187) found the combination of a treaty and a peace operation reduced the probability of civil war recurrence by 54 per cent. These peace impacts persist after peacekeepers leave. Doyle and Sambanis (2006: 336) found that, without a treaty and UN mission, the statistical prospects of successful peacebuilding in states of low capacity are extremely dim. Many other studies confirm a big statistical contribution of peace operations to building peace (Call 2012; Doyle and Sambanis 2000; Fortna 2003, 2008; Fortna and Howard 2008: 288–94; Gilligan and Sergenti 2008; Hultman et al. 2013; Nilsson 2006; Quinn et al. 2007; Riordan 2013; Sambanis 2008; Walter 2002). Fortna (2003, 2008) also found a large tendency for ceasefires overseen by international peacekeepers to be more effective than those without peacekeepers. Hampson (1996) argues that peace agreements are not self-executing: sustained third-party leadership, mediation, problem-solving and peacebuilding are needed as cement to hold the peace together. The wars that are more intractable and serious are the ones that attract the investment in a UN peace operation. Fortna's (2008) systematic quantitative data confirm this. When Gilligan and Sergenti (2008) corrected for the effects of non-random assignment with matching techniques, they found that the causal effect of UN peace operations in preventing war was even larger than would have been estimated had there been no correction for non-random assignment of UN missions. Walter et al. (2020) have completed the most systematic review of this evidence, while in addition showing that the mere *promise* that peacekeepers will arrive can dampen violence and encourage mediation and the signing of peace agreements: 'What is most striking about these studies is the consistency of their findings. Almost all of them find that peacekeeping is highly effective at preventing violence before it begins, reducing violence in the midst of war and preventing violence from recurring once it has ended. All else [being] equal, countries and regions that receive peacekeeping missions experience less armed conflict, fewer civilian and combatant deaths, fewer mass killings, longer periods of post-conflict peace and fewer repeat wars than those that do not receive peacekeepers. This relationship—between peacekeeping and lower levels of violence—is so consistent across large-n analyses that it has become one of the strongest findings in the international relations literature to date. The power of peacekeeping is all the more striking given that the UN tends to intervene in the toughest cases. Multiple scholarly studies have found that the UN Security Council tends to send peacekeepers to countries with more violence, particularly bad governments and ongoing conflict' (Walter et al. 2020: 2). On the other hand, the United Nations does not send peacekeepers to countries that refuse to accept a UN peace operation, and this is a methodological bias that cuts in the opposite direction. Moreover, countries that received peacekeepers during the past three decades almost always received UN human rights, gender rights and child protection staff; they received UN humanitarian assistance, housing for refugees, economic development, good governance, policing and security sector reform assistance, rolled into a peace operation package. Hence, it might be that what Walter et al.'s (2020) impressive and persuasive review demonstrates is the effectiveness not so much of peacekeepers, but of peace operations, especially UN ones, in preventing not only war, but also crime.

preventive effects at hotspots of conflict. In my limited observations of this kind of peacekeeping in these contexts, they do ask people to calm down when shouting starts; they do position themselves between fighters with weapons and the victims they might be interested in shooting; they do raise their eyebrows or gently raise their hand when people behave provocatively; they do enrol local respected religious leaders and ask them to help calm people; and they do set a calming example by 'acting like they are on vacation',[6] smiling back with gentle understanding at people who shout at them.

When peacekeepers or police act aggressively, however, that can make things worse—a lot worse—as we discuss in Chapter 9 with the violence that cascaded from the police bashing of Rodney King in 1992 and the killing of George Floyd in 2020. Spending more resources on policing can make crime worse when a broken-windows philosophy of arresting disadvantaged people for minor incivilities such as public urination can cause unemployment and contribute to the reproduction of inequality in the society. Spending on police can make crime worse when policing is stigmatising rather than reintegrative (Braithwaite 2002).

With business regulation, we have much more systematic ethnographic data on how street-level inspectors prevent violations of the law. Based on observations of 157 inspections and many other kinds of regulatory encounters in aged care homes in Australia, the United States, the United Kingdom, Canada and Japan, Braithwaite et al. (2007) revealed empirically no fewer than 27 strategies (in Table 6.1) that mainly were deployed through the guardianship work of soft corporate targets. Scholz and Gray (1990) showed that US Occupational Safety and Health Administration (OSHA) inspections contributed significantly to improving corporate compliance at a time when the average expected punishment cost of an OSHA offence could be measured in cents rather than dollars (because of low penalties, infrequent inspections and low detection probabilities). How could that be? How could it be rational to take any notice of an OSHA inspector when expected punishment costs were near zero? Surely firms should just wait for the unlikely occurrence of detection and then write a cheque? One reason inspection worked was that regulatory

---

6   Thanks to Clifford Shearing, who is the original source for this. For examples of it in peacekeeping in Timor-Leste, see Braithwaite et al. (2012).

inspection often delivered not by punishing people, but by reminding ethical people of their obligations to do things they knew they should do. Astute inspectors energised them to prioritise properly.

Our observational study of nursing home regulation in all Australian states, 30 US states and across the United Kingdom systematically revealed the 27 mechanisms in Table 6.1 through which regulatory inspection frequently enough had positive effects on compliance with the law. This helps us to see that organisational compliance with the law is achieved not only by impacting many soft targets, but also by impacting them at street level through many different mechanisms. This is how a combination of many mechanisms that are thin reeds can be woven together and deployed against many who are rarely criminal actors to prevent corporate crime more effectively than the single brittle reed of a prosecution.

Table 6.1 Strategies that improved nursing home compliance in certain observed contexts

Strategy	Process
Reminds	Tapping a staff member on the shoulder reminds of an obligation believed in but lost sight of.
Commits	Persuading someone who was not persuaded that compliance would benefit residents.
Shows	Shows how to do something necessary for compliance that the person does not know how to do.
Fixes	Inspector fixes something themselves (e.g. releases a restrained resident).
Incapacitates individual	Reports a professional to a licensing body that withdraws/ suspends their licence.
Incapacitates home	Withdraws/suspends licence for home.
Protects future residents	Bans new admissions until problem is fixed.
Management change	Orchestrates sale or management takeover of the home by signalling escalation up a regulatory pyramid.
Shames	Disapproves of noncompliance.
Exposes	Reports noncompliance to the public on a website or the nursing home notice board, inducing reputational discipline or market discipline, or both.
Praises	Congratulates improvement.
Deters	Imposes a penalty.
Wears down	Keeps coming back until the home wants closure to rid themselves of the inspector.

Strategy	Process
Changes resource allocation	Sanctions withheld only if there is a change in resource allocation.
Voluntary acceptance of responsibility on the spot	By asking a question, causes a professional to jump in and accept responsibility to put something right immediately. This and the next five are motivational interviewing effects.
Voluntary acceptance of responsibility in a plan of correction	Asking the right questions brings about a long-term plan that accepts responsibility.
Root-cause analysis	Asking the right questions induces an insightful root-cause analysis.
Trigger continuous improvement	Asking the right questions reveals the benefits of commitment to continuous improvement.
Trigger consultancy	Asking the right questions persuades the home to hire in help from a consultant.
Stimulate the home's deliberative problem-solving	Asking the right questions is a catalyst of problem-solving conversations at a staff meeting or other forum.
Triple-loop learning	Inspector spreads generative learning from mistakes in one part of a facility to another and to one facility from another.
Educates	Provides in-service training on the spot.
Builds self-efficacy	Helps management and staff to see their own strengths.
Awards and grants	Nominates the home or staff for an award or grant.
Empowers	Empowers friends of compliance within the organisation through some combination of the above strategies that puts pro-compliance factions of the organisation in the driver's seat.
Trigger pre-emption	The home fixes problems before the inspector arrives to pre-empt the deployment of any of the above strategies.
Trigger third-party engagement with any/all the above	A word to an advocacy organisation, a key shareholder, a lending bank, the media, a provider association, a tort lawyer, the ombudsman, the residents' council, relatives.

Schell-Busey et al.'s (2016) meta-analysis shows that regulatory inspection probably works in improving compliance with laws more than it should reasonably be expected to work based on a deterrence theory of corporate compliance. Indeed, their systematic review suggests that deterrence has no effect on its own; what works is a mix of regulatory enforcement strategies that inspectors deploy. Deterrence is often one of them. The same has been shown empirically to be true for peacekeeping; it does not always work, but it works best when it has a multidimensional regulatory and welfare mix (Doyle and Sambanis 2000, 2006; Walter et al. 2020). Thin reeds of enforcement directed against disparate forms of organisational power only work when they are bound together. This is not to deny that different regulatory strategies can be bound together in incompatible, counterproductive and mutually defeating, rather than mutually reinforcing, ways. Gunningham and Grabosky's (1998) *Smart Regulation* has given us a splendid beginning to understanding the particularities of where synergies in a regulatory mix are positive and where there is incompatibility among combined strategies. Notwithstanding the imperative for more fine-grained understanding, the possibility of productively binding together a mix of tools is good news for a theory of crime and freedom. It means that in corporate crime enforcement, peacekeeper enforcement against war crimes and reintegrative hotspot policing of street crimes, policymakers can do great things to reduce crime while rarely deterring through the clang of the jailhouse door, or even arrest.

This chapter argued that deterrence failure is a major impediment to effective control of organisational crime. It made a case for two strategies that can beat defiance, the deterrence trap and other corporate counterstrategies that make for deterrence failure:

1. Replace narrow, formal and strongly punitive responsibility (the 'find the crook' strategy) with broad, informal, weak sanctions (dialogic regulation) that touch many softer targets.
2. Separate enforcement targeting from identification of the actor who benefits from the wrongdoing.

Now a third strategy is added:

3. Rely heavily on street-level bureaucrats who mobilise what Peake and Forsyth (forthcoming) call the 'relational state'—a wide mix of preventive strategies, each of which is weak as a standalone strategy yet can be strong when woven into a fabric of relational prevention. These street-level relational regulators can be police, state, self-regulatory or NGO inspectors, state or NGO welfare supporters or citizens who mobilise collective efficacy at street level.

In fact, an astute, mutually supporting mix of these is needed. For confronting domination by the commanding heights of corporate power, while community groups are important third-party regulators (Braithwaite 2008), leadership from state regulators is imperative. Sometimes state regulators from developing countries who confront a global corporate colossus need backup from an international regulator like the International Labour Organization for labour rights abuses and from rights NGOs, the international trade union movement and more, in a web of networked governance that substitutes for weak state governance (Braithwaite and Drahos 2000; Braithwaite 2006b). For the most disadvantaged targets of law enforcement, who have suffered most discrimination by the state, a community-led mix tends to be superior to a state-led mix. Yet the state remains critical to any mix. State healthcare support is often critical to the mix. If a man pulls a knife and citizens of his community cannot persuade him to put it down, state police are also imperative.

At the macrolevel of the polity, the combination of these strategies means dialogic regulation combined with robust separations of powers within and between the public, private and community sectors. The number of third-party enforcement targets is greater to the extent that the organisational world and the political system have richer, more plural separations of powers. For example, under a plural separation of powers, the media baron who sells editorial support and biased reporting to a politician in return for the promise of a television licence or approval of a monopolistic media merger might, in a more effective republic, have their power checked by:

- courts of law
- a statutorily independent broadcasting authority that allocates licences only to fit and proper persons and has the capacity to investigate in cases of noncompliance
- industry association self-regulatory bodies
- a press council
- corporate charters of editorial independence
- a vigilant journalists' association that requires its members to comply with a journalists' code of ethics
- oversight committees of the legislature that investigate abuses of power by the executive, and other (separate) parliamentary committees that check diligent performance of the duties of independent regulators
- public interest groups that are granted standing to lodge complaints to all the foregoing institutions
- audit committees of boards of directors (all of whom are outside directors) with a remit to adjudicate complaints against management for ethical abuses

- corporate ombudsmen with public reporting capabilities
- ethical investment funds with an investigative capacity they use to put activist shareholders on notice about abuses of power in media corporations.

Separations of powers both within and between the private and public sectors are important to controlling such abuses of power, as is countervailing power from institutions of civil society that muddy any simple public–private division. Moreover, the more potential targets of third-party enforcement such separations of powers throw up, the better is the chance that one of them will be a caring soft target with leverage over the abuser of power. They can be sufficiently caring for the simple device of a regulatory dialogue to move that third party to use their leverage to stop the abuse. Because they care, they might trigger internal reforms to prevent recurrence or trigger the private justice system of the organisation to discipline those responsible for the abuse.

Thus, the richer and more plural are the separations of powers in a polity, the less the society needs to rely on narrow, formal, strongly punitive regulation targeted at the beneficiaries of the abuse of power. The more we can rely on a regulatory dialogue that appeals to the sense of social responsibility of all actors who share an overdetermined capacity to prevent the wrongdoing, the more persuasion can replace punishment. The reasons for this are that the more hands into which powers are separated: a) the more likely it is that one of those actors with power to prevent will be an ethically caring target, and b) the more third parties there will be who do not benefit from the abuse themselves, but who hold power over the abuser. Put another way, the more plural are the separations of power: a) the more overdetermined is the capacity to prevent abuse; and b) the more cases there are of disjuncture between an interest in the abuse and capacity to prevent it. All this means that societies can grow more points of engagement with responsible actors who can mobilise collective efficacy for prevention inside organisations and institutions. In this way, preventive relational public or self-policing more regularly becomes a strategy that works.

The final chapter of this book argues, furthermore, that these insights are critical to understanding how it is possible for weak social movement actors to defeat mighty states with large armies and wads of cash. Webs of reward and coercion are the master's tools that give masters an advantage over the dominated; webs of dialogue are where social movements enjoy comparative advantage over masters, partly because they can be mobilised to divide and conquer masters. Commitment to a politics of agonistic pluralism that is nonviolent is not only good for freedom; it is also good for political effectiveness in resisting hegemony.

Plural private separations; plural public separations

This chapter seeks to correct the bias of the republican tradition of political thought towards a focus on separations of *public* powers. Yet the arguments advanced are as relevant to the abuse of power by police as they are to the abuse of power by a private media organisation or internet platform. The head of state who rigs electoral boundaries is a hard target because nothing is more important to their career than the election outcome. Citizens who ask a judge to overturn the head of state's electoral rigging are approaching a softer target because the judge does not benefit from the election result in the way a head of state does. The traditional separation of powers between executive government and the judiciary can deliver the benefits revealed in our analysis of disjunctions between interest and preventive power.

Three separations of public power (executive, legislature, judiciary) are a narrowed plurality. Antifederalist separations of power (in some pre-revolutionary US state constitutions), as with the US federal constitution, aspired to avoid the concentration of power (as did its private-sector analogue in antimonopoly law). In the most uncharitable reading of this arrangement, each branch is left alone to abuse power without too much interference within its own sphere from the other branches of government; a strict separation of powers simply assures that the sphere of each is not too broad. This would be uncharitable, however, because in all the early

US state governments, while each branch had spheres of independence from the other branches, they also had spheres where their power was checked by the other branches of government (Flaherty 1996).[7]

Even so, the reconceptualisation of the rationale for the separation of powers in this chapter implies that in debates on the separation of public powers, attention is needed not just to assure the independence of honest judges from corrupt parliamentarians and corrupt executive governments (and vice versa). Attention is also needed to make corrupt, self-serving, nepotistic judges who flout the rule of law, patrimonial parliamentarians and corrupt executives vulnerable to the power of the other branches. One of the problems to confront if we are to make progress with some of our tougher problems, like police violence and corruption, is how to deal with pleas that any encroachment on the independence of the police via accountability to the elected government will take us back to a world in which the police lock up whomsoever the ruling political elite tells them is a troublemaker. How do we get universities that are fearless in undertaking research of which the state disapproves, yet that do not use this independence to become dominated by corporate interests that pay them fat research funding?

The answer proposed is to have a police force and a university that are sufficiently autonomous from state power, business power, church power, media power and the power of disciplines and professions to not be dominated by them. Part of their resilience in the face of any single source of domination will come from their very dependence on all those other sources of power. We need police that are vulnerable to publicly reported surveys of citizen satisfaction with the respect police show for rights (Braithwaite 1992), to meetings of police indigenous liaison committees,

---

7   Yet, late in his career, no less a republican figure than Thomas Jefferson—much influenced by John Taylor's (1950) book *An Inquiry into the Principles and Policy of the Government of the United States*—became an advocate of a total separation of the powers of the three branches, rejecting the dominant view of John Adams and the federalists that there should be some overlapping so there could be mutual checking of power. For Taylor, '[i]nstead of balancing power, we divide it, and make it responsible' (by which he and Jefferson meant all three branches must be responsible to the people by direct election) (Taylor 1950: 88; Vile 1963: 163–70). The late eighteenth-century French constitutions also rejected the idea of checks and balances in favour of a strict separation of powers, at least until the lessons of Maximilien Robespierre and Napoleon Bonaparte had been learnt. These were lessons about the fragility, adversarialism and vulnerability to tyrannical coups d'état of a purist democratic separation of powers (see Vile 1963: 198–99). Madison had foreseen that the best way to preserve the separation of powers was 'by so contriving the interior structure of government as that its several constituent parts may, by their mutual relations, be the means of keeping each other in their proper places' (Hamilton et al. 1963: 302–19).

vulnerable to losing some of their budget to night watch committees of indigenous elders, to meetings of the police–LGBTIQ liaison committee, to meetings with local businesses concerned about break-ins, to meetings of local citizen groups, to criticisms made at restorative justice conferences that a police officer used excessive force, to the ombudsman, to parliamentary committees, to royal commissions to investigate matters of extraordinary malfeasance, to a free and fearless press, to the council for civil liberties, to the judiciary and to an executive government that will sack the commissioner if there is reasonable suspicion that he or she is corrupt or recruits violent police. After 200 years of ugly tyranny in nations with beautiful constitutions, it is no longer persuasive to suggest that a separation of state powers will ensure the government 'will be controlled by itself' (James Madison, in Hamilton et al. 1963: 323).

In other words, a police service that is enmeshed in many webs of interdependence will be vulnerable to the many when it corruptly does the bidding of one or the few. This might be the way of resolving the dilemma of independence for different branches of government versus the checking of power between them. The checking of power between branches of government is not enough. The republican should want a world in which the different branches of business, public and civil society power are all checking each other. While the broad principles here are clear, the nuts and bolts of checks and balances, of independence and interdependence, require contextual deliberation for any given source of power. Clearly, there must be some sorts of power against which a police service must be protected by law ('Arrest this man or we will cut your budget'). Republican theory of the sort Braithwaite and Pettit (1990) endorsed requires detailed empirical investigation of the different ways of organising independence and interdependence to discover a set of institutional arrangements most likely to maximise freedom as nondomination. At the very least, a clear principle of separating powers is that there are enough actors with independence and preventive capacity such that one of them can be moved by dialogue to stop the abuse.

In the public arena, the literature on the separation of powers bequeaths to us a variety of reasonably well-understood heads of public power that might be separated: different houses of parliament, levels of government in a federation, lower versus appellate courts, administrative appeals tribunals, an independent public service commission, and so on. While it is a tricky business to put together or tinker with a robust public architecture of powers, at least we have some sense of the elements with which we might work. In contrast, the separation of private powers is comparatively under-researched. Here, most readers will need some elementary sense of what might be involved in separating private powers. The next section is a preliminary foray into what might be at issue.

How to separate powers in the private sector

The law review literature on corporate governance provides useful guidance on accomplishing separations of powers in the private sector, but not useful enough. The concentration tends to be on the separate powers of shareholders, directors and managers (Eisenberg 1975; Kiiwan 1995). Important separation of power issues are at stake here, such as whether a majority of members of the board of a company should be unrelated directors, meaning they have no business dealings with, nor a management position in, the company; whether the nominating committee for the appointment of new directors should have no management directors on it; whether it should be forbidden for the CEO to be chair of the board; whether there should be a bicameral board with a supervisory board as in Germany, France, the Netherlands and Indonesia; and generally how to give outside directors a role that is more than that of the CEO's 'pet rocks'. There is certainly merit from a republican point of view in engendering shareholder democracy, encouraging activist shareholders to call management to account, securing representation for minority shareholders on the board and effective monitoring of the board by institutional shareholders. When the New York Stock Exchange first required a board audit committee of nonexecutive directors as a condition of listing on the exchange in 1977, this was a significant step for the separation of private powers. It spread to many parts of the world. Long before that, in the English *Registered Companies Act* of 1862, a more important step was requiring companies as a matter of law to be audited by a professionally certified auditor. This is the well-understood end of the separation of private powers. A useful literature already exists on how to make these separations work better: how to improve shareholder accountability, restructure directors' duties, bring board audit committees to life and improve the performance and independence of auditors. The emphasis on the separation of powers between management and the two other branches of corporate governance neglects the main game, however, which is separation within management. With private power, more so even than with public power, the power in the hands of the other branches of governance is extremely modest compared with the concentration of power in the executive, the top management team.

Therefore, internal auditing within the firm that enjoys independence from line management is important. It must report to board audit committees rather than just management, for example. This is not just financial auditing, but auditing of equal employment opportunities, labour law more broadly, environmental, safety and competition law compliance, tax compliance, and more. In multinational corporations, the independence of local auditors, especially for compliance with matters like the US *Foreign Corrupt Practices Act*, can be best secured by auditors from one national subsidiary auditing auditors from another national subsidiary. Christine Parker (2002) showed how compliance professionalism inside corporations can be a bridge that is as accountable to a particular kind of compliance professionalism (for example, environmental) outside the firm as it is to the firm. Sensibilities and compliance techniques from outside the firm filter into the firm through the compliance professionalism network. Valerie Braithwaite and Janine Bush's (1998) research showed that Australian firms that had the best affirmative action compliance for the benefit of women were those in which the affirmative action officer of the corporation had the best feminist networks, particularly with other affirmative action officers across many firms.

This corporate compliance literature is rich on how collective efficacy is built in professional communities that stretch between professional associations outside and across subsidiaries within corporations. This is bridging capital, bridging professional collective efficacy. This bridging is fundamental to understanding how corporate compliance with laws works when it does work. One of the most effective programs for getting international corporations that were paying no tax in Australia to self-regulate their profit-shifting to avoid tax (for example, to tax havens) did not so much involve direct collaboration between the Australian Taxation Office and the culpable firms. Rather, the collaboration was between the tax office and the major outside accounting firms that were doing the firms' tax work. There was a new line of business in this for the accounting firms, so they were the soft targets. The tax office co-designed with them a responsive regulatory pyramid of enforcement escalations that would occur unless there was voluntary commitment from their clients to higher-integrity tax compliance. The research concluded that the program delivered an extra billion dollars in tax revenue for each million spent on the co-designed collective efficacy of the compliance program (Braithwaite 2005b: 89–100). On this view of collective efficacy for corporate crime prevention, the collective efficacy of epistemic communities of internal and external gatekeepers to corporate power delivered. They delivered through dialogue and the co-design of compliance systems that guaranteed a degree of independence for the gatekeepers of the separation of corporate powers. More detail on how this has worked in companies can be found in Fisse and Braithwaite (1993) and Braithwaite (1997).

The globalisation of business has enabled new separations of powers and new answers to the question: 'Who guards the guardians?' At Exxon, IBM and Big Pharma, Brent Fisse and I found that compliance auditors from one country regularly travelled to subsidiaries in another country to audit the quality of their auditing. The Asian regional office auditors might audit the head office audit group in New York. Arranging guardianship in a circle is an advance on the historical practices of organisations like Exxon and IBM, which, akin to many police departments, rotted like fish from the head down. Every Mafia boss knows if you corrupt the police commissioner, the rest of the organisation is not likely to be a problem. Braithwaite (2006a) has developed more fully the republican ideal of arranging guardianship in a circle (illustrated in Figure 6.1). The only hierarchical solution to the corruption of nth-order guardians is to add an n+1th-order guardian. Then what happens if the n+1th-order guardian is corrupted? If, instead, we arrange guardians of accountability in a circle (see Figure 6.1, right side), each guardian can be a check on every other guardian. We can escape from the infinite regress of hierarchical accountability. The more separated public and private powers there are in a polity, the richer can be the circular checking of one guardian by many others.

In the world of corporate governance, progress is slow to bring into the circle utterly external watchdogs who do not depend on the corporation for an income. In Australia, consumer movement nominees on the Banking Ombudsman Council have access to the consumer complaint records of private banks and have a public reporting responsibility, but this has been overwhelmed by the volume and secrecy of consumer abuses.

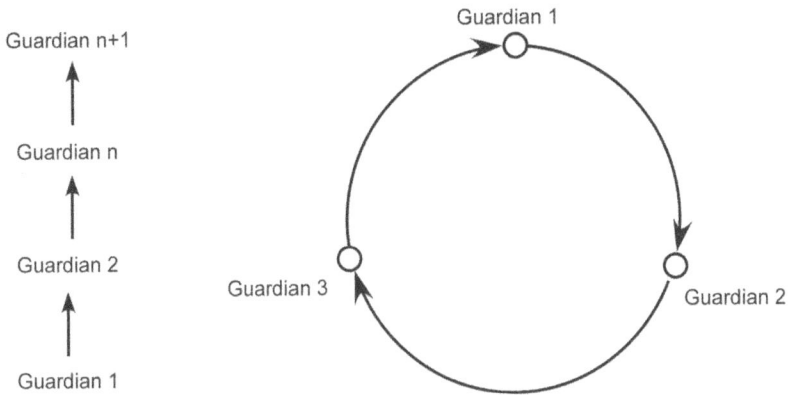

Figure 6.1 Models of hierarchical accountability and a circular republican conception of accountability

Accomplishments in widening the circle of guardianship to give outsiders a window into the audit performance of companies arose under the European Union's Eco-Management and Audit Scheme (EMAS) (EEC 1993). These were voluntary standards, yet they had significant force in a world in which many major purchasers and insurers required EMAS certification in environmentally high-risk industries. EMAS required companies to demonstrate continuous improvement in reducing environmental impact and product stewardship to an external environmental auditor. The report of that external auditor is generally publicly available and therefore can be examined by green groups on the lookout for environmental scandals. Unfortunately, some civil society auditing of environmental, fair trade, labour standards and animal rights compliance has tended to become captured, even dominated, by downstream retail interests (Sarfaty 2021). Some dominating retailers just want to sell more eggs via a low-cost path to labelling eggs 'free range' (Parker et al. 2017). Audit reports are sometimes less public than they should be. There is no need for despair about this; we must do more creative work to put in place more countervailing powers against retailer domination, against fraudulent retailer claims and for transparency. It requires pluralism that is more agonistic (Chapter 12).

There is a longer history of the empowerment of constituencies internal to the corporation, which have very different interests from management and affiliations to power bases outside the organisation. The leading example is elected union health and safety representatives who report both to management, which pays them, and the union, which legitimates them through democratic and deliberative accountability to workers, as discussed in the previous chapter. Rights of access to safety data have long been negotiated as a matter of contract between the union and the employer (Braithwaite 1985: 8), or as a matter of public law. These rights of access are sometimes checked by union-employed safety inspectors who conduct inspections of workplaces independently of state inspectors. In the case of large unions like the United Mine Workers of America during the 1980s, these could be many dozens in number (Braithwaite 1985). Empirical comparisons of high-accident and low-accident coalmines found that both safety directors and miners in mines with low accident rates reported that the union put greater pressure on management for safety through bargaining and dialogue (Braithwaite 1985). In Australian coalmines, elected worker inspectors do an independent check of a mine before a shift starts to double-check the assessment of company safety staff that levels of methane and other fundamental concerns are under control. Their assessment of the safety of the workplace is written in a record book at the entrance to the mine, which is available to all workers and to government safety inspectors. Union inspectors have a legal right to prevent or stop work at a mine on safety grounds until such time as a government safety inspector can come to the mine to adjudicate whether the safety stoppage is justified. This is quite an impressive separation of private powers that existed in the British Empire for more than a century and long existed in mine safety auditing in Japan, the United States, France, Romania and Poland (Braithwaite 1985: 9–10).

Professions are also important external–internal agents. A corporate circle of accountability is less closed to the extent that a general counsel who is a member feels an allegiance to the ethics of the legal profession that approaches in strength their allegiance to the corporation, or an accountant who feels ethical responsibility to accountancy's professional standards. Western nations are witnessing a proliferation of new professionalisms relevant to the penetration of corporate accountability by allegiances to values from outside the company. The 1990s in Australia saw a take-off of professionalism in environmental auditing, occupational health and safety and pharmacology (especially important in the pharmaceutical industry) and with the Society of Consumer Affairs Professionals in Business, the Institute of Compliance Professionals and the Regulatory Affairs Professionals Society (Parker 2002). In the United States, growth in corporate compliance staffing has been almost exponential during the past three decades (Haugh 2021).

Tempering power cannot work without a level of transparency that renders abuses in one area visible to another sphere of power. A recurrent abuse in the pharmaceutical industry occurs when the production manager of a plant, who is paid performance bonuses and promoted based on getting product out of the plant, overrules a finding of their quality-control manager that a batch of drugs does not meet specifications. The chances of a batch of drugs that just fails to meet specifications causing side effects that would be sheeted home to this failure are slight, while the payment of the production manager's bonus may be a certainty, but only if they get the batch at issue out on time. Hence, the incentive for the manager to break the law.

A simple solution to this problem was adopted by some of the more quality-conscious pharmaceutical corporations in the 1970s and has now been mandated in the laws of many countries. This is that a production manager is not allowed to overrule a quality-control judgement on a batch of drugs. It can only be done over the signature of the CEO. The effect is to make transparent the perverse incentives the firm creates for the production manager to break the law. Another effect is to taint the CEO and people who advise them with knowledge (the reverse of a policy of a vice-president responsible for going to jail). The final effect of this law is to strengthen the hand of quality control managers against the normally more senior production managers. CEOs in practice are reluctant to overrule quality control recommendations because the cost of redoing one batch of drugs is a comparatively minor matter to them and is a good way of sending a message to production managers to improve their performance on quality. The prospect of a batch causing a fatality, however remote, could be fatal for the CEO, as could the CEO tolerating a culture of sloppiness regarding quality. This, then, is an example of how a clever reporting architecture assures the separation of powers between quality control and production, prompts the need for dialogue on a quality culture that tolerates no errors on pharmaceutical specifications and shifts decision-making following the dialogue from a hard target with incentives to abuse power (the production manager) to soft targets with incentives to uphold the law (the CEO and the quality-control manager). These compliance dynamics of internally separated powers are possibly why the area of legal compliance that has improved the most, in a pharmaceutical industry in which corporate crime has generally worsened, is self-regulation of purity and sterility in drug manufacture (Dukes et al. 2014).

In a more generalised way, the reporting policies Fisse and Braithwaite (1983) discovered at Exxon in the aftermath of its international bribery scandals were exemplary in the way they ensured that the soft targets in the company who could be moved by ethical dialogue got to know about the temptations to which hardened crooks within Exxon were succumbing. We have no data on how rigorously these policies were implemented throughout and for how long, though we have doubts. As with collective efficacy in high-crime neighbourhoods, it does not continue keeping communities safe from crime after collective efficacy shuts down. Collective efficacy for compliance with the law in firms like Exxon is always at risk of being shut down by new-broom top management ruthlessly focused on short-term profits and pumping the stock price. Corporate collective efficacy is about internally independent kicking of the corporate tyres to ensure compliance. Once that independence is crushed, corporate crime returns.

During those moments of reform at Exxon, the 'controller' explained to Fisse and Braithwaite (1983) that effective control meant having an organisation full of 'antennas'. All units of the organisation had a responsibility to report not only confirmed violations of the 'Business Ethics Policy', but also 'probable violations'. 'Probable violations' were defined by corporate policy as 'situations where the facts available indicate that a violation probably occurred, even though there was insufficient information for a definite determination'. Hence, one could not sit on a matter on the strength of it being 'under investigation'. However, an obligation to report 'probable violations' is a less potent protection than a responsibility to report 'suspected violations'.

When violations were reported, there was an obligation on the recipient of the report to send back a determination as to whether a violation had occurred and, if it had, what remedial or disciplinary action was taken. Thus, a junior auditor who reported an offence and heard back nothing about it knew their report had been blocked—sat on somewhere. They were then obliged to activate the safety valve channel direct to the board's audit committee.

If they did not, they were in breach of the Business Ethics Policy for failing to ensure the problem was either resolved or put before the board. Many companies have policies requiring the reporting of ethics violations, but not many have policies that oblige the reporter to ensure the report is not blocked. This is important because one thing we know about criminal corporations is that they are expert at structuring communication blockages into the organisation to protect top management from the taint of knowledge. This had been true when Exxon was paying off politicians around the world. Fisse and Braithwaite (1983) cited memos from this era with statements like '[d]etailed knowledge could be embarrassing to the Chief Executive at some occasion on the witness stand'.

Summary of strategies for separating private powers

The strategies of generic importance for separating private powers discussed so far are:

1. Better securing the separation of the powers of the three major branches of corporate governance: shareholders, directors and managers.

2. Better separating powers within management: quality and production, environment and production.

3. Expanding audit capabilities to a range of areas beyond finance: safety, antitrust, ethics, environment, labour standards.

4. Professionalising audit so that internal auditors have an external professional allegiance to balance corporate loyalty.

5. Abandoning hierarchies of accountability in favour of circles of accountability so that auditors audit auditors, ensuring that someone guards the guardians.

6. Allowing into the circle of accountability outsiders with interests that diverge from corporate interests: unions into safety management circles, consumer group representatives into consumer complaints handling, greens into environmental circles by mandated public reporting of corporate environmental objectives, and public reporting of audits of whether the objectives are attained.

7. Guaranteeing transparency, tainting soft targets with knowledge by institutionalising a safety valve reporting route direct to a board audit committee, to a corporate ombudsman or both.

8. In domains where serious abuse of power is a risk, independent reports on compliance to the board's audit committee from separate powers: line management, legal, audit, unions.

9. Obligations on all employees to report suspected violations of law and violations of all corporate policies that involve an abuse of corporate power (for example, corporate ethics, environmental policies). Obligations to report the suspected violations directly to the board when the employee does not receive a written report that the matter has been satisfactorily resolved. Failure to meet this obligation must itself be an ethical breach that colleagues have an ethical obligation to report. In the context of corporate crime control, this is a key to collective efficacy that transcends the dominations of the extremely powerful.

For each of these strategies there is a debate to have about whether they should be mandated by the state, left to business or professional self-regulation or seen as demands that social movements must extract agonistically from private power.

Many soft targets and how social change works

As a general matter across the social sciences, the theory of persuading many soft targets may have its uses for understanding how social change works. My argument has been that the study of corporate and state crime has been afflicted with excessive pessimism grounded in the correct observation that it is difficult to deter an actor as powerful as the state, Amazon or Google. All states have their histories of criminalisation, periods when mafias, robber barons, drug lords or criminal stock market masterminds captured significant parts of the state. Equally, many states have put their criminalised past behind them, moving from a state with extractive institutions to states with inclusive and accountable institutions (Acemoglu and Robinson 2012), from predatory states to developmental states that institutionalise embedded autonomy (Evans 1995).

Realist international relations theorists are scathing about the irrelevance of international law. They ask why a state would ever comply with international law when it is against their interests; because there is no sovereign above states—the United Nations is not their sovereign; state sovereignty rules over the United Nations—states cannot be deterred by international law. International lawyers have found this realist challenge a dangerous one for their discipline. For the most part, their response has had little impact because they refuse in their rejoinders to reframe their referent. The problem of international lawyers is that they are just as wedded to the referent that international society is a society of sovereign states as are the realist international relations theorists. This is not to say that the rejoinders of international lawyers are without merit when they say that states are more than just rational actors pursuing their interests (for example, see the wonderful rejoinder of Chayes and Chayes 1998).

The more useful rejoinders, however, draw on work such as that of Ronald Mitchell (on the international law of oil spills at sea). Oil tanker owners often sailed under flags of convenience that made them undeterrable by the direct rule of any sovereign state. We saw how 98 per cent compliance with international law was achieved by broadening the range of regulatory targets to shipbuilders, classification societies, insurers and reinsurers, and more.

Putnam and Henning (1989) contributed an important reframing of the referent of international relations when they tackled the puzzle of how the G7—the seven most powerful sovereign nations on the planet—at its Bonn summit of 1978 could settle a trade and economic policy agreement that every one of those sovereigns strongly opposed. It was not even a compromise in which one country won on this and another won on that. It was, from the perspective of all seven sovereigns, a lose–lose agreement they had signed. Putnam (1988) resolved the puzzle by showing that each of the trade diplomats of the G7 was actually sitting at two tables. Putnam's contribution was called the two-table theory of international politics. Ministers were sitting at the G7 table with the trade ministers of six other sovereign states with whom they were implacably in disagreement. But as they did their deals, they were also turning around to their table of domestic politics, which included representatives of other state bureaucracies, domestic business and domestic civil society. For example, one Bonn summit agenda item was reducing global fiscal imbalances by all major states increasing taxes on oil. None of the trade ministries of the G7 wanted that, but the environment ministries represented at the second table of domestic politics did for each of the seven states—as did some business interests that were invested in other sources of energy (nuclear power interests, coal interests, paradoxically, and renewables investors in hydro, for example) and environmental NGOs. While the trade interests at the first table were opposing each proposal put up by the other six trade ministers, the pro–oil-tax interests around the seven second tables were joining hands to build strong domestic pressure for consensus in favour of higher oil taxes as part of the solution in each of their seven societies. The oil tax hike did become part of the agreement. In other words, a collaborative problem-solving politics among many weak players defeated a confrontational politics mobilised by the interests of all the strong players who were used to getting their way at the first table.

Braithwaite and Drahos (2000) describe in similar theoretical terms how a much more important environmental agreement was reached that criminalised conduct that was killing hundreds of thousands of people by widening the ozone hole. This was the Montreal Protocol of 1987, which was accomplished in a different way by dividing the opposition of the strong and persuading US President Ronald Reagan to defect from the strong to join the more unified environmental coalitions of the weak (discussed in more detail in Chapter 12). The most important and effective international agreement for crime control in human history, according to Braithwaite and Drahos (2000), was the agreement to ban the slave trade. It mobilised the same strategy of dividing the strategic trade interests of the most powerful sovereigns in the world, as just one strong sovereign, then two, joined more unified social movement coalitions of the weak against slavery led by Christian churches. This was the first great victory of global social movement politics that showed the way for others to follow, such as the women's movement in globalising the right for women to vote in the early twentieth century and the international trade union movement beginning the globalisation of labour laws from 1919 (Braithwaite and Drahos 2000).

The theoretical interpretation here is to see this paradoxical outcome of the weak using the jujitsu of the strong against them in international politics as reflecting the results of Schell-Busey et al.'s (2016) meta-analysis of what works in corporate crime control. In fact, it is this result writ large. Pure deterrence does not work as well as a regulatory mix of many thin reeds. Just as Christian churches could transform a world that was mostly not Christian in the antislavery movement against the most powerful corporations and states in the global system, so churches are a better hope than criminal law-enforcement decapitation strategies for regulating Latin American drug cartels. The more promising approach involves churches peeling off some of the most powerful cartel leaders to a deal in which they disinvest their capital from drugs and human trafficking and invest it instead in the legitimate capital market. They can live a comfortable life this way without passing on to their children a future fearing a hail of bullets. The caring and ethical soft targets here are organised crime bosses who want a more decent life for their children than the life they have led. The template for how to do this is not in the criminological literature on organised crime but in the peacemaking literature on how religious leaders working with women's groups have persuaded the wives of insurgency leaders to then persuade their husbands to lay down their guns (Braithwaite et al. 2010b). Critics rightly say there is not a lot of justice as proportionality in these deals. Murderous insurgency leaders tend to get rich out of the power-sharing deal that forges the peace while the victims of their murderous conduct get only crumbs from the table of the peace deal. In the long run of history, however, what both groups get is justice as a better future for all their children—a more peaceful future. Consider Froestad and Shearing (2012) on post-Apartheid South Africa taking on justice as a better future. None of this is to say that the transition from Apartheid, from slavery, war, domination by drug cartels or environmental domination by the G7 is easy. It is hard, agonistic work, but we can make more progress by mobilising the collective efficacy of many weak players than by deluding ourselves with simplistic strategies of decapitating or deterring domination.

In sum, we can think of the mistake the international relations scholars made as failing to reframe the referent, to use the language of Chapter 2. The referent needed to move from the state to bits of the state and bits of international society. This is a dialogue of many weak bits coordinating to accomplish a jujitsu that flips the strong. It does the jujitsu by turning some of its own strengths against itself. This way of thinking about social change is a way of reframing thinking about why collective efficacy and restorative justice should be seen as theoretically promising ideas that have encouraging evidence of effectiveness. Chapter 9 contrasts them with the theoretical framing of 'swift and certain deterrence' directed at individual offenders as the theoretical grounding for Operation HOPE. It is not that the intervention techniques of Operation HOPE lack promise. Its problem, according to the diagnosis of Chapter 9, is that it is hobbled by a myopic theoretical focus on deterring individual offenders. Operation HOPE can reframe its referent to a community of care, as restorative justice has done and collective efficacy does (Chapter 11), if it is to grasp the theoretical possibilities in its intervention strategy. The genius of collective efficacy exists at many levels, and this is just one of them. But in shifting from unpromising and costly deterrence interventions to collective efficacy interventions, we shift from a focus on hard targets who are committed to criminal subcultures to the larger numbers of caring, responsible citizens who surround them.

As collective efficacy is built, a majority of the most caring soft targets tend to be women; conversely, when we target dominating criminals who are hard targets, we mostly target men. This plays into Messner and Rosenberg's institutional anomie virtue of feminising the frames of aspirational reference for freedom and crime control. Poor communities do well when they learn to value more than grabbing the material possessions of others, when they learn to value collective community-building in which women are leaders in charting the better course. Likewise, in restorative justice circles, empirically, women do more of the speaking than men. Targeting a community of care in our interventions mobilises many soft targets and energises them through the 'collective effervescence' of the restorative circle (Rossner 2013).

Conclusions so far

A standard rationale for the separation of powers is deterring the abuse of power with countervailing power. Deterring the abuse of power, be it private or public, is not something societies are good at. Problems like police corruption, dumping of hazardous waste and corporate fraud bounce back after each wave of scandal and reform (Sherman 1978). An increasingly coherent theoretical and empirical literature can now make sense of why deterring the abuse of power so often backfires. Emotive defiance, cognitions of stigma and procedural injustice, psychological reactance, the deterrence trap, the retribution trap, the compliance trap and rational countermeasures are among the reasons big sticks often rebound (Braithwaite 1997; see also Chapter 9). This book shows that all of these mechanisms apply to powerful actors; several of them have more force with powerful than with powerless actors. Chapter 9 will show that defiance is greatest with the powers which the powerful care about most. Braithwaite (1997) shows that potent corporate counter-deterrence strategies are also most likely with the power corporations most care about dominating. This generally means defiance will be most potent with the commanding heights of organised power.

The first solutions to these problems considered are to:

1. replace narrow, formal and strongly punitive responsibility with broad, informal, weak sanctions that touch many soft targets
2. separate enforcement targeting from identification of the actor who benefits from the abuse.

Together, (1) and (2) imply: a) strong separations of power within and between both the public and private sectors, combined with b) another republican regulative ideal—problem-solving dialogue. The richer and more plural are the separations of powers, the more overdetermined will be the capacity to detect and prevent abuse of power. The more actors there are with this preventive capability, the more likely it is some of them will be soft targets who can be persuaded to check the abuse of power by simple and cheap discursive appeals to their virtue, or at least to interests different to those of the actors who are abusing power. The more that institutions for the control of abuse of power are based on moral reasoning rather than deterrence, the more public-regarding actors with preventive capability there will be to stand up against domination.

Deterrence is certainly needed when dialogue fails to control the abuse of power. Incapacitation is more strongly needed when deterrence fails (Chapters 9 and 10). But the more we can succeed in keeping deterrence and incapacitation in the background, the better are the prospects that separations of powers will check the abuse of power through moral suasion, and the better will be the chance that it will do so in a way that enhances rather than hampers economically efficient markets in virtue.

An interesting implication of this for republican political theory is that separations of powers and dialogic appeals to the virtue of citizens are not just separate republican ideals. Separations of powers create a world in which dialogue can displace sanctioning as the dominant means of regulating the abuse of power. These republican prescriptions are not only coherent in the sense that separations of powers and dialogic reconstitution of interests help secure freedom as nondomination. Deliberative democracy is causally dependent on separations of powers.

We have shown that if appeals to the virtue of soft strategic targets are to work, the form separations of powers must take is much more plural than the traditional separation of the legislature, executive and judiciary. The more richly plural are the separations of public and private powers, the more likely it is that the dependence of each guardian on many other guardians will secure their independence from domination by any one of them.

This theory of republicanism amounts to a rejection of the radical Jeffersonianism of the strict separation of powers that became influential in the early nineteenth century, and that was represented in the French Constitution of 1795. Simply dividing power and making it directly accountable to the electorate, preventing judges from meddling in the affairs of the legislature and vice versa, were part of a romantic theory even then—one that was bound to give birth to adversarial struggles for control that would deliver the likes of Napoleon Bonaparte. The romantic theory of this century has been that antitrust law could democratise the new private power simply by dividing it.[8] A pragmatic republicanism for the burgeoning private power of the twenty-first century will give more emphasis to the checking-of-power part of the republican ideal; it will pluralise the separation of powers, while rejecting any aspiration that each divided power be fully independent. Rather than having a few autonomous branches of governance, many semi-autonomous powers will recursively check one another. This means rejecting the status quo of the separation of powers, rejecting radical Jeffersonianism and creatively radicalising Madison for a world of new and disturbing concentrations of private power.

A good concluding illustration of how important these ideas are for crime reduction and freedom enhancement is reform in the United States in the early 1990s that steeply reduced the number of nursing home residents who were physically restrained: it declined from 42 per cent of all nursing home residents in the United States being physically restrained in the late 1980s to 4 per cent by early this century, with most of the decline occurring with the reforms in the first two years of the 1990s (Braithwaite et al. 2007: 44). Collective efficacy in the community of gerontological professionals to liberate the elderly was led by several innovative administrators who

---

8   Maximising the breaking up of private power through antitrust law might create inefficiently small firms. This is politically unsustainable in a world of intense international competition. Even if one could do it, why would one want to? In some senses, it is easier for state and civil society to demand the kinds of separations of power and dialogic justice discussed in this chapter from one profitable large firm than from a dozen small struggling firms. A conception of the separation of powers as simply dividing or breaking up concentrations is rarely attractive or realistic in the contemporary world. That is by no means to deny that there will be occasional contexts in which the best strategy to control domination is to break up a monopoly. This is also a strategy that the rule of competition law rightly provides.

built profitable 'restraint-free' nursing homes as a proof of concept. It was driven most importantly by an inspiring and agonistic social movement to 'Untie the Elderly' and by the retraining of street-level regulators to ask hard questions about why residents were being restrained. Inspectors recorded noncompliance when poor answers were given. There was also regulatory pressure during the 1990s to ensure that physical restraint was not replaced with chemical restraint. This vigilance meant that chemical restraint also halved in the early 1990s. In the twenty-first century, however, a new epidemic of chemical restraint crept back into the system and cascaded to take it over. Lobbying leadership of Big Pharma by Purdue Pharmaceuticals, who had a strategy to increase opiate addiction of the aged, was critical in this regress. The lesson here is that, on a regular historical cycle, regulatory parameters must be reset to counter whatever forms of gaming have entered the system since the last cycle of reform. Whether it is hotspot policing or nursing home inspection, street-level preventive strategies work, but they do not keep working if the guardians of freedom stop kicking the tyres at street level.

These new separations of powers that untied the elderly were economically efficient because it turned out that the corporations that sold restraints were peddling a false message that unless residents were carefully restrained, nursing homes would be sued for failing to prevent falls. The evidence showed that more nursing homes were sued by families after loved ones slid down in their chair and were strangled on their restraint than were successfully sued for falls of unrestrained residents (Braithwaite et al. 2007). Mercifully, Purdue Pharmaceuticals was ultimately bankrupted by suits and criminal enforcement over its creation of the opioid epidemic. These new separations of powers in aged care delivered one of the most unrecognised but fundamental advances of freedom in America in the twentieth century. Aged care accomplished this while reducing private litigation, while improving compliance with the law that reduced fines and while increasing efficiency and profitability. There is no doubt, however, that excess in separations of powers in other circumstances does reduce rather than increase efficiency. This is true for separations of powers in both the public sector and the private sector. This challenge is confronted in the next chapter.

Hence, in subsequent chapters, we must think more deeply about the character of what is required for a society that has low crime, low domination and that flourishes with freedom. The next chapter traverses the micro–macro in a more comprehensive way, putting emphasis on the importance of strong individuals for high freedom and low crime. But strong individuals do not appear from thin air. They come from strong families, strong schools, strong universities and collective efficacy in strong communities where it 'takes a whole village to raise a child'. More abstractly, these strengths require strong markets to be complemented and tempered by strong states, strong civil society and strong individuals.

Looking forward to a macro vision of collective efficacy for freedom

The next chapter argues that financial capital must be tempered by human capital, social capital, recovery capital and restorative capital. Collective efficacy is the most critical facet of social capital for crime prevention. Collective efficacy also does not appear from thin air. To deliver it at the level of all local communities, societies must get serious about scaling up recovery capital, restorative capital and prevention. The next chapter and Chapter 11 grapple with how the undominated, low-crime society moors a complex web of separated private and public powers to accomplish the scaling up of social capital. Chapter 7 considers Sun Yat-sen's thinking and leadership of a century ago when he was contemplating his Chinese republic. Authoritarian resistance to communism washed his republican vision into the bloodied soil of his beloved China. The key innovation of Sun Yat-sen's republican constitutions was a fourth branch of governance that drew on the wisdom from millennia of Chinese institutional history on how to complement an independent executive, legislature and judiciary. This fourth branch is an integrity and accountability branch of governance. I think of this fourth elected branch of non-party one-termers as the conductor of the richly separated powers of a society's orchestra. Its philosophy is to temper wisely the many separated powers arrayed in front of it. This is a complex and interesting art of government. Freedom's orchestra does not soar simply by getting each musician to play in tune.

Finally, Chapter 11 argues that the most extractive of states and economies are vulnerable to cascading civil wars and violent state crime. Wars do make strong states—a theme from Tilly discussed in Chapter 3. In contemporary conditions, strong states emerge in the aftermath of wars that escalate to the point of destroying old regimes. UN peacekeeping and peacebuilding can become for a period of transition perhaps the most important elements of the separation of powers. We have seen in this chapter that the effectiveness of UN peacekeeping in preventing war and crime is one of the strongest empirical relationships established by the discipline of international relations (Walter et al. 2020). This UN work is a profound source of hope for all societies. This is because, for example, if we want to look for the society that has the most inspiring institutionalisation of women's rights in its constitution, look to Nepal, where a vibrant women's movement institutionalised those constitutional rights in a 2006 peace agreement. That peace process put its polity in a more 'original position' with UN support—an original position where no political faction knew who would win the post-conflict election and all needed to sustain support from the women's movement by supporting the de-institutionalised domination of women (Braithwaite 2015).

One implication of understanding tempered and plural powers is that the next great innovations in the institutionalisation of freedom are most unlikely to come from stable, smug western democracies for reasons similar to why the next great genres of music that lift our souls may not be inspired by white westerners. What the West can do is become more cosmopolitan in the way it looks out to learn from the next Sun Yat-sen, the next Gandhi, the next Nelson Mandela, or the next Nepalese feminists.

7

Tempered and diverse forms of capital

Key propositions

- Competition policy is a good thing when it strengthens markets in goods, and bad when it strengthens markets in bads. The remedy is to temper Donor McDonor markets with strategic regulation.
- Markets in children's books, *Consumer Reports* magazine, pricing carbon, software markets that protect against property crime and markets for motor vehicle antitheft technologies are among examples of virtuous markets in crime prevention. Markets in compliance professionalism and the privatisation of criminal prosecution are particularly strategic for controlling corporate crime (Chapter 9).
- High-crime cities that have deindustrialised can be renewed by renewable energy and welfare, by a green welfare economy that opens the door to a low-crime information economy (in which black lives matter).
- Old socialism and 'old' neoliberalism cannot deliver this liberating outcome. Transformation requires a hybridity of strategic publicisations of the private and privatisations of the public with an eye on freedom as nondomination.
- Regulation of the financialisation of capitalism and of tech platform monopolies is particularly imperative.
- Economic capital must be strong to accomplish a low-crime, high-freedom society, but so must be human capital, social capital, recovery capital and restorative capital.

- While there are fertile distinctions among different forms of social capital, they are mutually constitutive. Each tempers the abuse of power by the others. This is also true of collective efficacy—a variant of social capital that is particularly strategic for crime control.

- When all these forms of capital become strong, the way they each check and balance one another creates a societal strength that is nuanced, nimble and dialogic rather than dominating.

- Mutually constitutive forms of capital in turn constitute CHIME (Connectedness, Hope, Identity, Meaning and Empowerment). CHIME controls crime.

- Without further strengthening all of the foregoing strengths, the superior capacity of authoritarian capitalism to pull levers may overwhelm liberal capitalism. A violent world dominated by authoritarianism, criminalised states and criminalised markets is our path unless we consider these hybrid paths not taken.

- Strong markets, a strong state, strong civil society and strong individuals with an agency that makes the personal political are all vital to more freedom and less crime, as are enculturating trust and institutionalising distrust in all key institutions.

- Contemporary capitalisms are highly internally variegated. Different variegations require different mixes of forms of capital and forms of regulation.

- A crucial art of freedom is to learn how to flip markets in vice to markets in virtue. Markets that control crimes of domination are an important part of that art of freedom. Institutional anomie theory is misguided if it neglects or dismisses this.

- Crashes in capital markets are connected in dangerous ways to security crises and environmental crises. Flipping to markets in virtue is one important approach to averting cascading crises.

- Markets such as Wall Street are constituted by communitarianism among traders; understanding this is a key to understanding how to flip them to markets in virtue via collective efficacy remedies such as restorative justice.

Markets in criminal bads and crime-prevention goods

This chapter resumes the theme of how to temper anomic financial capital with checks and balances. In this sense, it picks up the institutional anomie approach of previous chapters. Where it diverges sharply from that tradition, however, is that it argues for strengthening the institutions of the market to harness markets to control crime and expand freedom. Chapter 2 introduced the criminalisation of markets as a central issue for macrocriminology in conditions of contemporary capitalism. This chapter argues that financial capital is important in the era of the financialisation of capitalism. But financial capital, like all forms of capital, becomes a better tool of freedom when it is intertwined with all the other forms of capital the chapter discusses.

Competition policy under capitalism induces some effective competition in harnessing modern management techniques to the more efficient production of bads as well as goods. This problem is structurally general. It can be illustrated with many vices such as paedophilia and its mass marketing by competing commercial exploiters of this vice through the internet, sex shops and sex tourism. Indeed, it can be illustrated with a more competitive and more globally networked market in bodies of various ages and in body parts, not only for sexual exploitation, but also for illegal immigration and for medical, cosmetic and other uses. For republicans, few vices could be worse than this darknet-enabled reinvention of slavery. Starting with the liberation of Hebrew and other slaves by Cyrus the Great of Persia and culminating with the nineteenth-century globalisation of the ban on the slave trade, this was the greatest and the first successful global social movement for human liberation.

Examples such as the sex trade and the payment of bribes in countries where every business pays them bring into focus the question of who is to say what is vice and what is virtue? Liberal economic theory argues that more effectively competitive markets are good precisely because markets leave it to every citizen's taste to be enacted by them alone into preferences that drive the price mechanism. Why should this not apply to the price of sex or bribes, which could be economically efficient or productive in growing economies? The state, the church or political activists must not tell us what is good for us. Untrammelled choice, they say, is the essence of being a free citizen of a liberal society.

It nevertheless remains the case that all of us have views—albeit conflicting—about what are good and evil things to do as we indulge our preferences. Mostly, these normative judgements are bound up with obligations we believe citizens should have to be other-regarding. To the extent that competitive markets succeed in delivering the more efficient satisfaction of freely chosen preferences, they will more efficiently produce bads as well as goods—however bad and good are defined. Yes, we all have different views on what is good and what is bad, what is vice and what is virtue, what should and should not be criminal. However differently we define these things, it is analytic that more effective competitive markets will more efficiently produce bads and goods, legal and illegal products and services, alike.

A paradox of a more effectively liberal economy is that it forces us to make more judgements about the vices we want the state to regulate or criminalise. Because a perfectly competitive market economy more efficiently produces vice—indeed, innovation in vices yet to be invented (such as new designer drugs, killer robots and weapons of mass destruction)—it creates greater demand from citizens for state and global regulation. Markets that are widely viewed as markets in virtue often stimulate markets in vice. Hence, Braithwaite (2005b) shows that markets in tax law advice constantly generate new shelters to protect the rich from their tax obligations. They also engender insurance markets that cover their legal liability for tax penalties should the shelter be successfully attacked in the courts. Yet Braithwaite (2005b) also shows that in reaction to this, a market in reputable tax advice is created by accountants whose main asset is their reputation with tax authorities as law-abiding, ethical tax advisors. Software markets develop products that assist the evasion and/or avoidance of tax obligations; other software products help firms to check whether they have complied with the law. Capitalism thus engenders an ever more robust contest between markets in tax vice and markets in tax virtue. The regulator's challenge, according to Braithwaite (2008), then becomes what state and civil society can do to advantage markets in virtue and hobble markets in vice.

Braithwaite (2008: 52–60) and Dukes et al. (2014) developed several regulatory principles for how to flip markets in vice to markets in virtue. These devices can be purely economic, such as taxing sugary drinks (sugar as a market in vice) and giving cheaper health insurance to consumers who take out gym memberships (gyms as a market in virtue). Instead of criminalising the purchase of dangerous drugs by children (as with tobacco) or criminalising use by a person of any age, an option is to tax dangerous drugs very heavily and regulate their sale heavily (by banning advertising, requiring prescriptions, and so on). Regulatory devices for flipping markets in vice to markets in virtue can also involve webs of normative and social movement influences to shift the vice–virtue market balance.

These can be combined with incentives to draw whistleblowers from inside the market in vice across to support the market in virtue. One way is to pay whistleblowers a percentage of the fines imposed on sellers who break regulatory laws, as in the US *False Claims Act*. We discussed in the previous chapter the evidence that bounties for whistleblowers have been a major help in enforcement against corporate crime in the United States. Another strategy is shifting enforcement targeting from perpetrators of vice to marketers of vice and leaders who cover up vice in their institutions. This is the idea that a more effective way of shutting down paedophilia than prosecuting aged priests would be to prosecute the Pope or a cardinal who heads a national church as an individual, or the church as an institution, for a new criminal offence of covering up extreme domination.[1] The safety of air travel has improved so much in the past century even though pilots and air traffic controllers are very infrequently prosecuted for their mistakes or recklessness. Because the cover-up of near-misses or negligence is prosecuted, however, a culture of learning from mistakes has been nurtured (Braithwaite 2005a). The second half of this chapter adds a more structural approach to flipping markets in vice to markets in virtue through advocacy for creative balancing and tempering of financial capital with other forms of capital.

It does not matter to the analytic argument that both bads and goods are produced more efficiently by competition policies that engender vibrant markets, however good and bad are defined. This does not mean that how good and bad markets should be defined is unimportant. On the contrary, it demonstrates that criminology is dangerous without contested normative moorings. The previous chapter showed that markets stripped of a moral dimension are heartland concerns for a macrocriminology of freedom and of market anomie. Indeed, a world in which virulent markets produce vices more widely, more efficiently and more amorally is a threat to the normative order and therefore to the management of crime and unleashing of freedom.

---

1   Elizabeth Warren's proposal, discussed further in Chapter 9, of CEO criminal liability for negligent stewardship of a criminal corporation would be another path to prosecution of some future Pope.

Learning to diagnose criminal markets: The Philippines

Let us illustrate the diagnosis of criminal markets by considering one society, the Philippines, which turned out to have profoundly criminal markets. This is a macrocriminological illustration of why one society can have higher levels of many kinds of crime and threats to freedom than others. There are dozens of countries with a worse homicide rate than the Philippines, but at 8.8 per 100,000, its rate is as high as homicide gets in Asia. The estimate fails to count exceptional numbers of murders by the police. I will argue that the criminalisation of markets is an important contributor to police murders. The criminalisation of Philippine markets is a particularly important criminalisation because of the way it sustains high levels of poverty and pushes up rates of many other forms of crime.

I visited the Philippines 20 years ago with leaders of the ACCC and the Foundation for Effective Markets and Governance. Our mission was to assist the Philippines with introducing new competition and consumer protection laws and their enforcement. I came away cynical about our mission. My analysis was that there were so many higher priorities for the Philippines than getting competition and consumer law working effectively. Regulation of monopolies is a good thing, but the Philippines' problem, as I wrongly diagnosed it then, was that the country needed to focus on creating more flourishing businesses before it started worrying about businesses monopolising the economy. More fundamentally, the Philippines needed to focus on lifting poor people out of poverty and it was public investment in things like education that would achieve that.

In 2015 and 2019, when I visited the Philippines for the fourth and fifth times, I was impressed by the quality of the educational outcomes and the great progress that had been made, particularly in education for girls. The poor were still poor, however. Well-educated young people had no jobs to go to. So what was wrong now? It was my earlier analysis that was wrong. One profound poverty-inducing malaise in the Philippines was always monopoly. Companies that create jobs fail to grow in the Philippines because dominant monopolies crush competition from new competitors. Take Philippine Airlines. Why is it so much less successful, so stunted, compared with most Asian national airlines? You might think it has a massive commercial advantage over an airline like Singapore Airlines because it has a huge domestic air transport market of 100 million people separated across large islands. It should have been able to build a formidable international business with economies of scale on that domestic foundation compared with Singapore Airlines. The reason it has not is that political cronies long ago took over Philippine Airlines. Ex-Philippine Airline executives captured the airline regulators. The company's monopoly profits have been protected from competition; they line the pockets of political cronies.

The commercial opportunities to corrupt markets in this way are enabled in turn by political corruption. Criminalised markets induce criminalised states and vice versa. While we can easily see how one kind of corporate crime leads to another and to state crime, this hardly seems to explain high homicide rates. In fact, it does to a degree because the corrupted state often disappears people it does not like. Sometimes when the police or their political patrons do not like a little person or even a big one like a mayor, they kill them, claiming they were drug dealers or drug barons resisting arrest. Many cronies in the Philippines have become bosses of organised crime who buy impunity for their murderous activities in the market for votes that is Philippine democracy. Paul Hutchcroft (1998) described it as *Booty Capitalism*.

But the more fundamental connection between monopoly and murder is at the level of the *local* monopolies of booty capitalism. High-integrity criminal law enforcement is more important than competition law enforcement to breaking the grip of these local monopolies. Yes, there are people who dominate national monopolies, but there are other often totally different people who are local oligarchs. Frequently, this is the wealthiest businessman in a town, who buys votes to become mayor. He then uses his position to drive away any local competitor to his businesses. He drives them away either by using his political power as mayor or by threatening them with violence by a militia he controls. He also deploys their violence to keep winning elections. This means in the Philippines the monopoly power of the national airline is a small problem compared with hundreds of little local monopolies that make food, financial services, accommodation and many other things much more expensive for poor people than they would be if there were local competition. In very recent years, partial salvation for the poor who live under the yoke of these violent local monopolies of business power has been opened by e-commerce becoming more accessible to poor Filipino towns. Internet markets have therefore tempered the power of local oligarchs somewhat and have also contributed to crime prevention by helping to reduce poverty. I cannot think of many ways in which e-commerce dominated by the likes of Amazon is a market in virtue, but this is certainly one of them. Hence, after centuries of underdevelopment, this contestation of local monopolisation by a global market effervescence, combined with an excellent education system for girls and boys (many of whom return incomes from overseas) and natural blessings like the world's richest fisheries, began to cause job creation and growth to improve from 2005. Growth was particularly strong in 2018 and 2019. Now, local corruption and violence pose new threats to that accomplishment. An example is overfishing that is not regulated effectively by corrupt regulators. The imperative remains to incapacitate local oligarchs by criminal enforcement from monopolising local business power, political power and militia power.

Accommodating markets in virtue in institutional anomie theory

Institutional anomie theory (Messner and Rosenfeld 2013) is the extant macrocriminological tradition closest to the theory of tempered institutions developed in this book. It seeks to integrate institutional with classical (ancient and Durkheimian) and Mertonian anomie theories oriented to illegitimate opportunities and lure. The review of evidence supporting these perspectives as important to explaining crime proved encouraging in earlier chapters. The problem with institutional anomie theory opened up by the example of booty capitalism in the Philippines, however, is that it fails to consider where markets are virtuous and it fails to advocate the strengthening of virtuous markets.

The most important examples of markets in virtue are markets in decent jobs in which employees are treated with respect regardless of their race or sex. These are jobs that build the human and social capital of employees and what we describe in this chapter as CHIME (Connectedness, Hope, Identity, Meaning and Empowerment) in their journey of human capital formation. Not all jobs do this, of course. A homeless teenager who survives through sex work in oppressive conditions participates in a market in vice rather than a market in virtue. The criminalisation of markets in human trafficking is needed but is not likely to deliver as powerful a pathway out of the market in vice as programs that discover what sort of future the teenager seeks and then help place them into a job with training opportunities that open that pathway. Often a countervailing market in virtue offers the better pathway out of vice than the criminalisation of vice.

Many markets that constitute CHIME are quite banal, such as the market in children's books, which is not monopolistic. It is steered to virtue by wise parents sharing the good fun and developmental experiences they have with their child reading a particular book. It is a market buttressed by charities that sell such books secondhand to poor families at very affordable prices, and by a gift economy of passing on good books to those we love.

Then there are markets that are virtuous because they protect citizens from crime. At the western frontier of the United States in the nineteenth century, citizens could be terrified to enter a bank lest an armed outlaw arrive. Such unfreedom does not terrorise banking today. The banking market has restructured to diminish opportunities by holding less cash; the bank building is full of monitors, cameras and alarms that can make it impossible to escape with these modest amounts of cash. Markets in private security technologies have delivered this freedom to bank customers. As citizens prepare to drive away from the bank, theft-protection technologies make it less likely than it was half a century ago that they will discover their vehicle has been stolen. For example, private-sector automotive markets half a century ago started to perfect ignition systems that made it impossible for car thieves to steal a car without a key by 'hotwiring'. This assisted great reductions in car theft in the final decades of the twentieth century, even as car thieves began to adapt by stealing car keys from owners' homes. Car theft reduction was part of the great crime drop of the 1990s in western countries. Burglar alarm systems in cars and homes have also made contributions to preventing both kinds of theft, but much less so than hardening using engine immobilisers (Farrell et al. 2014; Weatherburn and Rahman 2021: Ch. 6). Markets in the virtue of target hardening have thus contributed much more to motor vehicle theft reduction than better deployment of police and increased imprisonment to increase deterrence (Chapter 9). The market in virtue was enhanced by consumer organisations and publications like *Consumer Reports* and *Which* around the world that produced shame lists of the brands of vehicles most prone to theft. This consumer-movement shaming motivated laggards in the market of target hardening to be more competitive and motivated government regulatory and insurer responses that mandated adoption by car manufacturers of technologies such as engine immobilisers. The growing efficiency of markets in electronic funds transfer has reduced the attractiveness of all forms of crime involving the grabbing of cash (Weatherburn and Rahman 2021). Markets in target-hardening technologies have made it much harder to steal from a bank, a business, a home or a car, to shoplift, to counterfeit banknotes, to steal a mobile phone, to fence stolen goods or to hijack a plane, contributing variably but substantially to the great western crime drop of recent decades. Most criminologists might acknowledge this, yet criminological theory has developed in a way that mostly marginalises it as a minor issue, which empirically it is not. Our understanding of these markets is still rather confused because the effects are undoubtedly nonlinear—that is, there probably are tipping points where property offenders consider that robbing a bank makes no sense, breaking into a wealthy person's home or car makes no sense and hardening higher proportions of those targets makes no difference. Criminology fails to inform our understanding of where those tipping points might be.

Ayres and Levitt (1998) found that Lojak, a hidden transmitter used for retrieving stolen vehicles, reduced fraudulent insurance claims[2] and caused a sharp reduction in motor vehicle theft, saving $10 in reduced theft costs for each dollar spent on Lojak. Consumers who paid to install Lojak in their cars obtained only 10 per cent of these benefits. Ninety per cent of benefits went to free riders through reduced risks of car theft in cities where Lojak attained significant levels of use. This led Ayres and Levitt (1998) to propose subsidising this market in crime prevention as a cost-effective policy. That kind of policy proposal is not the way criminal justice policymakers think, so policy ideas for markets in virtue are little pursued, even in this case when the work of elite researchers (Ayres and Levitt) was taken seriously in little-cited work by the absolute elite of criminological researchers (for example, Nagin and Weisburd 2013).

Ignition interlock devices for the incapacitation of drink-driving are another technological innovation that have been shown in systematic reviews to have one of the highest effect sizes among correctional measures (Weisburd et al. 2017: 427). The huge wave of terrorist hijackings of aircraft half a century ago was all but ended during the 1980s and 1990s through the effectiveness and continuous improvement of markets in scanning technologies for use before passengers board aircraft.

---

2   Personal communication with Ian Ayres.

While the private sector has driven anti-theft innovation, there has been public-sector innovation in markets in anti-theft virtue, such as the invention by the Reserve Bank of Australia of plastic banknotes that are difficult for counterfeiters to copy. Sadly, Australia's public-sector central bank adopted some private-sector vices when it sold this innovation to some countries by paying bribes to state decision-makers, including Saddam Hussein of Iraq! Credit cards also made counterfeiting a progressively less lucrative crime. But as is the story of all markets in anti-crime virtue, they inspire counter-markets in vice that are new forms of criminality. In this case, that is credit card fraud. So, we will see there is a great deal of contingency in how the competition between markets in virtue and markets in vice unfolds. The reality of contemporary capitalism is there is no escaping that competition, so there is no alternative but for societies to seek to get better at markets that design ever more effective incapacitation of access to sites of lure.

Clifford Shearing says we move from one bubble of private security to another as we travel from a bank to a shopping mall to a sports stadium to an airport or railway station, and then to our workplace. Public security provided by police comes into play only as we move between one bubble of private security and another. Under each bubble, markets in security technologies are often what protect us, though they can also be private policing markets. If a terrorist is lurking at the airport, this risk is more likely to be detected by the AI market in facial recognition than an alert police officer. It is more likely to be the private market in scanning technologies that detects their bomb or gun. These are markets that might slow our transit through the airport, but they are markets in private security that make us freer from the fear and reality of terrorism (at least in the context of boarding a plane). From reading criminology journals, one would not think those markets could be more important than prisons and police in protecting us from crime. Policing and punishment of drink-driving are less important in protecting us from drink-drivers worldwide than the global market in road construction technologies that make it impossible for the drink-driver to veer to the wrong side of the road and crash into oncoming traffic. This technology market protects us 24 hours a day from drink-drivers who used to do this a lot. Police patrols only protect us during those infrequent minutes when their patrols intersect with our journeys. Even forms of criminal victimisation that historically had large but largely financial impacts on us, such as insider trading in shares that we or our pension fund owned, are now detected from time to time by software that monitors micropatterns of share price movements. Software of this kind also makes it difficult to fix consumer prices through the simple expedient of secrecy in cartel meetings, because what used to be kept secret to the naked eye is more detectable as price-fixing patterns by price-monitoring AI.

Consider the markets of vice and virtue in the challenge of climate change. While the noble exceptions are many (for example, Gunningham and Grabosky 1998; Michalowski and Bitten 2005; Ayling 2013; Shover and Hochstetler 2005; Simpson et al. 2013; Haines and Parker 2017; White 2017; Holley et al. 2018; Pali and Biffi 2019), criminology mostly neglects the duty to make criminological contributions to this existential crisis. Carbon taxes and emission trading schemes are promising ideas that have performed poorly so far in realising their promise, for many reasons. One neglected reason is that a tax on harm cannot do all the regulatory work of criminal enforcement. Sophisticated businesses cheat on taxes on harm in the same way they cheat on any tax (Braithwaite 1981). Therefore, they must be sanctioned criminally when they fraudulently misrepresent the quantum of environmental harm they submit to the tax authority. The cross-national analysis of Best et al. (2020) revealed that the impact of increasing the price of carbon is statistically significant, but one would have to say disappointingly small compared with the predictions of economic theory. The average *annual growth* rate of carbon dioxide emissions from fuel combustion was found by Best et al. (2020) to be only 2 percentage points lower in countries that have a carbon price than countries without. Statecraft must do much more than reduce future carbon growth rates by this amount to create a liveable future for generations to come. We must move to substantial annual percentage reductions. Hence, we look the possibility in the eye that carbon fraud is one reason these estimates are not as large as economic theory predicts, and indeed the possibility that they are estimates inflated by carbon fraud. Beyond that, there is the problem that while the European market has been the leader, it has been used mainly as a financial market for hedging and speculation that Berta et al. (2017) described as 'a bubble of compliance in a whirlpool of speculation'. Criminologists of markets in vice and virtue have a massive contribution they must make for our children's future here—likewise with countering corruption and fraud in developing-country carbon market offsets for replanting rainforest.

Robert Agnew (2012) argues that climate change is likely to have catastrophic consequences for surging crime rates because it will push structurally anomic forces such as large population movements, armed conflicts over dwindling and contested water resources, the digging of illegal wells, illegal diversion of irrigation and attacks on those wells and irrigation systems, famines, fires, floods and other disruptions to social and normative orders. While anomie theory is highly relevant in Agnew's analysis, a limitation of the institutional version of anomie theory remains its neglect of the importance of prevention through markets in virtue. I refer, for example, to renewable energy startups who invent new technologies to harness solar power through improved panels and battery storage for electricity and new technologies to harness the power of wind, water and hydrogen. It is dubious to see nuclear power as a market in virtue; the problems of nuclear waste make it almost certainly a market in vice. But at least regulatory studies have made great contributions to showing how to reduce the risk of nuclear power production disasters through a move from punitive to regulatory controls that promote systemic wisdom about risk prevention—most notably, through the work of Rees (2009). Since the Three Mile Island incident, enforced self-incapacitation is what has made us safer from the corporate offences that cause a nuclear meltdown that could kill a million people (as discussed in Chapter 10).

With the climate change challenge, the imperative is so clear that we must develop a position on what are and are not markets in virtue, and then commit as a species to promoting those markets. Much can be learnt from how the national security state (Weiss 2014) in the United States promotes markets in the vice of more deadly weapons systems. This works not through pure market solutions but through strategic kinds of state–market hybrid collaborations/competitions among networks of firms and state agencies steered by the Pentagon (Dorf and Sabel 1998). The outcomes are mixed. This networked governance of markets has delivered markets in destabilising, anomic, new vices like killer robots to invade countries that might be produced in the millions by 3D printers. It also produced the internet, which is a market with many virtues (and vices). Sadly, the US Navy also developed a secure, encrypted way for its ships, submarines and the intelligence community to communicate (Swan 2016). The code for the encryption was released publicly for open-source development, but this technologically enabled the dark web to secretly sell hacking kits, drugs and sex slaves!

Competition policy, which increases the vibrancy of markets in goods, is a good thing and an institutional domain in which corporate criminologists have important contributions to make. Yet policies to increase the vibrancy of the production of goods are only a good thing if they are counterbalanced by regulatory institutions that regulate the consequential markets in bads. At one level, this is a quintessential institutional anomie theory point to make. At another level, it exposes the need for institutional anomie theory to accommodate the imperative of the aggressive promotion of markets in virtue. American antitrust policy has contributed profoundly to the greatness of the US market for job creation and has tempered corporate power somewhat at the commanding heights of capitalism (Braithwaite and Drahos 2000: 175–218).

Monopolisation by technology giants continues to be a massive risk to all economies and requires antitrust reforms that tackle that monopolisation. Firms like Facebook pose grave risks to freedom. In the long run, nevertheless, US competition policy has done a useful job of stoking the vibrancy of the American information technology (IT) sector. This started early on with the monopolisation cases in the United States (and Europe) against IBM, which once was number one on the Fortune 500 list of the largest corporations and once dominated IT as an unassailable colossus. Forty years ago, Fisse and Braithwaite (1983) interviewed key players in these accomplishments, like Nicholas Katzenbach, who was attorney-general in the Johnson administration. Katzenbach launched the early monopolisation cases against IBM. At the time of our interviews during the administration of Jimmy Carter, he was employed by IBM as its vice-president and general counsel! The accomplishments of this early antitrust enforcement more generally were criminologically profound, yet ignored by deterrence scholars in criminology. Waldman's (1978) research, reinforced by Fisse and Braithwaite's (1983) on IBM and other cases, showed there were profound specific deterrence effects that were achieved long before any penalties were imposed, and before cases went to court. Monopolists like IBM prepared for their impending antitrust cases by transforming their antitrust compliance policies and, in some instances, by divestitures in advance of cases that they feared could lead to forced divestitures by the courts. Specific deterrence worked in advance of punishment because enforcement strategy gave time for markets in virtue to rally and reconfigure markets in vice because of the anticipation of a possible future penalty from the regulatory state. Chapter 9 discusses the broader importance of deterrence that precedes rather than follows prosecution. IBM long ago ceased being an IT monopolist. The vibrancy of US competition in this sector allowed many new firms to enter the market and clip IBM's wings. Today, IBM competes with contemporarily more formidable monopolists by being a champion of machines integrated with open-source software, which is one best hope for breaking these latest monopolies.

Rose-coloured glasses cannot obscure the less illustrious accomplishments of US antitrust law under the Trump administration. Nor can we use rose-coloured glasses to look at regulatory state accomplishments against IT markets in bads more broadly. Yet, at a structural level, notwithstanding its neoliberal rhetoric, the US state has accepted the imperative that if it wants the benefits from the most vibrant IT economy in the world to continue, its capabilities for regulating cybercrime must be improved. Undoubtedly, it has not performed as well as consumers would like in keeping up with the entrepreneurship of cybercriminals with regulatory entrepreneurship. Yet it does accept the imperative for a regulatory state that works hard at the task of trying to catch up. And this is a general criminological imperative, not just one about cybercrime. Markets in virtue can do good for humankind, including in crime prevention, but it is an iron law of markets that markets in goods will be gamed into markets in bads. This means the benefits of markets in goods will be lost if the criminological imagination fails to mobilise to the challenge of regulating markets in bads.

This argument started with a consideration of the most virtuously important market for human survival and flourishing: new markets in renewable energy. These inspiring renewables markets are also making electricity available for the first time for students to do their homework at night in thatch-roofed houses in the most remote, impoverished villages of our planet. Lights and laptops are powered by tiny solar panels for each dwelling. Let me, then, conclude this section with a reminder of the virtues of a great environmental law enforcer from an earlier era, US President Ronald Reagan, who mobilised markets in environmental virtue. I refer to the regulatory accomplishment of President Reagan in ordering his ambassadors to persuade—or coerce, if necessary—other states to sign the Montreal Protocol on ozone-depleting substances in 1987. Thanks to the Reagan administration, and to American markets in virtue, the Montreal Protocol became the most effective international environmental agreement, the best enforced one and one that has saved hundreds of thousands of human lives (Kuttippurath and Nair 2017). How was this accomplished (Braithwaite and Drahos 2000: 261–67)?

In the first instance, it was an accomplishment of strong American civil society in the form of an environmental movement securing a ban on chlorofluorocarbons (CFCs) before Reagan came to power. Environmental movements in the rest of the world had been unable to accomplish this. The US chemical industry rose to the challenge of the regulatory ban by competing in a new market in the virtue of CFC-substitution technology. After DuPont won that competition, it went to Reagan with the argument that it would be good for US business to force the rest of the world to also ban CFCs. Failing to do that would mean US manufacturers would be disadvantaged by being hobbled with more expensive green technology. Conversely, forcing the rest of the world to follow the US to more demanding environmental standards would give DuPont (and upstream and downstream American suppliers) a strategic trade advantage over their European, Japanese and Chinese competitors. The chemical giants of these economies would be pushed to buy licences for the new CFC-substitute technology from DuPont. And so, a successful and implausible coalition of Reagan, the US chemical industry and environmental NGOs in Europe, Japan and the rest of the world assembled to lobby country by country to get signatures on the Montreal Protocol and then to enforce it after 1987. The lesson of Montreal is that the weak can prevail against the strong in the world economy when civil society groups harness strategic trade theory to divide the strong, turning markets in business virtue against markets in business vice, breaking off bits of business solidarity and harnessing them to projects of the good society. This is accomplished in harness with strong states with strategic trade interests aligned with markets in virtue.

A strategically comparable accomplishment also opened up in the previous chapter was that of Christian churches in the British Empire, at a time when North America was part of that empire, in the movement that banned the slave trade (Braithwaite and Drahos 2000: 498–501). Once Britain and its colonies surrendered to the political power of the churches among the ranks of the British Parliament's lawmakers, Britain had a strategic interest in defending the competitiveness of its colonial plantation economies by forcing the other colonial powers (Spain, Portugal, France) to cease international slave trading. One way it did this was by using the regulatory power of the British Navy to prevent foreign slaving ships from entering the harbours where new slaves were sold. This is theorised as an incapacitation accomplishment of the British Navy in Chapter 10, rather than a deterrence accomplishment.

A big conclusion of this book is dramatically illustrated by the Montreal Protocol and international slave trade case studies: few of the best things criminology can achieve occur through criminal punishment. Rather, they are achieved by harnessing strong state regulatory enforcement (which usually has a preventive quality) to strong civil society activism and to markets in business virtue—and sometimes to preventive international law as well. Because markets in virtue tend to be global in contemporary conditions, criminology, and institutional anomie theory in particular, must not only overcome its neglect of the possibilities for enhancing freedom by embracing markets in virtue, but also overcome criminological neglect of international law. To date, the limits of institutional anomie theory are profound in these respects. This is well illustrated by mixed results from studies that have used the Heritage Foundation's Index of Economic Freedom as a measure of institutional anomie theory's idea of the subordination of other institutions by markets (for example, Bjerregaard and Cochran 2008; Hughes et al. 2015). This is a variable that is a measure of neoliberal freedom that lumps together markets in vice and markets in virtue in one indiscriminate measure. It also rejects the regulatory state (seen in Heritage Foundation thought as an antithesis of freedom). This book argues that the regulatory state is central to securing freedom.

Balanced capital formation

All economies are mixed

Why would someone who values nondomination embrace a form of capitalism that is tempered by institutional checks and balances? The embrace macrocriminology must consider in contemporary conditions is simultaneously of market and public values or, more precisely, of balanced capital formation and balanced state growth, of balance in the mix between privatisation and nationalisation (or rather between tempered privatisation of the public and publicisation of the private) (Freeman 2003). Freedom is enhanced by rich and plural policy conversations about strategic publicisation of the private and privatisation of the public. This book aims to identify how to temper the dangers of capitalist markets that must be regulated when competition policy fails to energise markets in goods as much as markets in bads.

In the next section, we consider why those who believe in liberty have little choice but to sustain capital formation if they are to realise their political objectives. It argues that neoliberal capitalism faces serious competition from authoritarian capitalism, which has outperformed liberal capitalism in markets this century. The argument is that the way authoritarian capitalism can lose in this competition is for neoliberalism to transform itself into a more tempered form of capitalism with a stronger welfare state, effective regulation and redistribution and financial capital formation that is tempered by robust human, social, recovery and restorative capital formation. Conversely, if China wants to win, it must temper its authoritarianism by taking Sun Yat-sen more seriously. In short, what is necessary for the survival of liberal capitalism against authoritarian challenges is a republican freedom of tempered markets in vice and invigorated markets in virtue that also increase the likelihood of a low-crime society.

This balanced capital formation analysis appropriates much from Merton and from Messner and Rosenfeld. We have seen already that one difference is that it makes distinctions between markets in virtue and markets in vice, healthy and unhealthy exercise of state power and healthy and unhealthy forms of community and normative order in civil society. The ideal is for healthy power in markets, states and civil society that are each tempered by healthy power in the other institutions, where health is assessed in terms of the contribution to freedom as nondomination. Another difference of the freedom theory of crime is that market power so tempered is something that it is healthy to strengthen, just as it is healthy to strengthen tempered state and civil society power. The final difference with the freedom theory of crime is that theoretical value is found in distinguishing financial capital, human capital, social capital, recovery capital and restorative capital—all of which are deployed to strengthen the integration of normative theory and explanatory theory. This tempered amalgam dissolves fear of an overly strong state or excessive commodification by markets in favour of the promotion of a strong state, strong markets, strong civil society and strong individuals. Each of these must temper the excesses of the others.

Capital formation

Social democratic activists must be as seriously engaged as those on the right with the challenges of how to promote capital formation. This is required to be intellectually serious about reducing inequality and domination and the predatory crime these induce. Social democratic disappointments like Tony Blair and Bill Clinton did embrace markets. They were timid, however, about state regulation of markets, timid about a strong welfare state, about quality public housing and free education for the poor and about nurturing progressive social movement politics that offered critiques of their abuse of state power. Differential association theory might suggest their friendship networks were infected with markets in vice in the form of sometime-friends when in power like Rupert Murdoch.[3] Murdoch was Thatcher's key ally in the militarised union suppression that succeeded after the miners' strike in destroying British union power. Murdoch led the crushing of journalism with a social democratic sensibility; and Murdoch was George W. Bush's key ally in the military adventurism of Afghanistan and Iraq, which Blair and Hillary Clinton so pliantly supported. A small part of social democratic excellence is averting overregulation of capital; a much larger challenge for social democratic excellence is avoiding being overregulated *by* capital.

This chapter will first consider financial capital, then human capital, social capital, recovery capital and restorative capital. Crime prevention is difficult without the creation of more of all these forms of capital. Accomplishing this is not rocket science; most societies can point to many of their local communities that accomplish all these things rather well.

---

3   I say 'sometime' because Rupert Murdoch has been on and off in his support for Hillary Clinton, depending on who was in power, and has not returned calls to Tony Blair in recent years, allegedly because of a relationship that became too close between Blair and Murdoch's former wife Wendi Deng. Murdoch accuses Deng of being a Chinese spy who used him to get close to Donald Trump's daughter Ivanka. The FBI warned the Trump family about this, if one believes Murdoch's *Wall Street Journal* (O'Keefe and Viswanatha 2018). Bill Clinton, of course, had even more unsavoury differential associations with Wall Street vice in the form of Jeffrey Epstein, who offered him financial stabilisation advice when he was in the White House and frequently provided his corporate aircraft to Clinton for fundraising for the Clinton Foundation after he left the White House. Murdoch's influence across the West and beyond is based on two simple business insights. One is to befriend and support through media influence whoever is in power or is likely to win it (differential association of the power of capital with the power of political winners). The other insight is that there is more money to be made by telling media consumers lies they like to hear than there is in quality journalism. Facebook adapted this insight with even greater market success.

Crime prevention also requires changes in how we balance these different forms of capital and how we redistribute and regulate them so they are constitutive of virtuous institutions.

As robots and computers led by AI take over more functions previously undertaken by humans, some of us may struggle to find meaning from useful work that also lifts our family out of poverty, especially if we work for tech giants like Amazon. Rupert Murdoch also invented the idea that selling media lies to market segments that want to hear those lies is more profitable than selling truthful, quality journalism. That idea was then picked up by social media AI on platforms like Facebook and Twitter. AI was a market in virtue when it guided surgical robots to search for cancers more cleverly than could doctors, but a market in vice when it searched for lies more cleverly. It is a market in vice if it trains killer robots to kill every person in a militarised uniform (bus conductors, police, Salvation Army officers, hotel porters, firefighters). Learning to work with killer robots is a scary form of human capital because it is such a powerful joint product of a market in vice and what have to date evolved as disciplinary monocultures of AI in white western universities and tech firms, and Chinese versions of them. At the same time, we know that many decent scholars struggle to make AI more relational, more interdisciplinary, less monocultural, plurally grounded beyond lessons from neuroscience, and better regulated (for example, Lee 2020; Crawford 2021).

We saw in Chapter 4 that the evidence of the impact of short-term technological unemployment on crime is voluminous and contradictory. It is clearer that long-term unemployment induces lost hope and meaning and is therefore positively associated with crime even in time-series data. It is clearer still, according to Chapter 4, that individuals who come from families that experience long-term unemployment are more vulnerable to crime, and it is evident ecologically that those parts of cities where poverty, inequality and long-term unemployment are most concentrated are the areas where crime is high. Indeed, there is a multiplicative, not just an additive, effect on crime, of being a person cut off from opportunities created by capital formation and living in a community cut off from investment.

Technological change so far has not produced massive unemployment. It has casualised employment, helped reduce the share of wages in national income and produced reduced security for challenging jobs that require initiative. This happened with the loss of industrial and middle-class clerical and administrative jobs. Jobs with CHIME have been replaced with huge growth in the low-paid service industry work of a precariat who sell food and beverages to and clean the homes and hotel rooms of the minority who enjoy high pay. Jobs have also moved to those who work in private security to protect the valuables of those included in the new economy from the predations of those excluded. These employed people who live in poverty and have work with low meaning are a large part of the working-class political base built by Donald Trump and his breed of new far-right leaders across the West. While the new economy has not made jobs scarcer so far, it has made meaningful jobs scarcer and decimated those kinds of employment that save the humblest half of families from poverty and indignity. This book is partly about why such a world of growing inequality and declining meaning could pose a threat to the world's long-run decline in violence and crime rates (Chapters 2, 3; Pinker 2011). In the case of the Trump administration, that threat was mediated by several specific steps towards a criminalisation of the state and markets and corruption of the separation of powers. Another threat of predatory crime and unfreedom could come with economic crashes that crash more deeply.

The worst-case threat here is less crime than war. Economic crisis, particularly hyperinflation, fosters a resentful underclass and the rise of violent extremism. Braithwaite and D'Costa (2018) have shown that one thing crime and war have in common is they are cascade phenomena rather than displacement phenomena. If war were a displacement phenomenon, when we end a war in one country, this would cause war to be displaced to another country. War is not a displacement phenomenon in this way. At various points in this book, we show instead that war is a cascade phenomenon: unresolved wars cascade to more wars in that country and in neighbouring countries. Conversely, successful peace processes help neighbours to become more peaceful, enjoy lower crime rates and enjoy more employment through improved economic conditions. Bad neighbours who fight wars can cascade to us having a lot of war, crime and suicide. Crime is also not a displacement phenomenon: when we reduce crime in one locale, that tends not to increase crime in neighbouring locales, but to reduce crime there as well.

This macrosocial danger of a cascade from economic crisis to war, authoritarianism and crime is a theme that is discussed in more detail in Chapter 11.

Variegated capitalism and crime–war cascades

Today capitalism is more variegated than ever (Brenner et al. 2010; Peck and Theodore 2007; Dixon 2011; Jessop 2015). We have no alternative but to imagine a future form of capitalism quite different from that currently dominant because neoliberal capitalism has limited sustainability. Authoritarian capitalism, as in China, is an alternative that leaves little space for freedom. One possible context for macrocriminology is a suspicion that we may be approaching, or have already passed, peak globalisation and peak neoliberalism, as the world ponders lessons from the carnage of Covid-19.

The fastest-growing economies since the Global Financial Crisis have not been the neoliberal economies. That is not to say that the world will return to the lower levels of international trade and the higher levels of national industrialisation policies of the Keynesian decades after World War II. The fastest-growing economies since the Global Financial Crisis have been large authoritarian capitalist economies like China and Bangladesh, which for decades have been growing at two or three times the rate of neoliberal economies. Since the Global Financial Crisis, even more middle-sized authoritarian crony-capitalist economies—such as Cambodia, Vietnam and the Philippines—have also grown at two or three times the rate of the western economies. Many of the biggest countries, from China and Russia to Bangladesh and now Brazil, and many high-growth small economies as well, from the United Arab Emirates, Qatar and Israel to Singapore, have rejected liberalism in favour of their own versions of authoritarian capitalism. Shifts from neoliberal to authoritarian capitalism have been particularly sharp since the Global Financial Crisis in Eastern European economies such as Poland, Hungary and some former Yugoslavian republics. Some large economies are doing well as they move away from authoritarianism towards an intermediate position between liberal and authoritarian capitalism: examples of this kind of high-growth economy are Indonesia and India (at least until it was savagely devastated by the Covid crisis). Others, like the United Arab Emirates and the Philippines, are recording strong growth as they move in the opposite direction, towards a more authoritarian hybrid of capitalism. And Donald Trump rejected neoliberalism in favour of his distinctive version of a shift in a more authoritarian capitalist direction for fortress America.

Neither authoritarian capitalism nor neoliberalism is an attractive extreme from a crime-control perspective. Yet this book will argue that there are many versions of variegated capitalism on offer, some of which have more attractive features in terms of crime and domination prevention.

One macrocriminological argument of this book is the obvious one that growth in financial capital and redistribution of its fruits are critical to accomplishing a low-crime society. Most of the societies with the lowest homicide rates during the past half-century have been Western European and East Asian economies that have sustained high rates of capital investment and growth across many decades. At the other extreme are states that became so criminalised they were spurned by investors— domestic and foreign. An example is a country that for most of this century has been the poorest performer in economic growth and at the bottom of the Human Development Index: Democratic Republic of Congo (DRC). Capital investment collapse caused by criminalisation of the Congolese state cascaded from crime to war and then from war to more crime, particularly to exceptional levels of rape (Braithwaite and D'Costa 2018: Part I). We will never know the homicide rate or the robbery rate in DRC. Peacebuilding Compared fieldwork in DRC suggests most homicides and robberies in eastern rural areas, where so much of the population lives, are not recorded by the police. The survey evidence on the risk of rape in DRC is staggering, even though those who conduct the surveys cannot get to the remote rural villages that are not connected to cities by roads, where the risks of and impunity for rape by armed groups are most profound.

As well as mass unemployment leading to war–crime cascades, there are many familiar examples of hyperinflation having this effect, from Germany in the 1930s to Serbia in the 1990s (Braithwaite and D'Costa 2018: Part I). The cascade from hyperinflation to violence is mediated by classic anomie. Economic collapse is not the only macro-risk that can unleash crime–war cascades today. Environmental collapse or a nuclear exchange in Asia could also disrupt the normative order by inflicting famine on many hundreds of millions of people—mostly in China in the case of an unintended India–Pakistan nuclear exchange—and insecurity for an entire region.

If a catastrophic political crisis between North and South Korea, or India and Pakistan, happened to coincide with a stock market crash and an environmental crash, perhaps no power could hold back a global crime– war cascade. That is unknowable, just as it was unknowable until 2020 how global the economic destabilisation could be from a modern pandemic before our universities and drug markets discovered vaccines. Yet I still suspect it is not too late to reinvent capitalism, to reinvent environmental diplomacy, disease diplomacy and war diplomacy so that a coincidence of these kinds of catastrophes becomes an event of low likelihood. That is not to say it is probable that capitalism and diplomacy will be reinvented in these ways. It is just to say that political paths to transformation and prevention are available if active citizens have the wit to take them. Even if authoritarian capitalism is in the box seat to become the successor to neoliberal capitalism, the alternative somewhat less disastrous paths are many. These alternatives are paths that regulate capitalism to secure freedom to varying degrees.

China might be better able to recover from a financial or pandemic crash than the western economies that suffer the knock-on effects on world trade from a crash in China. The authoritarian regime in China may well have better control of the levers to direct the capital investment needed to quell the crisis. After a huge crash on the Shanghai Stock Exchange, China might wobble a bit, 100 million people might lose their jobs, but the regime might be prepared to do what it takes to keep control of those levers. The regime might not fall. In contrast, elected western governments could topple like dominoes in response to a future crash that is bigger than past crashes because China spikes down and does not save the day in the way it did after the 1998 Asian Financial Crisis, the 2008 Global Financial Crisis and the Covid crisis. Some of those western governments may fall into the hands of Chinese-style, Putin-style or Trump-style authoritarian capitalism, or even more radical despotism. The Chinese financial system has profound weaknesses in integrity that render it vulnerable to future crises. Yet the western assumption that China's vulnerabilities will increase the impetus towards democracy seems hard to justify when in significant ways China is becoming more rather than less authoritarian (especially with regard to the surveillance of its citizens) as it gets stronger.

This risk warrants reflection because trust in western governments has been declining steadily across the decades since trust has been measured (Citrin and Stoker 2018). In the United States, as discussed in Chapter 3, this decline in trust had an intergenerational dynamic that was particularly strong for the Vietnam War generation in the 1960s and 1970s and for the Iraq and Afghanistan war generation this century (van der Meer 2017: Fig. 4). Trust cannot decline forever without ultimately triggering a political crisis. Real wages cannot keep declining forever as workers watch the rich become the super-rich without this eventually catalysing a crisis. These are just some of the dynamics behind the empirical finding that economic crises destabilise democracies more than they destabilise dictatorships (Przeworski et al. 2000). 'What stands out first and foremost' from reviews of the evidence of the global decline of trust in governments 'is that political trust is highest in illiberal regimes such as Uzbekistan, China, Azerbaijan, Qatar, Singapore, and Malaysia. These high scores are a consistent finding' (van der Meer 2017: 7). While China is less buffeted by a blizzard of distrust than the United States, it is still vulnerable to the same dynamics. There has been some decline in trust in government in China and this is deepest in the regions where income inequality is most extreme (Yang and Xin 2020).

The risk of a mega-crash will persist unless working-class people get a lot more money in their pockets to maintain demand for job creation. More crashes like that in 2008 will be a risk unless working people are given enough income to avert a resort to overburdening themselves with debt that causes a crisis for them if they suffer a setback in their life, and a crisis for capitalism when enough of them suffer that setback at the same time. The risk is magnified further when the regulatory system mismanages this. Mercifully, wise economists did persuade many reluctant political leaders globally to put more money into the pockets of the poor immediately after the 2008 crash and the 2020 Covid crash. Without this, these crises would have been much more catastrophic. The decline in the capacity of states to collect tax from wealthy individuals and corporations cannot go on forever without causing a fiscal crisis and a deeper rebellion of the middle class than that described by Farrall and Karstedt (2019). US President Joe Biden's new Treasury Secretary, Janet Yellen, has now recognised this risk publicly and urged international agreement to increase taxes on corporations and the rich. When the next big crash comes in the later years of the 2020s or the 2030s, western states might have less capacity to deploy fiscal surpluses or reserves because debt levels have not recovered from the 2008 and 2020 crises. At the same time, the corporate sector might lack the capital reserves to privately reprime the pump (even though financial regulation since 2008 has done some invaluable work in mandating that the largest banks have bigger reserves).

Crises of demand can be averted by creating much needed jobs in the health, education and welfare sectors, but only if fiscal crisis is averted. States need to make their tax systems work better so they have the funds to hire those new workers as they pay down the debts from 2020–21.

Cross-nationally, the data suggest that societies with larger welfare states, controlling for other variables, have lower homicide rates (Lappi-Seppälä and Lehti 2014: 212; as discussed in Chapter 4). While collapses of capital formation are preventable, when they do happen, authoritarian capitalist regimes may survive them, while liberal capitalist regimes may fall. This means that sequences of crises—whether mediated by financial crime, a nuclear exchange, a pandemic or climate change—might ratchet the world in the direction of authoritarian capitalism. That in turn risks a positive recursive surge in corruption, various forms of state crime and unfreedom, in turn feeding back to more crime of other kinds on Wall Street and Main Street.

European criminology has been afflicted with a myopic kind of comparativism that is obsessed with comparing contemporary Western Europe with the United States and nowhere else, at no other time. This is too narrow a space-time lens for a rich macro-comparativism that comprehends crime and freedom. One problem with this European tradition is that the United States is a big place. There are larger differences within the United States than the differences between Western Europe and the United States on many variables that matter. This is true, for example, of how equitable is the distribution of the types of capital discussed in this chapter. There are small low-crime states like Vermont that are richer than Europe in restorative capital. Then there are larger states like Minnesota and Wisconsin that have higher levels of social capital, according to Putnam (2000), and richer restorative capital than most of Europe, lower unemployment rates, fewer people in poverty and large regions with crime rates lower than most of Europe. Putnam (1993: 35) conceives of social capital as the 'features of social organizations, such as networks, norms and trust that facilitate action and cooperation for mutual benefit'. Exceptions to the patterns Putnam (2000) identified are the deindustrialised districts of the largest cities of Minnesota and Wisconsin where there were such huge 'Black Lives Matter' uprisings in 2020. Minnesota abolished capital punishment in 1911 and Wisconsin in 1853, long before all but a couple of European states. Yet nearby are communities like St Louis and Detroit with among the highest crime rates of any cities in the western world, deindustrialised and devastated by the homelessness worsened by the Global Financial Crisis and the Covid crisis.

Imagine that it might be right that the world economy is passing peak globalisation. On the positive side, this could mean we move rapidly from economies that import oil, gas and coal in ships to economies that build new factories to produce hydrogen power, solar panels and storage batteries and lots of meaning-making blue-collar jobs in their maintenance and connecting them up to continuously improving batteries. Three-dimensional printing and factory robots could make these components cheaper to produce in Detroit, close to where the panels need to be installed. While there are fewer jobs in renewables than in Detroit's old industrial capitalism, there is still a good number of them. There is even a good number of low-skill jobs in tree planting and urban agriculture that must be surged at times of crisis, just as happened during the New Deal. Companies like Ford might go bankrupt in Detroit, but new companies building electric or hydrogen cars, or parts of them, might be encouraged by the state to invest in the city. And some of the public investment to build new driverless electric public transport systems might also intentionally be directed to Detroit because it is so desperately deindustrialised and because it has been the city in the US with the worst crime rate for a good part of the post-industrial period. Public investment in rebuilding the crumbling infrastructure of the United States, which President Trump made a good case for prioritising during his 2016 election campaign (without doing much once elected), can be concentrated in cities like Detroit that have been caught in a vicious spiral in which high crime rates deter investment and disinvestment further fosters crime. In this sense, as well as the sense of slavery legacies, Detroit's violence dilemma has much in common with the dilemmas of a country with the rich potential of the DRC.

Contra–Donald Trump, a reinvention of Detroit as a restorative city (which is happening) and a regenerative city can be complemented by the massive investment in the welfare state needed in the United States. This must be a central plank of transformation to make its economy a sustainably more flourishing lower-crime economy (as discussed in an evidence-based way in Chapter 4). This means building hospitals, health centres and aged care homes with improved investment in infection control (the need for which became evident during the Covid pandemic), which are highly labour intensive. It means investment in restorative justice programs and recovery capital programs that also intensively use the labour of local people. Public investment in the building of human capital by constructing new vocational training centres in disadvantaged communities is particularly imperative. The joint investment of a new type of capitalism in new-economy factory technologies, rebuilding depleted public infrastructure and building the welfare state can together attract a boom in service-sector jobs to revive deindustrialised cities. Once a developmental capitalist state jumpstarted a city like Detroit to become a safer place, it can attract droves of tourists to see the old industrial monuments of Henry Ford's production lines and the Motown creative scene born at its industrial zenith. Foreign students can be attracted to use its transport and service-sector infrastructure to enrol in Detroit's tertiary education institutions. Then a new entertainment Motown for a new century might be reinvented in Detroit as a restorative, regenerative city. Methodologically, what I am doing here is selecting Detroit as a least-likely case (Eckstein 1975) in the West for transformation to tempered, balanced capitalism, and then arguing that the needed transformation really could work well there.

Most readers will think it naive to conceive of massive reinvestment in the welfare state as politically possible. In the face of new technologies eliminating jobs and ever stronger challenges from authoritarian capitalist economies, it is hard to conceive of western capitalism surviving without a huge increase in job creation in health and welfare. So, we see the world today in a way that has similarities to the way Otto von Bismarck viewed it at that other highwater mark of economic liberalism in the late nineteenth century. Bismarck feared Germany was likely to descend into crime–war cascades, economic crises and ultimately into an authoritarian communist takeover unless it invested in building a welfare state. Hence, his government was indeed the first mover to build the welfare state in a serious way.

A more egalitarian world can also be helped by a viable strategy for gradually persuading more countries to sign International Labour Organization agreements to progressively increase their minimum wages, protect the labour rights of women and more (Marshall 2019; Quiggin 2019: 249–54), as also first happened soon after Bismarck's death. Today, it can be enhanced by a 'participation income' (Atkinson 2015; Garnaut 2021). The redistribution of profits from capital to labour would put more money in the pockets of workers to purchase more services from more service industry workers in depressed communities, as discussed in the pages that follow.

From a macrocriminological point of view, there is an imperative for macroeconomic reform and global regulatory reform, but also for state steering of investment to struggling communities like Detroit and for a local regenerative capitalism of cities, towns and villages. Growing the welfare state in a place like the Philippines or Detroit requires collecting more tax revenue. There are many ways this can be done. One way is through steeply progressive land and property taxes. For environmental sustainability, it is also imperative for the tax system progressively to steer the rich into smaller mansions and smaller downtown corporate offices. We know how to reverse the long-run decline in corporate tax revenue by reforming tax-enforcement policy (Braithwaite 2005b).

In the era of industrial capitalism, it was much harder to tax industrial firms heavily because of fear they might shift their factories offshore. Australia is like most economies in that the firms with the biggest market capitalisation are no longer industrial or mining firms. Nor are they global internet giants, as is true for the United States. They are all banks. The financialisation of capitalism means that, today, banks and other financial institutions such as pension funds own the industrial and service industry firms. So, it was good fiscal policy for Australia's conservative government led by a former investment banker, Malcolm Turnbull, to impose in 2017 a mega-tax only on Australia's five biggest banks, which own so much of the country's industrial and mining firms and which benefited from state largesse during the Global Financial Crisis. Australian banks cannot credibly threaten to move offshore in response to such taxes on capital. Hence, their wealth can be redistributed to build a stronger welfare state. Likewise, the wealth of those with multiple millions of dollars locked into defined-benefit pensions cannot be so easily whipped out of that pension fund and shifted offshore. It follows from the financialisation of capitalism that the largest banks in big economies are indeed too big to fail.[4] One reason is that banks create markets in virtue when they transfer money from savers to investors who make new ideas and opportunities happen. Yet we must prevent the steep multiplication of US political campaign contributions by banks in recent decades (Acemoglu and Robinson 2019: 481) from persuading politicians to privatise capitalism's profits and socialise its losses (to the tune of US$15 trillion in taxpayer support in 2008). The sheer size of the bailout of rich bankers by taxpayers of modest means was a huge new source of inequality, as former Bank of England Governor Mark Carney pointed out in his BBC Reith Lectures. In one important sense, Prime Minister Gordon Brown did a better job in the United Kingdom than President Obama in the United States of bailing out his banks during the Global Financial Crisis. Unlike the United

---

4   It can make sense for a tiny economy like Iceland to allow its banks to fail because of their exceptionally deep insolvency and to allow new banks to grow from their ashes. In general, however, confidence in the survivability of banks is good for capital markets and for long-run job creation.

States, the United Kingdom insisted on taxholder equity in failing banks like Lloyds; these shares could be sold when the market inevitably rose again. Even if the British taxpayer does later sell these shares at a loss, the shortfall can be made up later still by a special tax on banks of the kind Australia imposed in 2017. In their own ways, both Brown and Obama showed that a resort to socialist solutions can save capitalism in a major crisis—as leaders of all political hues showed again in their big-spending, big-state responses to the Covid economic shudder. This returns us to the point that if China and other authoritarian capitalist states are willing to pull socialist levers to deal proactively with smaller and larger crises, and neoliberal economies like the United Kingdom and the United States are reluctant or slow to do so, China will continue to recover from economic crises in better shape than the West, as it did in 2008 and 2020. The authoritarian capitalist economies may survive best and then dominate.

The optimistic point, however, is that in the new conditions of capitalism there is no longer a need for despair about the impossibility of a combination of tax policy, labour law and welfare policy creating much more egalitarian societies than we currently have. Chapter 4 assessed the evidence that societies with less inequality and less poverty have both less crime and less war than very unequal societies and are at less risk of crime–war spirals of the kind Europe saw in the 1990s in Serbia, Croatia, Bosnia and Kosovo. They also have better prospects of long-run capital formation, job creation and freedom.

To conclude on financial capital, we do need to grow it and to protect it from crises that might cause violence through mass unemployment or hyperinflation. Capital formation must be carefully attended to, and in a way that shakes off the shackles of old neoliberal and socialist ideologies, if we are serious about creating new job opportunities for the poor.

Creative new public–private hybrids, publicisations of the private and privatisations of the public are imperative for a form of capitalism that underwrites freedom. Chapter 9 argues that criminology must be part of this renewal when it argues that radical new privatisations of criminal prosecution are imperative for taming the enslavement of Main Street by corporate crime.

Part of the recurrent crisis engendered by financialisation is that debt substitutes for welfare. For example, instead of having nationalised health guarantees for all citizens, less than wealthy people are forced to borrow if they have a health catastrophe. Instead of guaranteeing public housing for the poor, credit is made more accessible for the poor to buy their own homes with backing from devices like derivatives in subprime mortgages. The problem is that when a crash occurs, a host of new problems afflicts the poor because they become homeless (and often unemployable) when they cannot pay these debts. Sadly, their children suffer even more from their parents' long-term unemployment. In the United States, there has been a dual pincer movement against the poor by substitution of debt for state welfare. It was followed by a collapse of the corporate welfare system of private pensions and health benefits that substituted for state welfare failure, as employment was deindustrialised and casualised for the working class. This coincided with a decrease in the share of wages in national income, especially the share of working-class wages. That in turn means financial capital keeps demand up to keep the economy growing by replacing demand from working-class income with demand from working-class debt. This accelerates a vicious spiral of welfare/wages to debt. The long-run formula for lower crime rates repairs this institutional damage not only by repairing the regulation of financial capital, but also by rebuilding the institutions of welfare and labour market rights. The minimum wage is at the heart of this, as is decasualisation that guarantees rights like sickness benefits.

Human capital

To reduce crime and imprisonment rates, societies must grow their human capital as well as their financial capital. The combination of strong human capital and strong financial capital should be greater than the sum of its parts, as illustrated in the earlier discussion of the strong growth of human capital in the Philippines but weaker growth in quality jobs for graduates as a strain factor for individualised anomie. So, financial capital formation is necessary for human capital formation, and vice versa. Doing well at school is a potent protective factor against delinquency (as we saw in Chapter 4). Going to university is a protective factor for preventing young people who are bullies at school from becoming physically violent young adults (Homel 2013). Societies that *redistribute* human capital so that more poor children do well at school and university, by simultaneously growing and redistributing human capital, can reduce crime even more. Correctional interventions that seek to improve educational, vocational and job-placement opportunities for offenders have good effect sizes in preventing crime (Weisburd et al. 2017: 425–27).

Reducing the number of children who fail in school is achieved not only at the microlevel, child by child; it is also achieved in a more macro way by transforming the institutional character of schooling. Chapter 4 argued that schools of a generation ago were less restorative and less redemptive than contemporary schools; they were more the mouse race that prepared us for the rat race. Perhaps in some ways disciplinary schools prepared workers for the discipline of the factory and prepared middle-class organisation men for clawing their way to the top of industrial capitalism. This is definitely not the way to prepare human capital for an information economy. While the divisiveness and demoralisation of this mouse race were extreme, much contemporary practice also structurally fosters hubris or despair. In redemptive schooling that builds the human capital of the poor, students compete against their own past performance more than against other children. They are motivated by the intrinsic rewards of learning that makes their life better. Restorative schooling, as discussed under the heading of restorative capital formation, is about children learning by supporting each other and learning to cooperate as democratic citizens (Hopkins 2003; Morrison 2007). No society can accomplish a transformation to redemptive schooling without overcoming economically irrational underinvestment in education, especially education of disadvantaged children. I say irrational because for decades states have been able to recover a return to GDP of increased education investment that is several times greater than the interest on state borrowing for that education investment. Restorative justice programs in schools struggle for sustainability because they involve work that dedicated teachers are asked to do as an extra gift to the children beyond the teaching that becomes a daily grind for all teachers at times (Burford et al. 2019: Ch. 14).

Education is at risk from neoliberal experiments to create competitive education markets. In countries where test scores determine access to educational opportunities, the educational effort of students can be diverted away from schools that educate a whole person. Instead, they sometimes put most of their effort into the 20 hours a week their parents pay for them to slave away in colleges that groom children to maximise test scores. As education becomes more commodified, private schools can show paths to new forms of educational excellence, but test-score factories can be new markets in bads. Universities are also becoming factories that commodify scores of various kinds for the education market. Increasingly, students become participants in this market in the vice of credentialism rather than in a virtuous pursuit of learning. Not in all respects, but for the most part, credentialism is a profoundly less worthy thing than learning how to learn. This is because credential markets require constant change. Education systems will never be good at keeping pace with the specificities of technological flux, but they can be good at promoting learning how to learn and how to lead from below. At all levels, only transformed regulation that moderates credentialism and quantitative indicators (particularly those based on test scores) is needed to ensure that markets in the vice of education factories do not dominate markets in virtue.

On the positive side, today in western universities there are more young women than men. American Ivy League institutions have many scholarships for poor students that they did not have a century ago, and many have senior faculty of colour. Affirmative action self-regulation and state regulation have delivered this kind of result in many countries. School education is also less violent, if not less exclusionary—a result that is directly important for crime control, because the evidence discussed in Chapters 4 and 5 suggests that physically brutal schooling with degrading initiation rituals has been a form of socialisation into violence and militarisation. The school bully becomes the workplace bully, the cyberbully, the war criminal, the *genocidaire* and 'ecocidaire'.

Social capital

Social capital is defined here as the structures of social relationships and social beliefs[5] that have productive benefits as well as being a social resource. This definition is broad enough to capture the features of the most influential definitions of social capital by Bourdieu (1986), Coleman (1990), Putnam (1995), Fukuyama (1995) and Inglehart (1997). Social capital is widely thought to have bonding elements among people with shared beliefs and bridging elements that connect diverse peoples (Putnam 2000; Dekker and Uslaner 2003). We have already seen that Confucian philosophy has elements that fit what today might be called social capital. Bonding and bridging combine with reciprocity norms to build social cohesion, linking capital that has both communal and economic benefits (Hong 2016). Like the World Bank, I conceive of linking capital here as institutional mechanisms that diffuse trust and dialogue

---

5   Beliefs are defined broadly to include attitudes, values and widely shared norms.

among institutions. As with human capital, social and financial capital are mutually constitutive. Social networks that are bonded and bridged allow the improvements in state and civil society governance that come from networked governance (Sørensen and Torfing 2016; Braithwaite et al. 2012). The core institution of the social capital literature is that goodwill among people that is built by social capital is a resource that assists the formation of financial capital, richer social relationships in civil society and therefore richer human capital and improved governance of the society.

These broad benefits might raise questions about the wisdom of using a concept (capital) that comes from the narrower economic tradition of thought. Relational goodwill formation may have been a better label than social capital formation. I choose, however, to go with social capital as the concept around which such a rich theoretical and empirical literature has developed. Besides, it is capitalism that future generations must transform if they are to survive.

CHIME (Connectedness, Hope, Identity, Meaning and Empowerment) is that cluster of social relationships and social beliefs that constitutes the subset of social capital that David Best called recovery capital. Best picked up the concept of CHIME as a way of summarising what is central to mental health recovery in meta-analyses (Leamy et al. 2011) and then applied it empirically to recovery from addiction and crime (Best and Laudet 2010; Best et al. 2015, 2018; Best 2017; Hall et al. 2018). The importance given in the CHIME literature to recovery from problems like alcoholism, drug addiction or a period in prison is also important to restorative capital, as discussed in the next two sections.

Trust is the most prominent dimension of social capital in the literature, though certainly not the only one (Braithwaite 1998). Hope is another dimension of social capital when it is collective hope with many of the virtues of trust that helps citizens survive war, unemployment, environmental catastrophes and anomic disruption of normative orders (Braithwaite 2004). Trust is both a social belief and a social relationship. When people trust each other in an economy, transactions are settled with lower transaction costs and with less monitoring, less auditing and less litigation for breach of trust. This is how social capital makes capitalist economies strong.

Social capital, human capital, recovery capital and restorative capital are unlike financial capital in that they are not depleted through use. When you spend your money from the bank, you deplete your capital. When you trust someone, you do not deplete trust; trust tends to be reciprocated and this engenders virtuous circles of trust-building. A politics of hope is likewise redemptive as we face adversity; it is infectious. In the same way, human capital is not depleted through use. When you *use* new human capital or recovery capital skills, this sharpens them, nourishes their future growth and allows others to learn from your use of your human capital. CHIME is not depleted through use; it is an investment that grows on its dividends. When we do restorative justice well, many want to do more of it. This is an old insight from Juliet in Act 2, Scene 2 of Shakespeare's *Romeo and Juliet*:

> My bounty is as boundless as the sea,
> My love as deep. The more I give to thee,
> The more I have, for both are infinite.

The evidence that social capital is important to crime control is considerable. Bob Bursik's (1999) research with various colleagues established a negative association between the social capital of communities and crime rates. Cross-nationally, Lappi-Seppälä and Lehti (2014: 188) showed that increased social trust is associated with reduced homicide rates. Marc Ross's (1985) multivariate analysis of data from 90 small-scale traditional societies showed that violence inside the society was low when there were strong crosscutting ties, meaning strong political links among communities and the resultant sense of intercommunal solidarity of a mini-league of nations (actually of communities in Ross's data). This means that internal violence is prevented by bridging capital.

Bonding capital, however, made things worse in Ross's (1985) research on small-scale societies. Societies with strong fraternal bonds—mainly strong solidarity ties holding together kinship groups—had higher violence. A simple way to illustrate this dilemma is to point out that in southern US communities where social capital was strong in the particular sense of strong bonding capital among members of the Ku Klux Klan, violence was and is still high. Where the strong social solidarity of an ingroup is mobilised by rejecting an outgroup, social capital promotes rather than reduces violence. Where strong kinship ties make it a matter of honour to exact vengeance against those who wrong one's kin, violent interfamilial violence and blood feuds can become common, as Ross's (1985) data reveal.

Some, but not many, European societies today still have this problem of strong bonding social capital among kin causing blood feuds and a male honour culture—for example, Kosovo and Albania (Marsavelski et al. 2018). Residues of collectivist honour cultures producing family feuds that deliver high rates of killing across the generations can even be found in the Appalachian Mountains not far south-west of Washington, DC.

Many developing economies outside Europe and North America still have large sections of the population in the grip of strongly bonded collective honour cultures that require males to use guns that are widely owned to kill a member of the family who wronged their family. Large parts of the Highlands of Papua New Guinea are like this, as are large parts of Pakistan (Braithwaite and Gohar 2014), and this is one reason Pakistan is an extremely violent society (Karstedt 2012a, 2014a). Indeed, this phenomenon remains so strong globally that Susanne Karstedt's data from this century for 67 countries show that collectivist values and authoritarian values are predictors of individual violence cross-nationally (Karstedt 2006, 2015) and state violence (Karstedt 2011b, 2014b). Her research shows starkly the dangers of highly collectivist and authoritarian forms of capitalism for violence, and against freedom (see also Karstedt 2001).

Karstedt explicitly interprets her cross-national results as showing that collectivist values increase bonding capital within groups and nations but deplete bridging capital between groups and nations, risking the deepening of divides between groups and nations (Karstedt 2003). She shows that this particular formation of social capital strengthens lethal violence, organised crime and corruption, particularly in transitional countries (Karstedt 2003). The long-run history of state formation mirrors Karstedt's cross-sectional late twentieth-century results in profound ways. In the historical process of state-formation, states mobilised violence to pacify ever-wider spaces, bonding nations with the Connectedness, Hope, Identity and Meaning parts of CHIME, even if not with Empowerment. These states encompassed widened pacified spaces where violence became progressively lower and long-run widening of pacification was accomplished (Pinker 2011). Yet in the process of widened internal pacification, states clawed at competing national identities that sought to widen *their own* internal spaces of pacification. In that dynamic, more unified ingroup national identities that prevented internal violence were accompanied by divisive outgroup identities. These outgroup identities were often identities pushing alternative visions of state boundaries that competed with our own. This is part of what Tilly (1975: 42) meant when he said 'war made the state and the state made war'.

Karstedt's data incorporate one clue as to how to keep the knot of internal unity strong while untying knots of hatred towards outgroups. This is her finding that it is the combination of collectivism and authoritarianism in patterns of cultural values that risks violence. Collectivist and authoritarian cultural patterns characterise societies with authoritarian state regimes and high homicide rates in Karstedt's data. Collectivism is benevolent when it is nested in ever-widening circles of identity to village, province, state, continent and as a citizen of all humankind. And it is benevolent when it rejects authoritarianism. Put another way, social capital is put into play in competitive struggles, just as are financial capital and human capital. Markets in social capital vice are not nested in more encompassing identities of inclusion and nondomination. Markets in social capital virtue become ever more inclusive, as banking networks historically have done, despite all their other vices (Burrough and Helyar 1991). Virtuous social capital cheers for the town's or the nation's team in a football match, but also cheers for the bridging bonds of sport that bring nations together in a World Cup or an Olympic Games, and even enjoys the accomplishments of other teams that win competitions against the home team. We all understand how this identity politics of sport can be nested in ways that reject a violent outgroup politics of the crowd, through friendly banter with opposition fans, building both bonding and bridging capital through the institutions of sport. The same nested nationalism–internationalism has played out at the World Trade Organization (WTO), where states stuck together to win good deals against other states, but also bridged with those competitors to defend the institution of the WTO as one that could put boundaries around that very competition. Families are rather better at this than states, though not always—that is, families are mostly good at sustaining their own bonding capital while respecting the role of other families to build their own bonding capital in their own way, building bridges to them without expecting other families to do as much for our children as we do for our own.

Hence, an important interim conclusion here is: not only are there markets in vice and markets in virtue, and in good and bad financial capital. There is also good and bad social capital, where good social capital is nested and anti-authoritarian, rejecting the domination of outgroups. While we did not discuss this explicitly in the human capital section of this chapter, obviously there is also good and bad human capital. The human capital induced by certain religious schools to have the piety, determination, self-sacrifice and resilience to be a suicide bomber is an obvious example of a bad form of human capital. Training bankers to be ruthless profit-seekers with no regard for commercial ethics is another.

More generally, all forms of capital formation can constitute markets in vice or markets in virtue. They can constitute violent, grasping cultures or nonviolent, generous cultures, locally and globally. We will see that even a form of capital that I have tended to characterise as virtuous, restorative capital, can and does contribute to oppression when its values are not clarified and when restorative justice is not enacted carefully to focus on inclusion and nondomination. Frankly, value-free positivist research on social capital has limited use for these reasons. This argument is pushed a bit further in Chapter 11, where it is suggested that one reason collective efficacy may be the form of social capital that best explains crime is that it is not a value-free conception.

Another important way of reading Karstedt's results is to focus on their reverse side: the result that homicide is lower in societies with a combination of strong individualism and strong egalitarianism in their cultural patterns (Karstedt 2001). This leads us not only to emphasise the importance of egalitarianism and nondomination through comparative equality, but also the importance of societies that constitute strong individuals. Structural equality, Karstedt concludes, is a strong predictor of high levels of generalised trust in a population. It is in inegalitarian, collectivist societies that people cling to their ingroup, failing to build trusting relationships with the other. Trust becomes generalised in its capability to build all forms of capital when individuals are strong and embedded in egalitarian cultural patterns that enculturate trust. This is the enculturation of trust versus institutionalisation of distrust theme we return to in the conclusion and throughout this book. Individuals who do not learn to trust never acquire the agency that is the stuff of making the personal political. At the microlevel, this book argues for restorative practices that empower the agency of strong individuals not only in the justice system, but also in families, schools, businesses and governance.

Reintegrative shaming theory can also be deployed to help sharpen the conceptual differences between good and bad social capital. Social capital prevents crime when it is reintegrative in its relationships with outgroups; social capital accelerates mobilisation for crime when it is stigmatising in its relationship with outgroups (Braithwaite 1989). That means respect and dignity being granted to outgroups and to those who wrong us. It means a politics of inclusion towards our enemies, be they family enemies, criminals or enemies of our religious group, ethnic group or country. In sum, whether social capital is a good or a bad thing in terms of crime prevention depends on eschewing the politics of stigmatisation through bridging capital that beats a path to a politics of inclusion. Valerie Braithwaite (2009b) would say it requires balances between security values (values about keeping us safe) and harmony values (values about a broadened politics of love and inclusion). Without that balance, we are at risk of being exploited by others or being the exploiters of others. We must be discriminating about what modalities of social capital might be protective against crime for communities (like collective efficacy, which we will now discuss). And we must be discriminating about which are dominating modalities of social capital, such as those constituted by the 'greed is good' subcultures of Wall Street.

Diverse studies now suggest collective efficacy may be the form of social capital that performs particularly well in protecting communities from crime (for example, Odgers et al. 2009; Hipp and Wo 2015). This may not be true in China (Zhang et al. 2017) where, perhaps, collective efficacy too often falls into Karstedt's authoritarian trap of being deployed to enforce domination by crime and by the state rather than freedom from crime and from the state (see Chapter 2). This danger is inherent in communal institutions that simultaneously secure the normative order of community safety and the order of party domination. Collective efficacy is a more specified form of social capital, an actively engaged form of community capital, which prevents crime in the West. Sampson et al. (1997: 918) define collective efficacy as 'social cohesion among neighbors combined with their willingness to intervene on behalf of the common good'. Collective efficacy that prevents crime is certainly a set of 'social relationships'; social relationships that make a community safer also have productive benefits because investment avoids unsafe environments. Collective efficacy is more than the sum of individual self-efficacy (Bandura 1986, 2000) in that it is also about hospitable social solidarity.

Our research team has shown empirically that collective combined with individual self-efficacy helps managers of organisations prevent regulatory offences by making corporate compliance systems work (Jenkins 1994). Hence, this form of social capital is relevant to preventing crime in the suites, just as it is to preventing crime in the streets (Braithwaite et al. 2007: 307–18). Interestingly, from the perspective of republican political theory, Bandura (1989: 1182) sees self-efficacy as defining freedom 'in terms of the exercise of self-influence'. Collective efficacy is also liberating for individuals who participate in it because it involves collective empowerment, including collective empowerment to resist domination. Bandura's self-collective efficacy view of freedom is at one with Amartya Sen and Martha Nussbaum's capabilities approach to freedom—that is, freedom as capabilities to enjoy the kind of life individuals have reason to value. An important part of such capabilities that can be destroyed by low income, among other things, is 'freedom to act' (Sen 1999: 86). This freedom to act as capability might alternatively have been conceived of as self-efficacy and collective efficacy as capabilities and freedoms to act.

Sampson et al. (1997) and Morenoff et al. (2001) found that greater race and class segregation in metropolitan areas meant smaller numbers of neighbourhoods absorbing the economic shocks of deindustrialisation and a more severe resultant concentration of poverty. I have argued that class segregation has long been associated with increased crime, and there is a long-demonstrated multiplicative, as opposed to additive, relationship between class and class segregation in their combined effects of crime (Reiss and Rhodes 1961; Braithwaite 1979). Deindustrialisation accelerated class concentration and its effects on the 'truly disadvantaged' (Wilson 2012). Sampson et al. found that the effect of class and race concentration in increasing crime rates is partly mediated by declines in collective efficacy. The geographical concentration of the collective loss of hope and meaning might also heighten a subjective sense of exclusion.

Local communities are better able to go about the business of building a neighbourhood with collective efficacy if distrust is institutionalised through a capacity to call in police who are trusted. A job of civil society in the good society is to enculturate trust through collective efficacy; a job of the police is to institutionalise distrust of criminality when there is a serious enough breach of community trust.[6] Of course, this division of labour fails when police in disadvantaged communities do not believe that black lives matter.

In Chapter 11, we will see that just as crime, violence and anomie are cascade phenomena, so is collective efficacy. When you spend social capital in the form of collective efficacy, this sends wider ripples of collective efficacy across society's pond.

Recovery capital

Groshkova et al. (2013) showed that recovery capital can be measured with acceptable concurrent validity and test–retest reliability that distinguishes it from social and human capital (see also Sterling et al. 2008). This result is not inconsistent with our conception here of financial, social, human, recovery and restorative capital being mutually constitutive when they eschew domination. Recovery capital prospectively predicts desistance from drug abuse and predicts life satisfaction (Laudet and White 2008; see also Mawson et al. 2015). Recovery capital is defined as structures of social relationships and social beliefs that have recovery benefits as well as being a social resource. Networks of social support are critical resources of recovery capital (Best et al. 2012). White and Cloud (2008) conclude from their review of the evidence that recovery is more about capital (the presence of strengths) than the absence of pathologies. Most recoveries from addiction need dollops of social support and collective hope as social capital because, ultimately, desistance from abuse is almost always preceded by a considerable number of concerted failed attempts at desistance (Laudet and White 2008). Recovery communities that constitute recovery capital are an important concept in this work.

Criminology has made a formidable contribution here, even when it does not use the language of recovery capital. Best and Laudet (2010) summarise the criminological literature as having a large overlap with what has been learned about recovery from mental illness, alcoholism,

---

6   Braithwaite (1998) developed the idea of the good society as one that enculturates trust in the foreground of social life and institutionalises distrust in the background. It builds on Yamagishi and Yamagishi's splendid Japanese program of research showing that a culture of trust builds social intelligence. One must learn from the culture how to take the risk of trusting others, learning about judgements of which contexts and people are trustworthy (Yamagishi 2001). These ideas will be further developed as this book proceeds.

overeating and various other non-crime problems. Best and Laudet (2010) approvingly cite Laub and Sampson's (2003) overview of what we know about desistance from crime as being central to what we know about recovery more broadly:

- attachment to a conventional person (spouse)
- stable employment
- transformation of personal identity
- ageing
- interpersonal skills
- life and coping skills.

Shadd Maruna's (2001) work on *Making Good* through redemptive scripts discovered implications for building recovery capital through programs that put old offenders who had made good, who had re-narrated themselves, into networks with younger criminals who have not learnt how to re-story their criminal career in a redemptive way. Evidence for this has since grown stronger (for example, Laudet and White 2008). Recovery capital scripts can be even simpler. Kenneth Polk (1994) found that young men convicted for murdering other young men had never learned that when one accidentally bumps into a person carrying drinks in a bar, it is best to say, 'Excuse me'. No-one had taught Polk's young male-on-male violent offenders such simple scripts. Recovery from something as terrible as conviction for a pub homicide can be assisted by these young men concluding, 'No, I am not an irredeemably violent person, but I am a man who needs to learn certain simple rituals of civility to become a more polite person.'

The most important findings from meta-analyses of recovery from a diverse range of dreadful life challenges—including mental illness, drug addiction, alcoholism and a criminal conviction—are that CHIME (Connectedness, Hope, Identity, Meaning and Empowerment) precedes recovery (Leamy et al. 2011; Best and Laudet 2010). Beyond access to the recovery version of social capital, access to economic capital is also important to recovery, particularly in the form of secure housing. This literature suggests that many interventions that are effective for people in secure housing are not effective for those without secure housing (Cano et al. 2017). This is so much the case that secure housing is an integral part of the scale to measure the recovery capital construct (Best et al. 2012; Groshkova et al. 2013).

Alcoholics Anonymous (AA) has an interesting strategy for scaling up recovery capital. Its step 12 is to pass on the gift of recovery, to help yourself by helping other alcoholics to learn the lessons to re-story themselves to recover. This happens at scale through 106,000 AA groups across 150 countries around the world. Chapter 11 argues that there is an AA insight here that might be applied to the challenge of cascading recovery capital, restorative capital and collective efficacy more broadly.

Clifford Shearing and Richard Ericson (1991) realised that organisations as well as individuals can be re-storied. They argue that police culture is a storybook rather than a rulebook. Changing a police organisation requires changing the stories police share about good policing in the lunchroom and the patrol car. It is also possible to re-story a nation. We have discussed how Nelson Mandela did this for South Africa, reassuring whites with the message that whether citizens were black, white or coloured, to be a South African was to be a victim of a terrible institution called Apartheid (Meister 1999). Likewise, Abraham Lincoln at Gettysburg redemptively re-storied a nation—a scaled-up form of narrative therapy for a nation. Whether South or North, black or white, Americans are all people who suffered from slavery as an institution. It was a noble meaning for the American identity to be one of struggling continuously against the violence of slavery; and for South Africans to be engaged with a lifetime struggle to purge the nation of the violence of Apartheid (Meister 1999). This is the nobility of recovery capital.

Restorative capital

Restorative capital is like recovery capital in being a form of social capital that is a relational resource constituted by a relational practice (relational restorative justice) (Llewellyn 2012). My big-picture proposition here is that societies that are more holistically just are likely to have less crime and less armed conflict. Societies that have more social justice, more procedural justice, more gender justice and more restorative justice are likely to be less violent. People with special gifts in how to communicate to others love, understanding, compassion, empathy or spiritual depth in a restorative justice circle are those with the most restorative capital for building all these kinds of justice. They have gifts in how to cascade relational gestures of healing around a restorative circle. Relational justice allows relational enforcement of recovery agreements. The Canadian

Department of Justice's meta-analysis of the effectiveness of restorative justice by Latimer et al. (2001) found that the biggest effect size was not related to the direct power of restorative justice to prevent crime, though that was statistically significant. It was the superior capacity of restorative justice to achieve compliance with restorative agreements to help victims. Control groups in which reparation to victims was ordered (for example, by a judge) accomplished less delivery of reparation to victims than cases where reparation was volunteered in the restorative circle. The superior enforcement power of restorative justice in getting compliance with restorative agreements is mediated not by the police, but by friends and loved ones at the restorative conference who commit to monitor and ensure compliance with the agreement they participate in defining. A special capability of restorative justice is that it is a superior delivery vehicle for securing compliance with and commitment to rehabilitation and future prevention interventions that work (Braithwaite 2002).

So, we need not think of restorative justice as a micro-intervention. It is macro in two ways. First, restorative justice institutionalises spaces such as restorative circles and restorative city networks in which all manner of more micro-interventions are given a better chance to work than they are given by judges ordering them or prisons institutionalising their captives. Second, restorative justice is a social movement that is about justice and that has things to say about big injustices—for example, the injustice of the financial crimes of the Global Financial Crisis and how they might have better been addressed and prevented (Braithwaite 2013a). Braithwaite's (2000) conception of restorative justice does embrace advocacy of social justice and, more widely, it advances social movement advocacy for a transformed normative order compared with the order embedded in extant criminal legal systems (Braithwaite 2002)—an order that emphasises healing and prevention with safety, deep listening and empowerment.

For many Christian, Jewish, Muslim, Buddhist and First Nations advocates of restorative justice, it is a spiritual social movement that goes deeper than the values articulated above. I am a spiritually shallow person for whom religious social movements hold little appeal. Yet my empirical experience of observing many restorative justice circles is that when a 'spiritually deep' person is in the circle, this does gently spread a contagion of care across the circle. I once said to Chief Justice Emeritus Robert Yazzie of the Navajo Nation: 'I do see that spiritual contagion in the circle from indigenous leaders with *mana*, but I am a spiritually shallow westerner. So, how can I learn from your indigenous wisdom?' I expected something like, 'You have no hope, white man.' But no, the wise Navajo leader said I could achieve personal spiritual deepening by taking my heart to a place in nature I most love—a place that resonates with my identity and my ancestors and takes me out of myself. I have taken that advice these past 20 years and I do improve as a person when I take myself to my loved spotted gum overlooking the Pacific Ocean. I hug that tree regularly! There is strong evidence now that spiritual belief and spiritual activities can give hope and strength and provide meaning, especially during times of stress (for example, Galanter 1997); can prevent substance abuse, especially of alcohol and cocaine (Bakken et al. 2014); and are associated with desistence from crime in cross-sectional studies, though less so in longitudinal data (Giordano et al. 2008). Randy Martin (2000) even speaks of the evidence that spiritual alienation as anomie contributes to crime. Underwood and Teresi (2002: 31) describe this as 'social support from the divine'. Indigenous people often fear spiritual enforcement after a breach of a restorative agreement 'after the stone is buried'. After *Breaking Spears and Mending Hearts* (Howley 2002), hearts stay mended for fear of breaching an agreement that implies sacred enforcement in various parts of Indonesia, Timor and Melanesia (Braithwaite et al. 2012: 216–23). The literature shows a strong and consistent inverse relationship between spiritual wellbeing (a multidimensional construct that incorporates existential wellbeing or life meaning and spiritual beliefs) and psychosocial wellbeing of diverse kinds (Ellison 1991). For criminologists, however, the evidence remains unsettled on whether the notable effects on offending rates are the preventive effects of spirituality or the social support and other benefits of being religious or churchgoing (Jang and Franzen 2013; Johnson and Jang 2011; DiIulio 2009; Baier and Wright 2001). Put another way, are these effects about the Connectedness or the Meaning facets of CHIME?

Restorative capital is constituted when large numbers of children have experiences of these values in their families and schools, and then later in their life in primary workgroups. The evidence is that social capital ripples out more strongly and more broadly from primary groups of family–school–work than it does from intermediate civil society organisations, though these are also important (Job and Reinhart 2003). In other words, restorative justice in the criminal justice system is a second-order reform for crime prevention and building freedom compared with restorative justice in families, schools and primary workgroups. What do I mean by saying that primary-group restorative capital is important for building freedom and not just for preventing crime? Children are not born free; they are not born democratic; they are born dependent and powerless. Restorative justice circles in families and schools can be venues where children learn to become democratic, how to become free citizens who can resist domination deliberatively. In other words, the hypothesis is that a society that invests in restorative justice takes a macrocriminological step towards constituting social capital, and therefore towards crime reduction.

Mutually constitutive variegations of societal capital

Braithwaite (2013a, 2019) argued in a detailed way for the implausible counterfactual that restorative capital could have been deployed preventatively before the Global Financial Crisis occurred. Some details of these regulatory reform arguments are discussed Chapter 10. Their implausibility or plausibility need not delay us in this chapter. The example is signalled to illustrate the general point that when all the foregoing forms of capital are strong and more justly distributed, they can be mutually constitutive and each can be mutually tempering of the power of the other. Furthermore, this is fundamental to preventing cascades of crises that include financial crises, ecological crises and wars. If our accounting schools do not produce professionally competent and ethical accountants as a crucial pillar of our human capital, financial capital will not flourish. Likewise, if trust and collective efficacy do not flourish on Wall Street and in the City of London, embezzlement will flourish. Without trust and collective efficacy on the street, financial capital corrodes and collapses from within. While the idea of collective efficacy comes from the streets of Chicago, we saw it on the streets of the financial City of London and on Wall Street a century ago at times when Baron Rothschild in London and J.P. Morgan in New York would act to prevent a run on a bank by marching to the front of the frenzied queue of customers waiting to make a withdrawal and ostentatiously deposit a huge pile of Rothschild or Morgan cash into that teetering bank (Braithwaite and Drahos 2000). This indeed was social cohesion of the financial street 'combined with their willingness to intervene on behalf of the common good' (Sampson et al. 1997: 918). The best ethnographies of Wall Street, such as *Barbarians at the Gate* (Burrough and Helyar 1991), have been written by experienced financial journalists who aimed to reveal the ruthless fabric of the street.

Yet a social fabric they do reveal is that Wall Street and the City of London are financial communities with communal qualities frequently affirmed by rituals of apology, forgiveness and reconciliation, even if rarely by fully repairing the harm done!

In Burrough and Helyar's (1991) rich ethnography of the greatest takeover up to that time, the battle for RJR Nabisco, the following passage shows Henry Kravis, the pre-eminent investment banker who won the takeover battle, acting to affirm the importance of ceremonies of reintegration in the Wall Street investment community:

> Wall Street is a small place, and in the interests of harmony Kravis wasted no time healing wounds inflicted during the fight. He made peace with Peter Cohen at a summit in February and actually hired Tom Hill to investigate the possible takeover of Northwest Airlines ... Kravis also moved to smooth relations with Linda Robinson. Soon after the Gerstner episode, Linda took a message that Kravis had called. She ignored it. Within days she received a small ceramic doghouse with a cute note from Kravis, suggesting he was in the Robinsons' doghouse. Linda Robinson waited a few days, then sent Kravis a twenty-pound bag of dog food. All was forgiven. She and Kravis still own 'Trillion'. Fees, of course, went infinitely further toward soothing Wall Street's wounds ... Kravis even spread the largesse to those whose feelings he might have bruised. Geoff Boisi's Goldman Sachs got the job of auctioning Del Monte, while Felix Rohatyn's Lazard Freres did the same for the company's stake in ESPN. (Burrough and Helyar 1991: 508)

These may be vulgar modalities of reintegration, yet they are practical means of nurturing vulgar communities of commercial excess. A standard observation in the business culture literature is that the City of London was historically much more communitarian than New York (for example, Wechsberg 1966: 41; Coleman 1990: 109). Clarke's (1986) book on the City of London was about the imperative for a shift to more formal regulation of the city because Wall Street 'cowboys' and other rapacious internationals like Rupert Murdoch and Conrad Black did not quite understand that they were being allowed into a gentlemen's club where 'a word is as good as a contract'.

The storm of the Great Depression was too great for even the reparative power of the Rothschilds and Morgans to mobilise collective efficacy on the street. Instead, it proved necessary from the 1929 experience to institutionalise distrust in bank imprudence through regulatory agencies that accrued ever-greater powers in the century since. Wall Street needs CHIME after it crashes. It needs connectedness on the street that can incubate new networks of trust. It needs realistic collective hope that recovery is possible. Wall Street needs a sense of identity, meaning and empowerment after a crash that has devastated its confidence and the self-efficacy and collective efficacy of its traders and its institutions. Unemployed traders need to recover the meaning they get from a job. On the ashes of the unethical trading that causes crashes like that of 2008, traders need to find a new professional identity and a new ethical meaning in their business lives that are connected to their redemptive responsibility to unfreeze lending and rebuild confidence in a more genuine integrity of markets so that the unemployed might find jobs. Some of the most successful investors of financial capital, like Warren Buffett, have been recurrently good at this as they survived one crisis of capitalism after another. Recovery capital as well as restorative capital are critical to rebuilding devastated capitalist markets after a crash.

Strong institutions for building human capital, social capital, recovery capital and restorative capital are also needed to check and balance economic capital. Without constant growth of economic capital, long-term unemployment is the result. Chapter 4 showed this is a crime risk. Yet, some shifts from private to public capital are also needed. An example is that the European Union might have established a public European ratings agency to contest the fraud of the major US private ratings agencies seen during the Global Financial Crisis. The crimes of Deutsche Bank during that crisis could have been sanctioned by 'capital' punishment— an equity fine in shares of the company, as discussed in Chapter 9—rather than a massive cash fine. Averting climate change catastrophe will not be achieved so much by punishing environmental criminals as by shifting capital from carbon to solar and hydrogen, and cars from petrol power to electric power. Then the fuel economy crimes of corporations like Volkswagen become less important.

Financial capital needs more checking than service-sector capital because banking is the most aggrandising and the least humble form of capital, and the most criminogenic. That means an imperative for freedom and crime prevention is the regulation of markets in goods and markets in financial bads. Criminal markets are conceived of as markets in domination, in unfreedom, whether they are markets in financial fraud, corruption, buying politicians with hidden campaign contributions, illicit drugs, fake Covid-19 vaccines, prostitution, organ trafficking, trafficking in endangered species or modern slavery. This chapter has argued that new sustainable markets are vital for rebuilding all forms of capital in devastated cities like Detroit because such cities can be seedbeds of transformation from neoliberalism to authoritarianism and thence to future crime–war cascades.

Creatively balanced capitalism

Capitalism has a mystique that suggests private capital is the creative engine that drives forward all innovation. Economic capital certainly is important to driving creativity, but of an importance frequently exaggerated by those who ignore our other forms of capital.

Consider food production, the most important productive activity humans do. Three-star Michelin restaurants cultivate the mystique that their chef keeps his secrets so we must go there. In practice, this is impossible as staff the chef mentors move to other restaurants where they might improve on those supposed secrets. They might decide to become even more famous than their mentor through a television show in which their recipes are shared. Most historical innovation in the production of food has occurred in non-market household economies; this is the intellectual property that three-star restaurants usually purloin. Women's labour for millennia experimented with new foods and new recipes. Women shared their recipes. Sharing accelerated when cookbooks—often assembled by women's organisations such as church groups—were enabled by new technologies of printing. The internet and television further accelerated the sharing of women's unremunerated human capital in feminised food innovation. Older readers appreciate how steep this acceleration has been. Before television, our experience of food was monotonous, monocultural. Change was driven by creative balance between the unpaid innovation of our mothers and its propagation in cooking columns and books. Growing wealth in service economies meant that, by the late twentieth century, we could afford to dine at restaurants where food was cooked by someone other than our mothers. Feminism enriched diversity in the human capital contribution to family food; sometimes there would be turn-taking of meals prepared by fathers or brothers. The human capital market in chefs was captured by men; it drew on men who had been active in family food preparation.

377

In sum, the massive surge in the creativity of food preparation in recent decades is a product of creative balance between market capitalism, the globalisation of emulated food innovation driven by the emergence of mass media and social media, the human capital of women, the community capital of the church cookbook and the social capital of feminism as a social movement that brought more celebrity female chefs to the fore. One might say the state had little to do with it. State-funded technical colleges did train chefs to special forms of culinary excellence, but this was hardly the main game. The problem today is that food innovation is no longer making us better off because state regulation is not playing a big enough role in food industries that have become overly commodified. The progressive struggle has been one of bringing more of the human capital back into food to supplant that takeover of factory food that is a market in vice. In sum, even the most important productive endeavour for the flourishing of humankind is not fundamentally an accomplishment of markets and, when the market did become more prominent, it was more a market in vice than a market in virtue.

The role of the state was always of more importance than people could see. As restaurants took off, fly-by-night cooks who cut corners on the freshness of their food proliferated under the protection of the anonymity of large cities. All states and local governments had to hire food inspectors. This improved things. Even so, millions of people suffer food poisoning that makes them awfully sick (and kills formidable numbers of them) every year in every society. Food poisoning is possibly the only crime of capitalism that virtually all of us suffer on multiple occasions during a lifetime. Criminology is myopic in the way it almost ignores food poisoning as a crime, merrily persisting with the fiction that crimes like theft are more important than food crimes—and more important by ratios of thousands of articles on theft to each one on food crime in criminology journals.

Poisoning by rotten food is not the most important harm of culinary capitalism. Imbalanced commodification of global processed food means that consumption of the same deadly cans of cola is a global pandemic. Commodification of sugary foods by processors and of fatty foods by global fast-food chains of Donor McDonor capitalism have built an obesity epidemic. This epidemic is a greater killer than Covid-19 or the cancer caused by the commodification of tobacco or alcohol. Japan is the developed economy least afflicted with obesity, where people live longer because it has been most resistant to global food. Although 7-Eleven stores can be easily found in the vicinity of international hotels in Japan, the food in their refrigerators is different than in other countries. More of it is unprocessed, fresh Japanese fare such as sashimi prepared by humans.

Hence, the creative balance of food production has tipped too far towards commodified food. This is a similar point to the claims made in the discussion of human capital about how the creative balance of education production has tipped too far towards commodified education. Now we realise that we were better off with the food that preceded the accomplishments of feminism in projecting women's human capital into food markets; children were better off with the food produced by the unpaid domestic labour of their mothers. The policy remedy here of course is not to reverse the gains of feminism but to accelerate the regulation of food markets by means such as sugar taxes and by investing in human capital that enculturates resistance to sugar; teaching boys as well as girls about fresh food preparation in primary school, in the mass media and on the internet, so the human work of preparing wholesome food is shared.

Untempered commodification of food profoundly worsens inequality. Markets in bads have become so efficient that processed food, fast food, fat and sugar (once a luxury) have become supremely cheap. They are cheap ways for hungry poor people to fill their stomachs. Repeatedly eating potato cooked as fries or processed crisps boiled in fat may be low-cost, but with long lags, this makes health and lives a misery. Poor nutrition has become a major structural driver of inequality. Poor health and visible obesity ultimately also affect the employability of the poor as they get older, reducing their ability to move their children to better circumstances.

Hence, food crime is directly responsible for widespread corporate homicide by food poisoning; imbalanced commodification of food is responsible for inequality that indirectly increases crime in communities sickened and impoverished by commodified food—less so in Japan, Italy or France, but more so in the societies most afflicted by global food. This is even more true in parts of those societies such as the working-class communities of Glasgow, where deep-fried fare flourishes and sugar surges, and where those who live in the city's middle-class suburbs live 28 years longer than those in working-class areas (Marmot and Friel 2008: 1096).

MACROCRIMINOLOGY AND FREEDOM

The most deeply structural conclusion of this chapter is that capitalism helps us to flourish and enjoy low-crime societies when financial capital is balanced by human, social, recovery and restorative capital. Food has been used to illustrate the more general phenomenon that unbalanced domination of money capital corrodes the creativity of human society. It is ultimately self-defeating because of its own contradictions of commodification. This was the brilliant and enduring insight of Karl Marx that sat alongside his many less-enduring insights that stemmed from the oppressive idea of a dictatorship of the proletariat.

Writing before the regulatory state rose in Victorian England (MacDonagh 1961), Marx failed to see how a regulated, mixed and balanced capitalism had the potential to regulate its crises, to sustain its creativity and to clear the smog from its cities by controlling environmental crimes. Still, Marx's enduring insights mean there is no inevitability that the human species is capable of rebalancing capitalism to prevent it from destroying our civilisation and our planet. Burgeoning commodification causes so much corporate and common crime because it is so dominant a structural force that it sometimes proves beyond our capacity to tame. Even if we succeed in saving the planet by punishing corporations that cheat on obligations to reduce carbon emissions, at some future point in history some state criminal, some mentally unstable military official with a finger on a button or a terrorist may destroy the planet by triggering a cascaded exchange of weapons of mass destruction after which safe crops will no longer grow across large swathes of the planet. The challenge of struggling to make this prediction false by effective regulation of capitalist markets in weapons systems, killer robots, carbon and deadly food is the challenge for human survival. Ultimately, humans are likely to fail at this challenge, but if the next generation builds sounder institutions of nondomination, extinction can at least be deferred for centuries. A criminology of capital formation for organisational crime prevention is at the heart of this politics of hope.

Dangers of trust in capital formation

To build social capital, we must enculturate trust. Trust is enculturated in civil society through the educative stories of families and schools on the virtues of trustworthiness, through the actual granting of more trust to children as they grow and through nurturing pride in virtue by honouring trust as an obligation. Hence, human capital formation in the education system both creates trust and depends on trust—as do recovery and restorative capital formation. Douglass North has contended that secure property rights and trust nurtured by merchant codes of behaviour enabled a striking decline of interest rates in the Dutch capital market of the seventeenth century and then in the English capital market in the early eighteenth century (North 1990: 43). There is an open debate, however, over whether it was the moral force of such codes or the monitoring and use of sanctions they enabled that was the more important influence (Greif 1989). Perhaps there was a bit of both.

Robert Putnam (1993) has shown that fabrics of trust arising from rich traditions of civic engagement characterise the regions of Italy that flourished economically and subdued the Mafia throughout modernity. Furthermore, the more economically backward regions, where distrust dominates, are also the regions where political corruption festers. Putnam was methodologically deft in showing that the direction of historical causality operating here was not that economic success generated a trust-based culture but that a strong fabric of trust, woven in strong institutions of civil society, had economic benefits. Putnam's results are the most tantalising empirical evidence we have that resilient trust simultaneously limits the abuse of power and expands economic growth. Putnam's work shows how we can be both freer from want and freer from organised crime and corruption when social capital is in plentiful supply. Yet undersupply is standard, unfortunately, because we all have an interest in free-riding on the efforts of others who work to build a rich civil society. Trust creates more wealth to tax and causes people to pay their taxes more honestly. Trust, for Putnam, is the most important feature of social organisation that facilitates coordination to solve collective-action problems. Putnam (1995) has also shown across 35 nations a strong positive correlation between 'social trust' and 'civic engagement' (the density of associational membership). Networks of civic engagement are where trust and norms of reciprocity and cooperation are learned and enculturated. Enculturating trust is a technique for controlling the abuse of power that not only averts a major drag on economic efficiency, but also actually increases efficiency.

The problem with interpersonally trusting people and civil societies is that ruthless people abuse their trust. In response to this problem, Braithwaite (1998) argued that the priorities are to enculturate trust and to institutionalise distrust. The crucial way to institutionalise distrust is to temper the power of one strong institution with other strong institutions. The republican dilemma is that while a stronger state risks bigger abuses of trust and has more power with which to crush freedom, a stronger state can also do more to increase freedom. The bigger the state budget, the more it can disperse to combat the unfreedom of poverty, for example. Strong states, strong markets and strong civil society (including strong families) are simultaneously the greatest resources we have for building freedom and the greatest threats to it. The challenge of institutional design is to realise fully their potential for building freedom while maximally controlling their potential for destroying freedom. The republican perspective is that we can trust the state to be stronger when there are robust separations of power. A state in which the judiciary is independent and the rule of law is strong can be more powerful than one in which they are not; a state with strong institutions of civil society to exercise countervailing power against the state can be stronger than one in which they are weak. We can allow markets to rule over more domains of resource allocation when state regulatory capacities are strong. When civil society is strong, the jeopardy to freedom from what Jürgen Habermas (1985: 305–96) called 'the colonization of the lifeworld' is checked. A danger of rampant markets is the commodification of things (like food) that better constitute freedom when they take a noncommodified form. Education and research are other good examples. Art is perhaps a more controversial one, given the impetus markets have so often given to artistic innovation. Even so, it seems clear that we can be much more relaxed about market encroachments on art when the elements of civil society that nourish the arts are strong. So long as local folk clubs continued to meet and play around campfires, at family pianos and in little pubs and cafes, we did not need to worry about Bob Dylan topping the charts.

Strong civil society is by no means always constitutive of freedom. Perhaps no institution does more damage to freedom than the domineering, engulfing family. While the prime countervailing power against domination in southern US civil society in the 1960s also came from civil society—from black churches and white college campuses—a strong attorney-general and a strong president who stood in the firing line were also important. We can trust families to be strong only when the state is willing to intervene in families in which women and children are brutally dominated. In comparatively egalitarian capitalist societies, where family monopolies of socialisation are contested by the state education system and electronic markets for information, and where job markets give women economic opportunities to escape, strong families are not quite as troubling as they are in feudal or tribal societies in which markets provide no exits, no counter-socialisation.

Similarly, there were good reasons to worry about the threat of the church to freedom when markets were so weak and the church so strong that it could dictate who could get employment and who should be denied it based on religious belief. Today, few societies fear another Inquisition. The power of the church to punish is so much more effectively checked by separated powers of the state. Public interest groups and social movements are less likely to become oligarchies when states require them to be run democratically and to respect human rights. Environmental groups are less likely to be captured or corrupted by the very business and state institutions against which they should be exerting countervailing power if their seats at negotiating tables with business and government are contested by competing environmental groups (Ayres and Braithwaite 1992: 54–100).

Beyond neoliberalism and socialism

Practical politics rarely works to enculturate trust and institutionalise distrust. Neoliberals and libertarians like to totalise their trust in markets and distrust of the state. They want strong markets that weaken the state. Socialists distrust the exploitation caused by markets; they are overconfident in the capabilities of a socialist state; they want a strong state that weakens markets. Incumbents of the institutions of the state and of markets want to weaken the power of civil society because civil society is always criticising the way they exercise their power. In response to this reality, there are some civil society activists, influenced by a mix of anarchist and green ideologies, who want markets to be weaker and the state to be weaker. Likewise, in academia, economists are misguided in seeing civil society as a sideshow because markets are what really matter; public policy scholars and some criminologists are misguided when they see civil society as unimportant because the state is where the action is. By civic republican lights, all these political ideologies are deeply misguided in all these ways.

Republicans, Braithwaite (1998) argued, want an enculturation of trust that enables strong markets, strong states and strong civil society. Because republicanism is a liberal philosophy, it also values strong individuals. This book argues that a strong United Nations also adds critical institutionalisations of distrust that advance freedom in international society. Republicans should not reject all aspects of neoliberalism and libertarianism, but they must reject their commitment to weaken a state that needs constant strengthening as a ship repaired at sea. Republicans should not reject all aspects of socialism, but they must totally reject the idea that markets should be weakened; markets in vice are what want weakening. Likewise, republicans must shun suggestions to weaken markets in some interpretations of institutional anomie theory. America's strong markets and strong individuals are prominent strengths, including in the discovery of new technologies for controlling cybercrime and every other form of crime. What we should want politically is to enculturate trust in those strengths while institutionalising distrust from a stronger US state, especially a stronger business regulatory state, and ever stronger US civil society.

These past two chapters have argued that strong markets, a strong state, strong civil society and strong individuals are all vital to more freedom and less crime. Both enculturating trust and institutionalising distrust in all these institutions are imperative. The practical way to accomplish this are prudent and radically pluralised separations of power. That means each institution of separated powers being strong enough and independent enough that it can deliver the trust-building work that is its contribution to the economy, the polity, the criminal legal system and the society. But it also means that its strength must be checked and balanced by the strengths of many other similarly strong institutions in the separation of powers. And it means that no institution—not the presidency nor the supreme court and especially not the military—must be so strong that it can shut down the power of all other institutions. The next chapter argues that when those checks and balances are settled, strong and subject to the continuous strengthening of all institutions, as opposed to unsettled by anomie, the ship of society can better plough through dangerous waters. Societies run on to the rocks when any institution makes a play for unaccountable domination over all others.

8
Tempering power through networked governance

Key propositions

- Most good things accomplished in social life require the exercise of power. Among the things power helps accomplish are protecting freedom and preventing crime.
- Hence, we do not seek to limit or curb power, but to enable good power by tempering it.
- Untempered power dominates. It is not constrained by other powers from being arbitrary.
- Constitutions and their implementation are imperative conduits to power, to protecting freedom and to preventing crime.
- Constitutions enable tempered power by separating and balancing powers while also enabling power to be decisive. Decisiveness accomplishes specialised purposes of power efficiently and semi-autonomously. Judicial power is decisive because judges, and only judges, can convict. Judges have clearly defined capacities to break gridlock between other separated powers because they have decisive powers. Conversely, it is the police officer, and not another judge, who has the power to arrest a judge for domestic violence, and a prosecutor who has the power to prosecute. Each power is channelled to its specialised purposes by checks and balances from other powers that prevent them from arbitrarily breaking banks beyond their channel. This gradually breaks down in the historical journey towards the criminalisation of states.

- Contestation, dialogue and science have important roles in channelling power to good purposes, and away from arbitrary excess. If security services torture suspects, claiming that this saves lives, citizens must rise up to contest the arbitrary authority for police to punish. Debate is required in the legislature of the propriety of police jumping outside their authorised channels of prevention and arrest. Prosecutors should monitor the debate and charge police with assault as appropriate. If participants in a restorative justice conference credibly uncover excessively brutal use of force in an arrest, prosecutors must also act in response to that democratic contestation to rechannel police power. Good science in independent universities tests claims that torture prevents terrorism.

- Sun Yat-sen's constitutional innovation of an elected accountability and integrity branch of governance that is independent of the judiciary, legislature and executive and has impeachment authority over them is a profound contribution to republican thinking about securing freedom and preventing crime. Business regulatory institutions, particularly the central bank, must be accountable and democratised, but independently democratised from the central government. Sun Yat-sen's thought holds one clue for how to accomplish this.

- Nodal power in civil society networks has a crucial role in coordinating bridging capital among the separated powers of a democracy to tame a rogue power. Without networked governance of tyranny led from civil society, there can be no freedom. Criminalised states and criminalised markets evolve when there is no networked governance of their dominations.

- Social democratic parties that embody civic republican values of nondomination in their platforms are important to championing freedom. Yet without networked governance of tyranny from civil society, they are as vulnerable to criminalised state power as any political party. An elected pro-freedom party governing under a pro-freedom constitution puts freedom at risk whenever there is a failure to institutionalise distrust.

- A paradox is that societies cannot enjoy long-run freedom from anomie and violence unless civil societies enjoy destabilisation rights to restore freedom by dynamic adjustment of the constitutional order.

- Summarising so far, lessons about liberal freedom and taming ancient anomie are important to tempering domination and reducing crime, but they are not enough. Blocked legitimate opportunities must be opened and illegitimate opportunities closed. Institutional anomie theory insights must be realised through strong institutions of the family, welfare and education. The data further suggest that religious institutions that resist tyranny can prevent violence, that institutions of tax equity are important, as are labour market institutions and other institutions that promote equality. Particularly fundamental are separations of micro and macro powers. The promise of institutional anomie theory also requires strong business regulatory institutions, strong markets in crime-control virtue, strong civil society, strong financial, human, social, recovery and restorative capital and strong individuals. The most brilliantly institutionalised freedom could not be freedom at all if it were a freedom of timorous individuals who allowed institutions to do everything for them. At the same time, free individuals are unlikely to survive the risks of nuclear genocide and ecocide across the next century or two without a stronger United Nations.

- Uncontested commodification of too many things is a risk of American capitalism. Uncontested state control of too much is a danger of Chinese communism. Getting the balance right between market power and state power is not the right way to think about this dilemma. After all, this book shows that crime and domination are caused by excesses of state control in America and by excesses of commodification in China. The imperative is the struggle for both markets and states to be stronger in ways that temper domination in both societies.

What does it mean to temper domination?

In considering what it means to temper domination, this opening section considers abstractly the theme of this entire chapter. Next, the greater part of the chapter makes these abstractions concrete using the history of war, crime and freedom in Timor-Leste as a case study. Finally, the chapter summarises where the book has taken us so far on what we would need to measure in testing the freedom theory of what shapes empirical patterns of crime and domination.

Bad power is conceived as domination in this book. It is arbitrary power that is unchecked by a rule of law and by a plurality of separated powers. My ambition is to understand how to temper power, how to transform bad power in a society through good, tempered power. The previous chapter argued that the form of unequal power called domination is checked by strong markets, strong states, strong civil society and strong individuals that empower vibrant financial capital, human capital, social capital, recovery capital and restorative capital. Nondomination, according to Chapter 7, is accomplished by a complex of forms of capital that builds successful societies through enculturated trust and institutionalised distrust.

Limiting or curbing power is less appealing than tempering power, according to Martin Krygier (2017, 2019). Power is a good thing; it is needed to enforce legal judgements, to keep the peace, to raise funds to build schools. It is untempered power that is bad because it is arbitrary power. Power that is tempered by the discipline of the rule of law and rich separations of power is more resilient. It grows authority that is trusted by citizens as legitimate because it can be distinguished from domination (untempered, arbitrary power) (Pettit 1997). Domination destroys the trust that the previous chapter argued is the yeast for flourishing contemporary economies. For Krygier, and for ancient Greek philosophers who advanced temperance as a virtue, temperance means a 'moderating balance of elements'—for example, legal justice tempered with the compassion of restorative forms of justice by ancients who interpreted justice as *shalom* in the Judaeo-Christian tradition and *salam* in the Islamic tradition. This is also interpreted to mean peace with justice (Krygier 2017: 47). Tempered steel is made tougher, less hard and less brittle as an alloy (a balance of more resilient metals) in a test of extreme heat. For Krygier, this tempering metaphor in governance means tempered power is less brutal and less brittle. Tempered power is not weakened by the rule of law, while arbitrary power in pursuit of whims is very much constrained by the rule of law. Tempered power is more enduring as a rule of law virtue than an arbitrary 'rule of men'.[1] Krygier (2019) asks why we should want law to rule; for what purpose is the rule of law a good thing? The answer he elaborates is tempering power so that arbitrary abuse of power is checked.

---

1   Likewise, when in common usage we temper justice with mercy, we strengthen justice. Soldiers who are tempered by combat are hardened, but also moderated through the wisdom and prudence of experience. When music is tempered, it becomes more powerful in the sense it can be modulated into other keys. Tempering a sauce in cooking means gently heating egg yolk or a dairy ingredient before adding it to improve the sauce. Usage of the concept of tempering has been in continuous decline since the late 1700s: 'Definition of "Temper"', *Collins Dictionary* (available from: www.collinsdictionary.com/dictionary/english/temper).

Using the example of state constitutions, Krygier quotes Stephen Holmes on the error of seeing constitutions only as a restraint on power. Constitutions are also empowering in that they enable the concentration of power for good purposes:

> Limited government is, or can be, more powerful than unlimited government.
>
> ... [T]hat constraints can be enabling, which is far from being a contradiction, lies at the heart of liberal constitutionalism ... By restricting the arbitrary powers of government officials, a liberal constitution can, under the right conditions, increase the state's capacity to focus on specific problems and mobilize collective resources for common purposes. (Holmes 1995: xi)

The idea that states, markets and other institutions both temper and enable one another is an old one. Karl Polanyi (1957: 140) articulated it most influentially: 'The road to the free market was opened and kept open by an enormous increase in continuous, centrally organized and controlled interventionism.' Half a century before Polanyi, Max Weber (2002) made the point that capitalism could neither take off in a dominating way nor flourish in a good way without a strong state bureaucracy. Peter Evans (1995) advanced on Weber and Polanyi in a way that resonates with the Timor-Leste case study in this chapter. Evans was worried about states that take a trajectory towards becoming predatory states, as in his example of Zaire, which became Democratic Republic of Congo. This was contrasted with societies like South Korea that lifted themselves above poverty and corruption through becoming developmental states.

As in the example of South Korea, to become a free and flourishing society, a strong state is needed that can be a 'midwife' to development. That state requires an autonomous professional bureaucracy that is competent and meritocratic. Long-term careers of dedication to public service are vocations that are valued. In addition, for Evans, it is essential that the state has embedded autonomy. It is the embeddedness of bureaucratic autonomy that prevents states from becoming predatory. Embeddedness is a key to tempering the power of bureaucrats from pursuing their own interests rather than public goals. For Evans, bureaucracies must not be insulated from civil society in the way they are in the Weberian vision of bureaucracy. They must be autonomous, but the autonomy must be embedded in 'a concrete set of social ties that binds the state to society and provides institutionalized channels for the continual negotiation and re-negotiation of goals and policies' (Evans 1995: 12). The apparently contradictory tempered alloy of state autonomy, strength and coherence, on the one hand, and embeddedness on the other, is, for Evans, the underlying structural condition for becoming a developmental state like South Korea rather than a predatory state like Congo. This is also present in this book's discussion of Peake and Forsyth's (forthcoming) relational state and in its diagnosis of the networked governance of freedom and predation in Timor. Relational embeddedness is key to the paradox of separated powers that have enough autonomy to exercise strong state power in a way that advances freedom and controls crime, while experiencing enough tempering of that power to prevent separated power from becoming a criminalised state or a criminalised bit of a state.

One reason that plural checks are the heartland of meaningful embedded autonomy that tempers power is that concentrations of power are so variegated and nimble in the conditions of contemporary capitalism. Without a networked governance of tyranny, without the embedded autonomy of a strong state, strong markets and strong civil society, countries like Congo will continue to suffer high rates of poverty, violence, theft and rape and the predations of a criminalised state that enables criminalised markets and criminalised crony networks that crush freedom.

The tempering approach to power grows from an understanding that there is no such thing as an all-powerful state, institution, corporation or person. The most powerful states—the United States, China, the United Kingdom, Germany and Japan—have all had historical moments when they have unravelled into anomie and devastation and will have them again in the future. The most balanced, powerful individuals experience depression, rage, hate, terror, gluttony, sloth and self-harm. The greatest universities lose their way into intellectual irrelevance and become seedbeds of relevance to evil. German universities did this when they were seedbeds of Nazi youth in the 1920s and 1930s and Anglo-American universities did this when they built the instruments of nuclear and biological warfare. Few of the greatest corporations in history survive more than a century before they crash, failing to rise again. No orchestra stays great for long if it fails to be attuned to feedback from audiences and conductors. They require a spirit of innovation that grows excellence with well-tempered claviers, conductors and critics.

How power was tempered in Timor-Leste

To make Krygier's abstractions practical, consider my attempt with Hilary Charlesworth and Adérito Soares in *Networked Governance of Freedom and Tyranny* (Braithwaite et al. 2012). In Indonesia, East Timorese student leadership was critical to the people-power movement on the streets of Jakarta that helped democratise the country and overthrow the crony-capitalist regime of President Suharto in 1998. This involved 270 million people in as genuine a transition to democracy as the world saw in the past 30 years. In the process, East Timorese people power won democracy for an independent Timor-Leste in 1999. Braithwaite et al. (2012) is about how that was accomplished by networked governance, after the fulcrum of struggle shifted from armed struggle to nonviolent civil society struggle. This nonviolence accomplished regime change at the commanding heights of an exceptionally dominating state (rather as in South Africa's transition from Apartheid). The transition was punctuated by moments of extreme authoritarianism and violence, especially in 2006 when UN peacekeeping was forced to return to Timor.

Acemoglu and Robinson (2019) point out that the first deep transitions to republicanism in the wealthiest region of Europe with the highest concentration of large cities between 1000 and 1300 CE, in Northern Italy, were also rocky in this way. Most Northern Italian republics at some time negotiated their conflicts by appointing *podestàs* (magistrates) from outside the republic who would be fully independent of the ruling families and factions. They often arrived with a formidable transitional administration. For example, one arrived in Siena in 1295 for a year with a staff of seven judges, three knights, two notaries, six squires and 60 police from his own province (Acemoglu and Robinson 2019: 148).

The problem in Timor-Leste was that once the new leadership group consolidated sovereignty over a newly independent country after the 1999 UN referendum, the leaders wilfully cut themselves off from the networks of marginalised people in civil society who had helped them humble power in Jakarta. This was rather like what happened with the consolidation of sovereignty into the hands of African National Congress leaders post Mandela. Our book displays how the weapons of the weak in civil society were mobilised a second time to temper the power of their president and prime minister and rebuild a distinctive and variegated hybrid of separated powers in a democratic Timor-Leste today. Like Krygier in his work on contemporary Eastern Europe (Krygier and Czarnota 2006; Krygier 1996), Braithwaite et al. (2012) focused on the concern that the forces organised against domination could become sources of domination from the moment they assumed sovereignty over a state.

We interpreted the problem with the Timor-Leste transition as being that it was not republican enough. Until 2006, transitional governance failed to keep working at institutionalising tempered power in the country. Yet, when their leaders directed arbitrary power back at civil society, especially at the Catholic Church, civil society remobilised and re-established a richer democracy with tempered power after 2006. That book's title, *Networked Governance of Freedom and Tyranny*, signifies that networks can restrain the excesses of realist international diplomacy and check the excesses of executive domination within a state to deliver republican freedom. Networked governance was defined as the action of plural actors linked by coordinating dialogue. Relational dialogue encompasses both interdependence and sufficient autonomy for different nodes of the network to check and balance other nodes of (tempered) power. Networks can only govern themselves in a nodal way (Shearing and Wood 2003; Drahos 2004; Burris et al. 2005). Inherent in that proposition is the claim that even sincere democrats who seize nodal control are at risk of corrupting the separation of powers to preserve their hard-won victories. While networked governance has a more variegated horizontal architecture than state governance (Castells 1996; Sørensen and Torfing 2016), networks of capacity and accountability can be linked to every level of multilevel governance. This includes every layer of subnational, national and international hierarchies. Sometimes they are coordinated by state regulation, and sometimes not.

Networked accountabilities that temper power enable regimes to change in ways that prevent one form of enslavement from replacing another. Domination can be continuously challenged by networks that renew themselves with novel ways of checking power that are not confined to enduring constitutional balances. Variegation in checks and balances is our theme here. I join others like Jamie Peck (2013; Peck and Theodore 2007; Jessop 2015; Zhang and Peck 2016) in valuing an understanding of variegated capitalism. As concluded in the previous chapter, the politics of how to temper power in such a world must involve variegated separations of powers. One of the more exotic variegations directly witnessed in the traditionalist, predominantly rural village society of Timor-Leste in 2006 was the ritual ripping out of the heart of a terrified pig in the presence of dead ancestors angered by the capricious exercise of power by the country's cabal of leaders. I had a ringside seat—unfortunately, next to the pig. There were genuine tears from these party hardmen that their people had found it necessary to humble their power under the wiser eyes of the ancestors in this way. As a result, these leaders genuinely did re-empower the institutions of traditional civil society presided over by the ancestors, as well as the church, opposition political parties and, to some degree, the courts and the constitution, at least for a period after 2006. Somehow, I fear that invocation of appalled ancestors might not have worked in Donald Trump's America. Nor would accountability to a UN transitional administration, which played an important part in preventing the resurgence of various dominations in Timor-Leste, especially war. For variegation to work, it must be responsively attuned to local meaning-making.

Previous chapters posited it as definitional of institutions that temper power and prevent anomie that they must have a degree of stability. They must also be able to adapt dynamically, however, repairing the ship of republican society at sea while keeping it afloat. Roberto Unger (1983, 1987) introduced the notion of 'destabilisation rights' as a way of thinking about this dilemma. Given that rights reside with the citizens of a republic, destabilisation is more likely to productively keep the ship afloat when it comes from the people, rather than from institutions such as the military, a political elite or an interfering foreign power. Charles Sabel and William Simon (2004) further developed the concept of destabilisation rights within the American pragmatist tradition of 'democratic experimentalism'. These are rights to unsettle and open up state institutions that persistently fail to fulfil their functions. Destabilisation rights are dynamic checks on failures of institutionalised accountabilities to do their job. For example, the right to private litigation can combine with street demonstrations to destabilise defunct structures of environmental regulation (Boyer and Meidinger 1985). Oppressed minorities can appeal for rights redress to UN institutions. Destabilisation rights enable a politics of dis-entrenchment. Networks can deliver experimental innovation by reinvigorating the separation of powers. The state is often dug too deep into ancient entrenchments for innovation and democratic experimentalism. Western doctrine on the separation of powers has stultified because it has not been open to learning from the democratic experimentalism in civil separations of powers revealed in non-western histories such as that of Timor-Leste.

The past three chapters showed that free republics with low crime must radically pluralise their vision of how to separate and temper powers within the state so the state has pluralised branches of separated powers rather than just the traditional three (legislature, judiciary and executive). How can we enliven a political imperative for separations of powers that progressively become more separated? The history of Timor-Leste can be read as one of progressive struggle for continuous improvement in securing ever more separated powers; not just for Montesquieu's (1977) tripartite separation of powers among an executive, legislature and judiciary, but also for much more variegated and indigenously attuned separations of ever more powers; not just separations of government powers, but division of both private and public powers. Braithwaite et al. (2012) documented dozens of separated powers in response to Timor-Leste's post-conflict dominations. Capitalism is a continuous process of creatively destroying old concentrations of power and constituting even more worrying ones. Hence, the struggle for freedom must be more than a struggle for a new democratic constitution that guarantees a conclusive separation of powers. It must be contestation of an evanescent constitutionalism that struggles to continuously deepen separations of powers at every stage of a nation's history.

A republic is an unfinished struggle towards a polity in which each separated power has sufficient clout to exercise its own functions with support from other separated powers. This is not a new perspective. Hannah Arendt (1963: 300) quoted Benjamin Rush complaining in 1787 of those who confuse the struggles of the

> American revolution with those of the late American war. The American war is over; but this is far from being the case with the American revolution. On the contrary, nothing but the first act of the great drama is closed.

A republic is a polity in which no one centre of power is so dominant that it can crush any other separated power without the other separated powers mobilising to push back that domination. The Timor-Leste case study showed that Holmes and Krygier are right about the imperative to have a positively empowering vision of the constitution:

> Republicanism does not require powers that are so diffused that separated powers cannot act decisively. The executive is empowered to declare war, the judge to declare guilt, the legislature to declare laws. Decisiveness for the judge is actually enhanced by the

knowledge that only an appellate court can overturn her decision on an error of law; she cannot be dominated by a prime minister who demands the acquittal of a political crony. Decisiveness for a constable on the street is knowing that she is the one with the power to decide whether to arrest a judge who appears to assault his wife; then it is no longer in her hands but in the hands of the separated powers of a prosecutor. Decisiveness for a general is knowing that once the executive declares war, she can conduct it in accordance with laws of war approved by the legislature, without interference from politicians who think of themselves as armchair generals.

Of course, a mature constitutional debate is needed to fine tune separated powers to ensure that each can decisively perform its function without domination from any centralising power and without confusion as to who exercises each separated power, and under what norms. None of this is to deny that democracies must at times debate trade-offs between greater accountability and greater efficiency. Separated powers of civil society and the media to speak assertively during those constitutional debates are critical elements of separated powers that get the separations clear and effective. (Braithwaite et al. 2012: 128–29)

When the separations are clear and effective, yet dynamically responsive to changing societal and global circumstances, they have a claim on the respect of citizens. This respect is a bulwark against the anomie and violence that characterised Indonesian society in the late 1990s (Braithwaite et al. 2010a). It is the antithesis of legal cynicism (Sampson and Bartusch 1998). Dynamism is a neglected topic in debates on the separation of powers. One of the things republican revolutions have done throughout history is dis-entrench powers. Destabilisation rights and 'democratic experimentalism' (Dorf and Sabel 1998) unsettle and open up state institutions that persistently fail to fulfil their functions. Networks are imperative for experimental innovation in the invigoration of separations of powers because of states' propensities to rigidify.

One risk of richly separated powers is that they can induce gridlock. Networked separations of powers are themselves the best ways of tempering the inefficiency of gridlock. The empirically grounded conclusion of Peacebuilding Compared's Timor-Leste and Indonesia books was about embedded autonomy (Evans 1995):

For most tasks of modern governance, networks get things done better than hierarchies. Well-designed networks of power are not only mutually checking upon bad uses of power; they are also mutually enabling of good capacities for power. Networks must be coordinated and sometimes—not always—the state is the best candidate to supply a key node of coordination. For most problems, strengthening state hierarchy to solve problems is not as effective as strengthening checks and balances on hierarchy as we also strengthen private–public partnerships, professions with technocratic expertise on that problem, civil society engagement and vigilance, and other networks of governance, while at the same time strengthening coordination of networked governance. The most effective governance is rarely centrally monopolised; it is usually messily attentive to multiple accountabilities. This is not to deny that there must be agreement on who will make the final call on matters that have not reached resolution after deep contestation under a separation of powers. Elections are one such state institution with this usefully ultimate capacity to break a logjam (without violence). So are state courts. On legal matters, as valuable as it is to have a rich tapestry of legal pluralism where the national rugby judiciary regulates most violence on rugby fields, it is also valuable to have state appellate courts that have the legitimacy to make ultimate decisions on the basis of a synoptic view of all the adjudication that has occurred across that tapestry ... Gridlock is a risk of separated powers. Often it is more important that things are settled than settled right. Paralysis and disengagement in the face of great problems are profound risks, not only in times of war. Executive government has an oversight responsibility for ensuring that really big problems do not fall between the cracks. This is not the same as saying the government should fix them. It is to say that the state has a responsibility to take a synoptic view of a society, and to catalyse action when lesser actors are paralysed by the enormity of the challenge. We see this need most acutely at times of great natural disasters when so many leaders of civil society are busy bailing out their house or looking for lost families. One of the great examples of a chief executive with synoptic vision in the twentieth century was China's Deng Xiaoping when he saw in 1978 that the institutions of state production were bogged down. He opened up the Chinese economy to private institutions that broke through many of the production bottlenecks and bureaucratic gridlocks that were grinding the economy to a halt. We might even say that the most important role of state political leaders is to be gridlock breakers: to get that budget through the legislative contestation process, to issue an ultimatum to an enemy state of a kind that has less meaning when only a general issues it. Yet the ultimate power to break gridlock resides with the people when they take to the streets in a revolutionary moment in which they persuade the media or the military to side with the revolution. Republicans hope these will be revolutionary moments that dis-entrench bad power and entrench new separations of powers that secure freedom from domination. (Braithwaite et al. 2012: 303–4)

In the short term, there is little guarantee of that. Chapter 11 grapples with the problem that transitions from the untempered power of communism or Apartheid to a more tempered constitutional order are inherently anomic during the transition. These moments of transition to tempered democracy can indeed be exceptional periods when elevated crime or war is the price of freedom, as opposed to something freedom's institutions can conquer in the *longue durée*. In that *longue durée*, we must be deeply suspicious of arguments that a dictator can get the trains to run on time or can increase economic efficiency by overruling a court or a regulator that needlessly slows investment that would benefit the people:

> The experience of history … is that autocrats more often exercise their domination for corrupt and patrimonial purposes that reduce the efficiency of national resource allocation. So in the long run many separations of powers that seem inefficient to the politically naive are in practice economically efficient.

> Part of the efficiency dividend from separations of powers that are attuned to local realities is from a more efficient division of labour. Because central bank board members focus their intelligence and training on the large and intricate challenge of securing monetary balance for an economy, they are likely to make better decisions of this specialist kind than are the generalist politicians of the cabinet. Because police training is in community policing that enrols the community to do most of the serious business of crime control, they become better at it than the military with their training and experience in the use of maximum force. Our Timor-Leste narrative has well illustrated the provocation and inefficiency that can arise when the military takes over public order policing. (Braithwaite et al. 2012: 300)

The most inspiring thing about the struggle that led Timor-Leste to become a free, low-crime society was that its political strategy was for Timorese students in Jakarta to be shock troops who made the most creative sacrifices for the democracy movement on the streets. Their courage caused Suharto to fall at the moment of economic crisis. Powerless students of tiny East Timor were fulcrums when this profound democratic transformation was levered in the world's fourth-largest country. A gift of networked governance of freedom and tyranny from the students of Timor-Leste to the people of Indonesia was the strategy that worked for ending the Indonesian military occupation of Timor-Leste.

Greening New Deal social democracy

Productive innovation is always ahead of redistributive innovation—through the tax system, for example—in untempered capitalism. Markets in vice are one step ahead of regulatory institutions. Regulatory institutions cannot respond to vices that markets have yet to invent, so they play catch-up, though B-grade economies can prepare themselves for the next wave of market abuse by watching closely the waves of abuse crashing over A-grade economies today (Braithwaite 2005b). Chapter 2 showed that derivatives markets come in forms that are markets in virtue and other forms that are markets in vice. In both their good and their bad versions, these markets have accumulated staggering wealth in the hands of the super-rich, who are cocooned in financially engineered shelters from obligations to pay their share of tax. This profoundly eroded the legacy of the New Deal in America. Large corporations that pay no tax have at the same time been beneficiaries of profligate corporate welfare in the form of subsidies, research and development grants, socialist bailouts of capitalism's losses, and the like. The US state has ceased being an institution to redistribute wealth from the super-rich to the rest of society through its tax and welfare systems in the way it did from the New Deal until the 1960s. Today, it redistributes wealth from the rest of society to the super-rich (Braithwaite 2005b).

This means that the old-fashioned social democratic politics that gave birth to the New Deal is as relevant today as ever. Versions of republicanism that see it as being about political equality as an ideal, but not economic equality (for example, Sunstein 1988), therefore do not have much more appeal than liberalism. Philosophers' debates about what level of inequality is or is not morally acceptable are unimportant in the context of a social system called capitalism that always drives already unacceptable levels of inequality to ever higher levels unless checked by redistributive politics. In the history of capitalism, no society has accomplished a level of redistribution that has triggered even the beginnings of a debate among social democrats that perhaps this was too much equality. Too much equality is something that might happen in some philosophically possible world, but never in any sociologically existing capitalist world. We can say the same about equality between men and women, rich and poor countries or people with and without disabilities.

If freedom as nondomination is your ideal, poverty and structured disadvantage make freedom impossible. Choices for the poor are dominated and constrained by those with the economic power to push them around (Pettit 1997, 2014). As social democrats play catch-up with the latest power plays, the financial engineering to escape obligations to the poor, the stock market fiddling, the tax shelters and the monopolisation of the intellectual commons, social democrats need not worry about being too successful in any future sociologically possible world. Indeed, social democrats will not be very successful at all if they are old-style New Dealers infatuated only with the politics of the welfare state. The statist politics of provider capitalism is insufficient to deliver social democratic objectives. Markets are too innovative in new vices, too internationally footloose, for statist regulation/redistribution to be capable of saving civic republican ideals. Nor can nondomination be effectively pursued through a single social democratic party or a single set of NGOs such as the trade union movement. Nondomination requires social democrats to be networked with the women's movement, human rights NGOs, green NGOs, indigenous rights groups, development NGOs and the National Citizens' Coalition for Nursing Home Reform (Chapter 6). That is one difference between the New Deal and a Green New Deal.

If it sounds like a politics of infinite complexity, we should remember the pragmatics of the nodal governance tradition (Burris et al. 2005). Because a networked society is more fluid, complex and indeterminate than older structures of government such as parties and ministries, understanding how governance unfolds is more challenging. This challenge has increased the appeal of nodal governance as a way of thinking about the possibilities for strategic regulatory action. The question becomes what are the nodes where networks can be organised, where the levers at the disposal of one network can be tied into the levers available to another or several networks? A node is a place where resources, ideas, deliberative capability and leadership are available to make networked governance buzz. These nodes are the focus of attention in this theoretical tradition because a synoptic understanding of how whole networks and sets of networks operate is beyond our grasp. What we may be able to grasp is whether there are effects when nodal governance is mobilised to bind networks together.

This is an old idea in Eastern philosophy. Sima Qian around 89 BCE quotes the following exchange with Confucius: 'Do you think me a learned, well-read man?' 'Certainly,' replied Zi-gong. 'Aren't you?' 'Not at all,' said Confucius. 'I have simply grasped one thread which links up the rest' (quoted in Castells 1996: 1). Each strand of a web of controls that seeks to govern some person or some phenomenon may be weak, and we may have a dim understanding of this complex web of governance. Yet, if we learn to pull the right strand at the right time, we might find that the entire fabric of the web of forces for liberation tightens to become quite strong. Conversely, we can learn that if we pull the wrong strand at the wrong time, the entire fabric can unravel. From a republican point of view, we should be interested in how to cause the unravelling of webs of control that dominate citizens in an arbitrary way, and how to secure webs of control that prevent domination. This can be accomplished by strategic deliberation at strategic nodes of networked governance.

A richly tempered republic gives us frequent opportunities to vote for people who represent our interests, plus many nodes of governance that give us opportunities to contest power and deliberate in our own voice at that node of governance. Tempering domination does not require that we all spend our evenings in meetings, just that enough of us assume responsibilities to temper power when we see injustices not being righted. It requires a learning democracy where enough of us learn to care to engage and learn to be democratic through early experiences of deliberation in schools, families and restorative justice conferences. In addition, citizens must learn how to convene nodes of governance at the strategic intersections of networks that can regulate abuse. Put another way, through these means, we learn the collective efficacy that prevents crime and defends freedom.

Manuel Castells (1996) was right in his networked governance insight that, while states still matter greatly, governance is becoming less statist and more networked across the spectrum of all public issues. If this is so, deliberative opportunities for nodal governance become increasingly central to the institutions of republican governance. Restorative justice is an example (as discussed further in Chapter 9). A combination of the nodal governance of networks from below and meta-governance of networks by institutions of representative democracy can provide superior accountability and superior transparency than either approach alone. The superiority comes from covering the weaknesses of hierarchical accountability with the strengths of horizontal accountability and vice versa. A republic nurtures a creative tension among electoral accountability, accountability to the rule of law, contestable accountability enabled by separations of powers and directly deliberative accountability of each to every other in circles of denizens. Accountability is accomplished by widening circles of deliberative accountability (for details, see Braithwaite 2006a). This bubbles up the justice of the people into the justice of the state. Meanwhile, the state takes responsibility for educating its citizens in a rights culture that filters the justice of the law down to the justice of the people. All nodes of separated private, public or hybrid governance need enough autonomy so they cannot be dominated by other nodes of governance. Equally, each needs enough capacity to check the abuse of power by other nodes so that a multiplicity of separated powers can network to check any node of power from dominating all the others.

When our vision of democracy is messy—and is of deliberative circles of accountability—there are many kinds of circles we can join that we believe actually matter in building democracy. Democracy is, then, not something we lobby for as a distant utopia when the tyrant is replaced with free elections; democracy is something we start building as soon as we join the NGO, when we practice responsively as a lawyer, establish business self-regulatory responses to demands from green groups, deliberate about working conditions with our employees and employers, educate our children to be democratic citizens or participate in politically serious global intercultural conversations on the internet. If, on the other hand, we believe only in the hierarchical model of accountability in Figure 6.1, and if we apply it to an institution like a police department, we discover eventually that a police department is like a fish that rots from the head down. Who guards the guardians? If our only solution to corruption by an nth-order guardian is an $n+1$th-order guardian, we can be saved the trouble of corrupting many and concentrate just on corrupting the $n+1$th guardian. That is why the jury is a good anticorruption institution; it is harder to corrupt 12 different citizens in dialogue around a table than it is to bribe a judge. The republican vision of accountability for a low-crime society is of circles of accountabilities that check hierarchies of accountability so that everyone is accountable to everyone else.

Constitutional meta-governance for freedom and against the criminalisation of societies

This section shifts focus to the role of constitutional law in tempering domination and enabling multiplicities of accountabilities to flourish in a society. Constitutional law may be more important than criminal law to the prevention of crime. Republican constitutional law can help enculturate trust and institutionalise distrust. With this challenge, there is much to learn from ancient Chinese wisdom from before the invention of criminal law institutions, and even more to learn from the republican thinking of Sun Yat-sen a century ago.

One ancient Chinese safeguard against the criminalisation of the state was the institution of an independent examinations branch of governance. To be appointed as a civil servant, prosecutor or judge, citizens had to pass an exacting examination tailored to the professional demands of the examinations branch. The branch served as an ancient Chinese method of constitutionally regulating bad governance and fostering competence. The idea of independent branches that could regulate the executive government was also evident in the office of the censor (御史; *yù shǐ*) under the Qin and Han dynasties, which influenced the modern constitutional thinking of Sun Yat-sen (Braithwaite 2016b). Later, the Sui and Tang dynasties established the office of the *tái* (臺), which supervised the conduct of civil servants and military officers.

In Sun Yat-sen's Republic of China Constitution that was voted for in 1928, but not implemented until 1947, this tradition was picked up in an innovative adaptation of western republican thought to regulate the anarchic conflicts for power in the early Chinese republic (Tung 1964). Two years after Sun Yat-sen's constitutional ideas came into force in China, the republic was swept away by Mao's communists. Chiang Kai-shek's civil war government ultimately fled to Taiwan with an authoritarian vision of how to implement this constitution.

Sun Yat-sen's constitution provided for five independent branches of government: a legislature, an executive, a judiciary, an examinations branch and an accountability and integrity branch called the Control Yuan. The Control Yuan was elected until a 1992 revision to the Constitution. Clause 90 of the 1947 Constitution defined it as 'the highest supervisory organ of the state'. Fundamental to thinking about the Control Yuan was that it would check the capture and abuse of power in regulatory agencies in the executive branch, but also in the legislature and judiciary. Instead of allowing these branches to impeach their own wayward members—something Sun Yat-sen rightly saw as a woeful weakness of western constitutions—the accountability and integrity branch would independently adjudge impeachment. The constitutional realities of the 1947 Constitution have meant that censure and 'corrective measures' are speedier and more potent than impeachment (Ma 1963). In the 30 years following the demise of martial law in Taiwan, there were only 541 impeachment cases (Caldwell 2017: 757). Sun Yat-sen's original thinking on the separation of powers had a sixth branch, the Auditing Yuan. In 1931, the Auditing Yuan was subsumed as the Ministry of Audit into the Control Yuan.

Contemporary reinvigorations of this Chinese republican thought could be considered for the next constitutional revolution that occurs in a western democracy. This is particularly so for the contemporary West where financialisation has captured politics and the regulation of capital in a way that is dangerous to the sustainability of freedom (Braithwaite 2019). The job of an independent regulation and accountability branch is the regulation of the state, meta-governance (the governance of governance) (Sørensen 2006) or meta-regulation (Parker 2002; Morgan 2003; Grabosky 2017). Consider the meta-regulation of central banks. Here, the thinking of Steven Klein (2020) is helpful. Klein concedes that central banks must be independent of elected governments. Independence helps avert an electoral cycle of monetary policy that excessively promotes inflation by priming the pump in election years. The other side of that policy folly is being dangerously contractionary to restore balance in the year after an election.

Yet for Klein, central bank independence has led to insufficient responsiveness in democracies overly governed by key performance indicators like inflation targets, which work well enough when markets are functioning well but work badly during those large proportions of time when markets are in crisis (Quiggin 2019). We saw clearly with the 2008 Global Financial Crisis and the 2020 Covid crisis that central banks must be key players in doing deals with big banks and other corporations to save them from collapse. Without being democratically accountable, while hiding behind a fiction of political independence, they sit down with presidents and prime ministers to decide, no, we will not bail out

Lehmann Brothers; yes, we will bail out Citigroup and Bank of America. Most importantly, according to Steven Klein, they decide to allow millions of impoverished mortgage holders to crash and burn. Central bankers in the United States come from Wall Street and return to Wall Street, which is why they see their accountability pressure as coming from Wall Street, not Main Street. So, Klein says, central banks must be democratised, but independently from the executive government. This, according to Klein, is the way to escape a dangerous trilemma of independence, versus crisis prevention, versus domination. The trilemma is, first, independence from democratic politics and from the electoral monetary cycle; second, dependence on the economic cycle that means a political imperative to save the society by priming the pumps during crises; and third, tendencies to enact those imperatives in ways that serve those who dominate and disserve the dominated.

An independent accountability and integrity branch like the Control Yuan that is elected for only one term is one possible pathway to an independently democratised governance of money and central banking. Otherwise, central banking is a system of domination that guarantees the value of the currency by promising to take money in demands for future taxation of citizens, without being accountable to those citizens who underwrite their decisions. Otherwise, central banks continue to drive a redistributive politics of dismantling welfare with a 'debt-fare' of predatory lending to the poor, an economics of debt and the financialisation of capitalism (Braithwaite 2019). Credit 'transforms money into power' (Klein 2020: 31). For Klein, and for me, an elected accountability branch of governance to meta-regulate central banks would hardly be enough. A vibrant civil society politics of agonistic contestation of financialisation is additionally imperative through social movements like Occupy Wall Street this century and the organised consumer movement inspired by Ralph Nader and many Progressive Era muckrakers during the previous century (Chapter 12). Klein (2020: 19) describes this as the imperative for Polanyian 'social freedom through democratic self-organization and collective struggle in the economy'.

Sun Yat-sen's five branches of governance persist in the Taiwanese (Republic of China) Constitution today.[2] During Chiang Kai-shek's long rule of militarised authoritarianism, Sun Yat-sen's ideals were gutted.

---

2   Office of the President of the Republic of China, *Constitution of the Republic of China (Taiwan)*, Chs V–IX (2005) (available from: english.president.gov.tw/Page/94).

The Control Yuan became a puppet of executive rule even as Taiwan turned back to democracy. While calls to weaken or abolish the Control Yuan are incessant, in recent democratic renewals of Taiwan, the Control Yuan has done some useful meta-regulatory work, such as implementing the Sunshine Acts to ensure transparency, regulating political donations and maintaining registers of assets held by public officials.[3] In addition to supervising what would be called the auditor-general function in the West, the Taiwanese Control Yuan has supervised the integrity and independence of the other four branches by way of the Control Yuan Committee on Anti-Corruption.

Other committees exist for other purposes. There is a Control Yuan Committee on Human Rights with functions similar to western human rights commissions. There is a Standing Committee on Judicial Affairs and Prison Administration, performing the functions of judicial self-regulation in the West as well as prison ombudsman and prison inspectorate functions. The Control Yuan also has an oversight Standing Committee for National Defence and Intelligence Affairs, as well as a committee with oversight of procurement by all branches of governance. A separate standing committee advocates for, checks and balances ethnic minority affairs. Although the Control Yuan, as in white-settler societies, has a class interest in upholding Han Chinese interests over those of the indigenous owners whose land was stolen from them, it does seem a visionary idea to have a sub-branch of governance with the job of holding the other branches to account on questions of First Nations rights and reconciliation—more so one that has a high proportion of indigenous staff and that is independent of the judiciary. An accountability branch might consider a new treaty with indigenous peoples that overturns doctrines of *terra nullius* long enforced by courts that have defended the land rights of the occupiers, including those of wealthy judges. Institutionalised independence from a legislature, judiciary and executive with histories of rejecting indigenous self-determination could be a way to open doors to a form of self-determination that delivers a more radical vision of indigenous collective efficacy: Connectedness, Hope, Identity, Meaning and Empowerment for first nations.

---

3   For a survey of the history of the Control Yuan and its changing powers, see Ernest Caldwell (2017).

The Control Yuan has been under threat not only from the authoritarianism of pre-democratic Taiwan and from ceasing to be an elected branch since 1992. The policy of the current Democratic Progressive Party government had been to abolish the Control Yuan and move to a more conventional tripartite liberal separation of powers. In 2020, it pulled back from this to repurpose the Control Yuan as a national Human Rights Commission. The chair of the Control Yuan as of 2020 is a former member of the Democratic Progressive Party, which is a slap in the face to Sun Yat-sen's view that the impeachment of political leaders and judges should be independent and totally removed from the hands of political partisans. Bills were being debated in the legislature during 2020, however, to return to strengthening the guarantees of political independence. For the most part, we could summarise by saying that Sun Yat-sen's vision for the Control Yuan has been overwhelmingly discarded by the two major-party machines. These machines see it as an encroachment on their power that they would rather do without.

Thailand is the only country to have emulated Taiwan's constitutional architecture of an accountability and integrity branch. The 1997 'People's Constitution' was a radical document in terms of public participation and rights accountability. It was dismantled by the 2006 military coup and the 2007 Constitution promulgated by the Council for National Security, which made it a crime to criticise the draft constitution (Sapsomboon and Khundee 2007). As I completed early drafts of this chapter in December 2020, student-led demonstrators were massing again on the streets of Thai cities with demands for a new people's republican constitution. Covid-19 then began to dampen this politics of the street. It is perhaps testimony to the virtues of this architecture that tyrants found it so dangerous and students found it worthy of endangering their lives to revive. Members of the fourth inspection branch of the 1997 Thai Constitution oversaw impeachment in the other three branches, the election commission, the human rights commission, the ombudsman and audit and anticorruption functions, as in Taiwan's Control Yuan. The 1997 Thai Constitution involved the further innovation that membership of this fourth branch was limited to candidates who were not members of political parties *and were for one term only*. This served as a prudent check against progressive capture by parties and business cronies that dominate the executive and legislature and stack the judiciary.

Business regulators such as competition authorities, food and drug administrations, securities regulators and banking regulators must be independent. This has proved an impossible ideal under crony-capitalist regimes. It is an ideal constantly white-anted under liberal capitalism by business leaders who make fat political campaign contributions. During the 10 years I was a part-time commissioner with Australia's most independent, credible and respected business regulatory agency—its competition, consumer protection and product safety authority—we nevertheless had a day when it was alleged on the front pages of the newspapers that our chair had taken a call from his minister, the Attorney-General, that had influenced our decision on the biggest merger in the country's history. Our chair issued an indignant press release saying that the commission was an independent authority that was not subject to political influence over merger approvals and that he had had no conversation with the Attorney-General about the matter. That was true; he had not taken the alleged call from the Attorney-General, but he had taken one from the Prime Minister on the merger and I had spoken to the Prime Minister about it myself. Hence, independent meta-governance of independence and integrity is imperative even for the most independent of regulators. What would be desirable is for all major independent business regulators to have a dotted-line reporting relationship with the executive government and a solid-line accountability relationship with an accountability and integrity branch like the Control Yuan. That fourth branch would be responsible for the meta-governance of all business regulation. It would impeach regulatory commissioners when they allowed their independence to be politically compromised by political donors.

There is something attractive about Sun Yat-sen's architecture of a fourth accountability branch of governance comprising many sub-branches. This is especially so for the challenges that white-settler constitutions have so badly mishandled, such as theft of land from indigenous custodians and righting the dominations of genocidal frontier wars to ethnically cleanse indigenous landowners. For societies in which settlers have forced indigenous landowners off their country, there is that special appeal in one of those branches being elected from indigenous peoples for oversight of the other branches in terms of the *longue durée* of reconciliation and treaty renegotiation. This has appeal in the context of histories of indigenous dispossession, mass atrocities, disproportionate contemporary imprisonment and all other indigenous rights abuses. Constitutionally empowering this kind of compassionate entrenchment of first nations regulatory authority is appealing and novel.[4] For societies ruled by bankers' power (Braithwaite 2019), the idea of independent meta-regulation of banking regulators, central banks and labour regulators to ensure they are not captured by capital or by politicians on the prowl for campaign contributions is an attractive one to pull from the top drawer of activists' constitutional reforms after the next crisis.

Summarising powers to be strengthened and separated to temper domination

What follows is a kind of summary of the theoretical induction of the past eight chapters about anomie and domination and their relationships to crime and freedom. Because the theoretical journey has involved considerable embrace of ancient anomie, then Merton, Cloward and Ohlin and, finally, Messner and Rosenfeld's synthesis of institutional anomie theory, we start by building on the now considerable evidence that supports their theoretical conclusions—first, with ancient anomie, then with institutions of family, welfare and education. The polity came in for special elaboration because it had too thin a treatment in Messner and Rosenfeld. In considering how we explore a theory of crime and freedom empirically, the aim is to test whether its key variables explain not only homicide, robbery and burglary, but also levels of corruption, tax compliance, banking crime and environmental stewardship. Unfortunately, criminologists are comparatively good at measuring crimes like homicide and incapable of measuring corporate crime with reliability and validity. When we try, we tend to allow the less serious to dominate the variance in the measure. This drives out the influence of the more important dimensions of the criminality of the powerful. That is not an argument against trying to get better at it.

The conclusion to Chapter 2 has already summarised how a cross-national test of the following hypotheses could be modelled in a stepwise quantitative analysis. Readers uninterested in testing criminological theory quantitatively may decide to skip quickly to the conclusion of this chapter.

---

4   It is also consistent with the proposals in the *Uluru Statement from the Heart*, which came about after a dialogue among Australian Indigenous leaders in 2017 (2017 First Nations National Constitutional Convention, *Uluru Statement from the Heart*, 26 May 2017, available from: www.referendumcouncil.org.au/sites/default/files/2017-05/Uluru_Statement_From_The_Heart_0.PDF).

Liberal freedom

The first hypothesis is that thin political freedom, as captured by measures such as the Political Freedom Index, predicts low crime, perhaps very weakly compared with republican freedom. This lays a liberal foundation on which to build a deeper republican freedom explanation based on a more complex view of freedom as nondomination.

Ancient anomie

Citizen commitment to the normative order can be measured adequately enough by indices such as the World Bank's rule of law indices, which Testa et al. (2017) have found to be positively associated with cross-national measures of homicide rates. Measures of legal cynicism, which are also widely associated with higher crime, are another measure of the strength of commitment to the normative order (Sampson and Bartusch 1998), though they can be as much a rationalisation as an explanation of crime (Nivette et al. 2015).

Mertonian closed opportunities

The section below on 'Labour market institutions and other institutions of inequality' outlines subsets of blocked legitimate opportunities, as seen through the theoretical lens of this book.

Open illegitimate opportunities

The indices of Cloward and Ohlin's illegitimate opportunities in cross-national comparisons include the various indicators of the size of underground economies (Schneider and Buehn 2018). A challenge of making them independent variables is that there is also appeal in using them as dependent variables that measure the extent of organisational crime. Where the channelling of funds into tax havens is high, drug empires are large, darknet trade is rife and smuggling is common, these can constitute illegitimate opportunities while they also are measures of the degree to which illegitimate opportunities are in fact being grasped. So, as researchers build models with them as measures of organisational crime, they might also create feedback loops in the model to conceive them as forms of crime that are rich in their capacity to create new opportunities for further crime of even more diverse kinds. The density of criminal gangs and their control of territory and markets are other measures of illegitimate opportunities.

Institutions of family, welfare and education

Messner and Rosenfeld's arguments for balancing dominations of market institutions with the countervailing strengths of institutions of the family, welfare and education have catalysed considerable evidence that these do indeed matter in preventing crime. We have seen that this literature has mobilised a rich diversity of measures of the strength of these institutions. Messner and Rosenfeld see a strong welfare state as, among other things, a fundamental support to the strength of institutions of the family that are of special importance to families with many children and one parent. There are other domains in which a strong welfare state tempers domination. This relates to mentally ill or drug-addicted persons who are totally estranged from all remnants of family, to people with a disability or the frail aged who need institutional support from the welfare state because further home care is beyond the skills and coping capacity of their family, welfare support for families who are strong and capable but who are put at risk when a financial crisis takes their home and puts them on the street or families who are strong and capable but are decimated by a deadly epidemic. There are such varied misfortunes to which the welfare state has become attuned to respond. This reinterpretation of Mertonian anomie theory means that we also interpret a strong welfare state as a fundamental bulwark against domination.

Religious institutions

Chapter 4 discussed how Messner and his co-authors launched international comparative studies suggesting that societies with strong religious institutions fare better than others in crime control. It is easy to understand why Messner and Rosenfeld did not include religious institutions in their original theory and why Messner concludes that adjustment may be needed in light of these data. In the long sweep of history in Chapter 3, we gained some insight into how religious institutions have been central to waves of anomie that destabilised whole societies and continents through war and the criminality of highwaymen and armed gangs. This refers, for example, to the devastation of the whole of Central Europe and beyond by the Thirty Years' War, in which wave after wave of Protestant and Catholic armies and armed gangs of predators ravaged the countryside. It refers to the cruel character of the state crimes of the Inquisition and to the genocidal religious campaigns of the Crusades and how they cascaded violence between Christians, Jews and Muslims to the present. Yet here is where theoretical adjustments that emphasise the tempering of domination come into their own. The horrors of religious cleansing in the Thirty Years' War, the Inquisition, the rise of the Caliphate and its attack by the Crusades—all arose when the most important dominations in these regions were religious, more than state or market, dominations. The globe has seen since those times a formidable tempering of religious dominations. Still, there are pockets of the planet where religious domination remains the most important domination in play. When a UN peacekeeping mission responds to a region of an African country where Boko Haram has been dominating the society, particularly its women and girls, the top priority of peacekeeping remains pacifying and tempering religious domination.

Our Peacebuilding Compared project requires more data collection for a balanced sample of armed conflicts. So far, only 67 post–Cold War armed conflicts are preliminarily coded. One telling variable is religious leaders as advocates of both nonviolence and violence at different historical moments: 'Qualitative coding of a sequence of religious leaders contributing to conflict by supporting violence, followed by religious leaders becoming advocates of peace.' Twenty-three (34 per cent) of the conflicts strongly fit this particular sequence; 18 per cent evidenced a mixed tendency towards this sequence, and just under half had no evidence of it.

Hence, in empirical evaluations of the theory of crime and freedom, the strength of religious institutions variable must be considered with historical and contextual nuance.

Institutions of tax equity

Another institution that more recent cross-national comparative work by Messner and his colleagues showed to be important was wealth redistribution through tax policy. Like the strength of the welfare state, this can be interpreted as simply another index of inequality in societies. On the other hand, there is specificity in the centrality of institutions of taxation to domination. In the history of colonialism, they have been vital to understanding armed uprisings against the British Empire, for example from India (Braithwaite and D'Costa 2018: Ch. 5) to the American

Revolution, stirred at the Boston Tea Party. Two millennia earlier, Julius Caesar, according to George Bernard Shaw (n.d.), opined about tax and domination by empire:

> Pothinius: Is it possible that Caesar, the conqueror of the world, has time to occupy himself with such a trifle as our taxes?

> Caesar: My friend, taxes are the chief business of a conqueror of the world.

Taxes on capital, wealth and real estate are particularly important to increased equality because the International Monetary Fund (IMF) has concluded that 'income Ginis, on average, are half the size of wealth Ginis' (Dabla-Norris et al. 2015: 16). This relates to Piketty's (2014) structural insight that inequality is driven up by returns to capital that are higher than overall economic growth ($r > g$, where r is the rate of return on capital and g is the growth rate of the economy).

In crony-capitalist societies, it continues to be the case that what Acemoglu and Robinson (2012) call extractive rulers extract everything they can from the populace. They also free themselves and their inner circle of cronies from any obligation to pay tax. There is no social contract in these states to share fairly the burden of paying for things like an education system and a welfare state; the system is one of extraction of obligations imposed on dominated citizens and freedom from obligations by rulers who are the beneficiaries of the extractive institutions. The more extreme the extractive inequality of the tax system becomes, the more likely it is that it will become a major driver of anomie in the society.[5]

Labour market institutions and other institutions of inequality

This lens on empirical work in the tradition of Messner and Rosenfeld sees egalitarian institutions of welfare and taxation as important. Institutions of the labour market that set a minimum wage that is a living wage for poor families, that take care of employees and their families when they are

---

5   Extraction, predation and inequality are the issues, not the size of the tax take. Alinaghi and Reed's (2020) meta-analysis of the impact of tax levels on economic growth shows that across 979 estimates of tax effects in Organisation for Economic Co-operation and Development countries a 10 per cent increase in taxes is associated with a decrease in annual GDP growth of –0.2 per cent when bundled as part of a TaxNegative tax–spending–deficit combination. But it is associated with a +0.2 per cent increase in annual GDP growth when part of a TaxPositive fiscal policy package.

injured at work or become sick, that provide for parental leave when new children are born into workers' families and that guarantee gender and racial equality in the labour market make up another important institution of equality. Particularly important are labour laws that were created under the New Deal and globalised by the International Labour Organization to guarantee the rights for trade unions to organise. These have been significantly deregulated since the 1980s. Their institutional importance arises from the conclusion of Quiggin (2019: 242) that 'the biggest factor determining the distribution of market income is the relative shares going to wages on the one hand and to capital incomes (rent, interest, dividends and capital gains) on the other', combined with the conclusion even of the conservative IMF that '[o]n average, the decline in unionization explains about half of the 5 percentage point rise in the top 10 per cent income share. Similarly, about half of the increase in the Gini of net income is driven by deunionization' (Quiggin 2019: 247).

Many strong economic studies now go to this conclusion. In today's conditions, what that giant of British economists Tony Atkinson (2015) called a 'participation income' is needed. This is based on the principle that everyone has a right to a living income and an obligation to contribute to society. A broader view of contribution to society is needed for a Green New Deal, such as contributions to the arts and volunteering for charities, both of which were enabled by Roosevelt's New Deal. Atkinson advocated the economic benefits of scrapping complex thickets of welfare benefit programs that can be gamed—one pension for the aged, another for people with disabilities, another for one-parent families, and so on—and replacing them with the same basic income guaranteed for everyone not in full-time work. For those in part-time work, the policy design must avoid the poverty trap of high effective marginal tax rates that arrive to deter work as eligibility thresholds are passed. The integration of the tax and welfare systems can be given a gradualism of cut-out of the participation income that avoids such poverty and work incentive traps (see Garnaut 2021).

There are a great many other institutions that make their contribution to the level of inequality in the society. These range from housing policies that go to the affordability of housing—be it public or community housing— to gendered rights, to bonus cultures that drive extreme wealth in financial markets that lure traders to defraud people of their savings, to effective competition laws and tempered intellectual property protections that are prevented from constituting new forms of monopoly by competition law enforcement (Drahos with Braithwaite 2003).

It can be best for empirical work to focus on overall measures of inequality that summarise the net effects of all the institutions that drive inequality even as the policy responses needed to fix inequality must involve a long march through all these institutions, policy by policy.

Merton's warning about why there will be profound contingency about the effects of poverty and inequality on crime remains of utmost importance. Most people living in conditions of domination decide to accept it, so they can concentrate on the struggle to care for their family. This has been true whether their families lived behind the Iron Curtain in the twentieth century, were oppressed by the exploitative taxes of the British East India Company in eighteenth-century India, lived in chains in the plantation economy of the nineteenth-century American South or on reservations impoverished by ecocide against buffalo and the buffalo economy of First Nations across the Great Plains of North America. We have shown how, when oppressed people do break out of their self-made emotional prison of reconciling their family to its condition of domination, there is no deadly simply mechanics about which of the many inequalities that afflict them might cause crime. The oppressed might follow agitators who rise in violence when the state shuts their local school or hospital, or if the price of fuel rises sharply, when these specificities are only a tiny part of their domination. We saw from Nepal et al.'s (2011) study that when neither levels of poverty nor levels of inequality nationally predict violence, the degree of inequality between local landlords and the peasants of a small community can be a driver of violence.

Hence, from a Mertonian point of view, we might be unimpressed by the endless parade of studies testing the effects of one measure of inequality against another in search of some holy grail of a law of positivist criminology that shows this kind of inequality is the one that matters, and that one is not. This is about studies showing whether the percentage of the population below the poverty line, the rate of long-term unemployment or the Gini coefficient predicts when some other measures do not. The search for an essence of inequality that is the truer driver of a law of criminology may not be the right search. In different places and times, in response to particular historical events, one social construction of inequality may be interpreted as oppressive, as a source of hunger that motivates theft of food or the murder of a landlord, and may be most damaging in the dynamics of that context.

Social democratic politics has a good grasp on this. The social democratic political insight is that political and economic institutions must be reformed to progressively reduce all forms of inequality. Republican social democrats who replace inequality with domination through this insight acquire an even better grasp. Because social democrats know that the powerful always fight back rather successfully against all efforts to redistribute wealth and power, they need not waste their time on philosophers' and economists' debates about what is the optimal level of inequality. For the social democrat, in every society that has ever existed, there is too much intersectoral inequality and poverty. If there is historical injustice between the indigenous owners of the land and white settlers, struggle politically to fix it and close the gap; if there is inequality between rich and poor, struggle to reduce it by many means; if there is an oppressed religious minority, struggle politically to lift their oppression; struggle relentlessly to reduce inequality between women and men, LGBTIQ and straight people, between people of one colour and another, and so on, endlessly and without ever ceasing or being satisfied that the good and fair society has finally arrived. If ever it did, it could not last once power again started to beget domination.

This social democratic intuition can be modelled in a more productive kind of quantitative criminology. In ecological studies of crime across census tracts, cities, villages, provinces, war zones or countries, instead of putting, say, poverty, Gini, black–white inequality or caste inequality in an unresolvable contest for the most essential form of inequality to explain crime, put them all in together as one block of inequality variables.[6] The important question for the social democrat is rightly (in terms of a republican normative theory) to seek to achieve as much reduction

---

6   Some measures of inequality will have so much multicollinearity with others that it is best to form composite measures to achieve data reduction with as multidimensional a theory as the theory of freedom and crime. But where correlations among different measures of domination are moderate, my preference is to enter them all as a block of variables. The deepest theoretical interest is in the variance explained by the whole block of variables. This is not to deny that there is merit in going on to replace the block with each single variable, in one reanalysis after another, remaining open to some facets of inequality proving more empirically important than others. Extant research suggests these facets will be quite different for explaining crime than for explaining war. This occurs even though the indirect effect on crime mediated through war, and on war mediated through crime, should be important, according to the theory.

as is politically achievable in the levels of all dimensions of inequality. What we are theoretically interested in is not the explanatory power, the correlation of each facet of inequality, but the multiple correlation of all facets of inequality with crime. So, mirror this normative insight in the explanatory test of the theory of inequality and crime. This is a good example of normative theory improving the power, the sense and the sensibility of explanatory theory.

This approach also problematises the overall summary in Chapter 4 that inequality is the better explanation of crime cross-nationally while poverty is the better explanation of war cross-nationally. I would rather conclude that a social democratically relevant implication of anomie theory is that domination (which encompasses many facets of inequality and poverty) increases the risks of both crime and war, particularly after crime and war cascade into each other (see Chapter 11). The risks arise at many different levels of the oppressive consequences of poverty and inequality depriving people of freedom from dominations such as hunger or an absence of decent education or health services, and the suffering involved in disparate social constructions of the dominations of diverse kinds of inequalities. Inequalities between people with disabilities and the able-bodied are different for vision-impaired people and people without limbs. The numbers of people involved in these different particularities are small, so they will never explain a statistically significant proportion of the variance in crime. Yet the social democratic political intuition is worth taking seriously: we need a well-funded welfare state that embraces repairing the harm of all kinds of domination, including these. If we push this on every front, our aggregated hypothesis is that, in producing a more just society, we will reap the collateral benefit of a more peaceful and less predatory society. At the level of empirical testing, we can capture the dominations of disability in our blocks of measures of inequality and poverty as criminology gets better at measuring the quantity and quality of welfare state guarantees.

Micro-organisational separations of power

What about the move from the commanding-heights politics of inequality to the micro-drivers of white-collar crime that opened the analysis in Chapter 6? It pointed out what every white-collar crime scholar has known since the first wave of white-collar crime scholarship: that micro-separations in organisational life between the power of one corporate officer to put an employee on the payroll and the power of another to issue the paycheque must be separated. Why? Because if we fail to do that there will be risks of members of the organisation using 'ghost' employees to enrich themselves. Chapter 6 traversed a wide range of these types of organisational micro-separations of power that reach up to rather higher levels of organisations (which are imperative to white-collar crime prevention). The way crony-capitalist economies work to enrich the few and exploit the rest is through the select group of cronies corrupting a whole gamut of such micro-separations to line their own pockets. Each one might be of modest consequence on its own, but it is the aggregation of the micro to a macro pattern that ultimately criminalises markets and states.

While criminologists need to understand these micro–macro dynamics of organisational domination and crime, we must also have a searing micro-focus on checking and balancing each and all micro illegitimate opportunities one by one. Chapter 10 argues that deft regulatory strategies that lever organisational self-incapacitation are a key policy abstraction for delivering this. Chapter 10 argues that it is difficult and demanding for the regulatory state to accomplish a line of sight into every organisation in an economy and then intervene to plug illegitimate opportunities one by one. Hence, a meta-regulatory strategy to lever self-incapacitation is needed. It delivers regulated self-regulation to incapacitate the exploitation of illegitimate opportunities. Markets in virtue also have a role here.

Consider our Peacebuilding Compared fieldwork on the armed conflict and rule of armed gangs on the streets and neighbourhoods of Guadalcanal in Solomon Islands between 1993 and 2004. Illegal logging in one of the remaining large areas of rainforest on the planet was an important root cause of this violence. It led to criminalisation of the state and armed overthrow of the state driven by illegal logging interests (Braithwaite et al. 2010c). State-building macrostructural remedies were important in Solomon Islands peacebuilding; forestry regulation reform should have been a more important macro-remedy than it was.

Yet, there were micro-elements of logging crime that were usefully remedied through the peace process. Some of the problematic logging was completely illegal, some was completely legal and some was undertaken with a legal licence secured by bribes to political leaders. Some timber could be more cheaply exported through legal shipping contracts; other timber via more expensive illegal shipping. When logs moved on regular legal shipping routes, there were customs duties to be paid. Fraud was rife in the customs service here in misrepresenting the value of logs or allowing illegal to be mixed in with legal logs through the payment of a bribe. Often this worked by a low-level employee putting the correct valuation in the customs database. Then a senior customs official in the pay of a political leader would change that valuation. In exchange for peacebuilding investments in improving the training and efficiency of the customs service, foreign donors insisted that new commercial customs software be installed that made it impossible for these practices to continue. Once the new software was installed, the senior officer's electronic signature would be indelibly recorded in the customs database after they changed the valuation of the timber. Audit would track the validity of these changed valuations and the corrupt customs official and their political master would be at risk of criminal conviction.

Let me use this not so trivial micro-separation of powers in Solomon Islands to reinforce the major methodological point about evaluation design that tests blocks of theoretically conceived policy measures rather than putting separately conceived variables in competition, as we saw with the empirics of which is more important: poverty, Gini or racial inequality. Similarly, there is no way that a micro-measure so specific as installing new customs software will predict crime rates in any quantitative comparison. But this customs reform is part of a large bundle of many such micro-reforms called multidimensional peacebuilding, where being multidimensional means being attentive to many of these diverse drivers of illegitimate opportunity structures for the economic predation that feeds armed violence. We have seen in Chapter 6 that the international evidence is that peace operations do work in ending wars and reducing the duration and severity of violence, and that these effect sizes are larger—indeed, they are very large—when these peace operations are multidimensional (Walter et al. 2020). Hence, part of the diagnosis of what is needed at the microlevel for the Solomon Islands peace operation to be effectively multidimensional is software that separates micro-powers to improve customs integrity. In international comparative studies of peace operations, the Solomon Islands peace operation is coded as a highly, though not completely, multidimensional peace operation. And so, at a blocked level of analysis, the customs reform that is ethnographically vindicated in our research (Braithwaite et al. 2010c) is also vindicated through its tiny contribution to macro-quantitative research on peacebuilding multidimensionality. Bovens and Wille (2020) made a helpful methodological contribution to how this might be tackled. They argued that to estimate the strength of accountability institutions in a society one would not want to simply count how many of a list of accountability institutions exist in that society. Bovens and Wille (2020) refine 19 measures of the quality of watchdog powers that go beyond the size of inspectorates, budgets and formal powers, to more informal qualitative assessments for each institution, such as its 'salience' (whether its reports grab attention, whether it is a marginal or central player in the accountability landscape), 'credibility' (captured by measures of recognition and legitimacy among the public and stakeholders) and 'creativity' (whether the search is creative for mobilising informal powers when formal powers fail to produce accountability).

Strong business regulatory institutions

Many countries do not have a national competition authority that enforces what Americans call antitrust laws. Until 1990, most did not, as can be seen in the dynamic model prepared by David Levi-Faur and Jacint Jordana that can be found on my website at johnbraithwaite.com/regulatory-capitalism/. The majority of regulators in countries that have a national competition regulator are captured by the interests they are supposed to regulate and are quite incapable of credible enforcement action. Hence, to measure this facet of the separation of powers, we must count how many of the key domains of business regulation are covered by adequately resourced regulators with large numbers of street-level inspectors—covering environmental and securities regulation, banking, food, drugs, occupational health and safety, consumer protection, competition, tax enforcement, human rights, discrimination, labour rights, and more. Second, we must code the enforcement credibility for each of these key regulators. Just as the evidence is now encouraging that effective policing reduces crime, so it is that effective street-level regulatory inspection works (Schell-Busey et al. 2016; Braithwaite 2008, 2021f). The difference is that expenditure on policing budgets is popular among politicians, and not only populist politicians. Neoliberal ideology, concern about 'business confidence' and business campaign contributions all make spending on more regulatory inspection much less fiscally favoured by politicians worldwide. The potential for increasing freedom and saving lives by regulatory inspection spending is almost certainly greater than through spending more on police, even though policing is still something that can save a lot of lives when done in an evidence-based way.

The number of criminal prosecutions a business regulator takes is not the best measure of the enforcement credibility of business regulatory agencies in light of the evidence of Schell-Busey et al.'s (2016) meta-analysis of 58 studies of corporate deterrence (see also Chapter 9). The existence of some big prosecutions that deliver big penalties and big changes in industry practices would be a relevant measure—although that would have to be coded qualitatively by a knowledgeable coder sophisticated in business regulatory realities. Chapter 10 argues that potent incapacitation remedies are more important to corporate crime prevention than long prison sentences or big fines. What is more important still is evidence that the regulator has a strong and continuously improving mix of regulatory sanctions and remedies available to it. That mix is a variable that Schell-Busey et al.'s (2016) meta-analysis suggests has an impact alongside formidable inspection.

Braithwaite (2016a) argues and cites evidence that their conclusions about the importance of a mix of strategies would have been even more strongly reached had Schell-Busey et al.'s (2016) outcomes of interest been broadened beyond 'reducing crime' to reducing workplace deaths, reducing environmental harm and similar regulatory outcomes, which are actually the outcomes more commonly and more importantly measured in the policy literature. Usually a measure like workplace deaths is also more important to freedom as nondomination than counts of workplace crimes. An impressive evaluation of stock market regulation by Choi et al. (2016) demonstrates the regulatory strengths that an accountability and integrity branch under a Sun Yat-sen–style constitution might meta-regulate regulators to deliver. Comparisons with controls revealed that a responsively mixed set of strategies is much more effective than having a single punishment or persuasion strategy. Choi et al. (2016) set out to test the effectiveness of the construction between 1992 and 2006 of a responsive regulatory pyramid by the Australian Securities and Investment Commission (ASIC). Choi et al.'s (2016) analysis showed that as successive law reforms progressively equipped ASIC with new layers of more varied arrows in its law-enforcement quiver, the effectiveness of its enforcement progressively increased. A difference-in-differences analysis (to mimic an experimental design) with the impact of New Zealand's securities and financial market regulation as a control reinforced this result. Choi et al. were interested in the effectiveness of securities regulation in making markets more transparent to investors and therefore more efficient and less prone to artificial bubbles that burst. The ASIC outcome of concern was whether the market was fully informed. Did regulation produce an improved information environment and market liquidity? Hence, Choi et al. measured the impacts of the Australian and New Zealand financial disclosure regimes by variables such as reduction in financial analysts' forecast errors, forecast dispersion, bid–ask spreads and increases in the turnover rate from the market liquidity test. ASIC's budget and enforcement intensity (measured by prosecution counts) helped analysts to reduce forecast errors for future profits. The responsive regulation effect more strongly increased predictive accuracy over and above those punitive impacts on the integrity of markets. The leverage in such data was formidable, with an Australian sample of 148,498 firm-month observations (with each observation based on the median for several analysts) and a New Zealand sample of 116,585.

Choi et al.'s (2016) research has the strength of a multiple construct, multimethod move to a pooled time-series, cross-sectional analysis of all major corporations in an economy on an outcome that securities enforcement is designed to deliver, combined with a difference-in-differences analysis of two whole economies. It delivers a larger n of observations than criminological research normally can manage.

Strong markets in crime-control virtue

Competitive markets in crime-prevention technologies like customs software are important to achieving a low-crime, low-violence society that is freed from corruption and criminalised states. Markets in virtue matter because they deliver the crime-prevention goods along many of the pathways to more richly separated private and public powers. Chapter 7 showed there are many of these virtuous market accomplishments of crime control. Not all of these are familiar to criminologists, though some are, such as reductions in car and bicycle thefts accomplished by locking devices, cybersecurity technologies and a galaxy of security technology markets that have made banks hard targets for anyone who does not own or dominate a bank (Farrell et al. 2014).

Strong civil society

We can use the Solomon Islands logging crime case study to illustrate the importance of a strongly independent power of civil society that is independent of a criminalised state and a criminalised logging industry.

Environmental advocacy groups lobbied the leaders of the Solomon Islands peace operation about why illegal logging was not only a major ecological catastrophe, but also a principal driver of the criminalisation of the Solomon Islands state. This had at least some impact in stirring the peace operation into some multidimensional action that included the customs software reforms discussed above. Feminist and church activists had an independent insight into the local secrecy of the problem that revealed another shocking dimension of it. Foreign loggers so economically dominated locales where they logged that they became a law unto themselves. Being above the law allowed them to traffic weapons and other illicit goods such as pornography on logging ships. Not only did they traffic pornography; they also produced it by exploiting indigenous children, according to the systematic research of The Anglican Church of Melanesia (Herbert 2007). It was found that village children were raped, sold into marriage and used for pornography on a remarkably wide scale by foreign loggers. Child prostitution was found in every village visited on the large island of Makira.

A Solomon Islander former logger told Herbert (2007: 25): 'Last year I worked at the camp. There were seven Malaysian men there, and everyone was married to a young girl—[aged] 13 or 14. They are not interested in the older girls—once they are 18.'

In other words, these crimes beyond the reach of a criminalised state were called to account by feminist church children's advocates. Qualitative coding is best when it can know about the capacity of a civil society actor like the Church of Melanesia to temper power, as opposed to the crudity of counts of the numerical density of NGOs present in a country. Indices of the strength of feminism as a social movement are a particularly strategic facet of civil society strength in this view of measuring what is most important.

Strong social capital

Evidence that there is an association between social capital broadly conceived and crime, and even more strongly an association between collective efficacy and crime, has been discussed. Robert Sampson and his co-authors make insightful points about why collective efficacy is the most important variant of social capital for crime prevention. Trust alone, for example, is not enough; to really make a difference, trust must be translated into the hands of collective efficacy to prevent, guard, warn or 'pick problems: fix them' (Sparrow 2000). This collective efficacy happens on the street (or in the suites, in the case of collective efficacy to prevent corporate crime). With certain more specific types of crime, one could make the claim that, for that kind of crime, recovery capital is more important than collective efficacy. One possible hypothesis could be that the level of investment in recovery capital programs that work would be a better predictor of drug use than collective efficacy.

Some ask whether investment in restorative justice cross-nationally would be a credible predictor of crime. One sensible answer is to think not, at least not in the immediate future, because all societies have some restorative justice programs but in no society does restorative justice approach the status of a mainstream approach to crime. It exists in every country but is a marginal fact on the ground in almost every country. This means its predictive power should be weak. Still, it might be part of a block of 'strength of multidimensional social capital' variables that would include recovery capital and restorative capital measures, social capital variables that could include trust in varied institutions of local, provincial and national government, trust in civil society institutions and trust in business and its institutions. Strong human capital as measured by various Human Development Index variables such as the education of girls cross-nationally is probably best separated from a block of social capital variables.

An interesting question for future empirical work on the freedom theory of crime is that an aggregated measure of reaching the UN Sustainable Development Goals might be a good predictor of crime, war and freedom cross-nationally. Exploring that macrocriminological hypothesis could be a valuable and challenging project. If our principles of crime control are to build freedom, temper power, eliminate poverty and reduce all forms of domination under a just, normative order, I have argued that this implies achieving the UN Sustainable Development Goals. These are: no poverty; zero hunger; good health and wellbeing; quality education; gender equality; clean water and sanitation; affordable and clean energy; decent work and economic growth; industry, innovation and infrastructure; reduced inequalities; sustainable cities and communities; responsible consumption and production; climate action; life below water; life on land; peace, justice and strong institutions; and partnerships for the goals. The UN Sustainable Development Goals enjoy global recognition and consensus. They are not a perfect fit to the criminological theory of this book, but the perfect must not be an enemy of the good in communicating ideas and testing and playing with them.

More broadly, the theoretical intuition of this section is that a block of multiple social capital formation variables is theoretically what matters more than competition among them.

Strongly separated powers inside the state and inside business

Based on 25 years of Peacebuilding Compared fieldwork, I am coding a variety of separation of powers ratings (high, medium, low) based on literature on that society that includes its constitution and its law in action, interviews on the ground and relevant quantitative data. They include an evaluation for that society of the separation of the legislature from the executive, the degree to which the electoral system is 'winner takes all' as opposed to one that delivers more proportional legislative balancing, the independence of the judiciary, the independence of the police and separation of the military from involvement in executive government and business. Peacebuilding Compared also codes the density, flourishing and independence of civil society organisations, which include specifically important ones such a free press, free trade unions and independent human rights and women's rights groups for the earlier block of variables representing the strength of civil society. It also codes state capabilities to regulate business, and civil society's capacity to regulate the state. For example, how hard is it in this society for an NGO to win a court case against the government (high, medium, low) and against big business (high, medium, low)? Another code is of what Hood et al. (1999) call *Regulation Inside Government*. Again, this is a high–medium–low code that is influenced in the rating of its level (before and after conflict) for Solomon Islands coding, for example, by fieldwork knowledge of the little customs reform mentioned above, drawn to our attention in interviews with peacebuilders, ministers responsible for customs and former prime ministers and officials of the customs agency itself. Then there are more objective variables based on codes of whether the state has an ombudsman, an independent audit office, an independent civil service commission, an anticorruption commission and what their budgets, powers and independence look like. Other variables go to human rights enforcement capabilities. Another set of Peacebuilding Compared qualitative separation of powers codes (pre-conflict and post-conflict) included:

- Is there a rich separation of powers between the judiciary and the rest of the state?
- Is there a rich separation of powers between prosecutors and the rest of the state?
- Is there a rich separation of powers between the police and the rest of the state?
- Is there a strong separation of the police and military from involvement in business (protection rackets count as involvement)?
- How politically powerful is the intelligence service(s)?
- Is there a rich and plural separation of powers between accountability institutions such as the ombudsman, auditor-general, inspector-general, civil service board, anticorruption commission and the rest of the state?
- Do some elites enjoy impunity from the rule of law?
- How strong are parliamentary institutions compared with the executive?
- Does the separation of powers create so much interference by one branch into the affairs of another that branches of governance have insufficient autonomy and discretion to be responsive to the needs of citizens?
- Is freedom to protest in the streets secured by the rule of law?
- How potent is anti-monopoly legislation?
- How monopolised/cartelised is the economy?

Peacebuilding Compared codes a considerable number of additional separations of powers variables beyond these. The aim is not to use each as an independent variable on its own but to include it in scales of blocked variables that measure, for example, 'strongly separated powers inside the state' and 'strongly separated powers inside business'. Again, the theory advanced is that any one of these policy measures is a thin reed for changing much on its own but, woven together, a clutch of thin reeds could have strength in the binding together of their weaknesses. This is not a theoretical intuition plucked from thin air. It is grounded in an appreciation of the empirical findings discussed in previous chapters that multidimensional peacekeeping works better than unidimensional peacekeeping, that problem-oriented policing works as a policy that plays out with many disparate dimensions of problem solving even though one particular street-lighting intervention might not work at all, that motivational interviewing works as a recovery capital intervention that follows unknowable and diverse individualised paths. The multidimensionality of motivational interviewing is so robust it can have some effectiveness in delivering recovery in the hands of practitioners who fail to grasp and implement most motivational interviewing principles (Best et al. 2009; Miller 2007)!

Through all of the above the hope is to have shown that it is possible to give more institutional meaning to Messner and Rosenfeld's idea of strong institutions of the polity that temper the power of markets. Messner and Rosenfeld have already admirably demonstrated the operationalisability and power of strong institutions of the family, education, welfare and religion. This book seeks to go beyond that to argue that macrocriminology can operationalise through blocks of more micro and meso variables the ideas of strong markets, a strong state and strong civil society, strong separations of public powers, strong separations of private powers, strong enculturation of trust and strong institutionalisation of distrust, strong economic capital, strong human capital and strong social capital. Together, this ensemble of strengths can form a resilient republican fabric that delivers freedom from domination and crime. Or so I hypothesise.

The empirical testing strategy for such a republican theory of crime control and freedom would involve, at a conceptual level, the stepwise addition of blocks of correlated variables with an institutional character, more than adding single variables. It would be bound to involve a mix of both.

What about strong individuals?

I am insufficiently the psychologist to have clear views about how to measure cross-national differences in the strengths of individuals. Dominated individuals include those who would never speak up in a critical voice to their boss and who always do what a patriarch, a parent or delinquent peers tell them to do even if that is an unhealthy choice. Dominated individuals can be enslaved—and even prefer to be a slave than to be free by speaking truth to power. Measuring the strength of individuals across societies by their suicide rates seems unsatisfactory. There may be circumstances in which suicide is enacted as a kind thing one can do for one's family and an individual must be strong to do it.

Susanne Karstedt has used Hofstede's cross-cultural study of a values scale that measures individualism, showing that in societies with high individualism, interpersonal lethal violence is lower (Karstedt 2006), as is state violence (Karstedt 2011b), corruption and organised crime (Karstedt 2012b). Smith and Robinson (2019) found bullying victimisation was lower among school-aged children in individualist societies. One of the problems with Hofstede's individualism as a measure of the strength of individuals is that one can endorse Hofstede's item 'Group success is more important than individual success' while being an amazing individual success. This indeed is what sporting coaches always say: if you want to become the biggest star on the team, play for group success rather than individual success. Likewise, you can have the strongest possible capacity to achieve and commitment to your individual goals while agreeing that 'Employees should pursue their goals after considering the welfare of the group'. Nevertheless, variants of Hofstede's individualism scale may be one option for the strength of individuals across societies.

At the end of the day, republicanism is about liberating individuals. No great social movement for freedom ever took off without the strength and self-efficacy of catalytic individuals who initially were small in number. For all that, I am content for the moment to be the macrocriminologist who sees strong individuals as being constituted by their own agency, by strong families, strong welfare rights (such as to secure housing), guarantees against being born into poverty, a strong healthcare system, communities with collective efficacy, strong recovery, restorative and relational capital, strong schools and human development in workplaces and strong women's rights—all enabled by the enculturation of trust and collective hope.

Conclusion

Braithwaite et al. (2012) studied the 1999 triumph of networked tempering of tyranny in Timor-Leste by inspiring social democratic leaders with pro-freedom values like Xanana Gusmão and José Ramos-Horta. After decades of war, domination and criminalisation, a peaceful, free, low-crime society was created. Through this national case study, we have been able to grasp the many blocks of variables and individual variables that can be specified in tests of the theory of freedom and crime, or simply in an elaborated and integrated version of classical and institutional anomie theory. The conclusion to Chapter 2 summarised how these variables and blocks of variables could be layered into some kind of stepwise quantitative test of the theory of crime and freedom on cross-national data on homicide rates, corruption levels, the size of the black market and other crime outcomes. Historical and ethnographic research based on more studies such as this one of Timor-Leste, and other studies of more global sweep such as Peacebuilding Compared, will also refute and revise the key propositions of the theory of crime and freedom in the decades ahead.

Braithwaite et al. (2012) wrote a story of how quickly the government led by exceptional Timor-Leste leaders became corrupted and criminalised. This happened because they excluded the very civil society networks that brought them to power. With equal historical speed, however, these civil society networks regrouped, independent journalism spoke truth to power, the UN transitional administration helped to resurrect constitutional checks and balances, UN peacekeeping worked (Walter et al. 2020). Priests and nuns protested from pulpits and on the streets and marginalised indigenous elders from remote villages brought the ancestors to the capital to discipline wayward national leaders in national rituals of restorative justice.

Good constitutions enable tempered power by separating and balancing powers. They also enable power to be decisive in accomplishing specialised purposes efficiently and semi-autonomously. Each power is channelled to its specialised purposes by checks and balances from other powers that prevent them from arbitrarily breaking the banks of their channel. The Timor-Leste case study illustrates how contestation, dialogue and science have important roles in channelling power to good purposes, away from arbitrary excess. When police intelligence tortured suspects claiming this saved lives, citizens rose up to contest arbitrary authority for the police to punish. Debate about the propriety of police jumping outside their authorised channels of prevention and arrest occurred in the Timor-Leste legislature. Prosecutors monitored the debate and threatened police with assault charges. The UN transitional administration was a channel of good policy science that disputed assertions that torture was a way to prevent terrorism and coups. Many other terrible tyrannies occurred along this fraught historical journey, however.

Adjusting channels that empower the legitimate exercise of power is fundamental to states, businesses and societies having the capacity to grow freedom and prevent crime. Acemoglu and Robinson (2019: 270) illustrate the problem of inept articulation of rules of state power with the impoverished Indian state of Bihar. Bihar would receive money from the national government, but then fail to spend it because any spending of more than US$55,000 had to be approved by the state cabinet, which could not wade through the backlog of decisions this mandated!

Nodal power in civil society networks has a crucial role in coordinating, bridging and linking capital among the separated powers of a democracy to tame rogue power. Without networked governance of tyranny led from civil society, there can be no freedom. Criminalised states and criminalised markets evolve unless there is networked governance of their tyranny. Social democratic leaders in Timor-Leste who embodied civic republican values of nondomination proved as vulnerable to criminalised state power as the brutal occupation they had supplanted when this networked governance of tyranny from civil society was pushed and fell away. Reliance on a revered pro-freedom leadership governing under a new pro-freedom constitution destroyed freedom. Then the brave people of Timor-Leste, still recovering from the trauma of the genocide that had been attempted against them, reorganised in a nodal way in civil society after 2006. They realised that democracy and nondomination are not things you put in place with a shiny new constitution and trusted leaders. They are things you lose if you fail to struggle continuously for them through civil society networks.

Perhaps as much as one-fifth of the Timor-Leste population lost their lives because of the violent occupation by Indonesia that ended in 1999. According to UNODC, the homicide rate in Timor-Leste was down to 12 per 100,000 per year in 2003–06, then halved by 2007, according to the World Bank, and halved again between 2007 and 2009 to become a country with a below-average homicide rate. Today, the gang violence that was out of control until 2006 is overwhelmingly pacified; Timor-Leste is a comparatively low-crime democracy, although perhaps not a model democracy in many ways. It still suffers its dominations. In 2020, it worsened on the Transparency International corruption perceptions list to 86 of 198 countries. Then again, few, if any, of the countries with a worse ranking were recovering from the level of domination and violent death per capita that Timor-Leste had suffered in the final decades of the twentieth century. Overall, its journey since 1999 has been determinedly towards freedom and away from cascading violence and crime.

Sun Yat-sen's constitutional innovation of an elected accountability and integrity branch of governance that is independent of the judiciary, legislature and executive and has impeachment authority over them is a profound contribution to republican thinking about securing freedom and preventing crime. This chapter has sought to argue that constitutionalism is important to the macrocriminological pursuit of a low-crime society. But sadly, unlike the South Koreans, the western constitutional imagination is bogged in western ruts that have given up on the idea that it is possible to impeach a president, a prime minister, or a chief justice. Westerners do not understand why the Thai students leading the protests on the streets of Bangkok at the time of writing have a bigger vision. It is a vision for the character of the people's struggle for a new people's constitution to restore freedom and tame a criminalised state and criminalised markets.

9

Minimally sufficient punishment

Key propositions

- For unusually oppressed people, like First Nations Australians, punishment is not a minor facet of their domination, but is central to the dynamics of domination.

- Deterrence works best when it is progressively reduced with the aim of growing freedom as nondomination. It must be reduced to the lowest level of deterrence that can avert the escalation of crime.

- Which strategy works best at crime control is not the most important question for criminology. More important is which meta-strategy is best in a given situation; which strategy for sequencing strategies best reduces crime and domination? Deterrence contributes best to meta-strategy design when punishment is low and decreasing, but detection is perceived to have high certainty, and escalation is seen as inexorable without desistance.

- Deterrence works best when escalation of deterrence is combined with escalation of social support to help offenders take paths away from punishment.

- Successful crime prevention persuades offenders that trouble hangs inexorably over their head, but caring people will support them to avert it.

- Freedom depends on escalating social support until desistance from domination is consolidated.

- Deterrence above minimal sufficiency blunts deterrence. Anything more than a minimally sufficient frequency of escalation to deterrence blunts deterrence for future cases.

- A preference for restorative justice over deterrence sharpens future deterrence of crimes of the powerless and, more surprisingly, future deterrence of crimes of the powerful.

- Deterrence usually fails because the criminal justice system always faces a system capacity crisis that is at its worst when and where the crime rate is worst. Responsive escalation helps solve the system capacity crisis by motivating most punishment to be self-punishment and most prevention to be self-prevention. Responsive regulation rations punishment to cases where ethical appeals for remorse, apology, reparation and self-prevention of future offending do not work.

- When intrinsic motivation to comply with the law is kept intact, responsive regulatory enforcement chooses not to crowd out intrinsic motivation with extrinsic threats.

- Responsive enforcement has a dynamic design to ensure that game-playing to avoid legal obligations inexorably produces escalation to deterrence and then incapacitation.

- Deterrence works best when it focuses on a line that should never be crossed after an announcement date, followed by progressive lifting of that line, raising our expectations of responsible corporate and individual citizens.

- Law enforcement works best when it averts stigmatisation, while communicating the shamefulness of predatory crime.

- Freedom is maximised when the structural punitiveness of the system is gradually reduced until punishment gets so low that insufficiency of punishment increases crime.

- Minimally sufficient punishment allows the least punitive societies to close most of their prisons while meeting the UN Standard Minimum Rules for the Treatment of Prisoners (the 'Nelson Mandela rules').

- This is best done with pride and publicity that educate citizens about why 'jailing is failing'.[1]

---

1   'Jailing is failing' is the campaign message of the Justice Reform Initiative in Australia, of which I am proud to be an ACT patron.

Dynamics of just enough deterrence

Threats to freedom must be deterred, but deterrence is overrated compared with other crime-control tools discussed in this book. The next chapter considers how incapacitation, especially self-incapacitation, is a more useful doctrine of prevention than deterrence. It also argues that when incapacitation is not mainly in the form of imprisonment, it can be a less dominating doctrine than deterrence. Captivity is not the best circumstance for cultivating capabilities for freedom. Most Aboriginal and Torres Strait Islander people in Australia are arrested by the police during their youth, often with deeply stigmatising consequences during their schooling and as they attempt to get their first job. This is something that happens to quite a small minority of white Australians. Aboriginal and Torres Strait Islander people are even more overrepresented in prison populations than African Americans in the United States. The intersection of a criminal record and race makes it impossible for a large proportion of the Indigenous population to sustain employment. Overreliance on deterrence and prison is thus central to the domination suffered by disadvantaged minorities. My contention is that there is little hope of tackling racial inequality without emptying prisons of 90 per cent or more of their occupants.

This chapter is about how to achieve just enough dynamic deterrence to secure freedom through minimally sufficient deterrence. For more, see Braithwaite (2008, 2018), on which this chapter expands and draws heavily.

Dangers exist in maximalist approaches to deterrence and in minimalist ones (such as that restorative justice can replace punishment). A minimal sufficiency strategy aims to avert these dangers. The objectives are to convince people that the webs of relationships within which they live mean that lawbreaking will ultimately lead to bad outcomes. These webs of relationships can also persuade offenders that predatory crime is simply wrong. The pitch to offenders is to abandon criminal careers because doing so assures desistance of the state and of loved ones from increasing intrusions in their lives. Social support lays a path to desistance that is also a path to freedom for the offender. Alternative support and control strategies should be attempted until desistance finally occurs. Communities can be helped to understand that this is how minimally sufficient deterrence works. By relying on layered strategies, this approach takes deterrence theory on to the terrain of complexity theory. It integrates approaches based on social support, recovery capital and collective efficacy, dynamic concentration of deterrence, restorative justice, responsive regulation, responsivity and indirect reciprocity. Deterrence is desolate in its failure as a criminological doctrine because of its rejection of complexity in favour of simple theories such as rational choice.

Some criminologists are inclined to ask why any role would be given to deterrence. The evidence for the power of deterrence in reducing crime is thin, after all (Nagin 2013; Chalfin and McCrary 2017; Tonry 2018). There are three answers to why deterrence should retain a significant role. One is that a good meta-strategy for crime control achieves strength through the convergence of weaknesses: deterrence can help to motivate crime-control strategies that are more effective. Second, deterrence is one weak strategy that can be tried after various less weak strategies have failed, strengthening the efficacy of a complex mix that is tied together as a bricolage of strategies. In other words, deterrence does work, but rarely on its own and mainly when deterrence is woven into a regulatory mix. Third, when deterrence of a specific offender fails, it might slightly strengthen the general deterrence of other offenders.

Sometimes a tax audit teaches a corporate chief financial officer more about what they can get away with in an audit than what they cannot. Sometimes punishment or the threat of punishment provokes defiant reactions that can make crime more, not less, likely. For most values of relevant variables, defiance effects exceed deterrence, but there are some contexts in which specific deterrence exceeds defiance. For these reasons, deterrence minimalism is rejected in favour of minimally sufficient deterrence.

Deterremce maximalism is also rejected. Zero tolerance and other political slogans that go to deterrence maximalism are common. They are doubtless helpful in some kinds of election campaigns but are rarely taken seriously by scholars who understand the evidence. Deterrence can never be the main game of crime control. Even so, it is reckless to fail to develop a view of the constructive role deterrence must have in crime prevention. The data on the limited effectiveness of deterrence and the cost of prisons (Nagin 2013; Durlauf and Nagin 2011a, 2011b; Travis et al. 2014; Petrich et al. 2021) demand disinvestment from locking up offenders. This is a cornerstone of 'justice reinvestment': disinvestment from prison and reinvestment in evidence-based social support pathways. It is easy to dismiss the prescriptions of maximalists who push for sentences that are as long as the political process can drive them.

Likewise, it is easy to dismiss maximising the shame aimed at offenders. While there are criminologists who argue that shame has power in crime control (Braithwaite 1989), these scholars do not advocate maximising the denunciation directed at offenders. The evidence is that this strategy leads to stigmatisation, which makes crime worse (Ahmed et al. 2001: 3–72; Braithwaite 2020c). Moreover, we now know that healthy pride management may be quantitatively as important as, or more important than, healthy shame management (Ahmed and Braithwaite 2006; Maruna 2001; Best et al. 2016). Intentionally directing unhealthy shame at offenders may crowd out healthy pride from the encounter. There is unhealthy shame that increases crime and healthy shame acknowledgement that helps prevent crime and repair harms. Likewise, there is unhealthy pride that fosters crime by vaunting superiority over others, and there is humble pride in doing things well with others that is vital to crime prevention—often via pride in the identity of being a law-abiding citizen who cares about the suffering of others (Ahmed and Braithwaite 2006). Humble pride in citizenship obligations is a building block of freedom. What is needed is an approach to deterrence that does not crowd out healthy shame acknowledgement and healthy pride in a law-abiding self. Indeed, a strategy that nurtures them is required. A virtue of minimally sufficient deterrence is that it minimises that stigmatic crowding out that is inherent in deterrence that brutalises.

Progressives who seek to minimise the quantum of fear or shame that criminal processes invoke are also a danger. For example, this chapter contends that it is dangerous to regard restorative justice as an abolitionist prescription that eliminates the need for punishment and deterrence. Restorative justice is a strategy to give an opportunity to all the stakeholders in a crime to participate in a process that discusses who has been harmed, who has needs and what might be done to repair those harms and meet those needs (Zehr 2015). It is about the idea that because crime hurts, justice should heal. A naive aspect of the view that restorative justice eliminates the need for deterrence is denial of the reality that if we gave criminal offenders the choice between agreeing to meet their victim in a restorative circle to discuss repair of the harm or doing nothing and forgetting about it, most offenders would opt to forget it. Offenders mostly agree to participate in restorative justice because the alternative has deterrent elements. We see from this that a useful role for deterrence is to motivate engagement with something that is more effective than deterrence: restorative justice and the rehabilitative and preventative measures for which restorative justice is a delivery vehicle. Indeed, wise integration of restorative justice and deterrence allows restorative justice to strengthen the preventive power of deterrence, in addition to allowing deterrence to strengthen restorative justice. This illustrates the ambition of identifying a good meta-strategy for crime control that achieves strength from the convergence of weaknesses: in this example, strength from the convergence of the weaknesses of deterrence and restorative justice.

Some restorative justice advocates are reluctant to see a positive role for shame or are minimalists about shame (for example, Maxwell and Morris 2002). A society in which rape, violence and corporate crime are minimally shameful will be a society with high rates of rape, violence and corporate crime (Braithwaite 1989, 1995, 2020c). Hence, it is also imperative to diagnose what minimal sufficiency of the right kind of shame might mean.

There are alternative paths between maximalist and minimalist approaches: a minimal sufficiency strategy of deterrence guides us towards them. Minimum deterrence and minimum shame are inferior to minimal sufficiency, which means just enough of the right kinds of deterrence and the right kinds of shame (which shun stigma as a criminal law doctrine or an objective of sentencing). Deterrence and shaming are more effective when combined with a dynamic theory of social supports partly because supports render shame more reintegrative. Communicating the shamefulness of predatory crime is more effective when combined with the reintegration of offenders (Braithwaite 1989). As with deterring crime, the evidence is that deterring warfare works better when armed fighters are simultaneously shown the costs of killing and shown a supportive peace dividend that benefits them, their family and their community (Braithwaite and D'Costa 2018: Ch. 3; Toft 2010). This is why there is strong evidence that peacekeepers prevent war when they do multidimensional peacebuilding that supportively delivers peace dividends (Doyle and Sambanis 2006; Walter et al. 2020). It is also why simplistic strategies of deterrence maximalism by backing threats to foes with investment in ever more battalions and bombs get countries into more, not less, war.

In business regulation, we have seen that perhaps the most cost-effective strategy is informal praise by inspectors when companies improve because a statistically significant improvement in compliance is achieved at near zero cost (Chapter 5; Makkai and Braithwaite 1993), along with benefits to morale, motivational postures (Braithwaite 2009a) and regulatory legitimacy. Data located at a radically different level from street-level encounters of inspectors also support the pivotal role of praise compared with shame.

The meta-analyses show consistent, statistically significant positive effects of the reporting of environmental stewardship on the financial performance of large firms, and even bigger effects for small firms (Dixon-Fowler et al. 2013). The effect sizes are not huge, but they are sufficient to make it generally rational for firms of all sizes to work hard at being good environmental citizens. The empirical work of Amato and Amato (2012) suggests, however, that these effects may not be about punishing dirty companies with adverse publicity, but about praising green leaders who attract business and investment. Amato and Amato found no negative effect on the stock values of the largest 500 US companies from being in the bottom quartile in *Newsweek*'s ranking of 'The Greenest Big Companies in America'. In the 10 days after the ranking was announced, however, the praise impact on the share price of firms in the top quartile was very large. Their share price performance was more than twice as good (less than half as negative during a bear market) as the other 75 per cent of US firms.

Criminological theory needs something better than cynicism driven by piling up empirical studies about the limits of deterrence. Few citizens think deterrence has no role to play in the prevention of rape, theft or corporate crime. In failing to develop a theory of deterrence that takes fear and shame seriously in social control, criminologists have handed the deterrence debate to neoconservative maximalists.

This is sad because deterrence maximalists justify a greatly increased level of suffering for incarcerated people and their families. Maximalism increases crime by skewing state budgets towards prisons that mostly worsen the criminality of those sentenced to them (Nagin et al. 2009). Yet maximalists make more sense to the community than criminologists who say only that punishment deters little. One way of seeing the imperative to take deterrence seriously, even if minimally, is that deterrence underwrites the greatest historical accomplishment of the justice system. As discussed in Chapter 3, Eisner (2003: 126) revealed sharply falling homicide rates between the sixteenth and seventeenth centuries across Europe—the period when some European states institutionalised courts to manage violence. The capability of courts in the eyes of citizens to deter and incapacitate violence was one reason they abandoned the private deterrence of blood feuds, thereby greatly reducing homicides (Pinker 2011).

A strategy of minimally sufficient punishment can increase the power of deterrence theory in crime prevention substantially if its empirical claims are more strongly verified by future research and if it can win the political debate against maximalists. It can increase the power of deterrence with a policy that involves the release of most prisoners even in societies with the lowest imprisonment rates. At the same time, it can tackle the unfreedom of overcrowded prison systems where viruses like HIV, tuberculosis, hepatitis, Covid-19 and violence itself proliferate, and human rights are compromised. Luckily, Ebola was contained in Africa before it caused terrible devastation inside the walls of overcrowded western prisons. Minimal sufficiency's claims are consistent with the limited existing evidence.

The aim in this chapter is to develop ideas towards a theory of minimally sufficient deterrence and to reflect on that evidence. To do that, the chapter discusses seven interwoven principles of a crime-prevention meta-strategy for minimally sufficient deterrence:

1. Escalate enforcement: Display intent to progressively escalate a responsive enforcement pyramid that involves progressive escalation of sanctions for wrongdoing and support for social responsibility.
2. Inexorability: Pursue inexorable consistency of detection of predatory crime. Communicate inexorable community commitment to stick with social support for those struggling with problems of lawbreaking until the problems are fixed.
3. Escalate social support: With repeated offending, increase social support. Even when there is escalation to a last resort of severe incapacitation, escalate social support further. Keep escalating social support until desistance is consolidated.
4. Sharpen the Sword of Damocles: Cultivate the perception that 'trouble hangs inexorably over my head; they want to support me to avert it'.

5. Dynamic concentration of deterrence: Focus deterrence on a line that should never be crossed after an announcement date. Then progressively lift that line, raising our expectations of socially responsible citizens and corporations.

6. Community engagement: Engage the community with offenders in widening restorative conversations that educate in the shamefulness of criminal predation for the many who participate in the conversations. Avert stigmatisation.

7. Modesty: Settle for the modest general deterrence delivered by this shamefulness and a minimal number of cases that escalate towards the peak of the enforcement pyramid.

This chapter first explains the idea of the responsive regulatory pyramid. It provides a scaffolding for these seven principles. Readers versed in the literature of restorative justice and responsive regulation may find much of the pyramid discussion familiar and can skip over it. Then the importance of inexorable response is explained, followed by the theory of dynamic deterrence and defiance and next how to constitute the shamefulness of the curriculum of crimes. The chapter concludes with an inductive conceptualisation of minimally sufficient deterrence.

The regulatory pyramid

The regulatory pyramid defines a meta-strategy of regulation, a strategy for how to sequence strategies (Braithwaite 2008). It is relevant to regulating crime by organisations or individuals. Figure 9.1 is an example of a regulatory pyramid elaborated in the next section. The presumptive strategy (a presumption that can be overridden) is to start at the base of the pyramid and escalate slowly. This is a strategy for keeping the power of deterrence sharp by making it rare to reach the pointy end of the pyramid. The rationale for keeping the Sword of Damocles sharp is discussed later.

Consistent with the evidence on what works with corporate crime enforcement from Schell-Busey et al.'s (2016) systematic review of 58 studies, this is a strategy that provides a wide mix of regulatory options before recurrently deterrent measures are reached that risk blunting the Sword of Damocles. At the bottom of the pyramid are restorative strategies that provide support to offenders and victims, and that meet needs and repair harms.

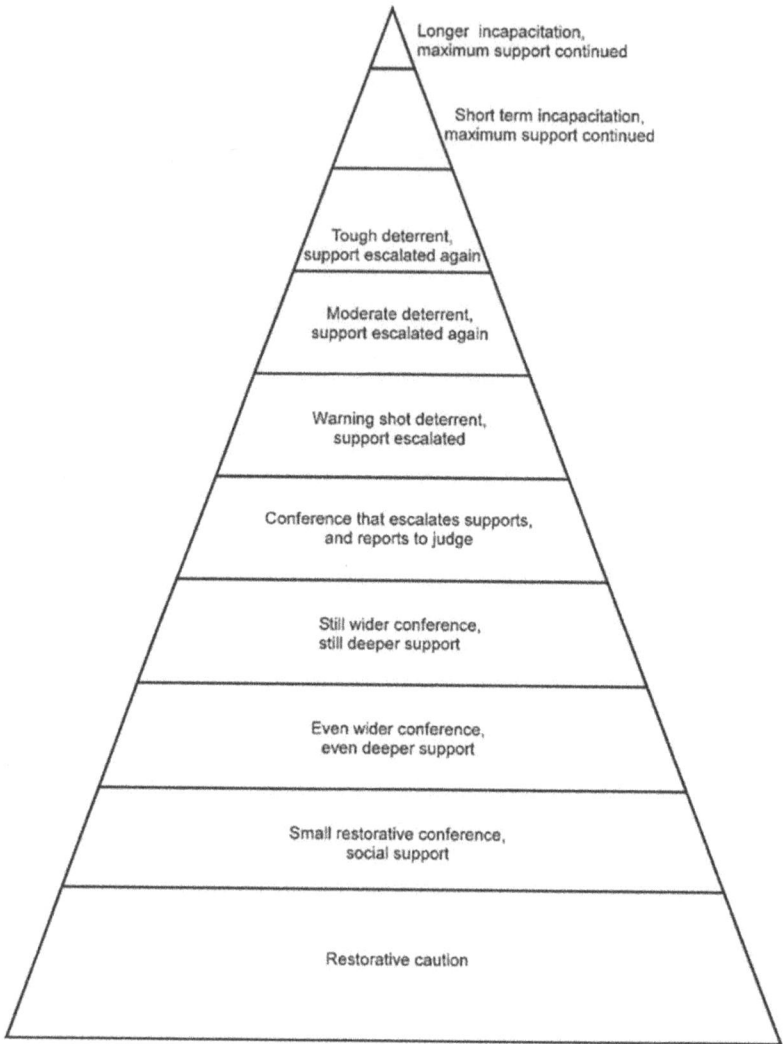

Figure 9.1 A responsive pyramid of minimally sufficient deterrence

Responsive regulatory theory says we should first look to the strengths of a lawbreaker and then seek to expand them. Mental health researchers led the way in showing that training in building on strengths improves quality of life and vocational and educational outcomes (Stanard 1999). When those outcomes are improved, recent econometric findings show more clearly than in the past that unemployment can be averted by vocational training and education, that this reduces crime and that wages for the poor can be increased, reducing crime by increasing the attractiveness of legitimate work compared with illegitimate work (Chalfin and McCrary 2017: 33–35). This path to crime reduction is resource intensive, though less so than a massive prison system, and it is a benefit to the economy in contrast to the economic deadweight of prisons. The idea is to absorb weaknesses by expanding strengths. Put another way, regulators should not rush to law-enforcement solutions before considering a range of restorative approaches that can be delivery vehicles for capacity-building and for collective efficacy (as discussed further in Chapter 11). As some offenders see their strengths expand to levels not previously considered possible, societies must celebrate their innovation, publicise it and support its extension. With corporate enforcement, research grants and prizes for rolling out new approaches that take internal compliance systems up through new ceilings for that industry offer an illustration. An example is involving young black men in Minneapolis in celebration circles. Victims join with the offender's loved ones to celebrate the way an offender has repaired the harm, righted the wrong and turned their life around (Braithwaite 2002: 103).

As we move up the pyramid through a first to a second to a third restorative conference, conference participants are likely to decide to escalate to increasingly punitive interventions. The policy idea is to persuade participants that they should also keep escalating to new ideas and resources for providing support for the offender. The philosophy of restorative justice is to empower stakeholders to take advice from experts. But then stakeholders should make their own decisions contextually attuned to the circumstances of their offender. This includes knowledge of the programs the community of care can persuade the offender to complete and the needs of their victim and other stakeholders in their circle. A problem with this is that it does lead to a bricolage of community responses rather than one that maps mechanically from 'what works' criminology. This is a complex relational and community empowerment process in which the problem is in the centre of the circle, rather than a stigmatised individual being put in the centre. The content of the pyramid is not prescriptive. The use of terms such as 'escalated support', 'wide' and 'wider' support and 'escalated deterrence' without specifying escalation 'to what specific measures' is intentional.

With complex phenomena, it is best to follow not the most evidence-based strategy, but the best meta-strategy. The research question of which strategy works best is not as fertile as which meta-strategy works best. Rarely will the first strategy attempted work in a complex context that differs from the conditions of any controlled evaluation trial. A good meta-strategy informs stakeholders of results from the 'what works' literature and presumptively tries the most supported strategy first and then the second most supported strategy (after the first strategy fails). That presumption can be overridden in light of particular circumstances. Clinicians, by analogy, try one therapy after another for a patient, informed by their knowledge of the outcomes of randomised controlled trials and their knowledge of particular cases, including what other medications patients are taking, their capabilities for surviving side effects, how strong their hearts are, and much more. As in restorative practice, clinicians can also decide what to recommend to catalyse community controls that will prevent spread of a contagion. In neither case does best practice involve a narrow focus on an individuated view of what works.

More detailed discussions of how to go about the process of deciding when and how to escalate up a responsive regulatory pyramid, and how to mobilise networked escalation as opposed to simple statist escalation, can be found in Braithwaite et al. (2007) and Braithwaite (2008, 2011). Intervention in complex phenomena like criminal careers should follow a trajectory that first assumes the answers are knowable and known. Therefore, evidence-based strategies can be applied (Braithwaite and D'Costa 2018: Ch. 12). When that fails, assume the challenge is knowable but unknown (and work to acquire at least some contextual qualitative understanding of the knowable). Then, if that repeatedly fails, assume one confronts a complex or chaotic phenomenon that is unknowable. In that situation, do not surrender to analysis paralysis; keep probing with new forms of social support that emerge from restorative conversations until a resonant response begins to produce positive change.

At the base of the responsive pyramid of sanctions are the most restorative, dialogue-based approaches we can craft for securing compliance with a just law. One reason for an approach that is deliberatively responsive to complexity is that a particular law, or its interpretation, may be of doubtful justice, in which case we can expect dialogue mainly to be about the justice of the law. This is imperative for the law of freedom (Pettit 1997). If excessive force was used during arrest, or if racism was in play, we can expect dialogue about whether it is the defendant or police who have committed the greater crime. As we move up the sanctions pyramid, increasingly demanding interventions are involved. The idea of the pyramid is that our presumption should always be to start at the base, and then escalate to somewhat punitive approaches only reluctantly and only when dialogue fails. Then we escalate to even more punitive approaches only when more modest sanctions fail.

Strategic use of the pyramid requires resistance to categorising problems into minor matters that should be dealt with at the base of the pyramid, more serious ones that should be in the middle and egregious crimes at the pyramid's peak. The presumptive preference, even for serious crimes, is to try dialogue first, overriding that presumption only if there are compelling reasons for so doing. There will be such reasons in exceptional cases: a violent first offender who vows to keep pursuing the victim to kill them may have to be locked up; a person who has never offended but attempts to blow themselves up in a subway may be killed by police who get a clear shot. The 2005 incident in which British police shot an innocent Brazilian man in a subway who was suspected of terrorist intent illustrates the justification for the responsive regulatory imperative always to consider, however quickly, the viability of interventions at lower levels of the pyramid.

As we move up the pyramid in response to repeated failures to elicit restorative reform and repair, in most cases, we eventually reach the point at which reform and repair are forthcoming, even if it is many years later. Whenever that point is reached, responsive regulation means that escalation is reversed; the regulator de-escalates down the pyramid. The pyramid is firm yet forgiving in its demands for compliance. Reform must be rewarded just as recalcitrant refusal to reform is ultimately punished.

A dramatic transformation of criminal law jurisprudence will be necessary if evidence supportive of responsive regulatory theory continues to mount. The imperative to de-escalate deterrence responsively when an offender rehabilitates means that every year a reformed person remains in prison is needless suffering. It is in addition a frittering away of society's scarce crime-control resources and a path to blunted power for deterrence.

If the empirical claims of responsive regulatory theory are right, this is also a missed opportunity to reduce crime and increase freedom by putting rewards for rejecting a life of crime alongside sanctions for embracing crime. In practical terms, when social support succeeds in helping prisoners serving long sentences to turn their backs on a life of crime, what is needed is a return to court for a hearing about the possibility of sentence shortening. The sentencing judge in such hearings should be obliged to consider the views of victims who in turn listen to the opinions of parole professionals, the offender and the offender's family. From a responsive regulatory perspective, a criminal law that keeps people in prison until they have paid the proportionate penalty for their wrongdoing is folly and a threat to freedom. It is an indefensible policy in terms of a dynamic theory of deterrence. It can make deterrent sense only under a passive deterrence theory, especially a maximalist one. This is the passive theory that minimally sufficient deterrence seeks to render obsolete.

The deterrent superiority of the active deterrence of the pyramid is opposed to the passive deterrence of a fixed scale of consistently imposed penalties. This is elaborated in Braithwaite (2002: 73–136; 2008). The current state of the evidence for the superiority of integrating restorative justice and responsive regulation to secure compliance with the law and other outcomes important to domination reduction is traversed in Braithwaite (2021f).

Consistently proportionate punishment is justified by just deserts theories of equal punishment for equal wrongs. Equal punishment for equal wrongs, however, is a danger to freedom and justice. It privileges punitive equality for offenders, while riding roughshod over the justice claims of future victims of crime who suffer because of an inferior crime-prevention policy. In addition, some present victims may not want equal justice for equal wrongs to apply in their case. For example, they may prefer more reparation, less imprisonment and more support of offenders' family members who suffer to variable degrees because of an imprisoned breadwinner (Braithwaite 2002, 2003). In any event, what kind of equality is expressed by a logic of equal punishment for equal wrongs when some offenders are lucky enough not to be raped or bashed in prison and others do suffer these horrors? There is little equality of justice when some are trapped in prison-induced contagions of drug addiction and others are not; when some acquire HIV, hepatitis or tuberculosis in prison systems that are the best-known incubators of these contagions, and some do not. This is not to disagree that maximum sentences should be set on the basis of seriousness; it is to say that the right sentence is the minimally sufficient one.

Responsive regulation has had some influence on business regulation policies, but almost none on policing policies. This would not have surprised Edwin Sutherland (1983), who 70 years ago first demonstrated the propensities to tolerate forgiving approaches towards crime in the suites that are seldom evident towards crime in the streets.

Restorative justice provides stakeholders with professional advice on the rehabilitation and prevention options they might choose. The community of care can then be mobilised to monitor and enforce compliance with whatever is undertaken. This is an approach informed by values that define not only a just legal order, but also a caring civil society. These values are derived from the foundational republican value of freedom as nondomination (Braithwaite and Pettit 1990; Pettit 1997). Some who share these restorative values derive them from different foundations, including spiritual ones.

Ordering strategies in the pyramid is not just about putting less costly, less coercive, more respectful options lower in order to preserve freedom as nondomination and to save money. It is also that use of more dominating, less respectful forms of social control only after more dialogic forms have been tried first helps law enforcement to be seen as more legitimate. When regulation is seen as more legitimate and more procedurally fair, compliance with the law is more likely (Tyler 1990; Tyler and Huo 2002). Nagin and Telep (2021) question this, while agreeing with the perceptual claim. They argue that there is a dearth of evidence that actual procedural fairness increases compliance. Astute business regulators often set up legitimacy explicitly (Dekker and Breakey 2016). During a restorative dialogue over an offence, the inspector says there will be no penalty this time, but they hope the manager understands that if they return to find the company has slipped out of compliance again, they will have no choice but to refer this to the prosecution unit. If and when the manager explicitly agrees that this is a reasonable approach, a future prosecution will likely be viewed as fair. Parker's (2006) 'compliance trap' will then be less likely to trip up enforcement. Under this theory, therefore, privileging restorative justice at the base of the pyramid builds legitimacy and therefore prevents crime (Tyler et al. 2007).

There is also a rational choice account of why the pyramid works. System capacity crises result in pretences of consistent law enforcement when the reality is that punishment is spread thinly and weakly (Pontell 1978; Pontell et al. 2014). Unfortunately, this problem will be worst when lawbreaking is worst; criminal justice is a sprinkler system that fails when the fire gets hot. Hardened offenders learn that the odds of serious punishment are low for any infraction. Tools like tax audits that are supposed to be about deterrence can backfire by teaching tax cheats how much they can get away with (Kinsey 1986).[2] The reluctance to escalate under the responsive pyramid model means that enforcement can be selective in a principled way. The display of the pyramid itself channels the rational actor down to the base of the pyramid. Noncompliance comes to be seen (accurately) as a slippery slope. In effect, the pyramid solves the system capacity problem by making punishment cheap. The pyramid says: 'Unless you punish yourself for lawbreaking through an agreed action plan near the base of the pyramid, we will punish you more severely higher up the pyramid (and we stand ready to go as high as we have to).' So, it is cheaper for the rational actor to self-punish (as by agreeing to payouts to victims or community service). Some Asian criminal justice systems, such as that of Japan, work this way much of the time, even for serious crimes such as rape, aggravated assault and murder, which are frequently resolved through compensation and remorseful apology rather than through prison time. Such reparative leniency does not cause crime to spin out of control in Japan (Ahmed et al. 2001). Once the pyramid succeeds in creating a world in which most punishment is self-punishment, there is no longer a crisis of capacity to deliver punishment when it is needed. One of the messages the pyramid provides to corporate criminals is that 'if you violate repeatedly without reform, it is going to be cheap for us to hurt you (because you are going to help us hurt you)' (Ayres and Braithwaite 1992: 44).

Paternoster and Simpson (1996) showed the limits of passive specific deterrence on intentions to commit corporate crime. When respondents held personal moral codes, these were more important for predicting compliance than were rational calculations of sanction threats (though the latter were important, too). Appeals to business ethics (for example, through restorative justice that exposes executives to the consequences for victims of a corporate crime) therefore may be a better first strategy than sanction threats (Parker 2004). It is best to succeed or fail with such ethical appeals first and then escalate to deterrence for the minority of contexts in which deterrence works better than ethical appeals. One of the psychological principles in play here is that when intrinsic motivation to comply with the law is intact, do not crowd out intrinsic motivation with extrinsic threats (Ayres and Braithwaite 1992: 49–50; Osterloh and Frey 2013; Frey 2017). This is another key to averting the deterrence

---

2   Mazzolini et al. (2017) found that, on balance, audits increased reported incomes by an average of 8 per cent, though audits that detected no extra tax liability reduced future reported incomes in the short term (see also Mendoza et al. 2017). In a meta-analysis, Dularif et al. (2019) found no effect of increased audits on tax evasion.

trap (Coffee 1981) and what Parker (2006) calls the compliance trap. Nine meta-analyses completed since responsive theory and behavioural economics picked up 'crowding out' and minimal sufficiency from developmental psychology have shown that there remains strong psychological evidence that crowding out does occur. They also show that both intrinsic and extrinsic motivations independently affect behaviour (Cerasoli et al. 2014).

According to responsive regulatory theory, what we want is a legal system in which citizens learn that responsiveness is the way our legal institutions work. Once they see the law as a responsive regulatory system, they know there will be a chance to argue about unjust laws or unjust enforcement (as opposed to being forced into a lower court production line or a plea bargain where such discussion receives short shrift). But defendants will also see that game-playing to avoid legal obligations inexorably produces escalation, as does failure to listen to arguments about the harms their actions are doing and what redress is required. The forces of law are listening, fair and therefore legitimate, but also ultimately might be viewed as invincible.

A paradox of the pyramid is that to the extent that we can guarantee a commitment to escalate if steps are not taken to prevent the recurrence of lawbreaking, escalation beyond the lower levels of the pyramid occurs in a low proportion of cases. This is the image of invincibility making self-regulation probable. Without commitment to escalation when reform fails to fix the problem, the system capacity crisis rebounds. A fundamental resource of responsive regulation is the belief of citizens in the inexorability of escalation if problems are not fixed.

Restorative justice works best with a spectre of punishment threatening in the background but never threatened in the foreground. When punishment is thrust into the foreground, even by implied threats, other-regarding deliberation is made difficult because offenders are pushed to deliberate in self-regarding ways—out of concern to protect themselves from punishment. This is not the way to engender empathy for the victim or internalisation of the values of the law or the values of restorative justice. The job of responsive regulators is to treat offenders as worthy of trust. When regulators do this, the law more often achieves its objectives (Braithwaite and Makkai 1994; Gangl et al. 2015; Haas et al. 2015). This ideal is one version of enculturating trust (in the foreground) while institutionalising distrust (in the background) through deterrence as a last resort.

Testing theories about dynamic interventions layered in a pyramid is more complex than testing the effects of passive policies like heavier sentences because the effects of sequences of interventions must be tested. How can a regulatory pyramid be tested when it involves an entire suite of sequenced dialogic, then deterrent and next incapacitating approaches? It has worked in raising an extra billion dollars in tax for each million spent on a program for multinational companies engaged in illegal profit shifting (for example, to tax havens; Braithwaite 2005b: 89–100). Evaluation in a tax compliance context requires, first, the creation of this whole pyramid of sequenced new policies for companies that have been paying no tax, and then observation of how much tax they pay after the new pyramid is put in place, as well as observing at what sequenced stage of the pyramid most tax payment starts to flow. The quality of information from the latter observations is instructive, yet low. This is because we do not know whether a compliance effect is the result of the last step up the pyramid or a combined effect of some subset of the whole sequence of escalations. A comparable evaluation challenge applies to problem-oriented policing as a meta-strategy. Randomising some police patrols to problem-oriented policing shows that problem-oriented policing works as a meta-strategy (Braga 2002; Weisburd et al. 2010; Hinkle et al. 2020), but it gives feedback of limited quality on which initiatives addressing which problems produced the result. Even so, evaluating meta-strategies is more important work for criminology than evaluating single crime-control strategies.

Braithwaite (2021f) has advanced an approach for how to think clearly about evidence in relation to dynamic theories of supports and sanctions. It argues that restorative justice and responsive regulation should each be viewed as constitutive of the other and both are dialogic forms of regulation. Restorative justice should be at the base of responsive regulatory pyramids and should be a practice of responsive listening. For both restorative justice and responsive regulation, motivational interviewing is an important evidence-based practice of active communal listening and active responsibility for problem-solving. Braithwaite (2021f) shows that both restorative justice and responsive regulation are meta-strategies; meta-strategies are strategies for deciding on and sequencing strategies of prevention.

Seven meta-analyses have all concluded that restorative justice has modest effectiveness in reducing crime. Braithwaite (2021f) argues that this is because it is a superior delivery vehicle for a great variety of strategies that work. Responsive regulation works for the more banal reason that it involves trying one prevention strategy after another until the problem goes away. Van der Heijden (2020) completed a meta-review of a mix of qualitative and quantitative evaluations of responsive regulation. He found a positive effect of responsive regulation in eight settings, no effect in one, a negative effect in six and in nine other data settings observed effects that were qualified and context specific. Van der Heijden's accurate but underwhelming answer to the question of whether responsive regulation is effective was: 'It depends.'

When responsive regulation is found to be effective, this is because it covers the weaknesses of one preventive strategy with the strengths of many other strategies that are redundantly layered above it in the regulatory pyramid. Braithwaite (2021f) follows the lead of earlier work on why restorative justice and responsive regulation are vindicated by some empirical evidence. In that work, restorative justice and responsive regulation are seen, like community policing at hotspots, as street-level strategies that are problem-oriented and responsive to dialogue that builds collective efficacy. The collective efficacy theme is developed further in Chapter 11.

The empirical effectiveness of restorative justice and responsive regulation in preventing lawbreaking in part is seen as a result of both doctrines being grounded in a principle of street-level responsiveness. Braithwaite's (2021f) conclusion advances a view about how social science understanding has failed to cut through to why policing is wrongly seen as ineffective when policing that is fair and responsive can be very effective, why UN peacekeeping is seen as ineffective when it is even more effective in saving lives than the best hotspot policing, why rehabilitative programs are wrongly seen as ineffective, why regulation for corporate crime control is wrongly seen as ineffective and why foreign aid investments in development are wrongly seen as ineffective when they make very small contributions to a profoundly large and widespread problem of global poverty. These perceptions are in error, especially when interventions are responsive and grounded at the street level, because normal social science fails to see why good meta-strategies are more fundamental than learning to pick the most evidence-based strategy:

> We can read the meta-analyses that suggest that problem-oriented
> policing works, that motivational interviewing works at the end of its
> iterated reframings of motivation, that positive deviance strategies

for improving village nutrition work, that a multidimensional mix of strategies works in controlling corporate crime (Schell-Busey et al. 2016) and that multidimensional UN peacebuilding works (Braithwaite and D'Costa 2018) as converging on a paradoxical insight. This is that, in a world of complexity, it is more possible to discover the meta-strategies that work best than it is to move single strategies from the realm of the knowable to the realm of the known. For example, the meta-strategy of 'search for positive deviance' may be more useful than learning what are the particular forms of positive deviance that worked to improve nutrition in particular villages. To use another example, it is easier to know that a vague, heterogeneous concept such as problem-oriented policing or motivational interviewing works than it is to know that it works because it fixes the street-lighting at hot-spots or discovers some specific motivation for losing weight. And this is a methodologically impressive paradoxical finding because it is harder to muster the statistical power to show the efficacy of heterogeneous than homogeneous interventions. (Braithwaite and D'Costa 2018: 553)

Inexorability of supports and sanctions

Inexorability has three elements:

- prioritising increased consistency of detection above tougher punishment
- always taking serious crimes seriously with a continuum of restorative responses to every detected serious crime; avoiding 'do-nothing' responses
- escalating the seriousness of response to a second, third and fourth offence; sticking with the problem until it goes away.

Prioritise detection

The inexorability piece of the theory of minimal sufficiency builds on the evidence from the deterrence literature that the perceived and actual severity of punishment are rarely good predictors of compliance with the law, while the perceived and actual certainty of detection are often useful predictors (Blumstein 2011; Robinson 2011; Friesen 2012; Nagin 2013). One reason for this is that detection mobilises not only formal punishment but also informal disapproval, which is a more powerful driver of compliance with the law (Braithwaite 1989). Theoretically, this is not just about the evolution of cooperation (Axelrod 1984) or the evolution of compliance when noncompliance is visible to a punisher. The newer theoretical insight is that it is also about indirect reciprocity through fear of reputational loss even without repeated encounters with the same people (Berger 2011; Nowak 2012; Braithwaite and Hong 2015; Hong 2016). Criminologists therefore tend to read the deterrence literature as showing that 'detection deterrence' and 'disapproval deterrence', both specific and general, are more powerful than deterrence by severe formal sentences. Minimally sufficient deterrence is based on this view that 'detection deterrence', indirect reciprocity and 'disapproval deterrence' are indeed thin reeds that can be combined to be more powerful than deterrence by severe state punishment. This conclusion runs contrary to the Nobel Prize–winning predictions of Gary Becker (1968), which enjoy little empirical support according to this reading of the evidence.

Always respond

Inexorability is absent in contemporary urban justice. Enforcement swamping and system capacity overload mean that young people picked up as minor first offenders learn that they do not receive significant punishments even if they are prosecuted. This is also likely to happen with their second, third or fourth minor offences during their teenage years. When the system does finally decide to hit youth offenders hard because someone decides they have 'had enough chances', offenders wonder 'why now?'. Legitimacy is a casualty of this policing strategy for muddling through system capacity crises. Tough punishment seems to repeat offenders to have unfairly come out of the blue, when they got away with worse in the past and when they see friends get away with even worse. Because this seems and is arbitrary, it is by definition a threat to freedom (Pettit 1997, 2014) and has shallow legitimacy in their eyes. These dynamics are quite comparable with Parker's (2006) compliance trap for corporate crime. The next section considers an alternative response approach to first, second, third, fourth and fifth offences.

Escalate responses

Critics might say the trouble with inexorability is that it is hard to reconcile with minimal sufficiency of punishment. Punishing everyone detected indeed would be maximal net widening rather than minimal sufficiency. The challenge of averting net widening is to craft a minimally sufficient response for a minor first offence. Police, teachers or parents who observe children hitting each other do well to pause rather than walk by. They must insist that the children stop fighting; they do best to say something non-stigmatising like, 'You guys are better than that', and then walk on after assuring themselves that fighting has ceased. This is a better way of taking violence seriously than looking the other way. It is more than 'nattering' as one walks by without stopping the violence (Patterson and Bank 1989), but less than net widening, which creates a recording of alleged wrongdoing and a formal decision on what to do about it.

Restorative theory can inform an inexorability that averts the perception of an arbitrary punishment lottery. The evidence is strong that restorative justice buttresses the legitimacy of the justice system (Tyler et al. 2007; Sherman 2014; Barnes et al. 2015; Miller and Hefner 2015). Prosecution is not the way to go with a first-offending child arrested for a petty offence. Nor is turning a blind eye. Wang and Weatherburn (2019) found that police cautions for minor youth offenders resulted in lower reoffending than arrest and referral to juvenile court. A restorative police caution with a degree of ritual seriousness is an option. Police can respond to a shopkeeper holding a child who has stolen something by ensuring the child returns the stolen property, taking the shopkeeper's contact details and then taking the child home to ask their parents or guardians what they intend to do. Or the child can be held at the police station until their parents arrive to take them home following a restorative caution.

The restorative caution gives the child and parent space to come up with the suggestion that they will visit the shopkeeper together to apologise, perhaps even baking a cake or bringing some flowers. Traditionalists see such idiosyncratic gestures of apology as strange elements to take seriously in criminal justice policy, yet that is the essence of trusting the community rather than the police with averting an offender's reaction that 'nothing happened, so breaking the law is no big deal'. Police tell the parents they expect a text advising what has been done to apologise. The police say they may check the shopkeeper is satisfied. In other words, most of the work of social disapproval is delegated away from the police. A reason for this as one approach to taking every crime seriously is the evidence that censure by families and closest friends is more likely to be a reintegrative form of shaming, while censure by criminal justice officials is more likely to be stigmatising (Ahmed et al. 2001: 157–76).

So, what to do about the teenager's second minor offence? The minimally sufficient deterrence suggestion is a restorative justice conference that the victim is invited to attend. The child's loved ones would be expected to sit in the circle for a serious family ritual involving parents, grandparents, siblings, perhaps aunts, uncles and a sports coach or a teacher trusted and nominated by the child. Communicating this expectation is important because a concern is to ensure that overburdened mothers do not shoulder all the burdens of social support. Wider circles of participation also enhance the effectiveness of restorative justice (Braithwaite 2002: 50–51, 55, 74, 252–65). This result is also evident in Wilson et al.'s (2017) meta-analysis finding that teen courts, impact panels and reparative boards are ineffective forms of what some loosely call 'restorative justice', but which in fact are programs that are thin on collective participation and collective efficacy.

Unlike a criminal trial that assembles people who can inflict maximum damage on those on the other side of the case, the restorative justice conference assembles people who can offer maximum support to their own side, be it the victim's or the offender's. At a meeting of two communities of care, the communication of disapproval comes from those personally affected by the crime but, more importantly, also from those who most love the offender. Nathan Harris's evidence from restorative justice conferences is that only disapproval communicated by people the offender most loves is effective in inducing remorse (Harris 2001: 157–76). People who are well liked but not loved are not potent at inducing remorse. Nor are the police. Albert Bandura (2016) made the point that self-censure for cruel conduct is switched off when others are stripped of the quality of being humanly important to us. Indeed, Bandura suggests that not only restorativeness but also responsiveness are 'capabilities' in Sen and Nussbaum's sense of capabilities being fundamental to freedom. Responsiveness is learnt through the loving social capital of families: '[I]nterpersonal experiences during the formative years, in which people experience joys and suffer pain together, create the foundation for empathic responsiveness to the plight of others (Bandura 1986)' (Bandura 1999: 200). Humanising those whom one might want to hurt or punish is fundamental to preventing moral disengagement (Bandura 2016). For Bandura, the psychological evidence shows that self-efficacy is a key to strong, free individuals resisting pressure from delinquent peers to dehumanise others so that crime and other predations might be inflicted on them (for example, Bandura et al. 1996).

While an informal police caution for a first offence is a minimalist response in terms of taking the crime seriously, a restorative justice conference for a second offence escalates to a longer family and community ritual with a trained facilitator and a wider circle of participation by people concerned about the child. Such a conference becomes a focused way of supporting children. Are they struggling in school? If so, what support can the conference mobilise? Are they struggling in their relationships? Are their friends leading them into trouble? Is there support from other friends who can steer them clear of such trouble? If there are problems with alcohol, drugs or anger management, proactive support may be needed. In this world of social support, every child leans on a 'youth support circle'. This is a restoratively elaborated version of parent–teacher conferences in schools that meet every year with every child aged over 12, with their extended family and with well-networked elders until the child is helped to get his or her first job or into university (Braithwaite 2001). The youth support circle is designed to reduce stigmatisation of crime by being universal; children who never do anything wrong have the circles. In that world of a better-funded, more communal welfare state, this conference for a second offence has no extra cost because it would be integrated into routine youth support conferences for building human capital, affecting only the timing of a conference that might normally be annual.

What about a third criminal offence? A longer restorative conference with a wider circle of participants is needed, usually with a follow-up conference to celebrate completion of an agreement. That would be more onerous than the conference for the second offence. More importantly, the next conference would see an escalation of social support for the child compared with the first conference. A child welfare worker could attend. The expertise a trained social worker brings would include knowledge of the range of options available in the town for rehabilitation of the young offender. The social worker should also have knowledge of the principles of risk–need–responsivity in evidence-based selection of rehabilitation options (Andrews and Bonta 1998, 2010), sound knowledge of the 'what works' literature of criminology and a good clinical capacity for responsiveness to the complexities of the specific case. In a restorative justice conference, it is not the job of the expert to dictate to a family (Pennell and Burford 2000). Restorative justice works by delivering stronger implementation of conference agreements enforced by the parties themselves than courts can achieve with police enforcement. This was the biggest effect size in the Canadian Department of Justice meta-analysis of restorative justice by Latimer et al. (2001). The effects of completion of restorative justice agreements were stronger than the statistically significant effect of restorative justice on reduced reoffending compared with control group members.

We can reconcile these results by understanding that if a restorative justice conference and a court both send a child to a counterproductive program, restorative justice will do more damage. The child will be more likely to complete the counterproductive program when it was agreed to by the family and other conference stakeholders than when the same outcome is ordered by the court. Restorative justice does greater harm than court when the circle agrees to counterproductive measures, and greater good than court when it agrees to effective measures. The reason is that restorative justice is a superior delivery vehicle for the completion of rehabilitation programs.

The idea is to strengthen this comparative advantage of restorative conferences by investing in experts who speak up when the family considers sending the child to a scared-straight program. The expert points to the evidence that scared straight is counterproductive (Weisburd et al. 2017: 428). It follows from this that a good way to reanalyse a meta-analysis such as that by Lipsey (2009) would be to assess whether effect sizes can be increased by the combination of highly effective interventions such as social cognitive programs with restorative justice as their delivery vehicle. Put more provocatively, it is not useful to compare effect sizes for restorative justice with those for other programs because restorative justice should be conceived of as a way of delivering multiple strategies—a meta-strategy (Braithwaite 2021f). It makes more sense to compare restorative justice with court as an alternative delivery vehicle for diverse correctional options, as in Strang et al. (2013). Likewise, the end of this chapter argues that it makes more sense to compare deferred corporate prosecutions with corporate convictions than to compare deferred prosecutions with some other approach to corporate reform. The bigger insights might come from teasing out which specific combinations of programs and delivery vehicles have positive and negative synergies, as is done in the smart business regulation literature (Gunningham and Grabosky 1998).

A conference for a fourth offence might allow the family to mobilise rehabilitative options from further afield or expensive options that are rationed. Critics might query why such an expansion of the quantum of social support would make a difference given that in Lipsey's (2009: 141) meta-analysis of youth justice programs, providing more hours of services, surprisingly, did not increase the effect sizes of interventions. Restorative justice programs were the big exception to this result; hours of restorative service provision strongly increased the already statistically significant effect size of restorative justice in reducing reoffending. Within the 'restorative justice' category of programs, those that included a mediation component, as opposed to simple restitution, also had an effect size more than one-third higher (Lipsey 2009: 142).

A conference for a fourth offence might also send the conference option to court for approval (or modification) by a judge, perhaps as a deferred prosecution. A meta-analysis from seven British studies led by Joanna Shapland concluded that restorative justice conferences have benefits that average eight times as much as their costs (Strang et al. 2013: 44–46). This result is a reason not to consider costly escalation to court until a fourth offence. Yet isn't escalation to something less cost-effective inept at any stage? Actually, there is a relevant complexity in the evidence that should leave us open to this. While Strang et al.'s systematic review found that court is clearly less effective in preventing crime than restorative justice, it also suggested that a combination of court and conference could be more effective than either on its own. More data are needed to assess whether this is robust. The quantitative transitional justice literature finds that war crime prosecutions, truth (and reconciliation) commissions and amnesties all have limited or contextual explanatory power on their own. However, when all three are used together, combining the punitive and the restorative, countries experience strong reductions in human rights abuses. This is particularly true when the truth commission's engagement with civil society is wide and deep and when amnesties are qualified rather than blanket (Olsen et al. 2010; Dancy et al. 2013; see also Sikkink 2011: 184–87). The combined cost of a restorative justice conference that then reports to court might also be less than the sum of its parts if the integration can be designed to streamline court processing. This is essentially how the most comprehensive youth justice conferencing program in the world operates, in New Zealand (Johnstone 2013).

At a fourth conference (for a fifth offence), when a young person and a victim are on the precipice of deeper trouble, escalated interventionist expectations can be assumed by the community of care. For example, in a 2014 interview, I was told of a teenager in an Irish Republican Army area of Belfast who had repeatedly assaulted his mother. The restorative conference was conducted by Community Restorative Justice Northern Ireland. One part of the community restorative justice agreement, which had many parts, was that four community members agreed to respond immediately to calls for help from the mother and participated in training on how they could respond. These were not civil servants living far away, arriving the next morning. They lived around the corner and committed to respond within minutes, 24 hours a day. This is a good example of how restorative justice can expand to a wider, more timely and more proximate web of social support and social control, while still providing a softer web of collective efficacy than court enforcement to protect the mother by locking up her child.

By this point in our inexorability narrative, deterrence maximalists are aghast that this is a fifth criminal offence with no formally punitive response presumed. The offender has had 'five free hits': the police restorative caution, followed by four restorative justice conferences and a first deferred prosecution that might involve a court appearance—all 'doing nothing' for punitive deterrence. Perhaps there will have been six 'free hits' if the first restorative caution was preceded by an informal warning on the run. All I advocate for these mostly disadvantaged fifth-offender children is that we give them five chances in the same way that we do for corporate criminals, as explained in the final part of this chapter.

Contrary to maximalist fears, offenders perceive restorative justice conferences not as 'doing nothing', but as gruelling experiences meeting their victims in the presence of their loved ones (Umbreit and Coates 1992; Schiff 1999). Deterrence maximalists are wrong to see imprisonment as the only kind of perceptually tough response. Perceptually, *The Process is the Punishment*, as in the title of Malcolm Feeley's (1979) book, especially when the process is designed with a ritual seriousness that is emotionally demanding.

If offending persists, repair of harm does not occur, but restorative justice achieves far from nothing because we resiliently stick with the problem. We refuse to take the easy path of putting the offender into a punishment production line that casts them out of our sight. The resilience to stick with the problem is accomplished by empowering those who most love the offender and the victim to stick with the problem with state and civil society support, especially from people who are passionate about the social movement for restorative justice. That passion is an ingredient that cannot be achieved without patient work to build a movement for restorative justice. Restorative justice people actually ask us to tarry with the problem in the centre of the circle. Many who had not been restorative justice people had this experience of seriously tarrying for the first time with the problem of white supremacy and black oppression in their emotional engagement with the killing of George Floyd in 2020 by the weight of a policeman's knee. In June 2020, after National Rugby League games in Australia, the two majority-white teams would mingle in a circle arm-in-arm, led by black-minority players to 'take a knee' together to remember Floyd and reflect in silence on how they were going to be actively responsible for confronting racism in Australia. Many around the world in that month would tarry for eight minutes and 46 seconds to represent the duration of the policeman's knee on Floyd's neck that stopped him breathing.

Building a social movement for restorative justice is a slow-food paradigm shift for injustice in which the passion to struggle against domination is accomplished by asking us to pause with the story of a single victim and perpetrator, or two. And then for an active politics of scaling up that reflection and commitment even across to so many rugby league teams in Australia. We scale up what Chantal Mouffe calls agonistic pluralism (Chapter 12) because of the power of the movement, the power of the story and the power of love for a suffering human being that makes us human. Without the narrative and the global anti-racism movement, we never renarrate the politics of denial of racism.

Dynamic deterrence and defiance

The Sword of Damocles is an ancient metaphor popularised by the Roman senator and republican philosopher Cicero (1877: 185–86). He based it on the story of a Sicilian king who hung a sword attached by a horsehair above the head of a courtier called Damocles, who envied the king. The ruler wanted to illustrate the insecurity of being king. Today, the Sword of Damocles generally refers to any ever-present peril hanging over a person. The existence of ever-present peril is an important element of minimally sufficient deterrence.

Preserving the sword

At a child or young adult's appearance for a sixth offence in a criminal career, the court might signal that a sword hangs over them. This is best done not as a threat. The power of the sword, according to Cicero, is not that it falls or is threatened; its power is that it hangs. The regulatory literature shows that the best signalling is for the judge to say at the outset of the court hearing for a sixth offence that its objective is to support the family and save them from having their child taken away. Perhaps only later than a sixth offence and only after a very serious crime would the judge ask whether the offender would think it reasonable that they be incarcerated to protect the community were they to commit another serious offence. Note the use of motivational interviewing techniques here, which are empirically established as effective and that avert threat-making (Rubak et al. 2005; Lundahl et al. 2010). The objective at that later trial is to open the mind of the offender to the reasonableness of the community protecting itself with a custodial sentence.

The idea at the next trial for the next serious offence would be to remind the offender that in their last appearance they said themselves that a custodial sentence would be reasonable if an offence of this seriousness recurred. The judge would then concede the offender's point of view but mobilise social support for one last chance to stay in the community, while making it clear that next time they were likely to agree with the incapacitation recourse that the offender themselves had concluded was reasonable in these circumstances. Lorana Bartels (2009) showed that a suspended sentence can be an effective Sword of Damocles here. She found that suspended sentences in Tasmania resulted in low reconviction rates compared with executed sentences.

At every stage, the minimally sufficient approach requires that the offender be led to see a new escalation of social support provided in response to a new transgression, but also a set of punitive options with a long prison term at the peak of the pyramid. Community service orders, fines, electronically monitored home detention, orders to a violent husband to transfer bank accounts to his wife so she has the financial capacity to leave him and a diverse variety of other options that are found lower in the pyramid are available as alternatives to prison. The sheer diversity of community gifts of support conveys a message of care when it includes, for example, the Royal Society for the Protection of Cruelty to Animals program in Australia that guarantees care to the pets of domestic violence victims who would otherwise stay in abusive relationships to care for those pets. The escalation of support as a life careens into deeper trouble is a way of increasing the legitimacy of more severe sanctions as a last resort when escalation to them does occur. It is also a strategy for combating the widespread perception by criminal offenders in many societies that the system lets you get away with it for years and then one day out of the blue locks you up. The proposal is inexorable both in escalating support and in the way it signals a move to escalating deterrence.

Why reserve court appearances until after a fourth or fifth officially detected offence? Why reserve serious sanctions for later still in a criminal career? One reason is the evidence from randomised controlled trials of restorative justice in Canberra led by Lawrence Sherman and Heather Strang. Offenders randomly assigned to restorative justice had greater fear of future criminal enforcement after restorative justice conferences than offenders randomly assigned to criminal prosecution had after their trial (Braithwaite 2002: 119–22). Offenders emerged from restorative conferences more fearful that they would be rearrested if they offended again, more fearful of family and friends finding out and more fearful of a future conference, compared with those assigned to court (Sherman and Strang 1997; Sherman et al. 1998). Minimally sufficient deterrence favours restorative justice for multiple early offences in a criminal career because these data show that restorative justice sharpens the Sword of Damocles, sharpening deterrence. Criminal trials blunt the sword hanging over the offender. After the courtroom sword is brought down, its mystique is lost. The criminal trial in current judicial practice blunts deterrence because in most non-serious cases the offender is surprised at how easily they get off as the court struggles with system capacity overload.

The minimally sufficient deterrence idea is to hold the trial in reserve until it is time to take the case seriously by projecting a clear trajectory of escalation to an ever-bigger Sword of Damocles that is being averted by more and more support. Among other objectives, this support is intended to make that sharpening of deterrence appear ever more just. Other kinds of criminological evidence support a Sword of Damocles effect (Sherman 1992, 2011), including Dunford's (1990) finding that a warrant for arrest deterred domestic violence substantially better than either actual arrest or nonarrest. Later, this chapter considers the possibility that deferred individual and corporate prosecutions may deter better than completed prosecutions. The theoretical perspective of minimal sufficiency is that warrants for arrest have great attractions over actual arrest and that deferred prosecutions are more powerful tools than actual prosecutions. These are problem-solving tools that can enable support to play a larger role than sanctions. Concluding that deferred prosecutions are in principle powerful tools is not to deny that their widespread use in corporate criminal law has often approximated doing nothing in matters of a seriousness that called for doing quite a lot (Eisinger 2017). Nevertheless, we will see in the final sections of this chapter that, empirically, restorative corporate justice can also sharpen deterrence while conviction of the corporation can blunt it, actually causing a criminal corporation's stock market value to rise.

Dynamic deterrence that accounts for defiance

Responsive regulatory theory argues that the passive deterrence thinking of the law and economics tradition, as in Gary Becker's (1993) Nobel Prize–winning work, has limited value. The reason is that real-world deterrence unfolds dynamically. Dynamic deterrence moves through sequences of threats; passive deterrence is static, involving levels of threat that are constant across time. International relations theorists have been more dynamically sophisticated than criminologists and economists of deterrence. They do not assume that, even though the United States has a bigger deterrent arsenal than the rest of the world's militaries, it works for America to say to another country: 'Do what we say or else!' There is evidence aplenty, from countries as close to the United States as Cuba, that threats are as likely to induce defiance as compliance. This is accepted even by conservative writers like Michael Rubin who oppose dialogue with 'rogue states'. Rubin (2014: 4) nevertheless conceived of Cuba, North Korea, Iran, Iraq and Libya as 'backlash states' that were 'defiant'. Former US defence secretary William Cohen tweaked this definition of rogue states to conceive of them as regimes 'immune to traditional deterrence' (Rubin 2014: 4). While demands for compliance backed by passive deterrence work poorly in international affairs, when the United States dynamically escalates its deterrent power towards a weaker country, as it did during the Cuban Missile Crisis, it can get a deterrent result (dismantled Cuban missiles). Dynamic escalation of deterrence in international affairs is a dangerous game because little Cuba might mobilise powerful friends to dynamic escalation of their deterrent capabilities in response. Little Serbia did manage to dynamically escalate catastrophic deterrence by triggering the escalation to World War I after the assassination of Archduke Franz Ferdinand by Serbian terrorists.

Psychologists of learning approach the way punishments work as dynamic learning sequences that are beyond the writ of static deterrence models. They demonstrated psychological reactance to threats (Brehm and Brehm 1981). Defiance is the more elegant term that Sherman (1992) deployed to describe this phenomenon.

461

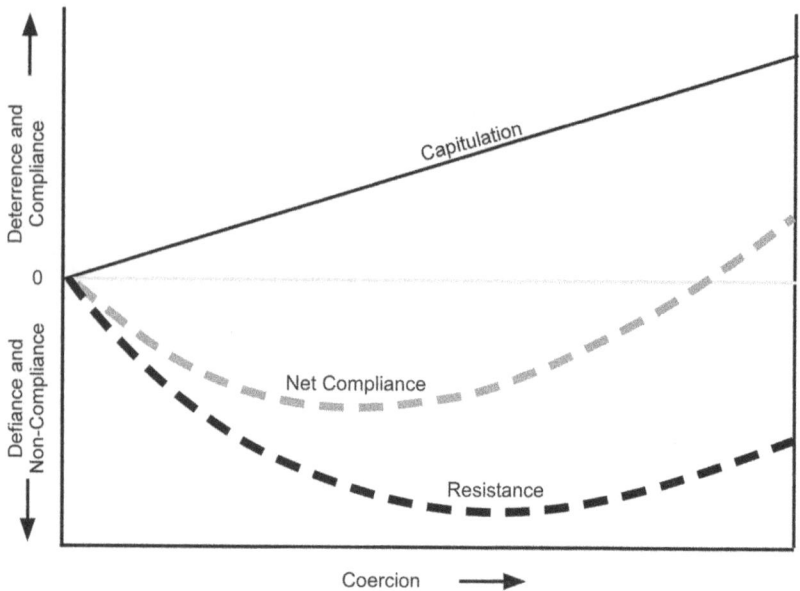

Figure 9.2 Theory of the effect of coercion on compliance as the net result of a capitulation effect and a defiant resistance effect

Sources: Based loosely on experiments summarised by Brehm and Brehm (1981) and subsequent research (Rains 2013).

A paradox of the pyramid is that by being able to escalate to tough responses at its peak, more of the regulatory action can be driven down to its deliberative base. Yet punishment, according to responsive regulatory theory, simultaneously increases deterrence and defiance. Figure 9.2 is a way of summarising the implications of more than 50 experiments on defiance originally conducted by Brehm and Brehm (1981) and their colleagues, and many more since (for example, Rains 2013). At low levels of punishment, defiance usually exceeds deterrence. Figure 9.2 expresses this as the resistance effect exceeding the capitulation effect at lower levels of coercion. The dashed line is the net compliance effect represented as a sum of the resistance score and the capitulation score. Only when punishment bites very deeply at the peak of the pyramid, resulting in many giving up on resistance, does deterrence exceed defiance.

Yet escalation only as far as the lower levels of the pyramid can elicit compliance when that first step up the ladder is seen as a signal of willingness to redeem regulators' promises to keep climbing until the problem is fixed. Put another way, the first escalation becomes a wake-up call that convinces offenders they are heading towards deterrence. Social support initiatives also help by signalling that paths away from deterrence are available. A perception of the dynamic inexorability of the pyramid does most deterrence work, not the passive general deterrent.

Redundancy in the design of the pyramid saves the day when defiance effects initially exceed deterrence effects. The redundancy idea is that all regulatory tools have deep dangers of counterproductivity. Therefore, one must deploy a mix of regulatory tools with heavy representation of dialogue and social support in the mix. The best way to deploy the mix is dynamically, so that, in sequence, the strengths of one tool have a chance to cover the weaknesses of another. For example, the pyramid in Figure 9.1 is about the strengths of one form of restorative justice covering the weaknesses of other forms of restorative justice, strengths of deterrence covering weaknesses of restorative justice, strengths of incapacitation covering weaknesses of deterrence and strengths of strong social support covering weaknesses of limp social support. Hipple et al. (2014) found that restorative conferences that avoided defiance by being strong on restorativeness and strong on procedural justice were more effective at reducing reoffending. The risk of defiance exceeding deterrence is one reason the peak of the pyramid should always be threatening in the background, but not directly threatened in the foreground. Making threats increases defiance, turning the resistance curve in Figure 9.2 more steeply downward. How, then, can lawmakers and business regulators be threatening in the background without making threats? One way is by being transparent that the pyramid is the new policy. Law enforcers must be the change they want to see. They achieve this by communicating openly with society about the policy design of the pyramid. By citizens being invited to be partners in the democratic design of different regulatory pyramids for responding to different crime problems, citizens also come to learn about the inexorability of escalation until the law redeems its promises. The ideal is to communicate the inexorability of deterrence in this way rather than by making threats in specific cases.

Dynamic deterrence as a remedy to enforcement swamping

A dependable, inexorable peak to the pyramid is a particular way of thinking about what Mark Kleiman (2009) calls dynamic concentration of deterrence—often called (in a misleadingly static way) focused deterrence.[3] For responsive regulation, the dynamic concentration of deterrence potency is at the rarely used peak of the pyramid. Kleiman, like David Kennedy (2009), reached a kindred conclusion to responsive regulatory theory about the superiority of dynamic over passive deterrence through contemplating how to respond to enforcement swamping as a challenge for thinly resourced policing agencies.

Kleiman's dynamic concentration theory shows why abandoning random targeting in favour of strategic concentration of targeting can work as long as monitoring works. In the simple case of scarce resources enabling the targeting of only one of two regulated actors, an erroneous intuition is that 'concentrating on Al would allow Bob to run wild'. If Al is promised certain punishment, a rational Al will comply if the compliance costs are less than the penalties. 'Then Bob, seeing that Al has complied, will himself comply; otherwise, Bob knows that he would certainly be punished. So, giving priority to Al actually increases pressure on Bob.' In this we see the dynamic elements of the strategy. Kleiman (2009: 54) shows that this initial insight holds for a variety of conditions such as promising certain punishment of the second mover rather than the first, and larger numbers of players. Dynamic concentration helps a little punishment go a long way.

Tax authorities likewise have learned how to respond to enforcement swamping when rich people, trusts and companies stampede into illegal tax shelters. This is to announce that while the tax authority lacks the resources to enforce the law against all who herd into shelters, they can prosecute the first risk-taker to jump into a shelter after the date of their announcement of intent to attack particular shelters in the courts. This can be extremely effective in ending cascades of risky tax cheating by high-wealth individuals and corporations (Braithwaite 2005b). Braithwaite (2012) discovered the same dynamic concentration in the wisdom of

---

3   The danger of describing the theory behind innovations like Operation Ceasefire as focused deterrence is that it will be understood as a static policy of identifying the highest-risk group for targeting. Even the principal authors of the strategy, who clearly understand its dynamic qualities, often describe a static deterrence targeting strategy, complemented by short breakouts into discussing its dynamic aspects (Kennedy et al. 2017). The most common mistake regulators make concerning responsive regulation is to understand it as a static policy of triaging the highest-risk groups for targeting with tougher deterrence. The point of reframing deterrence is to push criminologists away from such static ways of thinking. Minimally sufficient deterrence commends restorative justice as an alternative to prison even in the highest-risk circumstances such as creeping genocide, actual genocide or murders that risk further revenge killings (for example, Braithwaite and Gohar 2014).

generals who faced the biggest enforcement swamping challenge in the world at that time: small numbers of UN peacekeepers facing Africa's worst war in Democratic Republic of Congo.

As usual, practitioners here were ahead of theory. Tax officials were ahead of us, as were those generals in Congo and that Texas Ranger on the screen in our youth. The Ranger faces a lynch mob with one bullet in his gun. He turns them away with the promise that 'the first to step forward dies'. Kleiman (2009: 49–67) elegantly theorises why the dynamic concentration of deterrence by the Texas Ranger works. Systematic reviews of dynamic concentration found consistent effectiveness across studies and a medium-sized statistically significant crime reduction effect overall (Braga and Weisburd 2012, 2014; Weisburd et al. 2017; Braga et al. 2018, 2019). The intuition that concentrating deterrence on Max will allow Mary to run wild turns out to be wrong in terms of rational-choice theory (Kleiman 2009: 49–67) and empirically wrong according to Braga et al. (2013: 315), who found that with dynamically concentrated deterrence, 'vicariously treated gangs were deterred by the treatment experiences of their rivals and allies'. Dynamic focusing on the peak of a pyramid is just one way of concentrating limited enforcement resources that delivers dynamism to both specific and general deterrence.

Dynamically raising the bar serious offenders must jump

Boston's Operation Ceasefire is criminology's *locus classicus* of the dynamic concentration of deterrence in showing how an inner-city justice system overwhelmed by gang violence reduced homicide (Kennedy 2009). It was also 'focused deterrence' in that it did not attempt to deter all crimes perpetrated by gang members, only their gun crimes. My hypothesis is that the passively focused features of Operation Ceasefire may have some value, but its dynamic concentration of deterrence is more innovative and more germinal. It follows that rerunning and updating of Braga and Weisburd's (2012) encouraging meta-analysis are needed to compare those interventions that were simply focused and passive in their deterrence with those in which the intervention delivered a dynamic concentration of deterrence. The dynamic concentration aspect of Operation Ceasefire involved the Texas Ranger trope described above. Police sat down in meetings with gang leaders and members to let them know, in effect, that we know that you know that we have insufficient capacity to go after all of you for all your offences. But we do have the capacity to go after all the offences and all the parole and probation breaches of all the members of the next gang to use a firearm in a crime.[4] This means that instead of concentrating deterrence on the worst offenders, deterrence was dynamically concentrated on the first offender to use a firearm after the announcement date. The theory of the intervention was that all gangs would self-regulate gun carrying and use to avoid being the first gang to be targeted or the second gang to be targeted after the first. The ethnographic side of the evidence on the formidable desistence of these gangs from gun use seems to support this hope (Kennedy 2009). For proportionality theorists, it is a weakness of the program that it diverts resources from prosecuting the most serious offences to what might be minor parole violations after a gang uses guns. This critique also applies to responsive regulation. It has been eloquently advanced by Karen Yeung (2004).

Operation Ceasefire was in tension with the minimally sufficient deterrence model in two ways, however. First, the approach was thin on restorative justice and social support as approaches that strengthen a deterrence strategy into which restorative justice and social support are integrated. There was certainly dialogue with the gang members involved, and pathways out of the gang were discussed and even provided for some; but from the perspective of minimally sufficient deterrence, it was too narrowly oriented towards pulling levers to focus deterrence as more 'swift and certain' for a strategically targeted subgroup. There are reasons to suspect that in some of these programs this swift and certain deterrence may have been communicated with Trumpian threat. Such threats risk being counterproductive according to minimal sufficiency theory, defiance theory and the theory of motivational interviewing.

There was insufficient attention in Operation Ceasefire to a dynamic approach to support. Leaders of the innovation protest that this is not true (Kennedy et al. 2017). If moderately violent societies like the United States are to learn how to manage their hotspots better from experience with peacekeeping in extremely violent societies like Congo, we might

---

4   Papachristos and Kirk (2015: 536) describe the moderator of what they found to be the effective Chicago program opening before that with: 'This isn't a trick. Everyone gets to go home tonight. So relax a bit. We're here to talk to you about one thing: gun violence. No tricks. Just some straight talk, and an offer to help.' And, indeed, unlike some of these initiatives that put all the emphasis on deterrence, the encounter moves recurrently to: 'If you want help, it's here for you.' Service providers in the room explain what help they can offer, including health, mental health, housing, drug treatment, education and employment service providers (Papachristos and Kirk 2015: 537).

be able to build a consensus for the dynamic concentration of support to become more prominent. This policy lesson has been better learned in international peacekeeping and peacebuilding than in national policing to control organised violence (Braithwaite and D'Costa 2018: Ch. 3). That might be one reason for the conclusion in Chapter 11 that UN police are more effective than domestic police in saving lives (Hultman et al. 2013) The lesson is that desistance should not only cause a lifting of punishment; the strategy should also maximally concentrate rewards and supports at the moment of desistance. The rewards are not only tangible matters of vocational training and job placement, but also rituals of pride at celebration conferences in which loved ones eulogise peacemaking and rehearse redemption scripts (Maruna 2001).

Project HOPE is a drug court program in the focused deterrence tradition that initially seemed to have promising pyramidal features of escalated responses targeted at hard cases. HOPE stood for Hawai`i Opportunity Probation with Enforcement. It has been adopted in dozens of US locations with 'Honest' replacing 'Hawai`i', yet with mostly limited investment in creating job or other 'opportunities'. Intervention escalated as drug users went off the rails. Yet it may be the program that ran off the rails. Much of the rhetoric of its practitioners was maximalist, oriented to 'swift and certain' deterrence. This happened when the evidence is not supportive of criminal justice swiftness (Pratt and Turanovic 2018), though swiftness of a supportive parental firm hand in childrearing is important. Hawken and Kleiman (2009) entitled their evaluation *Managing Drug Involved Probationers with Swift and Certain Sanctions: Evaluating Hawaii's HOPE*. Duriez et al. (2014) raise the concern that the ideology driving the diffusion of Project HOPE has emphasised its 'swift and certain' character, ignoring other positive features such as motivational interviewing training for officers in the program—something for which there is a strong evidence base (Rubak et al. 2005; Lundahl et al. 2010), which is why motivational interviewing has become central to restorative and responsive justice (Braithwaite 2011). The findings of the literature reviews can be characterised as landing somewhere between HOPE showing great promise and being discouraging of HOPE (Lattimore et al. 2016).[5] As with Operation Ceasefire, the systematic reviews should

---

5   Lattimore et al. (2016: 1103) describe their HOPE program's four-site evaluation of a 'program that emphasizes close monitoring; frequent drug testing; and swift, certain, and fair (SCF) sanctioning. It also reserves scarce treatment resources for those most in need.' There is not much escalation of support in that description, nor any dynamic distinctiveness of the deterrence strategy to transcend the limits of static deterrence.

be reanalysed after some on-the-ground engagement with what each specific program does. They could be coded qualitatively or quantitatively according to four variables: how much deterrence is involved (HOPE's 'E' = 'Enforcement'), how much social support is involved (HOPE's 'O' = 'Opportunity'), how dynamically concentrated is the deterrence and how dynamically concentrated is the support. Meta-analyses might contribute more to science if they were more theoretically focused on what they evaluate and less focused on heterogeneous puzzles like HOPE that are in essence brands.

The second tension between minimally sufficient deterrence and Operation Ceasefire is that an approach that says your gang will be targeted intensively only if it uses guns challenges the inexorability principle. In an enforcement swamping crisis, however, we must confront the reality that priorities must be set that start where it is most important. In Democratic Republic of Congo, that priority was mass rape atrocities in which sometimes hundreds of women and children were raped, murdered or enslaved into mines (Braithwaite 2012). At least one peacekeeping commander was effective in reducing this seemingly impossible enforcement swamping crisis during the first decade of this century, according to our Congo fieldwork. He convinced assembled militant leaders that the next militant group to commit a mass rape atrocity would be the group on which peacekeepers would focus all their military capabilities to bring perpetrators to trial. In fieldwork trips to Congo during the past decade, I reproached the head of the UN Organization Stabilization Mission in the Democratic Republic of the Congo, the military commander, the deputy commander, the general in charge of the relevant region and the US ambassador for failing to implement this strategy against Colonel Cheka of Mai Mai Cheka, allegedly the worst perpetrator of mass rape atrocities, and some others like him. Within a year of the appearance of publications that discussed this (for example, Braithwaite 2012), the United Nations announced a policy shift in the direction of the dynamic concentration of deterrence, though this had nothing to do with the publications. This did improve the security of the people of Congo after 2014, particularly through the surrender of the M23 armed group that in 2012 captured Goma—a strategic city with a population of 1 million that is now liberated. In 2017, after almost three years of sustained military pressure to force surrender to face trial, Cheka turned himself in. That is no more than suggestive qualitative evidence for the dynamic concentration of deterrence from the least likely case (Eckstein 1975) of probably the world's most extreme and persistent enforcement swamping crisis of recent decades.

Gun violence was obviously an outstanding target for Operation Ceasefire. It produced a wonderful result in reducing shootings and homicides by more than 30 per cent—a result that continued to be supported in more recent work on the dynamic concentration of deterrence on US gang violence (Braga et al. 2013; Kennedy et al. 2017). The strategy, however, fails the inexorability test of minimally sufficient deterrence because inexorability happens only for the offence in focus (usually gun crime). Prioritising the greatest harm is desirable and might not deeply threaten inexorability as long as there is a strategy to move on to clean up one kind of gang crime after another, to move down to the B-list of gang harms and then a C-list, after the A-list of gun homicide harms has been tamed.[6] Then a strategy like Operation Ceasefire perhaps in the long run could pass the inexorability test.

Similarly, with the enforcement swamping crises with tax shelters that the United States and Australia faced in recent decades, Australia learned that it is possible gradually to raise the bar on tax compliance obligations. This was achieved by targeting the 10 worst tax compliers each year—a different 10 each year because last year's terrible 10 are no longer so terrible this year:

> When the judgment is made that there is a culture of tax cheating in a particular market segment, the industry norm revealed in the multivariate analysis is still used to target those furthest below the norm for audit and other compliance tools. But more of them can be targeted than in other industries. And when they are caught out by the audit, the bar they are required to reach before they are released from targeted surveillance can be raised a little higher than the industry norm. As a result of the worst 10 compliers in the industry moving from way below the old norm to above it, the norm of course is moved upwards. Then in the next year, a new set of the worst 10 in the industry is moved up above that higher norm. This raises the bar again. We can in this way keep raising the bar with problem industries until they are paying their fair share. (Braithwaite 2005b: 160)

6　At times, practitioners speak of A-lists and B-lists in static terms, by, for example, arguing that police go after an A-list of the most serious offenders for automatic prosecution, putting only the B-list into an Operation Ceasefire or a deferred prosecution program.

Stampedes of the wealthy into tax shelters do recede, as they did in Australia in the late 1970s and again around 2000 (Braithwaite 2005b). Cascades of open-air drug markets taking over great cities—even the stairs of the New York Public Library—also end, and that contributed to the downward cascade of homicide in Manhattan (Zimring 2011). Consider a brief list of accomplishments in reversing catastrophic cascades. The ozone hole was substantially closed even though it seemed unstoppable until the Montreal Protocol started to reverse the cascade into chemical use that was widening it (Kuttippurath and Nair 2017). Resources were provided to developing countries to comply with the Montreal Protocol after 1987, and there were diplomatic shots across their bows as well, particularly by US embassies (Braithwaite and Drahos 2000: 261–67). Today, we see substantial beginnings of reverse cascades from coal power to solar and wind energy. President John F. Kennedy predicted a cascade to 15–25 nuclear powers by the 1970s, yet half a century beyond the 1970s only the United States, Russia, China, the United Kingdom, France, Israel, India, Pakistan and North Korea have nuclear arsenals. This is thanks to civilising forces in international civil society that won a 2017 Nobel Peace Prize and dogged regulatory inspection in places like Iraq under the nuclear nonproliferation regime (Braithwaite and Drahos 2000: 318). Interminable civil wars in the places where the worst wars have cascaded for longest, such as Congo, will also one day reverse to cascades of peace (Braithwaite and D'Costa 2018; Walter et al. 2020).

The trend in regulatory theory is to seek ever greater sophistication in risk assessment and risk management as the main game of how best to cope with the seemingly impossible challenges of regulatory enforcement swamping (Black and Baldwin 2010). Though this is not totally wrong, there are also risks in shifting a high proportion of regulatory resources into deskbound risk analysis positions in a regulator's central office and away from street-level inspection. We may learn most from worst cases like Cambodia after its multiple cascades of genocidal violence beyond the 1970s. In the 1990s, and particularly since 1998, downward cascades of violence began to spread in Cambodia. Broadhurst et al. (2015, 2018) described this as a dynamic civilising process (Elias 1969; Pinker 2011). Broadhurst and his colleagues document that local police and UN peacekeepers did useful things to help trigger the reverse cascades. They show with Cambodia, as a least-likely case (Eckstein 1975), that it was not so much that Cambodian police were geniuses of risk analysis. Rather, they did something that Malcolm Sparrow (2000) describes simply as 'pick important problems; fix them'.

Cambodia was more a matter of a return to long-run momentum towards the civilising processes that citizens crave and governments pursue when they seek legitimacy from citizens and from the international community. This was combined with police and peacekeepers helping with an A-list of violence problems that they helped clean up, eventually moving on to B and C-lists. A-list criminality included robbery, homicide and kidnapping, with cattle theft being high on the B-list because this can be financially devastating in rural societies. Local police became quite popular, according to Broadhurst and his colleagues, and gradually moved away from putting bullets in the heads of desperadoes and towards peacetime community policing.

We can learn from local priests, mayors and elders in Rwanda who acted like Texas Rangers without even a single bullet in the midst of Rwanda's cascade of genocide. These leaders stood their ground—in most cases, stopping the genocide from spreading to their community through their emotional dominance in insisting that their church, their leaders, would not stand for this in their village (Klusemann 2012). Other brave priests who tried this were hacked down. Together, long-run civilising processes helped by dynamic concentrations of sanctions and support, combined with gradually raising the bar on what kinds of violence are intolerable, eventually can pacify even genocidal intent in Cambodia, Rwanda or Timor-Leste, as documented in the previous chapter. It can also close an ozone hole and end the slave trade to the Americas. All this can be accomplished without filling prisons.[7] Or so I hypothesise.

Conversations across the curriculum of crimes

Restorative justice principles are useful to a minimally sufficient deterrence strategy because defiance (Sherman 1992, 2011) is a critical risk. Defiance is reduced when communities of care do most of the work. Nathan Harris found that perceived informal disapproval from those most loved inside

---

7   Rwanda did fill its prisons with 126,500 people charged with participation in its 1995 genocide. Many were children who were then raped in prison and died from HIV/AIDS. Many others were innocents forced to participate after seeing their family members hacked to death for refusing. Defendants were executed on the judgements of second-year law students. In the end, that tiny, poor society did not have the capacity to deliver justice to 126,500 defendants for such serious crimes. Most were released to face traditional *gacaca*, which much of the time was somewhat restorative in approach (Clark 2010).

restorative justice conferences, not from criminal justice actors, does the work of persuading offenders that their crime is shameful, persuading them to remorse and repair of the harm to victims and to their own family (Harris 2001: 157–76). In restorative justice, there is no need for anyone to invoke the concept of shame, nor for anyone directly to shame offenders. Loved ones discussing how concerned they are about the consequences of the crime, the suffering of victims and what the family can do to help repair the harm is the way to elicit remorse without defiance. Motivational interviewing of these loved ones can draw this out.

Conversely, there is evidence that stigmatisation (as opposed to reintegrative shaming) increases crime in criminal justice processes (Ahmed et al. 2001; Braithwaite et al. 2006; Tyler et al. 2007; Braithwaite 2020c) and in business regulation (Makkai and Braithwaite 1994b; Harris 2017). Stigmatised offenders are treated as bad people who have done bad things, while reintegratively shamed offenders are treated as essentially good people who have done a bad thing. Stigmatised offenders are cast out from the community of the law-abiding without paying attention to reintegration rituals that might have drawn them back into the law-abiding community. Aversion of stigmatisation is critical to an effective package of minimally sufficient deterrence.

The theory of reintegrative shaming concludes that shame is important to crime control and to problem-solving (Leach and Cidam 2015; Spruit et al. 2016; Braithwaite 2020c). Societies in which rape is not shameful have a lot of rape. Societies in which feminist politics communicates the shamefulness of rape and domestic violence can enjoy steeply reduced rates of these crimes, as Pinker's (2011: 196–201) analyses of declining rates of rape and domestic violence and the growing shamefulness of these crimes in certain western societies suggest. Broadhurst et al. (2015: 310–13) likewise diagnose repeated surveys in Myanmar since 1996 to show declining domestic violence, growing disapproval of wife beating and growing public awareness campaigns about why it is wrong. Feminist politics is just one kind of engagement around the shamefulness of certain crimes.

One of the virtues of deliberative forms of justice such as restorative justice is that they increase the active participation of citizens in their democracy through the judicial branch of governance, through children's participation in antibullying programs in schools and through the involvement of environmental activists and fishers in the regulation of environmental crimes. Restorative justice therefore has a role to play in educating citizens in the curriculum of crimes and why they are shameful, through their participation in restorative conversations about the crimes of their classmates, their neighbours, their family members and themselves.

Existing criminal justice institutions by contrast are overly professionalised. One consequence of this is they provide no space for democratic deliberation with the young about why crimes that affect people are wrong and what should be done about them. Democratic citizens can sit in the public gallery for criminal trials, but few do; and if they try to participate in the conversation about the rights and wrongs of the matter from the gallery, they are silenced.

Penal populism that increases punitiveness is certainly a risk within contemporary criminal law jurisprudence (Lacey 2008). Advocacy for minimally sufficient deterrence, however, is advocacy of quite a radical transformation of these dysfunctional institutions. Ordinary people are more punitive than the courts when they read accounts of cases and sentences in the media. When they read about the rich complexity of the same case as the judge hears it, they recommend sentences similar to those of the judge. The more information they have, the less punitive they are (Doob and Roberts 1983, 1988). In Warner et al.'s (2017) survey of jurors in Australian cases, they were twice as likely as the judges in their cases to recommend a noncustodial sentence. When citizens have the chance to engage even more directly with offenders and the complexity of their circumstances in a restorative conference, their punitiveness and vengefulness reduce even further (Strang et al. 2013: 40–42). This helps explain why restorative justice conferences produce less-punitive outcomes on average than do traditional criminal justice processes (Braithwaite 2002: 146–48).

In sum, the restorative justice component of minimally sufficient deterrence calms defiance,[8] helps educate offenders and the entire community about the shamefulness of crime and the curriculum of crimes, while laying foundations for minimally sufficient punishment that can defeat penal populism's maximalist politics. A utopian world can be imagined in which each year 1 per cent of the population takes some responsibility for an offence in a restorative justice conference conducted

---

8   This also means that restorative justice and the escalation of deliberative supports help provide an exit from what Christine Parker (2006) calls the compliance trap, as discussed earlier and later in this book.

by the criminal justice system, a school, a university or a workplace. If 10 supporters of victims or offenders attend each conference, conversations about the curriculum of crimes would ripple across 10 per cent of the population each year. Because humans are storytelling animals, we learn the shamefulness of the curriculum of crimes through participating in, and retelling, stories of which we are a part. This retelling can do most of the work of constituting the curriculum of crimes, especially when newer crimes such as profit-shifting by multinational corporations become transparent. Consciences are formed by operation of 'the criminal law as a moral eye-opener' (Andenaes 1974: 116–17), especially when shamefulness is suppressed through a politics of domination with crimes such as torture and gendered violence.

Minimal sufficiency of general deterrence

The preceding section was partly about the general deterrence that arises from citizens talking with one another about why crimes like rape or torture are wrong. Reintegrative shaming theory advances the idea that general deterrence by means of the internalisation of shame (anticipated self-shaming rather than shame sanctions) combined with a path out of shame (Leach and Cidam 2015; Spruit et al. 2016; Braithwaite 2020c) are more important than deterrence by sentences handed down by courts (Ahmed et al. 2001). It is also about restorative justice's political strategy for community support for a less punitive justice system. Satisfaction with the justice, with the respect for victim rights and with the effectiveness of restorative justice in crime prevention is high (almost always over 80 per cent, and normally over 90 per cent) for citizens who sit in on restorative justice conferences (Braithwaite 2002: 45–71; Wilson et al. 2017). Part of the practical politics of driving punishment down to minimally sufficient deterrence is convincing politicians who see restorative justice as a soft option to sit in on a circle and chat afterwards with participants. This is important because democratic politics is the key constraint on whether and how judges or police can move to minimally sufficient deterrence.

The literature on the consequences of police strikes (Andenaes 1974) has long persuaded criminologists that crime spikes when deterrence is taken off the table. The contention of minimally sufficient deterrence is that courts will have limited work to do in delivering minimally sufficient general deterrence if citizens are empowered conversationally about the shamefulness of the curriculum of crimes (Braithwaite 1989: 77–79). Courts must ensure through some form of incapacitation that the community is protected from the modest number of people who are a severe danger to the community. The hypothesis is that minimally sufficient punishment will be provided by general deterrence resulting from imprisonment in such incapacitation cases. These are combined with other general deterrence effects when repeated failures of social support and moderate deterrence escalate to more severe deterrence towards the peak of a pyramid.

So long as deterrence does not fall to zero, increasing average prison terms does not have much effect in reducing crime (Nagin 2013; Chalfin and McCrary 2017). It seems unlikely that any society will face crime risks from insufficient passive general deterrence if it takes seriously shame management and education about the curriculum of crimes and if it puts in place a credible peak as a last resort in its pyramid of dynamic deterrence. We cannot completely do without passive general deterrence, but a minimally sufficient quantum of it delivered by the model proposed here may be enough to achieve the limited work general deterrence can do.

My proposals can be accomplished only incrementally; learning through monitoring is important to reveal any explosion of crime driven by a deficit in passive general deterrence (Braithwaite and Pettit 1990: 140–55; Dorf and Sabel 1998). If and when empirical evidence suggested this was happening, incremental movement could be halted and adjusted to bolster passive general deterrence. The prediction, however, is that as societies such as the United States and Russia, with imprisonment rates of more than 600 per 100,000, reduce their passive general deterrence towards that of societies such as India, Indonesia and Japan, with imprisonment rates in the thirties to forties per 100,000, passive deterrence deficits will not cause crime waves. This view is encouraged by cross-national comparisons of crime that show that low-incarceration societies, many of which are in Asia, often have low crime rates.

Restorative justice strengthens deterrence of corporate crime?

This chapter has explained how responsive regulatory escalation makes it rational for corporations to punish themselves at lower levels of the pyramid to avert more punitive measures higher up the pyramid. I have already explained how restorative justice near the base of a regulatory pyramid can reduce what Parker (2006) calls the compliance trap.

It attempts this through the deep listening and motivational interviewing restorative justice requires and by minimising the degree to which extrinsic threats crowd out intrinsic motivation to comply with the law. Chapter 6 argued for softening the defiance and legal cynicism of the compliance trap by levering soft targets who do not benefit from the crime to secure compliance. Abandoning hierarchies of accountability in favour of circles of accountability was another important part of this argument. All this in turn is enabled by greatly pluralising the separation of private and public powers. Chapter 7 argued for social capital strategies of CHIME for securing compliance dialogically most of the time. Inspectors and auditors explaining initial forbearance from deterrence means deterrence is more likely to be perceived as fair when it does come. At the same time, clear signalling that escalation to deterrence and incapacitation is inexorable deters gaming that undermines the regulatory order for everyone. This includes those who perceive others to be playing the regulator like a fiddle. In this chapter, explanation of the power of restorative and responsive justice has moved to how rationing corporate deterrence can avert a blunted power of deterrent escalation through overuse, instead allowing restorative justice to sharpen deterrence, as it has been shown by some limited empirical evidence to do.

But there is more than all of these points involved in why restorative justice embedded in wisely implemented responsive regulation can strengthen the deterrence of corporate crime. The system capacity crisis is more profound with corporate crime than with crime in the streets because business regulators receive less funding than the police—even though corporate crime investigations are more complex and expensive (Coffee 2020). Acquittals for corporate crime are more common partly because not all lines of inquiry receive the investigative work they need. What restorative justice delivers here at the base of the regulatory pyramid is an invitation to a deferred prosecution or a prosecution forgone in favour of an enforceable undertaking if the defendant adopts various self-enforcement measures.

Spalding (2015) perceives US sentencing guidelines as encouraging restorative justice in deferred corporate prosecution agreements. We will see that one problem is that deferred prosecutions and enforceable undertakings became too routine in failing to honour the restorative principle of earned redemption. Coffee (2020: 147) has discussed the imperative for deferred prosecutions to be 'truly earned'. Laying a charge, but formally deferring prosecution, is the quintessence of the Sword of

Damocles. The US Department of Justice's policy has stated in various ways at various times that it will not proceed from deferred to actual prosecution if the corporate defendant:

- voluntarily discloses the corporate offence and responsible individual offenders
- disgorges illicit gains
- makes a 'credible and authentic commitment to remedy wrongdoing and promptly self-report future violations of law' (Baer 2021: 351)
- 'invests significant resources in compliance-related activities' (Baer 2021: 351)
- cooperates fully with the government's investigation
- repairs the conditions that caused or promoted the alleged offence (Arlen and Kahan 2017).

Declining to move to an actual prosecution from formal notice of a deferred prosecution is supposedly the practice only if the corporate defendant makes a fair fist of these conditions. In the Corporate Enforcement Program under the *Foreign Corrupt Practices Act*, self-disclosing companies also avert Stanley Sporkin's disliked innovation of a third-party monitor appointed by the Justice Department. These benefits of self-enforcing justice are denied in theory to 'recidivists', though recidivism is a loosely defined concept. In practice, recidivists frequently receive deferred prosecution agreements as separate subsidiaries of a mega-corporation that is too big to nail. On an extremely wide front, they get non-prosecution.

There is experimental evidence (Bigoni et al. 2012) that cartel formation can be deterred when what the Justice Department's policy calls 'leniency' is offered to the first reporting party combined with high fines for parties that fail to voluntarily report offences. The problem in practice is whether firms that do not meet the Justice Department's requirements for corporate leniency are prosecuted. Generally, the answer is they are not. Often there is no reality to the inexorability of escalation to the tough peak of the enforcement pyramid. Hence, critics reasonably opine that leniency is a terrible name for the Justice Department's policy.[9] Its beautiful theory

---

9   We might welcome Baer's (2016: 1113) plea for parsimony and clarity in corporate criminal prosecutions rather than 'leniency'. Of course, I often will prefer 'restorative' corporate prosecutions.

of principled contingency of leniency has become an ugly practice of consistent leniency towards corporate criminals, particularly during the Trump administration (Garrett 2020: 116).

Defenders of the policy say that even under President Trump a benefit of the leniency program has been that it has motivated massive growth of corporate investment in internal compliance programs. There is little doubt this is true; corporate compliance staff and the compliance consultancy market have accelerated almost exponentially (Baer 2021). Defenders of leniency include a high proportion of corporate law practitioners who point out that it has always been true that a tiny proportion of corporate wrongdoing is detected by the state and put into the hands of prosecutors. Most of the corporate wrongdoing that is detected, stopped, punished by action against responsible executives and then leads to repair for victims and prevention of recurrence is a result of detection accomplished by corporate compliance staff. Alternatively, detection is by internal whistleblowers who refuse to report to outsiders but will report noncompliance to compliance staff or a board ethics/audit committee. This is also undoubtedly true, though it is also a reason Sporkin's innovation of a government-mandated third-party monitor with a desk inside the firm should not have had its momentum reversed as much as it has.

In the 1980s and 1990s, a network of reformers of which I was a small part in Australia, associated with the Australian Competition and Consumer Commission and some other regulators, became heavily involved in seeding the corporate compliance market and corporate compliance professionalism in Australia. It seeded corporate compliance courses in law, business and accounting schools, formed professional associations for compliance and successfully urged Australian regulators to give more emphasis to this in their regulatory strategies. While we still take some pride in that networking, the critiques of our work 30 years on in Australia seem correct to me, and much the same as the US critiques.

Baer (2021) argues that the corporate compliance market is a market in lemons. Soltes (2021) captures the voices of critics of the compliance market who say it is one that 'finds loopholes to circumvent obstacles' or is a market in 'schooling executives in cover-up rather than compliance'. In Australian aged care regulation, Braithwaite et al. (2007) had been advocates of the growth of an aged care compliance consultancy market that assisted nursing homes to innovate to achieve 'continuous improvement' in the Australian regulatory regime that required quality of care beyond compliance with static standards. Empirically, Braithwaite et al. (2007) found this innovation corroded to become regulatory ritualism. Ritualism is another way of describing Baer's market in lemons or Parker and Gilad's (2011) corporate compliance 'window-dressing'. The compliance consultants would arrive with ritualistic checklists that would not provide long-term improvements in the quality of care. For example, some short-term, unsustained reform that aged care residents would notice as an improvement might be put in place. Then a slipshod piece of survey research would be administered to residents or their families that would show the residents subjectively perceived a short-term improvement in their quality of care. This was compliance on the cheap, tick-the-box, short-term and short on integrity. Inspectors would find the same problem a year or two later. It was the antithesis of corporate restorative justice. Rather, it was a crude transaction of non-enforcement in exchange for compliance ritualism that saved criminal corporations losses they would have sustained under tougher enforcement. This reveals a problem with narrowly economistic theories of why deferred prosecutions are good policy in circumstances of enforcement swamping and scarce prosecutorial resources (as in Leone et al. 2021).

This is a general problem across a diversity of domains of corporate compliance. One impressive regulatory initiative in the United States has been regulators orchestrating sanctions and incentives to motivate corporations to put in place internal whistleblower policies. Decades on, Soltes (2020) found that regulatory mandates that organisations have whistleblower hotlines (for example, under the *Sarbanes–Oxley Act*) resulted in regulatory ritualism. Soltes made field inquiries regarding alleged misconduct to the whistleblower hotlines of 250 firms. Receipt back of clear and specific answers and action on the inquiries were disappointingly infrequent. Worse, Soltes (2020: 429) found that one-fifth of firms had 'impediments that hinder reporting'—for example, disconnected phone lines, email bounce-backs, incorrect directions to a website. These hotlines not only fail to have a no-wrong-door policy, they also have a shunt to a wilfully closed door. In these cases, beautiful paper policies on whistleblowing were an ugly practice of deadend accountability. This is why the *qui tam* policies discussed in Chapter 6 that motivate insiders to blow the whistle on cover-ups of corporate crime by paying them a percentage of the fine are a vital inexorability-inducing reform. It is why that reform has proved effective in the face of such weaknesses of corporate compliance reforms.

When Baer (2021) coins the idea of a compliance market in lemons to describe these developments, she tracks Nobel Laureate George Akerlof (1970) on how the used car market works. Buyers struggle to discern the difference between lemons and good used cars. Owners of cars in good shape drop out of the market because buyers do not trust their claims about the car and will not pay what it is worth. Thus, the market unravels to a point of market failure in which only crooks who tout lemons are willing to play. It is not an exaggeration to say that some markets in corporate compliance services are kindred criminalised markets in smoke and mirrors. Modern regulators monitoring compliance systems suffer an information asymmetry similar to buyers of used cars, especially the large number of regulators who have moved away from street-level inspections that kick the corporate tyres, in favour of desk auditing or algorithmic compliance. This is why Baer (2021) insightfully diagnoses the compliance market as having unravelled from an idealistic practice of late twentieth-century reformers from within corporations, regulators and civil society with an incipient restorative justice imaginary to a market in compliance lemons.

There are things that can be done to repair this market by a combination of market and regulatory means. For example, when an Australian aged care compliance consultant pushes away regulatory enforcement with a flawed compliance innovation that is poorly evaluated, the regulator should mandate the lodging of the evaluation report on the *My Aged Care* website. Then family and residents in the home can complain to the regulator that as soon as the regulator went away, the so-called reform amounted to nothing and long-term compliance worsened. Even more importantly in market terms, when compliance monitoring reports are put up on public websites, we know from programs like registered self-certification of software programs for tax compliance (Braithwaite 2005b: 87–89) that competitors in the compliance market go to the regulators to tell them that particular evaluations of compliance improvement are flawed. More often the reputable compliance practitioner goes to the firm that has hired the slipshod compliance professional to suggest that the job could be done more professionally by replacing their existing compliance consultant. When they do this in the market for compliance services, the firm that has bought a compliance lemon might see a risk that this competitor in the compliance consultancy market could alert the regulator to the corrupted compliance work. Unfortunately, most compliance evaluation reports in contemporary regulatory practice are not transparently posted on accessible websites. A case can be made for internal compliance reports to be confidential when they relate to matters that are unknown to regulators. The argument is that if they were made public, firms would have less incentive to invest in internal detection and remediation. But there is no such argument in cases where a compliance report is produced pursuant to an enforcement action over noncompliance known to the regulator.

Baer (2021) points out that the evidence is encouraging that voluntary self-reporting of foreign bribery has become relatively common in the United States. In the theoretical terms of this chapter, the offer of deferred prosecution or non-prosecution has increased the inexorability of detection. After a corporation's counsel voluntarily discloses to a regulator or prosecutor that bribes have been paid, the prosecutor must decide if this has been a prompt and complete disclosure.

This, in turn, requires a fair amount of verification. The prosecutor might ask the corporation's counsel for a list of employees who have already been interviewed, for documents that have already been searched, and so on. The government might subpoena documents independently to corroborate the information it has received or conduct its own interviews of relevant witnesses. Verification is costly (Baer 2021: 359).

The more time and energy governments invest in testing the corporation's claims, the less valuable deferred prosecutions become as a solution to enforcement swamping and the system capacity crisis (Pontell 1978). Eventually, the regulator or prosecutor therefore decides to truncate their verification of voluntary reporting.

Public interest in the deferred prosecution bargain can erode because of adverse selection akin to the used car market Akerlof described. Ethical or remorseful corporate leaders can decide that disclosure is not worth the trouble and is against the interests of shareholders. Unethical executives continue to game the voluntary compliance system with compliance ritualism or compliance corrupted into sophisticated cover-up.

Major punitive prosecutions of firms that corrupt voluntary compliance professionalism and of firms that cover up are one important remedy. Another is requiring firms to evaluate the effectiveness of their compliance programs—something evident in only 55 of 255 US deferred prosecution and non-prosecution agreements (Garrett 2014: Ch. 3).

It remains a fundamental point that if that remedy is inexorably executed, restorative justice for genuinely contrite and reforming corporations could save more prosecutorial resources for those corporations that do game the law. This more strategic use of finite deterrence resources can make deterrence more potent. If restorative justice can genuinely deliver corporate compliance in those cases where contrition and reparation are volunteered because the justice is more genuinely restorative, the sword of corporate deterrence can be sharpened by putting more resources into the cases that need the most deterrence, the cases in which corporations are most dangerous because they are the least contrite and the most disposed to cover up.

Most fundamentally of all, Chapter 6 argued that it is wrong to evaluate corporate deterrence by how well it deters offenders. Corporate deterrence works best when it deters soft targets who are third parties with the power to prevent corporate offences rather than when it seeks to deter offenders before or after their offence. This was illustrated in Chapter 6 by Mitchell's (1994a, 1994b) work on the almost total ineffectiveness of the regime designed to deter shipping companies criminally responsible for oil spills, compared with the 98 per cent effectiveness of the regime that deterred the firms that insured and 'classified' those ships. It was illustrated by the Australian Taxation Office's campaign against profit-shifting by multinationals that raised $1 billion in extra tax for every $1 million spent on the program by targeting major accounting firms as gatekeepers rather than the offending firms themselves (Braithwaite 2005b: 89–100). Deterrence repeatedly is shown to work well by moving the corporate targeting away from a tough-nut corporate deterrence target and on to a soft but strategic gatekeeper or other third-party target with the capacity to prevent. This is because in corporate life the capacity to prevent is overdetermined and not primarily in the hands of individual offenders. As Cumming et al. (2021) and Dyck et al. (2010) argue, it takes a whole village to detect financial crime, which includes auditors, compliance and ethics staff, analysts, short sellers and institutional investors. Perhaps it is wrong to call this targeting deterrence.

That critique may be of no concern when the objective here is not to defend deterrence in any narrowly conceived way. On the other hand, when the International Maritime Organization as regulator says to the insurer that it will not be authorised to issue ship insurance unless it gets ships to do certain things, the regulator withholding the licence to insure ships from an insurer is a form of deterrence. Likewise, it is a kind of deterrence when the insurer says to the ship owner that if you fail to do this, your insurance is void.

Another important thing to say about how corporate deterrence works is that it mostly works *before* sentences are imposed when cases do go to court. Chapter 6 discussed Waldman's (1978) and Fisse and Braithwaite's (1983) early research on this. It showed that the costliest things convicted corporations do in response to a prosecution are done prior to trial to improve their case for corporate responsibility presented at the trial. This is also why the stock market impact of state enforcement tends to come with the announcement of the prosecution or the investigation or even rumours of investigation of irregularities (Carberry et al. 2018), while 'the public corporation's stock price usually goes up on the announcement of the sanction' (Coffee 2020: 66). Karpoff et al. (2008b) support this pattern of a reputational effect of investigation rather than a sentencing effect in SEC cases in the United States. They further found that

> the expected loss in the present value of future cash flows due to lower sales and higher contracting costs—is over 7.5 times the sum of all penalties imposed through the legal and regulatory system. (See also Karpoff 2012)

This reality opens the door to creative future use of restorative justice in research and development on deferred prosecutions and enforceable undertakings (Parker 2004). This is a particular instance of the more general point made about the Sword of Damocles in this chapter. The deferred prosecution process can be designed to sharpen deterrence, while imposition of a criminal sentence by a court blunts it with surprising frequency.

A final important point is that with occupational health and safety inspections and low-level fines, the evidence points to an almost total absence of general deterrence, but formidable specific deterrence (Scholz and Gray 1990). This may be because of the range of semi-formal and informal inspection compliance levers discussed in the context of Table 6.1. These levers can be readily enabled by backing inspectors with restorative circles that demand repair and future prevention, mostly of the self-incapacitation kind discussed in the next chapter. Likewise, regulators can be enabled to underwrite them by prosecutions (and indeed enabled to underwrite restorative justice). More precisely, the specific deterrence and other preventive effects of inspections in Table 6.1 may be better underwritten by an integration of restorative justice and punitive prosecutorial justice than by either alone.

Too big to fail; too big to nail?

In the earliest days of restorative innovations in Australian Competition and Consumer Commission enforcement (Parker 2004), some of us at the ACCC did have the view that the victim compensation and other remedies agreed to in enforceable undertakings often had higher costs for the firm than would have been obtained by a prosecution. This was not because we saw ourselves as oppressive in our negotiation of these undertakings; we saw ourselves as tough negotiators who were firm but fair. And we as regulators were the initiators of Australian law reforms that sought more accountability in enforceable undertakings to ensure the terms were neither captured nor oppressive, and satisfied the rule of law. In early cases like the consumer frauds in remote Queensland Aboriginal communities by global insurance corporations, we believed the outcomes were tougher than judges would have imposed in a prosecution because top management, CEOs or board chairs of some of these companies had become genuinely ashamed of what their company had done. That was partly because there were some criminal convictions of individual insurance company executives as well. Top management had not started with remorse; that was an accomplishment of restorative elements of the process when CEOs sat with Aboriginal elders in 'yarning circles' (Parker 2004). Defendants often started with ridiculous techniques of neutralisation of responsibility that accused the accusers of oppressive enforcement and that blamed Aboriginal victims. These neutralisations fell away quickly when they sat in the circle with victims and elders. These are the senses in which restorative justice theory married to the economics of responsive regulatory theory can offer a better explanation than the narrowly economic theory of deferred prosecutions in Leone et al. (2021).

By the late 2000s, however, conversations within our ACCC reformers network were about enforceable undertakings becoming a soft option in the hands of many Australian regulators who allowed defendants to get away with saying, 'We didn't do it, but we won't do it again.' This became a national conversation when the Royal Commission into Misconduct in the Banking, Superannuation and Financial Services Industry found in 2019 that enforceable undertakings negotiated by ASIC and the

Australian Prudential Regulation Authority had been consistently soft on bank criminality. Dukes et al. (2014) extended this critique to US corporate prosecutions concerning our longstanding work on corporate crime by Big Pharma. We found that recidivist pharmaceutical giants showed a pattern across four decades of paying bribes both inside the United States and globally and committing other serious corporate crimes, while settling with prosecutors one corporate integrity agreement, then another, then another. They scandalously breached its intent each time without being prosecuted.

Much as I continued to be attracted to restorative corporate justice, an inescapable conclusion was that the view had become widespread that corporations were 'too big to fail' or nail: law enforcement was captured by the concern that big banks must survive for the sake of the stability of the financial system and Big Pharma recidivists like Pfizer must survive because they hold patents to lifesaving drugs, as we saw with the huge contribution Pfizer made to building on government-funded university research on Covid-19. Pfizer needed to be a 'fit and proper person' to participate in government pharmaceutical benefits programs. Pfizer has long been by far the biggest, most important and most politically influential pharmaceutical corporation in the world. It negotiated one corporate integrity agreement with a restorative US state, offended again and negotiated a new corporate integrity agreement and then, when further offences were revealed by very senior Pfizer whistleblowing, US prosecutors negotiated a third corporate integrity agreement (Dukes et al. 2014: 339) and then a deferred prosecution agreement over alleged corrupt practices in eight countries (Paul Hastings 2012). In 2020, the US Department of Justice Foreign Corrupt Practices Unit opened yet another investigation over new possible breaches of this agreement in Russia, then China (FCPA Professor 2020). This followed another renewed line of litigation against Pfizer by US service and civilian personnel killed or wounded in Iraq and their families, alleging that corrupt payments by Pfizer to the Jaysh al-Mahdi terrorist group helped fund this group that attacked them (FCPA Professor 2020).

In the United States, there was a particular political history that drove this concern about enforcement capture. After Arthur Andersen was convicted and then had this conviction overturned by the Supreme Court for its role as the auditor of Enron and other corporations bankrupted during the stock market crash of 2001, Arthur Andersen itself effectively collapsed because of the adverse publicity surrounding the indictment, with 28,000

US employees losing their jobs. George W. Bush's administration drew the lesson that it was unfair that these innocent Arthur Andersen employees had lost their jobs. Australia had an identical debate when thousands of innocent Australian Arthur Andersen employees lost jobs against the background of some Arthur Andersen responsibility in major corporate crimes of 2001—in particular, the jailing of the CEO of the Australian insurance giant HIH.

Deferred corporate prosecutions were rare before the Arthur Andersen collapse. Coffee (2020: 38) found 419 deferred and non-prosecution agreements between 2002 and 2016, but only 18 in the previous 10 years up to the Arthur Andersen case. This section considers the possibility that deterrence may have been enhanced overall, at least in the terms that matter in the analysis of this chapter, and at least until the arrival of the Trump administration. That was because Garrett (2007: 855) found that prosecutors were laying charges in larger numbers of cases in the early twenty-first century than in the twentieth century; it is just that the increase was in deferred rather than completed prosecutions. Alexander and Cohen (2015) concluded empirically that the rise of deferred prosecution agreements has not suppressed other forms of corporate liability. Corporate cooperation with the individual accountability aspects of expanded deferred prosecutions has also meant that while there are reduced convictions of corporations, there is a small contribution to increasing convictions of individuals for corporate crimes in the United States (only 414 individual prosecutions across 306 deferred and non-prosecution agreements) (Garrett 2015: 1791) and some increased convictions in other countries with foreign corporations (Garrett 2014), plus some leveraging of foreign law reforms that could enable expanded future global enforcement (Garrett 2011: 1852). After the Global Financial Crisis, the Obama administration persisted with the shift from corporate crime prosecution to deferred prosecutions combined with compliance agreements. There were many unconscionable Obama administration failures to prosecute. Dukes et al. (2014: 185) wrote:

> Restorative justice is important when it can lead to Corporate Integrity Agreements that genuinely confront and transform cultures of manipulation. Yet Corporate Integrity Agreements are not at present very searching;[10] they fail to confront corporate cultures of manipulation. To date, they are no more than a tiny

---

10   This analysis cited the work of Ford (2008), Ford and Hess (2009, 2011) and Hess and Ford (2008).

step towards crafting a less manipulative industry that respects the spirit of the law in preference to gaming it. This is the reason [for taking] on the challenge of reforming Corporate Integrity Agreements by embedding them in a more robust framework, comprising tougher hybrid public and private law enforcement, restorative justice and transparent reporting and accountability for corporate integrity that transforms manipulation.

Changes to the board and the top management team are very common in deferred prosecution cases because of the adverse publicity in the financial press and as a consequence of the enforcement action, whether it is a prosecution or a deferred prosecution agreement. Corporate monitors were also appointed in 30 per cent of deferred prosecution cases (Arlen 2016). Regulators also often mandated corporate monitors pursuant to civil enforcement action. A chief compliance officer was often appointed to the top management group as part of the mandate. It may be that what Brandon Garrett (2007) called 'structural reform deferred prosecutions' that pursue 'deep governance reforms' indeed can transform. Garrett (2007: 855) illustrated transformation with the 2005 KPMG agreement to shut down its entire private tax practice, cooperate fully in the investigation of former employees and retain a former SEC chairman as an independent monitor for three years to oversee an elaborate corporate compliance program. The next chapter argues that the most important of such deferred prosecution undertakings go to corporate self-incapacitation rather than deterrence and that this is where their preventive potential mainly resides.

At least when it comes to big banks and Big Pharma, my professional experience of these organisations since the 1970s is that they have often remained recidivist criminalised corporations. If it is right that many of the organisations subject to deferred prosecutions that demand deep structural reforms are firms systemically criminalised across more than one kind of corporate crime, the governance and compliance reforms mandated by the deferred prosecution agreement may shut down other kinds of crime that have nothing to do with the offence for which the firm has been charged.[11]

---

11   This was an early discovery of Stanley Sporkin's voluntary disclosure program after the Lockheed bribery scandals (Coffee 1977, 1981; Braithwaite 1984). External monitors of companies that had off-the-books slush funds for paying bribes found that criminal executives also used those accounts to rip off their company. For example, while Adnan Khashoggi may have persuaded ministers in foreign governments to buy Lockheed aircraft with bribes, he also gamed its slush funds to perpetrate massive fraud against Lockheed (Fisse and Braithwaite 1983, 1993).

If all this is so, why do CEOs not rationally defend this loss of sales and the sustained hit on the stock price by opting for a prosecution? One hypothesis is that CEOs do not defend the rational interests of the firm because cooperating with the prosecutor may be one path to their own survival. A CEO who keeps control during a negotiated settlement is likely to protect themselves and their board chair from losing their jobs and from prosecution by cooperating constructively and offering a lot of reform and repair to make the regulator, the prosecutor and civil society critics in the media happy enough. Even if a senior individual is going to be prosecuted, by cooperating to stay in control of events, the CEO can wield power to ensure the fall guys are vice-presidents responsible for going to jail (Braithwaite 1984; Garrett et al. 2019). Prosecutions are also expensive, and some ethical CEOs genuinely prefer to see money spent on victims rather than putting that money into the pockets of lawyers. CEOs also like negotiated settlements because they do not drag out as long as prosecutions, ending the distracting, debilitating uncertainty in their lives and in the market from high-profile enforcement. The deal can also do something to end the reputational damage quickly, which Fisse and Braithwaite (1983) found to be important to CEOs for its own sake, independently of the financial consequences of a reputational hit.

In the very first restorative justice case at the ACCC 30 years ago, the CEO refused to cooperate with the restorative justice process. The ACCC widened the restorative justice circle to include the chair of the board, who fired the CEO and then agreed to much more formidable undertakings than would have been imposed by a court (Parker 2004). Regulators grasped from the beginning that the rational CEO is a cooperator who, if pressed hard enough by victims, activist NGOs and the regulator, can give up a bigger financial loss in an enforceable undertaking than the maximum financial penalties in the law. Of course, that does not happen when the regulator is captured and victims and NGOs are quiescent, as predicted by responsive regulatory theory (Ayres and Braithwaite 1992: Ch. 3). There have been countless occasions during this century in the United States and Australia when this capture and quiescence have been present.

Alexander and Arlen (2018) concluded that convictions do not increase reputational damage beyond that imposed by deferred prosecution agreements, as long as the conviction does not reveal extra information about the firm's riskiness. This is true, among other reasons, because reputational damage does not depend on a plea of guilty. Extremely large agreed payouts to harmed victims, a restorative justice of corporate contrition and revelations of facts to the media can do the reputational damage. These factors can also do reintegration through reform just as well, or better, than guilt conferred in the dock.

A final important datum from a restorative justice point of view is that corporations convicted by a judge in the United States pay an average of $3 million in restitution to victims; in deferred prosecution agreements negotiated by prosecutors, the average is $94 million, though this partly reflects the fact that larger corporations are more likely to receive deferred prosecution and smaller companies more likely to be convicted (Garrett 2014: Ch. 5). On average, victims get much more from civil suits arising from corporate crime than from public enforcement (Garrett 2014). All this says something shocking about how dismissive extant criminal sentencing is of victims' rights to restorative justice. Better integration of restorative victim compensation and prosecutorial punishment is another missed opportunity in how restorative justice could contribute to corporate criminal deterrence. This is not the most important defect of corporate criminal law from a restorative justice point of view. Much more attention to empowering victims with a voice, deep listening, apology, healing and prevention of further harm is required.

The largest criminal fine in Garrett's (2014) dataset was US$1.26 billion against BP for the Deepwater Horizon oil spill. Probably more than $28 billion was ordered in a combination of $4.5 billion in civil penalties paid to the Justice Department and the SEC, civil suits or voluntary payments in compensation or for cleanup before this was demanded by any prosecutor or judge. Much of this is the old Waldman (1978) effect of delivering corporate self-enforcement to avert conviction or soften public enforcement. The US courts were stunningly kind and gentle to Halliburton and extremely tough on BP, if not as tough as BP was on itself. More importantly from a restorative justice point of view, while no great transformation in the corporate conscience of Halliburton has occurred, BP has sought to to sell the story that it will transform itself from a carbon Goliath into a renewables David, committed to carbon neutrality by 2050, to become the oil major with the most transformative vision for the planet (Reed 2020). BP in turn sought to survive by filing $40 billion in suits against the rig owner, Transocean, the rig cementer, Halliburton, and the blowout-preventer manufacturer, Cameron International. Pre-emptive self-punishment is also fundamental across all the data discussed. This involves investment in new compliance systems, appointing new chief compliance officers and independent monitors of reform and firing senior managers. So much of this is done defensively as self-incapacitation (Chapter 10) in advance of demands that the self-punishment be done.

The most important point from an Australian restorative justice perspective about the Deepwater Horizon and Arthur Andersen cases is that cosmopolitan restorative justice in Australia could have prevented these catastrophes before they befell the United States. This is argued in the next chapter in relation to the power for the global corporate self-incapacitation of Halliburton in particular that was in the hands of Australian law enforcement. The Timor Sea oil spill, which was uncappable for 75 days and which occurred just a year before the 86-day Deepwater Horizon spill, which was uncappable for the same reasons at the hands of the same cement base contractor, Halliburton, should have produced a cosmopolitan restorative response for justice for future victims. Australian environmentalists should have demanded that the Australian regulator or courts require corporate monitoring reports of the cementing of all oil rigs around the world undertaken by Halliburton. Chapter 10 argues that the evidence is clear that this would have revealed a worldwide pattern of catastrophic risks with deepwater wells that were screaming to be fixed. Chapter 10 argues that, likewise, in the late 1990s, Australian regulators, particularly the Australian Taxation Office, were detecting a catastrophically criminal transformation of Arthur Andersen that might have catalysed cosmopolitan demands for global compliance and culture change, including at its Chicago headquarters.

One puzzle is why judges seem not to be as creative in their sentences as prosecutors working with regulators to impose compliance monitoring under deferred prosecution or non-prosecution agreements. There is no reason the judiciary could not become more creative custodians of corporate crime prevention in their sentencing.[12] One view is that law reform should force the judiciary into this role by requiring them to oversee the justice of both prosecution and non-prosecution agreements and the enforced self-regulation imposed by so many Australian regulatory agencies through enforceable undertakings. Then, perhaps, this limitation of corporate sentencing is because judges are not bureaucracies. Regulatory agencies (such as the Environmental Protection Agency with environmental crime and the Internal Revenue Service with tax crimes) working with prosecutors' officers have the better bureaucratic capacities

---

12   I am grateful to Brent Fisse for posing the question to me in this way.

to check the reports of corporate monitors, vet the suitability of the new chief compliance officer and oversee the rigour and transparency of their work in restoring integrity to the corporation. Moreover, there is the danger that activist judges who mimic regulatory bureaucracies will be accused of overreaching to usurp the policymaking responsibilities of elected officials, prosecutors who are accountable to elected officials but professionally independent, a politically accountable but professionally independent civil service and regulatory commissioners in the separation of powers (Baer 2016). Reasonably fearing this accusation, judges may always be too timid, too stretched, for the magnitude of a challenge so vast that they can never make the inroads required as the planet burns and financial systems unravel.

With deferred prosecution agreements and restorative corporate justice, the justice principles still seem the same as those Fisse and Braithwaite (1993) articulated. Most fundamentally, all who are responsible should be held responsible, be they individuals, firms or subunits of firms. That does not mean judges sentencing all of them to prison. If we have a president who gropes staff or a professor who gropes students, likely the university is responsible, the department is responsible, the head of the department is responsible and the groping professor is responsible. Fisse and Braithwaite (1993) have a lot of useful things to say about how to guard against scapegoating by powerful CEOs and how to hold CEOs individually accountable in appropriate ways while giving them credit for cooperation and for reactive acquittal of their fault (Fisse 1982). CEO fault is almost always something that societal collective efficacy demands as a remedy under Fisse and Braithwaite's accountability model—at least, managerial fault for the failings of operating procedures in a corporation they lead, but often criminal fault and civil liability under regulatory laws as well.

Given the power of CEOs to orchestrate smokescreens of diffused accountability to absolve themselves, societies do need to discuss the proposal of Harvard law professor Elizabeth Warren. She proposed during her 2020 presidential campaign that negligence should be the standard for CEO criminal liability inside criminalised banks that have catastrophic impacts on economies. Perhaps, however, Warren's objectives can be accomplished by tweaking what criminal recklessness means in the context of the power of a bank CEO. Perhaps given the pivotal importance of both CEOs and board chairs, remorse and accountability at those levels should also be encouraged by criminal law reforms that require them normally to be in court for corporate criminal sentencing and at the press conference when the results of a deferred prosecution agreement are announced.

Corporate crime enforcement was wound back dramatically under President Trump. In the 15 years to 2017, aggregate corporate criminal fines increased from less than $1 billion to $10 billion a year, but they fell off a cliff in the next two years to one-fifth of what they were (to $2 billion) (Garrett 2020: 116). Corporate convictions, convictions of individuals for corporate crimes and deferred prosecutions all declined during the Trump administration. Under President Biden, America could do worse than return to building on the limited progress that was being achieved through deferred prosecutions and *qui tam* actions for whistleblowers during the first decade of this century.

Misplaced optimism here could be a risk because the track records of the Clinton and Obama Democratic administrations were of beating the enforcement drum in press releases but muffling it during corporate negotiations that became politicised at times. The trajectory of the data on the stringency of deferred prosecution agreements post Enron suggests the same pattern of evolution towards a market in lemons described for Australian enforceable undertakings since 1990. Leone et al. (2021) created a cooperation score that combined corporate volunteering for self-investigation, timely reporting, prominent disclosure and the replacement of executives. Consistent with the Australian history, for the period 2002–10 (under the administration of George W. Bush), deferred prosecution negotiations left firms worse off: a 1 unit increase in a firm's cooperation score increased the probability of enforcement by 4.2 per cent and increased penalties by $2.04 million. This result reversed during the Obama period of 2011–14, with 1 unit of higher cooperation reducing the odds of enforcement by 4.6 per cent and resulting in $2.55 million less in fines (Leone et al. 2021). Firing allegedly culpable executives was particularly rewarding for firms during the Obama era, raising the scapegoating concerns that were such an issue in Fisse and Braithwaite (1993). Leone et al.'s (2021) results were consistent with an earlier study by Files (2012) that found cooperating with the SEC in deferred prosecution negotiations made firms worse off *before* 2010.

Untangling recursive causality in these data is difficult. Nevertheless, the data, combined with the Australian historical experience of enforceable undertakings, are sufficient to conclude that the pursuit of some static, evidence-based set of optimal deterrent policy settings is folly. Much depends on how tough regulators and prosecutors are in deferred prosecution negotiations. That constantly shifts with the political winds, the excellence of regulatory leadership and shifts in corporate cultures of responsibility. The interactions among corporate, CEO and lower-level sanctions that may target executive scapegoats are complex, as are interactions between deterrence and preventive incapacitation. This is no warrant for nihilism. It justifies carefully monitored dynamic responsiveness, more genuinely restorative and responsive participation of third parties (particularly victim representatives) in the sanction negotiations, rather than state–corporate deals behind closed doors. The imperative remains unrelenting citizen and social movement vigilance against regulatory capture and corruption (Ayres and Braithwaite 1992: Ch. 3).

It also justifies consideration of further strengthening enforcement with Coffee's (2020) ideas on equity fines and the privatisation of corporate criminal enforcement, but informed by a more restorative and responsive philosophy of prevention and punishment. Coffee is surely right that access to potent equity fines would strengthen the negotiating clout of the public interest against corporate power in deferred prosecution negotiation. Baer (2016) may be right that the challenge of prosecuting every guilty corporate criminal to fix the crisis of 'too big to fail, too big to jail' is a mission 'too vast to prevail'. Yes, we can spend a good bit more on corporate prosecutors, but funding more street-level regulatory inspectors, fraud examiners, environmental NGOs and activists in networks like Citizens for Tax Justice may be a higher priority for reducing the suffering and domination caused by corporate crime than funding more lawyers and building more prisons.[13] More conceptually, my hypothesis is that the collective efficacy, the bridging and linking social capital of a society against corporate crime, may be what matters most.

---

13   As Coffee (2020: 93) himself concedes: 'Civil enforcement dwarfs criminal enforcement, whether in terms of manpower allocated, aggregate damages collected, or numbers of actions brought.' With banks, Coffee (2020: 93) points out that the six worst bailed-out US banks had experienced 'more than 350 "major legal actions" that had imposed approximately $182 billion in sanctions and settlements'. While the Global Financial Crisis did not produce major successes from criminal prosecutions until the final years of the Obama presidency, in the years immediately after the crisis, civil regulatory actions against banks peaked at 2,208 per year (Coffee 2020: 94). In turn, the financial recoveries from civil and criminal regulatory penalties combined were dwarfed by recoveries from securities class actions (Coffee 2020: 104). In my terms, regulators, internal compliance actors and civil society actors are the ones who deliver most of the detection and the diversity of control mechanisms in Table 6.1.

Deterring police departments as criminal organisations

Reflexivity is in scarce supply in criminology. Obviously, we must study police as both preventers and perpetrators of crime. Chapter 8 discussed the implications of Lawrence Sherman's (1978) evocative study of police scandal and reform. One reason prosecutors are reluctant to prosecute police is that they are hard targets who are expensive to nail. They are sophisticated witnesses, adept at orchestrating reasonable doubt and smokescreens of diffused accountability for wrongdoing. Police chiefs who seem corrupt to many in the community rarely go to jail; police constables who seem to many in the community to have murdered suspects are rarely convicted of murder. It makes little sense for the community to even attempt to punish itself by fining police departments that rely on the community's taxes. Police departments may be too big and too politically connected to fail, and too street smart to nail.

Nevertheless, police organisations are like other public sector organisations such as universities in that their leaders care about their reputation for its own sake, quite independently of any financial implications of a reputational hit. Chappell (2017) found that consent decrees settled with 23 agencies subject to US Department of Justice litigation for police misconduct produced a 23–36 per cent reduction in subsequent filings for further alleged civil rights violations. It is impossible to say whether this might be a deterrence effect mediated by police leaders' concern for their reputations. Based on Sherman's (1978) research, we might conjecture that reform was more likely to be a self-incapacitation effect negotiated under the consent decree. Internal police integrity testing was particularly important in the corruption scandal and reform cycles studied by Sherman. These are questions that are hard to answer, but we might do best to consider criminal police organisations as just one kind of criminal organisation. We should be open to the frame that criminalised police are just one bit of criminalised states, as we consider the potential of enforced organisational self-incapacitation in the next chapter.

Conclusion

Inexorability is a core principle of minimally sufficient deterrence: pursue inexorable consistency of detection and disapproval of predatory crime. This implies fusing the debate on dynamic concentration of deterrence with the debates about less prison and more and better street-level state monitoring and collective efficacy in civil society.

The move away from the nihilism about policing effectiveness prevalent at the time of the Kansas City Preventive Patrol Experiment has lessons for criminologists (Nagin et al. 2015); as has the shift from nihilism about rehabilitation prevalent at the time of the 'Nothing Works' slogan (Lipton et al. 1975). Policing and rehabilitation are useless or dangerous only if they are unresponsively deployed. For example, evidence-based refinement of the responsivity of rehabilitation can improve the menu of options in the pyramid of supports in Figure 9.1 (Andrews and Bonta 1998, 2010; Manchak and Cullen 2015). Weisburd et al.'s (2017) systematic review of 118 separate systematic reviews finds that a wide variety of interventions are quite effective in reducing crime when they strengthen what have here been called human capital, social capital, recovery capital and restorative capital, and a wide variety of other interventions to improve policing, diversion and mentoring or to close off criminal opportunities. The exception to this widely variegated pattern of greater and lesser effectiveness was the ineffectiveness or harmfulness of punitive sentences. Developmentalists convincingly showed that social support is important to crime prevention long before the first offence occurs (Cullen 1994). This is a vital piece for any integrated theory of crime prevention. Deterrence is therefore far from the most important element of a sophisticated strategy to protect citizens from crime and guarantee their freedom. Deterrence is less important than sound management of anomie and building plural forms of social capital, as discussed in previous chapters. Deterrence is less important than incapacitation, especially of the crimes of the powerful, as discussed in the next chapter.

'Less prison, more police' (Durlauf and Nagin 2011a) is not convincing as a slogan; nor is 'defund the police'. Having more police is an unpersuasive idea when so much policing in the United States and Australia is racist in ways that reduce freedom and increase crime. Meta-analyses such as that of Pratt and Cullen (2005) show that increased funding of police, police per capita and arrest ratios are at the bottom of their list of macrolevel predictors of crime, often engendering defiant backlash that makes crime worse (Sherman 1993). Having more police is only a good idea when policing is not racist, is evidence-based and steeply reduces arrest as its default strategy. In the end, this book also argues that transformed police, and more of them, could be a small part of a shape-shifting reform for reducing the environmental destructiveness of economies that avert the crises that most threaten freedom and violence (Chapter 12). Evidence-based policing can be part of a strategy for achieving economic growth in human services rather than in consumer durables. More police can also save surprisingly large numbers of lives when deployed to UN peacekeeping operations (Hultman et al. 2013).

A better slogan than 'Defund the police' on my analysis is 'Less prison, less arrest'. One reaction to many of the police killings that motivated the 'defund the police' movement was: 'Why were the police seeking to arrest this citizen in the first place, why did they pull out a gun when there was some resistance and why were they armed in the first place?' Bad criminological ideas like broken-windows policing that have been implemented in racist ways have contributed to the overuse of arrest to the point where 'in our society liberty is not the norm and detention prior to trial or without trial is not the carefully limited exception' (VanNostrand and Keebler 2007: 23). Police arrest policies have paved this path to tyranny.

Braithwaite's (1989) theory argues that when police are reintegrative, they can reduce crime; when they are stigmatising and violent, they increase it, which is why having more police does not currently lead to less crime. Kennedy (2017) rightly argues that there are US police departments that have reduced the number of arrests, reduced the number of complaints against them, reduced incarceration rates and reduced crime through evidence-based policing. They are exceptions at this point in history. Minimally sufficient arrests are a path to crime reduction and to enhancing freedom. Engel et al. (2017), for example, show persuasively how the Cincinnati police accomplished this after the Queensgate Correctional Facility was closed. Street-level police were persuaded to a cultural transformation whereby arrest should be used sparingly. Violent crime, arrests and imprisonment were simultaneously reduced by a combination of the evidence-based policing strategies discussed herein: hotspot policing, dynamic concentration of deterrence of the Operation Ceasefire variety, problem-oriented policing and expanded welfare resourcing of partnerships with social service and health agencies.

Suggestive evidence has been introduced that an inexorably supportive firm hand might help in preventing crime, in preventing the collapse of welfare states that struggle to deter corporate tax evasion and in addressing many other challenges of crime control. The white-collar crime piece of this is important. Any theory of crime that provides an account of crimes of the powerless but not crimes of the powerful is troubling and, indeed, misleading. It might be credible as a theory of something more specific than crime. Moreover, the dominance of theories in criminology that fail this test means criminology buttresses oppression when it normalises prisons that hold tiny numbers of wealthy white criminals.

The evidence adduced in support of minimally sufficient arrest, minimally sufficient prosecution, minimally sufficient imprisonment and minimally sufficient deterrence is no more than suggestive. It is common for criminological theories to have something going for them while being wrong in most contexts. Until minimally sufficient deterrence is subjected to an array of different kinds of empirical investigations, this may be as true of it as it is of the theories of passive deterrence that currently dominate thinking. I have attempted to show that minimally sufficient deterrence has promise as a strategy for moving from passive to dynamic deterrence because it starts from what we already know about deterrence and defiance and because it integrates insights from other relational theories that each enjoy a body of empirical support. These are theories of social support (Cullen 1994), social capital (as discussed in Chapter 7), responsivity (Andrews and Bonta 1998, 2010), responsive regulation (Braithwaite 2021f), sharpening the Sword of Damocles (Dunford 1990; Sherman 1992, 2011), dynamic concentration of deterrence (Kleiman 2009), shame and pride management (Ahmed et al. 2001), combined with indirect reciprocity (Berger 2011; Nowak 2012), and motivational interviewing (Lundahl et al. 2010). The imperative, grounded in complexity theory, for abandoning applied social science that tests specific parsimonious theories in favour of applying meta-theories has been explored. These are theories about how to organise multiple theories and meta-strategies—strategies about how to sequence many strategies.

While minimally sufficient deterrence is based on what we know about deterrence and defiance, that knowledge base has wide gaps of complex unknowns (Braithwaite and D'Costa 2018: Ch. 12). The future gap-filling research agenda can be framed under the seven policy principles of minimally sufficient deterrence:

1. Escalate enforcement: Display intent to progressively escalate a responsive enforcement pyramid that involves progressive escalation of sanctions for wrongdoing and support for social responsibility.

This has been the heartland research priority of Valerie Braithwaite's and my research group since 1980—for example, see Braithwaite's (2021f) review essay and more than 100 empirical evaluations of the application of responsive regulation to tax compliance by the Centre for Tax System Integrity (ctsi.org.au/; more broadly, see johnbraithwaite.com/responsive-regulation/).

2. Inexorability: Pursue inexorable consistency of detection of predatory crime. Communicate inexorable community commitment to stick with social support for those struggling with problems of lawbreaking until the problems are fixed.

Critical research contributions here bring together the established agenda of measuring the effects of perceived certainty of detection with the belief that supporters of offenders will deliver them unconditional support, sticking with offenders' problems until they are fixed. While increasing consistency of detection will increase deterrence, police being everywhere at all times risks undermining legitimacy and motivating defiance, especially when some police are stigmatising or inflame racial injustice. Lawrence Sherman has coined the idea of a sweet spot of intensity of just enough deterrence through police presence at hotspots. Gibson et al. (2017) found such an optimal sweet spot of minimally sufficient patrols in Merseyside, in the United Kingdom. Though it is well established that intensive patrolling at hotspots can reduce crime (Braga et al. 2014), Gibson and her colleagues are the first to explore the possibility of reducing the intensity of hotspot patrolling without increasing crime, perhaps even reducing it somewhat through optimising each sweet spot. This work opens a path to understanding cost-effective, minimally sufficient patrolling.

3. Escalate social support: With repeated offending, increase social support. Even when there is escalation to a last resort of severe incapacitation, escalate social support further. Keep escalating social support until desistance is consolidated.

Perhaps the most critical research needed here is macrosociological and economic work on strategies for sustaining a more credible welfare state, a topic re-joined in the final chapter. It is feasible to be politically effective in struggling for a return to progressively improving the welfare state.

4. Sharpen the Sword of Damocles: Cultivate the perception that 'trouble hangs inexorably over my head; they want to support me to avert it'.

Here, the 'less prison' research agenda shows the kind of work that illuminates Sword-of-Damocles possibilities (Sherman 2011). This is illustrated through Slothower et al.'s (2017) 'West Midlands Police experiment, Offender Management by Turning Point (Deferred Prosecution with a Plan)'. Random assignment to deferred prosecution combined with social support substantially reduced criminal harm (by 34 per cent) though not the incidence of crime, reduced the cost of the justice system and increased victim satisfaction with outcomes when compared with prosecuted cases. Moreover, the deferred prosecution 'did something'—something constructive that reduced costs, averting a world in which 'nothing' happens until one day a lot happens. This lot that happens then seems arbitrarily harsh. From the perspective of this chapter, a tempered 'something' that happens is also a better approach to constructive structural sharpening of the Sword of Damocles.

5. Dynamic concentration of deterrence: Focus deterrence on a line that should never be crossed after an announcement date. Then progressively lift that line in high-crime contexts, raising our expectations of socially responsible citizens.

Research in this tradition led by David Kennedy and Mark Kleiman has not been linked to evidence-based learning on restorative justice and responsive business regulation, nor to the dynamic concentration experience of international peacekeepers regulating war zones and negotiating gang surrenders to create peace zones. A more interdisciplinary research imagination is required to see the complex of strategies, including escalated social support and reconciliation, to embed dynamic concentration. This can increase the effectiveness of deterrence and justice. Future research must distinguish static, focused deterrence effects from dynamic concentration effects.

6. Community engagement: Engage the community with offenders in widening restorative conversations that educate about the shamefulness of criminal predation for the many who participate in the conversations. Avert stigmatisation.

The research required here includes the intersection of work on community engagement with crime control (for example, Sampson et al. 1997; Pratt and Cullen 2005; Odgers et al. 2009) and on the Connectedness, Hope, Identity, Meaning and Empowerment (CHIME) conclusion reached by Leamy et al. (2011) in their review of recovery capital research (Best 2017). The CHIME conclusion is that connectedness, hope, identity, meaning and empowerment are needed for freedom as capability (Sen 1999), for recovery from problems such as drug addiction, alcoholism, suicide attempts and arrest. It is important to integrate the best psychological and criminological research on pride and shame dynamics and on shame acknowledgement as offenders re-narrate their lives (Leach and Cidam 2015; Spruit et al. 2016; Braithwaite 2020c). The community best learns the shamefulness of corporate crime through media coverage of stories of corporate harm and restorative contrition, apology and repair.

7. Modesty: Settle for the modest general deterrence delivered by this shamefulness and a minimal number of cases that escalate towards the peak of the enforcement pyramid.

This is the 'decremental' research strategy commended by Braithwaite and Pettit (1990) for republican freedom and criminal justice. It means evaluating research on how low imprisonment can go without crime beginning to increase. When we have no choice but to lock up extremely dangerous people, we can be justifiably pessimistic that this will deter those specific people when they are released. Yet others noticing that imprisonment does sometimes happen may deliver a modest quantum of general deterrence of the rest of the population. Braithwaite and Pettit's (1990) decremental research agenda has gone nowhere in 31 years. No country pursued progressive reductions of imprisonment rates until evidence emerged that serious crime problems were the result. This is a measure of how wide the gap is in every country between minimally sufficient deterrence and criminal justice policy.

10

Why incapacitation trumps deterrence

Key propositions

- Criminological thought must become more punitive in incapacitation terms. New laws should announce execution dates for entire industries. Dates for the banning of internal combustion engine cars and aircraft and coal, oil and gas-fired power plants establish a renewed relevance for capital punishment in criminology. Companies that were once number one on the *Fortune 500* list—the old General Motors, the old Exxon, the old Boeing must be reborn or die. There are drug pushers of Big Pharma that must be incapacitated. Detroit must be reborn with social support for regenerative capitalism.

- The art of republican regulation is the art of steering self-enforcement democratically, deliberatively and relationally with motivational interviewing.

- An important revision of responsive regulatory theory for crime is that self-incapacitation should normally be sequenced before deterrence in an enforcement pyramid.

- Self-incapacitation generally has more preventive power than deterrence and incapacitation by the state—for organisational crime and for individual crime when individual offenders are responded to through restorative justice.

- Much self-incapacitation can be as simple as the Plimsoll line, which made it impossible for dangerously overloaded ships to leave port without being stopped.

- Self-incapacitation of war crime can be catalysed by a simple letter from an International Criminal Court prosecutor to a military commander warning that if he fails to disarm a militia under his control that begins to ethnically cleanse a region, he is on notice of potential personal war crime culpability.

- Self-incapacitation agreed to in a restorative justice circle can achieve a more global reach with organisational crime prevention. Cosmopolitan collective efficacy can demand global self-incapacitation. Restorative justice can scale up to help prevent global crises this way.

- Self-incapacitation agreed to in restorative justice circles can make contributions to the prevention of crimes that cause financial crises, environmental crises, wars and war crimes. Restorative circles can also help self-incapacitate street offenders from access to gambling if that is a root cause of their offending, from internet access to pornography for child sex offenders released from prison, and more.

- When deferred prosecutions result in restorative self-incapacitation, they can be more effective at corporate crime prevention than actual prosecutions. Self-incapacitation can deliver structural reform that is beyond compliance.

- With corporate crime and war crime, there is a case for nailing the minnows, then offering them effective immunity when they testify against the sharks. Then there is a case for a restorative conference with the sharks to secure their cooperation with self-incapacitation to prevent further corporate crime or war crime. After this organisational crime wave ends, the sharks who committed to self-incapacitation might then be pressured to testify against worse sharks who refused to comply with the self-incapacitation agreement.

- In a prosecution strategy, it can be much more important to be punitive when there is a cover-up of horrifically collective criminality than to prosecute individual participation in crime. Focusing punishment where there is a cover-up can enable structural prevention through collective incapacitation of future horrors and can enable learning cultures about recklessness (as illustrated with child sexual abuse in churches).

Corporate capital punishment laws now

For the world to achieve its Paris Climate Agreement objectives, carbon dioxide emissions must be halved during the current decade. At the time of writing, this appears unlikely. For many parts of the world, Paris was already too late—for example, islands in the Pacific that have already been abandoned by human habitation because of the rising ocean.

Capital punishment is now a crucial criminological remedy to past indecisiveness. It is imperative for each country to enact a law that announces a date when sales of internal combustion engine vehicles will be banned, and a later date when they will be banned from the roads. These dates must not be far into the future. This amounts to corporate capital punishment for the old auto firms that built Detroit. What has been good for General Motors is now bad for America. As discussed in previous chapters, that corporate capital punishment mentality must be accompanied by an escalation of social supports for regenerative economic growth in cities like Detroit, which have comparative advantages in building most of the components for electric vehicles and, for that matter, hydrogen-powered planes—from wheels, tyres and suspension systems to comfortable seats and enclosed vehicle sound systems. Detroit must grow a battery industry of a different kind from the acid batteries of its gas guzzlers. Another date further into the future should be legislated for ending the production of all aircraft fuelled by gasoline, and then a further date for grounding that fleet. The Boeing of the present cannot be closed before new hydrogen-powered competitors (including, hopefully, a renewed Boeing) can realistically emerge. While the dates must be later, the law and the announcement must be now, to steer renewable energy markets at tomorrow's opening of trade on the stock exchanges. Boeing will probably die, but we must not rule out the possibility of a renewed Boeing. Climate policy requires more than killing off the brown and renewing the green; it compels 50 shades of corporate green.

Another law is needed to announce a date when all the highest power-plant emitters of carbon dioxide are closed, another when all coal-fired plants are closed and then a later date when all oil and gas-fired power plants suffer corporate capital punishment. These dates must be attuned to realistic assessments of the differential feasibility for national renewable power programs to come on stream to fill these gaps in supply. A paradox of such command-and-control regulation for corporate capital punishment is that it will create regenerative markets in virtue. Financial capital will take note of the signal that these draconian laws are required and inevitable if we are to survive. Australian university professors are already taking note of such possible futures, shifting increasing proportions of their UniSuper pension investments into the Global Environmental Opportunities Fund. Between 2013 and 2021, we enjoyed a 330 per cent return on investment in these environmental opportunities.

This is the sense in which markets in virtue will be, and in limited ways already are, the proximate drivers of transformative shapeshifting in the economy towards regenerative growth. Corporate capital punishment is a more distal driver. It only has power because of the signal it gives to markets about where future profits will be made, and future losses (in coal, oil, internal combustion engines). This is the recurrent message of this book that markets in virtue are fundamental to regenerative social democracy and a regenerative version of institutional anomie theory.

This left criminology of renewable markets is of course strangely at odds with the critical criminology of the old left in its emphasis on incapacitation, punitive new capital punishment laws and the virtuous commodification they can drive (of batteries, hydrogen, wind and solar power and environmental futures financial capital).

What is incapacitation?

This chapter on incapacitation and self-incapacitation is devoid of the lists of quantitative studies and systematic reviews of previous chapters. Rather, it relies on many ethnographic studies of crimes of domination that may not seem very criminological. My method is induction from deeply disparate ethnographic sources on a long history of cases of some of the dirtiest polluters, dirty money banks, state murder, nuclear safety offenders, bribery, antitrust, organised crime, armed insurgencies, state military criminals, corporate crime in the pharmaceutical industry, securities fraud, tax fraud, child abuse across diverse religious organisations and indigenous communities, and the self-incapacitation of family violence by families. We start by considering the incapacitation of the safety crimes of airlines and pilots, hospitals, nursing homes and doctors.

The sweep through many specific case studies may be tedious to those with a quantitative bent, so please skip over those of lesser interest to you. Just as meta-analysis is important to quantitative inference, so is the breadth of ethnographic referents for inductive inference imperative to ethnographic macrocriminology. This is especially true for discovering different limitations of incapacitation in different applications of the concept. One aim is case study dot points that create a pointillist portrait of crime across a broad canvas of the planet. This is particularly so for this chapter because the potency of the inference is grounded in the sheer diversity, the strange unfamiliarity, yet the criminal seriousness of the archipelago of cases that underwrites the theory. A big policy inference is that restorative justice can deploy self-incapacitation to prevent banks, economies and environments from collapsing. A policy inference of interest to mainstream criminologists is that these insights can then be applied to restorative self-incapacitation of bread-and-butter youth offending. This is an essence of the conclusions of this chapter that move from the macro back to the micro.

Incapacitation is generally understood in a broad way in criminology as constraining the capacity of an individual to commit crime. The word 'depriving' the offender of the capacity to commit crime is sometimes used. The constraining conception is better because murderers still commit murder in prison, rapists still rape and thieves steal things from others while inside prison, so incapacitation only constrains the capacity to commit these crimes, as opposed to depriving the offender of that capacity. Far from incapacitating drug crime, today's prisons capacitate it; so many prisoners who enter institutions without a drug habit leave them as addicts.

In this chapter, I go just a little broader by defining incapacitation as constraining the capacity of individuals and organisations to commit crime. The tweak is important because much of my focus is on incapacitating organisations. If we wish to incapacitate drug crime in prisons, for example, the key imperative is to use prisons less and incapacitate prison administrations from allowing their employees to take bribes and import drugs into prisons.

While broad in conception, in practice, the discussion of incapacitation in criminology is obsessed with imprisonment of individuals. Execution as a form of incapacitation is usually discussed in the introduction to textbook discussions of incapacitation along with cutting off the hands of thieves, handcuffs, the stocks and castration of sex offenders as instances of the doctrine from other places and times. Criminological practice has always tended to narrow incapacitation to implementation with extreme punitiveness and physicality. Is it not incapacitation when we ground our child because they have been consuming illicit drugs if the confinement cuts them off from their suppliers and their community of users? This certainly fits the definitions of incapacitation used by most criminologists, and by me.

Then it becomes reasonable to ask whether there is really any point to the concept of incapacitation in criminological theory. Perhaps not, because, broadly conceived, incapacitation is hard to distinguish from the blocking of illegitimate opportunities, as discussed in Chapter 6.[1] This might not matter greatly if what we are concerned about are the practical implications of the ideas. The important thing about this chapter is the idea of enforced self-incapacitation as a strategy for reducing crime and protecting freedom. If critics like that idea but want to call it enforced self-reduction of illegitimate opportunities, that's fine.

One reason incapacitation continues to do useful work for responsive regulatory theorists is that what we want to say theoretically is that while deterrence cannot do the work that many judges and prosecutors would like it to (Chapter 9), incapacitation is a much more useful doctrine of criminal law jurisprudence. It is just that judges, lawmakers and the entire institutional infrastructure of justice backed the wrong institution of incapacitation when they built archipelagos of prisons.

---

1   Prominent Australian strategic thinkers sometimes make a distinction between containment and 'constrainment' (Varghese 2020). The genealogy of containment begins with US diplomat George F. Kennan's influential approach to containment of the Soviet Union and communism. This was the dominant, and ultimately successful, doctrine of a succession of US presidents during the Cold War. Constrainment but not containment is how some Australian diplomatic leaders want to interact with China today. They do not see containment of China as being in the interests of the world economy, of ecocide prevention or of a possible future transition to democracy in China. They believe in principled engagement with China, but they do want to constrain it from dominating the Indo-Pacific region. The West wants a regional balance of power with capacity to push back against Chinese demands that weaker states submit to China's will. I do not see great theoretical value in separating incapacitation into containment and constrainment, partly because deterrence and engagement are involved in both. Containment of the Soviet Union worked in halting the spread of its domination and worked in ultimately contributing to a transition to democracy in Russia, but it worked only because it was deployed in combination with engagement, especially during Ronald Reagan's tenure, and earlier, as the nuclear nonproliferation regime was developed collaboratively. This is consistent with the theoretical discussion of regulatory pyramids in Chapter 9 that says, as we escalate from deterrence to incapacitation, at every stage engagement is critical.

The macrocriminological project of this chapter is to take the standard conception seriously in the broad sense in which it was drafted. So, we define our key concepts as:

- Incapacitation is an order to constrain the capacity of an individual or an organisation to commit crime.
- Self-incapacitation occurs when an individual or an organisation voluntarily chooses to constrain their own capacity to commit crime. A seven-year-old who agrees to confine himself to his room when he has been hitting his sister engages in self-incapacitation, as does his father if he agrees to move out of the house because he has been hitting his partner.
- Enforced self-incapacitation occurs when the state requires an individual or an organisation to choose between self-incapacitation and escalated state sanctions. The state then sanctions noncompliance with self-incapacitation agreements that have the force of state law.

Chapter 9 concluded that the deterrence benefits of putting an extra person in prison, or even a lot of them, are modest. This chapter argues that incapacitation should be the main reason we strip citizens of their freedom by placing them in prison. Nevertheless, by the lights of republican theory, judges should rarely do so (Braithwaite and Pettit 1990). From the republican viewpoint, prison is for serial rapists, serial killers and serial paedophiles; it is for people who, having attempted to kill someone, are saying: 'I will get you next time.' Prison is for serial domestic violence offenders who are awaiting their rehabilitation and who are unsafe to rehabilitate in the community. Even though rehabilitation and incapacitation in the community will be more effective for mobilising restorative capital in most cases, and therefore better for their families, in small numbers of domestic violence cases, prison becomes, at least for a time, the best way to prevent domination.

Even though republican criminologists see incapacitation as the most common justification for imprisonment, they do not count imprisonment among the more important institutions for the prevention of crime. The previous chapter showed why republicans want to see most of the people currently in the prisons of western societies—even in societies with the lowest imprisonment rates—released to the care and reform that recovery capital and restorative capital can deliver in the community. At the individual level, republicans see crime prevention and rehabilitation as doctrines that do much more work than incapacitation. We saw in the previous chapter that one reason the republican criminologist is interested in restorative justice as a superior delivery vehicle for rehabilitation and prevention is that, paradoxically, restorative justice might increase deterrence more than punitive justice—because restorative justice sharpens deterrence, while overuse of imprisonment blunts it. In extremis, it has this effect by so imprisoning people that they are reluctant to face the world of freedom. Another reason is that restorative justice might deliver superior incapacitation in the community. For example, a vigilant family might be more effective at incapacitating drug abuse than a vigilant prison officer. That is a big theme of this chapter.

The chapter moves decisively from how to respond to an individual to a macrocriminological frame. In that move, it argues that incapacitation proves a more powerful tool than deterrence. The chapter also argues that, through a macro lens, incapacitation does more macro crime-prevention work proactively than rehabilitation can do reactively. Experience with the incapacitation of organisations is the key that unlocks an understanding of the broader uses of incapacitation in criminology. First, the chapter advances macrocriminological strategies that might have prevented the Global Financial Crisis of 2008, building up to that by showing how incapacitation implausibly made it safer to get from A to B by flying than by travelling on the ground (with mining and nuclear power being other important examples). Then it argues that these strategies are based on a synergy between state incapacitation and the self-incapacitation of criminal organisations. The limits of corporate self-incapacitation and the dangers of 'rituals of comfort' (Power 1997) are then considered, as well as responsive regulatory remedies to this problem. A revision is proposed to the conventional responsive regulatory pyramid whereby self-incapacitation comes lower in the pyramid than deterrence, with deterrence then being followed at the highest level of the pyramid by state incapacitation. This a major revision to all previously published responsive regulatory theory. War crimes are then considered as preventable by self-incapacitation catalysed by networked responsive regulation of war crime.

Finally, the chapter returns to individual street crime and the disorganised or semi-organised crime of local gangs. This discussion involves some minor reconceptualisation of the reflections on restorative justice in the previous chapter by applying to it the major rethink of incapacitation theory in this chapter. The chapter reconceptualises Operation Ceasefire as a germinal innovation in the control of gun violence that is an accomplishment of self-incapacitation. All gun surrenders in crime control and peacekeeping and the nuclear nonproliferation regime are also examples of self-incapacitation.

The focus of the chapter can be well illustrated by policy choices about the location of gambling machines in areas with widespread poverty. There are competing views, but this can be viewed as a market in vice that increases crime, suicide and poverty in Australia, which has the highest level of use of gambling machines in the world.[2] The ways to tackle this problem as a market in vice are about incapacitation. We can quite significantly incapacitate this sector of the gambling market by withdrawing all licences for gambling machines in working-class communities. Or, we can incapacitate with more moderation and freedom of choice. As state governments in Australia do, there can be campaigns for people suffering a gambling addiction to self-register to be prohibited access to the gambling areas of licensed premises. In turn, it becomes an offence for the gambling provider to fail to self-incapacitate the market in vice in this respect. That is, they can be prosecuted if they fail to prohibit entry to a person who has registered to exclude themselves from their local gambling den. Debates swirl in Australia about whether families whose incomes are being spent by the addicted gambler should be able to apply for exclusion, perhaps after a family group conference, and whether access to gambling areas should require the kind of smartphone technologies used for access to bars during the Covid-19 epidemic. For this market in vice, incapacitation by the state is one option; layering of individual self-incapacitation, corporate self-incapacitation and incapacitation enforced by the state is another.

Self-incapacitation for airline safety, medical malpractice and street crime

Most readers have had painful experiences of airline self-incapacitation. We sit on the aircraft ready to depart. The captain announces an obscure safety imperfection. We stream off as the captain calls in engineers to check if this is a false alarm. Sometimes we experience a shorter delay

---

2   Non-Australians find it hard to believe that the average Australian adult spends US$9,200 during one year (2017–18 data) on gambling, most of it in gambling machines.

because a passenger's luggage has been loaded, but they have not occupied their seat. Even in this circumstance, we might miss a connecting flight, as we wait for the luggage to be removed.

No regulator has ordered the captain or the engineer to make these decisions that frustrate us but keep us safe. Informed by the self-incapacitation obligations of air safety law, the airline voluntarily decides to abort the flight. Such self-incapacitation is fundamental to understanding why airlines have been so successful in saving lives. Flight moved from being an exceptionally dangerous form of travel in the early and middle decades of the twentieth century to become the safest form of travel—safer than any mode of travelling across the ground or the sea—by the late decades of the twentieth century. This is surprising given the larger number of things that can go wrong and how much more technically demanding it is to travel through the air than across water or land. The safety gap is not small. Driving a car for more than 400 km or a motorbike for 10 km is more dangerous than flying a plane for 10,000 km (Vally 2017).

This is an accomplishment of a regulatory system that refrained from punishing safety breaches by pilots, engineers or air traffic controllers, but is punitive towards cover-ups—particularly the cover-up of near misses. It is important here to note the pivotal role that minimally sufficient deterrence plays in motivating airline self-incapacitation. It is critical to build an airline safety culture of engineering and pilot professionalism such that if a flight gets away with ignoring a safety alert, or if the flight gets away with a separation error (getting too close to another aircraft), and this is covered up, the whistle is blown. Then those who participate in the cover-up are incapacitated by ejection from the industry. Therefore, a related virtue of air safety systems are the self-incapacitating qualities of airlines that are triggered by the voluntary decisions of highly professional staff. Self-incapacitation might be the main driver of safety, but only because of the way it is responsively bundled with deterrence, professionalism and social rewarding of whistleblowers.

Braithwaite (2017b) argued that civil aviation regulation responded more effectively to prevent hijacking following the 11 September 2001 attacks on New York and Washington, DC, than other regulators with responsibility for terrorism prevention. This was a replay of air safety regulation effectiveness through electronic scanning that ended the 1970s epidemic of airline hijacking.

The conclusion of many evidence-based health system designers is that one reason progress in air safety in the twentieth century was even more remarkable than progress in health care was that air safety systems were even more determinedly committed to correcting mistakes, as opposed to punishing them (Wilf-Miron et al. 2003). When a pilot does something wrong that causes a near miss or a separation error, in general, there are no sanctions for reporting this; indeed, there are professional rewards for contributing to a learning culture of air safety by confessing. Airline pilots are rewarded for triggering prevention. Cover-up, in contrast, is punished because it prevents prevention. Cover-up is also hard to do because of the ethic colleagues have of exposing error to analysis.

Healthcare collegiality has learnt from airlines to become more committed to open analysis of poor-quality diagnosis and treatment, especially when there are no consequences visible enough to threaten litigation. Nevertheless, the commitment to error reporting and analysis continues to be more total and more rigorous with air safety than with health. The cover-up of medical error remains endemic on the part of physicians and other professionals who fear acknowledging and apologising for errors that could threaten their licence or reputation. Yet a sea change is occurring in western health-quality institutions because of the empirical evidence that acknowledgement and apology for medical error do more to discourage litigation than to encourage it, reducing litigation costs by one-third (Gallagher et al. 2003). The Australian, British and US health systems are among those that are being transformed by increasingly systematic approaches to recording adverse incidents, quantitatively analysing patterns in such incidents, crafting interventions to attack the risks revealed and researching the impact of those interventions. The momentum in health care is shifting from a blame culture to a learning culture. If my analysis is right, it will assist health systems to build on the formidable record they already have of evidence-based reduction of risk (Braithwaite et al. 2007).

The trouble with criminal justice in this analysis of how health systems have learned from air safety systems is that justice systems encourage cultures of denial. The preventive imperative to tackle an underlying problem of substance abuse is not grasped because offenders and their family and friends cover up the crime and the substance addiction that drives it. The anger-management problem or the patriarchal domination that drives a pattern of violence is a truth covered up instead of discussed and confronted.

My conjecture is that we can arrange these institutions along a continuum according to how committed they are to eliminating the fear of punishment that induces cover-up. Air safety administration is the most committed to learning through errors and non-punitiveness; second is health administration and the last is criminal justice with its commitment to punitiveness. The further conjecture is that this is a reason air safety administration has made the greatest strides in safety improvement, followed by health administration and criminal justice administration in the rear, with the most dismal record of accomplishment.

Christopher Hodges (2015: 326–29) considers another possible reason for the remarkable effectiveness of British civil aviation in making air travel so safe. This is that it has been so responsive. He refers to the pyramid model from the flexible enforcement policy of the British Civil Aviation Authority (Figure 10.1).

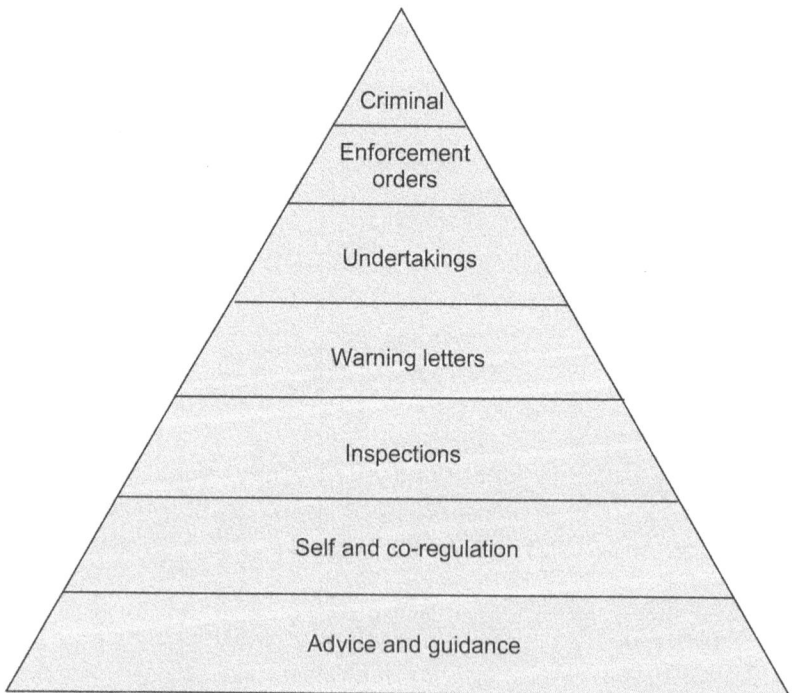

Figure 10.1 British Civil Aviation Authority responsive regulatory pyramid
Source: Hodges (2015: 326–29).

Spectrum of enforcement

Collaboration and faciliation	Advisory	Formal enforcement tools (from the CAA's overall perspective)
Day-to-day interaction with those we regulate.	Guidance to regulated parties. Verbal warnings. Using publicity to highlight issues and encourage compliance.	Prosecution Statutory demands Undertaking Suspension of license, approval etc. Variation of license,approval etc. Cessation of work On notice No fly directions License conditions Audit findings Letters before action

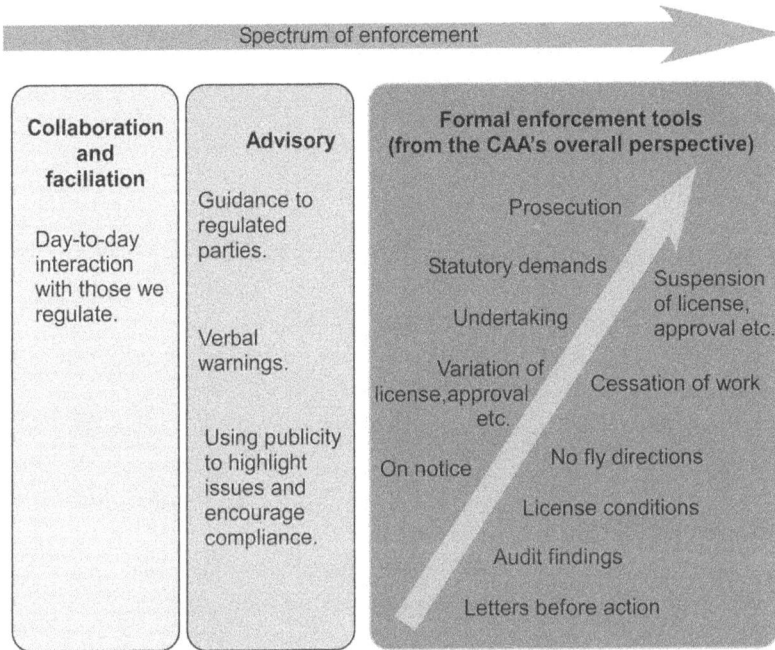

Figure 10.2 British Civil Aviation Authority responsive 'Spectrum of Enforcement'

Source: Hodges (2015: 326–29).

In addition, the British Civil Aviation Authority used the interesting diagram in Figure 10.2 for its rather responsive 'Spectrum of Enforcement'.

Hence, it is possible that civil aviation regulators, even in the poorest countries,[3] are comparatively effective in securing our safety not only because they are less captured than other kinds of regulators like financial regulators, but also because they are more responsive than financial regulators. They do use punishment, even the corporate capital punishment of licence revocation, when they must, but as a last resort. And they tend to be careful to reward confession of error, while being sharp in punishing the cover-up of recklessness. This seems plausible also because of the evidence that when financial regulators do become more responsive, they also become more effective in controlling financial crime (Choi et al. 2016; Braithwaite 2005b, 2008).

---

3   There are developing countries in which we are a hundred times more likely to be murdered than in some western countries and more than 10 times more likely to suffer sepsis if we are hospitalised. But there are no poor countries where we are 10 times more likely to die in an aircraft accident than in developed economies.

Self-incapacitation in coalmines, nuclear plants and Operation Ceasefire

Coalmines counted among the most-deadly workplaces in the history of capitalism. At the beginning of the twentieth century in both the United Kingdom and the United States, there were single years when 1,000 coalminers lost their lives to accidents—often big ones in which methane gas blew up an entire mine (Braithwaite 1985). Even more lives were lost to the occupational health disaster of black lung disease. By the later decades of the twentieth century, the US and UK were no longer leading coal exporters; Australia was by far the largest coal exporter. It produces far more coal than the UK and US did in those years when they were killing 1,000 coalminers in one year of accidents and thousands more because of black lung. But after the mid-twentieth century, black lung was almost eliminated as a cause of death among Australian coalminers. For many years in the twenty-first century in Australia, there have been zero deaths from coalmine accidents as well.[4] How was this accomplished?

Many of the health and safety reforms that accomplished this result were self-incapacitating. Modern mining machines vacuum up dust at the coalface where the coal is cut. The miners who operate and check the machine are seated in protected environments back from the coalface. Even so, if the geology or the poor maintenance of the mining machine is such that significant dust does escape from the coalface, dust detectors automatically shut the machine down. Miner safety from black lung was secured by this self-incapacitation technology of automated shutdown. Other self-incapacitating mechanisms are more social than technological. Since the nineteenth century in Australia, miners' unions enjoyed the right under mine safety law to elect full-time employee safety inspectors from among the miners at each mine. In Queensland, these union salaries were paid by the state. Before every shift, the miner-elected safety inspector

---

4   When I launched Neil Gunningham and Darren Sinclair's (2012) book on coalmine safety, I gently goaded them to be more upbeat about these long-run safety accomplishments as they pointed to so many weaknesses in contemporary Australian coalmine safety systems. Their reply was that one reason they had written the book was that the industry was becoming complacent about these safety improvements, the regulatory pressure was relaxing as a result and they believed this created a risk of older health and safety concerns returning. Sure enough, in the years immediately after the release of their book, the first major cascade of new cases of black lung disease among Australian coalminers for many decades was recorded and there were some bad fatality years in which as many as seven miners lost their lives in accidents. Gunningham and Sinclair's point proved right: when regulatory inspectors cease kicking the tyres, safety risks return.

checks the mine shaft for levels of coal dust, tests for methane in the mine and checks unsafe roof conditions. If the miner-elected safety inspector finds that the shaft fails any test, they forbid the next shift from entering. The mine owner incapacitates itself from taking any action against miners who then refuse to go in. This is another part of the self-incapacitating architecture of mine safety law. The logic is similar to the logic of air safety law that makes the pilot accountable for the lives of passengers on their flight, as opposed to some faceless bureaucrat safe at corporate headquarters. Because the captain loses their life as well if the plane goes down—just as the miner-elected safety inspectors may lose their lives if the mine explodes during their shift—the incentives for self-incapacitation are assured by this self-enforcing aspect of the regulatory architecture.

The Chernobyl incident in the Soviet Union in 1986 showed that nuclear power plant disasters are potentially far more dangerous than mine disasters, killing many thousands in that case, and potentially millions in a worst-case nuclear reactor meltdown. Luckily, Chernobyl occurred after President Mikhail Gorbachev started to open the Soviet Union to transparency and accountability. Though there were cover-ups that cost uncounted lives in the early stages of managing Chernobyl, they were less pernicious than would have happened under the domination of Gorbachev's predecessors. The openness that did ultimately prevail allowed formidable international technical assistance to pour in.

Many of the safety systems that were strengthened after the Three Mile Island disaster in the United States (in 1979) and after Chernobyl rely on the same genre of self-incapacitation logic that we saw in coalmines and air safety. 'SCRAMS'—automatic shutdowns of nuclear reactors after the reactor passes one of a number of thresholds—became more central to nuclear safety self-incapacitation. Most interestingly, SCRAMS became widely reported and an important part of the accountability architecture. In the decades immediately after Three Mile Island, SCRAMS were reduced to less than 1 per cent of what they had been in the United States and then worldwide (Braithwaite and Drahos 2000: Ch. 13). Joseph Rees (2009), a scholar in the Philip Selznick tradition of responsive and relational regulation, diagnosed the problem of the old nuclear industry as being that it put too much faith in doctrines like deterrence and a rule-bound 'autonomous law'. Rule-bound nuclear safety law meant that if the regulator saw a new problem, they wrote more rules. Because the risks were catastrophic, they were inclined to be punitive with swift and certain regulatory punishment of any infraction, however minor.

The problem this induced at the moment of crisis was that as Three Mile Island approached reactor meltdown, staff were running around covering themselves by ensuring they had complied with all of these thousands of rules instead of reflecting on the systemic wisdom they had of their nuclear safety system so they could craft a redundant strategy for trying one solution after another to steer the system to safety. Rees (2009) and the commission of inquiry into Three Mile Island became champions of shifting regulatory strategy towards taking self-regulation more seriously. This is redescribed here as a plea for enforced self-incapacitation. After lessons learned from major disasters on offshore oil rigs, the self-incapacitation learnings of Three Mile Island morphed into the 'safety case' regulatory reform movement that extended to multiple regulatory domains. For example, an oil rig would prepare a safety case based on a particularistic analysis of how the '100-year wave' in its region of the ocean was sometimes much bigger than the peak wave threat for other rigs. This demanded that it write its own distinctive set of self-regulatory rules. It would then seek the approval of the regulator for the systemic wisdom of this safety case and this set of self-regulatory rules. The operative rules would be privately written but publicly ratified. And the state could then publicly enforce them; the oil rig operator could be prosecuted criminally for failing to comply with its privately written rules.

The communitarian mechanism that Joseph Rees saw in play here was that the nuclear industry became a community of shared fate. It came to believe that if another Three Mile Island occurred, the whole industry would be shut down in the United States. Globally, after Chernobyl, the industry came to believe that another Chernobyl, and nuclear energy would end worldwide. The same German social capital and collective efficacy that delivered it a low rate of crime and a high degree of freedom post war came to the rescue of the former Soviet nuclear industry. Every nuclear power plant in the Soviet Union was twinned with the superior safety engineering team of a German nuclear plant. All manner of specialist safety staff moved back and forth between a plant in Belarus and their twin in Bavaria. This was a rather formalised collective efficacy of the community of shared fate among nuclear power producers. It worked in making the world a hundred times safer from a nuclear power disaster than it was four decades ago (Braithwaite and Drahos 2000: 297–319).

While the offshore oil and nuclear power industries saw the safety case as innovative in the 1980s and 1990s, it was actually applying old ideas from coalmine safety. Braithwaite (1982) called them enforced self-regulation—privately written, but publicly ratified and publicly enforced rules—which became part of responsive regulation (Ayres and Braithwaite 1992). Today, enforced self-incapacitation seems more apt because self-incapacitation is the conceptual driver of the safety outcome.

Let me be less abstract about how enforced self-incapacitation has worked for more than half a century in coalmine safety law. Roof falls that kill one or two miners at a time are worldwide the major cause of modern underground mine fatalities, much more so than the methane gas explosions that were the devastating killers a century ago. The problem is that the geological conditions in the roofs of all mines are radically variable and even differ in some parts of old mines dug a century ago from those in tunnels dug into newer seams. The responsive regulatory ideal is for mines to draft their own particularistic roof-control rules, sit down with their union and their mine-level safety committee, with the coalmine safety inspectors who know that mine best and with independent engineering consultants to receive critical feedback on their draft rules. Then management, with the support of the local miners' safety committee, submits the roof-control rules for that mine to the regulator, who ratifies or strengthens them. If a state inspector subsequently detects a breach of those roof-control rules, a court can uphold a criminal prosecution even if they are rules that constrain no other mine in the country. Responsive regulation argues for this approach because it encourages collective efficacy (Sampson et al. 1997) in the cause of a locally, contextually grounded systemic wisdom that combats legal cynicism (Sampson and Bartusch 1998) about the rules. Cynicism is suppressed through the collaboration in these rules being drafted together by local miners and local managers. The rules suffer less from cynicism and less from the compliance trap (Parker 2006) because they are designed outside-in rather than written inside-out (from inside the regulator to the industry outside) (Braithwaite 2005b: 156).

Even though Operation Ceasefire (see Chapter 9) has never been theorised as enforced self-incapacitation, it can be retheorised as fertile with enforced self-incapacitation insight. Consider what happens when local gangs agree to new rules (new for them) about desisting from ever firing a gun as they go about their business. Whether it is in domestic crime control or international peacekeeping, when the police subsequently raise the bar to rules about gangs actually surrendering their weapons and attending local ritual events at which their weapons are destroyed or melted into a sculpture by a local artist, these are rules written in a process that gave them local voice. If Operation Ceasefire builds local collective efficacy of which the gangs themselves are a part in this way, the program is more likely to have a large impact according to the theory of enforced self-incapacitation. The regulatory pyramid character of Operation Ceasefire, as discussed in Chapter 9, means that pyramidal escalation makes it rational for the gang to incapacitate itself. The police delegate this regulatory enforcement work to the gang because the state has made it rational for the gang to control its own members should some of them become trigger-happy.

Averting global financial crises by preventing crime

The next two sections develop an argument that, with the wisdom of hindsight, we can see how the crimes that fuelled major economic crises in the first decade of this century might have been prevented by enforced self-incapacitation of financial crime.

In the immediate aftermath of the Global Financial Crisis that spun out of control in 2008, Wall Street sought to persuade Main Street that the crisis was caused not by crime, but by forces that were difficult for anyone to control or even understand. Main Street never believed Wall Street's narrative. In retrospect, with the vast evidence we now have on the criminal conduct by banks and nonbank financial institutions that contributed to the crisis, we can say that Main Street had reason to reject Wall Street's narratives about the crisis. In an era of cynicism about democracy, this fact, and the surge of visible resistance to Wall Street narratives in the 'Occupy Wall Street' movement, was a credit to the American demos. This was especially so when the political elite of the Clinton–Bush–Obama eras and the regulatory elite, who did not want to be blamed for allowing a wave of macrocriminality, endorsed Wall Street's narratives. This drew countless gullible journalists and intellectuals into those elite narratives. It was a glorious democratic moment when the proletariat got it right and sophisticates like Alan Greenspan,[5] other gurus of the Federal Reserve and

---

5   Greenspan was the Federal Reserve chairman from 1987 to 2006. He had been perhaps the most revered financial regulator in recent American history until the crisis. Greenspan said in 2008 that he erred in not insisting on more regulatory distrust in banks: 'I made a mistake in presuming that the self-interests of organisations, specifically banks and others, were such that they were best capable of protecting their own shareholders and their equity in the firms' (Greenspan 2008).

financial regulatory agencies, Nobel Laureate economists like Robert C. Merton and current and former presidents and prime ministers of Anglo-Celtic countries were proven wrong. Years later, Greenspan was not alone among these sophisticated commentators in admitting he had erred.

Part of the false Wall Street narrative of 2008 was: 'If you were so smart about seeing the dangers in the predatory culture of Wall Street and the City of London, why were you not predicting the crash and warning people about it in 2006 and early 2007?' We now know that there were not only many who were predicting the crash, but also many who made fortunes by acting on this prediction, as popularised in the film and book *The Big Short* (Lewis 2010). It is true that this author, like most scholars of corporate crime, did not predict that a global financial crisis would peak in 2008 to push North America and Europe into recession. Yet prediction of the precise timing and precise form of the unravelling of a financial crisis is not what corporate crime scholars are supposed to be good at.

Consider the wider question of how the best financial minds think about how to make money in markets. Warren Buffett would be a candidate for the most respected and successful long-run investor in American markets. Buffett says he is not smart enough to get the timing right to sell when the market is about to crash and buy when it is about to boom. He thinks those investors who get rich through beating the market by timing bulls and bears tend to be luckier rather than smarter than those who lose money that way. Buffett conceives of the safer path to long-run wealth accumulation as having a good analysis of why particular companies will do well in the long run. Success then lies in investing in those companies, riding out the bulls and bears, holding them for the long haul and reaping the benefits of good analysis of what will be rewarding long-term investments.

Crime is like many complex phenomena that have this quality of root causes being knowable while the timing of their effects is unknowable, even chaotic. Oncologists cannot predict when you will die of cancer. They can advise that if you do not stop doing something, cancer will be more likely to kill you. Motor mechanics cannot predict how long your car will run before a defective part causes a breakdown; they can advise that if you replace that part, it will not break down for that reason. Business regulators are like Warren Buffett, oncologists and mechanics. They are quite capable of diagnosing risks that ought to be fixed and opportunities to strengthen systemic security that ought to be grasped. They have the tools to demand that these risks be seized and fixed. Prominent among them are the tools of enforced self-incapacitation.

The cynics challenge by asking whether they really have the tools, the competence and the political independence to pick weaknesses and fix them (or to pick strengths and expand them)? No-one says it is easy to be a mechanic, an oncologist or a regulator who gets it right. We can say, however, that competent mechanics, oncologists and financial regulators can make a huge difference to human flourishing. Their jobs are hard but far from pointless. To be effective, oncologists and regulators must be evidence-based in a way that allows them to detect snake oil. Regulators should not have accepted putting numbers into Robert C. Merton's models and receiving a good outcome as evidence that risk was being tamed just because his quantitative risk models had allowed the firm he advised, Long-Term Capital Management, to make stupendous profits during the four years before he won the Nobel Prize in Economics. The company crashed through massive losses the year after he won the prize. In addition to the Nobel Prize for those models, Merton was named Financial Engineer of the Year by the International Association of Financial Engineers in 1993. *Derivatives Strategy* magazine admitted Merton into its Derivatives Hall of Fame and *Risk* magazine to its Risk Hall of Fame. Robert C. Merton was no Warren Buffett.

What we know now about various influential quantitative risk models that legitimated short-term super-profits but endangered a long-term crash is that the regulators did not understand them, but also Wall Street CEOs did not understand them, nor did corporate crime scholars like me master them. The models read as credible legitimation for allowing the beautiful ride of super-profits to continue. They did not pass the test of being evidence-based. They were mathematical models premised on the assumption that behaviour in markets is economically rational. Yet one of the learnings from Keynes' (2018) general theory, as advanced before and after the Great Depression, was that markets are often driven less by rational calculation than by following the herd, by the 'animal spirits' that drive the emotions of charging bulls and retreating bears. In such a complex world, why would we not rid ourselves of regulators who trusted models that are simply untested theories—indeed, theories based on math they did not comprehend and math that does not capture rising confidence, tipping points where confidence crashes and cascades downwards along undulating nonlinear paths? We can and must replace them with regulators who, like good auto mechanics and alert consumers, kick the tyres. We need banking regulators who refuse to renew the licence of a bank that cannot provide evidence for the empirical validity of a risk model it depends on to place bets with other people's money, regulators who will not renew the licence of a bank with a risk analysis they do not understand. In the theoretical language of criminology, the good regulator will incapacitate a bank through its licensing power until the bank explains how its risk analysis works and provides the evidence for why its claims are right.

Poland was one state that did not have to recapitalise any of its banks, and was the only country in Europe that avoided recession in every year of the Global Financial Crisis: its GDP grew by 6.8 per cent in 2007, 4.8 per cent in 2008, 1.7 per cent in 2009, 3.8 per cent in 2010 and 4.4 per cent in 2011 (Pleitgen and Davies 2010; Strauss-Kahn 2010). There were various factors in this remarkable performance. One was that the prudential regulators in Poland were humble in recognising that they did not understand certain complex financial products to which fellow European banks in countries like the United Kingdom, Ireland, Iceland and Spain were becoming heavily exposed. So, they simply refused to allow their banks to become exposed to them. Dr Stanisław Kluza, then chairman of the Polish Financial Supervision Authority, had some cynicism about whether risk modelling based on assumptions that markets would be driven by rational action could provide assurance because: 'No country can feel safe when a crisis hits, regardless of the fundamentals. Emotions determine investors' behavior.'[6] Rather, what was needed was 'conservative prudential supervision performed by an integrated and independent authority'. At the top of Dr Kluza's list of the most important anti-crisis measures taken by the Polish authorities during the crisis were: prudential regulation of the Polish Financial Supervision Authority and tight cooperation of the supervisory authority with banks and their foreign owners. Kluza's learning for middling economies is: 'In a crisis, you need to rely on yourself.' Regulatory self-sufficiency means the 'quality of *supervision* at the *local* level determines the stability of the markets' (emphasis in the original). Dr Kluza advocated the old-fashioned principle of street-level responsiveness that is a recurrent theme of this book.

---

6   All quotes in this paragraph from Dr Kluza were sourced from a World Bank presentation, accessed from: siteresources.worldbank.org/FINANCIALSECTOR/Resources/Day1KluzaFinancial CrisisPanelPoland.pdf [page discontinued].

Polish financial regulators were without hubris; they adopted the view that theirs was not a financially sophisticated economy and their regulatory capacities were less developed than in big economies.[7] While it possibly made sense in the United Kingdom and the United States for regulators to license banks that traded in complex derivatives, it was more prudent for Poland to tell its banks that it would not renew their licences if they traded significantly in complex financial products that their regulators did not understand. These decisions left Poland's banks less touched by derivatives tainted with sliced and diced US subprime mortgages than those in the rest of Europe.

Many individual banks in Canada, Australia and Asia (where so many had been burnt by the 1998 Asian Financial Crisis) had a humility similar to the Polish regulators. Mark Carney, the Governor of the Bank of Canada during a crisis that Canada weathered so much better than its nearest neighbours, proved himself in his subsequent tenure until 2020 as Governor of the Bank of England to be as sophisticated as a central banker can be, yet still evinced that Polish-style humility during the crisis:

> Something I learned early on in my career in finance from a gentleman named Bob Hurst, who was then one of the partners at Goldman Sachs. Bob's rule was if something doesn't make sense, it doesn't make sense. Beneath the sort of Popeye-esque tautology was real wisdom. His point was that if someone explains something to you in finance, such as a flashy new product or why a company's valuation should be orders of magnitude higher than others in their sector and it doesn't make sense, ask the person to repeat the rationale, and if that response still doesn't make sense, you should run. (Carney 2020)

In the case of Australia, there was a high level of securitisation of housing loans by the big banks, but these were overwhelmingly Australian loans that were well-understood and prudent by world standards in 2008. In one critical precursor of the Global Financial Crisis, BNP Paribas froze

---

7   The Polish financial regulators managed risks instead of shifting them. Godziszewski and Kruszka (2013) point out that, unlike more sophisticated European banking systems, Polish banks were required to verify the incomes of those taking out loans. Godziszewski and Kruszka (2013: 33) note that '[d]espite weak labour market conditions, the number of non-performing loans did not rise sharply' during and after the crisis, and Polish banks had 'virtually no OTC [over-the-counter] derivatives'. Polish banks remained well capitalised during the crisis; none failed or required recapitalisation using public funds.

three of its funds, indicating it had no way of valuing the complex assets inside them known as collateralised debt obligations (CDOs) or packages of subprime loans.

Even at Lehman Brothers in the 2000s, there were a few prominent humble senior bankers who asserted the firm was becoming too highly leveraged into too many derivatives that were not sufficiently transparent in their relationship to complex risks in real estate markets. These people were marginalised, with their views seen as a danger to short-run profits and bonuses; in some instances, they left the organisation because no-one was listening to their pleas to temper the hubris (Phillips 2018). The most sophisticated, aggressive, bonus-driven and liberal financial markets in New York and London are the ones that are most difficult to temper. They pose the deepest global risks. Yet even within the United States there are more and less aggressive and more and less innovative and risk-taking institutions. In tempering banking power, one size cannot fit all. Responsive regulatory theory suggests that a relational species of regulation with a significant portion of restorative justice and enforced self-incapacitation can be helpful for strengthening the hand of the temperate, ethical insiders who always exist in corporate life, before they are pushed towards the door.

The crisis certainly refined our understanding of what was broken and needed a regulatory fix. But the basics of that understanding were already in place from previous crises such as the Savings and Loans scandal of the 1980s in the United States, the 'greed is good' Wall Street crash of 1987, the Asian Financial Crisis in the 1990s, the dotcom (tech-wreck) crash of Enron, WorldCom and Arthur Andersen in the United States and of Australia's biggest insurer, HIH, and Australian telecommunications corporation One.Tel, also in 2001. Indeed, learnings about the need for financial regulators to tame the 'animal spirits' as well as the rationality of markets had long been with us.

Corporate crime scholars have important professional responsibilities in macrocriminology and as public intellectuals. As one of its practitioners, I use myself as an example of failing to meet our collective responsibilities in the mid-2000s in relation to the major contribution of derivatives to the Global Financial Crisis. The US Senate's Levin–Coburn Report did a reasonable job of summarising the importance of derivatives in a cluster of causes. It concluded that the crisis was the result of 'high risk, complex financial products; undisclosed conflicts of interest; the failure of regulators, the credit rating agencies, and the market itself to rein in the excesses of Wall Street' (Permanent Subcommittee on Investigations 2011: 1).

Before the Global Financial Crisis arrived, I finished writing a book that was released at the end of 2007 called *Regulatory Capitalism: How it Works, Ideas for Making it Work Better* (Braithwaite 2008). As with this volume, I had been publishing working papers from which *Regulatory Capitalism* was compiled for a decade. There was no great originality in the way the book used the work of Frank Partnoy (1997, 2000, 2003) and other scholars to lament the way derivatives were being used to financially engineer firms around all manner of regulatory restraints.

I discussed this aspect of the book at a meeting of the Law and Society Association in Berlin in May 2007. This was nine months before the British Government announced its 'temporary' nationalisation of Northern Rock and 16 months before Lehman Brothers filed for bankruptcy. The session was well attended by many of the brightest and best regulatory scholars. There were great social scientists and great lawyers in the audience who were not regulatory scholars. They are not named for fear of implying that they share my culpability for failing to make a better contribution to crisis prevention. I do name the distinguished Australian securities lawyer Professor Peta Spender. She asked the right question and I gave the wrong answer. Peta responded to the presentation by saying that financial regulatory experts mostly agreed with me that unregulated derivatives were a desperate systemic risk. The challenge was how to write rules that could effectively regulate something whose reason for existence was to cleverly bypass rules. So far, this was proving beyond us. So, inquired Peta Spender, what are your thoughts on how we would rise to that challenge? My weak answer was that however difficult it is to meet the challenge of regulating derivatives that we do not fully understand, we must do so. Unfortunately, I was not smart enough, certainly not as smart as Peta Spender, in her capacity to contribute to that. We needed to bring together those with the best regulatory minds who have the best understanding of the intricacies of derivatives to do so. What was wrong with that answer?

The problem was I failed to add: 'And until we succeed in rising to that regulatory drafting challenge, where regulators do not understand the derivatives trading risks of a particular financial institution, states should decline to renew the licence of that institution.' That was the critical thing that regulators in the United States, the United Kingdom, Ireland and other countries failed to do. And it was what regulators in Poland did do. There would have been no brilliant insight in adding that to my answer because, as I spoke, prudential regulators in many countries such as Poland were indeed saying to their banks:

> You say the most sophisticated regulators in New York and London are allowing financial institutions to trade in these kinds of complex financial products. I say I may not be as smart as them because I don't understand the systemic risks such trading might pose to our banks. So, until you can explain to me in ways I can understand that they do not pose systemic risks, I am not going to allow you to trade in them (or I am going to suspend a decision to renew your banking licence until I can see you have a plan to actively reduce your exposure to them).

This is no different from what we regulatory scholars expect of an occupational health and safety regulator responsible for the safety of workers on an offshore oil rig:

> I will not allow production to proceed until you can provide me with a safety case that explains the oceanographic evidence of large-wave risks in this part of the ocean in ways I can understand. Prove to me why this rig can survive the 100-year wave.

Not only were there regulators in many countries like Poland that did not have any banks collapse during the Global Financial Crisis who messaged in this way; but also, worldwide, there were CEOs of many financial institutions who were as close to New York as Toronto and who said to their traders that they were not going to allow trading in major ways in derivatives whose risks they could not comprehend.

My responsibility as a regulatory scholar in the historical moment of the mid-2000s should likewise have been to consistently message in that way. I should never have missed the opportunity to say that the job of the state is to only renew banking licences when its regulators understand the risks its banks are running with the economic security of their nation. I was persistently failing to do that—and not just in Berlin in May 2007. When I later shared this self-criticism with two distinguished regulatory scholars who had been in the audience in Berlin, using the example of the virtuous incapacitation of reckless derivatives trading by Polish banking regulators, one answered in the following way. Yes, the Polish banking regulators did the right things by their economy and the British regulators did the wrong thing. But the British regulators had to survive in an environment in which their political leaders expected 'light-touch' regulation that was making the financial sector the lifeblood of the British economy. Banks were not the lifeblood of the Polish economy in quite that way. My answer was bank profits are still far from unimportant to the Polish economy, and therefore to Polish politics. But more fundamentally, a criticism of that response is that it allows us in the regulatory scholarly community to excuse something we should not excuse.

In any economy, a prudential regulator's job is to assess prudential risks. If they felt political pressures put them in a position with no choice but to sanction risks they did not understand, they should have resigned for that reason, putting the pressure back on the politicians. Regulators move on quietly more frequently than people think because they feel they are being put under commercial pressures mediated through their political masters. Such resignations help if rumours spread about the reasons for their quiet resignations. It helps more when they make public that they are resigning because they are not able to refuse to renew licences to financial institutions that are taking risks the regulator cannot be assured are prudent. Our role as regulatory scholars is to help create a climate of conversation around systemic risks that pressure regulators in an untenable political position to resign if they cannot do their job, and to give that political untenability as the reason. After all, most top financial regulators can make more money and enjoy a less stressful life by resigning. In the case of the Global Financial Crisis, the regulatory scholarly community was too sympathetic to the difficult position of the regulators during the era of 'light touch', both prospectively and retrospectively.

And we did not do enough to honour the calls made by the humbler Polish regulators. What was the regulatory instrument deployed by the Polish regulators? It was incapacitation. The Polish banks were incapacitated from reckless derivatives trading. And at the firm level, all the major Australian banks and most banks from Canada and many countries across Asia incapacitated themselves (self-incapacitation) from reckless derivatives trading.

Most of the world's financial institutions proved sufficiently prudent to survive the great shock that washed across from the United States in 2008, as did most financial institutions within the United States itself. While financial institutions and regulators alike around the world learnt that they needed deeper capital reserves for the future than in the past, most did have adequate reserves to survive the years immediately after 2007, though in some cases that was only because their state treasuries stood behind them as banks that were 'too big to fail'. Most CEOs of financial institutions had sufficiently constrained their traders from exposing the firm to risks they did not understand from complex financial products. In many countries, this CEO prudence was nurtured by insistence on prudence from regulators who demanded from those firms risk analyses that the regulator could understand. The next section argues that this was enforced self-incapacitation of financial fraud.

If we look at a map of the countries around the world that entered the deepest recession in 2009 as a result of the crisis, we see that while almost every economy in North America and Europe (Poland being the only significant exception) was in recession in 2009, most economies everywhere else in the world were not, including financially dominant economies like China and financially sophisticated economies like Japan, South Korea and Australia.[8] This included the BRICS (Brazil, Russia, India, China and South Africa) economies and other major G20 economies. These economies—particularly but not only China—kept the world economy pumping and prevented it from plumbing the depths of the 1930s depression. There were only 60 notable financial institutions around the world that failed during the crisis, the overwhelming majority of them from the Anglo economies, where the worst bonus culture of short-termism had taken hold, and only one of these was in Asia, the Philippine American Life and General Insurance Company.

My conclusion here is that the preventability of catastrophic financial crime through enforced self-incapacitation delivered by markets in banking virtue was everywhere to be seen. North Atlantic criminologists were blind to this and learnt no lessons from it.

A second self-incapacitation lesson is about seeing the glass half-full in crisis prevention. As I write, the Covid crisis rages. In Australia, no fewer than 80 per cent of Covid deaths in 2020 have occurred in aged care facilities. Yet 95 per cent of aged care homes have had zero infections among their high-vulnerability residents. All the expert regulatory diagnoses have been that what the 95 per cent were doing right was investing in infection-control protocols and infection-control professionalism. The protocols were forms of self-incapacitation, which included physical forms of incapacitating contact with Covid through

---

8   'Financial Crisis of 2007–2008.' *Wikipedia*. Available from: en.wikipedia.org/wiki/Financial_crisis_of_2007%E2%80%9308#/media/File:GDP_Real_Growth.svg.

masks, gowns and channelling movement around the institution to accomplish segregation. It was not rocket science; nor was it state incapacitation because, shockingly, many inspectors remained at home because their agency decided it was too hazardous for them to venture into aged care facilities! A Royal Commission into Aged Care concluded that, what was needed for the lawbreaking 5 per cent who were failing to meet their regulatory obligations to mobilise their infection-control committee during an epidemic was an inspector reminding them of their legal obligations under the infection-control standards for aged care facilities. Regulation and self-incapacitation may matter more in contexts that permit reframing the preventive behaviour of banks and aged care facilities as glasses 95 per cent full, rather than just half-full.

Incapacitation lessons from financial crises

The Global Financial Crisis seemed at the time to be an unmitigated global catastrophe, but in fact it was contained because Asia in particular had learned self-incapacitation lessons from the Asian Financial Crisis a decade earlier. Economies like Indonesia and Australia that had some problems with collapsing banks and insurers in the late twentieth century have had no bankruptcies of major financial institutions during the past two decades (Braithwaite 2019). Even within North America and Europe, the glass was far more than half-full because most financial institutions remained solvent. In a comparison of which banks around the world did and did not face solvency problems during the crisis, Beltratti and Stulz (2009: 1) concluded:

> Banks in countries with stricter capital requirement regulations and with more independent supervisors performed better ... After accounting for country fixed effects, banks with more loans and more liquid assets performed better during the month following the Lehman bankruptcy, and so did banks from countries with stronger capital supervision and more restrictions on bank activities.

Their results, however, did find that bank-level variables explained more variance than state-level regulatory variables, though not in the way predicted by the conventional wisdom of 'shareholder-friendly' governance. Beltratti and Stulz's (2009) results from 231 financial institutions with assets of more than US$10 billion in 2006 do not support the conclusion that financial institutions with 'good governance'—in the neoliberal sense of institutionalised responsiveness to shareholders—performed better. Quite the reverse:

> An OECD report argues that 'the financial crisis can be to an important extent attributed to failures and weaknesses in corporate governance arrangements' (Kirkpatrick 2008). We find no evidence supportive of such a statement in our data. There is no evidence that banks with better governance, when governance is measured with data used in the well-known Corporate Governance Quotient (CGQ score) perform better during the crisis. Strikingly, banks with more pro-shareholder boards performed worse during the crisis. Such a result does not mean that good governance is bad. Rather, it is consistent with the view that banks that were pushed by their boards to maximize shareholder wealth before the crisis took risks that were understood to create shareholder wealth, but were costly ex post because of outcomes that were not expected when the risks were taken. (Beltratti and Stulz 2009: 2–3)

Responsiveness to shareholder and trader short-termism turned out to be a market in vice (Chapter 7). Good regulators steered this to a market in virtue through measures that relied on incapacitation. That market in virtue was responsive to long-term shareholder interests and to taming the systemic risks of the national economic system that supplied the oxygen without which their bank could not keep breathing. Good regulators incapacitated their banks from exposure to complex financial products whose risks they did not understand. Good bank CEOs self-incapacitated their banks and their traders from exposure to derivatives vulnerable to bad American housing loans.[9] Beltratti and Stulz's (2009) research suggests that one reason for such effective private self-incapacitation was the public incapacitation of banks by regulators.

---

9   Commonwealth Bank of Australia Director Harrison Young expressed caution about the excessive reliance on poorly understood risk models that fuelled the Global Financial Crisis as follows: 'A potential message people might take from the stream of scholarly papers flowing out of Basel is that a competent bank can *measure* the risk the enterprise as a whole is taking. In my view, it cannot. If you are looking at a single line of business, and you have good data, it is possible to build a model that tells you the probability distribution of outcomes. But risks interact. Credit losses kill a bank because of their impact on liquidity. Operational failures damage reputation. Building a model that accurately reflects the probability of such chain reactions among multiple businesses is impossible. To be clear, banks can and do, through an *ad hoc* mixture of quantitative analysis and common sense, get their arms around the risks they are running. Stress tests and scenario exercises help a board and senior management explore hidden linkages and transmission mechanisms. Most of all, they are a vehicle for discussion, which is the best way to pool experience and refine judgment.' (Accessed from: www.ethics.org.au/on-ethics/our-articles/may-2015/this-com-bank-board-member-thinks-all-aussie-banks [page discontinued]).

Years earlier, American regulators should have done a better job of managing the expansion of residential housing credit to avert a mid-decade real estate bubble. That macroeconomic mistake having been made, its consequences need not have been so disastrous had the easy credit been withheld from borrowers who made fraudulent claims about their ability to repay loans. Citigroup's Richard M. Bowen testified before the US Financial Crisis Inquiry Commission that, by 2006, 60 per cent of mortgages purchased by Citibank from 1,600 different mortgage companies were 'defective' (not underwritten to policy or did not contain all policy-required documents) and, by 2007, 'defective mortgages (from mortgage originators contractually bound to perform underwriting to Citi's standards) increased … to over 80% of production' (FCIC 2010). In its testimony to the same commission, Clayton Holdings—the largest residential loan due diligence and securitisation surveillance company in the United States and Europe—testified that its review of more than 900,000 mortgages issued from January 2006 to June 2007 found that only 54 per cent of the loans met their originators' underwriting standards. Clayton's analysis further showed that 39 per cent of the loans that did not meet *any* issuer's minimal underwriting standards were subsequently securitised and sold to investors (Morgenson 2010; The New York Times 2010).

Knowledge of this epidemic of dud loans was not limited to corporate insiders like Clayton and Citibank. A 2006 report by the US federal Financial Crimes Enforcement Network showed a 1,411 per cent increase in mortgage-related suspicious activity reports between 1997 and 2005, 66 per cent of them involving material misrepresentation or false documents. There was a further 44 per cent increase between 2005 and 2006 (Nguyen and Pontell 2010). BasePoint Analytics' (2007) work on 3 million loans suggested 70 per cent of early payment defaults had fraudulent misrepresentations on their original loan applications. The fraudulent loans were five times as likely to go into default (Nguyen and Pontell 2010). There were public warnings from the FBI starting in 2004 that they were seeing a spike in mortgage fraud (Black 2005).

As with the reporting by FBI agents of the suspicious behaviour of Al-Qaeda operatives who wanted to learn how to fly a plane but not how to land it, local FBI agents did their job in detecting the tidal wave of mortgage fraud that was the proximate cause of the Global Financial Crisis. In both cases, the FBI as an institution failed in its macrocriminological imagination. Instead of seeing the suspicious flight training as an opportunity to prevent the macro-disaster of the 9/11 attacks, FBI leaders constrained by a micro-imagination could not see how this intelligence could lead to the conviction of individuals. Their regulatory imagination in 2001 was focused on individual deterrence rather than preventive incapacitation of Al-Qaeda as a criminal organisation. In 2004, their intelligence on 'liar loans' in which mortgage brokers and local banks encouraged people to misrepresent their financial circumstances was read as evidence of minor criminality for which conviction would be difficult because the borrower of fraudulent loans could blame the bank for the misrepresentations. The bank could blame the borrower or broker.

With the onset of America's two greatest crises of the twenty-first century before Covid-19, the FBI should have connected the dots of systemic risk to physical security (with 9/11) and financial security (with the mortgage fraud epidemic). The FBI in the 2000s should have initiated a dialogue with banking regulators on the need for incapacitation, as opposed to a prosecutorial approach. This could have involved regulators meeting one by one in 2004 with the banks that had the worst incidence of loan defaults in their city or state. Regulators could have required them to demonstrate that their loan portfolios were not infested with fraud. When bank self-investigation reports found in most cases that they were riddled with fraud, the bank could have been required to craft a plan to prevent the issuance of further fraudulent loans and a management plan to regularise as many current dubious loans as possible. Instead of doing that, what banks did was slice and dice their bad loans into securitised financial products that were then sold on to other financial institutions in the United States and Europe, globally diffusing systemic risk. Because regulators allowed them to pass the parcel, banks shifted their risks on to other banks instead of managing that risk. This regulatory failure created a risk-shifting culture that was a systemically devastating cascade of risk. One aim of a self-incapacitation approach to enforcement is a step back from risk-shifting to risk management.

Prosecutions after the event of individuals who assisted with the 9/11 attacks on New York and Washington, DC, contribute little—probably nothing—to deterring future terrorism. Prosecutions after the event of little local bankers, brokers and borrowers for mortgage fraud contribute little to deterring the next financial crisis. Incapacitation before the event rather than deterrence after the event was the remedy a macrocriminological imagination should have inspired. Criminologists can learn to see war (Chapter 11) and mass unemployment (Chapter 4) as crime-prevention challenges. Preventive incapacitation is the most crucial macrocriminological response required. President Obama repeatedly made the same point following mass murders with automatic weapons. Prosecution of those responsible will do little to prevent the next mass gun murder. More promising are incapacitation strategies to get automatic weapons out of people's hands across the society, as Canada, Australia, New Zealand and the United Kingdom have adopted after mass killings.

This is preventive incapacitation in making it physically difficult for a potential offender to hijack an aircraft, slice and dice fraudulent loans or acquire automatic weapons. Sometimes it is possible to incapacitate terrorists, criminal bankers and potential mass shooters by putting them in prison. That only incapacitates a horse that has already bolted. With the kind of corporate crime that was a proximate cause of the Global Financial Crisis, the regulatory incapacitation that counted was the kind that Polish regulators deployed. It involved regulators signalling to banks that if they were considering increasing their exposure to complex financial products involving bad loans—the effects of which were not clearly understood—think again. To go down that track could jeopardise their banking licence. The licensing power—licence deferral, suspension or qualification—was the decisive tool for motivating self-incapacitation. This is not to say that regulatory threats achieved these outcomes; rather, they were accomplished by regulatory conversations implicitly backed by licensing powers.

The more important lesson from the Global Financial Crisis is that corporate self-incapacitation was more effective still than state incapacitation. Australian, and most Canadian, bank CEOs did not need a regulatory conversation or a threat to their licence to incapacitate their traders from the excesses of exposure to derivatives they did not comprehend. They voluntarily constrained themselves from such exposure because they prioritised the long-run solvency of their banks above the short-term profits delinquent derivatives traders could deliver until late 2007.

Likewise, the self-regulation of mosques can contribute more to the incapacitation of young members of that mosque contemplating terrorism than can prisons that might preventively detain them (Wardak 2018). One reason is that the mosque can communicate restoratively to a whole network to incapacitate its violence; a prosecution targets just one or two members of that network and tends to engender defiance effects that result in the replacement of those arrested. Likewise, an Operation Ceasefire that enrols gang leaders to the project of incapacitating gang members from using guns can contribute greatly to reducing gun homicide. Operation

Ceasefire is not interpreted by its authors as a macrocriminological insight into incapacitation. A contribution of this book is to so reframe it. According to a macrocriminological imagination, prison is an institution that makes a very small contribution to incapacitation. Incapacitation by nonstate organisations to eschew crooked loans or incomprehensible derivatives, to disarm gang members or to disable terrorist hijacker training has more preventive promise.

In the history of regulation, from Lloyd's of London insisting that ships not be allowed to sail if they were loaded above the Plimsoll line painted around the hull to the New York Stock Exchange rejecting corporations for listing if they had no external auditor, and later a board audit committee with a majority of outside directors, regulation by private organisations often laid down regulatory policies that were later mandated by states (Braithwaite and Drahos 2000). This empirical finding was that the globalisation of self-incapacitation by many self-monitoring techniques like Lloyd's Plimsoll line preceded the globalisation of state laws to require such forms of self-incapacitation.

At the same time, it is naive in the extreme to hope that all mosques, all gangs and all banks will voluntarily opt for self-incapacitation. They sometimes need to be threatened with state incapacitation—closure of the bank, arrest of its terrorist leadership, imprisonment of the gang's leadership—to motivate the softer path of self-incapacitation. This is where the responsive regulatory pyramid has an important insight to offer.

Nevertheless, this chapter's diagnosis of the Global Financial Crisis as being, in part, a macrocriminological challenge implies a new way of thinking about the place of incapacitation in a responsive regulatory pyramid.

In the past, I always placed incapacitation above deterrence in the pyramid. There is something to this insight. If a doctor persists in defrauding Medicare, in prescribing dangerously, in treating patients who have conditions they are not qualified to treat, after a sequence of educative and deterrent regulatory engagements with the doctor, their licence to practice medicine should be threatened. This incapacitates them from all these professional abuses. For a bank that persists in fraudulent conduct, after courts have failed and failed again to deter the fraud with successive criminal convictions, corporate capital punishment is an incapacitating option—revoking its banking licence. For a domestic violence offender too livid with 'righteous rage' to be deterred, it may be necessary to incapacitate him in prison.

The macrocriminological insight of this chapter is that for many well-designed regulatory pyramids for responding to crime problems, organisational self-incapacitation will appear lower in the pyramid than deterrence. Then state incapacitation may come higher in the pyramid as an ultimate sanction (as in Figure 10.3). Figure 10.3 is no more than illustrative of a possible pyramid. State bailout and forced acquisition of bank shares, as the United Kingdom and Germany imposed during the Global Financial Crisis, might be a better option than closing a bank at the peak of the pyramid.

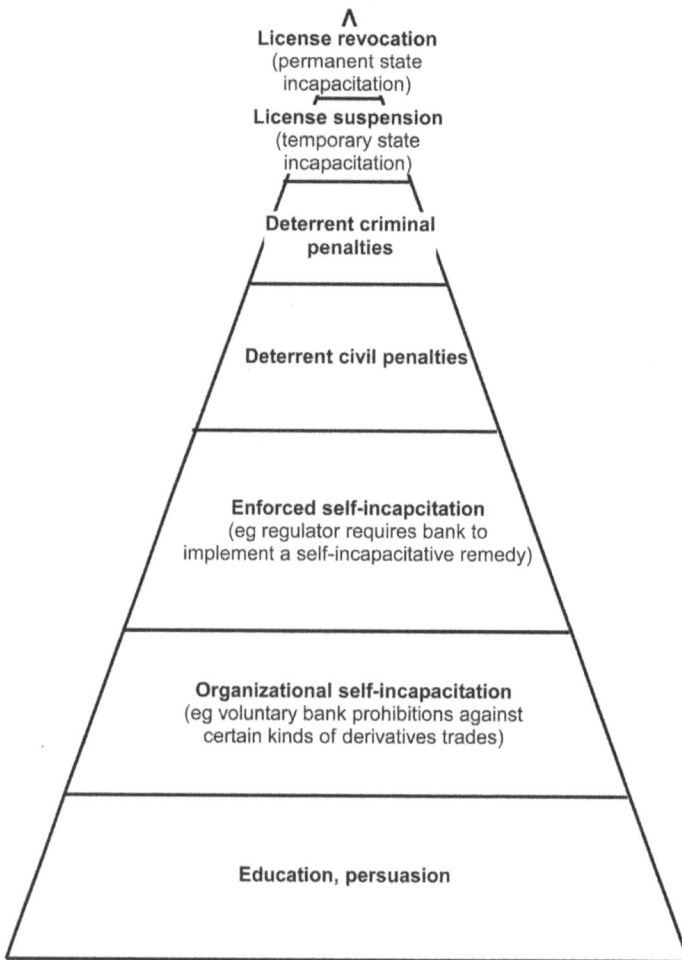

Figure 10.3 One possible responsive incapacitation pyramid

The power and limits of corporate enforced self-incapacitation

Across observations at hundreds of aged care homes, it is clear that a small proportion of the regulatory work is done by government inspectors (Braithwaite et al. 2007). Relatives and friends, or the residents themselves, complaining to management are more common forms of effective regulation than inspectors. Management complaining to staff, or one staff member horizontally tapping another on the shoulder, is more common still when someone is seen not fulfilling some obligation to residents.

Notwithstanding the catalytic power of inspectors arriving at the site and of infrequent court cases, the main game of standards improvement includes nursing home self-inspection, informal peer review and consumer complaints that trigger a self-regulatory response. Indeed, this is true of most or all domains of regulation. Government inspectors never have the budgets to be a greater regulatory presence than internal corporate self-regulators. Seung-Hun Hong (2016) has brilliantly developed the theory of indirect reciprocity. He shows that even though direct regulatory inspections by the state are infrequent, firms have reason to care that their responsiveness to other regulators, to consumer complaints, to self-regulatory complaints and to complaints from their own staff matter. The indirect responsiveness matters because it helps to build a reputation for responsiveness that is visible to inspectors on the rare occasions when they do arrive to kick the tyres. Seung-Hun Hong's theory of indirect reciprocity is about the way regulators are responsive not so much to how firms respond to iterated encounters with the regulator itself, as to how firms have been responsive to other parties, including internal self-regulatory parties, in meeting their obligations. In other words, the reputation of the firm for responsiveness to its obligations in interactions with many parties is more important than its iterated responsiveness to the regulator itself. These insights draw on the theory of indirect reciprocity in the natural sciences (Berger 2011; Braithwaite and Hong 2015).

It follows that the art of regulation is the art of steering self-enforcement. In addition, it is the art of responding with state enforcement to self-enforcement weakness that becomes visible to the state. The theory of restorative justice with youth crime is likewise about the idea that the police do little of the direct steering of young people away from crime (Karstedt-Henke and Crasmoller 1991; Braithwaite 2002: 116–20).

Rather, their important role is guiding the more iterated forms of steering with which families, peers, neighbours and schools regulate young people every day of their lives. They are the actors 'in the know' about matters unknown to the state.

With corporate crime, this means that a crucial strategy is deferred prosecutions during which corporate integrity agreements or enforceable undertakings are negotiated between the regulator and the firm. While this is true in theory, in practice, these agreements often follow standard templates and are feebly and ritualistically implemented and inadequately followed up by the regulator to remedy such ritualism (Chapter 9). Responsive regulation's remedy to this ritualism is to embed any corporate risk analysis within a pyramid of escalated state and nonstate networked accountabilities (Braithwaite 2008). Within responsive regulation, self-regulation is never totally voluntary as it is enforced and called to account by the prospect of escalation up the pyramid.

John J. McCloy's (1976) report into the pattern of foreign bribery indulged in by executives of the Gulf Oil corporation in the 1970s first provoked policy thinking about self-investigation reports by outside counsel (Coffee 1981; Fisse and Braithwaite 1983; Gruner 1988). Some Australian experiments with self-investigation and self-incapacitation in competition and consumer protection law enforcement did begin to show McCloy-style promise decades ago (Fisse and Braithwaite 1993; Parker 2004). Often, they involved disciplining culpable officers, restructuring of management, compensation of victims and, in some cases, leadership of trade associations and industry-wide leadership for improved corporate social responsibility. At their best, they saw companies transforming their cultures, their policies, their compliance systems and their willingness to take consumer protection to new levels of excellence. In some of these cases, the corporate compliance innovations helped inform law reform. By taking industry standards up through a new ceiling, emerging industry leaders sometimes helped drag the standards of laggards up towards them. Clever regulators in some places and times have latched on to the opportunity in this dynamic to ratchet up standards. John Mikler's (2009) *Greening the Car Industry* showed that Japanese regulators outperformed European and American regulation of automobile fuel efficiency, even though US regulation had tougher rules and was more prosecutorial. The Japanese regulatory accomplishment was delivered by requiring manufacturers to jump over the new bar set by any other Japanese auto maker that invented an improved technology for fuel efficiency. The less innovative auto makers were encouraged to invent their own even better technology to raise the bar further, but if they could not, they might have to pay to license their competitors' improved fuel efficiency technology.

Over time, self-incapacitation edge and innovation were lost in the United States with corporate integrity agreements (Ford and Hess 2009, 2011), and in Australia, with the spread of enforceable undertakings settled with companies in antitrust, consumer and environmental protection, securities fraud and occupational health and safety. Enforceable undertakings have become routinised in Australian business regulation, templated by compliance practitioners who take clients in trouble with a regulator through hoops to be jumped ritualistically. Part of the problem has been an absence of third parties in the process insisting that it be more demanding in taking self-incapacitation up through new ceilings of innovation. This is a theme re-joined in the final chapter, where we consider the need for the institutionalisation of distrust to be complemented by an active democratic politics, an agonistic politics (Mouffe 2013, 2018) of distrust. Environmental groups have been little involved in the meetings at which enforceable undertakings for environmental offences have been agreed, to consider just one example of truncated contestation. An innovative, continuously improving, networked imaginary of self-incapacitation is still a long way off in Australia and every country.

Notwithstanding these reservations, the previous chapter discussed some evidence suggesting that Spalding (2015) may be right that restorative justice can be a meaningful way of reconceptualising deferred prosecutions. Moreover, this may be about dialogue that leads to agreement with regulators on corporate self-incapacitation more than on self-deterrence (as by voluntarily paying fines). The final sections of Chapter 9 showed that it is common for deferred prosecution agreements to require companies to appoint a chief compliance officer, to supply personnel to new corporate compliance systems and policies, to transform corporate governance in major ways, to remove certain top managers from their positions and to appoint independent monitors approved by the prosecutor to oversee these self-incapacitation reforms.

Further, Chapter 9 argued that independent monitors should provide monitoring reports on a publicly accessible website. All this chapter does is slightly reinterpret Brandon Garrett's (2007) calls for 'structural reform deferred prosecutions' as self-incapacitation reforms aimed at deep governance transformation. Rituals of comfort to placate anger on Main

Street fail to deliver this. In other cases, deferred prosecution works in preventing crime through deep governance reforms. One of the reasons Stanley Sporkin said to Brent Fisse and me that *Fortune 500* companies went along with his voluntary disclosure program on foreign bribery was the dawning realisation that off-books accounts to pay bribes were also slush funds used by the criminals they bred to rip off their own company. More research is needed to explore these synergies.

Cosmopolitan collective efficacy

In making links between the dynamic concentration of deterrence (Chapter 9), enforced self-incapacitation, Operation Ceasefire in Boston and peacekeeping in Congo, this book seeks to catalyse the criminological imagination towards a more cosmopolitan vision of collective efficacy. We take this a step further in the next chapter on the contribution collective efficacy makes to the project of jointly preventing crime and war.

A staple of cynicism about the impossibility of controlling the high crimes of financial capital is the fact that global banks have a coherence in their law-evasion strategies that is international while regulators have only national coherence. Most regulators inhabit a national jurisdiction, a national regulatory mission and a national regulatory imagination even when the problem is global. There is no inevitability about this. In the regulation of epidemics, the best national health regulators in all countries have a global regulatory imagination; especially before a virus first arrives on their shores, their strategies are oriented as much to containing the international as to the national spread of epidemics. The regulation of violence (as discussed in the next chapter)—indeed, of many forms of lawbreaking—can be more effective with a more cosmopolitan regulatory imagination in which enforced self-incapacitation is a fundamental strategy for the global diffusion of regulation.

The preventive potential of cosmopolitanism will be illustrated with examples of how Australian cosmopolitanism might have prevented northern hemisphere catastrophes (only because that is where my experience resides). We have already seen how the enforced self-incapacitation of the Gulf Oil report of John J. McCloy incapacitated bribery in many countries. In Chapter 6, we saw how a similar self-investigation report incapacitated bribery rings that included heads of state and defence ministers, including Prime Minister Tanaka of Japan, who lost their jobs as a result. Now the chapter illustrates how Australian regulators might have prevented the criminality of Enron and other companies that collapsed in the dotcom crash of 2001. Then it shows how Australian alarm bells about dirty-money banks might have prevented crooked bank scandals that destabilised the governments of Australia's North Atlantic allies. Finally, it returns to the Gulf of Mexico to show how Australian regulators could have prevented the Deepwater Horizon disaster.

Arthur Andersen

Braithwaite (2005a) argued that the collapse of Enron and WorldCom, as well as of major Australian corporations audited by Arthur Andersen, might have been prevented by the Australian Taxation Office (ATO). How? When Arthur Andersen's partners came to senior ATO officials in the 1990s to apologise for the conduct of a 'rogue partner' who had enabled serious tax fraud, that was the time to sit in the restorative circle with the firm's senior partners to discuss the culture of compliance and business integrity within Arthur Andersen. It would have been revealed that the 'rogue partner' was not a rogue partner at all, but in fact manifested the core culture of Arthur Andersen. The 'rogue partner' would have defended themselves by explaining this was what they were trained and expected to do. Some of their friends within the firm might have supported them in this. Perhaps, more importantly, some retired old hand who had mentored the 'rogue partner' could be brought into the restorative circle by that partner as a supporter. They might argue in the process of supporting the rogue partner that the compliance culture at Arthur Andersen had changed for the worse (which it definitely had). The idea is that this might have triggered agreement in the regulatory circle for a thorough internal investigation into the compliance culture of Arthur Andersen conducted by outside counsel, akin to what John J. McCloy did two decades earlier with bribery in the oil industry. This in turn might have caused Arthur Andersen to meet its legal obligations as a gatekeeper to the fraudulent accounting of companies like Enron that crashed some years later. It might have averted the bankruptcy of Arthur Andersen itself because of the criminal prosecution targeting its accounting practices at Enron and other US corporations.

Because what restorative justice does in this circumstance is hold off on a national criminal prosecution in return for a voluntary corporate self-investigation report that recommends effective reforms for self-incapacitating future crimes by the organisation globally, the cosmopolitan regulator does something of greater moment than a narrowly national prosecution. It does this by inviting a wayward organisation to reform itself globally, as the regulator hangs national punishment over the company's head. Corporate leaders in the United States tend to leave an Australian criminal case to its Australian lawyers and management, but the worldwide report of an outside counsel into patterns of corporate criminality across jurisdictions, triggered in Australia, causes leaders in the United States to sit up and take notice. Hopefully, the outside counsel would also send a copy of their report to the US Securities and Exchange Commission. Australia had early warning of the criminal turn in the corporate culture of Arthur Andersen. One hope is that in future regulatory cultures that are more cosmopolitan, this might force the hand of US regulators to prevent a similar catastrophe. Not every outside counsel is as gifted and gilded with political aura as John J. McCloy in the Gulf Oil case. On the other hand, cases with this global importance are opportunities for leaders with the stature of McCloy to leave another legacy in their retirement years to make the world a better place.

Nugan Hand Bank, to BCCI, to Iran–Contra, to nuclear weapons proliferation

Likewise, Fisse and Braithwaite (1993) argued that the Bank of Credit and Commerce International (BCCI) was a case where regulators in many countries, probably including Australia, could have acted preventively. In many places around the world, criminal cases were launched against the bank for a wide variety of commercial offences. Each of these national cases created an opportunity for regulatory cosmopolitanism. BCCI is remembered by the CIA as the 'Bank of Crooks and Criminals International' (Passas 1997). They should know. The CIA used the London-based bank extensively. By some measures the seventh-largest bank in the world, BCCI had the greatest part of its real banking in London. In the end, the bank destabilised the government of UK Prime Minister John Major, pushing large numbers of British businesses into bankruptcy, when US$15 billion disappeared.

As it cultivated the bank, the CIA was insistent that mergers of American banks with BCCI and the investment of Bank of America in BCCI be reversed, but the CIA allowed its allies to carry the financial can. Two of the top-four shareholders in BCCI were the former head of Saudi intelligence and the Sheik of Abu Dhabi (in the United Arab Emirates). White House staffer Oliver North used BCCI for the Iran–Contra deal— as did Manuel Noriega, Saddam Hussein, Colombian cocaine cartels, Syrian gun runners, Palestinian terrorists, the Afghan opium trade, the Afghan Mujahideen and Osama Bin Laden. What the CIA may not have known was that BCCI financed the purchase of illegal US materials for the Pakistan Atomic Energy Commission. Or perhaps when the CIA did get to know this in an era when Pakistan was developing nuclear weapons and refusing to eschew first use of them against India, BCCI was allowed to crash.[10]

Australia should have been alert to the regulatory dangers of BCCI to the global financial system because it had hosted the allegedly CIA-sponsored dirty-money predecessor of BCCI, the Nugan Hand Bank. It was much smaller than BCCI, but it caused reputable Australian investors to lose a lot of money when it crashed in 1980. One principal of Nugan Hand, Michael Hand, disappeared after he and other bank employees were indicted for destruction of bank records. The other principal, Frank Nugan, was found with a self-inflicted gunshot wound to the head on a remote dirt track. His body was surrounded by the footprints of other men, leading police to speculate that he had been given an opportunity to shoot himself or suffer a more unpleasant end. A good vehicle of cosmopolitan incapacitation would have been an independent Australian royal commission into drug money, weapons smuggling and dirty-money banks, jointly into Nugan Hand after it collapsed and BCCI, as its successor in this market in vice, before BCCI reached the peak of its criminality. Commission findings could have caused international regulators to incapacitate BCCI in their countries before the Bank of Crooks and Criminals International did more damage.

Nugan Hand and BCCI might have been convenient for the CIA, but creating banks that specialised in dirty money was a deeply dangerous idea that cosmopolitan regulation should have mobilised to end. The sad

---

10 During the Cold War, Pakistan had been more aligned with the United States, and India more with the Soviet Union. After Pakistan acquired nuclear weapons in dangerous circumstances, India and the United States became more closely aligned. Pakistan's nuclear program carried a high risk of an actual nuclear exchange that could tip the global climate. Its nuclear weapons were designed to be mobile, driven around Pakistan's highways, and therefore vulnerable to capture by the terrorist groups that were plentiful in Pakistan. Western intelligence also suggested that Pakistan discussed renting these weapons to fellow Muslim states, in the event they were to confront a showdown with nuclear-armed Israel.

sequel to their historical contribution is that, four decades on, a larger proportion of the most reputable banks in the world are criminalised in the twenty-first century than was the case in the twentieth century. BCCI showed mainstream banks how much money could be made by moving dirty money around the globe. Many 'reputable' banks, including some in Australia, were enticed by the lure of those profits and wilfully allowed themselves to be used to improve the efficiency of those markets in vice controlled by drug kingpins, weapons traffickers, armed groups, and worse. Nugan Hand and BCCI also taught 'reputable' banks that a good way to secure their impunity from money-laundering excess was to be 'useful' to the most powerful national security states when some of their spookier agents needed to launder money. Huge banks with fine reputations that are criminalised are too big and too dangerous not to fail. When they refuse to shut down criminality that can run to something as dangerous as the flow of cash to secret nuclear weapons programs, huge equity fines could be needed that build up to shift most shares in the bank under public control. That may be the appropriate ultimate outcome at the peak of a regulatory pyramid.

Deepwater Horizon

Australia has had opportunities to prevent foreign environmental catastrophes through restorative environmental justice. A cosmopolitan restorative approach to the Timor Sea oil spill, uncappable for 75 days, could have prevented the Deepwater Horizon spill a year later in the Gulf of Mexico that repeated this problem (for 86 days), caused by the same reason as the Australian spill, at the hands of the same offending contractor, Halliburton.

On 21 August 2009, a drilling platform offshore from Australia in the Timor Sea suffered a blowout and oil spill that could not be capped. The diagnosis was that the defective concrete base of the oil well installed by the Houston-headquartered Halliburton caused the blowout (Bradshaw 2010; Gold and Casselman 2010). This revelation was not publicised internationally at the time. An Australian criminal prosecution was launched that resulted in a conviction and a fine of just US$380,000 two years after Deepwater Horizon. The Australian regulator could have insisted, as part of its enforcement response, that Halliburton retain independent engineering consultants to investigate whether other offshore wells it had cemented across the oceans of the world posed similar risks.

The historical record shows that the Australian regulator did not do so and the next year a BP deep-sea drilling base cemented by Halliburton also failed, causing a similar environmental catastrophe in the Gulf of Mexico. Given that Halliburton dominates the world's well-cementing business with one other company, the Timor Sea tragedy might have helped connect the dots and drawn attention to the magnitude of the risk flagged by 'a 2007 study by three U.S. Minerals Management Service officials [that] found that cementing was a factor in 18 of 39 well blowouts in the Gulf of Mexico over a 14-year period' (Gold and Casselman 2010). It is a measure of the poverty of our global conversation about how to make business ethics work in contemporary conditions that those living around the Gulf of Mexico did not protest Australia's failure to adopt a more cosmopolitan ethic in its contribution to regulating environmental crime.

So, a positive side of the globalising tendencies for crises to cascade from one country to another is that when corporate enforcement fails in one country, there are opportunities for ethically entrepreneurial enforcement to cascade from other countries that might be less captured by firms like Halliburton, Enron or BCCI.

Rudolf Giuliani and the macrocriminological imagination

Rudolf Giuliani, the former mayor of New York, is a vivid figure in the public imagination because of his role as Donald Trump's lawyer. He is discussed in criminology primarily because of the apparent success of New York in reducing crime in the 1990s and early 2000s, particularly its homicide rate, during his mayoralty. This discussion is about whether this was accomplished by hotspot policing that reduced gun carrying (Sherman 1995; Fagan et al. 1998; Wintemute 2000), the CompStat methodology of mapping risk patterns and accountability for police leaders to get improved crime outcomes on their patch or 'broken-windows' policing and the ethos of 'zero tolerance' (Harcourt 2001; Karmen 2000; Eck and Maguire 2000; Taylor 2001). These are important debates because it seems likely that at least some of New York's policing innovations were positive (Zimring 2011), even if others may have resulted in discrimination against minorities, and even if some other cities may have more successfully implemented the positives than New York itself.

Giuliani is inclined to see the policing of incivilities such as graffiti in subways as a 'broken-windows' policing accomplishment, but we do not know whether the undoubted accomplishment of the subways becoming safer was not simply a hotspot policing accomplishment of greater police presence at subway locales that were crime hotspots. In recent years, Giuliani has advanced projects of crude transplantation of some of the worst aspects of the New York innovations to contexts like El Salvador. These aspects of the contest for credit over the contribution of Giuliani and his police chiefs to crime prevention are not the focus here. It is important to be open-minded about Giuliani and New York criminal justice, so we can see his administration as innovative in contributing some very positive things and others that were very negative.

Here the focus is on James Jacobs' important book with Coleen Friel and Robert Raddick (2001), *Gotham Unbound: How New York City was Liberated from the Grip of Organized Crime*. This is about clearing the Mafia out of a variety of markets in New York City under Giuliani's watch as mayor. After decades of failed punitive law enforcement against members of organised crime groups who were simply replaced when imprisoned, the strategy that Jacobs et al. describe as finally working was in substantial part a business regulation strategy, particularly one that targeted licences, though still a strategy with an important place for criminal punishment. One way to stop the Mob from fixing prices in the New York garbage collection cartel was to withdraw the waste collection licences of Mob associates. In some markets corrupted by the Mob, suppliers were required to hire an auditing firm that specialised in certifying that the business was Mob-free. The court appointment of trustees to clean up (restore workers' democratic control of) Mob-controlled unions was another important strategy. The effectiveness of such preventive organisational incapacitation compared with purely retributive enforcement came as no surprise to those who worked on business regulation. Jacobs et al.'s findings are reminiscent of the placement in US coalmines of resident inspectors at the least-safe mines in the country to reform their management practices and thereby improve safety dramatically (Braithwaite 1985: 82–83). One reason is that they refused to allow miners to enter the mine on days when methane gas levels were too high or enter areas where the geology was too unstable. On these days and in these tunnels, the resident inspector was incapacitating the mine owner from murdering its miners.

Jacobs et al.'s research showed that a responsive regulatory approach with business regulatory licensing, monitoring, auditing and restructuring, moving up from the base of an enforcement pyramid that has stiff terms of imprisonment at its peak, can work against the most entrenched, sophisticated and ruthless organised crime groups in the world. Jacobs et al. argued that political will and enforcement imagination were required to accomplish this. The strategy was, first, to prevent the Mafia from taking over new markets, then closing their control of the markets they were already in, one by one. Incapacitation that crippled the influence of the Mafia in New York City was no small enforcement accomplishment. It was a macrocriminological accomplishment of decriminalising markets.

Another area of Giuliani's innovation was in the 1980s when he was a federal prosecutor in New York. After the Wall Street crash of 1987, Giuliani led criminal enforcement against some of the greatest corporate criminals of that era—a story told in the movie *Wall Street* in which Michael Douglas utters the famous words of one of those mega-criminals: 'Greed is good.' After Giuliani's prosecutions on Wall Street three decades ago, there was reason to be hopeful that public prosecution was on an upward trajectory for corporate crime. Some of Giuliani's techniques were crude but effective. His team would come across evidence of the crime of some comparatively minor malefactor within a targeted corporation. They would sit him down, say gotcha, you are in deep trouble and promise immunity if he could provide testimony against a bigger fish; then that bigger fish would turn on an even bigger fish, who would be turned against a shark. This approach led Giuliani's team up to Ivan Boesky, Donald Levine and Michael Milken. Milken was the inventor of the junk bond, perhaps the greatest genius of his time on Wall Street and still one of the richest people in the world today. Moving up from protecting minnows to netting sharks was also used with less stunning, but significant, success against organised crime.

We glimpse a remarkable failure to follow this approach after the Global Financial Crisis peaked in 2008 in the documentary *Inside Story*, in which the madam of a Wall Street brothel disclosed that she had credit card authorisations from major Wall Street firms to record prostitution services as 'payments to compliance consultants'! She goes on to reveal that no law enforcement authorities had asked to examine these credit card records. If law enforcement was serious about putting Wall Street criminals behind bars, it would have used Giuliani's strategy. A comparatively minor credit card fraud of this kind is ideal for sitting someone down to say you will be going to jail for the fraud unless you help with evidence of more major fraud against a bigger fish in your organisation (then hopefully moving up to a genuinely major predator). During the first Obama administration, the Justice Department was simply not interested in such Giuliani-style tactics.

Australia tended to reject the Giuliani approach to corporate crime enforcement after its corporate mega-crimes of the 1980s because it viewed the method as crude, unprincipled and unsophisticated. It certainly comes with risks that small fish in the hot seat will fabricate or exaggerate evidence against others to secure their freedom. What Australia did instead was to set up royal commissions and crime commissions populated with teams of top lawyers. These produced sophisticated synoptic analyses of the nature of Australia's corporate crime and organised crime problems, with some recommendations for where prosecutions might occur. This did not convict big fish on major charges with anything like the success rate of the crude Giuliani strategy.

The accomplishment of Giuliani's strategy was not so much that the likes of Michael Milken were convicted to prison and paid billions of dollars in fines. The key thing was an incapacitation accomplishment. This was more than the fact that the doors were closed at the powerful criminal organisations they controlled; the junk bond was dead, as were the firms that invented them. Traders were incapacitated from buying junk bonds because there were none to buy. Milken's firm, Drexel Burnham Lambert, was also bankrupted. Killing off criminogenic kinds of markets, at least for a while, was the important incapacitation accomplishment.

The other aspect of the incapacitation of Milken as a Wall Street criminal is that he has kept himself out of trouble since completing his prison sentence by shifting his considerable and growing capital from the promotion of fraud to the formation with his brother of the Knowledge Learning Corporation. It is the largest for-profit provider of childcare in the United States and a provider of online learning. He has redeemed himself by philanthropy that turned his financial genius to assisting developing countries avert banking and debt crises—a rejected community service offer he had proposed as a plea agreement to avoid prison in 1989, but that he went on to do anyway. Milken also applied his innovative mind to venture philanthropy. *Fortune* magazine had him on its cover as 'The man who changed medicine' (Daniels 2004):

> Michael Milken 'changed the culture of [medical] research,' says Andrew von Eschenbach, director of the National Cancer Institute. He created a sense of urgency that focused on results and shortened the timeline. It took a business mindset to shake things up. What he's done is now the model.

Few could have made a more catalytic or financially larger contribution than Milken to the 53 per cent reduction in prostate cancer deaths in the United States between 1993 and 2017. It is disappointing that criminology does not hold up Milken's transformation and self-incapacitation more than it does in its research on organisational crime control.

The quantitative evidence is now very strong that the decapitation of drug cartels has made a huge contribution to increasing the Mexican homicide rate in the past 15 years (Calderón et al. 2015; Dell 2015; Phillips 2015; Ríos 2013; Atuesta and Pérez-Dávila 2018; Lessing 2018). As battles cascaded among successor leaders to take over the markets of decapitated leaders, so many innocent citizens suffered from escalating levels of homicide. A better solution may prove in future to be an enforcement-driven self-incapacitation pitch:

> Do you want to bequeath to your children an empire they can only defend by a life dodging bullets? Divest from drug markets and extortion and reinvest your capital in something really secure, profitable and worthwhile for your country.

Drug cartel bosses are capable of the same smarts that Milken showed in chairing the Knowledge Learning Corporation, becoming a respected philanthropist who can look back from his deathbed on how he turned around a life of crime. We have seen unsophisticated experimentation with this kind of strategy in Latin America led by Catholic priests, but not sophisticated experiments led by criminologists with strong political support.

Averting the Global Financial Crisis with self-incapacitation enforced by restorative justice

Let us turn our criminological imagination to how the Global Financial Crisis might have been prevented in 2004, 2005 or even later. We have argued already that the FBI failed to show a macrocriminological imagination with the evidence it had about both 9/11 and the subprime mortgage fraud that were preventable proximate causes of the major crises of the presidency of George W. Bush.

What could have been made of all that FBI evidence that banks across America were allowing mortgage brokers to write fraudulent loans? How could the banks be so stupid, the forensic minds of 2004 might have asked? The answer was they were not stupid, of course. They could make more money by shifting risks than by managing them. Wall Street invented complex financial instruments that sliced and diced bad loans for banks. Bits of those bad loans were then sold across the financial system by hedge funds and others to players who usually did not understand that they were buying bad debts. So, this always had the whiff of Wall Street fraud driving it. High-level culpability is hard to nail, however, as so many players are just slicing and dicing the risk they buy themselves and then passing it on to others. Such figures do not make great collars because many of the fraudsters might turn out to be also victims of fraud themselves. But surely such widespread mortgage fraud as we see in the FBI data means that the proliferating game of pass the parcel was pumping up systemic risk. So why were the ratings agencies not calling some of these hedge funds for the junk they were? Why weren't Moody's and Standard & Poor's calling some of their bank and insurance companies for the large exposures they were building up to these bad loans through CDOs? Go and find out why not, prosecutors should have been saying to their staff. They would have returned with the news that the creation of so many new financial entities and businesses in this game of passing the parcel was creating a lot of business for Moody's and Standard & Poor's, the two ratings agencies that do most of the ratings on Wall Street and globally. The prosecutor might have said, sniff around on the street and see if you can pick up any evidence of significant business irregularities of any kind by anyone working for Moody's or Standard & Poor's.

That task would have been no harder than it was for New York prosecutor Rudolf Giuliani with the 'greed is good' Wall Street frauds of the 1980s. The success of his team in the Southern District of New York in locking up Wall Street's greed-is-good brigade of 1987 was what made Giuliani's reputation and laid his pathway to becoming the Mayor of New York. From 2005, putting criminally culpable small fish under the bright lights with the choice of going to jail or revealing how sharks were misrepresenting the realities of systemic risk on Wall Street would have exposed what subsequently appeared on the public record and in enforcement actions many years after the Global Financial Crisis. Standard & Poor's and Moody's were proved to have made an appalling contribution to the onset of the crisis. Standard & Poor's was afflicted with an executive who could say: 'Let's hope we are all wealthy and retired by the time this house of cards falters'; another who said: 'We rate every deal. It could be structured by cows and we would rate it'; and yet another, who said: 'Profits were running the show' (O'Brien 2009: 75).

This might have led regulators to demand urgent repair work to stabilise Wall Street's house of cards before it collapsed. Luckily, the junk bond house of cards was incapacitated before it caused massive damage to the real American economy, which recovered extremely quickly from the 1987 stock market crash. Tragically, more than 50 million people across the North Atlantic lost their jobs in the more savage consequences of the 2008 crash. A similar number lost their homes.

Incapacitation steps could have transformed ratings from a market in vice back to its historical role as a market in virtue. The European Commission might have established a public ratings agency to compete with Moody's and Standards & Poor's. A Wall Street market in ratings vice could have been incapacitated from ever emerging again in a new world in which a European public ratings competitor was on the street watching their abuses and competing with them.

This chapter argued earlier that regulators could have met one by one in a restorative circle in 2004 with the banks that had the worst incidence of loan defaults in their city or state. Regulators could have required them to demonstrate that their loan portfolios were not infested with fraud. When bank self-investigation reports found in most cases that they were riddled with fraud, the restorative conference could have required the bank to craft a plan to prevent the issuance of further fraudulent loans and a management plan to regularise as many current dubious loans as possible. As these restorative conferences revealed the scale of the problem, they would have revealed the imperative to scale up a macro-regulatory transformation.

Giuliani in Belgrade

Structural incapacitation is as important with war crime as it is with corporate crime. It cannot be delivered by prosecutions of small fish. In 2015, Aleksandar Marsavelski and I interviewed longstanding Serbian war crimes prosecutor Vladimir Vukčević, who had prosecuted 170 war crimes cases—probably more than any other prosecutor, living or dead.[11] We explained to him Giuliani's strategy on Wall Street and the Australian strategy of a commission with special investigative powers that synoptically reviews all possible targets and recommends the highest priorities for state prosecution. As a war crimes prosecutor who has had a lot of success in convicting serious Serbian war criminals, Vukčević quickly replied that Giuliani's strategy 'is the only strategy that can work'. Having said that, he and other war crimes prosecutors we have interviewed point out that it is more complex to make the Giuliani strategy work in war crimes cases and in civil law jurisdictions (Marsavelski and Braithwaite 2020).

The history of the mother institution to the national Serbian war crimes prosecutor, the office of the prosecutor of the International Criminal Tribunal for the former Yugoslavia (ICTY), reveals the greater complexity with war crimes than with corporate crime prosecution. The ICTY and its prosecutor were much criticised in their early years, during the mid-1990s, for prosecuting relatively minor war criminals. The reason they started small was so they could build confidence in international justice with quick impacts. It is doubtful whether this worked because all sides in Yugoslavia ended up believing that The Hague was prosecuting their little fish and letting off their enemy's big fish (Nickson and Neikirk 2018). One advantage, nevertheless, of these lower-level cases early on was that many of the lower-level war criminals who were targeted sought to save themselves or to soften their sentences by providing evidence to prosecutors against bigger fish. This allowed the ICTY to move up to middle-level and top-level targets. Over a long period, and at great cost, the ICTY was successful in moving right up to prosecutions of President Slobodan Milošević and top-level political, military and militia leaders of most of the armed factions of the former Yugoslavia.

One reason national prosecutors' offices were established in the successor states of the former Yugoslavia was that the states funding the ICTY through the United Nations began to signal that they would not finance many more prosecutions. Finally, donors insisted that only the prosecutions currently under way could be completed. The pressure this created for the institution of national war crimes prosecutors to complement the

---

11 I am in deep debt to Aleksandar Marsavelski for the development of some of the thinking in this chapter, and in Chapter 5, during our richly rewarding Peacebuilding Compared fieldwork together (Marsavelski and Braithwaite 2018, 2020).

work of the international tribunal was a good thing. Once prosecutors in The Hague moved up to prosecuting figures as senior as Milošević and the commander-in-chief of the Croatian armed forces, little fish who were being tapped on the shoulder for questioning by prosecutors were being advised by their lawyers not to worry because the ICTY was no longer in the business of prosecuting little fish like them. The advent, in particular, of the Serbian national war crimes prosecutor's office in 2003 again made it unwise for legal advisers to tell low-level war criminals not to worry; the national war crimes prosecutor might get them. So, if international justice can learn how to get the synergy right between the justice of national, international and hybrid (national/international) war crimes courts, the Giuliani strategy can be more or less delivered (Marsavelski and Braithwaite 2020).

Over time, international criminal law has developed a capacity to build evidentiary linkages between bottom-up and top-down cases. The investigation strategy of the International Criminal Court's Office of the Prosecutor (OTP) was revised in its 2012–15 strategic plan:

> The required evidentiary standards to prove the criminal responsibility of those bearing the greatest responsibility might result in the OTP changing its approach due to limitations on investigative possibilities and/or a lack of cooperation. A strategy of gradually building upwards might then be needed in which the Office first investigates and prosecutes a limited number of mid- and high-level perpetrators in order to ultimately have a reasonable prospect of conviction for those most responsible. The Office will also consider prosecuting lower level perpetrators where their conduct has been particularly grave and has acquired extensive notoriety. (OTP 2013: Executive Summary, Point 4)

Incapacitating war crime

War crime prosecutions are mainly important to an incapacitation strategy for preventing war crime through the way the threat of prosecutions can help motivate self-incapacitation by parties to conflict. Fear of war crime prosecutions is less important, however, than diplomatic and military pressures. Consider the slaughter of the scorched-earth policy that began to unfold after the people of East Timor voted for independence from Indonesia in the UN-supervised plebiscite of 1999 (Braithwaite et al. 2012). There was a clear root cause of this escalation of armed conflict: the decision of the Indonesian military to lead and pressure civilian militias loyal to Indonesia to wipe out independence supporters. An effective incapacitation remedy to end this war crime before the killing escalated to genocide was put in place: the removal of the root cause, the Indonesian military, and the removal of its capacity to coerce civilian murders. A UN resolution required all Indonesian troops to leave East Timor. Peacekeeping troops of the International Force East Timor (INTERFET) arrived quickly to monitor the completeness of the Indonesian troop withdrawal. Thanks to a huge amount of international diplomatic and military pressure, 24 years of Indonesian military killings of more than 100,000 East Timorese abruptly ended in that historical moment.

Cantonment is another incapacitation strategy frequently successfully deployed in peacekeeping. When an army cannot leave a war-torn territory in the way the Indonesian Army left East Timor, because that army has no place to go, peacekeepers can negotiate cantonment camps for armed groups. These are in areas where they are well away from their enemies; peacekeepers patrol the cantonments to ensure the former combatant armies do not break out to prey on civilians. In Nepal's peace agreement, the Maoist army insisted that it would not put its troops in cantonment unless the Royal Nepal Army submitted to the same. This became a case where both insurgents and state forces were put in cantonment as a precursor to a security sector reform process through which many Maoist fighters were integrated into the new Nepal Armed Forces.

In the 1990s, cantonment came to be part of a package of policies called DDR: Disarmament, Demobilisation and Reintegration. Later, this was elaborated into variants such as DDRRR (Disarmament, Demobilisation, Repatriation, Rehabilitation and Reintegration) and with other Rs such as Reconciliation, and transformative security sector Reform. Only the two Ds and the first R (Repatriation, as with the Indonesian troops in Timor) are about incapacitation. With Disarmament, the debates bear many similarities to debates over the empirical evidence on gun control and domestic crime in the West. Are gun buybacks the best path to disarmament, for example? Or do buybacks create a moral hazard (as in Afghanistan, where the Taliban received money for an old gun and then used it to buy a new gun)?

Very partial forms of incapacitation of access to guns are often contextually wise elements of peace processes that are riddled with distrust. For example, in the Bougainville secessionist civil war with Papua New Guinea (PNG), the Bougainville Revolutionary Army (BRA) agreed to lock their weapons in containers to which both their commanders and the United Nations had keys. While this was a relatively weak assurance against the containers being broken into, it succeeded in getting the guns out of the villages. It reduced crime. It has an interesting resonance with the domestic criminology literature on the effectiveness of regulating gun *carrying* at hotspots of crime, as opposed to attempting to end gun *ownership* (Sherman 1995; Fagan et al. 1998; Wintemute 2000). The reason for the Bougainville approach was that the BRA did not trust either the government forces or the forces of a spoiler BRA group that did not join the peace. They worried they would be killed if they completely removed the option of retrieving their guns. Trust-building and commitment were constructed brick by brick through an architecture of commitment in the Bougainville peace process (Regan 2010; Braithwaite et al. 2010b). Staged disarmament commitments, from locking guns in containers through to their ultimate destruction, were only implemented after the PNG Government complied with its milestones in the agreed sequence of the architecture of commitment to peace.

Disarmament of the Irish Republican Army (IRA) was also a partial process with some similarities to Bougainville. The UK Government persuaded the Loyalist side of the conflict that it would ensure the IRA fully disarmed before power-sharing was put in place in the Stormont parliament. Years of wilful duplicity passed in which the British state did not force the IRA (or the Loyalists) to fully disarm (McEvoy and Shirlow 2009: 36–37). This may have been a pro-peace duplicitousness as there is reason to suspect that had the IRA disarmed too quickly they might not have been able to prevent the Real IRA and other spoiler factions from derailing the peace.

The least empirically fraught part of the incapacitation of war through the Disarmament part of DDR is de-mining. All sides, and especially the children of all sides, benefit from de-mining. It is an unsung part of peacebuilding across the globe that always saves lives. It can also contribute greatly to overcoming postwar hunger in devastated agricultural economies by allowing farmland planted with mines to return to production after its fallow years of war. It can open up mined transport routes to the postwar economy. Theoretically, then, de-mining not only contributes to the incapacitation of war, but also delivers through a reward mechanism, by enabling this agricultural peace dividend.

Overall, the evidence that incapacitation through DDR contributes to peace is quite strong, especially when that incapacitation is integrated into a credible, contextually attuned architecture of commitment to peace (Braithwaite et al. 2012; Braithwaite and D'Costa 2018). Even more convincing is the evidence that UN peacekeeping—especially when crucial elements like DDR are integrated into a multidimensional peacebuilding package to support the transformation of a war-torn society—reduces the prospects of another war (Doyle and Sambanis 2000, 2006; Walter et al. 2020).

The nuclear and chemical weapons nonproliferation regimes have also been remarkable accomplishments of war crime incapacitation. Who would have thought after half a million people were gassed in World War I that so few lives would be taken by chemical weapons in the unusually terrible and numerous wars of the next 100 years, when chemical weapons were within the technical capacity of even weak states?

When President Kennedy predicted in a press conference in 1963 that the world could see 15 to 25 new nuclear weapons states by the 1970s,[12] who would have thought he would be proved wrong by the incapacitation accomplishments of the nuclear nonproliferation regime? When the US and UK governments argued at the United Nations in 2003 that weapons inspections had not worked in disarming Saddam Hussein's weapons of mass destruction, western publics were gullible in believing this, when the truth was what the weapons inspectors themselves perceived: their inspection activities were working.

Through a macrocriminology lens, it is important to see the nuclear attacks on Hiroshima and Nagasaki as war crimes, just as it is to see as crimes the more devastating firebombing of Tokyo and of cities like Dresden in Germany, as well as the devastating bombing campaigns by Germany and Japan in China, the United Kingdom and beyond. As terrible as late twentieth and early twenty-first century bombing campaigns have been, it is also important to understand them as mostly less systematically criminal since the end of the Vietnam War than they were in the mid-twentieth century. It is important to see that if the incapacitation of nuclear, chemical and biological warfare had not worked as well as it has since 1945, many of those reading this book today might have perished from war crime falling from the sky.

---

12   Reported in *The New York Times*, 23 March 1963.

Self-incapacitation of war crime

The diplomacy of the great powers has been important in persuading lesser states like Australia not to acquire nuclear weapons. After World War II, there was considerable support for the acquisition of nuclear weapons in the wake of French and British acquisition, as a safeguard against feared resurgent Japanese power and rising Chinese communist power in Asia. Equally important in incapacitating the Australian state from the use of nuclear, chemical and biological weapons has been the work of civil society—the peace movement, activist doctors, the Campaign for Nuclear Disarmament—in motivating Australian renunciation of weapons of mass destruction. Any political party that campaigned for the nuclear arming of Australia's military would lose because the polling evidence is clear that Australians have long been opposed to this. Australia is like many countries in the power of its civil society leadership in guaranteeing the incapacitation of nuclear war crime. More remarkable accomplishments of this civil society potency for incapacitation include those in South Africa, which was already effectively a nuclear power when the pro-Apartheid National Party regime made it politically popular with the white electorate to renounce nuclear weapons. South Africa complied with the nuclear nonproliferation regime years before Apartheid was dismantled. Three decades later, it is hard to overstate how profound an accomplishment this was. It has underwritten Africa—the planet's most war-torn continent— becoming a nuclear weapons–free zone. South Africa's renunciation of its ambition to be an African regional nuclear power helped Nelson Mandela in persuading his friend and supporter in his long struggle, Muammar Gaddafi, to dismantle Libya's nuclear weapons program.

The incapacitation record of civil society here is patchy. Nuclear arms are extremely popular in Pakistan. The failure of international diplomacy to solve the festering oppression of Muslims (and other religious groups) in Kashmir from the 1940s not only led to an incapacitation failure of the nuclear nonproliferation regime across the Subcontinent, but also made a substantial contribution to the long-run rise of jihadist terror (Braithwaite and D'Costa 2018).

State self-incapacitation of weapons of mass destruction has, overall, been the most profound contribution of incapacitation to creating a less violent world and one less oppressed by war crime (Chapter 11). At the same time, this is the most fragile accomplishment of incapacitation in protecting our life and liberty. In more micro ways, let us now also illustrate the power and potential of self-incapacitation.

Self-incapacitation in asymmetric warfare

The odds of any combatant going into a modern war and securing total subjugation of the enemy are low, whether the combatant is an insurgent group or a state. Since World War II, even the most potent combatant, the United States, found in major deployments of air power and masses of ground troops in Korea, Vietnam, Indochina, Afghanistan and Iraq that unconditional victory was less likely than exit with a return to political negotiation of a conflict that continued. That was also true of more minor American military commitments to wars that included those in Libya, Syria, the various conflicts of the former Yugoslavia, Somalia, the war on drug cartels in Latin America and even more limited engagements where military force was aimed more at changing the nature of a negotiated outcome than permanent conquest of an enemy. What is true of the greatest military power in the world is even more true of lesser powers. Realising the limited and expensive gains to be garnered from military deployment in contemporary conditions, the period since World War II has been unique in that the number two and three economic powers— China and Japan in the twenty-first century, Germany and Japan in the twentieth—almost totally eschewed military deployments in favour of diplomacy as the way to advance their objectives.

Whether what is negotiated are the terms of a surrender, a victory, a ceasefire or a compromise peace agreement born of military stalemate, the parties to contemporary conflicts—whether they are as powerful as the United States or a minor insurgent—need the support of the international community for terms around which they can mobilise diplomatic support. This imperative for building international support is the context for all types of combatants to be open to diplomatic entreaties for self-incapacitation. Even warmakers as ruthless as Stalin, Hitler, Mussolini and Tojo, when millions of their citizens were perishing, could still agree to self-incapacitation against the use of chemical weapons and indeed to a variety of other Geneva protocols for self-incapacitation against different kinds of war crimes against civilians, enemy combatants and prisoners of war. Sadly, implementation was often imperfect, yet it was sufficient to be game changing.

The ICTY Prosecutor Louise Arbour in March 1999 showed the way to a potentially important new strategy for triggering the self-incapacitation of war crimes. She wrote to several Serbian leaders, including Deputy Prime Minister of the Federal Republic of Yugoslavia, Nikola Šainović. They were in effect 'be aware' warning letters on specific war crime risks. The letters had the intent and effect of putting leaders on notice to take steps to prevent these war crimes from proceeding. In particular, the individual leaders were warned to exercise authority over their subordinates to prevent war crimes and to punish subordinates who committed serious violations of international humanitarian law in Kosovo. The letters may not have overwhelmingly succeeded in motivating self-incapacitation. Later, however, the ICTY Trial Chamber relied on Arbour's letter to Šainović to find that he was a politician who had received information that crimes were being committed—a reliance affirmed by the Appeals Chamber of the ICTY (Brammertz and Jarvis 2016: 423–24).

Obviously, one reason for sending such letters is to sharpen the Sword of Damocles, which Chapter 9 argued does more deterrence work than the actual imposition of punishments. The potential of such prosecutor warning letters seems greatest in those situations, as in Syria at the time of writing, where it is well to consider the even greater promise of this approach in terms of motivating self-incapacitation. Consider the work of the NGO Geneva Call. It built on earlier one-off initiatives such as the 1981 agreement of the South-West Africa People's Organization (SWAPO) insurgents with the International Committee of the Red Cross to comply with all Geneva conventions[13] and the 2002 agreement of the Moro Islamic Liberation Front to end kidnapping in the Philippines.[14]

Geneva Call started with dialogue engaging 158 nonstate armed groups to persuade them to comply with international humanitarian law with respect to antipersonnel mines. By 2019, Geneva Call had signed 65 deeds of commitment with nonstate armed groups in Africa, Asia and the Middle East, with 54 of these banning totally the use of antipersonnel mines and committing to cooperation on mine action (Geneva Call 2020). Bongard and Somer (2011) found that compliance with these

---

13 'South West Africa People's Organisation—SWAPO Declaration to the International Committee of the Red Cross—ICRC', 15 July 1981, available from: theirwords.org/media/transfer/doc/na_swapo_1981_01-c69993289a437a48ccd467ea42798b25.pdf.

14 'Moro Islamic Liberation Front Central Committee Resolution', 26 February 2002, available from: theirwords.org/media/transfer/doc/ph_milf_biaf_2002_06-6bd99b91fd576e25a44bcdf18e43af9d.pdf.

agreements has been good. Only one case revealed conclusive evidence of violation of the prohibition on the use, production, acquisition and transfer of antipersonnel mines. On the positive side, monitoring found widespread mine action activities in areas under the control of signatory armed groups. Between them, the first 49 armed groups had destroyed more than 20,000 stockpiled antipersonnel mines by 2011 along with thousands of improvised explosive devices (IEDs) and abandoned explosive ordnance. The deeds of commitment are signed by the nonstate armed group's leadership and countersigned by Geneva Call and the Government of the Republic and Canton of Geneva—in most cases, in a ceremony in Geneva's City Hall, where the first Geneva Convention was adopted in 1864. The symbolism here is about Geneva Call's work as a remedy to the deficiency in international humanitarian law that enforcement mechanisms and implementation obligations rest in the hands of states.

Bongard and Somer (2011) concluded that signatory nonstate armed groups have been quite responsive to investigations of allegations of noncompliance with deeds of commitment, conducting their own investigations, allowing field visits by third-party monitors and agreeing to recommendations of third-party investigations for coming into compliance. The argument of this chapter as to why nonstate armed groups would do this is that they seek to build international legitimacy if and when the time comes for a diplomacy of negotiated resolution of their grievances or an end to their war. Geneva Call requires all signatory armed groups to establish self-monitoring mechanisms for their deeds of commitment and to report to Geneva Call on the measures put in place to implement them. Geneva Call's independent monitoring of compliance is undertaken by gathering information from a range of third-party actors present on the ground (such as media and international and local organisations) and through field missions by Geneva Call on a routine basis to follow-up on implementation or verify compliance in the event of allegations of noncompliance. Geneva Call claims that in Iraq, Sudan and other war zones, the commitments made by nonstate armed groups were instrumental in the accession of the states concerned to the Anti-Personnel Mine Ban Convention.

While Geneva Call started with a focus on antipersonnel mine commitments, recent years have seen a considerable broadening in the coverage of deeds, their self-enforcement and NGO enforcement, and international enforcement in the context of ceasefire and peace agreements (for example, by the United Nations). Geneva Call's more recent priorities have expanded to protecting children from the effects of armed conflict, prohibiting sexual violence in conflicts and working towards the elimination of gender discrimination. Many nonstate armed groups have engaged in dialogue with Geneva Call on what they might specifically do in their circumstances to protect children from the effects of armed conflict. Twenty-nine have signed a deed of commitment on protecting children and have implemented measures to enforce these obligations (Geneva Call 2020). A deed prohibiting sexual violence and gender discrimination has been signed by 25 groups, which have taken specific measures to enforce these obligations. This specificity can be illustrated by a deed of commitment for a protected space for 60 young girls at risk from armed violence with local partner Nashet Association in Palestinian refugee camps in Lebanon. Since its creation in 2000, Geneva Call has engaged in dialogue, training in local languages and monitoring with nonstate armed groups across this wider range of topics, including in the most challenging of contexts such as Syria. It maintains a directory of 576 commitments and agreements made by nonstate armed groups that occasionally also go to some more specific issues such as protection of health care and cultural heritage and displacement during armed conflict. They also cover commitments to training measures that include specifics like posting key rules in camps.

The Geneva Call agreements might be criticised in some cases for following a standard template. The mistake was failing to come to terms with the specificities of matters on which armed groups need to self-incapacitate in their theatre of war. In the history of international agreements before the arrival of Geneva Call and kindred NGOs, where there was no specificity of commitment by nonstate armed groups, we can see in retrospect that agreements to comply with international law were not honoured or, worse, were even tragically counterproductive. Examples were the agreements with armed groups operating in the former Yugoslavia in the 1990s to honour safe havens for civilians. These agreements actually facilitated the passive herding of civilians into concentrated slaughter in UN-sanctioned safe havens in Bosnia and may have prolonged the war, which is also one way of interpreting the effect of UN-sanctioned safe havens in Syria (Cerkez 2012). Safe havens were also used as bait to trap civilians for mass slaughter in Democratic Republic of Congo (Braithwaite and D'Costa 2018: 138–40). Humanitarian aid to starving people was used to lure them into killing zones. Once humanitarian agencies discovered the whereabouts of refugees who had fled their former camps, they sought permission from military units to let them in to provide aid. 'Facilitators' who advised refugees where to go to receive aid were repeatedly the agents of their murderers who lured the vulnerable to slaughter (Reyntjens 2009: 96–97). These were preventable disasters of faux self-incapacitation that should have resulted in the criminal conviction of those responsible for gaming safe havens to commit war crimes. The international community should also have been more insistent on disciplining the military leaders of international peace enforcement whose weakness allowed such catastrophes.

We have seen that the worst cases of failed self-incapacitation by corporate integrity agreements and enforceable undertakings involve 'rituals of comfort' (Power 1997) that are mere symbolism. The worst cases of failed self-incapacitation in peace processes are even worse than that. They involve the amplification of criminality rather than failed containment of it. They involve armed groups in eastern Congo being integrated into the Congolese state army in ways that enable them to rape and pillage the civilian population more effectively than before, and with the legitimacy of acting as part of the state (Vlassenroot and Raeymaekers 2009). Such power-sharing can also induce a moral hazard: nonstate predators stake a claim by causing grief in a region of a country so they can negotiate a power-sharing deal that gives them state sanction for a monopoly over predation across what becomes their patch.

Both the disasters and the successes of self-incapacitation should direct our attention to the need to reform international law in two ways. On the positive side, reform would credit combatants who sign meaningful agreements to incapacitate themselves from engaging in specific kinds of war crimes and for genuinely engaging in self-enforcement against their own troops to deliver compliance. On the negative side, loss of life or sexual violence that arises from failing to honour specificities in deeds of commitment with organisations like Geneva Call should have legal consequences. Both positive and negative assessments of self-incapacitation could/should inform International Criminal Court decisions on whom to prosecute and whom to decline from prosecuting. It could inform arguments that international criminal law considers in submissions from prosecutors and defence counsel on the degree of criminal culpability. This means reforms to sentencing and prosecution guidelines for international criminal law institutions to give due recognition to self-incapacitation and to its abuse by combatants who game it. Perhaps even more so, it requires judicial leadership in international appellate courts to evolve a case law that helps harness the potential of international criminal law to promote forms of self-incapacitation that it finds saves lives when there is compliance. All these arguments are developed more fully in Marsavelski and Braithwaite (2020).

We have seen such developments in national regulation of corporate crime in recent decades, with enforced self-regulation meaning that corporations and their executives can be convicted criminally for breaches of privately written rules that have been publicly ratified because such private rules implement the principles in the law in the specific circumstances facing that corporation (Braithwaite 1982; Ayres and Braithwaite 1992). Translating into international criminal law the enforced self-regulation doctrine that we discussed with the regulation of roof control or methane in mines might see the International Criminal Court statute nominate a particular UN agency as responsible for ratifying agreements for securing compliance with international law. These could be negotiated by an organisation like Geneva Call in accordance with the principles of international law. To date, we have an international criminal law excessively obsessed with impunity and deterrence and insufficiently responsive to the potential of self-incapacitation. There is a need to make an example of military commanders who make agreements to protect safe havens that they then abuse through civilian slaughter. The international community should send clear signals that certain generals have not been targeted for prosecution because they went the extra mile to attempt to incapacitate their forces from war crime, while others are targeted for prosecution because they failed to do that.

Restorative justice and self-incapacitation

One of the important things that happens in restorative justice is the mobilisation of the collective efficacy of the circle to help offenders regulate themselves. That is the idea of motivational interviewing as an evidence-based practice that we have seen can be adapted as a collective restorative and responsive practice as opposed to an individual-on-individual practice. The circle rolls with resistance from the offender until the offender defines a redemptive path along which to re-narrate themselves in nonviolent and nondominating ways. Relational care for victims and offenders and a collective desire of the community of care to help the victim recover and repair the harm to the victim help the offender to self-discovery of how they can recover. This has complex and variable dynamics. For example, one path occurs for offenders who manage to cut themselves off from allowing themselves to feel remorse, even on hearing about terrible suffering from their victim, when their mother breaks down in the restorative circle on hearing the victim speak of their suffering. The offender's affection for their mother is what gets behind the shield that protects them from shame acknowledgement, remorse and repair. The self-regulation that matters most often has a social cognitive character; it involves re-narrating the self as a good person who has done something bad. This transforms their self-talk from talk of hitting back at people to talk of repairing the harm they have done, repairing themselves and sometimes incapacitating themselves.

Circles of support and accountability are one form of restorative justice with a very particular history. This approach was initiated nationally by Canadian prisons desperate to come up with a solution for the problems of child sex offenders due for release. Sadly, this is a category of offenders with high reoffending rates on release to the community. A political failure of evidence-based penology is one reason for this. With higher-risk parolees from prison, we do best to gradualise their release from prison: allow them a toe in the water of freedom to see how they adjust to it. For example, in the months before full release, we might trust them with day leave to attend a job, an apprenticeship or a university course in the community. If they break and run or commit some new offence during this conditional release, breach conditions may put more time on their sentence. Sometimes highly prisonised offenders near the end of a long sentence have a learned helplessness that leaves them afraid of freedom. They reoffend so they can return to the only world where they have learned to cope with choices because it is a world of someone else making those choices. They suffer *The Fear of Freedom*, as Erich Fromm (1942) titled his book. Such toes in the water of freedom through graduated release are particularly apt for child sex offenders. But the politics of parole is that no-one in a parole system may be willing to take responsibility for the early release of child sex offenders because of their fear of blame should something go wrong. Child sex offenders consequently serve maximum possible terms and are released only when the opportunities for graduated or conditional forms of release are exhausted.

What to do to try to create a journey of release that is safe for the community and for the offender? Enter circles of support and accountability. The journeys of child sex offenders who have been locked up for a long time for horrific crimes are politicised. Journalists get to know their release date, film their exit from prison, find out where they live, film them there and interview the neighbours about how they feel about child safety. This often triggers repeated episodes of discovery by the cameras that torment parolees, then flight from one residence to another, making reintegration fraught.

Instead of community rejection, circles of support and accountability find a community that will accept the child sex offender. In Canada, this was often a volunteer church group that was part of the prison chaplain's religious network. With a First Nations offender, it might be a First Nations community that is best placed to deliver CHIME (Connectedness, Hope, Identity, Meaning and Empowerment) through the leadership of its elders. Like so many restorative justice approaches, circles of support and accountability also build what David Best et al. (2018) call community capital through assertive linking to prosocial groups and activities.

Circles of support and accountability tend to develop self-incapacitation agreements of the following form: in the restorative circle, the child sex offender confesses that certain events tend to be contexts of temptation, such as visiting sex shops, watching internet pornography, hanging around outside schools or drinking alcohol. So, it is agreed that should any of these triggers arise, released offenders will call a member of the circle to go to their home immediately to have a coffee with them until this period of anomie or drift into danger passes. The intervention is resource-intensive in community volunteerism, with daily meetings/monitoring with warm support from at least one volunteer at first. Graduates of the program are successfully volunteering as wounded healers (Wager and Wilson 2017).

The evidence that the regular social support of Canadian circles of support and accountability is effective is encouraging, with Wilson et al. (2009) reporting an 83 per cent reduction in sexual reoffending and more moderately encouraging results in earlier research. A subsequent US randomised controlled trial showed the intervention to be effective and strong in cost–benefit terms (Duwe 2013)—updated on a larger sample with the same conclusion by Duwe (2018). A similar cost-effectiveness result was replicated in the United Kingdom by Elliott and Beech (2013). These studies do have methodological limitations, however; a systematic review by Clarke et al. (2017) cautiously supports the cost-effectiveness but cautions that sample sizes have usually not been sufficient to be statistically significant. Larger samples are needed to deliver confidence in these generally positive results.

Hollow Water and the prevention of child sexual abuse

Many of the principles that informed circles of support and accountability were pre-dated in Canada by the holistic healing circles for child sexual assault offenders of the Manitoba Ojibway community of Hollow Water (Lajeunesse 1993; Ross 1996; Bushie 1999). In Hollow Water, ex-offenders are not shunned and excluded from the community, even though they may be incapacitated by exclusion from homes where children they have abused and who are afraid of them still live. Ex-offenders are seen as important resources for 'getting under the skin' of new offenders and disturbing the webs of lies that have sustained their criminality. Better than anyone, ex-offenders understand the patterns, the pressures and the ways to hide from the obligations to incapacitate themselves. As they tell their personal stories in the Hollow Water circle, ex-offenders talk about the lies that once shielded them and how it felt to face the truth about the pain they caused. It is done gently but inexorably (Chapter 9). The circles signal to offenders that their behaviour has roots that can be understood, but there are no such things as excuses (Ross 1996: 183). Indeed, at Hollow Water, before they met their own victim in a healing circle, sexual abusers met other offenders and other offenders' victims, who would simply tell their stories as a stage in a process towards breaking down the tough guy identity that pervaded the dominating relationship with their own victim.

Just as a pilot would be less likely to report a near miss if they felt they might go to prison, so a serious street offender will be more likely to confess if the result will be a restorative resolution rather than prison. Hollow Water was also ahead of its time in learning the self-incapacitation lessons that we have already drawn from airline safety regulation: that it is more important to punish cover-up of offending and the refusal to learn how to incapacitate oneself in the aftermath of abuse than it is to punish abuse. The circles began to deal with what many at first thought to be an epidemic of alcohol abuse. As citizens sat in circles discussing the problems in 1986, they realised there was a deeper underlying problem: they lived in a community that was sweeping child sexual abuse under the carpet. Through a complex set of healing circles to help one individual victim and offender after another, they discovered eventually that most of their citizens were at some time victims of sexual abuse. Most of the leading roles in identifying child abuse were taken by women of Hollow Water (Bushie 1999). Jaccoud (1998) reported that 52 adults in a community of 600 formally admitted to criminal responsibility for sexually abusing children—50 as a result of participating in healing circles and two as a result of being referred to a court of law for failing to do so (Ross 1996: 29–48; Lajeunesse 1993). Ross (1996: 36) claimed that the healing circles succeeded by having only two known cases of reoffending. Five years later, Couture et al. (2001: 23) reported that 91 offenders had been charged (with 107 processed through the project) with still only two reoffending since 1987 when the first disclosure occurred. What is more important than the crime-prevention cost-effectiveness of Hollow Water (Native Counselling Services of Alberta 2001) is its crime-detection outcome. When and where has the traditional criminal process succeeded in uncovering anything approaching 91 adults confessing criminal responsibility for child sexual abuse in a community of just 600 people?

As we have seen from the systematic exposure of centuries of abuse in the Catholic Church, cover-ups work (Edelman 2020). The imperative in the Catholic Church, just as at Hollow Water, is not so much to put tens of thousands of abusing priests in prison, but to prosecute bishops who persist in covering up the activities or who move abusive priests around, spreading their predation from parish to parish, rather than confronting and incapacitating them into roles separated from children. Criminalising this domination by cover-up effectively may require criminal law reform. Hollow Water perpetrators who refused to participate in the restorative circles did go to prison. Those who apologised to the community and their victims, incapacitated themselves from future offending and worked for the community to help prevent future offending by others were not formally punished.

Conclusion

One implication of macrocriminology is a shift from obsession with convicting individual offenders to the flipping of markets in vice to markets in virtue. This led to the insight of this chapter that incapacitation is more important in criminology than deterrence. Moreover, self-incapacitation is more important than incapacitation by the state.

Macrocriminological theory is a corrective in criminological thought, illustrated by the neglect of a broader vision of incapacitation as a concept that has little to do with incapacitation's conventional focus on imprisonment. It is, however, just a corrective. Prison is an unappealing form of incapacitation because it has such devastating effects on the freedom of families and the confined family member. This chapter proposes the important adaptation of responsive regulatory theory that self-incapacitation will often be more effective in preventing macrocrime when it is used before deterrence, lower in a regulatory pyramid, than with state incapacitation deployed when both self-incapacitation and deterrence fail. There is no purity of distinction between organisational and individual incapacitation in this because organisations are made up of individuals. The regulation of powerful organisations is a micro–macro project.

The pyramid of self-incapacitation and enforced self-incapacitation in Figure 10.3 is worthy of reflection for some common forms of individual offending. Consider a family with an adolescent recurrently in trouble at school for drug use. At the base of the regulatory pyramid, families may pour on a lot of social support and educate the child in how to self-regulate for desistance and recovery. As risks of serious trouble with the police escalate, parents might well apply lessons from business regulatory responsive pyramids, using motivational interviewing with the child after perhaps explaining honestly how they are reacting to other parents being critical of them for failing to totally ground their child. They may explain that what worries them is if something terrible happens to their child because of their drug use, and how they fear they will never forgive themselves for the failure to discipline the child. The aim here in the journey of motivational interviewing is to reach a point where it might be agreed that the child will not be grounded after this infraction and the child undertakes to destroy the drugs and commit to it never happening again. Then the parent asks: 'With my anxiety about being an uncaring parent for failing to ground you, and my terror of future regret, what do you think would be a fair thing if this happens again?' As in business regulation, the hope is that the child will actively agree that self-incapacitation, self-grounding, would be fair in the unlikely event that drug use happens again. When it does happen again, grounding and other measures like rehabilitation program attendance agreed to last time are, as in business regulation, likely to seem more legitimate and to be affirmatively supported by the child. All this seems to have more promise than the usual command-and-control drug regulation by families: 'You're grounded. Period.'

When internet pornography is a trigger for child sexual abuse or internet gambling is a root cause of street offending and suicidal thoughts, blocking offenders' access to relevant sites can be the relevant form of self-incapacitation. Self-incapacitation by gambling providers and by problem gamblers themselves then becomes a series of intersecting pathways to crime prevention that must be joined up in societies like Australia that are most widely afflicted with problem gambling. To ponder these concluding micro examples, consider the hypothesis that macrocriminology implies applying lessons from the macro sphere of understanding to the micro. This is a reversal of the normal trajectory of criminology of applying a micro approach like individual prosecution to a more macro strategy like corporate criminal prosecution.

There is no decisiveness in the distinction between the new concepts of self-incapacitation, enforced self-incapacitation and old concepts of self-regulation and enforced self-regulation in responsive regulatory theory. This is because self-incapacitation is simply one form of self-regulation that has more specificity of meaning than the more general term. In practice, however, self-incapacitation will be implemented in combination with other forms of self-regulation, just as macro-regulation will often be implemented in combination with individual regulation. Self-incapacitation is a specific form of crime prevention, just as gun surrenders are an even more specific form of both crime prevention and self-incapacitation.

Conventional criminology has focused considerable research resources on whether sentencing policy could be reformed to better prevent crime through individual incapacitation in prison. It is hard to see how such research could show a way to save lives. This chapter has attempted to show that self-incapacitation of organisational crime may have saved millions of lives during the decades since Edwin Sutherland first urged us to focus on organisational crime. At the same time, the chapter has argued that the self-incapacitation glass is more than half-empty. So, there are millions more lives macrocriminologists could have been saving from corporate crime in the pharmaceutical industry (Dukes et al. 2014), from future risks of weapons of mass destruction, from war crimes, and more. Many will die on this planet if a nuclear war breaks out between Israel and Iran or Saudi Arabia (with mobile nuclear weapons supplied by Pakistan), or if terrorists purloin a mobile nuclear missile in Pakistan and fire it in a fashion that appears to indicate a US–Russian nuclear exchange. If we do not persuade Pakistan and India to give up their nuclear weapons on the back of a lasting peace in Kashmir, hundreds of millions could die from a Pakistan–India nuclear exchange—more of them in China than in South Asia from mass starvation when crops subsequently fail. The empty space of a half-empty glass of self-incapacitation is an important opportunity for a macrocriminology that makes a difference for humankind. The next chapter re-joins this theme of war crime prevention by coming to an understanding of war and crime as cascade phenomena.

11

Tempered cascades
of crime

Key propositions

Crime cascades to more crime through the following common dynamics:

- Modelling (often conceived as emulation, diffusion).
- Commercial interests cascade particular forms of crime (for example, cocaine franchising) and particular kinds of soft targets for crime (for example, Facebook, Tinder users).
- The crimes of parents cascade to crime by their children; the crimes of children cascade to crime by their friends; differential association cascades.
- Hopelessness, loss of identity and closure of opportunities tend to cascade, particularly at hotspots of concentrated disadvantage in conditions of extreme inequality and policy failure in providing decent housing for all.
- War and pro-violence politics cascade to domination, anomie, hopelessness, closed opportunities and more crime; crime cascades to more war; war cascades recursively to more crime.
- War, crime and anomie are often entangled in mutually reinforcing cascades.
- War cascades to criminalisation of states and criminalisation of markets by armed groups or in pursuit of corruption by shadow states that support armed groups.

Crime prevention cascades when:

- Respected actors have the self-efficacy to transform cultures by modelling anti-crime norms; self-efficacy scales to collective efficacy through explicitly connecting evidence-based microcriminology to a macrocriminology of cultural transformation.
- Norms of civility and nondominating collective efficacy at one locale spread like ink spots that connect up, ink spot to ink spot, covering whole societies with norms of civility.
- Parents and schools mobilise collective efficacy to reject stigmatisation yet communicate to their children why violence and stealing are shameful.
- This enables redemption scripts for offenders to help themselves, and to grasp self-efficacy as wounded healers who cascade help to other offenders.
- An inclusive politics of hope, identity formation and opening of legitimate opportunities cascades to embrace formerly disadvantaged communities (collective efficacy becomes part of CHIME and helps constitute CHIME).
- Civil society obligations to pass on CHIME become an integral part of recovery and a structural way of cascading recovery.
- Institutionally embedded primary groups—families, schools, workgroups—that cascade nondominating collective efficacy alongside other forms of social capital can deliver prevention in the criminology of place; conversely, this prevention can depend on hotspot policing and peacekeeping that make streets safe for collective efficacy, and the planet safe for collective efficacy as ink spots of nondomination spread globally.

Cascading crime and crime prevention

Major institutional renovation to reduce domination is required to accomplish a world with less crime of the powerless and of the powerful. The final chapter draws on the thinking of Chantal Mouffe on the challenges of transforming cascades of hegemony around the globe that are sometimes neoliberal and sometimes authoritarian, and that make transformation a politically fraught project. This chapter lays theoretical foundations that might open our eyes to seeing how both domination and nondomination can cascade, how hegemonic projects and counterhegemonic projects can cascade, through social movement politics.

It argues, for example, that feminist politics has helped to reduce gendered violence. This chapter contends that the anomie discussed in Chapter 3 is a cascade phenomenon, and so is normative order, whether the orders are hegemonic or counterhegemonic orders that cascade at critical junctures. Domination, and the hegemony that justifies it, can never be utterly conquered, but it can be tempered. This chapter lays a foundation for that wider political hope by plugging away at the more modest claims that crime is a cascade phenomenon and so is crime prevention. Crime prevention does not cascade as much as it could, however, with a more visionary institutionalisation of crime prevention.

Braithwaite and D'Costa (2018) deployed mainly South Asian data to conclude that war tends to cascade across space and time to further war,[1] crime to further crime, war to crime and crime to war. Braithwaite (2020a) built from that an analytical sketch of crime as a cascade phenomenon. This chapter draws heavily on both works. Examining crime through a cascade lens helps us to imagine how to more effectively cascade crime prevention. Braithwaite and D'Costa (2018) show how peacemaking can cascade nonviolence, how it cascades nonviolent social movement politics, and vice versa. Seeing crime through the cascade lens opens up fertile ways of imagining macrocriminology. Self-efficacy and collective efficacy are hypothesised as catalysts of crime-prevention cascades in this macrocriminology. Australian successes with gun control and drink-driving point to the importance of explicitly connecting evidence-based microcriminology to a macrocriminology of cultural transformation. More structurally, building collective efficacy in families, schools and primary workgroups may cascade collective efficacy into neighbourhoods and vice versa. The microcriminology of hotspot policing might be elaborated into a macrocriminology of ink spots of collective efficacy that cascade and connect all forms of social and human capital.

---

1   In their update of the evidence on the effectiveness of peacekeeping, Walter et al. (2020) also reached this conclusion. In terms of cascading across space, Walter et al. (2020: 5–6) add value by explaining well how studies like that of Beardsley and Gleditsch (2015) use geo-referenced conflict polygons to show that peacekeeping missions that deploy at least 1,000 peacekeepers can prevent violence from spreading from one locale to another *within* a country, as opposed to from hotspot to hotspot across the borders of countries, as other studies demonstrate through event history analyses. This becomes more strongly the case as the number of peacekeepers deployed increases.

Braithwaite and D'Costa's data unfortunately also reveal that while violence tends to cascade fast, nonviolence cascades slowly. A politics of patience is needed for projects of peacebuilding and crime prevention because they require so many kinds of institutional architectures to be rebuilt.

Criminology's neglect of cascade explanations

The assassination of President Kennedy in November 1963 was followed by a steep, sudden increase in violent crime (Berkowitz and Macaulay 1971). At the time, this seemed out of the ordinary. Yet, we might look back at the history of American violence since as a cumulative sequence of cascade shocks in which this assassination, that of Martin Luther King Jr, which sparked fires across America, and other acts of racial violence, *From Reverend King to Rodney King* (Gale 1996), counted among many important moments that were mostly more local triggers of cascades. The state violence deployed against civil rights and anti–Vietnam War activism formed perhaps other 1960s cascades in the early years of the US crime rise that stretched from the 1960s to 1992 (Chapter 3). It included unprecedented forms of violence such as the National Guard firing on protesting white college students, murdering them in cold blood. The 2020 cascade of violence after the police murder of George Floyd was different from the incidents in Watts or Detroit in the 1960s in a way that is theoretically central to the analysis of this chapter. A politics of violence on the streets was progressively overwhelmed by a politics of nonviolence as the days of protests turned into weeks across America (and globally). The cascade of nonviolent resistance to police violence was slower moving than the early days of escalating violence on the streets, but clearly became the more majoritarian and inclusive ethos of the politics triggered by the initial violence against George Floyd. The 2020 nonviolent movement may not have produced a leader as revered as Martin Luther King, but it produced a more diffused movement that had political consequences— locally in Minneapolis, nationally for the Trump administration and even globally for the 'Black Lives Matter' movement. As weeks of protests turned into months, right-wing extremists raised the temperature of violence. They were encouraged in this by President Trump. He decided to take a page out of Richard Nixon's successful law and order election campaign of 1968, using the violence to stoke a politics of white fear.

So many of the attempted arrests that ignited racial conflict during 2020 should never have been arrests, according to the analysis of Chapter 9. Criminologists must own some responsibility for contemporary excess in the use of arrest because of the overly charitable hearing we gave to broken-windows policing arguments that actually conduced to racist policing. The trajectory of the Arab Spring from 2011 has much in common with the Black Lives Matter trajectory of 2020, even though Black Lives Matter will not cascade to half a dozen civil wars that kill hundreds of thousands of people, as in Libya, Syria and across northern, then central, Africa and the Middle East. What is common between both is that the Arab Spring started with the arrest of an impoverished street vendor in Tunisia who should never have been arrested. His suicide by self-immolation sparked the cascade of nonviolent protest that was the Arab Spring. The nonviolence of the streets was corrupted, and then captured, by a politics of violence, promoted by arms funding by foreign provocateurs. This cascaded to civil wars that brought to power regimes that were even more authoritarian than those that existed before the uprising.

This section contemplates and challenges the limited interest of criminology in cascade explanations compared with other sciences. Then the chapter specifically puzzles over the limited interest in hotspot policing as a cascade phenomenon after it was found mostly *not* to displace crime to nearby communities. Brief consideration is then given to the analytic advantages of reframing gun violence as a cascade phenomenon, then drink-driving, drug dealing, burglary, intergenerational transmission of criminality, life-courses of crime, looting, rioting, corporate crime and war crimes.

This opens our eyes to crime-prevention cascades. Can we catalyse a criminological imagination for purposively nurturing cascades of crime prevention? Special note is taken of the US National Rifle Association's mobilisation of cascades of information and political interests to promote gun culture. Braithwaite and D'Costa (2018) analysed Islamic State's exploitation of the stigmatisation and humiliation of Muslims with information cascades to promote murder. These activist imaginaries are interpreted as models for how crime prevention and nonviolence might also be cascaded. Alcoholics Anonymous (AA) is then diagnosed as a model because of the way its twelfth step involves volunteering to help others recover. AA was influenced by Christian ministry and volunteering for missions of macro-cultural transformation. Christianity was itself a globally massive cascade phenomenon after all. Its cascades—violent and nonviolent—were often called 'crusades'. From a crime-prevention perspective, however, the genius of the AA cascade is that it connects self-efficacy to collective efficacy.

What are cascades?

Cascades are defined as phenomena that spread to multiply instances of themselves or to spread related phenomena. These related phenomena that cascade might be objects like guns that spread simply as objects in markets rather than as social or biological contagions. The guns may cause an epidemic or a cascade of violence but not a contagion in the sense of something that spreads person to person (Fagan et al. 2007). All contagions are cascades and they are the most important kind of cascade. This book interprets cascades as the more general diffusion phenomenon. Cascade explanations are staples across the physical and biological sciences: the cascading of particles in particle physics; the cascading of particles called bacteria and viruses with infectious contagions; environmental cascades to climate change; and the cascading of liquids (lava, water) in the geological formation of planets (Kun et al. 2014). In the social sciences, cascade explanations have also been common. Examples are Rosenau (1990) in international relations, Sunstein's (1997) norm cascades, Kuran's (1998) repetitional cascades, Hale's (2013) regime change cascades, Sikkink's (2011) cascades of criminal enforcement for crimes against humanity and Gladwell's (2000: 7) cascades past 'the tipping point' that spread 'like viruses do'. Contagion in biology and cascades in the social sciences have a shared core of meaning: the existence of a phenomenon induces the diffusion of more phenomena of that type (or mutations of it). In both cases, an analytical shift is demanded from exogenous to endogenous explanation as a priority—to the reversal of cascades and the triggering of counter-cascades.

With crime, we have long known that people are more likely to cheat on their taxes if they perceive a lot of cheating among others (Sheffrin and Triest 1992; Frey and Torgler 2007) and if tax haven and tax shelter opportunities are cascading (Braithwaite 2005). It has long been known that contagion effects are particularly likely with crimes that have a high profile in the media such as hijacking, assassination, kidnapping and serial killing (Bandura 1973; Berkowitz 1973; Landes 1978). Hijacking took off in the 1970s, then virtually ceased in the two decades before 2001, whence it cascaded to a more diverse multiplicity of terrorist scripts. Generations of developmental psychologists have been interested in how phenomena like aggressive disruptive events in classrooms can cascade to one life-course setback after another that spiral to leave young people in desperate situations (for example, Masten et al. 2005). Crane (1991) scales up this kind of microprocess to a macro-contagion model of ghetto formation, showing how cascading social problems pass ecological tipping points. Peer influence is Crane's critical mediating mechanism for these cascading problems, which is also central in differential association theory in criminology alongside cultural cascades of normative meaning. These are also posited as key cascade mechanisms in the theory of collective efficacy in the analysis of this chapter.

Cascade mathematics

Non-criminologists have been more fascinated than criminologists by cascades. Mathematician Adolphe Quetelet (1842) was puzzled by the high statistical variance in crime across space and time. Economists Glaeser et al. (1996) puzzled further over why this variance is so huge compared with variables that are seen as candidates for explaining variation. This leads to the hypothesis that cascading on itself might provide a better explanation than exogenous change. This is illustrated by Miranda Forsyth's (2018b) contemporary fieldwork on sorcery contagions in Papua New Guinea. A district that has never experienced sorcery-related violence suffers one accusation against one sorcerer and, in a short time, violence is being directed by against many who are accused of sorcery. The history of sorcery-related violence in the United States and the United Kingdom has similarities, with most places and times having none and then sudden convulsions into cascades of violence that can be pondered in great art such as Arthur Miller's *The Crucible*. Chapter 2 discussed the case of the Gebusi, among whom all violence, most of it sorcery-related, decreased many times more than a hundredfold for the period 1989–2017 compared with 1940–75 (Knauft and Malbrancke 2017).

When we inspect homicide rates for different years and different countries, Quetelet's (1842) pattern is still evident. There are annual rates recorded of more than 100 homicides per 100,000 population. Chapter 2 explained that El Salvador reached 142 per 100,000 in 1995 and the Gebusi many times higher than that. Then we find more than 50 countries that have had rates of much less than 1 in recent decades. Domestically, we find census tracts with crime rates much more than 100 times the rates for the lowest tracts within a country. Some western societies also seem to have had hundredfold differences between peak and trough homicide rates across the past millennium; England recorded a rate of 100 in the mid-1300s and below 1 for much of the past century, for example (Eisner 2014: 80). Finally, I have concluded that the most dominating organisations, be they Big Pharma or Big Brother police, can kill a thousand times as many citizens as nondominating organisations. At the intersections of these hundred and thousandfold differences, macrocriminology seeks to learn from criminalisation of the worst spaces at the worst times, where 100 times 100 differences may sometimes exist. Why is it inside Democratic Republic of Congo at the beginning of this century that we find villages where a lot of the men and boys and most of the women and girls have been raped, often many times, and mostly gang raped? Why were there many towns and villages in Libya in 1911 where almost all the civilians were slaughtered, and why in Carthage 2,000 years earlier where every house was burnt to the ground and every man, woman and child murdered apart from the 50,000 sold into slavery by Roman legions?

Glaeser et al. (1996) argued that differences in crime rates are huge compared with differences in the variables most commonly used for explaining variation. This is true if we think for western societies about the comparatively modest percentage differences in demographic profiles, in average incomes or in the percentages of people unemployed between high and low areas, and indeed in more sociological variables like collective efficacy. As economists, Glaeser et al. reason that the variance in crime rates is too high to be explained by exogenous changes in rational incentives, by variation in the costs and benefits of crime. They find variance to be too high to be rationalised 'as the outcome of independent decisions to engage in crime' (Glaeser et al. 1996: 542). Criminologists can reasonably dismiss this concern as a consequence of economists being too narrowly focused on the rational calculation of absolute numbers. Yet perhaps criminologists should not be as dismissive when economists turn to the kind of absolute numbers that *could* explain huge variances. Glaeser et al. point out that interactions among people could cascade to explain the variance. If one crack-cocaine dealer interacts with five others to persuade them that becoming a dealer is smart, and each of them so persuades five others, and so on, simulations show this dynamic can multiply huge space-time variance between a point in space-time where that process takes off and places and times where there has been no trigger of the cascade. On the downside of exit from the crack epidemic, Kennedy (2020) interprets the evidence of the spread of negative attitudes towards crack as a cascade of the shamefulness of crack use.

Cascade criminologies

Loftin (1986) is one criminologist who argued that in cities like Detroit in the 1960s fear from rising crime cascaded gun ownership, which in turn fed into the cascading of rapidly rising homicide rates (note also the cascades of fear, disorder and decay in Skogan 1990). Public health scholars used to connect rising crime in New York's disadvantaged communities to an accelerating contagion of social disintegration up to 1992 (Wallace and Wallace 1990). Criminologists had tended not to theorise the reverse crime drop in New York after 1990 as a reversal downwards of that cascade when the city's opportunity structures recovered, readjusted and took off again, recovering from the shocks of the era of deindustrialisation.

Then Fagan et al. (2007) articulated a cascade explanation of the great New York crime rise and fall that is consistent with what is known about these dynamics in a good number of other US cities. In many cities, the trends were not as steep as for New York. Their argument follows in the footsteps of William Julius Wilson's (2012) *The Truly Disadvantaged*. Fagan et al. showed that there was nothing general about it. It was overwhelmingly about young African-American males in neighbourhoods devastated by the deindustrialisation that peaked in the 1980s:

> As middle- and working class African American families moved away from the inner cities when their jobs left, there remained behind a disproportionate concentration of the most disadvantaged segments of the urban populations: poor female-headed households with children and chronically unemployed males with low job skills. The secondary effects of this exodus created conditions that were conducive to rising teenage violence: the weakness of mediating social institutions (e.g. churches, schools), and the absence of informal social controls. (Fagan et al. 2007: 702)

Deindustrialisation was not confined to New York, but was quite a general phenomenon in the West, as was the crime rise from 1960 (Chapter 3). Neither the particular chronology of this crime rise nor the deindustrialisation was general beyond the West (not in developing countries that had not industrialised, and still have not, and not in the tiger economies to which the western factories initially fled). Economists now are on board Wilson's evidentiary bandwagon that the shock of deindustrialisation disintegrated black families, driving up black male unemployment, loss of meaning, insecurity, unwed motherhood, single-parent families and many other social challenges (Autor et al. 2018). Fagan et al. interpreted the rise and fall of violent crime in New York since the 1960s as

> indicative of a nonlinear pattern in which the phenomenon spreads at a rate far beyond what would be predicted by exposure to some external factor and declines in a similar pattern in which the reduction from year to year exceeds what might be expected by linear regression trends. This leads to the second perspective: the factors leading to its spread are not exogenous factors, as in the case of contamination or disaster. Instead, the nonlinear increase and decline suggest that the phenomenon is endemic to the people and places where its occurrence is highest and that this behavior may be effectively passed from one person to another through some process of contact or interaction. (Fagan et al. 2007: 689)

At the macrolevel, the qualification is in order that the US national crime trends are steep but rather linear, both in the crime rise from 1960 to 1992 and in the drop since (Sampson 2019: Fig. 1). Fagan et al. (2007) covaried neighbourhood social and economic characteristics with temporal homicide trends. This identified gun homicides as the key contagious agent. Gun homicides were what 'diffused across New York City neighborhoods, and gun homicides ... [were what] retreated just as quickly' (Fagan et al. 2007: 690). Fagan et al. interviewed young males active in gun violence. This showed qualitatively that diffusion arose in a dynamic process of social contagion. They connect the gun homicide cascades quantitatively and qualitatively to three sub-epidemics in retail drug markets: one of heroin that peaked in 1972; a second of powder cocaine, peaking in 1981; and third, crack cocaine, peaking in 1991. Golub and Johnson (1996) confirmed empirically that the crack cocaine epidemic was indeed a cascade phenomenon. It was a word-of-mouth diffusion of innovation that saw existing powder cocaine snorters move to crack in a huge surge between 1984 and 1986. Guns cumulatively became the basic tools of routine business activity in these booming drug markets. This in turn infected everyday disputes with an 'ecology of danger' (Fagan and Wilkinson 1998). Fagan et al. (2007) concluded that guns were at first an exogenous factor in cascading violence but became an endogenous cascade within socially isolated neighbourhoods of the deeply disadvantaged.

Quantitatively, Fagan et al. (2007) discovered that the occurrence of at least one adolescent homicide in a census tract significantly increased the likelihood of adolescent homicide in surrounding neighbourhoods. It was actually only gun homicides (and not non-gun homicides) that were contagious in producing other gun homicides, controlling for neighbourhood characteristics. In the 1990s, the declining economic opportunities of 1960–92 gradually improved in the neighbourhoods that had driven the crime rise; disadvantage became somewhat less ecologically concentrated; and crack became much less appealing to young people, perhaps to the point where small initial reductions in gun homicides then accelerated to a cascading crime drop.

Mohler (2013) showed that contagion effects explained more than half of property and violent crimes in Chicago. Mohler concluded also that half of the increases in terrorist events in a Northern Ireland dataset could be explained by contagion. In Fallujah in Iraq and in Israel, the civilian terror and conflict death contagion effects were much smaller, explaining only 23 and 12 per cent of the violence, respectively (Mohler 2013). Papachristos et al. (2015) revealed gun-crime patterns in Chicago consistent with Fagan et al.'s (2007) New York cascade patterns; they found that 70 per cent of all nonfatal gunshot victims during the observation period could be located in co-offending networks that comprised less than 6 per cent of the population of the city. A 1 per cent increase in exposure to gunshot victims in one's network increased the risk of becoming a victim oneself by 1.1 per cent, holding all else constant (Papachristos et al. 2015).

Mennis and Harris (2011) revealed spatial cascades, measured as the rate of recidivism for specific types of delinquency. Proximity to a youth offender's residence increased the likelihood of a cascade to others innovating with that type of offending, with the cascading of neighbourhood delinquency specialisations being especially strong for drug offences. Their results support peer contagion in crime specialisation. Differential association theory always identified such patterns as contagiously causal, but there have always been critiques that challenge this with counter-dynamics of birds of a feather flocking together or shared third variables as explanations.

Information cascades in which people make decisions based on their observations of other people's actions seem to be particularly attractive for explaining why criminal behaviours like looting or rioting are normally near zero but can multiply quickly once someone starts a stampede (Ellis and Fender 2011). Herding into illegal tax shelters is likewise an information cascade phenomenon (Braithwaite 2005b). As they sought an integrated explanation of crime–war clusters, Braithwaite and D'Costa (2018) noted that more common kinds of crime also behave like wars in this regard. They point out that, in many countries, the best explanation of whether one's house will be burgled in the next six months is whether it was burgled in the previous six months (Pease 1998); and likewise, the best explanation of whether one's country will suffer a war this year may be whether it suffered a war in the past three years (Braithwaite and D'Costa 2018). Likewise, coups predict more coups and genocides more genocides at the intercountry level of analysis.

When criminologists found that most crime could be concentrated at 3 per cent of the addresses in large cities (Sherman et al. 1989) and policing strategies concentrated at those hotspots could substantially reduce crime at them (Weisburd et al. 2011; Braga et al. 2014), the natural reaction of criminologists was cynical. How could simply 'putting cops on the dots' be effective? Cynicism steered criminologists to the hypothesis that criminals will respond by shifting their crime from old hotspots to nearby locales or by creating new hotspots. Subsequent research did not bear out this displacement hypothesis (Weisburd et al. 2011; Hinkle et al. 2020). Indeed, it showed that hotspot policing not only reduced crime at the hotspot, but also had positive spillovers in reducing crime to lesser degrees in surrounding areas (Weisburd et al. 2011). Recent research with a strong design in Bogotá, Colombia, shows more modest impacts of hotspot policing strategies (Blattman et al. 2018), and Nagin and Sampson (2019) raise important questions about how to correct for the effects of reduced policing at non-hotspots. But the issue that interests me is why did criminologists not proceed from more evidence for diffusion than for displacement with a sense of excitement at the surprise of having their expectations reversed? Why not explore and develop a converse theory that there may be cascade effects of crime-prevention success? Why not build the model of targeted hotspots into a model of ink spots of civility and reintegrative policing that spread? Criminologists tend not to respond to overturned cynicism with excitement. They do not jump at the opportunity to build dynamic theory on new inductive insights.

They prefer to move on to cynicism about something else that they can test with static methods. The tendency of criminology to discipline young minds with an exogeneity obsession is just an example of a wider pathology of recursiveness as something to be controlled rather than savoured and developed, and dynamic theory development as something to push aside in the rush to test first statements of static new theories. To be fair, medicine also had an exogeneity bias, clinging for centuries to beliefs that contagions were a result of the exposure of human populations to the same exogenous factors in the atmosphere.

Modelling macro-cultural shifts

What other cascade clues are evident in emergent patterns of criminality? What facts might be reinterpreted through a cascade lens? Consider the high level of mass shootings in the United States this century, compared with Australia. One way of seeing this, popularised by the American filmmaker Michael Moore, has been that this is a result of the contrasting response of Australia when it had a mass shooting in 1996. Australia toughened its gun laws and funded a national gun buyback in 1996. Australia has not had a mass shooting since 1996 and greatly reduced its rates of gun shootings, so this inference is reasonably warranted within the limits of a comparison of two countries (Chapman et al. 2018). Even if true, it is also true that Australia was galvanised by the shock of the 1996 Port Arthur massacre to cascade a transformational rejection of gun culture across society, whereas in the United States, this has not yet happened. The societal consensus behind the transformation was strong in Australia; it was led by the most conservative prime minister Australia had had in half a century. No Member of Parliament voted against the new gun laws. That is, a cultural cascade might be the operative variable more than the gun buyback per se. And this might explain why the meta-analysis effects of gun buybacks alone are weak (Makarios and Pratt 2012).

American political elites have historically extended their hands to the National Rifle Association (NRA) to cascade ambivalence about gun culture. Albert Bandura (2000) draws together the criminological findings on collective efficacy with a variety of experimental studies to sustain the more general conclusion that groups with high perceived collective efficacy achieve higher motivational investment in their undertakings, stronger staying power in the face of setbacks and greater accomplishments in collective search and pursuit of pathways to change. Bandura (2000: 75) conceives of collective efficacy as 'shared beliefs in the power to produce effects through collective action'. Bandura's insights about collective efficacy are relevant to the counter-hegemonic cascades against domination in the reflections on Chantal Mouffe in the next chapter. Across recent US history, the NRA has been effective in cascading a counternarrative of collective efficacy, partly through an information cascade on social media that insists society needs more guns to protect itself. Indeed, after mass shootings, gun sales often spike (Wallace 2015).

Is there also a cascade in the imaginaries of mass shooters—an emulation effect as one disturbed person takes the lead from other disturbed persons? Is this a diffusion of the idea that a way to resolve anger at their school or workplace is to start shooting? Towers et al. (2015) showed a substantial contagion effect in the United States, with each mass shooting estimated to incite 0.3 extra future incidents. We know high-profile celebrity suicides cascade to increased suicides by ordinary people (Stack 2005) and that media coverage of suicide generally contributes to cascades of suicide (Gould 1990). In China, suicides also temporally cluster in ways statistically associated with the prominence of media reporting of previous suicides in the cluster (Cheng et al. 2011). The fact that media reporting is a mediating mechanism increases the plausibility of the interpretation that a social cognitive cascade is in play rather than an exogenous factor simultaneously stressing contiguous actors. One reason indiscriminate shooting at a purported source of grievance has not gripped the imaginaries of disturbed young Australian men is that a cascade of this imaginary never gained momentum because of the macro-cultural character of the response to the 1996 mass shooting.

Since 2001, suicide bombing is another kind of purposive killing that has cascaded (Braithwaite and Li 2007). Part of the 'strategy of savagery', the 'management of savage chaos', of Islamic State in Naji's (2004: 11) canonical ideological text is to appeal to mentally disturbed young people, among other targets, to become mass killers. Again, information reproduction on social media is an important part of the intentional strategy to cascade savagery, as is the collective efficacy that Muslims can transcend centuries of humiliation and tyranny by infidels to rebuild the Caliphate. With certain cascades that take off—such as suicide bombing and paedophilia-related violence—the problem might be that before the internet, these violent networks were insufficiently dense to cascade. Cyberspace perhaps delivered the density and the darknet the secrecy to cascade furtively (Kennedy 2020). Racist hate speech is greatly enabled by internet amplification. These two cascade reframings go to why cascades of violence are rarely best understood as individualistic forms of human emulation. Whether it is gun culture promoted by the NRA or suicide bombing by Islamic State, we might best build our understanding by looking for purposive action by those with an interest in promoting the cascade. We see this with cascades from war to more war. When one country directs warlike action towards another, this creates opportunities for hawks to break out of the cages that mostly contain them in civilised societies. The hawks seize such moments to purposively use the warlike actions of the other to demand aggression in response. The search for the interests that lie behind cascades of violence has not been prominent in macrocriminology.

The hotspot policing finding that crime-prevention success can cascade violence reduction is evident in many places, including war zones, should criminologists care to see it through a cascade lens (Walter et al. 2020). Some criminologists have argued that the historical data on rates of domestic violence support the conclusion that feminism as a social movement has made a global contribution to cascading reductions of violence against women. Ahmed et al. (2001) and Braithwaite and D'Costa (2018) argue that feminist social movement politics has constituted violence against women as shameful. Pinker (2011) and Broadhurst et al. (2015) put more emphasis on this happening through a feminist form of collective efficacy. For Pinker, there is purposiveness of political action at play in these cascades of violence reduction—the purposive collective efficacy of anti-domination feminist politics.

When levels of gun carrying in public places reduced in the 'Wild West' of the United States, when duelling cascaded downwards towards extinction a century earlier in the United Kingdom, there were purposive moral entrepreneurs of norm cascades behind the scenes. They were local sheriffs who mobilised community support to ban sidearms in saloons and push ordinances prohibiting concealed weapons in cow towns by the 1870s (Utter and True 2000). They were aristocrats who insisted that honour be redeemed in better ways than by challenge to a duel. An example was the way the eighteenth-century reign of Beau Nash at Bath banned the wearing of swords at balls and other social occasions in the aristocratic nightlife capital (Trevelyan 1985: 385). These sheriffs and aristocrats cascaded preventive collective efficacy.

Ross Homel's (1988; Homel et al. 2017) research reveals a purposive campaign to cascade deterrence combined with a norm change. So far, it would seem to have saved more than 10,000 lives since the introduction of police random breath-testing for drink-driving in Australia.[2] Rather like the Australian gun buyback example, Homel found that the effectiveness of the Australian introduction of random breath-testing was much more profound than reported from other countries in the wider evaluation literature. Homel did not interpret this as a pure deterrence effect. He struggled to understand why the introduction of random roadside breath-testing had such a large effect in reducing drink-driving in Australia. Homel fingered the marriage of deterrence to the cultural purposiveness of the norm-building of the Australian campaign. Australian group-drinking norms had long supported drinking and driving. The combined deterrent and normative campaign persuaded drinkers to offer to drive friends home when they had had too much to drink and to save friends from having to do this for them by moderating their drinking and driving. Note that a cascade of self-efficacy is involved (you can make a difference to save your friend's life) as well as a cascade of collective efficacy (a conscious strategy to make the helping behaviour of drinking groups more interventionist). We return to this theme. Deterrence was in the mix because one was being a friend not only to save the lives of friends, but also to prevent their arrest under the new random testing laws. We baby boomers imbibed Australia's heavy drinking culture. We were brought up to believe that drinking to excess on a night out and driving home with your mates were accepted, so we were amazed by the cultural transformation of our children, who became more responsible than ourselves, finding it unacceptable to do that and shocked that their parents had behaved in such an irresponsible way in their youth.

This illustrates how reframing crime as a cascade phenomenon opens new ways of seeing what can work in crime prevention. It had to be accomplished against political mobilisation by liquor industry interests. Mercenary interests in drug abuse can be reframed by a cascade lens on the history of illicit drug abuse. Since opium took off as a mass addiction for the first time in China in the second half of the nineteenth century, we have seen subsequent periods in the histories of many countries when opium or heroin became uncool among most young people. There were

---

2   In the state of New South Wales alone (where Homel focused his research), alcohol-related traffic deaths were around 400 a year up to 1980 and, despite great growth in population and car ownership, have been far fewer than 100 per year every year in the current decade, hitting a low of 45 in 2015 (Centre for Road Safety 2018).

periods of impressive mobilisation against the opium trade in the West and India by the collective efficacy of women's movements networked with the Women's Christian Temperance Union, the Society for the Suppression of the Opium Trade and the Women's Anti-Opium Urgency Committee (Braithwaite and Drahos 2002). We saw an even greater transformation with the largest mass addiction event ever at the turn of the twentieth century in China. Neither opium use nor heroin use is cool for most young Chinese today, nor was it by the middle decades of the twentieth century. Heroin, which had cascaded to increasingly widespread levels of addiction and death across the West from the 1960s, also became more uncool there well before the turn of the twenty-first century. Those with a purposive interest in addiction fought back, however, in some countries, with reconfigured street marketing campaigns for heroin, but more commonly with new products of mass addiction such as crack cocaine, which initially was more appealing to the young; then, when cocaine's appeal faded, ice and new generations of synthetic drugs were marketed as cool party drugs.

Markets in vice that cascade

MacCoun and Reuter (2001) surveyed the evidence on many drug policy experiments worldwide. One conclusion was that the legalisation of illicit drugs does not have a great effect in worsening drug abuse, at least not on its own. Legalisation is mostly associated with sharp increases in drug abuse only when it moves on to aggressive commercialisation. Allowing people to grow their own pot of marijuana and smoke it privately does little to cascade marijuana use. The existence of networks of retail outlets and street pushers linked to substantial commercial producers backed by sophisticated marketing, on the other hand, does cascade drug abuse. Purposive commercialisation of drugs of addiction has throughout history been necessary for genuine mass addiction events to break out, for cascades of vice to defeat the reproduction of virtue (Braithwaite 2005b). There was no evidence of opium being a drug of mass addiction for thousands of years of Egyptian, Mediterranean and Indian opium eating. Then the British East India Company, which was importing shiploads of Chinese goods, searched for something to return in empty ships to China. The company struck on the idea of research and development of how to market opium as a drug of mass appeal in the Chinese market. It improved the delivery system from eating to the more appealing method of smoking opium combined with tobacco. It encouraged triads and other localised criminal entrepreneurs to establish opium dens across China and, later, globally, spreading to locales like the west coast of the United States, Vancouver, New York, London, French port cities and Australia. When China pushed back to protect its young from this commercially driven scourge by banning opium imports, the British state defended its opium interests by fighting China in two devastating Opium Wars. This was a classic case of a cascade of crime cascading to successive wars (in 1839–42 and 1856–60).

The opium mass addiction cascade resulted in Big Pharma (particularly Bayer) subsequently innovating into more efficient injectable opium. This was heroin as a market in vice (Braithwaite and Drahos 2002). Cocaine epidemics were likewise induced by pharmaceutical industry innovation in adding cocaine to cough medicines and other dangerous and ineffective patent medicines. These products were fraudulently promoted as safe and effective. Corporate food interests collaborated with the pharmaceutical industry to put cocaine into Coca-Cola, among countless other mass consumption fads. These were commercially purposive cascades of mass addiction. They were preceded historically by a worse commercial dynamic of mass addiction to tobacco. It is important to note how these cascades of addiction were arrested during the 1920s through a combination of women's movement activism and incorporation of the 1912 International Opium Convention into the Treaty of Versailles peace agreement in 1919. This had the effect of driving Big Pharma out of the opiate, heroin and cocaine markets it had created. It was not prohibition that worked, but the uncoupling of drug marketing from corporate power and from Big Pharma research and development that dampened drug markets. McCoy (1972: 268) found global opium production fell from 41,600 tonnes in 1906 to 7,600 by 1934, to 1,000 in 1970, rising again to 4,200 tonnes by 1989 with renewed commercialisation by organised crime marketing. Heroin exports likewise collapsed in the 1920s. Yet the commercialisation dynamic in cascades of drug addiction continues to innovate and bounce back. There is today's opioid epidemic, which has taken half a million lives, driven by wilful Big Pharma recklessness in the marketing of the pain medication Oxycodone, for which there have been some corporate criminal convictions, a US$8 billion Justice Department settlement in

2020 with Purdue Pharma and a Justice Department suit against Walmart for its alleged role in pushing drugs as a retailer of suspicious prescriptions (Quinones 2015; Humphreys 2017).[3]

American First Nations peoples had been using tobacco in a way that was regulated by ritual and moderation for centuries. When the French Ambassador to Portugal Jean Nicot first imported tobacco from the New World to the French Court in 1556, the beginnings of a commercialisation dynamic saw smoking become fashionable in the West. As with cocaine, the commercialisation of tobacco was fraudulently promoted as good for one's health, to the point where schoolboys at Eton in the seventeenth century were flogged if they failed to smoke for the sake of their health (Walker 1980). As with the British East India Company's research and development into a more commercially appealing delivery system than opium eating, the research and development of the Imperial Tobacco Corporation, which became the biggest corporation in the British Empire, and Duke's American Tobacco Trust created the more appealing drug delivery system of the compact cigarette. In harness with European tobacco corporations, Duke was also a pioneer of mass marketing campaigns to portray smoking as suave, first for men, then for women seen smoking their sleek cigarettes in sophisticated locales like Monte Carlo in Peter Stuyvesant ads. Elegant women attracted the attention of jet-setting males lighting their smokes. Men were classically conditioned by campaigns like the Marlborough Man to associate smoking with a self-image of rugged masculinity. Simple micro-dynamics of classical conditioning were cascaded to scale by commercially purposive mobilisation of culture change.

The difference between emulation and modelling, according to Bandura (1986), is that modelling is not mere habitual mimicry, but emulation with transformative cognitive content. It is emulation that cascades meaning and social identity for those who participate in the modelling.

---

3   The $8 billion payment by Purdue Pharma to victims of OcyContin incapacitated the company through bankruptcy, but an appeal by victim litigants succeeded with the argument that the Sackler family, who owns Purdue, had siphoned almost $11 billion out of the company before the bankruptcy, shifting much of it to off-shore tax havens. Now an appeal of that decision is on that will decide whether victims access any of the personal Sackler wealth as well. Unfortunately, OxyContin addiction became a gateway to a new wave of addiction to heroin or heroin laced with OxyContin, and then to a worse wave of fentanyl or OxyContin laced with fentanyl. Long before they created Purdue Pharma, the Sacklers had been the most aggressive advertisers, marketers and lobbyists for deregulation of marketing psychotropic drugs. This started from a 1960s wave of addiction for Librium and Valium. The paradigm-shifting brand appeal a Sackler business genius invented for Librium was decidedly republican—a hybrid of liberty and equilibrium.

Model mercenaries are commercial organisations with the entrepreneurial flair to cash in on these addictive substitutes for lost meaning and identity in modernity (Braithwaite 1994). Whether the model mercenary is a British trading empire, Chinese triads or their western organised crime successors, the NRA, gun manufacturers, Big Pharma, big tobacco or marketers of tax havens and tax shelters, cascades of commercial fraud are central to the dynamics of crime as a cascade problem. Scholars publishing in the top finance journals have shown greater interest than criminologists in financial fraud as a cascade phenomenon. They reveal fraud contagion effects at the corporate and geographical levels that are associated with the geographical concentration of political corruption (for example, Parsons et al. 2018). Individual offending contagion effects are also demonstrated—for example, mergers that heighten differential association with fraudulent advisors from merging firms increase advisor misconduct by 37 per cent (Dimmock et al. 2018). All this goes to the importance of a macrocriminology of how capitalism constitutes corporations with stunning levels of collective efficacy for good or ill. Corporate collective efficacy can cascade vices or virtues that remake the world.

Intergenerational cascades of crime

This chapter seeks to provoke criminologists to see macrocriminological patterns differently through a cascade lens. So, we shift from unfamiliar to utterly familiar ways of seeing among criminologists. Criminologists are taught, and generally accept, that children whose parents have serious criminal records are more likely to acquire criminal records themselves, as are children who have friends with criminal records. More specifically, children and adults who are exposed to violence, by witnessing it or being subjected to it, are more likely subsequently to engage in violence themselves (Widom 1989; Reitzel-Jaffe and Wolfe 2001; Ehrensaft et al. 2003; Guerra et al. 2003; Kokko et al. 2009; Roberts et al. 2010; Sharkey 2018). Theoretically, criminologists accept that Sutherland and Cressey's (1984) differential association theory and Akers and Jensen's (2011) social learning theory have explanatory value. A meta-analysis by Pratt et al. (2010) supports this. Criminologists argue endlessly, however, about whether to interpret these associations in terms of control theory or differential association.

For its theoretical purposes, this chapter interpolates a third theoretical possibility that this is a temporally and spatially concentrated cascading of criminality from one generation to the next and from child to child at specific locales. The cascade insight here reads as banal in the same way that critics of differential association theory say this theory is banal. What is argued in the concluding sections of this chapter, however, is that by reframing mainstream findings and theory through a macrocriminological cascade lens, through the mechanism of integrating micro self-efficacy with macro-cultural collective efficacy, more interesting insights might follow about how to cascade crime prevention. Chapter 12 takes this further to consider counter-hegemonic cascades of social movement politics, inspired by the writing of Chantal Mouffe (2013, 2018), to transform institutions of domination.

Cascades of anomie and hopelessness

Braithwaite and D'Costa (2018) developed their analysis of violence as a cascade phenomenon from Peacebuilding Compared data on how crime cascaded in conditions of armed conflict. War, in particular, was found to unsettle the normative order; citizens did not know what the rules of the game were, nor who was in charge in a conflict zone (Braithwaite et al. 2010a). This was anomie in the classic sense of an absence of norms and of authority to set them. Braithwaite and D'Costa (2018) concluded from their data that anomie cascades to war and war to anomie. The normative vacuum of anomie attracts the most tyrannous of forces, so domination also cascades. Braithwaite and D'Costa (2018) found that as ordinary citizens become more dominated by warlords and the corrupt politicians in their pay, a sense of hopelessness and loss of identity tend to spread. Political corruption decimates economies in combination with the ravages of war itself so that legitimate economic opportunities are increasingly closed off to the poor. The poor resort to illegitimate opportunities to eke out survival (Cloward and Ohlin 1960). To summarise, not only do anomie and hopelessness come to cascade, but also domination, criminalisation of states, loss of identity and collapse of legitimate opportunities. This is how it is possible in a short space of years for a country like Democratic Republic of Congo to tumble from being second only to South Africa in African industrialisation, and richer than almost all countries in resources and future economic opportunities, to dead last in the world rankings of human development and GDP per capita (Braithwaite and D'Costa 2018: Part I).

Most sociological variables do not cascade, but Braithwaite and D'Costa argue that crime, war, anomie, domination and concentrated disadvantage are critical variables that do. Even with variables like violence that do cascade in contexts like war, gang competition or ethnic competition, there are many contexts in which violence does not cascade. For example, Randall Collins (2008: 9–11) makes the point that, contrary to one-in-all-in barroom brawl scenes in Hollywood movies, where there is no antagonistic group identity under threat in a barroom altercation, the empirical evidence is that bystanders overwhelmingly tend to fearfully shy away from the fight. A huge resource for organisations whose mission is to cascade nonviolence, such as Nonviolent Peaceforce (Gray forthcoming), UN peacekeepers or violence interrupter programs, is the fact that most people in most conditions want to see violence de-escalate rather than escalate and they personally find violence hard to do, even when they are professional soldiers (Collins 2008: Ch. 3; Klusemann 2012).

The dynamics of cascades of armed conflict prevention are mirrored in less devastating ways in the communities of societies at peace identified in the research program of Robert Sampson and his co-authors. They found an association between crime and a collapse in collective efficacy, a more specific form of anomie and corroded social capital. Where collective efficacy was low, crime was high. Pratt and Cullen's (2005) meta-analysis of more than 200 studies of neighbourhoods and crime rates found a mean effect of 0.3 for collective efficacy—results further reinforced by many subsequent studies from other continents.

In communities within wealthy western societies decimated by deindustrialisation, this research showed how cascades of unemployment and concentrated disadvantage cascaded hopelessness and loss of identity and this cascaded to lower levels of collective efficacy (Sampson et al. 1997; Morenoff et al. 2001; Odgers et al. 2009; Hipp and Wo 2015; but see Zhang et al. 2017). Again, this chapter just redescribes criminological findings in the dynamic language of cascades. Cascading collective efficacy prevents crime. Fagan et al. (2014) showed that collective efficacy also ameliorates the negative effects of exposure to violence on substance abuse and the perpetration of violence. There is even some evidence that neighbourhood collective efficacy and rejection of norms of non-intervention may help with the prevention of child abuse (McLeigh et al. 2018) and intimate partner violence through disclosure outside the home to third parties in high collective efficacy neighbourhoods.[4] Aubrey Jackson (2016)—like most research in Footnote 1 in Chapter 12—found that neighbourhood collective efficacy reduces intimate partner violence, but only in neighbourhoods where women have at least a modicum of neighbourhood control over resources. This is a result that reinforces the case we make later for broadening the target beyond collective efficacy to the forms of social capital most relevant to the specificities of particular social problems. Jackson's result that social support from families was the strongest protective factor against intimate partner violence also goes to a somewhat broader kind of social capital.

A theme of *Cascades of Violence* (Braithwaite and D'Costa 2018) is the way anomie and war allow money politics and business corruption to flourish with little restraint. This happens because of the ways money power is connected to the military power needed for survival. Criminalised states and the business cultures thus engendered create few opportunities for the poor, entrenching hopelessness. Poor people who understand these realities of their domination sometimes use it to excuse seizing whatever illegitimate opportunities they can in their wartime struggle to eke out family and personal survival. Indigenous peoples who have their lands stolen by invaders not only struggle to regain the sense of identity that tends to be so connected to their land; they may also struggle to find fault with stealing something back from the occupying majority. That loss of identity for dispossessed first nations peoples is often transmitted intergenerationally. In various ways, cascade dynamics are therefore reinforced by tendencies for crime in the suites to cascade to crime in the streets (Braithwaite 1991). Farrall and Karstedt's (2019) research shows how anomie in the middle-class heartland of societies spreads middle-class crime and anomie right across the social landscape.

War–crime–war cascades

Braithwaite and D'Costa (2018) offer a sweeping but only partially systematic study of micro and macro dynamics from across one large region of the world of how armed conflict cascades to crime, crime cascades to further crime and further armed conflict, and how one war cascades to another. This is part of a more general phenomenon of one kind of violence

---

4   See Browning (2002) and Dekeseredy et al. (2003); though Capaldi et al. (2012) and Wright and Tillyer (2020) reviewed the evidence as mixed.

cascading to other forms of violence (Institute of Medicine and National Research Council 2013). This chapter will not retrace that South Asian evidence. The discussion simply skates through the quantitative evidence on these intertwined cascades of violence that are discussed in more detail in that book. Archer and Gartner (1984) were the first to demonstrate systematically an association between the involvement of a nation in war and the subsequent elevation of its homicide rate (results replicated by Stamatel and Romans 2018). Thorsten Sellin (1926), half a century earlier, discussed less systematic data consistent with this conclusion, and before that Bonger (1916: 518), in 1905, diagnosed war as legitimating violence and neutralising norms of nonviolence (see Gartner and Kennedy 2018).

Ghobarah et al. (2003) confirmed Archer and Gartner's (1984) result cross-nationally for suicide as well as homicide increasing after war. They found that homicide also spikes after war for countries contiguous to the country that experienced civil war. Much of this domestic violence and self-violence cascade is perpetrated by the children of fighters as much as, or more than, by the fighters themselves. In addition to the negative effects on the sons of Australian Vietnam War veterans, their daughters also experienced sharply heightened risks of PTSD, depression, drug abuse and sexual assault (O'Toole et al. 2018). The extremely high rates of rape and sexual assault victimisation for daughters of Australian Vietnam veterans seem to hold a key as to why the contagion effects are stronger for the daughters than for the sons of Vietnam vets. For Israel and Palestine, there is a strong time-series association between spikes in conflict-related violence and spikes in homicide and other forms of violent crime (Landau and Pfeffermann 1988; Landau 1997, 2003; Huesmann et al. 2017). Clark et al. (2010) found an association between the exposure of Palestinians to conflict violence and domestic violence in their families, while Dubow et al. (2010), Landau et al. (2010) and Boxer et al. (2013) discovered an association between Israeli and Palestinian children's exposure to conflict violence and their subsequent PTSD symptoms and violence within their own community. Miguel et al. (2008) revealed an association between being a professional soccer player who suffered different degrees of exposure to civil war in their home country and the receipt of yellow cards for aggressive behaviour on the field. The Institute of Medicine and National Research Council (2013: 66) discussed the evidence for a link between African child soldiers' experiences of violence and subsequent peacetime violence, though this effect was greatly ameliorated by good postconflict reintegration, family support and economic opportunities.

Braithwaite and D'Costa (2018) argue that there is something of theoretically general importance about violence in all of this. As discussed in Chapter 3, violent death rates often go up after a war 'ends' in cases like Iraq, El Salvador and many in Africa (Boyle 2014: Ch. 8; Duffield 2001: 188), as can gender-based violence such as sorcery accusations (Forsyth 2018a).

Sambanis (2001, 2004) found that a country that has neighbouring states at war is more likely to experience a civil war itself, as did Gleditsch (2002, 2007), Salehyan and Gleditsch (2006) and Ward and Gleditsch (2002), but not Hegre et al. (2001). Alex Braithwaite (2016) and Houweling and Siccama (1985, 1988) showed that interstate militarised conflicts cluster in both space and time to produce hotspots. Braithwaite and Li (2007) showed quantitatively that terrorist incidents cascade and cluster at and from geographical hotspots. Braithwaite and Johnson (2012) further found that within one country (Iraq), IED attacks were clustered in space and time and these hotspots behaved in a manner similar to that observed in the spread of disease and crime. Terrorism is also exacerbated by hotspots in the sense that the exit of foreign fighters from hotspots is associated with heightened terrorism at home (Braithwaite and Chu 2018). Similarly, the exit of state troops back to the homeland after foreign wars is associated with heightened homicide at home—much of it domestic violence. Wilkinson's (2004: 44–45) Indian data show that Hindu–Muslim riots and casualties in them are predicted by the incidence of riots in that town in the previous five years. Finally, Chenoweth and Perkoski (2017) concluded that one of the best predictors of countries experiencing mass crimes against humanity was the experience of mass killings in their past, and Harff (2017) found that past genocide in a society increases the likelihood of a cascade to a future genocide. In civil wars, the number of civilian killings per month is a good predictor of the number of civilian killings in future months (Hultman et al. 2013: 887).

Tambiah (1996: 214) interprets the Indian evidence as showing that 'intermittent ethnic riots form a series, with antecedent riots influencing the unfolding of subsequent ones'. This is also true of Braithwaite and D'Costa's (2018) inferences about the cascading of nonviolence. Here, global imaginaries of nonviolence and freedom from tyranny are important alongside local and national ones. Alex Braithwaite et al. (2015) showed statistically that nonviolence, like violence, is a contagion phenomenon reproduced globally by feeding on itself. In the Arab Spring, however, the global cascade of freedom and nonviolence was not the only global imaginary in play. In all the Middle Eastern and Arab uprisings, from the 1979 Iranian Revolution and Egypt and Syria in 2011 to the 'new Arab Spring' in Lebanon, Sudan, Algeria and Iraq in 2019–20, tyrannical jihadist imaginaries of a caliphate imposed by force were competing toe to toe with peace-loving pluralists for leadership of a nonviolent revolution.

All this evidence about the way that war and other forms of violence cascade reveals similar dynamics to the way Sampson (2012) shows in Chicago that both crime and the preventive power of collective efficacy cascade across space (from neighbourhood to nearby neighbourhood) and time (from decade to decade across a century of Chicago crime data).

Pondering how to cascade crime prevention

Respected actors model anti-crime norms

The Australian campaign to transform drinking and driving norms illustrates the importance of respected friends cascading crime prevention by modelling anti-crime norms, perhaps combined with messaging in television advertising and school road safety campaigns. Feminist social movement politics led mothers to lead their sons and daughters to gradually cascade normative prevention of domestic violence. There have been many social movements that have cascaded crime prevention of macrocriminological importance. Since the publication of Rachel Carson's *Silent Spring*, the environmental movement has advocated for environmental crime enforcement and encouraged at least some respected business leaders to model pro-environment norms that take their industry through new ceilings of excellence in environmental compliance systems (Braithwaite and Drahos 2000). In earlier periods of history, the trade union movement began to secure similar accomplishments for crimes against workers. Earlier still (in the eighteenth century) churches constituted the collective efficacy of the antislavery movement that globalised the criminalisation of slavery (a case study re-joined in the final chapter).

Sharkey's (2018: 51) research on the great crime drop since 1992 shows the importance of a 'wave of community mobilization that spread across US cities in the early 1990s, after decades in which community organizations struggled for public support'. Community-based organisational mobilisation against violence was complemented by diffusion across the country of an ethic of responsibility to keep every member of a community safe. Sharkey et al. (2017) analysed longitudinal data (over 20 years across 264 cities) with an instrumental variable strategy to deal with endogeneity for the formation of community-based organisations to find that 'every new organization formed to confront violence and build stronger neighbourhoods led to about a 1 percent drop in violent crime and murder' (Sharkey 2018: 53). This was in the 1990s, when in some of the largest US cities thousands of new organisations of this kind were formed. A 9 per cent reduction in the murder rate was associated with 10 additional organisations focusing on crime and community life in a city of 100,000 people (Sharkey et al. 2017). While foundation funding and funding by multilevel governance for this kind of community-based mobilisation may be common exogenous factors here, rallying around them at the neighbourhood level may be more of a cascade phenomenon, and the spread of this funding priority among foundations may also involve emulation. As in the empirical literature on the cascading of jihadist imaginaries (Braithwaite and D'Costa 2018), the cascading of the imaginary can be more resilient, resourceful, innovative and adaptive than the cascading of specific actions, such as specific forms of terrorism.

Collective efficacy to cascade ink spots of civility that connect up

Peacekeeping operations often confront a seemingly impossible enforcement swamping challenge of anomie and violence. One way they rise to this challenge to become effective in reducing postconflict violence (as documented in Chapter 6, Footnote 5) is to start wherever it is feasible by creating an ink spot of security and civility somewhere, then somewhere else. Once this process of intervention passes a tipping point, a self-sustaining cascade of peace and civility spreads; the ink spots connect, eventually merging into one another to pacify a society more holistically with norms of civility (Braithwaite and D'Costa 2018). It is not exactly the reverse of a hotspot strategy in that the priorities for the first ink spots of pacification tend to be the most strategic sites for institutional stabilisation: areas around the parliament, courts, banks, hospitals and UN headquarters itself. The hottest hotspots of war tend to enter late into the cascade of pacification, though hotspots for atrocities against civilians behind the front lines are often deployment priorities to maximise the protection of civilian lives. One dynamic that underpins this cascade is that neighbouring communities look across to the new peace zones to envy the greater progress they have made in renewal, trade and development, peacefully working together to rebuild schools and health centres. They decide they want this, too. Their neighbouring ink spot gives them AMP: Awareness of what they need to do to build local peace; Motivation to do it; and shows them a Pathway to become the next ink spot of civility (Honig et al. 2015). The Peacebuilding Compared team has documented this conscious ink spot strategy of peace operations in Timor-Leste (Braithwaite et al. 2012), Bougainville (Braithwaite et al. 2010b) and Democratic Republic of Congo (Braithwaite and D'Costa 2018). Local actors may have the awareness and motivation needed to build peace in their community, but they may not mobilise their collective efficacy until peacekeepers secure a safe pathway to manifest that collective efficacy.

It is not just that (notwithstanding many case-specific failures) UN peacekeepers are statistically highly cost-effective in reducing the incidence of war (Chapter 6). It is also that UN police and military peacekeepers are more potent in crime prevention than western domestic police (Hultman et al. 2013).[5] One reason for this potency might be that hotspots of civilian murder during civil wars tend to be extremely hot and comparatively small in number at any point in time, even though they may be large in number across the duration of the war as front lines move across wide swathes of territory. Each region of frontline action takes its turn to become a transiently anomic space.

Hotspot policing policies in western societies can build out their policy imagination for how to cascade hotspot successes. We might be optimistic that this could work with similar success to peacekeeping because, naturalistically, as discussed above, there are positive spillovers of hotspot policing successes in reducing crime in neighbouring locales. What seems to be required of the analysis here is to connect several separate policy ideas. One is to continue to deploy scarce police resources to patrol high-crime hotspots where they can make the biggest difference. The next

---

5   In the multivariate and matching analysis of Hultman et al. (2013) across all African armed conflicts between 1991 and 2008, the movement from zero to just 200 UN police in a peace operation, conditioned by controls on other variables, was associated with a reduction in the expected number of civilian killings from 96 per month to 14. Given this is a monthly estimate, and the average duration of deployments is 65 months, small contingents of police seem to save very large numbers of lives.

might be connected to the cascade literature and the collective efficacy literature. This connection is made in part on the simple basis that police patrols in high-crime areas can give residents the confidence to walk the streets to build collective efficacy (Kochel and Weisburd 2019). Collective efficacy scholars rightly say that citizens simply being on the street is not enough; dense street networks are not enough until the networks are mobilised to be active with preventive interventions. Citizens feeling safe to venture on to the streets of a hotspot can be interpreted as a necessary but not a sufficient condition for crime prevention.

Neighbourhood disorder (which reintegrative hotspot policing might dampen) also threatens other facets of social capital such as generalised trust (Intravia et al. 2016). It is not necessarily the police who will be effective in building collective efficacy, though it is a possibility (Weisburd et al. 2015) for which there is some evidence (Weisburd et al. 2012; Kochel et al. 2015). Support for groups like Moms UNITE for Health, which has a collective efficacy philosophy of offering help in walking groups around the neighbourhood with practical objectives like health education messaging, could be a more participatory and practical approach (Dlugonski et al. 2015), as could simple sociality like shared supervision of children and attractive conditions of access to shared community gardens (Teig et al. 2009; Comstock et al. 2010). Shur-Ofry and Malcai (2021) showed that community gardens are an institution for collective action (Ostrom 1990) that scales from a micro initiative to a macro transformation of a city as a social contagion without central regulatory direction. Quantitatively, they show that new gardens boost the increase in the spread of gardens, and the diffusion of gardens displays a fractal pattern[6] and clustering. These three attributes are cascade features in self-organised complex systems. While gardens expand without top-down intervention, Shur-Ofry and Malcai (2021) suggest that municipalities can be bridging institutions that nudge and trigger self-amplifying processes. Sampson (2012: 350) likewise concludes that nonprofit organisations can weave a web of mundane routine activities that can lubricate collective life in an unplanned way as social capital formation in pursuit of some public good.

---

6   Fractals are objects that manifest self-similarity. This means geometrical features of similar structures across a range of scales.

First, there is an empirical question. After hotspot policing succeeds in reducing local crime, we must understand whether and how collective efficacy grows naturally. Are there local initiatives or policy settings that help it grow faster? With that evidence in hand, criminology could be ready to change policy settings, not only to cascade hotspot policing, but also to cascade capacity-building outwards for collective efficacy in its wake. This can transform the hotspot into an expanding ink spot that will eventually connect to other expanding ink spots—ultimately to reduce crime across a whole city and then a society. Put another way, it becomes a good investment to intervene to accelerate small cascades of naturally occurring civility. The hope is to nudge cascades past the tipping point beyond which collective efficacy, security and civility continue to cascade to cover an entire society. Rauktis et al. (2010) show that a good predictor of the adoption of restorative child protection programs is whether such programs exist in neighbouring communities. Policy thinkers such as Gale Burford use this study to argue that the best way to scale up restorative programs and restorative capital is not to disperse pilots all over a country but to invest in quality programs in adjacent neighbourhoods so they might become nodes to diffuse ink spots of innovation out from a supportive cluster (Burford et al. 2019).

CompStat accountabilities of police leaders currently fail to nurture a cascade policy imagination. Police leaders are evaluated and rewarded in CompStat in terms of how well they perform in reducing crime in their own patch, so much so that when they succeed in cascading their success to another precinct, they may help that area's patrol leader to promotion ahead of them! Combined with the incentives CompStat creates for the non-reporting of crimes in one's own precinct, the potential for cascading benefits outside that precinct makes a case for a more nuanced and less statistical peer review of the performance of police leaders in how they leverage hotspot policing. They need to pile in support for their peers who are having success on the peer's patch—success that is currently eluding them. The hope and the collective belief are that ink spots of success elsewhere will ultimately be encouraged to spread to their own patch and to every patch.

Linking these three ideas—hotspot policing, collective efficacy and cascades—is only illustrative of a more general cascade policy imagination. Focused deterrence is another policy idea shown to work well on focused places and problems, such as gun crime by gangs in a particular city (Braga et al. 2018). Once success is secured in persuading a gang that operates in one area to desist from gun crime, what are the new policy levers to cascade this success to other forms of crime committed by that gang? Restorative and responsive policing have a raise-the-bar strategy as one possible answer to this question (as discussed in Chapter 9).

This raise-the-bar strategy has also been applied to reversing stampedes into tax havens and other financially engineered shelters (Braithwaite 2005b), causing cautious corporations to cascade out of shelters. Far from Wall Street, in Yangon, in 2016 Peacebuilding Compared fieldwork, I was intrigued to see the Milken Foundation providing helpful assistance with regard to how Myanmar's fragile financial system might avoid a systemic crisis. This was redemptive work of the ex-prisoner Michael Milken, portrayed by the Michael Douglas 'greed is good' character in the film *Wall Street*. In this work, there were shades of the stellar contribution of Watergate criminal Charles Colson to the restorative justice movement through his establishment of Prison Fellowship International after his release from prison. Crime prevention can go corporate with this kind of Wall Street collective efficacy, conceiving of the deepest harms in society as no longer matters of individual action but matters of corporate action. Corporate compliance systems and cultures of corporate social responsibility sometimes do cascade social licences for integrity and justice. They are a path to crime prevention insufficiently discussed as an option for a better future.

Cascading redemption; cascading self-efficacy

How might crime-prevention policy respond to the phenomenon that the crimes of parents cascade to crime by their children; and the crimes of children cascade to crime by their friends? Reintegrative shaming theory (as revised in Ahmed et al. 2001) offers one possible approach. It picks up the insight from Albert Cohen (1955) that if the justice system stigmatises a family, a peer group, a gang, a school, an ethnic or religious group, a corporation in corporate crime enforcement or, one might add, a jihadist group, this can foster the formation of criminal subcultures. Stigmatisation motivates humans to reject their rejectors. Once this subculture formation sets in, it cascades because a law-abiding value promoted by my rejectors will be rejected and reversed. Doing so is a subculturally reinforced way of rejecting my rejectors. Cohen might suggest today that cascades of mass shootings in schools can be understood as young people being rejected by a school that rejects violence, and then rejecting the values of their rejectors through turning mass violence against the school community.

A remedy, according to reintegrative shaming theory, is schools that suppress stigmatisation by hating violence and loving perpetrators of violence. This sounds vague and platitudinous, yet the social movement for restorative justice prioritises schools over the justice system and has worked through detailed, practical reintegrative programs with which there is now vast experience and some encouraging evidence of effectiveness (Hopkins 2003; Morrison 2007; Augustine et al. 2018; Open Society Institute 2020). McCold's (2008) study of 1,636 children with behavioural problems sent to a restorative school program found a 58 per cent reduction in reoffending, as discussed in Chapter 4.

Shadd Maruna's (2001) research emphasises the importance of redemption scripts in restorative dynamics and desistence from crime more broadly. Serious offenders who made good had to find a new way of making sense of their lives—a theme also taken up by Giordano et al. (2002). Desisting offenders re-storied their life histories. They defined a new ethical identity for themselves that meant they were able to look back at their former criminal selves and believe they were 'not like that anymore' (Maruna 2001: 7). They found appeal in the Jesse Jackson ethos: 'You are not responsible for being down, but you are responsible for getting up' (Maruna 2001: 148). Those in Maruna's persistent reoffender sample, in contrast, were locked into 'condemnation scripts'; they saw themselves as irrevocably condemned to their criminal self-story. Maruna's desisting offenders had re-storied themselves to believe that their formerly criminal self 'was not me'. The self that did it was, in William James's terms, not the I (the self-as-subject, who acts), nor the Me (the self-as-object, who is acted on), but what Petrunik and Shearing (1988) called the It, an alien source of action (Maruna 2001: 93). Restorative justice might therefore help wrongdoers to write their It out of the story of their 'true' ethical identity. Maruna (2001: 13) concluded that communal processes he called 'redemption rituals' were important in this sense-making because desisting offenders often narrated the way their deviance had been decertified by important others such as family members who said Johnny was now his old self. Zehr (2000: 10) makes the point that whether we have victimised or been victimised, we need social support in the journey 'to re-narrate our stories so that they are no longer just about shame and humiliation but ultimately about dignity and triumph'. This is therefore a self-efficacy effect that complements at an individual level the collective efficacy effect demonstrated by Sampson et al. (1997).

Another feature of Maruna's (2001) 'generative scripts' that characterised desisting offenders was their desire to help others as part of defining a renewed positive identity for themselves. LeBel et al. (2015) assessed more recent progress with implementing this 'wounded healer' strategy. An impressive body of evaluations is yet to accumulate, though there is encouraging research (Perrin et al. 2017). Heidemann et al.'s (2016) mixed-methods study of desisting wounded healers among formerly incarcerated women is encouraging. Another study, by Lee et al. (2017), of drug offenders, found that two 'spiritual virtues'—service to others and the spiritual experience of love—contributed to reduced recidivism and did so through greater humility. Defiance, in contrast, 'was associated with higher incarceration, while the combination of service and love predicted lower incarceration and mediated the impact of defiance' (Lee et al. 2017: 161). Lee et al.'s (2017: 168) results were interpreted as support for the claim of the co-founder of Alcoholics Anonymous that AA's 12-step process boiled down to two core principles: love and service. The twelfth step of AA recovery explicitly involves helping to heal the suffering of fellow alcoholics. The evidence from systematic reviews of the effectiveness of AA's 12 steps as a package is encouraging on accomplishing abstinence (Kaskutas 2009; Humphreys et al. 2014; Kelly 2017). While this is contested, the lesson I draw here from AA is not so much about its evidence base as about its strategy for scaling up collective efficacy from self-efficacy. AA may be effective, but not as effective as holistic multisystemic family therapies (Spas et al. 2012) that engage and empower whole family systems with evidence on effective approaches for multiple risk factors. This is because such therapies have that multidimensionality of holistic peacekeeping, problem-oriented policing, restorative justice, responsive regulation, motivational interviewing and positive deviance approaches to human development, as discussed throughout this book.

White (2014) expresses this as 'recovery is contagious and recovery is spread by recovery carriers'—a multiplicative networked dynamic of the shift from 'I story' to 'We story' (White 2015). The cascade point here is that if each healed addicted person sought to pass on their healing to help multiple others, there might be a multiplicative cascade of prevention. If each recovering criminal offender imbibed self-efficacy and joined in the collective efficacy to seek to help a number of troubled youths in the neighbourhood where their history gives them street credibility, where they will not be rejected as rejectors, there is the prospect of a multiplicative cascade of freedom-building crime prevention. This only becomes true if wounded healers mobilise widely and if the evidence continues to be encouraging that they, and those whom they help, experience reduced offending. To date, the interest of policymakers in mobilising wounded-healer cascades of freedom and prevention has been modest. So, we must await further evidence that such a virtuous cascade could scale up. AA has institutionalised the scaling up of wounded healing with flare for alcoholism. Some 106,000 AA groups exist in 150 countries and countless hybrids of AA with distinctive brands have proliferated (White and Kurtz 2008). AA is a massively scaled up NGO that cascades collective efficacy overwhelmingly into the hands of volunteers inspired by its twelfth step of helping others to recover. Wounded healers do not have to be wounded by addiction or crime to be interpreted as wounded healers by their community. Sharkey's (2018: 174–79) discussion of Noongar night patrols in Australia valorises the preventive work of Aboriginal people wounded by colonial dispossession and the stripping of their identity. Identity is retrieved in part through a Noongar approach, relying on embedded cultural authority, walking the streets to prevent and de-escalate community conflicts before they escalate to violence. Harry Blagg's estimate that there are 130 such First Nations night-patrol programs in Australia is now a considerable underestimate and there is a rich tradition of research by Aboriginal scholars on the hybridity between First Nations night patrols and state policing that emphasises the criticality of fluency in local Indigenous languages, cultural knowledge and skills and cultural respect to persuade without domination (Langton 1992; Porter 2016, 2018; Blagg and Anthony 2019).

The hypothesis advanced here is that both self-efficacy and collective efficacy can be helped to cascade through well-known strategies. The contours of these strategies are conceptualised in the recovery capital literature (Best and Laudet 2010; Best et al. 2015, 2018; Best 2017; Hall et al. 2018) that defines CHIME (Connectedness, Hope, Identity, Meaning and Empowerment) as an intertwined cluster of social relationships and social beliefs that constitute recovery capital (Chapter 7). Recovery capital and CHIME are hopeful candidates for cascade effects because they have a key characteristic that they share with collective efficacy, social capital, human capital and recovery capital. Unlike financial capital, recovery capital, social capital and human capital are not depleted through use. When you manifest collective efficacy by helping someone, you do not reduce help because helping behaviour is contagious. People do pass on acts of kindness (Tsvetkova and Macy 2014); experimentally, cooperation reproduces itself (Fowler and Christakis 2010).

Institutionalised contagions of collective efficacy

There are more deeply institutionalised sites than AA programs that can cascade collective efficacy. These are called families, schools and primary workgroups inside organisations. Good families, schools and workplaces do encourage their members to pass on acts of kindness, to pay forward trust and collective efficacy, to help others recover from problems from which they themselves have recovered, to be wounded healers who multiply their own healing, especially as they grow into family and organisational leaders, and to intervene when they see an opportunity to prevent predation. There is much that we can do to further educate, motivate and show pathways to these benefits for people inside these institutions. A macrosociological imagination requires that we ask whether these institutions might provide the most effective ways to cascade collective efficacy because they are more institutionally embedded primary groups than neighbourhood groups. This is not to cast doubt on the importance of place in inscribing disadvantage and anomie that was so convincingly revealed by Sampson (2012), Shaw and McKay (1942) and other urban ecologists. Yet families, schools and workgroups might provide more fertile soil for the spread of the social roots of collective efficacy across geographical places than places themselves because of their more institutionalised character and the multiple levers they can mobilise.

Community that is liberated from place—indeed, that connects communities across very long distances—is important in the internet age. The rising creative class that Richard Florida (2014) contends is the engine of twenty-first-century growth is concentrated through sites in cyberspace as well as at physical locales like Silicon Valley and Manhattan. The other side of the coin is that digital divides concentrate disadvantage just as do neighbourhood and international divides. The internet can connect the collective efficacy of grandparents as well as parents into school communities to help with children's journeys of learning; it can connect up families increasingly separated by geographical mobility. Combined with the installation of solar panels in the remotest villages of rural Africa currently without electricity, the internet can help connect the nodes of concentrated disadvantage on the planet to educational opportunities.

Australian work in the social capital literature shows that trust in government and voluntary taxpaying mostly spread out from primary group trust in families and workgroups, more so than from civil society (as in the theories of Putnam 2000; and Skocpol 2013) (Job and Reinhart 2003). The dynamics emphasised by Putnam and Skocpol are shown in this empirical work to be important in Australia, but less important than the rippling out of social capital from primary groups. Primary-group social capital (which includes, but is a more general concept than, collective efficacy) can be a platform for cascading collective efficacy and other benefits of social capital such as improved health and education outcomes, which in turn also help reduce crime, with the crime reduction then further improving health, education and employment outcomes. This is because exposure to horrific violence can derail learning and wellbeing for years (Sharkey 2018: 93–94, 111).

Reconfigured hotspot policing might have most impact when it cascades macrosociological effects and when they pacify dangerous spaces to the point where citizens are enabled to return to the streets to spread collective efficacy. Yet the healthy effect sizes of strengthened collective efficacy on organisations attaining their objectives,[7] and the strong effects with achieving educational outcomes and reducing educational disadvantage in schools (Eells 2011; Leithwood and Sun 2012), suggest that places are not necessarily the only or the most fertile sites for planting the seeds of self-efficacy and collective efficacy. Then there was Lackey's (2016) result that neighbourhood collective efficacy in Ohio's *rural* neighbourhoods had a strongly significant effect on self-reported delinquency, but school collective efficacy had an even stronger coefficient when added to her model and caused the neighbourhood collective efficacy effect to fall below significance.

The collective belief of teachers that by working together they can deliver better educational outcomes may even be the strongest school-level predictor of those outcomes, ahead of predictors that most of us might have expected to be stronger, such as socioeconomic status, parental involvement, prior achievement, motivation and teacher–student relationships (Hattie 2009, 2012; Donohoo 2017). The collective efficacy of students encouraging one another not to give up on solving mathematical problems can also have strong impacts on improving the

---

7   These include Stajkovic et al.'s (2009) and Gully et al.'s (2002) meta-analysis effects of 0.35 and 0.41, respectively.

outcomes for difficult skills (Katz and Stupel 2015). Goddard et al. (2017) likewise found that teacher collective efficacy strongly improved student mathematics and reduced the mathematics achievement gaps suffered by African-American students by 50 per cent. Bryk and Schneider's (2002) more Putnamesque study of social capital in schools showed that schools with high levels of 'relational trust' delivered reduced truancy and improved learning outcomes. Finally, Tian et al. (2017), in a wonderful Chinese study, showed that classroom collective efficacy helped students to become more active and effective learners, better at self-regulating their self-efficacy. The combination of high classroom collective efficacy *and small class sizes* delivered collaborative, relational learning that simultaneously produced improved learning and reduced delinquency and aggression (Tian et al. 2017).

Therefore, the best solutions to crime problems may not be found in either place or criminal justice system variables. The best paths to crime prevention may maximise benefit–cost ratios because they cascade broader forms of social capital than collective efficacy; these broader social capital cascades help explain collective efficacy and help solve other deep social problems through the impacts of collective efficacy on many of the problems that concentrate disadvantage—like health disadvantage (Ahern and Galea 2011; Gilbert et al. 2013), suicide (Maimon et al. 2010), obesity (Cohen et al. 2006) and even environmental collapse (Jugert et al. 2016; Thaker et al. 2016). People need to believe in their collective capability to make a difference to the environment before they will make a difference. Other facets of social capital beyond collective efficacy may be more effective in delivering other public goods like mental health that in turn contribute to crime prevention. Hardyns et al. (2016) found that social support—whether from families, schools, workplaces, neighbourhoods or beyond—was the facet of social capital most important to sustaining mental health, while neighbourhood levels of social trust, disorder and collective efficacy had negligible effects.

A broad macrosociological policy imagination for expanding social capital might also have a wider array of benefits than collective efficacy. Collective efficacy has the strength of being a form of social capital attuned to direct crime prevention. Yet trust, reciprocity, collaborative skills, social support skills and hope might all be forms of social capital that nourish one another and support collective efficacy. On the other hand, however effective are families, schools, workgroups and other primary groups as seed beds of social capital, self-efficacy and collective efficacy, if citizens dare not venture on to the streets to manifest collective efficacy at dangerous hotspots, that macrosociological potential can be cut off. Policing at places might be important in this way, even though places may be relationally thinner sites for building collective efficacy than primary institutions that enjoy thicker institutional fabrics for relationality. And we discussed earlier that there is evidence that both police in high-crime neighbourhoods and peacekeepers in war zones make it safe for community leaders to venture on to the streets so they can build collective efficacy. When cascades of collective efficacy enabled by hotspot policing that is not racist complement more holistic, multidimensional strategies for cascading social capital and tackling concentrated disadvantage, micro-policing policies might connect to a macro-strategy that not only reduces crime, but also improves health, homelessness, educational and employment outcomes, workforce productivity and an array of other forms of social wellbeing. If all this is true, narrowly micro criminal justice policies are never likely to be as attractive in cost–benefit terms as macrosocial ideas that are liberated from policy silos like the criminology of place.

A puzzle for criminology is why collective efficacy is such a central variable in the criminology of place, but less so in life-course criminology, especially when Robert Sampson (2012) himself has always emphasised these links and is a towering figure of both fields. Arguably, the more foundational institutional building of cultural habits of collective efficacy in families and schools is more important than building collective efficacy in workgroups. Yet in western economies it is business that has seen the biggest macro-cultural shifts towards collective efficacy. This started well before World War II with Elton Mayo's relational school of organisational studies, with its critiques of machine bureaucracies and Fordist production lines. The transformation greatly accelerated in the 1970s, and more strongly in the 1980s, with American business soul-searching that Japanese business productivity was outperforming that of US corporations. Japanese quality circles delivered collective efficacy for improving quality; they were then widely emulated in the West. Half a century ago, US corporations applied lessons drawn from Japan and from the successes of autonomous workgroups in Swedish companies like Volvo that broke out of the top-down discipline of Fordist production systems. Business energised transformative leadership for change. This was powerfully demonstrated by Jung and Sosik's (2002) finding from 47 South Korean workgroups that transformational leadership could empower members, build cohesiveness and collective efficacy and thereby improve workgroup effectiveness in achieving business goals. A meta-analysis shows that trust in the local work team is a particularly critical variable across 112 studies, improving performance substantially over and above trust in leaders, past performance and other key controls, moderators and mediators (de Jong et al. 2016). This could be the most important domain where markets in virtue have contributed more to domination reduction than virtuous states or virtuous civil society actors.

Arguably, the United States, better than any society, translated these lessons into the challenge of collective efficacy for innovation in the new information economy. The evidence is strong from US business that 'transformational leadership' works when it persuades semi-autonomous workgroups that they can work together and the collective efficacy to discover, innovate and learn. Systematic reviews conclude that training programs to improve teamwork and helping behaviour do improve teamwork and team performance (McEwan et al. 2017). Western schools and families have not shifted to transformational leadership for collective efficacy to the same degree. Paradoxically, they remain more rooted in individualistic philosophies than do business institutions. Schools and families tend to be more focused on building the self-efficacy of individual children as the path to their success in life. 'The child can do it' remains a more important trope than the idea that 'the classroom can do it' or 'the family can do it'. Only in explicitly collective activities such as performances by choirs or bands, or team performances in sport, do most schools fully emphasise collective efficacy. Professional development for teachers tends to be individual professional development rather than professional development that builds the collective efficacy of teaching teams.

Restorative justice in schools and families is one movement that seeks to transform this. Restorative group decision-making in nuclear and extended families and in school classrooms often starts with building out from strengths by asking a family to list their greatest strengths as a family, a classroom to list their greatest strengths as a class. The facilitator then writes them up for the group on a flipchart. Then a family group is enabled to continually return to the theme that instead of focusing on their children's many problems, these problems might begin to fall away if they will only believe in, and build out from, the strengths their family supports can deliver.

Hence, the hypothesis of this section is that visionary policy shifts that drive all major institutions in the society to educate themselves in the importance of social capital formation will make it easier for hotspot policing to make a big difference in preventing crime as it applies lessons from the criminology of place. These will also be collective efficacy policies with higher benefit–cost ratios because there is evidence of their relevance to improved educational outcomes, improved employment, more rewarding work lives, heightened productivity, improved health, reduced alcoholism, smoking, obesity and suicide, and collective efficacy in transforming environmental impacts (Muller et al. 2018). The macro-policy imagination involves holistically strengthening both the recovery capital that enables the rehabilitation of offenders through CHIME and the social capital that prevents crime before it occurs. It is about building social capital in the intermediate civil society institutions such as bowling leagues, choirs and clubs that so impressed Putnam (2000) and in the encompassing civil society organisations that once had millions of members that so impressed Skocpol (2013), such as the Women's Christian Temperance Union and lodges with millions of members.[8] But most importantly, it means holistically building social capital in the primary groups of the institutions with the deepest cultural roots: families, schools and workgroups in business and government. And, yes, neighbourhoods as well.

Kirk (2009) made the important contribution of showing that school-based, family-based and neighbourhood-based collective efficacy, when combined, substantially reduce juvenile arrests and student suspensions from school. Simons et al. (2005) delivered the equally profound contribution of showing that neighbourhood collective efficacy encouraged authoritative parenting among African-American caregivers. Authoritative parenting is warm and supportive but insists that boundaries are not crossed; it is distinguished from authoritarian and laissez-faire parenting. The evidence has long been overwhelming that authoritative parenting is a key to crime prevention (Wright and Cullen 2001). So, it is an inspiration for a holistic vision of cascading social capital formation to understand Simons et al.'s (2005) finding that the collective efficacy

---

8   Fortunately, some of these mass participation organisations still exist in which most members take their turn to be president of their little local branch. An example in Australia is the Country Women's Association (CWA), which, when I led the Consumers' Federation of Australia, was its most effective member in campaigns to hold corporate Australia to account. At that time, in the 1980s, the CWA still had 2 million members.

of a community amplifies the benefits of authoritative parenting for delinquency reduction. The result is profound because the effect sizes of authoritative parenting on delinquency reduction are generally stronger than those of collective efficacy, even though the latter also tend to be strong (for example, Simons et al. 2005: 1019). All of this is just another way of describing how a macrocriminological imagination shifts the focus away from criminological silos and towards cultural and structural transformation that is multidimensional in its cascading of complex, often mutually reinforcing, processes of social capital formation.

Social capital or collective efficacy?

The more transformative shifts towards the collective efficacy of business compared with social institutions also illustrate the dilemma that caused Robert Sampson to sharpen the focus of social capital on to collective efficacy. US business has done brilliantly in unleashing the collective efficacy of its information-age technology corporations to solve so many previously unsolvable challenges. Yet the collective efficacy of tech giants like Facebook has also been mobilised to abuse the privacy rights of its customers and to collaborate with the authoritarian security services of many states to threaten freedom. More broadly, all forms of corporate malfeasance and crime are difficult to hold together, as revealed by another Chicago School empirical literature on how hard it is to hold business cartels together. Criminalised cartel discipline requires highly developed forms of collective efficacy. At the same time, the managerial self-efficacy of leaders that is grounded in the collective efficacy of their organisation is central to efforts by organisations to control corporate crime (Jenkins 1994; Braithwaite et al. 2007). So, we should applaud mention by Sampson (2012: Ch. 15, fn. 21) of the hypothesis that the crimes of Wall Street during the Global Financial Crisis might have been prevented by a combination of transcending legal cynicism towards financial laws and building collective efficacy to regulate and self-regulate in respect of those laws. Sampson is tuned in to this kind of dilemma. He worried that sometimes in the urban ecologies he studied, the strong communities with strong social capital were white communities that mobilised social capital to exclude black entry to their neighbourhoods—in the worst cases, even by violence or firebombing their new homes. Sampson is alert to the work of William Foote Whyte (1943) and Suttles (1968) showing that criminogenic organisations such as youth gangs often mobilise their collective efficacy to prevent 'young hotheads' from needlessly bringing heat on the gang. Street leaders regulate the criminal adventurism of younger gang members. We see the dilemma sharply in the public health literature: in communities where norms are tolerant of smoking, collective efficacy increases smoking; in communities where norms are intolerant of smoking, collective efficacy reduces smoking (Ahern et al. 2009). When policymakers disperse slums, they disperse both some positive and some negative collective efficacy dynamics (Skogan 1990).

This is one reason Sampson's theoretical move is to specify his definition of collective efficacy to a focus on social cohesion combined with the willingness to intervene on behalf of the common good (Sampson et al. 1997: 918). His measures follow this specification with its biggest cluster of four items being about helping behaviour oriented to youth crime prevention. These are expectations that neighbours would act if: 1) children skip school and hang out on a street corner; 2) children spraypaint graffiti; 3) children show disrespect to an adult; and 4) a fight breaks out in front of their house. There are several other items that are about the social cohesion part of collective efficacy in the composite concept. These include items with a classic social capital character in the Putnam sense, such as: 'People in this neighbourhood can be trusted'; 'People around here are willing to help their neighbours'; and 'This is a close-knit neighbourhood' (Sampson 2012). All this in turn is highly correlated with the density of civil society associations. With such a composite index we can never rule out the interpretation that the impacts of the 'willingness to intervene to prevent' items are proxies for the causal effects of more general social capital and social cohesion variables (as in Bursik 1999; Lederman et al. 2002) or vice versa.

The extant literature never puts Sampson's conception of collective efficacy in competition with Bandura's. Bandura's conception is both more general and more specific than Sampson's. On the one hand, Bandura's collective efficacy is more general in that it is not narrowed to the willingness to intervene in ways relevant to crime prevention. Bandura's collective efficacy goes more generally to the belief of groups that they can act together with effectiveness to solve a problem conjointly, be it crime, helping children to learn or hurting people who are whistleblowers against organisational malfeasance. Bandura's collective belief within disadvantaged school communities that all students can be helped to grow, learn and flourish may be more relevant to defeating disadvantage there than Sampson's collective efficacy as a willingness to intervene to prevent bad behaviour.

On the other hand, Bandura's collective efficacy is more narrowly a social cognitive belief of groups; it does not combine cognitions shared in groups with the preventive actions taken by groups (or expectations of preventive action as a proxy for preventive action) in the way Sampson's conception does. The strength of Sampson's conception is its focus on ties strongly tethered to collective actions, contrasted with the wide range of other forms of ties that are weakly tethered to action that prevents crime.

We might say that Sampson's move is helpful in specifying that the activities of the Ku Klux Klan or the NRA are not collective efficacy. On the other hand, there can be no guarantee that in a world in which the collectivism of the social cohesion facet of his measure is high, the collective efforts of authoritarian groups will not also be structurally strengthened. Alongside the efforts of community groups that do by Sampson's lights promote the public good, the collective capabilities of the Ku Klux Klan and the NRA might also be strengthened. It may be that collective efficacy is vital to hold together drug cartels and the communities that tolerate them and that paramilitary cartels build community and regulate low-level criminality as part of their strategy for enabling higher-level criminality, or violence may be exogenous to the formation of gangs for protection. These may be reasons for Cerda and Morenoff (2009) finding the counter-theoretical result in Medellín, Colombia, that neighbourhoods high in collective efficacy have higher concentrated disadvantage and higher rates of homicide and perceived violence.

We see this dilemma in systematic studies at the cross-national level of analysis that Sampson does not consider. Societies whose citizens score high on collectivism in their social values have higher levels of violence (Karstedt 2006, 2015). Karstedt is not measuring collective efficacy here but a collectivism scale that has been replicated as stable. This can be interpreted as the risk that highly collectivist societies can be more prone to stigmatising outgroups (and more dominated by an honour culture for ingroups), thus enabling violence against outgroups at times of social stress. Honour cultures—not only in collectivist societies, but also among gangs and paramilitary groups inside individualistic societies—have strong but short bonds that cut off the embrace of outgroups, according to Karstedt. Collectivism, as understood in Karstedt's research, emphasises bonding to the exclusion of bridging, cutting off Granovetter's (1973) strength of weak ties because people's obligations, alignment and honour reside with their own group.

At times of great societal stress, extremists can take charge and enrol collective efficacy to projects of exclusionary violence. There is also a great deal of qualitative evidence in the armed conflict literature for Karstedt's view that there can be a recursive loop between extreme violence and collectivism. When a society is afflicted with extreme violence, people seek shelter in loyalty to collectives that embrace protective duties towards them and that cut off outreach to perceived enemies (Karstedt 2011a). This is what Karstedt means by cutting off the strength of weak ties. We saw this danger with the way President George W. Bush could mobilise the formidable (if not sustained) collective efficacy the United States has been able to mobilise at times of war, especially the collective efficacy of all media barons in 2001, but also embracing the opposition Democratic Party, in a way that was easy to understand after the shock of the 9/11 attacks on the United States. This collectivism and collective efficacy at a time of threat, in a society that is not normally highly collectivist, justified the invasions of Afghanistan and Iraq that in the opinion of many international lawyers were crimes of aggression (Braithwaite and D'Costa 2018). We saw it with the formidable collective efficacy of the Tutsi leadership of Rwanda in a counter-genocide against Hutus inside Congo in the aftermath of the 1994 Hutu genocide against Tutsis inside Rwanda (Braithwaite and D'Costa 2018).

For the above reasons, I do not think Sampson can be fully convincing that specifying collective efficacy as a combination of social cohesion and intervention to promote a liberal Rawlsian public good resolves the challenges. Yet this is not the only theoretical move Sampson makes to help with these challenges. His other move is to integrate legal cynicism into his empirical and normative analyses. He finds that the spatial concentration of collective inefficacy and legal cynicism together explains crime (Sampson 2012: Ch. 9). In other words, if societies promote a world with equally strong collective efficacy and respect for laws (that include the human rights of outgroups), collective efficacy is more likely to be a force for good. By my lights, this is the more promising of his two theoretical moves to counter the problem of the Ku Klux Klan as a historical instantiation of American collective efficacy. Naturally, I would say that because it is kindred to the moves in the theory of shame and reintegration (Ahmed et al. 2001). This theory specifies bad shame as not only stigmatisation as opposed to reintegrative shaming, but also shame that mobilises disapproval of those who seek to break away from or blow the whistle on criminal groups or criminal subcultures. Good shame is reintegrative shaming that prevents domination and reinforces the values of just criminal laws that protect against domination. Those anti-domination criminal law values help prevent collective and individual actors from participating in criminal subcultures.

Likewise, we should read Sampson's theory as steering us towards seeing good collective efficacy as that which motivates individuals and collectives to prevent crime and respect the rights of others. My inclination is to theorise this as nondominating collective efficacy. Collective efficacy, in contrast, that motivates the abuse of rule-of-law values such as human rights is bad collective efficacy. Or, as I would theorise it, cultures and structures of collective efficacy against domination are phenomena that social activism should seek to cascade. Those cascades should only be encouraged, however, when that mobilisation is checked and balanced by cultures of reintegrative disapproval of collective efficacy that dominate others. More structurally still, until we have clearer evidence of how highly specified forms of collective efficacy do good, we do better to be scholars who point to the likely virtues of strengthening all forms of social capital in all kinds of places and institutions, but in combination with struggle against the politics of domination. Whether the domination takes the form of criminal domination of others or domination through concentrations of disadvantage, the struggle against it must be advanced through cascading many forms of social capital. At the end of Sampson's journey, I read this as the most important essence of his theoretical destination (and also Bandura's). Republican freedom as nondomination requires much more than this. It requires mutual checking and balancing among strong individuals (with self-efficacy), strong communities (with collective efficacy), strong states, strong markets, strong international institutions and strong legal institutions (all of which draw on collective efficacy).

Conclusion

A criminology that neglects cascades seems as silly as a medicine that is uninterested in containing contagion. Macrocriminological explanation must come to terms with deeply institutionally structured endogeneity of crime and crime prevention. Reframing crime as a cascade phenomenon implies a shift from research on individual offenders to macrocriminology. The contribution of this chapter is just a sketch of options for catalysing cascades of crime prevention. Developing a well-formed theory of crime cascades, let alone marshalling the evidence for such a theory, is a future project; it is not an accomplishment of this chapter. Braithwaite and D'Costa's (2018) study of cascades of violence across South Asia was a considerable empirical undertaking that could be submitted as a proof of concept—but no more than that. The 10 propositions of that book about cascade mechanisms towards war and peace are more important than those about crime, particularly in showing what can be done with the insight that the best way of protecting ourselves from future wars is to stop getting into current ones. Yet a neglected reason for the importance of that policy work is that war and crime cascade into each other so profoundly. If we follow a cascade analysis, a strong United Nations can be seen as an institutional path towards lower long-run crime in our neighbourhood. Below is a recap of starting hypotheses for a reconfiguration of criminology based on the way this chapter has built on D'Costa's and my earlier book.

Crime cascades to more crime through the following common dynamics:

- Modelling.
- Commercial interests cascade particular forms of crime and particular kinds of soft targets for crime.
- Differential association cascades.
- Hopelessness, loss of identity and closure of opportunities tend to cascade, particularly at hotspots of concentrated disadvantage in conditions of extreme inequality and policy failure in providing decent housing for all.
- War and pro-violence politics cascade to domination, anomie, hopelessness, closed opportunities and more crime; crime cascades to more war; war cascades recursively to more crime.
- War, crime and anomie are often entangled in mutually reinforcing cascades.
- War cascades to the criminalisation of states and the criminalisation of markets by armed groups and the growth of shadow states.

Then it was argued that crime prevention cascades when:

- Respected actors have the self-efficacy to transform cultures by modelling anti-crime norms; self-efficacy scales to collective efficacy through explicitly connecting evidence-based microcriminology to a macrocriminology of cultural transformation (the lessons from Australian gun and drink-driving control).

- Norms of civility and nondominating collective efficacy at one locale spread like ink spots that connect ink spot to ink spot, covering whole societies with norms of civility.

- Parents and schools mobilise collective efficacy to reject stigmatisation yet communicate to their children why violence and stealing are shameful.

- This enables redemption scripts for offenders to help themselves, and to grasp the self-efficacy to cascade help as wounded healers to other offenders.

- An inclusive politics of hope, identity formation and the opening of legitimate opportunities cascade to embrace formerly disadvantaged communities with CHIME.

- Institutions of civil society, following the model of Alcoholics Anonymous, institutionalise obligations to pass on CHIME as an integral part of recovery and as a structural way of cascading recovery.

- Institutionally embedded primary groups—families, schools, workgroups—that cascade nondominating collective efficacy alongside other forms of social capital can deliver prevention effects in the criminology of place; conversely, these prevention effects can depend on reintegrative hotspot policing and peacekeeping that render streets safe for collective efficacy.

- Awareness of these possibilities for prevention is complemented by Motivation and efficacious Pathways that actors can see. AMP is imperative for preventing cascades of crime.

Braithwaite and D'Costa's (2018) cascade of norms of nonviolence provides a ninth explanation of when and why crime prevention cascades. Specific antiwar norms that can be encouraged by social movement politics also cascade, such as the global norms against torture, against the use of chemical weapons, against wars of aggression and the anti-mercenary norm. Braithwaite and D'Costa argue for universities to collectively organise a preventive diplomacy wiki for sharpening diagnostic capabilities in conditions of local and global complexity. If Braithwaite and D'Costa are right that war cascades to more war and more crime, war-prevention cascades might cascade to crime prevention. They advocate a macrocriminology of how to ride this tiger.

Apparent contagion effects may in fact be contiguous actors being exposed to the same exogenous factor at the same time. This discussion has not grappled with the best methodologies for separating such exogenous causation from cascades. These are methodological challenges in which sciences like medicine are more advanced than criminology, and challenges which this author would not tackle impressively. An implication of the analysis is that criminology must become methodologically stronger in that regard. Like medicine, criminology can learn to temper its hang-up with exogeneity to see the importance of research for understanding how to dampen contagions, even when it does not yet understand the micro-mechanisms that drive their spread.

The foregoing dot points are suggested as a framework for the kind of macrocriminological reframing that might make a good fist of big patterns in the evolution of crime. These include:

- Explaining why western societies have less violent crime than they had centuries ago (Eisner 2014).
- Explaining why so many Latin American societies have so much more criminal violence than other regions and have not experienced the post-1992 crime drop of their northern neighbours (Nivette 2011).
- Explaining why East Asian societies have continuously experienced dramatic reductions in violence since the onset of the steep crime rise in many western countries from 1960.
- Explaining why in the same period the United States has had higher crime and war-participation rates than other western societies.

The cascade analysis of this chapter therefore directly connects to the analysis of how these patterns are shaped by shifting normative orders in Chapter 3. Conversely, how could control theory be seen by criminologists as one of the most empirically supported of all theories without confronting it with the difficult macro questions and with alternative cascade explanations? Does it makes sense to say that the United States has so much more crime than Canada, Europe or Japan because Americans are less able to control their impulses? Explaining crime as a cascade phenomenon is a path that might deploy Bandura's (2000) distinction between self-efficacy and collective efficacy and Robert Sampson's analyses of concentrated disadvantage and social support for transformation from anomie to collective efficacy. Hope resides there for renewed prospects of micro–macro theoretical synthesis.

12

The art of struggle for
free societies

The art of complexity

To be a serious social democratic leader in a democracy has always been demanding. You must make the tax system more progressive, build social housing, revitalise the welfare state, grow a more redemptive and inclusive education system, increase the minimum wage, reduce discrimination based on gender, sexuality, race, age, disability and more, shift the shape of the economy so people grow in a wealth of human services while shrinking their wealth in consumer durables and other activities that burn carbon and other pollutants, strengthen dozens of regulatory institutions, energise peace diplomacy, care for refugees, revive the United Nations and be advocates within it for nuclear disarmament, and more.

To be active social democratic citizens, however, in one sense demands much more than we demand of our leaders. Social democratic citizens must hold our leaders' feet to all these fires that could see them burned by entrenched interests. On top of that, we must keep social movement politics in good condition. We hit the streets to support youth leaders on 'School Strike 4 Climate' day. We are active in showing that Black Lives Matter and in resisting all manner of dominations and wars. In a second sense, active citizenship is not so demanding. It is a labour of love that sustains our souls. And we know we must not and cannot diffuse our energies into every cause. Rather, we select some concentrated contributions that matter, growing the hearts of activists who CHIME with Connectedness, Hope, Identity, Meaning and Empowerment. Good activism is like good scholarship in being a gift of joy that nourishes our being alongside our fellow earthlings.

The theory of crime and freedom is a theory of what to do to build a society that subdues domination and subdues crime. What is to be done? Such an enormous list has accumulated in the key propositions listed in Appendix I. There is so much to do only in making minimally sufficient deterrence work, just to enliven so many separations of private and public powers. Yet they are actually a long list of tributaries of practical work that give meaning to rivers of transformation. These rivers are:

- Reduce all dimensions of domination.
- Separate and temper powers.
- Strengthen institutions of the market, state and civil society, and strengthen individuals.
- Maintain a normative order that nurtures collective efficacy to resist domination.
- Strengthen financial capital, human capital, social capital, recovery capital and restorative capital.
- Prevent wars before they begin to cascade violence, anomie and domination.

These six rivers with all their tributaries then combine to form a particular flow for macrocriminology. This is the recursive flow of strengthening freedom to prevent crime and preventing crime to strengthen freedom. The many tributary propositions show what it means for freedom to be a wide and powerful waterway. Freedom is socially embedded in many not so minor flows of institutions. This vision is contrasted with thin liberal freedom. The argument is that thin liberal freedom perhaps helps in crime prevention, but only weakly, whereas thick republican freedom helps mightily.

My empirical analysis is complex about when and how crime is increased or decreased by wars, markets, states, civil societies, inequalities of different kinds, pluralised separations of powers, normative orders of diverse kinds and varied forms of capital. These structural features cannot be reduced to a small number of simple empirical understandings; the normative dot points are simple and sweeping, even as they are grounded in an empirical analysis that is complex. Because of that empirical complexity, the political sense-making of the six dot points will be radically different in different times, places and circumstances.

I hope readers who reject republican social democracy in favour of liberalism, socialism, or conservatism can still find the odd inference of value to them in this book, as well as some good issues for conversation and the waging of political contestation. While you do not have to be a republican social democrat to find value in the theory of freedom and crime, this is the political philosophy that gives coherence and direction to what is otherwise a jumble of propositions for a complex world. Rejecting republican social democracy just renders my long list of propositions devoid of its pretences of elegance, coherence or parsimony.

A paradox of what this book has accomplished is that it shows how a nuanced grasp of empirical complexity can motivate empirically informed normative inferences that are simple enough to be rallying cries for populist political struggles. A good example of this is the empirical understanding that most forms of inequality and poverty do not explain most crime most of the time, but that *some* form of inequality or poverty or discrimination helps explain crime (and war) most of the time. This empirical understanding motivates the normative inference to 'reduce all dimensions of domination', even when particular dimensions in particular circumstances do not explain crime or war. Hence, the art of complexity that averts policy paralysis by analysis is the art of putting normative propositions in conversation with explanatory claims and vice versa. Finally, I hope criminologists who believe normative theory is something scientists should not do will nevertheless find some empirical insights in the macrocriminological reframing of the field.

The final pages of Chapters 2 and 8 attempted to create the rudiments of a roadmap for quantitative researchers to begin to knock over the many unknowns to inform our understanding of what makes all these institutional tributaries flow. There is much for historians of crime and freedom to do. Great challenges lie ahead for ethnographers of crime and freedom. When that is done, many of my tributaries will prove to be creek beds that have run dry, particularly in nuanced application to contingent local institutional histories. New tributaries, however, may be found that run deeper to make crime prevention flow with freedom and freedom flow with crime prevention.

In this work, criminologists should not be too humble that the work of political theorists of freedom is so much more profound than that of criminologists. The political philosophers, lawyers, economists and historians do contribute to grand intellectual challenges that give meaning to freedom. But if criminologists play their part badly, financial crimes will cause financial crises that might cascade to war. If they do not play their part in showing how to regulate environmental crimes, there will be ecocide. Surviving political philosophers will then be back doing their work in dark caves. If criminologists do not discover how to prevent cyberwarriors, cyberterrorists and cybercriminals from doing foolish things that destabilise weapon control systems, that polarise previously listening democracies into digital tribes that disengage from their enemies, genocide or ecocide awaits humankind. We may suffer an unintended nuclear war between India and Pakistan next year, or next century. It might cause an unprecedented impact on the ozone layer, a nuclear winter and famine for decades across the entire planet (Mills et al. 2014; Hess 2020) or there might be no global nuclear winter and only regional environmental impacts (Reisner et al. 2019), depending on whose model you choose to believe. Whatever was the correct assessment of the extremes of these risks during the 2010s, they are bound to be higher during the 2020s and 2030s as India and Pakistan expand the number and sophistication of nuclear weapons they are capable of launching. This book has explored a journey of belief that macrocriminology matters because it has worthy contributions to make to preventing ecocide and genocide and preserving freedom and democracy.

As the speed of missiles increases, panicked generals have fewer minutes to decide whether their screens reveal a false alarm or an imperative to use or lose their missiles. Gone are the good old days of the Cold War when nuclear powers had 30 minutes to decide whether to launch in response to the multiple occasions when false evidence of attack secretly shook the planet. Ecocide and genocide are preventable; criminologists have obligations to their descendants to get to work on crime-prevention projects that inspire hope with their relevance to these challenges. The next section discusses how criminological theory must become more adaptive to a dynamic world normative order with the example of AI crime.

AI crimes

Control over Artificial Intelligence (AI) renews powers to dominate. AI enables crimes that leverage domination, as in control of swarms of killer robots on ground, air or sea. One standard answer to this risk is to say that ethicists as well as engineers must be involved in design of AI algorithms. Yet no one in the social sciences or in public administration ever felt it wise to entrust anything totally to ethicists. The insights of ethicists have great value, but must be checked and balanced by a galaxy of other traditions of understanding found across universities and societies that offer different kinds of insights about complex realities.

Algorithms are defined as sets of rules (usually procedurally sequenced, step-by-step sets of rules (for example, first do A, then if B, do not do C, and so on)). All socio-legal scholars understand that the rule of law cannot work justly as a rule of rules that can be read off by one actor placing their lens upon complex realities to decide how a set of rules applies to a set of facts. Nor can AI work justly when decisions are made by one pre-programmed machine. A method for reconciling rules and principles is needed to render the rule of law just. This must be combined with a method of multifaceted dialogue between judges and prosecutors, judges and defence lawyers, defence lawyers and prosecutors, among different judges in appellate courts, among all these professional actors and witnesses, defendants and jurors, and in dialogue with legal scholars who reflect and write on long and paradoxical histories of case law. The more powerful are the actors contesting the interpretation of rules (as in corporate tax law, securities law), the more the body of rules evolves towards complexity and thickets of contradiction that allow the interpretation of one sub-set of the rules to evolve to challenge the logic of other sub-sets of the wider fabric of rules. Then the rule of law must be tempered with a rule of principles, dialogically applied. An example is Braithwaite's (2005b: 144–55) theory of legal certainty by transforming the relationship between rules and principles, and outside-in regulatory design.

The more AI succeeds in extending power, the more it will fall under the control of powerful corporations and national security states. This can mean computers gaming rules to advance the objectives they are programmed to pursue—be they profits on trades, or kills. A kindred evolution of algorithmic gaming and loopholing of complexity and contradiction will accelerate to render the wider fabric of the ethical rule of rules unserviceable. Propensities of machines, and of powerful actors who own them, to game rules requires more than tempering the rules by principles and by dialogue and appeals, as in the practice of the rule of law. Most defenders of AI will say that 'a regulator' is also needed. While that is definitely true, this book has shown that regulating corporations doing business actually requires hundreds of regulators. In the less complex business environment of the 1980s, Grabosky and Braithwaite (1986) studied 103 major business regulators operating in one country (Australia), without including international regulators in the study. The present book concluded that corporate and national security state power must be tempered by hundreds of separations of powers within institutions and between them. In addition to state checks and balances, AI domination must be tempered by trade unions, consumer groups, environmental groups, Citizens for Tax Justice, Shareholders' Associations, professions such as health, architecture, engineering, accounting, compliance professionalism, and more. They also need to be tempered by the work of parliaments, elections and referenda, by political parties, by a complex array of public service bureaucracies, which in turn are regulated by public service commissions and inspectorates, Ombudsmen, anti-corruption commissions, human rights commissions, by international law enforced by treaty secretariats, UN agencies, and other international institutions like the International Civil Aviation Authority meta-regulating flight by drones just as they do for piloted flight. In sum, we might want AI to be tempered by all the institutions discussed in this book, and for all these institutions to learn to adapt to this challenge. Therefore, it is facile to say that to avoid glitches AI should be regulated by 'an AI regulator'. We can assume that AI regulated by one regulator would be as large a folly as corporate conduct would be if regulated by just one corporate regulator. While it is too early to comprehend how criminal entrepreneurship in domination through AI will evolve, we might assume that most of the principles for tempering power to control organisational crime discussed in my 150 propositions will apply to AI crime, and that many extra principles will be needed that are AI-specific.

The military-industrial complex leads lobbying for unregulated AI as it gathers around itself well-funded ethicists it can live with. As we see with preliminary use of drone warfare in Libya and attacks inside Saudi Arabia, it can considerably destabilise and unbalance balances that serve peace.

In time, the drone swarms may arrive to attack strategic laboratories on university campuses we love, mimicking the Israeli method of extra-judicial assassination of Iranian nuclear physics professors. However worried we should be by that risk, we cannot, should not, kill off the power of AI. Superior AI capabilities to detect cancer and detect fraud in carbon markets are urgently needed. AI constitutes new markets in virtue, new markets in vice, and new capabilities for extreme domination in ways that render most of the theoretical spadework of this book relevant.

National security states and the most richly capitalised corporations are the actors seizing control of the AI assets that most extend wealth and power. What this means is that AI creates a new frontier of hegemony. It therefore calls out a new hegemonic contest from civil society, for example to ban algorithms for killing human beings, criminalise them, socialise them as shameful. The key phenomenon to understand for those who care about freedom is exactly how does AI transform hegemonic settlements, exactly how, in detail, can AI power be tempered, and what should be the nature of struggle for a new hegemonic settlement. That is a topic for many books beyond this one. Because domination is voracious in the way it grows new modalities and frontiers of domination, the question of how to struggle for new hegemonic settlements to temper this expansion is a natural way of conceiving the central political question. Having illustrated its importance with the example of AI, this is the question that animates this concluding chapter.

Peace and the local turn to freedom

A problem with the approach of this book is that there is little prospect of achieving freedom and crime prevention during a civil war or a foreign invasion along any of the institutional rivers its chapters have followed. The second part of the problem is that it is unsatisfactory for me to keep referring the reader to another recent book with Bina D'Costa, another vast literature, on that part of the macro picture about how to pursue and moor workable institutions of peace. The fact is that there is much to learn from peace research concerning the limits of all 150 macro conclusions. Most wars and the war crimes that fester within them are rendered complex by many local cleavages that feed and transform master cleavages, often through joint action by local and supralocal actors (Kalyvas 2003, 2006). Civil wars are neither feuds writ large nor local manifestations of macro cleavages. Rather, wars are phenomena that, like crime, can only be pacified with justice, hotspot by hotspot, right across national–global landscapes. This is because wars spread violence through mechanisms of local, national and international cleavage and alliance.

What we learn about how to do peacebuilding well has lessons of more general import about how to struggle for better institutions. After Cambodia was ravaged by genocide, civil war and invasion by a foreign power, the United Nations could simply install a peace operation to build better institutions on its ashes. The United Nations did that with great success in consolidating peace with dramatic reductions in crime from the extreme levels of murder and theft that prevailed during the genocide, as discussed through the research of Broadhurst et al. (2015, 2018). The Cambodian peace operation, however, was a failure in institutionalising freedom. The legacy of war since 1985 has been one of despotism by a former Khmer Rouge communist battalion commander, Hun Sen, who defected to support the invasion by Vietnam. He institutionalised an authoritarian one-party state that pretends to hold free elections.

What we learn from peacebuilding research is that it does not work for the United Nations to march in and start building institutional superstructures of separated powers, such as a professional judiciary. It does not matter how well the United Nations trains the judges because the despot fires them if they act with genuine independence. We learn that the better strategy is to ask what institutional building blocks for the foundations of a better society have survived in the ashes or are beginning to sprout from them. This approach applies to the green shoots of the agonistic pluralism discussed in the next section. Without civil society contestation of hegemony, hegemony cascades horrors of domination.

This way of thinking is apt for judicial institutions. Peacebuilders, local and international, must ask themselves: 'What is already working around here to deliver justice and safety from violence for these people?' Wardak and Braithwaite (2013) and Braithwaite and Wardak (2013) concluded that in Afghanistan the answer was local tribal *jirga*s (assemblies of elders) and *shura*s (consultations). Survey research indicated that these were the local institutions that people most trusted for these purposes. The least trusted institutions were the state courts funded by international aid; their judges were corrupt and captured by the will of warlords or opium kingpins. The police were viewed as organised thieves. These US-run surveys showed that the Taliban courts were more popular and were seen (accurately) as less corrupt. But the most preferred justice was local justice under the stewardship of village or tribal elders that delivered *jirga*s and *shura*s (forms of restorative justice). They were deeply imperfect, dominated by male greybeards. We have seen how Ali Wardak and Ali Gohar's work is about different ways of bringing the greyhairs (female elders) into prominence in *jirga* justice (Braithwaite and Gohar 2014). Some local *jirga*s accept foreign aid to support their work with the string attached that they must empower greyhairs in the process. In other local contexts, this kind of foreign interference is spurned, but funding support for separate circles of greyhair *jirga*s is embraced by the women, and in time greybeard *jirga*s often reach a rapprochement with growing greyhair assertiveness. Peacekeepers and local police sometimes play vital roles in protecting these green shoots of justice reform, protecting them from men with guns who aim to uproot them.

While I will not re-summarise all the empirical experience and literatures traversed in Peacebuilding Compared, it is vital to make the point that a problem with my macrocriminology is that it is too much about institutional superstructure and too little about socially embedding foundations for them. I keep paying lip-service to micro–meso–macro linkages throughout this book, providing but a thin veneer of institutional texture and nuance to how that does or does not work from the bottom up. There is a need for ethnographic critiques of this book for its top-down deficits. I hope to do more of that in resuming Peacebuilding Compared fieldwork in new locales post Covid.

'Best practicitis' (Ramalingam 2013: 33) and evidence-based policy can be curses on good governance. They indoctrinate policymakers to persist with 'evidence-based policy' when it is demonstrably failing in new contexts. Best practice might work when local contexts are well understood—as Green (2016) explains in *How Change Happens*. Usually, top-down reformers and agonistic resisters alike do not understand local contexts well. Randomised controlled trials show that 'positive deviance' in development practice—for example, searching for deviant rural village practices of positive nutrition and encouraging modelling of these practices by others in the village—works. It works better than village education programs on nutrition best practice (for example, Bradley et al. 2009). This can be the positive deviance of a loved cook in their village or the agricultural practices of a respected local farmer. Positive deviance, again, is something that can work even though it is unknown or little understood by anyone from outside the village. It is radically variable because it is 'deviant' (Green 2016). In part, positive deviance works by the power of model-mongering and localism. In part, it works because it appeals to tastes adapted to unique circumstances. It energises because someone in the community has identified the solution, so it focuses on their assets and knowledge rather than on their deficits compared with a 'best practice', which tends to come from the North Atlantic.

The idea of positive deviance can be scaled up from the village to macro projects of transformation like China's, for good or ill! The Communist Party of China could be interpreted as adopting what is, from its point of view, a positive deviance approach to Confucianism. Under Mao Zedong, Confucianism was seen as ruling-class feudal thinking that had to be stamped out. This century, the party leadership concluded that half a century of stamping it out had failed, so they shifted strategy by asking themselves what are the good aspects of Confucian ideology for creating the harmonious communism they crave after their rejection of Mao's divisive Cultural Revolution? Second, they sought to revitalise the paternalistic bond between citizen and state that in Confucianism is modelled on the bond between a dutiful son and a father (Tu 1998; Ebrey 1991). Reframed in this way, Confucianism is now back in China, taught in schools again.

The discussion of Sun Yat-sen's constitutionalism and of Dennis Wong's (2014) advocacy of the suppression of Confucianism's Three Bonds and promotion of its Five Norms had a purpose. That was contestation of the Communist Party's appropriation of Confucius with a civic republican appropriation of Confucius. While the West can learn some good things from Confucius, Sun Yat-sen and Dennis Wong, any project of finding 'positive deviance' in Confucian practices that prevent crime and domination is, of course, bound to have more resonance in China than in Europe. That is fine because what has resonance in East Asia is more important than European resonance. This is not only because there are so many more East Asians than Europeans. It is also because East Asia is more important to preventing ecocide than Europe—with China accounting both for more carbon and for several times as much investment in green technological innovation as Europe (Drahos 2021), and even Japan accounting for about as much investment in renewables as all of Europe (Braithwaite 2020a). Europe is important, too, especially through the diplomatic bridge it is best placed to build between China and the Americas. The risks of triggering an accidental nuclear genocide that could wipe out all freedoms and all civilisations with a global famine are bigger from East Asia than from Europe. That also makes questions about what resonates in China, the Koreas and Japan of special importance.

This attempt in the present to be less pathologically western than in my past is still limited. The aspiration of evidence-based western social science to reveal 'what works' is a common criminological pathology compared with more eastern and southern searches for positive deviance in what is already working better in particular spaces. We should relish the paradox of randomised controlled trials that show positive deviance is 'what works' better than evidence-based application of 'what works'! A local turn away from best-practice universals is crucial to the art of freedom.

We can learn from Tom Scheff (1990) that the macro-methodology of freedom is abductive. It involves induction from a grand canvas, from a pointillist painting of a map of the planet, with a bright dot here from a *jirga* of greyhairs under fire from Islamic State in Afghanistan, another bright dot in Rolpa, Nepal, where feminist Maoist peasants develop their proposals for a feminised postwar constitution, another in a restorative justice training course in which New Zealand Prime Minister Jacinda Ardern soaked up Polynesian wisdom about how to heal and prevent violence, an AA meeting in a Christian community from which wounded healers fan out to scale up collective efficacy and recovery capital for substance abuse by gang foot soldiers, war crime trials in Colombia in which a military commander from the Revolutionary Armed Forces of Colombia (FARC) and a state general confess their crimes and undertake as sentences five-year programs of dangerous work clearing mines to protect the next generation of children.

While there is so much contextual diversity in the bright colours of each dot, the inductive method is to look for macro-patterns in the dots of positive deviance, and deviant swerves away from domination. We can watch especially for dots that become ink spots expanding to connect to other ink spots of freedom to flow across a landscape of liberation. Then we must shuttle from such induction to deduction: on peacebuilding, yes, we need the United Nations and we need to temper its power to make it stronger. This tempering and strengthening include vernacularising lessons from local dots of wisdom (Merry 2006). The United Nations has a major role to play in scaling up mine clearance across the planet. One of the things it can do to make us freer from violence is persuade war criminals to tell us not only where the bodies are buried, but also where the mines are buried, and to self-incapacitate the planting of more. While I apologise for a book that is too heavily weighted towards top-down deductive institutionalism and too light on embeddedness, I am unrepentant about how important the macro-institutional superstructures are. My remorse is about insufficient micro-texture in how I have shuttled between deduction and induction.

For agonistic pluralism

This book has certainly argued for big savings in state expenditure through release of 90 per cent of people currently in prison. It also argues for shapeshifting the economy from goods to services through huge increases in state and community expenditure on a great variety of institutions. More tax, environmental and other regulatory inspectors; greatly expanded health, welfare and education budgets; and radical redistributions of wealth and power are particularly important. Australia can shapeshift to grow its recycling sector, which currently generates 9.2 jobs per 10,000 tonnes of waste, compared with only 2.8 jobs for the same amount of waste sent to landfill (Beringen 2021). At the time of writing, the world needs a post-Covid care-led recovery with more investment in state funding for child care that becomes more educative and enables more women to work who want to, care-led restoration of the land and the environment, restoration of an aged care system that has been ravaged by Covid and state neglect, and total elimination of extreme poverty by education and health guarantees, social housing (Braithwaite 2021b) and a participation income (Atkinson 2015; Quiggin 2019). The next section argues that this kind of institution-building grounded in institutional anomie theory is desirable not only for freedom and crime control, but also for the survival of species on this fragile planet. That does not mean it is politically feasible to do it. The agency of all species ultimately finds it impossible to prevent themselves from becoming extinct.

A fair criticism of the book to this point is that it articulates no theory of power and politics that might inform grappling with how elites resist so many of the ideas in the book, however essential they might be to human freedom and flourishing. Critics will say all it has is a criminological theory of how to escape the deterrence trap, the compliance trap and the retribution trap and a commitment to transform republican and social democratic politics to accomplish long lists of reforms. It does have more than that to say about political strategy. Yet the thrust of the criticism is fair that its political strategy is not up to transcending my defeatism in suspecting that human civilisations will be destroyed in an unintended cataclysm in the next century or two. The hopeful paradox here is that the very crises with known risks for taking us to the brink are the kinds of near-crises that can bring about the agonistic struggles discussed in this book. These struggles might prevent crimes of reckless civilisational suicide triggered by genocidal nuclear conflict or climate catastrophe.

How might we think more deeply about these dangers and alternative politics of freedom? We cannot rethink the institutional domain without energising the democratic. We cannot avoid stirring political passions in a renewed way. This renewal must be different from the way the right mobilises affect through a populism that is about nationalist and racist exclusion and the exclusion of a narrowed kind of criminal class. Technocratic institutionalism, in which contemporary criminology is mired, opens the door to the unfreedom of exclusionary populism. Mouffe could equally be critiquing the professional criminology of experts (Loader and Sparks 2013) when she chastises the Third Way as a 'technocratic form of politics' freed of partisan confrontation in a supposedly neutral management of public affairs (Mouffe 2018: Introduction).

In spite of confessing to being a card-carrying social democrat, I am attracted to Chantal Mouffe's (2005: 56–63, 2013, 2018) 'post-social-democratic' critique of Third Way social democracy. That critique targets the writing of Anthony Giddens and Ulrich Beck, for example, and the political practices of Tony Blair, Bill Clinton and Barack Obama. Blair in important ways consolidated hegemonic terrain conquered by Margaret Thatcher, and the Clintons consolidated a hegemony of Wall Street and rentier capitalist inequalities installed by Ronald Reagan and affirmed with Clinton's 'it's the economy, stupid' brand of politics. Thatcher boasted that Blair was her greatest accomplishment—something with which Blair seems to agree. In light of everything said about republican imperatives to regulate Wall Street and the City of London, to rebuild public support for welfare housing, to make the tax system more redistributive, there can be no attraction to the stewardship of these institutions by many so-called social democratic regimes of recent decades. Mouffe reasonably sees ideological surrender to neoliberal thought in Third Way social democracy. That Third Way found virtue in keeping taxes low, governments small, unions weak and markets liberated as inevitabilities that social democrats must accept. This is not to say that civic republicanism is on the same page as

Mouffe's post-Marxist thought in many respects. I was never attracted to Marxism and always to markets, but always wanted more richly and deeply separated powers within and against states and markets to check and balance their dominations.

Where Mouffe and I are on the same page is in rejecting Third Way social democracy that is captured by finance capital. We are also at one in rejecting the left's disengagement from projects to transform state institutions that we see in the thinking of some theorists and activists of developments such as the Occupy Wall Street movement (for example, Negri and Hardt 2000). Leftists who want to drain the swamp will bequeath us undrained swamps and unregulated malaria just as surely as will rightist swamp-drainers. Like Mouffe, I argue for a politicised social science that engages with projects of state, market and civil society transformation to begin the process of repairing the problems that flow from crusted hegemonies, but particularly the hegemony of finance capital. We have also seen that the hegemony of monopolist tech giants backed by potent state sponsors is a threat emerging as a rival domination to finance capital.

Like Mouffe, I do not think populism need be a dirty word for what should be a wholesome politics of the people confronting oligarchy or, as Laclau (2005) sees it, the 'underdog' resisting 'those in power'. Populism should not be gifted to the right by the left because the left thinks it should be dispassionately technocratic rather than passionately political. While the kinds of institutional projects advocated in this book attempt to be evidence-based and technocratically wise, they cannot be progressed without engaging the passions of democratic politics. This means social movements, the women's movement, postcolonial struggles, the labour movement, the environment movement, the human rights movement and social movements that are more specific but particularly strategic such as Citizens for Tax Justice, the social movement for restorative justice and our 'jailing is failing' movement of the Justice Reform Initiative. Engagement with such social movements has been meaningful in motivating me. I commend that path to young scholars and hope it enriches them.

Many of our most insightful criminologists today cultivate circumspection about populism as inherently dangerous. Russell Hogg (2013: 118), with Laclau, cautions against excising the insurgent crowd from history and from political theory, and offers these thoughtful reflections on the writing of Sparks:

Richard Sparks argues that we should not (as others have done) see managerialism and populism as competing trends or influences, but consider the possibility that a populist political rationality and an administrative rationality can be mutually necessary and simultaneously in play: one operating in the political foreground— the domain of representation—and the other backstage—where the logic of pragmatic, managerial calculation prevails. If Sparks is correct, one reason for the struggling political fortunes of the left is that it has become suffused by a rationality of politics as administration and is seemingly incapable of articulating a credible, progressive political vision.

It is hard to imagine a hegemonic shift in China away from the politics of domination in criminal justice, toward more democratic settings with tempered, separated powers, without insurgent crowds playing a significant political role. Our political imagination can go to scaling up participation in the restorative circle as a micro-platform for a future where marginalised Chinese youth learn how to be democratic because restorative circles tend to be an overwhelmingly popular experience among participants (Braithwaite 2021e), and in China restorative reforms have already helped reduce incarceration rates (Zhang and Xia 2021).

A message for criminologists has been that if you wish to be more than just scholars and to be politically active, the best way might not be law reform tinkering (even though that can be helpful); it is to be an active feminist, a peace activist, a First Nations' rights activist, a welfare rights activist, a tax reform and environmental activist and a campaigner against criminalised corporate dominations of markets and states. Criminological activism in these social movements has helped persuade citizens to be more concerned about the corporate crimes of Big Pharma and banks, about the patriarchal crimes of men against women, about war crimes, and more. Agonistic contestation can only be effectively counter-hegemonic for Mouffe if it connects to identities, projects and discourses that resonate with people affectively.

One contribution has been to argue for averting stigmatisation as crucial to resonating effectively (Braithwaite 1989, 1995; Ahmed et al. 2001). Many violent men in Australia, for example, reject their feminist rejectors as man-haters. Australian feminism in general eschews the stigmatisation of men. It manages to communicate disapproval within a continuum of respect. Occasional stigmatic excess, however, has been fuel for the fire of the patriarchal authoritarian right, which does so much damage by sustaining moral ambiguity about gendered violence.

Historically, hegemonic inequality has allowed all manner of crimes of domination to thrive because powerholders have been able to sustain immunity from community disapproval. Reintegrative shaming theory is useful in showing how a society of censorious individualist busybodies can be profoundly counterproductive, while social movement shaming of structural evil can be transformatively productive. It shows why cancel culture was a passing fad that lit no road to freedom; cancel culture wanted for redemption and eschewed the grace that is the better path to nondomination and nonviolence.

Mouffe has clear thinking on the imperatives for these movements to achieve outcomes that fall far short of conquering hegemony. Rather, the purpose of political struggle is occasional victories that reset a new hegemony that is somewhat less dominating and freer than the one it replaces. 'Society is always divided and discursively constructed through hegemonic practices' (Mouffe 2018: Ch. 2); hegemonic practices are 'the practices of articulation through which a given order is created and the meaning of social institutions is fixed' (Mouffe 2013: 13; Laclau and Mouffe 1985); 'any order is of a hegemonic nature, i.e. it is always the expression of power relations' (Mouffe 2013: 7). According to this approach, nevertheless, 'every order is the temporary and precarious articulation of contingent practices'. Major change becomes possible at regular conjunctures (Mouffe 2013: 14). In macrocriminology, these conjunctures are anomic crises of disorder on the streets, wars, ecological crises and financial collapse. The formation of an antislavery movement, a trade union movement, 'first-wave' feminism and an environmental movement were also important conjunctures constructed from below. There is no final point of arrival at a society freed of domination. But crises are conjunctures that enable a reset from one vulnerable hegemony to another that might open a better pathway for life on the planet to survive its own violence.

There is massive variation between the kind of hegemony that exists in China versus hegemony in the United States, versus that in New Zealand under Jacinda Ardern. Mouffe finds virtue in imperfect struggles for the less-dominating hegemonies that create more space for liberty and equality. At the same time, Mouffe believes in agonistic pluralism whereby even though social movements struggle for the more benign hegemony of Ardern's New Zealand in preference to Trump's United States, it remains imperative for plural social movements to position Ardern's regime as an adversary flawed by diverse failures to tackle domination. An adversary in Mouffe's language of pluralistic agonism has certain ideas that should be contested but is not an 'enemy' to be destroyed as in the language of 'antagonism'. Furthermore, adversaries must not be seen as irrelevant, as in some discourses of anarchic disengagement from state institutions. Mouffe rejects liberal theorists' imaginaries of politics as a field where different groups compete to occupy positions of power. There is no appeal in the objective of displacing others from a seat they might take 'without putting into question the dominant hegemony and profoundly transforming the relations of power' (Mouffe 2013: 19). Politics is about agonistic questioning more than competition among elites. Practitioners of agonistic pluralism advance counter-hegemonic struggles for ideas 'under conditions regulated by a set of democratic procedures accepted by the adversaries' (Mouffe 2013: Ch. 1). Something in common is needed among citizens of a polity: a framework of 'conflictual consensus' that is a precondition for agonistic contestation to flourish.

Mouffe conceives of Hannah Arendt's and particularly Jürgen Habermas's ways of thinking about the rule of the people and the rule of law as fundamentally misguided in the character of their advocacy of deliberative democratic consensus. There is no enduring consensus around the new articulation of institutions settled after a partially successful counter-hegemonic struggle for institutional transformation, just a new hegemonic formation, a revised benchmark of hegemony to contest in the next struggle of agonistic pluralism against domination. Agonistic struggle proceeds with a politics of hope that '[e]very hegemonic order can be challenged by counter-hegemonic practices, which attempt to disarticulate the existing order' (Mouffe 2013: 124). This is another way of formulating the paradox of destabilisation rights as necessary for a less anomic social order, as discussed in Chapter 8.

While I agree with Mouffe on this at the level of macro-institutional politics, at the more microlevel of institutions, I throw in my lot with deliberative democracy theorists. Hence, as explained in previous chapters, the aim of a restorative justice conference is an undominated dialogue that leads to a workable consensus—not one where everyone feels they got exactly what they wanted, but one where they feel 'that's good enough for me' (to quote Tim Chapman, who in turn quotes Northern Irish victims from restorative conferences). Chapman means they believe their perspective has been listened to and taken seriously and they accept that the other perspectives in the room likewise had to be fairly accommodated in the final conference outcome. When the deliberative democracy of the restorative circle fails to reach a workable consensus, the matter is settled in the more adversarial justice of the rule of law interpreted by a judge. Moreover, representative democracy should be more deliberative than it currently is at the microlevel. University councils, faculty meetings or the cabinet of an elected government should make decisions via undominated dialogue and, if they can, reach the kind of workable agreement described above for a restorative justice conference. If they cannot, the alternative becomes, first talk, then vote (Goodin 2008). Then the losers of the vote return to the contestatory politics (Pettit 1997) of agonistic pluralism.

The agonistic politics of struggle for more equitable taxation is an example of a marginalised struggle, yet one punctuated with moments when social movements like Citizens for Tax Justice have some influence in reshaping new national and even global tax orders (van der Walt forthcoming). One new conjuncture arrived with the election of the Hawke Labor government in Australia in 1983. I worked with Treasurer Paul Keating on a small committee of business and civil society leaders from the 1983 National Economic Summit (which had more than 100 participants) to move forward the summit's agenda by establishing a 16-member Economic Planning Advisory Council. As the CEO of an active NGO, I was selected by Prime Minister Bob Hawke as a civil society representative on the council that met with the prime minister and other national leaders from government, business and trade unions for at least one full day every month. Hawke was a reformer, though a liberal rather than a left-wing Labor leader, but he had enormous strengths in nurturing deliberative processes that could work meaningfully in a room of 16 people. A rare day of counter-hegemonic progress arrived in 1985 when Hawke and Keating (who succeeded Hawke as prime minister in 1991) announced they were minded to propose options for new taxes on wealth and/or capital gains at the National Tax Summit (another summit of around 100 people). The business leaders on the council insisted this was a bad idea. That was expected and cut little ice with a government that was also willing to cut company tax as part of the reform package. The most politically energised resistance in the room came from the head of the National Farmers' Federation. He made good points about how Australian agriculture on our big brown land could only be internationally competitive if farms were massively larger than in other countries. A problem with taxes on death or wealth would be that in times of drought when the only wealth left was the value of the land that was being taxed, the sole path to paying the tax would be to break away a parcel of the land, reducing agricultural efficiency.

Hawke then said that he wanted him to assume that the government was so strongly determined to introduce some sort of tax on wealth or capital that farmers had no hope of stopping it. If the prime minister then gave him the opportunity to design such a tax in a way that would minimise the breakup of family farms at moments of intergenerational inheritance, how would he design it? What we had here was a long-term agonistic struggle over taxes on wealth and capital that reached no deliberative consensus at this moment of Australian history, nor at any point since. Yet there was meaningful deliberative democracy in the micro-conversation of the 16 council members. The council made some useful progress in understanding what might be more destructive forms of tax for the comparative advantage of Australian agriculture. On this and other issues that arose during my four-year term, the council provided many useful moments of micro-timeouts from agonistic politics of the social movement variety. The main game remains one of agonistic pluralism, but micro-moments of consensus-building around a table on particular issues have a worthy place in a sensibly hybrid democracy. Other moments are about softening up in faint hope of future consensus-building moments. An example from that 1983–87 term was softening up business, trade union and political leaders to accept why a carbon tax would be in the long-run interests of business, workers and governments. This was not at all agonistic; it was smiling banter about my crazy ideas that everyone knew would go nowhere in the 1980s. I would send them copies of 1980s economic publications on carbon taxes; they would return them with pleasant jibes to humour me. Thirty years later, after the secrecy of cabinet minutes was lifted, I learnt that the Labor Cabinet actually discussed a new carbon tax as a way of managing its fiscal deficit. It was rejected but had attracted support from a substantial minority around the table.

The deliberative democracy of the workplace meeting, the kinds of safety committee meetings in mines and of residents' or relatives' councils in care homes much discussed in this book can offer a hybrid of micro-deliberative democracy. They can be combined perhaps with some citizen participation in deliberative polling processes that elected politicians take seriously,[1] with deliberative democratic participation in the local branch of

---

1   I do agree with Mouffe (2018: Ch. 3) that because deliberative polling is an individualised form of politics, it is not as important as the contestation of collective projects. Then, as long as deliberative polling does not displace collective political contestation, it can add some richness to the deliberative texture of a hybrid political order. It also empowers individual agency structurally if a large proportion of the society gets their turn to shape politics in this way.

one's chosen political party, and other hybrids. At the macrolevel, a hybrid of representative democracy, contestatory democracy and agonistic pluralism can be the light on a social democratic hill. Agonistic pluralism can be energised to contest the way these other forms of contestation fail to work in a representative democracy. All these other forms of hybrid democracy and all the separated powers of local society, business society, national society and international society have parts to play in the contestation. It is important not to believe that the only game, or the main game, of agonistic pluralism must be contesting the decisions of elected governments. A Mouffean hybrid of micro–macro democracy averts the dangers of technocratic sanitisation of democracy that kills off passion for progressive politics. Technocratic governance leaves populism in the hands of authoritarian populists who threaten new eras of political domination (Mouffe 2018). While we have seen that authoritarian capitalism has been on the rise in recent history, from Moscow and Beijing to Dhaka and much of the West, so are agonistic social movements led by the young; the latter are the republic's remedy to the former.

Ordinary people can enjoy a less alienated life if they experience some real influence over how their part of their workplace is run, how their school is run, how their child is sanctioned if they get into trouble with the police, how their parents are cared for in an aged care home, how an environmental group they are passionate about sets its priorities and even how the political party of their choice makes decisions at the local level that bubble up local political impulses to higher echelons of the party. This is not to say that to be a good citizen you should get active in a social movement, a political party or restorative justice conferences. It is just to say that we should want enough people to get active at these levels for the democracy to energise and accomplish a progressive populism that resists authoritarian populism. Second, we should want all citizens to be able to avail themselves of the opportunities for agonistic contestation in forums of these kinds that matter to them most. Then they can become citizens with the social capital of Connectedness, Hope, Identity, Meaning and Empowerment in a democracy that CHIMEs. CHIME might have technocratic roots in meta-analysis, but it implies more opportunities to jump in and get meaningfully politically active. Moreover, democracy that CHIMEs should begin with children learning how to be democratic. This book has argued that restorative justice in families, schools and the justice system can contribute to learning how to become agonistic pluralists. It happens when restorative justice delivers a 'that's good enough for me' outcome rather than perfect healing.

Ecocide and genocide as likely futures

There are aspects of contemporary hegemonic formations that are existential threats, as well as threats to freedom. If criminology in universities can discuss politically creative ways of confronting and contributing to turning back existential threats that are such a heavy burden on the very being of young people, criminology can be found to have something to offer that is appealing to students who seek to make a difference. Criminology might take pride when some of its students sally forward to be leaders of social movements for counter-hegemonic transformation. Of course, all political traditions should flourish in a university. Criminology will never have many of the answers to questions about how we might build a future society together that is free from threats to the very existence of our fellow species and our own. Throughout, this book has attempted, nevertheless, to uncover more ways in which criminology might contribute to saving the ecosystems of this planet from cascading past tipping points.

Insufficient environmental enforcement

Much pathbreaking research is done on environmental enforcement. Yet Edwin Sutherland would be disappointed by what a low proportion of excellent environmental compliance research is undertaken by criminologists. The deterrence of environmental crime is not minimally sufficient (Chapter 9) and incapacitation (Chapter 10) is even more woeful. Chapter 10 discussed the historically amazing self-incapacitation accomplishments of aviation safety in reducing fatalities, as documented by authors like Wilf-Miron et al. (2003) and Hodges (2015). For all that, we must also see that air travel is insufficiently deterred for the environmental damage it does. International flights are the great carbon guzzlers of the world of travel. I put much less carbon into the atmosphere in a year of driving my 14-year-old car than in one economy international flight from Australia to the northern hemisphere. Travelling business class takes up twice as much of the space on the flight and twice the share of the flight's carbon emissions. Carbon screams for a higher price so that the cost of that international travel might double or triple, so I am deterred from doing too much of it and so airlines are motivated to move to flight powered by renewably produced hydrogen, for example. Chapter 10 discussed the stunning work of the coal industry in reducing fatalities.

But, really, carbon today must be priced at a level that deters mining companies from digging it up at all or, if they cannot be deterred by the market, incapacitates them by corporate capital punishment.

In May 2020, the operating company of the Hazelwood Power Station in Victoria's Latrobe Valley, Australia, and the open-cut coalmine that fired it was fined A$1.9 million for occupational health and safety and environmental protection offences associated with a terrible fire that ignited the massive mine. The mine's pit had an 18-kilometre perimeter. The major corporate owner and operator of the mine was the largest private-sector energy corporation in the world, the French company ENGIE (formerly Suez, which built the Suez Canal). It had revenue of A$83 billion in the year before sentencing (2019). Most estimates of the cost of the fire to the nearby town of Morwell were more than $600 million. So, was a fine of $1.9 million minimally sufficient (Chapter 9)? One of the things environmental activists in Morwell wanted was at least $10 million in seed funding to start a large solar farming industry in Morwell to replace employment in coal with jobs in renewables. They did not get this out of a sentencing process that took seriously none of the restorative justice principles discussed in Chapter 9.

The more fundamental point here is that this mine and its power station should never have existed. Regulation should have revoked its licence decades ago. This never happened, but mercifully, self-incapacitation did, when ENGIE, pursuant to a new policy of shifting energy production to renewables, voluntarily closed both the power plant and the coalmine in 2017. Corporate power ultimately took the most decisive step towards repairing harm after state regulatory power endlessly failed to do so. This was a mine that was always going to have this kind of catastrophic fire one day. During the life of the mine, the number of fires that broke out and triggered regulatory notification was reduced from 250 a year to 100—still an unacceptable risk. But more fundamentally, this brown coal plant was one of the dirtiest electricity plants in the entire world. It should have been escalated to responsive state incapacitation many years before the voluntary self-incapacitation of closure occurred, with the blowing up of the smokestacks televised.

A reforming new Paris-based CEO, Isobel Kocher, was appointed in 2016 to transform Suez to become ENGIE, a greener organisation that shifted its investment to renewables.[2] It was Kocher who took the decision to decommission the Hazelwood plant and mine in 2017, to sell the nearby Loy Yang B brown coal power station in 2018 and to announce on the company's website an intent to close or divest 'all emissions-intensive coal-fired power generation facilities'. This induced internal conflict on her board; she was replaced in late 2020. A good restorative strategy would have been to ask Kocher during this 2016–20 window of opportunity to come to meet the citizens of Morwell, rather as the ACCC did in its early restorative justice cases in the 1990s (as discussed in Chapter 10). Morwell activists could then have made their pitch to Kocher for ENGIE to fund $10 million or more towards their massive solar farm development and other new green employment opportunities in Morwell to compensate for the impending loss of jobs from the community's historical commitment to coal. This was the kind of project that interested Kocher; she opened a large wind farm in Australia in 2019. It would have been a good kind of innovation for the prosecutor or the judge to enable a restorative encounter with the CEO long before conviction and sentencing to allow an agonistic pitch from the people of Morwell to Isobel Kocher to start funding that green investment that was so aligned with her values and her company's new corporate strategy at that historical juncture.

A restorative corporate law imagination requires conversations with reformers inside corporate wrongdoers to open the door to the contestation of big agonistic and restorative ideas. It is a tragedy for Morwell and for the planet that such a conversation was not attempted at Hazelwood. The reason was a misplaced fear of being anything less than totally punitive towards the corporate offender. Precisely what Morwell needed was massive investment in renewable energy jobs by investors with pockets as deep as ENGIE's and with support from all levels of Australian government for a renewed Morwell.

---

2   In August 2020, the ENGIE website explained: 'What are we doing? Inventing a new reparative growth model. At ENGIE, we are convinced that "the common good is good for business". Our role as a leader in the zero-carbon transition is to show that this necessary transformation creates value and that it can combine performance and the common good. To live up to this ambition, we rely on the commitment of the Imaginative Builders community, formed by the Group's employees and all those who work with ENGIE (cities, startups, suppliers, NGOs, students, customers, etc.). This is why ENGIE is offering its customers a new approach to support their progress towards the challenge of a zero-carbon transition. Unique on the market, our "as a service" approach aims to make the zero-carbon transition accessible through integrated, tailor-made and co-financed solutions.' (Available from: www.engie.com/en/news/engie-positive-impact-strategy).

Chapter 10 discussed the hundredfold reduction in safety risks achieved in nuclear power plants. Even so, another century of production delivers to our dear earth the risk it faced during 1986, when Chernobyl put the planet on the brink and killed an unknown, extremely large, number of people. And every year even the safest of nuclear plants produces nuclear waste that will still be with us when humankind becomes extinct. The Fukushima disaster showed in 2011 that tsunamis can be a mega-risk of the *longue durée* to nuclear plants. Again, the nuclear industry may present such a risk that anything short of total incapacitation is insufficient—a dispensation the majority of societies have settled on by deciding not to build any nuclear power plants or to de-license existing ones. The United Nations has demonstrated that it can reduce the risks of ecocide through climate agreements. It has demonstrated it can greatly reduce war and crime and increase freedom through small investments in peacekeeping (Walter et al. 2020). Therefore, study of the impact of the United Nations on crime and freedom rivals the centrality to macrocriminology of the study of states.

Ecocide and Green New Deal politics

Some criminologists today write about the imperative to mirror the ultimate crime of genocide against our own species with a crime of ecocide against many species (Zierler 2011; Higgins et al. 2013; White and Kramer 2015; Pali and Biffi 2019). This is motivated by evidence that late modernity has already seen the extinction of 680 vertebrate species and thousands of invertebrates and a million species now face extinction risk (IPBES 2019). It is an ethical duty of criminology to make a better contribution to how environmental enforcement policies can stem the tide of extinctions before it cascades to human extinction. The big insights of this book about how to reshape the institutions of regulation, enforcement and state and corporate accountability can be combined with growth in the institutions of welfare to help prevent ecocide. To pick up Chantal Mouffe's theme, the current hegemonic formation is on a trajectory that leads to the extinction of the hegemons. This makes it a less resilient hegemony than reformers have tended to think. In a more immediate way, a megacorporation like ENGIE can realise after a disaster like Hazelwood that it is on a faster path to corporate extinction than it realised if it keeps feeding coal into power plants. Its survival path is to step up massively its investments in renewables. We have seen that BP confronted this survival shift after its Deepwater Horizon fiasco.

A US path to survival is to help avert the extinction that could come from an unintended escalation to a nuclear weapons exchange with Russia or China by building cooperation with them on new regulatory technologies to avert ecocide (Drahos 2021; Braithwaite 2020a). Chinese and Russian paths to survival are collaboration with the United States on a global Green New Deal. Part of what needs to be done to that end is to make the United Nations more effective in preventing crime, war, ecocide and genocide by tempering the veto of the great powers. Post-Covid, we can see that a World Health Organization with strengthened institutional capacities can help prevent global economic crises and the authoritarianism and therefore wars they might cascade to. The United Nations has demonstrated it can reduce the risks of ecocide through climate agreements (for example, closure of the ozone hole). We saw in Chapter 7 that strategic social movement activism can deploy strategic trade theories to divide and conquer ecocidal states and markets and slave-trading states and their markets.

While slave-trading is by definition a market in the vice of domination, this book has not generally been prescriptive in defining lists of markets in vice and markets in virtue. That is a topic for another book. The focus here has been on more meta-conclusions about the importance of agonistic contestation of what citizens should contest as markets in vice, and how. However we define vice and virtue, the globalisation of markets has proliferated both markets in vice and markets in virtue. Globalisation has also driven a race to the bottom in regulatory standards to control certain markets in vice, with states competing for investment by promising less onerous demands on business. This race to the bottom has been an especially large problem in driving down tax collections from corporations. At the same time, we have seen that organisations like Citizens for Tax Justice and Oxfam have had their victories in contestation for a more equitable tax system (van der Walt forthcoming).

Strategic trade accomplishments involve a social movement persuading a hegemon like the United Kingdom to ban the slave trade. Then the social movement levered British strategic trade interests to coerce other states into levelling the playing field in their plantation economy competition with the United Kingdom by also banning their slave trade. Working ratchets up at different levels is a totally different way to defeat markets in vice with markets in virtue. For example, when President Trump came to power and refused to implement the Paris Climate Agreement, social movements got to work with campaigns for states, cities, corporations and universities to make their own Paris commitments. This means that when the national ratcheting up of standards has broken down, lower levels can be ratcheted up. At a later date, this will increase the pressure on and possibilities for the national ratchet to get moving—and vice versa: in periods of history when the corporate ratchets for regulating markets in vice are stalled, national ratchets can move up with reasonable hopes that this will get corporate ratchets moving again after a lag. When that happens, even President Trump in his strategic trade competition with China could find it helpful to use these accomplishments of lower-level US ratchets to attack China for putting more carbon into the environment than the United States. When Trump did this, he was being an agent of the social movement for climate change, just as Ronald Reagan was more profoundly so in lobbying for the Montreal Protocol after US business had been forced by its environmental movement to be an early mover in banning chlorofluorocarbons. Meanwhile, the European Union was a more virtuous strategic trade actor that was negotiating trade agreements with China that committed the EU and China to bigger loops of ambition than Trump's United States. Both loops bore promising fruits of EU and Chinese commitments at the 2021 Glasgow climate meeting.

Social movement accomplishments like the Forest Stewardship Council (FSC) sought to put ratchets in a sequence. That is, the institutional design was that if the standards in a provincial or a national law went up, the FSC standard went up. If the International Organization for Standardization (ISO) 14001 voluntary international standard went up, the FSC standard ratcheted up. Furthermore, there was lobbying for 'continuous improvement' approaches within all of these regulatory ratchets so that the ratchets in series would be one-way, each constantly driving the other towards upward movement. None of these continuous improvement ratchets worked smoothly and often they worked badly. They clunked agonistically, with business lobbyists constantly throwing spanners into the works. More fundamentally, the coverage of the FSC remained small; most business opted out and forests continued to disappear. It is not the purpose of this book to evaluate such particularities. Readers can go to the johnbraithwaite.com website to search the word 'ratchet' to find accounts of global continuous improvement ratchets in series on nuclear power plant safety and many other domains in e-publications. The purpose here is only to show that there are social movement strategies of agonistic contestation that at conjunctures of crisis can deliver small or large victories.

Serious intellectuals such as Robert Reiner (2020) like to say it is easier to imagine the end of humankind than the end of capitalism. Yet Reiner also points out that social democrats want more than Blair and Obama's Third Way and less than the end of capitalism. They want radical transformation along the lines of the opening paragraph of this chapter. My argument has been that critical junctures of crisis do make this transformation possible, and therefore human survival is possible.

Even the world's most powerful banks supported extreme Keynesian pump-priming and a surging regulatory welfare state in 2008 and 2020 (Levi-Faur 2014; Braithwaite 2021c) and turned off many investment taps to carbon. That was because bankers were the biggest beneficiaries of this momentary surge of regulatory welfare capitalism. Within variably short spaces of years after 2008, they were off life-support, making massive profits again. Then banks captured state policies to shift back to austerity, to substitution of debt (to banks) for welfare. There was no inevitability that this conjuncture would turn back to the advantage of banks. Reiner (2020) points out that British Prime Minister Gordon Brown in 2008–09 proposed to President Obama what amounted to the foundations of the Green New Deal for which Obama had campaigned in 2007. The proposal was in effect a new Bretton Woods agreement that would renew global institutions for the regulation of capitalism. Obama spurned Brown. Obama appointed Wall Street apparatchiks to key economic posts. They believed that banks should be global and capitalist in life, but national and socialist in death.

Main Street hated this and hated the Wall Street policy elite who infiltrated Washington. Their resentment sadly laid a foundation for Trump's authoritarian populism rather than Mouffe's left populism. Chapter 7 showed how Brown also favoured share acquisitions that partially nationalised private banks rather than bailouts. Obama's chief of staff opined that the state should never waste a good crisis. Sadly, as Reiner (2020) points out, it was finance capital that did not waste a good crisis, securing a stream of debt into the future that was better proofed against future crises. Left populism utterly failed to surge behind Brown at this point and to persuade key moderate conservatives like Germany's Angela Merkel against austerity. The global left at this point liked Obama much more than Brown (whom they saw as pivotal in the failed Blair administration rather than a counterpoint to it). It could have been otherwise, but the left populism of the Occupy Movement—of which

I confess to have been a part—marching along Wall Street in 2008, made a tactical mistake in that moment to fail to mobilise behind Brown as a practical hope for Mouffean counter-hegemonic progress.

Because the upshot was the Trump presidency, more might have been lost than gained. Still, what was gained was a global reopening of the minds of econocrats to Keynesianism and the regulatory welfare state. This reopening of a Keynesian social democratic imaginary was reinforced by the Covid crisis of 2020–22. Authoritarian capitalist states like Trump's United States, Jair Bolsonaro's Brazil and Narendra Modi's India fared particularly badly for their own citizens in responding to Covid-19. Together with neoliberal states, they expanded a massive new inequality in the world system through a patent regime that prioritised vaccines for low-risk citizens in wealthy and powerful states over high-risk citizens in the least-developed economies. Semi-authoritarian, populist neoliberal regimes, like Boris Johnson's United Kingdom, likewise failed in these ways. They failed for the same reason of Hayekian aversion to state plans and state command centres ready to surge into action. They failed to save lives because of their embrace of the hollowing out rather than the strengthening of the welfare state. All these states were forced by the terrible realities of the pandemic to reverse these policies, at least partially, to more Keynesian pump-priming and the strengthening of regulatory welfare capitalism.[3] This wedged more libertarian factions of their own support base to turn against their leaders. Hopefully, this will lead to policy learning during the 2020s that East Asian states all suffered lower death rates than these western states, even though they were so much more proximate to the initial pandemic take-off and at least until the end of 2021 relied on less expensive and less effective vaccines. This was because East Asian state command centres were ready to jump in January 2020— for some states, with more than 100 policies in their pandemic prevention plan. East Asian societies were more educated to don their masks and had welfare states better primed to surge support for the suffering (Braithwaite 2021c). The formerly neoliberal profession of economics should find reason in the 2020s to return to a more Keynesian and social democratic dispensation if I am right in predicting that the evidence will continue to show that the states that were most ideologically Hayekian tended to fare worst in the two biggest crises of the past 15 years.

---

3   Similarly, more social democratic Sweden was forced to reverse its empirically misplaced hope of early 2020 that freedom and herd immunity would quickly deliver less suffering.

Reiner (2020: 156) may be correct that a kindred crisis that will follow Covid in the next decade or two will be a crisis of the failure of liberal capitalism to deliver the antibiotics that will tame future epidemics. Vaccines and antibiotics are mostly not very profitable drugs. Big Pharma long ago shifted their research and development portfolios away from them. There are many reasons that need not distract us here. One is simply that most epidemics are like Ebola, HIV, SARS, MERS, polio and Covid-19 in that they do not experience their initial outbreaks in the western markets where Big Pharma's profits are made. Very often they are like Ebola and are tamed in unprofitable African markets before they spread to the West. When they do spread to wealthy countries, often the West tames them quickly, while elimination lags by many decades in poor countries where demand for unprofitable drugs persists.

Socialism is an important part of the solution to this problem. Excellent state-funded universities and unprecedented state research funding for Covid cures, tests and symptom amelioration strategies remarkably reduced Covid death rates as infection rates surged. At the time of writing, expectations for vaccine effectiveness are higher than the pessimistic forecasts of immunologists up to October 2020. Covid demonstrated some virtues of a strong state coupled with strong markets with vaccines that vanquished suffering (at least for the rich). It also demonstrated the flaws of western monopolisation for serving humankind in the Global South.

Basic research into cures for orphan diseases and antibiotics for diseases with insufficiently large outbreaks among rich drug purchasers will require ever more innovation supported by strong states. A minor example for most westerners, but a light on the hill for Australians, was the creation of the Commonwealth Serum Laboratories (CSL) by its government in 1916. One reason for its founding was that Australia has many of the most venomous snakes in the world and some distinctive spider venoms. Bites are sufficiently rare that there have never been profits for Big Pharma in Australian antivenoms. So, a socialist pharmaceutical corporation was established to research and produce Australian antivenoms, the CSL, in what is now the Walter and Eliza Hall Institute building in Melbourne. 'Commonwealth' was a suitably socialist descriptor for the brand. As happens when researchers undertake brilliant science with novel basic research, unexpected commercial applications also evolved. Indeed, as long as a state hedges with a high volume of intellectually plural excellence in basic research innovation, it is likely to produce a bounty of profitable science. This is what happened with CSL.

CSL became sufficiently profitable that the state succumbed to cashing in its investment, privatising to help with the debts of the 1991 recession. CSL continued to produce a mix of profitable and important unprofitable products that saved countless lives worldwide. This continued until its latter years as a public corporation with, for example, a pioneering heat treatment to protect plasma and blood products from infection with HIV. CSL was privatised cheaply at a share price of $2.30 in 1994. By the turn of the century, it became the second Australian company to exceed $100 a share. Quiggin (2020) showed that, by 2020, CSL investors enjoyed a 500-fold increase in the stock market value of CSL—10 times as rewarding as the still impressive fiftyfold increase in the value of shares in the larger privatisation of the Commonwealth Bank. Strategic socialism enjoyed underestimated profitability in countries with a well-governed public sector—profitable for taxpayers and private investors alike.[4] As a private corporation, CSL produced the first vaccine for the swine flu epidemic in 2009 and became a world leader in influenza vaccines that are recommended by the World Health Organization. One of its promising current projects is a novel plasma-based compound as a therapy for acute coronary syndrome. In 2021, it was the socialism that seeded CSL that enabled Australia to have at least some industrial capability to manufacture onshore some of the vaccines needed for its citizens. Likewise, when in 1955 Dr Jonas Salk's laboratory at the University of Pittsburgh saved millions of lives worldwide by making the polio vaccine available to humankind without payment for a patent—in contrast to Covid profiteering today—CSL stood ready to produce 25 million vaccines for Australia. CSL delivered this without causing the 40,000 infections of children with polio that occurred through defective private manufacturing in the United States (Fitzpatrick 2006).

In retrospect, Quiggin (2020) is right that all the major Australian privatisations of the 1990s were underpriced. I was shocked by the breadth of this privatisation agenda in 1987 when discussion began on the Economic Planning Advisory Council. I queried fellow council members on how they would value the public health return to humankind of the invention of drugs for orphan diseases. With Qantas, I asked what the value to humankind was of Qantas as an international exemplar of

---

4   Between them, privatised Australian state corporations the Commonwealth Bank, CSL, Telstra, Qantas and Medibank Private are worth almost 20 per cent of the value of the ASX 200 (Denniss 2020: 11).

safety excellence? Qantas had the best safety record of all international airlines. Perhaps that worry was misplaced because the privatised Qantas continued to enjoy that distinction.

Reiner's (2020) social democratic hero Clement Attlee was prime minister not only during the decline to the lowest homicide rates ever recorded in UK history (Eisner 2017: 580); he also delivered world leadership in safety innovation and safety outcomes with the nationalisation of British coalmines (Braithwaite 1985, 2013b). Accident fatalities had been more than 1,000 in some single years of the early twentieth century and fell to near zero per annum after nationalisation—in addition to a large reduction in the number of health-related fatalities, mainly through the elimination of black lung disease. Even so, Margaret Thatcher's privatisation of the coalmines proved to be good green policy and good fiscal policy. The social democratic imaginary is not doctrinaire on privatisation; it advocates strategic privatisations, strategic nationalisations and strategic renationalisations. A new Commonwealth pharma corporation that specialises in research and development on multiple drug-resistant antibiotics is a good idea for similar reasons to why CSL was good Labor policy in 1916. With banks, Braithwaite (2019: 557–78) made a case for less oligopolistic banking by the state investing in a particular pathway to a new Commonwealth bank to compete with the old privatised Commonwealth Bank, including socialist finance that ratchets up investment in green innovation. This might create a more competitive, greener Australian economy, with an improved capacity to ride out future financial crises. Fraudulent conduct by the major private ratings agencies before the 2008 crisis should have motivated the European Union to establish a public European ratings agency with a tough integrity charter, to compete globally with Moody's and Standard & Poor's and to ensure higher integrity in environmental accounting (Braithwaite 2019).

Crises might open opportunities for such social democratic remedies. Reiner (2020: 16) considers, however, Michael Kalecki's (1943) warning to Keynesian social democrats that if they are too successful in reducing unemployment, lifting the wages share of national income to the point where indebtedness to banks is low and the profit share is low, to the point where unions become strong and militant, finance capital will fight back in alliance with media barons like Rupert Murdoch (and carbon barons threatened by a Green New Deal). To be fairer to the Obama presidency, this is perhaps what the Clintons were warning him about after they experienced such a potent conservative fightback against the modest expansion of the welfare state in their torpedoed national health insurance plan.

On the positive side of the ledger, however, Greta Thunberg–style youth are flocking to a green politics that is building resistance to neoliberalism and authoritarianism among the young. Just as Thatcher was able to scheme successfully to crush trade union movements through militarised confrontations with them, so it is possible for international unionism to reinvent itself in ways that surge back to relevance in its response to new crises. This goes to the importance of the new vision for an internationalised green trade union movement in the work of Shelley Marshall (2019).

Sweden has one of many social democratic parties around the world that has been checked and balanced by a Green Party that has been more responsive to these social movement forces. The Swedish Social Democrats were early movers in having communist unions split away from them in 1917 to form a separate communist party. They achieved the most formidable early welfare state accomplishments of any social democratic party in the middle decades of the twentieth century with a corporatist model that rejected nationalisations. Instead, they favoured negotiations between unions and business that tempered excesses in wage rises in times of inflation. Swedish business so liked this deal, and their seat at the table when it was shaped, that they became supporters of the Swedish welfare state and even its redistributive tax exceptionalism (Acemoglu and Robinson 2019: 467–74). By the 1980s and 1990s, this corporatism had become too cosy and neglectful of civil society concerns that were prioritised by neither business nor union cronies of the Social Democrats. Consequently, contestation by and collaboration with the Green Party (the coalition partner in government at the time of writing) has become a healthy tempering of the Social Democrats' model and has allowed them to respond to the decline in their vote since peaks in 1940, 1968 and 1994. The above analysis of strategic publicisations of the private is something Swedish social democracy with its Green Party partners might consider today.

Today, we have learnt that contextually attuned hybrids, which are neither total privatisation of the public nor total publicisation of the private, often serve freedom best. A purely private-sector model is not the way to conquer something like Covid-19. Publicly funded research in universities—at its foundation, in this case, by Chinese university research in Wuhan that made public the genetic sequence of Covid-19—will always provide much of the research grunt with such big challenges. The private pharmaceutical industry will always provide most of the grunt in scaling up the production of therapeutic breakthroughs needed at great scale. Private–public partnerships with extremely heavy doses of public funding are what invented the internet, and are what works best for building new generations of aircraft carriers or putting a human on the Moon. Social democratic parties today must work with green parties—with all parties—on bold state investments with different priorities than those of hybrid socialist production by the Pentagon, NASA and NATO. They might emphasise reinventing renewable technologies at greater scale and regulatory technologies for preventing accidental wars and protecting ecosystems. It makes no sense for social democracy to return to any general aversion to privatisation nor to an ideological commitment to nationalisation of the commanding heights of economies. Social democracy must be diagnostic and open about what forms of ownership best catalyse domination reduction.

The United Nations has proved it can reduce war, thereby reducing crime and growing freedom through cheap investments in peacekeeping (Braithwaite and D'Costa 2018: 494–501; Walter et al. 2020). A United Nations that has its power tempered by the power of states is imperative to the survival of humankind and the planet. That does not mean domination by great power vetos. The next section turns to genocide as the kind of crisis such tempered power must tackle.

Genocide

Few leaders are as admired as British Prime Minister Winston Churchill. He believed that one way to win World War II was to break the morale of German civilians by pulverising their cities with carpet-bombing and firebombing. Churchill was minded to do what Hitler was not: use chemical weapons to defend the United Kingdom against a German invasion. Churchill wrote to his chiefs of staff in February 1943: 'In the event of the Germans using gas on the Russians … We shall retaliate by drenching the German cities with gas on the largest possible scale' (Pruitt 2017). Drenching at scale would have been a crime of chemical genocide. President Roosevelt did not buy this. In 1939, he urged his allies against the approach Churchill came to execute in Hamburg and Dresden and to attempt in Berlin. Roosevelt said after the terror-inducing bombing of the civilians of Shanghai by Japan in 1937 and of Guernica by the European fascists:

> The ruthless bombing from the air of civilians in unfortified centers of population during the course of the hostilities ... has sickened the hearts of civilized men and women ... I am therefore directing this urgent appeal to every Government which may be engaged in hostilities publicly to affirm its determination that its armed forces shall in no event, and under no circumstances, undertake the bombardment from the air of civilian populations or of unfortified cities, upon the understanding that these same rules of warfare will be scrupulously observed by all of their opponents. (Ellsberg 2017: Ch. 14)

Well before the end of World War II, the United States had abandoned this ethical stance and joined the western descent into barbarism. It embarked on a nuclear weapons program of mass civilian destruction. Hitler decided not to devote resources to this because he rightly believed that Germany's war would be won or lost before such weapons could be used. Churchill and China's Chiang Kai-shek pressured US President Harry S. Truman to use its nuclear weapons against Japan. Most Americans believe the dropping of atomic bombs on Hiroshima and Nagasaki was a terrible but necessary evil because it ended the suffering of World War II. Credible historians of World War II do not believe this today and most members of the Joint Chiefs of Staff did not believe so at the time and opposed their use. Among the distinguished American military naysayers on dropping the bomb in 1945 were Dwight D. Eisenhower, Douglas MacArthur, Paul Nitze, Carter Clarke, William D. Leahy, Chester Nimitz, William Halsey Jr and Curtis LeMay (Ellsberg 2017). The firebombing of Tokyo had killed much larger numbers of civilians than were killed in Hiroshima, instilling terror at the centre of power, so most leading US strategists and scientists involved with the bomb favoured gradual acceleration of this terror—for example, by destroying shipping just outside Tokyo Harbor with an atomic blast or just a submarine blockade.

None of this was the main game of ending the war, however. The war was about to end because Russia had begun to attack and was set to invade Japan, and Japan was poised to surrender when they did. Truman did not want this to happen, and the atomic bomb was aimed at deterring the Soviets for the purposes of the impending Cold War as much as or more than deterring Japanese civilians. Criminologists of war crimes have contributed nothing to moving NATO's opinion away from the view of nuclear weapons as the necessary evil that ended World War II. Hiroshima and Nagasaki were war crimes directed at civilian terror, contrary to President Roosevelt's more ethical plea of 1939. Since then, US and Russian presidential criminality has worsened and deepened. US presidents became inured to threatening other countries with complete destruction of their cities. If international courts rightly found the events in Srebrenica and Rwanda to be genocides then threats of nuclear launches with contemporary warheads threaten much more massive civilian genocides. Indeed, what all nuclear powers—including smaller ones like the United Kingdom, France, Pakistan, India, Israel and North Korea—threaten against their enemies by pointing their nuclear arsenal at them is a genocide of larger proportions than Hitler perpetrated in World War II.

A distorted noble narrative of World War II is that the Allies fought it to end a genocidal regime. On the ashes of that victory, the Allies built a world order based on mutual threats of genocide, even a 'doomsday machine' on both sides, which guaranteed genocidal responses to any nuclear attack (Ellsberg 2017). Progressive American criminologists can be comfortable with allegations that George W. Bush was a war criminal, but they are not always comfortable when it is said that Clinton, Obama and Biden ruled and defended a world order based on mutual threats of genocide against all other societies, including non-nuclear states who renounce such threats as criminal.

Preventing genocide–ecocide cascades

Even nuclear wars between lesser powers like Israel and Iran, Pakistan and India, North Korea and China could all cascade to be ecocidal in their environmental impacts. We have seen how cyberwarfare or cybercrime that is intended to disable a satellite that targets conventional missiles might accidentally and coincidentally disable an entire nuclear arsenal (Ellsberg 2017; Beebe 2019; Perry and Collina 2020). These expert strategic authors explain how this might cause an imprudent state, fearing loss of its nuclear defences, to use them rather than lose them to their wrongly presumed enemy. Braithwaite and D'Costa (2018) show that there are strong tendencies for economic crises to cascade to wars, be they crises of mass unemployment or hyperinflation. Or the problem can be the likes of a slightly unhinged Pakistani general who once said Pakistan would interpret an inexplicable crash of the stock exchange in Karachi as an act of war by India. Further, Chapter 7 argued that nuclear war between Pakistan and India might cause a real global economic crisis and a climate crisis. If a catastrophic political crisis between India and Pakistan happened to coincide with a stock market crash and an environmental tipping point, perhaps no power could hold back a global crime–war cascade. Risks that might cascade from cybercrime to nuclear alerts are not reducing if it is true that China has been contracting cybercriminal organisations at scale to hack the West, and Microsoft specifically (Kanno-Youngs and Sanger 2021).

When pandemics break out in the aftermath of mutual cascades of ecosystem collapse, economic collapse and nuclear war, few of the most powerful states on the planet would be left with the logistical capability to combat a pandemic in the way they did in 2020 and 1918. Cascades from ecosystem collapse to diseases that jump from animals to humans are already increasingly common because of surviving wild animal populations being crowded to live closer to humans. In Australia, several new viruses have afflicted humans as a result of deforestation driving bats to refuge in the trees of urban parks, and after the bats themselves became more susceptible to disease because of ecosystem crises that afflicted their health. Anomic collapse of freedom might occur everywhere after a nuclear war. All this is an unknowable, unpredictable risk of crisis cascades. Yet it is not too late to reinvent capitalism, to reinvent environmental diplomacy and war diplomacy, to regulate cybercrime and AI that overreaches or goes awry. A coincidence of these kinds of catastrophes can then become an event of low likelihood.

My contention has been that while criminology does not bear the main responsibility for finding alternative paths to regulate the planet, it has a more important part to play than it has had the vision to see. This is because the fabric of prevention of cascades of crises has many strands. Some of these are better understood by economists or international relations scholars, but many strands are best understood by criminologists—for example, the corruption of regulatory institutions, the criminalisation of states, cheating within markets in virtue designed to temper markets in vice and cybercrime that coincidentally cascades to nuclear weapons being put on alert.

Chapter 7 argued that much can be done to increase welfare and wages to prevent crises of insufficient demand and to keep markets pumping during crises. Inspiring regulatory initiatives can be launched to strengthen the self-incapacitation of toxic corporations and of states armed to the teeth with weapons of mass terror. It is possible to shift the shape of economies so they stoke demand while softening their environmental impact. In the medium term, economies can be reshaped so that jobs are created less by investment in the production of material things than by growth in human services. Shifting the shape of the economy so more of the jobs are for nurses, teachers or carers reduces emissions (Denniss 2017; Burford et al. 2019). Financialised capitalism pushes workers and whole economies into levels of debt they cannot manage when crises arrive. Understanding these dynamics helps us grasp why authoritarian capitalist economies accomplished a wider economic growth lead over liberal economies this century and, in the case of China, a lead in green innovation (Drahos 2021; Braithwaite 2020a). This is a different pattern from previous centuries. Investing in more jobs to steer capitalism and expand welfare sits alongside creating more jobs in human services as an imperative to avert cascades to ecological, security, health and economic crises, and to authoritarianism. While there is enormous path-dependence of momentum towards extinctions, it might be countered by strategies for mutual interpenetration of growth path-dependencies among institutions of the market, welfare and regulation (Braithwaite 2021a).

Green growth is possible for an economy that consumes more of the services of aged care, childcare and disability care workers, doctors, nurses, educators, regulatory inspectors, UN peacekeepers and serving staff. Care workers do not burn carbon in the way factory workers do. If growth can be fuelled by further accelerating the shift to a services economy, driven in part by growing the welfare state, growth can be green. Likewise, debt that funds investment in renewables is economically fertile debt for growing an economy. A state that ran up debt by investing in expanded secondary or higher education during the 2010s borrowed at interest rates less than one-third of the return to GDP of increased investment in education (Psacharopoulos and Patrinos 2018); this differential widened after Covid. Taxes can be increased to improve education, health and welfare benefits. This helps green growth in economies that can allow lower taxes at a future time when the nation collects dividends on that social investment.

Likewise with welfare investment in modest but secure housing for the poor or regulatory investments that prevent disruptions in access to housing. Recovery programs for the hugely expensive burdens on states of alcoholism, addiction to illicit drugs and recovery from crime and prison are less likely to succeed with people who have insecure housing—so much so that secure housing is part of the scale to measure recovery capital (Best et al. 2012; see also Cano et al. 2017). Welfare state investment in secure housing for all can enhance the effectiveness, and the growth dividend, of all investments in the welfare state. This conclusion will not pile on more examples that go to the feasibility of markets that flourish because the shape of economies is shifted away from the consumption of large cars, large houses and corporate towers of big offices overflowing with consumer durables, fast furniture and fast fashion. A hegemonic shapeshift of this kind is beginning in the world's largest economy, China, where services consumption and health, welfare, education and regulatory workforces are all growing steeply (Braithwaite 2020a). While China is still by far the world's largest emitter of carbon dioxide, a steeply growing proportion of its factory production is in producing most of the world's electric cars, solar panels, wind turbines and other essentials of global carbon-neutrality. If China can shapeshift as part of its UN commitments to halve its emissions this decade, perhaps hegemonic shapeshifts are not beyond western economies.

Agonistic social movement model-mongering

Nonviolence is the ethos of protest politics critical to effectiveness and freedom. Activists need the wisdom to see that social movements are better able to ride waves of history than to create them. Opportunities to think cleverly about how to do this will be more frequent as existential crises press perilously upon us. Events like Australia's mega-bushfires of 2019–20 drove a substantial shift away from recalcitrant Australian climate denial on the backs of the three billion vertebrates that perished. Such events will recur more frequently. Waves of political unrest that are directly connected to climate change and drought in the manner of the Australian bushfires are just one kind of wave of history to ride. While the risks of a nuclear power plant meltdown have greatly reduced, one day there will be another Chernobyl. We have seen that global pandemics create another opportunity that social movements mostly had no strategy to ride. They, too, are historically common; modernity has seen dozens, though most in the recent past have not hit the West in a devastating way. HIV/AIDS and polio in the late and mid-twentieth century had health, though not economic, impacts of a scale that compared with Covid-19, with enduring and devastating impacts on young survivors. For several

African countries, Ebola was also tragic this century. Economic crises that result in recession or hyperinflation are even more common; the past eight centuries have seen 350 of them (Reinhart and Rogoff 2009).

Then there are micro-events that erupt into waves of history; a poor man in Tunisia self-immolates after a last straw of state oppression, catalysing the Arab Spring to cascade across a dozen countries. The killing of George Floyd by Minneapolis police in 2020 sparked a wave that surged anger and sorrow across 51 US states and dozens of other countries.

Environmental activists are no less in denial than the rest of the community. They are similarly unprepared to ride the wave of environmental concern that will arise when a city like Tokyo, Beijing, Pyongyang or New Delhi is erased in a never-before-seen cloud that rises into the atmosphere as a result of the failure to dismantle the reckless nuclear weapons programs of North Korea, Pakistan or, worse, Russia, or some other country. My fear is that our grandchildren are quite likely to see something like this happen during their lifetimes or that of their children. A random spark like the political assassination of a president in Taipei, Beijing or Washington might cascade risk. We know this because war happens in response to such sparks in defence strategists' war-gaming and scenario simulations of escalations (Allison 2017: 155). We prudently fear this because in the past great powers often got into wars they never wanted, and genuinely worked to avoid, in response to sparks like the assassination of Archduke Ferdinand of Austria-Hungary (Clark 2012).

Does the social movement against climate change really have contingency strategies in its top drawer that result from its scenario planning (as opposed to that of state defence ministries) about how to ride the kind of climate crisis wave induced by a nuclear war? History instructs us about what happens when social movements have failed to do their scenario planning well with much less dramatic events than a nuclear weapons exchange. Martin Luther King was strategically wise about the greater power of nonviolent compared with violent social movement politics. He was central to building an effective civil rights movement in the 1960s with Gandhian strategies. He predicted his own assassination privately to his colleagues and even publicly. When he was assassinated, this sparked a great wave of protests that saw many US cities in flames. The nonviolence of the uprising was poorly managed by an unprepared social movement. Cascading riots, looting and killing opened the door to Richard Nixon to win the 1968 election on a racist platform of law-and-order politics.

The wave of mobilisation that swelled after the murder of George Floyd was better harnessed by the Black Lives Matter movement. Instead of the forces of violent protest progressively displacing nonviolent protest (as occurred in the 1960s), in 2020, the forces of nonviolent protest were well enough prepared to progressively displace the politics of violence and this in turn helped *close* the door on the authoritarian law-and-order presidency of Donald Trump. Even so, the Black Lives Matter movement was not as prepared as it might have been for armed right-wing racists who enjoyed encouragement from President Trump to act as provocateurs of violence on the streets. The early tide of political resilience of nonviolence turned and the political advantage seesawed back towards Trump for a worrying period in late 2020. Scenario planning in social movement politics could be more detailed, resilient and nimble.

We can learn to make agonistic pluralism more diagnostic of when protest subdues violence, expands freedom, escalates violence and advances domination. The largest Arab Spring movement in Egypt surged liberal democrats and leftists, but it was captured by the Muslim Brotherhood, who swept to power electorally because they were better organised and had an organisational power base spread throughout the nation. The Muslim Brotherhood had done their scenario planning during their years in prison about how to swoop at that moment of regime weakness. The lesson of history is that they executed it well, even if they failed to hold their capture of the state against the return to power of militarised authoritarianism. In Syria, most Arab Spring protesters were also peaceful and progressive, but they, too, were outflanked by opponents of the regime who were committed to violence, to Islamic State and to Al-Qaeda. Again, the proponents of violence and domination had better organisational power bases, better scenario planning that they had gamed in their preparation and wealthier international support networks that were ready and waiting. The tragic outcome was half a million lost lives and a more militarily muscular Syria, Iran and Russia.

These Arab Spring failures repeated the failures of the Iranian Revolution of 1979, which was also mostly led on the streets by liberal democrats and leftists. But the ayatollahs were the ones who had the powerbases in the mosques and the Islamic educational institutions and who put the socialists, the liberals and the political leaders of Kurds, Arabs and other oppressed minorities of the revolution in prison. The 2009 Green Revolution, when millions of opponents of that Iranian regime occupied Azadi (Freedom) Square, was full of promise to overthrow the ayatollahs.

The leaders were inadequately prepared university intellectuals who failed to mobilise the marginalised ethnic minorities; they elected a committee in the square that foolishly advised the assembled millions to go home while they met to formulate a strategy to put to them the next day. As they made their way in small groups back to Azadi Square the next day, the security forces were able to pick them off, shooting, arresting and dispersing them. The uprising was over.[5] Social movements for transformation stand little chance if their adversaries do crisis scenario planning and they do not. Agonistic pluralism is a politics of riding waves of history with organisational bases and scenario planning. It is about being a model-monger, with most of your transformational plans for a moment of crisis waiting in the top drawer, a few others on the backburner, with all activist energy shifting to the front-burner a plan that is responsive to today's crisis (Braithwaite and Drahos 2000: Ch. 25).

Neither Mandela, Gandhi nor Gusmão in Timor-Leste totally renounced violence. What they demonstrated is that violence is the tool that favours the masters; a switch to nonviolence as their strategy of struggle increased the prospects of success for the dominated. Chenoweth and Stephan (2011) showed this systematically across 323 political struggles for maximalist transformation (such as regime change) since 1900. Nonviolent struggles were twice as likely to achieve most of their objectives in the long run compared with armed struggles. Their research also reveals that violent victories against domination are more likely to create dominating, undemocratic successor regimes (Braithwaite and D'Costa 2018: 59). This book advances further reasons why committing to nonviolence is committing to freedom. Braithwaite and Drahos (2000) showed that in global campaigns to regulate business domination, webs of dialogue were more valuable to the weak than to the strong, while webs of reward and coercion were more valuable to the strong than to the weak. This was not, however, full vindication of Lorde's (1984) 'the master's tools will never dismantle the master's house'.

Chapter 7 found social movement politics to be recurrently effective by turning the masters' tools against the masters. Adept social movements enrolled business organisations to defect to their projects (Latour 1986). The first great social movement was one of the most successful for this reason. The social movement against the slave trade in the eighteenth and

---

5   This interpretation is based on Peacebuilding Compared interviews with uprising leaders in Iran, Iraq and across the diaspora.

nineteenth centuries was nonviolent. Church leadership in England was particularly potent in mobilising electoral support for parliamentarians who supported bills to ban the slave trade and for causing those who opposed them to lose their seats. After this campaign succeeded in the United Kingdom, British business and the British state had a strategic trade interest in persuading other states to join a global ban (Chapter 7). British naval domination pursued the ban violently at times, blowing slaving ships out of the water in the Harbour of Rio de Janeiro. Likewise, we saw that after the US environmental movement succeeded in its campaign for a legal ban on CFCs because of the ozone hole they were opening, DuPont responded by inventing CFC-substitute technology. DuPont and President Reagan then decided they had a strategic trade interest in licensing DuPont's technology to the rest of the world. Then Reagan and his diplomatic corps became the most unlikely climate wolf-warriors the world has seen, but also the most successful, in implementing the Montreal Protocol on Substances that Deplete the Ozone Layer. This is what is meant about the power of enrolling the masters' tools to divide and conquer the masters. Activists must be politically honest about the fact that bad power cannot be defeated without broad alliances for good power. When allies are masters who use the masters' tools, the principled social movement must be clear that these are the masters using the masters' tools, not the movement's tools, but reap the benefits of their use nevertheless.

Rebalancing postwar social democratic virtues

The great powers, the United States and China, each interpreted the failures of the other in response to the 2020 Covid crisis as evidence of the weaknesses of the social and political systems of the other. Both were right to contend that we live in an era when crises are more globalised. In a world that has become tightly coupled, the globalisation of economies, of disease, of environmental crises and of war are all global risks. The West tends to credit the long peace between great powers since 1945 to nuclear deterrence. Russian analysts think differently. They see plenty of fellow analysts on both sides who contemplate ways of surprising the enemy to win a nuclear war. But Russian belief is that great powers are *unwilling* to gamble on winning, because after a nuclear exchange their logistical capabilities would be so depleted they would lack the capability to mobilise an army to capitalise politically by pacifying a massive society in another hemisphere (Chekov et al. 2020: 32).

For this to happen, a victorious army would have to arrive and restore a desired order in a defeated country. In the Russian view, however, to support large-scale long-term activities in another hemisphere is practically impossible (Kosolapov 2008).

My addendum is that a country weakened as a decisive nuclear war winner might struggle to contain the epidemics that historically so often plague continents after huge wars. The nuclear war winner's economy might lose out to a third power that is less devastated by the nuclear exchange.

China and the United States were right in their critiques of each other's systems in their Covid responses. The US was right to castigate China for a cover-up and the failure of its institutions of science and transparency to be independent in sounding the alarm to the world in a timely fashion. China was right to allege that the United States lost a hundred times more lives than China because its hollowed-out state lacked the institutional capacity to respond adequately to a crisis it knew in advance was coming.

But these were not the only two systems that were tested by this conflict. Eastern hemisphere economies—from more liberal ones like New Zealand, Australia, South Korea, Taiwan and Japan to more authoritarian ones like Vietnam, Cambodia, Malaysia and Singapore—performed much better. The latter group may not be transparent about the vices of their ruling parties, but, as the World Bank's 'Asian Miracle' report pointed out long ago, even the most authoritarian tiger economies are surprisingly transparent in allowing the contestation of evidence and public policies, as long as these do not threaten governing families and parties. They were transparent about Covid-19. Their states and civil societies were prepared to deal with it, and they pulled the levers to prevent its spread before it cascaded out of control. Those countries closest to the original outbreak, including China's neighbours Taiwan, Vietnam and South Korea, were among the countries that fared best during Covid's first year at containing the pandemic for these institutional reasons.

Their Third Way was not that of Tony Blair's or Bill Clinton's hollowing out of the state under a social democracy false flag that was in fact captured by finance capital and patrimonial capitalism (Piketty 2014). The most successful western government in its management of Covid, however, so far has been Jacinda Ardern's in New Zealand. Crisis responsiveness there was rapid, decisive and impeccably transparent. It was the first country to achieve first-wave elimination of the virus within its borders. In the 1980s, New Zealand became infatuated with the neoliberal Washington Consensus, which lasted many years. Ardern's New Zealand has moved to a hybrid of rediscovering old virtues of Keynesian social democracy and newer virtues of the Asian tiger economies, but with wider transparency, stronger commitment to evidence-based policy and less domination than these traditions of governance.

To a degree, all countries were forced by the imperatives of managing Covid to become more like New Zealand. Even China was forced by international scrutiny to become more transparent, opening itself to data collection by foreign medical scientists. Even the United States was forced to consider state 'planning' of the economy as no longer a dirty word. The Trump and, more so, Biden administrations opened up to Asian tiger–style capability to ensure that for this crisis, and the next, they had enough strategic industrial capacity to reverse deindustrialisation, at least to the point where it could rapidly scale up the personal protective equipment, ventilators and vaccines that were central to the crisis response.

Learning macrocriminology lessons from macroeconomic failures

Covid-19 is not the only crisis that has shifted policy thinking about the imperative for strengthening more diverse and tempered institutions. The economics profession, which—in the footsteps of Hayek, Robert C. Merton and Thatcher—supplied the ideas that fuelled financialised capitalism ruled by money politics, is still divided. Yet it has seen widespread changes of heart. Many economists now favour moving away from the radically privatised US health system of high-quality (but expensive) health care for the rich and early death for the poor. They favour tax collection that repairs hollowed-out state infrastructure, from health to highways, bridges and schools. Many agree with Piketty's (2014) interpretation of the evidence that requiring the rich to pay more tax will not significantly reduce incentives to work, though that continues to be contested. The most dramatic change is that most economists today see a strong evidence-based case for higher wages, especially for the poor, to sustain demand and temper indebtedness. The evidence no longer supports their former belief that upwards movement in the minimum wage increases unemployment (Quiggin 2019: 251–54). It is hard today to find economists in China or the United States who think that fighting wars is in the national interest because they drive creative destruction of unresponsive production systems (Quiggin 2019: 125–28).

Some of the privatisations of this era were good policy; others were not. The global movement to deregulate state price-setting in aviation markets and privatise national carriers has delivered cheap, safe flights for cut-price travellers. During the highwater mark of neoliberal thought, however, buyers of underpriced privatisations made large political donations or bribed public officials, particularly in Eastern Europe. Economists came to see it as a paradox of late twentieth-century privatisations that a hollowed-out state inadequately regulating privatisations delivered economically irrational, criminogenic, monopolistic and anti-freedom privatisations.

Remarkably, criminologists had little interest in warning against this outcome, nor in advocating regulatory reforms on the back of these corruption disasters. Russian President Vladimir Putin was the actor with the imagination to 'never waste a good crisis' by sweeping to power to clean up the oligarchs.

What these recent hegemonic shifts mean is that it is no longer pointless to advocate tougher regulation of corruption, of the military-industrial complex, financial capital, antimonopoly laws and environmental protection and tougher taxation of capital and the wealthy, more relentlessly responsive tax enforcement and street-level enforcement by labour rights inspectors who enable significant re-unionisation and globalisation of a living wage, following Marshall (2019) on how to deliver this.

Strengthening trade unions and regulation of labour standards as a strategy of redistribution and empowerment are a good case study of disenchantment with a tired old social movement that can be reversed. This is not politically utopian. Political centrists like Bill Clinton and Tony Blair in some ways sustained and even strengthened the anti-union reforms of Ronald Reagan and Margaret Thatcher. We can now see trade unions again as one of the transformative and earliest global social movements. We can reconsider their decline as not inevitable, but contingent and reversible. As Quiggin points out, unions had terrible decades with the global inflationary upsurges of the 1960s and 1970s:

> In retrospect, it is clear that the acceleration of inflation was primarily the result of mistakes in macroeconomic policy. At the time, however, it seemed more plausible to place the blame on [a] wage–price spiral caused by the greed of unions and big corporations, acting in concert. Because the process of keeping wages ahead of inflation required virtually continuous strike action, unions came to be seen (and to some extent to see themselves) as being in conflict with society as a whole. By contrast, attempts to control increases in prices, most notably during the Nixon wage–price freezes from 1971–73 ended in ignominious failure. (Quiggin 2019: 246)

As Reiner (2020) explained, crushing union power was also a conscious strategy in the way Thatcher worked with the Murdoch press to militarise the suppression of the miners' strike (Green 1990). Prime Minister John Howard in Australia deregulated labour law on the back of crushing the maritime union's strike. Union corruption and capture by organised crime further undermined union legitimacy and played into the hands of conservative conspiracies against unions. Royal commissions into union corruption became a stock in trade of Australian conservatives.

Second-wave feminists abandoned the unions that first-wave feminists had embraced in mutually beneficial networking because unions had been so incorrigibly patriarchal. That situation has recently radically reversed in some societies such as Australia, and indeed globally at the International Confederation of Free Trade Unions. This is necessary when the most oppressed unionised workforces are feminised. This book has argued that feminism is a social movement that is important to so many of the tributaries of reform proposed for a low-crime, low-domination society. Gender equality is a fundamental macrocriminological strategy for suppressing crime–war cascades (Braithwaite and D'Costa 2018: 525–26). Its potential might not be fully realised without returning to an alliance with feminised trade unions and welfare rights movements.

As Quiggin (2019) points out, casualisation and labour law deregulation can be repealed. Many workers crave the protection of unions but are simply afraid to sign up because they will be victimised by employers who should be prosecuted for such victimisation. Marshall's (2019) vision for how to accomplish this globally, and how to transform and reboot a globalised union strategy, is an inspiring one.

Some will question whether such economic policy analysis has much to do with criminology. Macrocriminology might learn from Keynes and New Deal macroeconomics. The austerity of the 1920s and 1930s that it displaced was at its worst in Weimar Germany and Japan; this was a macroeconomics of hyperinflation and mass unemployment that was causally implicated in the worst crimes of human history that threatened freedom globally. The world, and even Ronald Reagan's Republican Party, learnt from Keynes and the New Deal that incurring state debt to pump up employment is a better response to recession than austerity. The world applied that lesson somewhat to the Global Financial Crisis of 2008, but not well enough. Return to neoliberal austerity was too rapid, especially for countries like Greece. With the Covid recession of 2020, again, even the US Republican Party learnt that second lesson. The learning was from qualitative, historically and macro-theory–informed, evidence-based macroeconomics.

A world of better macro-settings

What criminology might ponder from its shared experience with the macroeconomics of violence is that criminology would do well to crave and craft its own historically and theoretically informed macro imagination. Ways to do this could include the proposals listed in Appendix I.

Appendix I is the book's actual conclusion. The conclusion to this chapter asks readers not to be dispirited by its warnings that the challenges of freedom and crime are complex and fraught with hegemony that repeatedly trumps liberation. It cannot be said that freedom and crime are variables that all societies have in similar measure. Today's freest societies have periods of great domination in their histories. Just as the differences in domination between the most and least free societies today are huge, the differences in crime are more than 100-fold between the highest and lowest by society, neighbourhood and period of history.

Cornucopias of micro-measures like better drug rehabilitation cannot eliminate 99 per cent of crime and domination on their own. What this book argues is that macro transformation can and does. That level of elimination is what 100-fold differences mean. In Congo for the past 30 years, rates of murder, rape, the burning of homes and looting have easily been a hundred times as high as in Germany. But, during the Thirty Years' War, Germany was rather like the Democratic Republic of Congo of the past 30 years in terms of crime and domination (and probably worse; see Chapter 3). One need not go back that far. When the Soviet army was sweeping across Germany in 1945, following Stalin's advice to rape women and take what they needed, domination and crime were not so greatly different from the Thirty Years' War. Germany's recovery from its postwar anomie, violence and domination was as rapid as Congo's descent into it. My thesis is that Germany was able to conquer crime and domination because it made a good fist of making the 150 tributaries of Appendix I flow into six rivers of freedom. Today, Germany CHIMEs with intertwined varieties of capital; it is rich in the collective efficacy to secure order and freedom; its institutions are strong, variegated and relatively autonomous. In recent years, even its institutions of finance have been somewhat tempered. Still, it can do much better. Indeed, many countries do better than Germany on almost all 150 of freedom's tributaries.

Germany did not need as much help as Congo, but it got more help than Congo will ever get, through the Marshall Plan—the finest moment of the American century. I have shown strong evidence that postwar peacekeeping and peacebuilding do work in helping societies to CHIME and conquer domination, war and crime. As the Montreal Protocol and the regime for oil pollution at sea have shown (Chapters 6–7), environmental agreements can and do work. There is no inevitability of ecocide. I have argued that the risks of nuclear genocide would be many times worse without the nuclear nonproliferation regime, even within the depressing limits of its regulatory capabilities. Anti-domination politics is politically rewarding, even though hegemony recurrently trumps liberation.

Appendix I: Tributary propositions; rivers of meaning

Without a hint of irony, it might be said that this book has accumulated a sufficiently long and detailed list of 150 propositions to give both empirically and normatively oriented scholars sufficient ideas to refute or revise. Six propositional rivers have been induced from the 150 tributaries that are now listed chapter by chapter. The six propositional rivers into which they converge are:

1. Reduce all dimensions of domination.
2. Separate and temper powers.
3. Strengthen institutions of the market, state and civil society, and strengthen individuals.
4. Maintain a normative order that nurtures collective efficacy to resist domination.
5. Strengthen financial capital, human capital, social capital, recovery capital and restorative capital.
6. Prevent wars before they begin to cascade violence, anomie and domination.

The reason this is an explanatory and normative theory of crime and freedom is that these six normative rivers, with all their tributaries, then converge to power a light on the macrocriminologist's hill that is both normative and explanatory: strengthen freedom to prevent crime; prevent crime to strengthen freedom.

The tributaries

Chapter 2: Reframing criminology

Crime control is fundamental to the constitution of freedom.

Freedom strengthens crime control.

Thin liberal freedom helps, but is brittle compared with thick republican freedom.

It is freedom as nondomination that holds a key to crime control. Nondomination means the tempering of arbitrary power over others.

Freedom from patriarchy, poverty and state and corporate tyrannies is central to nondomination.

Freedom tempers power, making power less brittle and more responsive to justice in tackling challenges like crime.

Macrocriminology demands a methodological pluralism of micro–meso–macro explanation that transcends methodological individualism.

Macrocriminology reveals more when it integrates explanatory and normative theory.

Macrocriminology reframes the referent beyond individual offenders to an integrated explanation of criminalised markets, criminalised states, criminalised norms, criminal organisations, criminalised spaces, times and life-courses, and macro-historical trajectories.

The book argues for a macrocriminology that asks not only how to treat individuals, markets, states and civil society to prevent crime, but also how to be responsive to them to increase freedom and prevent domination.

Therefore, the best solutions to crime problems are not found in the justice system. The most cost-effective solutions to crime are cost-effective partly because they help solve other deep problems like health disadvantage, suicide and environmental collapse.

Chapter 3: Macro-patterns of normative order

Globally, crime is a much more deadly and destructive problem than war (so far), and suicide is much more deadly than war and crime combined (though less destructive of cities, civilisations and ecosystems). Yet the fertile path is to see war, crime and suicide as part of the same cascade of problems—all partially shaped by complex cycles of anomie that are difficult to steer, but that can be steered.

Anomie is conceived in ways more ancient than those popular in contemporary criminology. Anomie means widespread uncertainty about the normative order, about what are the rules of the game and about whose authority is legitimate. Confusion about the arbitrary enforcement of arbitrary rules is domination by definition. Uncertainty about what the rules are also makes it harder for defenders of freedom to attack bad rules and bad rule, and easier for despots to obfuscate, saying the rules are X to one group but not X to another.

Legal cynicism about the rules of the game is a related concept and, like anomie, it correlates with crime.

Anomie is recurrently a factor in the onset of waves of crime and war.

In a wide range of circumstances, anomie accelerates crime and, at times, other forms of dominating disorder, including civil war and terrorism.

Anomie is one of the mechanisms that explains why crime risks cascades to more crime, and to war, and war risks cascades to more war and more crime.

When an invading army or internal insurgency smashes a society apart, its normative order tends to shatter, cascading to further violence and anomie.

Law enforcement that imprisons or kills the leaders of organised crime, terrorist or insurgency groups can also create an anomic fragmentation of those illegal groups that makes violence worse rather than better.

However, when a social order that is not reeling from an invasion does hold together during war, war can result in survivor societies rallying behind their normative order.

Moreover, after wider spaces are pacified by a war than were pacified before the war, settled sovereignty over wider territories can diffuse peaceful coexistence.

Vast empires of conquest have historically not only widened the zones of pacification of violence; they also quite often created spaces where the rule of law, human rights and the tempering of power could mature. So, war that transcends anomie with peaceful sovereignty can result in less crime, less domination and more freedom.

Durkheim helps us see complex contingency and recursivity of anomie contributing to violence. At one historical juncture, anomie promotes violence. This then loops contingently to alternative cycles. One contingency is a cascade of anomie and violence in the next historical moment that shatters a society, creating cycles of more anomie and more violence. Then a communal revival from violence rises from the ashes to conquer anomie, even with nonviolence. If cascades of violence can be paused, prevented from becoming endless, the social order can hold under fire. During wars that are not too long or devastating, the social order often becomes more unified. This is more likely when the societies involved in wars are not invaded and occupied. Another loop can occur when violence establishes a monopoly of force and peaceful sovereignty over a swathe of territory that pacifies violence and anomie.

A different loop arises when that monopoly of force dominates and excludes. When a monopoly of force is untempered, it risks unravelling that sovereignty in a return to cycles of anomie and violence (as Russia illustrates throughout its modern history to the present). All these are potential turning points that good governance can steer to the peaceful waters of freedom with low levels of crime. Most developed democracies have achieved these outcomes reasonably well since World War II—from small ones like Denmark, Norway and New Zealand to large ones like Germany, Japan and South Korea since it democratised. This is less true for the most militarised powers of this era: the United States and Russia. They have recurrently used their muscle in anomic and destabilising ways. At other times, the great powers have cooperated to support the United Nations and help it sustain the international normative order in the cause of peace and freedom.

The complex ways in which the foregoing list of propositions interact give a helpful account of why violent crime has been in long-run decline in Europe for the past 800 years. At the same time, the propensity of anomie effects to pass tipping points can be understood to explain major reversals from that trajectory in and beyond Europe during those 800 years.

More recently, the complex ways in which these propositions interact account for why there was a short-term but steep reversal to increases in crime across most of the West from 1960 to 1992. They also give an account of why France is a major exception to that reversal to crime trending in this western way, why violence in Latin America, the Caribbean and Africa continued to increase during the post-1992 western crime drop and why the great East Asian crime drop preceded the western crime drop by more than four decades and continued to fall during the 1960–92 period when crime was rising in the West.

The big-picture story of war, crime and normative order that Chapter 3 tells demonstrates not a unidirectional civilising process, but human agency in making peace and making war, in making institutional choices that cascade crime and violence or that cascade nonviolence.

Chapter 4: Opportunities for freedom and for domination

Anomie Américaine is not a substitute for *anomie ancienne*; it complements it.

Within *anomie Américaine*, Merton, Cloward, Ohlin, Cohen, Messner and Rosenfeld all add decisively to cumulate an institutional anomie theory of a plurality of institutions that temper domination.

The evidence grows increasingly suggestive that a rich plurality of institutions that temper the hegemony of economic institutions, and that temper commodification, can reduce crime and increase freedom.

When legitimate opportunities and opportunities for freedom are open; when illegitimate opportunities and opportunities to dominate others are closed, crime is reduced and freedom is enhanced.

Domination is a more fertile concept than inequality for explaining violence, with militarised domination and criminalised domination of governments and markets particularly critical. Yet struggles against domination and discrimination must be contextually attuned and responsive to what are subjectively salient inequalities.

Local micro-dominations (for example, between landlords and peasants) can be more important to explaining violence than more macro or more national inequalities. Because it is hard to predict which levels of domination will fuel raging fires of subjective oppression and violence, and which will not, societies do well to aim at tempering all kinds of domination.

It is common for multicollinearity to produce the result that inequality explains crime, but poverty or racial discrimination does not; or that poverty explains crime, but inequality does not; or that child mortality but none of these other measures explains crime. Often what is true in individual or ecological data is not true in time-series studies, or at least not true in time-series with short lags. We do best to read these literatures with a spirit of openness to domination effects that are socially constructed as oppressive at different times, places and levels of analysis in different ways with different lags. We must be wary of a selective positivism that, after failing to find a particular linear effect, empowers analysis paralysis over inequality effects. Likewise, we must be wary of selectivity in attention to the data by social democrats like me on questions of inequality.

Racial, gender, religious and caste discrimination and discrimination against children who perform poorly at school count among the recurrent contributors to domination and crime. Empirically, discrimination that is sanctioned by the state poses the gravest danger to societies.

Reducing national inequality on its own is less likely to have an impact than an integrated struggle against local, national and global inequalities of the kinds that the oppressed perceive as most destructive and humiliating. This is because intersectional domination explains violence better than a thin conception of inequality measured by a national Gini coefficient. The integrated social justice strategy required involves making power accountable at all levels and tackling domination and humiliation at the level of the school, the local community, the refugee camp, the bank, the national level and at the level of global imaginaries and global institutions. Most importantly, these strands of a web of justice, peace and nondomination must be joined up. That is difficult work requiring patience for weavers of a fabric of peace and nondomination.

Redemptive schooling can contribute to a less anomic society by assisting every citizen along the journey of discovering valuable ways they can excel.

Societies and schools that institutionalise failure, and societies afflicted with a commodified and militarised vision of what success and failure mean, suffer high crime rates and domination.

Inequality and poverty relate differently to crime and war and along different pathways. Because war tends to cascade to crime and crime to war, a helpful strategy for indirect prevention of crime–war cascades is to reduce extremes of poverty and inequality, particularly those most salient to the subjective sense of domination of a people in an incendiary situation of oppression.

Explaining crime–war as a cascade can be attractive to the point of perceiving violence and crime as variables that evolve together, collectively: from world wars, to international wars, civil wars, 'small-town wars', drug cartel wars, street gang wars, tiny terrorist cells, to mass and individual shootings by individuals. There are also important distinctions among these types of violence. The criminalisation of states and markets is so responsive to organised criminality and militarisation that crime and war cannot and should not be completely separated in historiography and violence research.

Domination grows in radically unequal societies. The rich tend to enjoy unaccountable power, while the poor can be desperate in their powerlessness. A narrow elite can put in place extractive political institutions that concentrate power in their hands; they disable constraints on the exercise of that power. Therefore, no topic is more critical for criminology than understanding how states and markets become criminalised.

The times and places where women are more dominated tend to suffer more war, more crime—particularly sexual assault and violence against women—and less freedom. This is not because feminised armies cascade wars that cascade to postwar sexual assault and violence by female veterans. Feminised armies are exceptionally rare; Nepal is the only case where female fighters approached a majority at the core of a post–Cold War conflict. There is no feminist Frantz Fanon espousing the cleansing power of violence against male oppressors. Understanding exceptions is important to macrocriminological method. It is notable that pacified postwar Nepal achieved more major feminist constitutional transformations than any other society, postwar or without war, and a female Maoist general who became president. Like Nepal, the genocide against Yazidis in Iraq was started by men but finished with women playing prominent roles in another instructive and liberating exception.

It is important to understand in a Durkheimian way that industrialisation contributed to anomie and crime, as did *de*industrialisation (see also Chapter 11). This complements the understanding we gain from Mertonian anomie.

Durkheim, Messner and Rosenfeld were astute to see that well-tempered institutions temper appetites. They temper dangerous ambitions for narcissistic acquisitiveness. Plural institutions can shape aspirations for a humble pride that eschews vaunting pride.

Commodification—market values that reduce all other values to their worth in markets—is a danger to freedom and to the tempering of crime.

Militarisation—martial values that colonise other institutions, reducing other values to their worth for making the state great in order to dominate other peoples, or making the faith great to dominate other faiths— is a danger to freedom and to the tempering of crime.

Chapter 5: Tempering inequality that empowers crimes of the powerful

Middle-class crime is stupendous in volume, increasing, but mostly minor in seriousness compared with crimes of the powerful and of the powerless.

The middle class often appears more criminal than they are because of systematic patterns of passing organisational accountability downwards in the class structure.

Middle-class complicity in crimes of the powerful and how to prevent this are major issues, however.

A less anomic, less legally cynical middle class is one key to civilising capitalism and tempering the domination of national security states.

Crimes of the powerful are the biggest crime problem. While they are enabled by concentrations of wealth and power, they cannot be fixed by killing off wealth and power. A challenge of this book is to show how greater equality in the distribution of wealth and power can strengthen capital accumulation. It is to show how tempering of state and market power can make states and markets more powerful builders of social and financial capital for distribution to the poor.

Economists are generating growing evidence suggesting that income inequality can explain proxies for environmental crime and corruption cross-nationally and by province. Corruption induced by higher levels of inequality is in turn associated with terrorism and organised crime. Corruption and organised crime criminalise states and markets, rendering both extractive, rather than inclusive and enabling.

Chapter 4 concluded that redemptive schooling is important to anomie prevention; this chapter concludes that schooling is a foundational institution for creating a society in which all citizens find how they can work at things at which they excel.

There can be no freedom in societies that send some citizens to the scrap heap as children or elderly citizens, or in between because they are a person with disabilities. There is a feasible politics for delivering every citizen a responsive education, freedom from hunger and decent housing supported by constant contestation for greater redistribution of wealth and power in favour of the marginalised.

Extreme inequality and the politics of domination are structurally humiliating and stigmatising for the dominated. This domination and stigma drive crime.

More wealth *for use* in the hands of the poor increases wealth creation overall even as it takes wealth away from the rich *for exchange*. More extreme concentrations of wealth for exchange in the hands of the rich also worsen the most dominating forms of illegitimate opportunities.

By heightening domination, more inequality means more crimes of the exploited and more crime by those who exploit.

Crimes of exploitation require tempering of wealth and power for exchange by the rich through pluralising separations of powers.

Chapter 6: Closing illegitimate opportunities by separating powers

The way to control the abuse of power is not to destroy power but to share it and temper it.

A separation of powers into the legislature, the executive and the judiciary is insufficiently complex for the contemporary division of labour.

In the world of contemporary capitalism, the separation of private powers is as important as the separation of public powers.

Corruption is controlled by continual reinvention of new ways of sharing separated organisational powers so that domination is always being put off balance.

Separated institutional powers must be able to pursue power up to the point where the power of one is not so strong as to overcome the power of the others. Each separated power must be strong enough, however, to secure the exercise of its own power from being dominated by any other institutional power.

Workplace democracy has an important niche in a separation of powers.

The deterrence trap means that sanctioning of an organisation sufficient to deter it may risk crippling it and crippling innocent citizens who depend on it.

One escape from the deterrence trap is to replace narrow, formal and strongly punitive responsibility (the 'find the crook' strategy) with broad, informal, weak sanctions.

A second escape from the deterrence trap is to separate enforcement targeting from identification of the actor who benefits from the abuse of power. Together, this escape and the one above constitute a strength of weak sanctions.

A third escape from the deterrence trap is to rely heavily on street-level bureaucrats who mobilise the 'relational state' and a wide mix of preventive strategies, each of which is weak as a standalone strategy, but strong when woven into a fabric of relational prevention. These street-level relational regulators can be police, state, self-regulatory or NGO inspectors, state or NGO welfare supporters or citizens who mobilise collective efficacy at street level.

Separations of private power can be crafted to prevent corporate domination through the following:

- Better securing the separation of the powers of the three major branches of corporate governance: shareholders, directors and managers.
- Better separating powers within management—for example, quality versus production, environment versus production.
- Expanding audit capabilities to a range of areas beyond finance—for example, safety, antitrust, ethics.
- Professionalising audit so that internal auditors have an external professional allegiance to balance corporate loyalty.
- Abandoning hierarchies of accountability in favour of circles of accountability so that auditors audit auditors, ensuring that someone guards the guardians.
- Allowing outsiders with interests different from corporate interests into the circle of accountability: unions into safety management circles, consumer group representatives into consumer complaint-handling circles, greens into environmental circles by mandated public reporting of corporate environmental objectives and public reporting of audits of whether the objectives are attained.
- Guaranteeing transparency and tainting soft targets with knowledge by institutionalising a safety valve reporting route direct to a board audit committee, to a corporate ombudsman or to both.
- In domains where serious abuse of power is a risk, independent reports on compliance to the board audit committee from separate powers, such as line management, legal, audit, unions.
- Obligations on all employees to report suspected violations of law and violations of corporate policies that involve the abuse of corporate power (for example, ethics, environmental policies). Obligations to report the suspected violations direct to the board when the employee does not receive back a written report that the matter has been satisfactorily resolved. Failure to meet this obligation must itself be an ethical breach that colleagues have an ethical obligation to report. This is crucial to corporate collective efficacy that can temper the dominations of the extremely powerful.

Most fundamentally, crime prevention must shift its focus from hard targets who are committed to criminal subcultures to indirectly leveraging change through caring and prosocial actors who surround them—such as their daughters, the priests of Mafia bosses or the accountants of Wall Street predators alike.

Chapter 7: Tempered and diverse forms of capital

Competition policy is a good thing when it strengthens markets in goods, bad when it strengthens markets in bads. The remedy is to temper Donor McDonor markets with strategic regulation.

Markets in children's books, *Consumer Reports* magazine, pricing carbon, software markets that protect against property crime and markets in motor vehicle anti-theft technologies are examples of virtuous markets in crime prevention. Markets in compliance professionalism and the privatisation of criminal prosecution are strategic for controlling corporate crime (Chapter 9).

High-crime cities that have deindustrialised can be renewed by renewables and welfare, by a green welfare economy that opens a door to a low-crime information economy (in which black lives matter).

Old socialism and 'old' neoliberalism cannot deliver this liberating outcome. Transformation requires a hybridity of strategic publicisations of the private and privatisations of the public with an eye on freedom as nondomination.

Regulation of the financialisation of capitalism and of tech platform monopolies is particularly imperative.

Economic capital must be strong to accomplish a low-crime, high-freedom society, but so must be human capital, social capital, recovery capital and restorative capital.

While there are fertile distinctions between different forms of social capital, they are mutually constitutive. Each tempers the abuse of power by the others. This is also true of collective efficacy—a variant of social capital that is particularly strategic for crime control.

When all these forms of capital become strong, the way they each check and balance one another creates a societal strength that is nuanced, nimble and dialogic rather than dominating.

Mutually constitutive forms of capital in turn constitute CHIME (Connectedness, Hope, Identity, Meaning and Empowerment). CHIME controls crime.

Without further strengthening all of the foregoing strengths, the superior capacity of authoritarian capitalism to pull levers may overwhelm liberal capitalism. A violent world dominated by authoritarianism, criminalised states and criminalised markets is our path unless we consider these hybrid paths not taken.

Strong markets, a strong state, strong civil society and strong individuals with an agency that makes the personal political are all vital to more freedom and less crime, as are enculturating trust and institutionalising distrust in all key institutions.

Contemporary forms of capitalism are highly internally variegated. Different variegations require different mixes of forms of capital and forms of regulation.

A crucial art of freedom is to learn how to flip markets in vice to markets in virtue. Markets that control crimes of domination are an important part of that art of freedom. Institutional anomie theory is misguided if it neglects or dismisses this.

Crashes in capital markets are connected in dangerous ways to security and environmental crises. Flipping to markets in virtue is one important approach to averting cascading crises.

Markets such as Wall Street are constituted by communitarianism among traders; understanding this is a key to understanding how to flip them to markets in virtue via collective efficacy remedies such as restorative justice.

Chapter 8: Tempering power through networked governance

Most good things accomplished in social life require the exercise of power. Among the things power helps accomplish are protecting freedom and preventing crime.

Hence, we do not seek to limit or curb power, but to enable good power by tempering it.

Untempered power dominates. It is not constrained by other powers from being arbitrary.

Constitutions and their implementation are imperative conduits to power, to protecting freedom and to preventing crime.

Constitutions enable tempered power by separating and balancing powers while also enabling power to be decisive. Decisiveness accomplishes specialised purposes of power efficiently and semi-autonomously. Judicial power is decisive because judges, and only judges, can convict. Judges have clearly defined capacities to break gridlock between other separated powers because they have decisive powers. Conversely, it is the police officer, and not another judge, who has the power to arrest a judge for domestic violence, and a prosecutor who has the power to prosecute. Each power is channelled to its specialised purposes by checks and balances from other powers that prevent them from arbitrarily breaking banks beyond their channel. This gradually breaks down in the historical journey towards the criminalisation of states.

Contestation, dialogue and science have important roles in channelling power to good purposes and away from arbitrary excess. If security services torture suspects, claiming that this saves lives, citizens must rise up to contest the arbitrary authority for police to punish. Debate is required in the legislature of the propriety of police jumping outside their authorised channels of prevention and arrest. Prosecutors should monitor the debate and charge police with assault as appropriate. If participants in a restorative justice conference credibly uncover excessively brutal use of force in an arrest, prosecutors must act in response to that democratic contestation to rechannel police power. Good science in independent universities tests claims that torture prevents terrorism.

Sun Yat-sen's constitutional innovation of an elected accountability and integrity branch of governance that is independent of the judiciary, legislature and executive and has impeachment authority over them is a profound contribution to republican thinking about securing freedom and preventing crime. Business regulatory institutions, particularly the central bank, must be accountable and democratised, but independently democratised from the central government. Sun Yat-sen's thought holds one clue for how to accomplish this.

Nodal power in civil society networks has a crucial role in coordinating bridging capital among the separated powers of a democracy to tame a rogue power. Without networked governance of tyranny led from civil society, there can be no freedom. Criminalised states and criminalised markets evolve when there is no networked governance of their dominations.

Social democratic parties that embody civic republican values of nondomination in their platforms are important to championing freedom. Yet without networked governance of tyranny from civil society, they are as vulnerable as any political party to criminalised state power. An elected pro-freedom party governing under a pro-freedom constitution puts freedom at risk whenever there is a failure to institutionalise distrust.

A paradox is that societies cannot enjoy long-run freedom from anomie and violence unless civil societies enjoy destabilisation rights to restore freedom by dynamic adjustment of the constitutional order.

Summarising so far, lessons about liberal freedom and taming ancient anomie are important to tempering domination and reducing crime, but they are not enough. Blocked legitimate opportunities must be opened and illegitimate opportunities closed. Institutional anomie theory insights must be realised through strong institutions of family, welfare and education. The data further suggest that religious institutions that resist tyranny can prevent violence and institutions of tax equity are important, as are labour market and other institutions that promote equality. Particularly fundamental are separations of micro and macro powers. The promise of institutional anomie theory also requires strong business regulatory institutions, strong markets in crime-control virtue, strong civil society, strong financial, human, social, recovery and restorative capital and strong individuals. The most brilliantly institutionalised freedom could not be freedom at all if it were a freedom of timorous individuals who allowed institutions to do everything for them. At the same time, free individuals are unlikely to survive the risks of nuclear genocide and ecocide across the next century or two without a stronger United Nations.

Uncontested commodification of too many things is a risk of American capitalism. Uncontested state control of too much is a danger of Chinese communism. Getting the balance right between market power and state power is not quite the right way to think about this dilemma. After all, this book shows that crime and domination are caused by excesses in state control in America and by excesses of commodification in China. The imperative is a struggle for both markets and states to be stronger in ways that temper domination in both societies.

Chapter 9: Minimally sufficient punishment

For unusually oppressed people, like First Nations Australians, punishment is not a minor facet of their domination, but central to the dynamics of domination.

Deterrence works best when it is progressively reduced with the aim of growing freedom as nondomination. It must be reduced to the lowest level of deterrence that can avert the escalation of crime.

Which strategy works best at crime control is not the most important question for criminology. More important is which meta-strategy is best in a situation, which strategy for sequencing strategies best reduces crime and domination? Deterrence contributes best to meta-strategy design when punishment is low and decreasing, but detection is perceived to have high certainty, and escalation is seen as inexorable without desistance.

Deterrence works best when escalation of deterrence is combined with escalation of social support to help offenders take paths away from punishment.

Successful crime prevention persuades offenders that trouble hangs inexorably over their head, but caring people will support them to avert it.

Freedom depends on escalating social support until desistance from domination is consolidated.

Deterrence above minimal sufficiency blunts deterrence. Anything more than a minimally sufficient frequency of escalation to deterrence blunts deterrence for future cases.

A preference for restorative justice over deterrence sharpens future deterrence of crimes of the powerless and, more surprisingly, future deterrence of crimes of the powerful.

Deterrence usually fails because the criminal justice system always faces a system capacity crisis that is at its worst when and where the crime rate is worst. Responsive escalation helps solve the system capacity crisis by motivating most punishment to be self-punishment and most prevention to be self-prevention. Responsive regulation rations punishment to cases where ethical appeals for remorse, apology, reparation and self-prevention of future offending do not work.

When intrinsic motivation to comply with the law is kept intact, responsive regulatory enforcement chooses not to crowd out intrinsic motivation with extrinsic threats.

Responsive enforcement has a dynamic design to ensure that game-playing to avoid legal obligations inexorably produces escalation to deterrence, then incapacitation.

Deterrence works best when it focuses on a line that should never be crossed after an announcement date, followed by progressive lifting of that line, raising our expectations of responsible corporate and individual citizens.

Law enforcement works best when it averts stigmatisation, while communicating the shamefulness of predatory crime.

Freedom is maximised when the structural punitiveness of the system is gradually reduced until punishment gets so low that insufficiency of punishment increases crime.

Minimally sufficient punishment allows the least punitive societies to close most of their prisons while meeting the UN Standard Minimum Rules for the Treatment of Prisoners (the 'Nelson Mandela rules').

This is best done with pride and publicity that educate citizens about why 'jailing is failing'.

Chapter 10: Why incapacitation trumps deterrence

Criminological thought must become more punitive in incapacitation terms. New laws should announce execution dates for entire industries. Dates for the banning of internal combustion engine cars and aircraft and coal, oil and gas-fired power plants establish a renewed relevance for capital punishment in criminology. Companies that were once number one on the *Fortune 500* list—the old General Motors, the old Exxon, the old Boeing—must be reborn or die. There are drug pushers of Big Pharma that must be incapacitated. Detroit must be reborn with social support for regenerative capitalism.

The art of republican regulation is the art of steering self-enforcement democratically, deliberatively and relationally with motivational interviewing.

An important revision of responsive regulatory theory for crime is that self-incapacitation should normally be sequenced before deterrence in an enforcement pyramid.

Self-incapacitation generally has more preventive power than deterrence and incapacitation by the state—for organisational crime and for individual crime when individual offenders are responded to through restorative justice.

Much self-incapacitation can be as simple as the Plimsoll line, which made it impossible for dangerously overloaded ships to leave port without being stopped.

Self-incapacitation of war crime can be catalysed by a simple letter from an International Criminal Court prosecutor to a military commander warning that if he fails to disarm a militia under his control that begins to ethnically cleanse a region, he is on notice of potential personal war crime culpability.

Self-incapacitation agreed to in a restorative justice circle can achieve more global reach with organisational crime prevention when national jurisdictions confront limits. Cosmopolitan collective efficacy can demand global self-incapacitation. Restorative justice can scale up to help prevent global crises this way.

Self-incapacitation agreed to in restorative justice circles can make contributions to the prevention of crimes that cause financial crises, environmental crises, wars and war crimes. Restorative circles can also help self-incapacitate street offenders from access to gambling if that is a root cause of their offending and from internet access to pornography for child sex offenders released from prison.

When deferred prosecutions result in restorative self-incapacitation, they can be more effective at corporate crime prevention than actual prosecutions. Self-incapacitation can deliver structural reform that is beyond compliance.

With corporate crime and war crime, there is a case for nailing the minnows and then offering them effective immunity when they testify against the sharks. Then there is a case for a restorative conference with the sharks to secure their cooperation with self-incapacitation to prevent further corporate crime or war crime. After this organisational crime wave ends, the sharks who committed to self-incapacitation might then be pressured to testify against worse sharks who refused to comply with the self-incapacitation agreement.

In a prosecution strategy, it can be much more important to be punitive when there is cover-up of horrifically collective criminality than to prosecute individual participation in crime. Focusing punishment where there is a cover-up can enable structural prevention through collective incapacitation of future horrors and can enable learning cultures about recklessness (as illustrated with child sexual abuse in churches).

Chapter 11: Tempered cascades of crime

Crime cascades to more crime through the following common dynamics:

- Modelling (often perceived as emulation or diffusion).
- Commercial interests cascade particular crimes (for example, cocaine franchising) and particular kinds of soft targets for crime (for example, Facebook or Tinder users).
- The crimes of parents cascade to crime by their children; the crimes of children cascade to crime by their friends; differential association cascades.
- Hopelessness, loss of identity and closure of opportunities tend to cascade, particularly at hotspots of concentrated disadvantage in conditions of extreme inequality and policy failure in providing decent housing for all.
- War and pro-violence politics cascade to domination, anomie, hopelessness, closed opportunities and more crime; crime cascades to more war; war cascades recursively to more crime.
- War, crime and anomie are often entangled in mutually reinforcing cascades.
- War cascades to criminalisation of states and criminalisation of markets by armed groups or in pursuit of corruption by shadow states that serve the purposes of armed groups.

Crime prevention cascades when:

- Respected actors have the self-efficacy to transform cultures by modelling anti-crime norms; self-efficacy scales to collective efficacy through explicitly connecting evidence-based microcriminology to a macrocriminology of cultural transformation.
- Norms of civility and nondominating collective efficacy at one locale spread like ink spots that connect ink spot to ink spot, covering whole societies with norms of civility.
- Parents and schools mobilise collective efficacy to reject stigmatisation yet communicate to their children why violence and stealing are shameful.
- This enables redemption scripts for offenders to help themselves and to grasp self-efficacy as wounded healers who cascade help to other offenders.
- An inclusive politics of hope, identity formation and opening of legitimate opportunities cascades to embrace formerly disadvantaged communities (collective efficacy becomes part of CHIME and helps constitute CHIME).
- Civil society obligations to pass on CHIME become an integral part of recovery and a structural way of cascading recovery.
- Institutionally embedded primary groups—families, schools, workgroups—that cascade nondominating collective efficacy alongside other forms of social capital can deliver prevention effects in the criminology of place; conversely, these prevention effects can depend on hotspot policing and peacekeeping that make the streets safe for collective efficacy, and the planet safe for collective efficacy as ink spots of nondomination spread globally.

Bibliography

Aaltonen, Mikko, John M. Macdonald, Pekka Martikainen and Janne Kivivuori. 2013. 'Examining the generality of the unemployment–crime association.' *Criminology* 51(3): 561–94. doi.org/10.1111/1745-9125.12012.

Abolafia, Mitchel Y. 1985. 'Self-regulation as market maintenance: An organization perspective.' In Roger Noll (ed.), *Regulatory Policy and the Social Sciences*. Berkeley, CA: University of California Press, pp. 312–43. doi.org/10.1525/9780520313651-012.

Acemoglu, Daron and James A. Robinson. 2012. *Why Nations Fail: The Origins of Power, Prosperity and Poverty*. London: Profile Books.

Acemoglu, Daron and James A. Robinson. 2019. *The Narrow Corridor: How Nations Struggle for Liberty*. New York: Penguin.

Adler, Andrew. 1964. *Individual Psychology of Alfred Adler*. New York: Harper Collins.

Adler, Freda. 1983. *Nations Not Obsessed with Crime*. Littleton, CO: Rothman.

Aebi, Marcelo F. and Antonia Linde. 2014. 'The persistence of lifestyles: Rates and correlates of homicide in Western Europe from 1960 to 2010.' *European Journal of Criminology* 11(5): 552–77. doi.org/10.1177/1477370814541178.

Agnew, Robert. 1992. 'Foundation for a general strain theory of crime and delinquency.' *Criminology* 30(1): 47–88. doi.org/10.1111/j.1745-9125.1992.tb01093.x.

Agnew, Robert. 2012. 'Dire forecast: A theoretical model of the impact of climate change on crime.' *Theoretical Criminology* 16(1): 21–42. doi.org/10.1177/1362480611416843.

Agnew, Robert. 2016. 'Strain, economic status, and crime.' In Alex R. Piquero (ed.), *The Handbook of Criminological Theory*. Oxford, UK: Wiley, pp. 209–29. doi.org/10.1002/9781118512449.ch11.

Ahern, Jennifer and Sandro Galea. 2011. 'Collective efficacy and major depression in urban neighborhoods.' *American Journal of Epidemiology* 173(12): 1453–62. doi.org/10.1093/aje/kwr030.

Ahern, Jennifer, Sandro Galea, Alan Hubbard and S. Leonard Syme. 2009. 'Neighborhood smoking norms modify the relation between collective efficacy and smoking behavior.' *Drug and Alcohol Dependence* 100(1–2): 138–45. doi.org/10.1016/j.drugalcdep.2008.09.012.

Ahmed, Eliza and Valerie Braithwaite. 2006. 'Forgiveness, reconciliation, and shame: Three key variables in reducing school bullying.' *Journal of Social Issues* 62(2): 347–70. doi.org/10.1111/j.1540-4560.2006.00454.x.

Ahmed, Eliza, Nathan Harris, John Braithwaite and Valerie Braithwaite. 2001. *Shame Management through Reintegration*. Cambridge, UK: Cambridge University Press.

Akbaba, Yasemin and Zeynep Taydas. 2011. 'Does religious discrimination promote dissent? A quantitative analysis.' *Ethnopolitics* 10(3–4): 271–95. doi.org/10.1080/17449057.2011.561988.

Akerlof, George A. 1970. 'The market for "lemons": Quality uncertainty and the market mechanism.' *The Quarterly Journal of Economics* 84(3): 488–500. doi.org/10.2307/1879431.

Akers, Ron L. 1998. *Social Learning and Social Structure: A General Theory of Crime and Deviance*. Boston, MA: Northeastern University Press.

Akers, Ron L. and Gary F. Jensen. 2011. 'Social learning theory and the explanation of crime.' In F. Adler and William S. Laufer (eds), *Advances in Criminological Theory. Volume 11*. New Brunswick, NJ: Transaction Publishers, pp. 9–38.

Alexander, Cindy R. and Jennifer Arlen. 2018. 'Does conviction matter? The reputational and collateral effects of corporate crime.' In Jennifer Arlen (ed.), *Research Handbook on Corporate Crime and Financial Misdealing*. Cheltenham, UK: Edward Elgar Publishing, pp. 87–150. doi.org/10.4337/9781783474479.00011.

Alexander, Cindy R. and Mark A. Cohen. 2015. 'The evolution of corporate criminal settlements: An empirical perspective on non-prosecution, deferred prosecution, and plea agreements.' *The American Criminal Law Review* 52: 537–93.

Alinaghi, Nazila and W. Robert Reed. 2020. *Taxes and economic growth in OECD countries: A meta-analysis*. OECD Working Paper No. 12/2020. Paris: Organisation for Economic Co-operation and Development.

Alkire, Sabina, Florent Bedecarrats, Angus Deaton, Gael Giraud, Isabelle Guerin, Barbara Harriss-White, James Heckman, Jason Hickel, Naila Kabeer, Solene Morvant-Roux, Judea Pearl, Cecile Renouard, Fancois Roubaud, Jean-Michel Servet and Joseph Stiglitz. 2018. 'An open letter from fifteen leading development economists.' *The Guardian*, 6 August.

Allison, Graham. 2017. *Destined for War: Can America and China Escape Thucydides's Trap?* New York: Houghton Mifflin Harcourt.

Alves, Luiz G.A., Haroldo V. Ribeiro and Francisco A. Rodrigues. 2018. 'Crime prediction through urban metrics and statistical learning.' *Physica A: Statistical Mechanics and its Applications* 505: 435–43. doi.org/10.1016/j.physa.2018.03.084.

Amato, Louis H. and Christie H. Amato. 2012. 'Environmental policy, rankings and stock values.' *Business Strategy and the Environment* 21(5): 317–25. doi.org/10.1002/bse.742.

Ambler, Wayne (trans.). 2001. *Xenophon: The Education of Cyrus*. Ithaca, NY: Cornell University Press.

Amir, Eli, Adi Lazar and Shai Levi. 2018. 'The deterrent effect of whistleblowing on tax collections.' *European Accounting Review* 27(5): 939–54. doi.org/10.1080/09638180.2018.1517606.

Andenaes, Johannes. 1974. *Punishment and Deterrence*. Ann Arbor: University of Michigan Press.

Anderson, Craig A. and Brad J. Bushman. 2002. 'The effects of media violence on society.' *Science* 295(5564): 2377–79. doi.org/10.1126/science.1070765.

Anderson, Frederick R., Allen V. Kneese, Phillip D. Reed, Russell B. Stevenson and Serge Taylor. 1977. *Environmental Improvement through Economic Incentives*. Baltimore, MD: Johns Hopkins University Press.

Andrews, Donald A. and James Bonta. 1998. *The Psychology of Criminal Conduct*. 2nd edn. Cincinnati: Anderson.

Andrews, Donald A. and James Bonta. 2010. 'Rehabilitating criminal justice policy and practice.' *Psychology, Public Policy, and Law* 16(1): 39–55. doi.org/10.1037/a0018362.

Apergis, Nicholas, Oguzhan C. Dincer and James E. Payne. 2010. 'The relationship between corruption and income inequality in US states: Evidence from a panel cointegration and error correction model.' *Public Choice* 145(1–2): 125–35. doi.org/10.1007/s11127-009-9557-1.

Applin, Samantha and Steven F. Messner. 2015. 'Her American dream: Bringing gender into institutional-anomie theory.' *Feminist Criminology* 10(1): 36–59. doi.org/10.1177/1557085114525654.

Archer, Dane and Rosemary Gartner. 1984. *Violence and Crime in Cross-National Perspective.* New Haven, CT: Yale University Press.

Arendt, Hannah. 1963. *On Revolution.* New York: Viking Press.

Ariel, Barak, Cristobal Weinborn and Lawrence W. Sherman. 2016. '"Soft" policing at hot spots: Do police community support officers work? A randomized controlled trial.' *Journal of Experimental Criminology* 12(3): 277–317. doi.org/10.1007/s11292-016-9260-4.

Aristotle. 1932. *Politics.* J.E.C. Welldon, trans. London: Macmillan. doi.org/10.4159/DLCL.aristotle-politics.1932.

Arlen, Jennifer. 2016. 'Prosecuting beyond the rule of law: Corporate mandates imposed through deferred prosecution agreements.' *Journal of Legal Analysis* 8(1): 191–234. doi.org/10.1093/jla/law007.

Arlen, Jennifer and Marcel Kahan. 2017. 'Corporate governance regulation through nonprosecution.' *The University of Chicago Law Review* 84(1): 323–87.

Atata, Scholastica Ngozi. 2019. 'Aged women, witchcraft, and social relations among the Igbo in south-eastern Nigeria.' *Journal of Women & Aging* 31(3): 231–47. doi.org/10.1080/08952841.2018.1436415.

Atkinson, Anthony B. 2015. *Inequality: What Can Be Done?* Cambridge, MA: Harvard University Press. doi.org/10.4159/9780674287013.

Atuesta, Laura H. and Yocelyn Samantha Pérez-Dávila. 2018. 'Fragmentation and cooperation: The evolution of organized crime in Mexico.' *Trends in Organized Crime* 21(3): 235–61. doi.org/10.1007/s12117-017-9301-z.

Augustine, Catherine H., John Engberg, Geoffrey E. Grimm, Emma Lee, Elaine Lin Wang, Karen Christianson and Andrea A. Joseph. 2018. *Can restorative practices improve school climate and curb suspensions? An evaluation of the impact of restorative practices in a mid-sized urban school district.* Research Report No. 2840. Santa Monica, CA: RAND Corporation. doi.org/10.7249/RR2840.

Autor, David, David Dorn and Gordon Hanson. 2018. *When work disappears: Manufacturing decline and the falling marriage-market value of young men.* NBER Working Paper No. 23173. Cambridge, MA: National Bureau of Economic Research. doi.org/10.3386/w23173.

Axelrod, Robert M. 1984. *The Evolution of Cooperation.* New York: Basic Books.

Ayling, Julie. 2013. 'What sustains wildlife crime? Rhino horn trading and the resilience of criminal networks.' *Journal of International Wildlife Law & Policy* 16(1): 57–80. doi.org/10.1080/13880292.2013.764776.

Ayres, Ian and John Braithwaite. 1992. *Responsive Regulation: Transcending the Deregulation Debate.* New York: Oxford University Press.

Ayres, Ian and Steven D. Levitt. 1998. 'Measuring positive externalities from unobservable victim precaution: An empirical analysis of Lojack.' *The Quarterly Journal of Economics* 113(1): 43–77. doi.org/10.1162/003355398555522.

Bacher, William. 1911. 'Hillel.' *Encyclopaedia Britannica. Volume 13.* 11th edn. New York: Encyclopaedia Britannica, Inc.

Baer, Miriam H. 2016. 'Too vast to succeed.' *Michigan Law Review* 114(6): 1109–35.

Baer, Miriam H. 2021. 'Designing corporate leniency programs.' In Benjamin van Rooij and D. Daniel Sokol (eds), *Cambridge Handbook of Compliance.* Cambridge, UK: Cambridge University Press, pp. 351–72. doi.org/10.1017/9781108759458.

Baier, Colin J. and Bradley R.E. Wright. 2001. 'If you love me, keep my commandments: A meta-analysis of the effect of religion on crime.' *Journal of Research in Crime and Delinquency* 38(1): 3–21. doi.org/10.1177/002242 7801038001001.

Bailey, William C. and Ruth D. Peterson. 1994. 'Murder, capital punishment and deterrence: A review of the evidence and an examination of police killings.' *Journal of Social Issues* 50(2): 53–74. doi.org/10.1111/j.1540-4560.1994. tb02410.x.

Bakken, Børge. 1993. 'Crime, juvenile delinquency and deterrence policy in China.' *The Australian Journal of Chinese Affairs* 30: 29–58. doi.org/10.2307/2949991.

Bakken, Nicholas W., Whitney DeCamp and Christy A. Visher. 2014. 'Spirituality and desistance from substance use among reentering offenders.' *International Journal of Offender Therapy and Comparative Criminology* 58(11): 1321–39. doi.org/10.1177/0306624X13494076.

Balint, Jennifer. 2011. *Genocide, State Crime and the Law: In the Name of the State.* London: Routledge. doi.org/10.4324/9780203806272.

Ball, Patrick, Paul Kobrak and Herbert F. Spirer. 1999. *State Violence in Guatemala, 1960–1996: A Quantitative Reflection.* Washington, DC: American Association for the Advancement of Science.

Bandura, Albert. 1973. *Aggression: A Social Learning Analysis*. Englewood Cliffs, NJ: Prentice-Hall.

Bandura, Albert. 1986. *Social Foundations of Thought and Action: A Social Cognitive Theory*. Englewood Cliffs, NJ: Prentice-Hall.

Bandura, Albert. 1989. 'Human agency in social cognitive theory.' *American Psychologist* 44(9): 1175–84. doi.org/10.1037/0003-066X.44.9.1175.

Bandura, Albert. 1999. 'Moral disengagement in the perpetration of inhumanities.' *Personality and Social Psychology Review* 3(3): 193–209. doi.org/10.1207/s15327957pspr0303_3.

Bandura, Albert. 2000. 'Exercise of human agency through collective efficacy.' *Current Directions in Psychological Science* 9(3): 75–78. doi.org/10.1111/1467-8721.00064.

Bandura, Albert. 2016. *Moral Disengagement*. New York: Worth Publishers.

Bandura, Albert, Claudio Barbaranelli, Gian Vittorio Caprara and Concetta Pastorelli. 1996. 'Mechanisms of moral disengagement in the exercise of moral agency.' *Journal of Personality and Social Psychology* 71(2): 364–72. doi.org/10.1037/0022-3514.71.2.364.

Barak-Corren, Netta. 2021. 'Regulation for integration by behavioral design: An evidence-based approach for culturally responsive regulation.' *Regulation & Governance*. doi.org/10.1111/rego.12385.

Barnes, Geoffrey C., Jordan M. Hyatt, Caroline M. Angel, Heather Strang and Lawrence W. Sherman. 2015. 'Are restorative justice conferences more fair than criminal courts? Comparing levels of observed procedural justice in the reintegrative shaming experiments (RISE).' *Criminal Justice Policy Review* 26(2): 103–30. doi.org/10.1177/0887403413512671.

Barnet, Richard J. and John Cavanagh. 1994. *Global Dreams: Imperial Corporations and the New World Order*. New York: Simon & Schuster.

Bartels, Lorana. 2009. 'The weight of the sword of Damocles: A reconviction analysis of suspended sentences in Tasmania.' *Australian and New Zealand Journal of Criminology* 42(1): 72–100. doi.org/10.1375/acri.42.1.72.

BasePoint Analytics. 2007. *New early payment default: Links to fraud and impact on mortgage lenders and investment banks*. White Paper. Carlsbad, CA: BasePoint Analytics.

Bauman, Zygmunt. 1989. *Modernity and the Holocaust*. Ithaca, NY: Cornell University Press.

Baumer, Eric P. and Regan Gustafson. 2007. 'Social organization and instrumental crime: Assessing the empirical validity of classic and contemporary anomie theories.' *Criminology* 45(3): 617–63. doi.org/10.1111/j.1745-9125.2007. 00090.x.

Beardsley, Kyle and Kristian Skrede Gleditsch. 2015. 'Peacekeeping as conflict containment.' *International Studies Review* 17(1): 67–89. doi.org/10.1111/ misr.12205.

Beck, Ulrich. 1992. *Risk Society: Towards a New Modernity.* New York: Sage.

Becker, Gary S. 1968. 'Crime and punishment: An economic approach.' In Nigel G. Fielding, Alan Clarke and Robert Witt (eds), *The Economic Dimensions of Crime.* London: Palgrave Macmillan, pp. 13–68. doi.org/10.1007/978-1-349-62853-7_2.

Becker, Gary S. 1993. 'Nobel lecture: The economic way of looking at behavior.' *Journal of Political Economy* 101(3): 385–409. doi.org/10.1086/261880.

Beebe, George S. 2019. *The Russia Trap: How Our Shadow War with Russia Could Spark into Nuclear Catastrophe.* New York: Thomas Dunne.

Bell, Brian, Anna Bindler and Stephen Machin. 2018. 'Crime scars: Recessions and the making of career criminals.' *Review of Economics and Statistics* 100(3): 392–404. doi.org/10.1162/rest_a_00698.

Beltratti, Andrea and René M. Stulz. 2009. *Why did some banks perform better during the credit crisis? A cross-country study of the impact of governance and regulation.* NBER Working Paper No. 15180. Cambridge, MA: National Bureau of Economic Research. doi.org/10.3386/w15180.

Bennett, Patrick and Amine Ouazad. 2020. 'Job displacement, unemployment, and crime: Evidence from Danish microdata and reforms.' *Journal of the European Economic Association* 18(5): 2182–220. doi.org/10.1093/jeea/jvz054.

Benson, Michael L. 1990. 'Emotions and adjudication: Status degradation among white-collar criminals.' *Justice Quarterly* 7(3): 515–28. doi.org/10.1080/ 07418829000090711.

Berg, Julie and Clifford Shearing. 2018. 'Governing-through-harm and public goods policing.' *The ANNALS of the American Academy of Political and Social Science* 679(1): 72–85. doi.org/10.1177/0002716218778540.

Berger, Ulrich. 2011. 'Learning to cooperate via indirect reciprocity.' *Games and Economic Behavior* 72(1): 30–37. doi.org/10.1016/j.geb.2010.08.009.

Bergère, Marie-Claire and Janet Lloyd. 1998. *Sun Yat-sen*. Janet Lloyd, trans. Stanford, CA: Stanford University Press.

Berghel, Hal. 2018. 'Malice domestic: The Cambridge Analytica dystopia.' *Computer* 51(5): 84–89. doi.org/10.1109/MC.2018.2381135.

Beringen, Helen. 2021. 'CSIRO'S Circular Economy Roadmap charts path to triple job creation.' News release, 25 January. CSIRO, Canberra. Available at: www.csiro.au/en/News/News-releases/2021/CSIROS-Circular-Economy-Roadmap-charts-path-to-triple-job-creation.

Berinsky, Adam J. 2007. 'Assuming the costs of war: Events, elites, and American public support for military conflict.' *The Journal of Politics* 69(4): 975–97. doi.org/10.1111/j.1468-2508.2007.00602.x.

Berkowitz, Leon. 1973. 'Studies of the contagion of violence.' In Herbert Hirsch and David C. Perry (eds), *Violence as Politics: A Series of Original Essays*. New York: Harper & Row, pp. 41–51.

Berkowitz, Leon and Jacqueline Macaulay. 1971. 'The contagion of criminal violence.' *Sociometry* 34(2): 238–60. doi.org/10.2307/2786414.

Berliner, Joseph. 1957. *Factory and Manager in the USSR*. Cambridge, MA: Harvard University Press. doi.org/10.4159/harvard.9780674188273.

Berta, Nathalie, Emmanuelle Gautherat and Ozgur Gun. 2017. 'Transactions in the European carbon market: A bubble of compliance in a whirlpool of speculation.' *Cambridge Journal of Economics* 41(2): 575–93. doi.org/10.1093/cje/bew041.

Besançon, Marie L. 2005. 'Relative resources: Inequality in ethnic wars, revolutions, and genocides.' *Journal of Peace Research* 42(4): 393–415. doi.org/10.1177/0022343305054086.

Best, David. 2017. 'Developing strengths-based recovery systems through community connections.' *Addiction* 112(5): 759–61. doi.org/10.1111/add.13588.

Best, David, Tracy Beswick, Steve Hodgkins and Matt Idle. 2016. 'Recovery, ambitions, and aspirations: An exploratory project to build a recovery community by generating a skilled recovery workforce.' *Alcoholism Treatment Quarterly* 34(1): 3–14. doi.org/10.1080/ 07347324.2016.1113105.

Best, David, Ed Day, Bill Morgan, Tina Oza, Alex Copello and Michael Gossop. 2009. 'What treatment means in practice: An analysis of the delivery of evidence-based interventions in criminal justice drug treatment services in Birmingham, England.' *Addiction Research & Theory* 17(6): 678–87. doi.org/10.3109/16066350802447090.

Best, David, Jane Gow, Tony Knox, Avril Taylor, Teodora Groshkova and William White. 2012. 'Mapping the recovery stories of drinkers and drug users in Glasgow: Quality of life and its associations with measures of recovery capital.' *Drug and Alcohol Review* 31(3): 334–41. doi.org/10.1111/j.1465-3362.2011.00321.x.

Best, David and Alexandre Laudet. 2010. *The Potential of Recovery Capital.* London: Royal Society for the Arts.

Best, David, Trish McKitterick, Tracy Beswick and Michael Savic. 2015. 'Recovery capital and social networks among people in treatment and among those in recovery in York, England.' *Alcoholism Treatment Quarterly* 33(3): 270–82. doi.org/10.1080/07347324.2015.1050931.

Best, David, Amy Musgrove and Lauren Hall. 2018. 'The bridge between social identity and community capital on the path to recovery and desistance.' *Probation Journal* 65(4): 394–406. doi.org/10.1177/0264550518790677.

Best, Rohan, Paul J. Burke and Frank Jotzo. 2020. 'Carbon pricing efficacy: Cross-country evidence.' *Environmental and Resource Economics* 77(1): 69–94. doi.org/10.1007/s10640-020-00436-x.

Bhattacharyya, Sambit and Rold Hodler. 2009. 'Natural resources, democracy and corruption.' *European Economic Review* 54(4): 608–21. doi.org/10.1016/j.euroecorev.2009.10.004.

Bianco, Lucien. 2016. 'Comparing Mao to Stalin.' *The China Journal* 75(1): 83–101. doi.org/10.1086/683126.

Bible Hub. 2004–21. '458. anomia. Strong's Concordance.' *Bible Hub.* [Online.] Available at: biblehub.com/greek/458.htm.

Bigoni, Maria, Sven-Olof Fridolfsson, Chloe Le Coq and Giancarlo Spagnolo. 2012. 'Fines, leniency and rewards in antitrust.' *The RAND Journal of Antitrust* 43(2): 368–90. doi.org/10.1111/j.1756-2171.2012.00170.x.

Bircan, Cagatay, Tilman Brück and Marc Vothknecht. 2010. *Violent conflict and inequality.* DIW Berlin Discussion Paper No. 1013. Berlin: German Institute for Economic Research. doi.org/10.2139/ssrn.1639826.

Bittle, Steven, Laureen Snider, Steve Tombs and David Whyte (eds). 2018. *Revisiting Crimes of the Powerful: Marxism, Crime and Deviance.* New York: Routledge. doi.org/10.4324/9781315212333.

Bjerregaard, Beth and John K. Cochran. 2008. 'Cross-national test of institutional anomie theory: Do the strength of other social institutions mediate or moderate the effects of the economy on the rate of crime?' *Western Criminology Review* 9(1): 31–48.

Black, Julia and Robert Baldwin. 2010. 'Really responsive risk-based regulation.' *Law and Policy* 32(2): 181–213. doi.org/10.1111/j.1467-9930.2010.00318.x.

Black, William K. 2005. *The Best Way to Rob a Bank Is to Own One: How Corporate Executives and Politicians Looted the S&L Industry.* Austin: University of Texas Press.

Blagg, Harry and Thalia Anthony. 2019. *Decolonising Criminology: Imagining Justice in a Postcolonial World.* London: Palgrave Macmillan.

Blattman, Christopher, Donald Green, Daniel Ortega and Santiago Tobón. 2018. *Place-based interventions at scale: The direct and spillover effects of policing and city services on crime.* NBER Working Paper No. 23941. Cambridge, MA: National Bureau of Economic Research. doi.org/10.3386/w23941.

Blumstein, Alfred. 2011. 'Approaches to reducing both imprisonment and crime.' *Criminology and Public Policy* 10(1): 93–102. doi.org/10.1111/j.1745-9133.2010.00694.x.

Blumstein, Alfred and Joel Wallman (eds). 2000. *The Crime Drop in America.* Cambridge, UK: Cambridge University Press.

Boggs, Sarah L. 1965. 'Urban crime patterns.' *American Sociological Review* 30: 899–908. doi.org/10.2307/2090968.

Bongard, Pascal and Jonathan Somer. 2011. 'Monitoring armed non-state actor compliance with humanitarian norms: A look at international mechanisms and the Geneva Call Deed of Commitment.' *International Review of the Red Cross* 93(883): 673–706. doi.org/10.1017/S1816383112000197.

Bonger, Willem A. 1916. *Criminality and Economic Conditions.* H.P. Horton, trans. Boston, MA: Little Brown.

Boulton David. 1978. *The Grease Machine.* New York: Harper & Row.

Bourdieu, Pierre. 1986. 'The forms of capital.' In John G. Richardson (eds), *Handbook of Theory and Research for the Sociology of Education.* New York: Greenwood Press, pp. 241–58.

Bovens, Mark and Anchrit Wille. 2020. 'Indexing watchdog accountability powers a framework for assessing the accountability capacity of independent oversight institutions.' *Regulation & Governance*. doi.org/10.1111/rego.12316.

Bowen, James. 2017. 'China, global peacemaker?' *IPI Global Observatory*, 25 September. Available at: theglobalobservatory.org/2017/09/china-belt-road-xi-jinping-peace/?mc_cid=3e3a7b6e87&mc_eid=5a83d8a219.

Box, Steven. 1971. *Deviance, Reality and Society*. London: Holt, Rinehart & Winston.

Box, Steven. 1983. *Power, Crime and Mystification*. London: Tavistock.

Boxer, Paul, L. Rowell Huesmann, Eric F. Dubow, Simha F. Landau, Shira Dvir Gvirsman, Khalil Shikaki and Jeremy Ginges. 2013. 'Exposure to violence across the social ecosystem and the development of aggression: A test of ecological theory in the Israeli–Palestinian conflict.' *Child Development* 84(1): 163–77. doi.org/10.1111/j.1467-8624.2012.01848.x.

Boyer, Barry and Errol Meidinger. 1985. 'Privatizing regulatory enforcement: A preliminary assessment of citizen suits under federal environmental laws.' *Buffalo Law Review* 34: 833–964.

Boyle, Michael J. 2014. *Violence after War: Explaining Instability in Post-Conflict States*. Baltimore, MD: Johns Hopkins University Press.

Bradley, Elizabeth H., Leslie A. Curry, Shoba Ramanadhan, Laura Rowe, Ingrid M. Nembhard and Harlan M. Krumholz. 2009. 'Research in action: Using positive deviance to improve quality of health care.' *Implementation Science* 4(1): 25. doi.org/10.1186/1748-5908-4-25.

Bradshaw, Keith. 2010. 'Relief well was used to halt Australian spill.' *The New York Times*, 2 May.

Braga, Anthony A. 2002. *Problem-Oriented Policing and Crime Prevention*. Monsey, NY: Criminal Justice Press.

Braga, Anthony A., Robert Apel and Brandon C. Welsh. 2013. 'The spillover effects of focused deterrence on gang violence.' *Evaluation Review* 37(3–4): 314–42. doi.org/10.1177/0193841X13518535.

Braga, Anthony A., Andrew V. Papachristos and David M. Hureau. 2014. 'The effects of hot spots policing on crime: An updated systematic review and meta-analysis.' *Justice Quarterly* 31(4): 633–63. doi.org/10.1080/07418825. 2012.673632.

Braga, Anthony A. and David L. Weisburd. 2012. 'The effects of focused deterrence strategies on crime: A systematic review and meta-analysis of the empirical evidence.' *Journal of Research in Crime and Delinquency* 49(3): 323–58. doi.org/10.1177/0022427811419368.

Braga, Anthony A. and David L. Weisburd. 2014. 'Must we settle for less rigorous evaluations in large area-based crime prevention programs? Lessons from a Campbell review of focused deterrence.' *Journal of Experimental Criminology* 10(4): 573–97. doi.org/10.1007/s11292-014-9205-8.

Braga, Anthony A. and David L. Weisburd. 2020. 'Does hot spots policing have meaningful impacts on crime? Findings from an alternative approach to estimating effect sizes from place-based program evaluations.' *Journal of Quantitative Criminology*: 1–22. doi.org/10.1007/s10940-020-09481-7.

Braga, Anthony A., David Weisburd and Brandon Turchan. 2018. 'Focused deterrence strategies and crime control.' *Criminology & Public Policy* 17(1): 205–50. doi.org/10.1111/1745-9133.12353.

Braga, Anthony A., Greg Zimmerman, Lisa Barao, Chelsea Farrell, Rod K. Brunson and Andrew V. Papachristos. 2019. 'Street gangs, gun violence, and focused deterrence: Comparing place-based and group-based evaluation methods to estimate direct and spillover deterrent effects.' *Journal of Research in Crime and Delinquency* 56(4): 524–62. doi.org/10.1177/0022427818821716.

Braithwaite, Alex. 2016. *Conflict Hot Spots: Emergence, Causes and Consequences.* New York: Routledge. doi.org/10.4324/9781315573380.

Braithwaite, Alex, Jessica Maves Braithwaite and Jeffrey Kucik. 2015. 'The conditioning effect of protest history on the emulation of nonviolent conflict.' *Journal of Peace Research* 52(6): 697–711. doi.org/10.1177/0022343315593993.

Braithwaite, Alex and Tiffany S. Chu. 2018. 'Civil conflicts abroad, foreign fighters, and terrorism at home.' *Journal of Conflict Resolution* 62(8): 1636–60. doi.org/10.1177/0022002717707304.

Braithwaite, Alex and Shane D. Johnson. 2012. 'Space-time modeling of insurgency and counterinsurgency in Iraq.' *Journal of Quantitative Criminology* 28(1): 31–48. doi.org/10.1007/s10940-011-9152-8.

Braithwaite, Alex and Quan Li. 2007. 'Transnational terrorism hot spots: Identification and impact evaluation.' *Conflict Management and Peace Science* 24(4): 281–96. doi.org/10.1080/07388940701643623.

Braithwaite, John. 1978. 'An exploratory study of used car fraud.' In Paul R. Wilson and John Braithwaite (eds), *Two Faces of Deviance: Crimes of the Powerless and Powerful*. Brisbane: University of Queensland Press, pp. 101–22.

Braithwaite, John. 1979. *Inequality, Crime and Public Policy*. London: Routledge.

Braithwaite, John. 1979–80. 'Merton's theory of crime and differential class symbols of success.' *Crime and/et Justice* 7–8(2): 90–94.

Braithwaite, John. 1981. 'The limits of economism in controlling harmful corporate conduct.' *Law & Society Review* 16(3): 481–504. doi.org/10.2307/3053371.

Braithwaite, John. 1982. 'Enforced self-regulation: A new strategy for corporate crime control.' *Michigan Law Review* 80: 1466–507. doi.org/10.2307/1288556.

Braithwaite, John. 1984. *Corporate Crime in the Pharmaceutical Industry*. London: Routledge.

Braithwaite, John. 1985. *To Punish or Persuade: Enforcement of Coal Mine Safety*. Albany: State University of New York Press.

Braithwaite John. 1989. *Crime, Shame and Reintegration*. Cambridge, UK: Cambridge University Press. doi.org/10.1017/CBO9780511804618.

Braithwaite, John. 1991. 'Poverty, power, white-collar crime and the paradoxes of criminological theory.' *Australian and New Zealand Journal of Criminology* 24(1): 40–58. doi.org/10.1177/000486589102400104.

Braithwaite, John. 1992. 'Good and bad police services and how to pick them.' In Peter Moir and Henk Eijkman (eds), *Policing Australia*. Melbourne: Macmillan, pp. 12–29.

Braithwaite, John. 1993. 'Shame and modernity.' *The British Journal of Criminology* 33(1): 1–18. doi.org/10.1093/oxfordjournals.bjc.a048257.

Braithwaite, John. 1994. 'A sociology of modelling and the politics of empowerment.' *British Journal of Sociology* 45(3): 445–79. doi.org/10.2307/591658.

Braithwaite, John. 1995. 'Inequality and republican criminology.' In John Hagan and Ruth D. Peterson (eds), *Crime and Inequality*. Palo Alto, CA: Stanford University Press, pp. 277–305.

Braithwaite, John. 1997. 'On speaking softly and carrying big sticks: Neglected dimensions of a republication separation of powers.' *University of Toronto Law Journal* 47: 305–61. doi.org/10.2307/825973.

Braithwaite, John. 1998. 'Institutionalizing distrust, enculturating trust.' In Valerie Braithwaite and Margaret Levi (eds), *Trust and Governance*. New York: Russel Sage, pp. 343–56.

Braithwaite, John. 2000. 'Restorative justice and social justice.' *Saskatchewan Law Review* 63(1): 185–94.

Braithwaite, John. 2001. 'Youth development circles.' *Oxford Review of Education* 27(2): 239–52. doi.org/10.1080/03054980125611.

Braithwaite, John. 2002. *Restorative Justice and Responsive Regulation*. New York: Oxford University Press.

Braithwaite, John. 2003. 'Domination, quiescence and war crime.' In Stuart S. Nagel (ed.), *Policymaking and Peace: A Multinational Anthology*. Lexington, MA: Lexington Books, pp. 213–26.

Braithwaite, John. 2005a. 'Between proportionality and impunity: Confrontation ⇒ truth ⇒ prevention. Sutherland Award Presentation to American Society of Criminology Meeting, Nashville, November 2004.' *Criminology* 43(2): 283–306. doi.org/10.1111/j.0011-1348.2005.00009.x.

Braithwaite, John. 2005b. *Markets in Vice, Markets in Virtue*. Sydney & New York: The Federation Press & Oxford University Press.

Braithwaite, John. 2006a. 'Accountability and responsibility through restorative justice.' In Michael Dowdle (ed.), *Rethinking Public Accountability*. Cambridge, UK: Cambridge University Press, pp. 33–51.

Braithwaite, John. 2006b. 'Responsive regulation and developing economies.' *World Development* 34(5): 884–98. doi.org/10.1016/j.worlddev.2005.04.021.

Braithwaite, John. 2008. *Regulatory Capitalism: How it Works, Ideas for Making it Work Better*. Cheltenham, UK: Edward Elgar Publishing.

Braithwaite, John. 2011. 'The essence of responsive regulation.' *University of British Columbia Law Review* 44: 475–520.

Braithwaite, John. 2012. 'Cascades of violence and a global criminology of place.' *Australian and New Zealand Journal of Criminology* 45(3): 299–315. doi.org/10.1177/0004865812456857.

Braithwaite, John. 2013a. 'Flipping markets to virtue with qui tam and restorative justice.' *Accounting, Organizations and Society* 38(6–7): 458–68. doi.org/10.1016/j.aos.2012.07.002.

Braithwaite, John 2013b. 'Strategic socialism, strategic privatisation and crises.' *Australian Journal of Corporate Law* 28(1): 35–59. doi.org/10.2139/ssrn.2249544.

Braithwaite, John. 2015. *Gender, class, resilient power: Nepal lessons in transformation.* RegNet Research Paper No. 2015/92. Canberra: School of Regulation and Global Governance, The Australian National University. doi.org/10.2139/ssrn.2685495.

Braithwaite, John. 2016a. 'In search of Donald Campbell.' *Criminology & Public Policy* 15(2): 417–37. doi.org/10.1111/1745-9133.12198.

Braithwaite, John. 2016b. 'Learning to scale up restorative justice.' In Kerry Clamp (ed.), *Restorative Justice in Transitional Settings*. London: Routledge, pp. 173–89. doi.org/10.4324/9781315723860-10.

Braithwaite, John. 2017a. 'Criminal justice that revives republican democracy.' *Northwestern University Law Review* 111(6): 1507–24.

Braithwaite, John. 2017b. 'Hybrid politics for justice: The Silk Road of restorative justice II.' *Restorative Justice* 5(1): 7–28. doi.org/10.1080/20504721.2017.1294795.

Braithwaite, John. 2018. 'Minimally sufficient deterrence.' *Crime and Justice* 47(1): 69–118. doi.org/10.1086/696043.

Braithwaite, John. 2019. 'Tempered power, variegated capitalism, law and society.' *Buffalo Law Review* 67(3): 527–94.

Braithwaite, John. 2020a. 'Crime as a cascade phenomenon.' *International Journal of Comparative and Applied Criminal Justice* 44(3): 137–69. doi.org/10.1080/01924036.2019.1675180.

Braithwaite, John. 2020b. 'Regulatory mix, collective efficacy, and crimes of the powerful.' *Journal of White Collar and Corporate Crime* 1(1): 62–71. doi.org/10.1177/2631309X19872430.

Braithwaite, John. 2020c. 'Restorative justice and reintegrative shaming.' In Cecilia Chouhy, Joshua C. Cochran and Cheryl L. Jonson (eds), *Criminal Justice Theory. Volume 26.* New York: Routledge, pp. 281–308. doi.org/10.4324/9781003016762-12.

Braithwaite, John. 2021a. 'Authoritarian under-labouring?' In Stefaan Pleysier and Tom Deams (eds), *Criminology and Democratic Politics*. London: Routledge, pp. 25–41. doi.org/10.4324/9780367821906-3.

Braithwaite, John. 2021b. 'Housing, crises and crime.' *Journal of Criminology* 54(1). doi.org/10.1177/00048658211011500.

Braithwaite, John. 2021c. 'Meta-governance of path dependencies: Regulation, welfare and markets.' *The ANNALS of the American Academy of Political and Social Science* 671(1): 30–49. doi.org/10.1177/0002716220949193.

Braithwaite, John. 2021d. *Regulatory capitalism, extinctions and China.* SSRN Working Paper. doi.org/10.2139/ssrn.3767372.

Braithwaite, John. 2021e. 'Scaling up prevention and justice.' *Crime and Justice: A Review of Research* 50(1). doi.org/10.1086/716093.

Braithwaite, John. 2021f. 'Street-level meta-strategies: Evidence on restorative justice and responsive regulation.' *Annual Review of Law and Social Science* 17:205–25. doi.org/10.1146/annurev-lawsocsci-111720-013149.

Braithwaite, John, Eliza Ahmed and Valerie Braithwaite. 2006. 'Shame, restorative justice and crime.' In Francis T. Cullen, John Paul Wright and Kristie R. Blevins (eds), *Taking Stock: The Status of Criminological Theory.* New Brunswick, NJ: Transaction Publishers, pp. 397–417. doi.org/10.4324/9781315130620-15.

Braithwaite, John and Valerie Braithwaite. 1980. 'The effect of income inequality and social democracy on homicide: A cross-national comparison.' *The British Journal of Criminology* 20(1): 45–53. doi.org/10.1093/oxfordjournals.bjc. a047131.

Braithwaite, John, Valerie Braithwaite, Michael Cookson and Leah Dunn. 2010a. *Anomie and Violence: Non-Truth and Reconciliation in Indonesian Peacebuilding.* Canberra: ANU Press. doi.org/10.22459/AV.03.2010.

Braithwaite, John, Hilary Charlesworth, Peter Reddy and Leah Dunn. 2010b. *Reconciliation and Architectures of Commitment: Sequencing Peace in Bougainville.* Canberra: ANU Press. doi.org/10.22459/RAC.09.2010.

Braithwaite, John, Hilary Charlesworth and Adérito Soares. 2012. *Networked Governance of Freedom and Tyranny.* Canberra: ANU Press. doi.org/10.22459/ NGFT.03.2012.

Braithwaite, John and Bina D'Costa. 2018. *Cascades of Violence: War, Crime and Peacebuilding across South Asia.* Canberra: ANU Press. doi.org/10.22459/ CV.02.2018.

Braithwaite, John, Sinclair Dinnen, Matthew Allen, Valerie Braithwaite and Hilary Charlesworth. 2010c. *Pillars and Shadows: Statebuilding as Peacebuilding in Solomon Islands.* Canberra: ANU Press. doi.org/10.22459/PS.11.2010.

Braithwaite, John and Peter Drahos. 2000. *Global Business Regulation.* Cambridge, UK: Cambridge University Press. doi.org/10.1017/9780521780339.

Braithwaite, John and Peter Drahos. 2002. 'Zero tolerance, naming and shaming: Is there a case for it with crimes of the powerful?' *Australian and New Zealand Journal of Criminology* 35(3): 269–88. doi.org/10.1375/acri.35.3.269.

Braithwaite, John and Brent Fisse. 1985. 'Varieties of responsibility and organizational crime.' *Law and Policy* 7(3): 315–43. doi.org/10.1111/j.1467-9930.1985.tb00356.x.

Braithwaite, John and Ali Gohar. 2014. 'Restorative justice, policing and insurgency: Learning from Pakistan.' *Law & Society Review* 48(3): 531–61. doi.org/10.1111/lasr.12091.

Braithwaite, John and Seung-Hun Hong. 2015. 'The iteration deficit in responsive regulation: Are regulatory ambassadors an answer?' *Regulation and Governance* 9(1): 16–29. doi.org/10.1111/rego.12049.

Braithwaite, John and Henry G. Law. 1978. 'The structure of self-reported delinquency.' *Applied Psychological Measurement* 2(2): 221–38. doi.org/10.1177/014662167800200205.

Braithwaite, John and Toni Makkai. 1994. 'Trust and compliance.' *Policing and Society* 4(1): 1–12. doi.org/10.1080/10439463.1994.9964679.

Braithwaite, John, Toni Makkai and Valerie Braithwaite. 2007. *Regulating Aged Care*. Aldershot, UK: Edward Elgar Publishing. doi.org/10.4337/9781847206855.

Braithwaite, John and Christine Parker. 2003. 'Regulation.' In Peter Cane and Mark Tushnet (eds), *The Oxford Handbook of Legal Studies*. Oxford, UK: Oxford University Press, pp. 119–45.

Braithwaite, John and Philip Pettit. 1990. *Not Just Deserts: A Republican Theory of Criminal Justice*. Oxford, UK: Oxford University Press.

Braithwaite, John and Philip Pettit. 2000. 'Republicanism and restorative justice: An explanatory and normative connection.' In Heather Strang and John Braithwaite (eds), *Restorative Justice: From Philosophy to Practice*. Burlington, VT: Ashgate, pp. 145–63.

Braithwaite, John and Ali Wardak. 2013. 'Crime and war in Afghanistan: Part I— The Hobbesian solution.' *The British Journal of Criminology* 53(2): 179–96. doi.org/10.1093/bjc/azs065.

Braithwaite, John and Yan Zhang. 2017. 'Persia to China: The Silk Road of restorative justice I.' *Asian Journal of Criminology* 12(1): 23–38. doi.org/10.1007/s11417-017-9244-y.

Braithwaite, Richard W. 2016. *Fighting Monsters: An Intimate History of the Sandakan*. Melbourne: Australian Scholarly Publishing.

Braithwaite, Valerie. 2004. 'The hope process and social inclusion.' *The ANNALS of the American Academy of Political and Social Science* 592(1): 128–51. doi.org/10.1177/0002716203262096.

Braithwaite, Valerie. 2009a. *Defiance in Taxation and Governance*. Cheltenham, UK: Edward Elgar Publishing. doi.org/10.4337/9781848449077.

Braithwaite, Valerie. 2009b. 'The value balance model and democratic governance.' *Psychological Inquiry* 20(2–3): 87–97. doi.org/10.1080/10478400903028367.

Braithwaite, Valerie and Eliza Ahmed. 2005. 'A threat to tax morale: The case of Australian higher education policy.' *Journal of Economic Psychology* 26(4): 523–40. doi.org/10.1016/j.joep.2004.08.003.

Braithwaite, Valerie and Janine Bush. 1998. 'Affirmative action in Australia: A consensus-based dialogic approach.' *NWSA Journal* 10(3): 115–34. Available at: www.jstor.org/stable/4316604.

Brammertz, Serge and Michelle Jarvis (eds). 2016. *Prosecuting Conflict-Related Sexual Violence at the ICTY*. Oxford, UK: Oxford University Press.

Brandt, Willy. 1971. 'Willy Brandt quotations.' *Quotetab*. [Online.] Available at: www.quotetab.com/quotes/by-willy-brandt.

Brehm, Sharon S. and Jack W. Brehm. 1981. *Psychological Reactance: A Theory of Freedom and Control*. New York: Academic Press.

Bremner, J. Douglas, Steven M. Southwick, David R. Johnson, Rachel Yehuda and Dennis S. Charney. 1993. 'Childhood physical abuse and combat-related posttraumatic stress disorder in Vietnam veterans.' *The American Journal of Psychiatry* 150(2): 235–39. doi.org/10.1176/ajp.150.2.235.

Brenner, Neil, Jamie Peck and Nik Theodore. 2010. 'Variegated neoliberalization: Geographies, modalities, pathways.' *Global Networks* 10(2): 182–222. doi.org/10.1111/j.1471-0374.2009.00277.x.

Briant, Pierre. 2002. *From Cyrus to Alexander: A History of the Persian Empire*. Winona Lake, IN: Eisenbrauns. doi.org/10.5325/j.ctv1bxgwdk.

Briceño-León, Roberto, Andrés Villaveces and Alberto Concha-Eastman. 2008. 'Understanding the uneven distribution of the incidence of homicide in Latin America.' *International Journal of Epidemiology* 37(4): 751–57. doi.org/10.1093/ije/dyn153.

Broadhurst, Roderic, Matthew Ball and Chuxuan Jiang. 2020a. *Availability of COVID-19 products on Tor darknet markets*. Statistical Bulletin No. 24. Canberra: Australian Institute of Criminology.

Broadhurst, Roderic, Matthew Ball and Harshit Trivedi. 2020b. *Fentanyl availability on darknet markets*. Trends & Issues in Crime and Criminal Justice No. 590. Canberra: Australian Institute of Criminology.

Broadhurst, Roderic, Thierry Bouhours and Brigitte Bouhours. 2015. *Violence and the Civilising Process in Cambodia*. Cambridge, UK: Cambridge University Press. doi.org/10.1017/CBO9781316271339.

Broadhurst, Roderic, Thierry Bouhours and Brigitte Bouhours. 2018. 'Violence and Elias's historical sociology: The case of Cambodia.' *The British Journal of Criminology* 58(6): 1420–39. doi.org/10.1093/bjc/azx072.

Browning, Christopher R. 2002. 'The span of collective efficacy: Extending social disorganization theory to partner violence.' *Journal of Marriage & Family* 64(4): 833–50. doi.org/10.1111/j.1741-3737.2002.00833.x.

Brush, Jesse 2007. 'Does income inequality lead to more crime? A comparison of cross-sectional and time-series analyses of United States counties.' *Economics Letters* 96(2): 264–68. doi.org/10.1016/j.econlet.2007.01.012.

Bryk, Anthony and Barbara Schneider. 2002. *Trust in Schools: A Core Resource for Improvement*. New York: Russell Sage Foundation.

Buhaug, Halvard, Kristian Skrede Gleditsch, Helge Holtermann, Gudrun Østby and Andreas Forø Tollefsen. 2011. 'It's the local economy, stupid! Geographic wealth dispersion and conflict outbreak location.' *Journal of Conflict Resolution* 55(5): 814–40. doi.org/10.1177/0022002711408011.

Buhaug, Halvard and Jan Ketil Rød. 2006. 'Local determinants of African civil wars, 1970–2001.' *Political Geography* 25(3): 315–35. doi.org/10.1016/j.polgeo.2006.02.005.

Burdett, Kenneth, Ricardo Lagos and Randall Wright. 2003. 'Crime, inequality, and unemployment.' *American Economic Review* 93(5): 1764–77. doi.org/10.1257/000282803322655536.

Burford, Gale, John Braithwaite and Valerie Braithwaite (eds). 2019. *Restorative and Responsive Human Services*. New York: Routledge. doi.org/10.4324/9780429398704.

Burris, Scott, Peter Drahos and Clifford Shearing. 2005. 'Nodal governance.' *Australian Journal of Legal Philosophy* 30: 30–58.

Burrough, Bryan and John Helyar. 1991. *Barbarians at the Gate: The Fall of RJR Nabisco*. New York: Harper.

Bursik, Robert J. 1999. 'The informal control of crime through neighbourhood networks.' *Sociological Focus* 32(1): 85–97. doi.org/10.1080/00380237.1999. 10571125.

Bushie, Berma. 1999. *Community Holistic Circle Healing: A Community Approach. Proceedings of Building Strong Partnerships for Restorative Practices Conference, Burlington, VT*. Pipersville, PA: Real Justice.

Calavita, Kitty, Henry N. Pontell and Robert Tillman. 1997. *Big Money Crime: Fraud and Politics in the Savings and Loan Crisis*. Berkeley, CA: University of California Press.

Calderón, Gabriela, Gustavo Robles, Alberto Díaz-Cayeros and Beatriz Magaloni. 2015. 'The beheading of criminal organizations and the dynamics of violence in Mexico.' *Journal of Conflict Resolution* 59(8): 1455–85. doi.org/ 10.1177/0022002715587053.

Caldwell, Ernest. 2017. 'Widening the constitutional gap in China and Taiwan: History, reform, and the transformation of the control yuan.' *University of Illinois Law Review* 2: 739–66.

Call, Charles T. 2012. *Why Peace Fails: The Causes and Prevention of Civil War Recurrence*. Washington, DC: Georgetown University Press.

Cancino, Jeffrey M., Sean P. Varano, Joseph A. Schafer and Roger Enriquez. 2007. 'An ecological assessment of property and violent crime rates across a Latino urban landscape: The role of social disorganization and institutional anomie theory.' *Western Criminology Review* 8(1): 69–87.

Cano, Ivan, David Best, Michael Edwards and John Lehman. 2017. 'Recovery capital pathways: Modelling the components of recovery wellbeing.' *Drug and Alcohol Dependence* 181: 11–19. doi.org/10.1016/j.drugalcdep.2017.09.002.

Cao, Liqun. 2004. 'Is American society more anomic? A test of Merton's theory with cross-national data.' *International Journal of Comparative and Applied Criminal Justice* 28(1): 15–32. doi.org/10.1080/01924036.2004.9678714.

Capaldi, Deborah M., Naomi B. Knoble, Joann Wu Shortt and Hyoun K. Kim. 2012. 'A systematic review of risk factors for intimate partner violence.' *Partner Abuse* 3(2): 231–80. doi.org/10.1891/1946-6560.3.2.231.

Caprioli, Mary. 2000. 'Gendered conflict.' *Journal of Peace Research* 37: 51–68. doi.org/10.1177/0022343300037001003.

Caprioli, Mary. 2003. 'Gender equality and state aggression: The impact of domestic gender equality on state first use of force.' *International Interactions* 29(3): 195–214. doi.org/10.1080/03050620304595.

Caprioli, Mary. 2005. 'Primed for violence: The role of gender inequality in predicting internal conflict.' *International Studies Quarterly* 49(2): 161–78. doi.org/10.1111/j.0020-8833.2005.00340.x.

Caprioli, Mary and Mark A. Boyer. 2001. 'Gender, violence and international crisis.' *Journal of Conflict Resolution* 45(4): 503–18. doi.org/10.1177/00220 02701045004005.

Caprioli, Mary and Peter Trumbore. 2006. 'Human rights rogues in interstate disputes, 1980–2001.' *Journal of Peace Research* 43(2): 131–48. doi.org/ 10.1177/0022343306061356.

Carberry, Edward J., Peter-Jan Engelen and Marc Van Essen. 2018. 'Which firms get punished for unethical behavior? Explaining variation in stock market reactions to corporate misconduct.' *Business Ethics Quarterly* 28(2): 119–51. doi.org/10.1017/beq.2017.46.

Carcach, Carlos and Evelyn Artola. 2016. 'Disappeared persons and homicide in El Salvador.' *Crime Science* 5(1): 1–13. doi.org/10.1186/s40163-016-0061-x.

Carlson, Susan M. and Raymond J. Michalowski. 1997. 'Crime, unemployment, and social structures of accumulation: An inquiry into historical contingency.' *Justice Quarterly* 14(2): 209–41. doi.org/10.1080/07418829700093311.

Carmichael, Fiona and Robert Ward. 2001. 'Male unemployment and crime in England and Wales.' *Economics Letters* 73(1): 111–15. doi.org/10.1016/ S0165-1765(01)00466-9.

Carney, Mark. 2020. 'Reith Lectures 2020: How we get what we value.' *BBC Radio 4*, December. Available at: www.bbc.co.uk/programmes/ articles/43GjCh72bxWVSqSB84ZDJw0/reith-lectures-2020-how-we-get-what-we-value.

Carrington, Kerry, Russell Hogg and Máximo Sozzo. 2016. 'Southern criminology.' *The British Journal of Criminology* 56(1): 1–20. doi.org/10.1093/bjc/azv083.

Castells, Manuel. 1996. *The Information Age: Economy, Society and Culture. Volume 1: The Rise of the Network Society*. Oxford, UK: Blackwell.

Cederman, Lars-Erik, Nils B. Weidmann and Kristian Skrede Gleditsch. 2011. 'Horizontal inequalities and ethnonationalist civil war: A global comparison.' *American Political Science Review* 105(3): 478–95. doi.org/10.1017/S0003 055411000207.

Centre for Road Safety. 2018. 'Random breath testing.' *Alcohol and Driving*. Sydney: Transport for NSW. Available at: roadsafety.transport.nsw.gov.au/stayingsafe/alcoholdrugs/drinkdriving/rbt/index.html.

Cerasoli, Christopher P., Jessica M. Nicklin and Michael T. Ford. 2014. 'Intrinsic motivation and extrinsic incentives jointly predict performance: A 40-year meta-analysis.' *Psychological Bulletin* 140(4): 980–1008. doi.org/10.1037/a0035661.

Cerda, Magdalena and Jeffrey D. Morenoff. 2009. *The Limits of Collective Efficacy*. Ann Arbor: Department of Sociology, University of Michigan.

Cerkez, Aida. 2012. *Safe Havens in Syria? They Failed in Bosnia*. Washington, DC: Atlantic Council.

Chakrabarty, Bidyut and Rajat Kumar Kujur. 2009. *Maoism in India: Reincarnation of Ultra-Left Wing Extremism in the Twenty-First Century*. London: Routledge.

Chalfin, Aaron and Justin McCrary. 2017. 'Criminal deterrence: A review of the literature.' *Journal of Economic Literature* 55(1): 5–48. doi.org/10.1257/jel.20141147.

Chamberlain, Alyssa W. and John R. Hipp. 2015. 'It's all relative: Concentrated disadvantage within and across neighborhoods and communities, and the consequences for neighborhood crime.' *Journal of Criminal Justice* 43(6): 431–43. doi.org/10.1016/j.jcrimjus.2015.08.004.

Chamlin, Mitchell B. and John K. Cochran. 1995. 'Assessing Messner and Rosenfeld's institutional anomie theory: A partial test.' *Criminology* 33(3): 411–29. doi.org/10.1111/j.1745-9125.1995.tb01184.x.

Chamlin, Mitchell B. and John K. Cochran. 1997. 'Social altruism and crime.' *Criminology* 35(2): 203–26. doi.org/10.1111/j.1745-9125.1997.tb00875.x.

Chamlin, Mitchell B. and John K. Cochran. 2007. 'An evaluation of the assumptions that underlie institutional anomie theory.' *Theoretical Criminology* 11(1): 39–61. doi.org/10.1177/1362480607072734.

Chamlin, Mitchell B. and Beth A. Sanders. 2013. 'Falsifying Merton's macro-level anomie theory of profit-motivated crime: A research note.' *Deviant Behavior* 34(12): 961–72. doi.org/10.1080/01639625.2013.800419.

Chapman, Bruce, Don Weatherburn, Cezary A. Kapuscinski, Marilyn Chilvers and Sandra Roussel. 2002. *Unemployment Duration, Schooling and Property Crime*. Sydney: NSW Bureau of Crime Statistics and Research.

Chapman, Simon, Michael Stewart, Philip Alpers and Michael Jones. 2018. 'Fatal firearm incidents before and after Australia's 1996 national firearms agreement banning semiautomatic rifles.' *Annals of Internal Medicine* 169(1): 62–64. doi.org/10.7326/M18-0503.

Chappell, Allison T. 2017. 'Consent decrees and police reform: A piece of the puzzle or a puzzling policy.' *Criminology & Public Policy* 16(2): 571–73. doi.org/10.1111/1745-9133.12302.

Chatterjee, Pratap. 2005. 'Meet the new interrogators: Lockheed Martin.' *CorpWatch*, 4 November. Available at: www.corpwatch.org/article/meet-new-interrogators-lockheed-martin.

Chayes, Abram and Antonia Handler Chayes. 1998. *The New Sovereignty.* Cambridge, MA: Harvard University Press.

Chegg Inc. 2003–21. 'Economics questions and answers.' [Online.] Santa Clara, CA: Chegg Inc. Available at: www.chegg.com/homework-help/questions-and-answers/graph-shows-unemployment-rate-united-states-1960-2016-average-unemployment-rate-lowest-the-q34909662.

Chekov, Alexander D., Anna V. Makarycheva, Anastasia M. Solomentseva, Maxim A. Suchkov and Andrey A. Sushentsov. 2020. 'War of the future: A view from Russia.' *Survival* 61(6): 25–48. doi.org/10.1080/00396338.2019.1688563.

Chen, Chung-wen, Hsiu-Huei Yu, Kristine Velasquez Tuliao, Aditya Simha and Yi-Ying Chang. 2021. 'Supervisors' value orientations and ethics: A cross-national analysis.' *Journal of Business Ethics* 170: 167–80. doi.org/10.1007/s10551-019-04254-0.

Cheng, Qijin, Feng Chen and Paul S.F. Yip. 2011. 'The Foxconn suicides and their media prominence: Is the Werther effect applicable in China?' *BMC Public Health* 11(1): 841. doi.org/10.1186/1471-2458-11-841.

Chenoweth, Erica. 2016a. The major episodes of contention dataset, V.1. Unpublished dataset. Denver: University of Denver.

Chenoweth, Erica. 2016b. *The rise of nonviolent resistance.* Policy Brief 19. Oslo: Peace Research Institute of Oslo.

Chenoweth, Erica and Evan Perkoski. 2017. *How risky is nonviolent dissent? Nonviolent uprisings and mass killings.* SSRN Papers, 1 February. doi.org/10.2139/ssrn.3045189.

Chenoweth, Erica and Maria J. Stephan. 2011. *Why Civil Resistance Works: The Strategic Logic of Nonviolent Conflict.* New York: Columbia University Press.

Cheong, Tsun Se and Yanrui Wu. 2015. 'Crime rates and inequality: A study of crime in contemporary China.' *Journal of the Asia Pacific Economy* 20(2): 202–23. doi.org/10.1080/13547860.2014.964961.

Choi, Ka Wai Stanley, Xiaomeng Chen, Sue Wright and Hai Wu. 2016. *Responsive enforcement strategy and corporate compliance with disclosure regulations.* Working Paper. Sydney & Canberra: Macquarie University & The Australian National University. doi.org/10.2139/ssrn.2722923.

Chomsky, Noam. 1969. *American Power and the New Mandarins.* New York: Pantheon.

Cicero, Marcus Tullius. 1877. *Tusculan Disputations.* C.D. Yonge, trans. New York: Harper & Brothers.

Citrin, Jack and Laura Stoker. 2018. 'Political trust in a cynical age.' *Annual Review of Political Science* 21: 49–70. doi.org/10.1146/annurev-polisci-050316-092550.

Clark, Cari Jo, Susan A. Everson-Rose, Shakira Franco Suglia, Rula Btoush, Alvaro Alonso and Muhammad M. Haj-Yahia. 2010. 'Association between exposure to political violence and intimate-partner violence in the occupied Palestinian territory: A cross-sectional study.' *The Lancet* 375(9711): 310–16. doi.org/10.1016/S0140-6736(09)61827-4.

Clark, Christopher. 2012. *The Sleepwalkers: How Europe Went to War in 1914.* New York: Harper.

Clark, Phil. 2010. *The Gacaca Courts, Post-Genocide Justice and Reconciliation in Rwanda: Justice without Lawyers.* Cambridge, UK: Cambridge University Press. doi.org/10.1017/CBO9780511761584.

Clark, Phil. 2014. 'Bringing the peasants back in, again: State power and local agency in Rwanda's gacaca courts.' *Journal of Eastern African Studies* 8(2): 193–213. doi.org/10.1080/17531055.2014.891782.

Clarke, Martin, Susan Brown and Birgit Völlm. 2017. 'Circles of support and accountability for sex offenders: A systematic review of outcomes.' *Sexual Abuse* 29(5): 446–78. doi.org/10.1177/1079063215603691.

Clarke, Michael. 1986. *Regulating the City: Competition, Scandal and Reform.* Milton Keynes, UK: Open University Press.

Clegg, Stewart. 1975. *Power, Rule and Domination.* London: Routledge & Kegan Paul.

Clinard, Marshall and Peter Yeager. 2006. *Corporate Crime.* Piscataway, NJ: Transaction Publishers.

Cloward, Richard A. and Lloyd E. Ohlin. 1960. *Delinquency and Opportunity.* New York: Free Press.

Cochran, John K. and Beth Bjerregaard. 2012. 'Structural anomie and crime: A cross-national test.' *International Journal of Offender Therapy and Comparative Criminology* 56(2): 203–17. doi.org/10.1177/0306624X10396071.

Cockburn, Cynthia. 2001. 'The gendered dynamics of armed conflict and political violence.' In Caroline O.N. Moser and Fiona C. Clark (eds), *Victims, Perpetrators or Actors? Gender, Armed Conflict, and Political Violence.* New York: Zed Books, pp. 13–29.

Coffee, John C., Jr. 1977. 'Beyond the shut-eyed sentry: Toward a theoretical view of corporate misconduct and an effective legal response.' *Virginia Law Review* 63(7): 1099–278. doi.org/10.2307/1072549.

Coffee, John C., Jr. 1981. 'No soul to damn, no body to kick: An unscandalized essay on the problem of corporate punishment.' *Michigan Law Review* 79: 413–24. doi.org/10.2307/1288201.

Coffee, John C., Jr. 2020. *Corporate Crime and Punishment: The Crisis of Underenforcement.* Oakland, CA: Berrett-Koehler Publishers.

Cohen, Albert K. 1955. *Delinquent Boys: The Culture of the Gang.* Glencoe, IL: Free Press.

Cohen, Deborah A., Brian K. Finch, Aimee Bower and Narayan Sastry. 2006. 'Collective efficacy and obesity: The potential influence of spatial factors on health.' *Social Science and Medicine* 62(3): 769–78. doi.org/10.1016/j.socscimed.2005.06.033.

Cohen, Lawrence E. and Richard Machalek. 1988. 'A general theory of expropriative crime: An evolutionary ecological approach.' *American Journal of Sociology* 94(3): 465–501. doi.org/10.1086/229027.

Coleman, James S. 1982. *The Asymmetric Society.* Syracuse, NY: Syracuse University Press.

Coleman, James S. 1990. *Foundations of Social Theory.* Cambridge, MA: Harvard University Press.

Collier, Paul. 2007. *The Bottom Billion: Why the Poorest Countries are Failing and What Can Be Done About It.* Oxford, UK: Oxford University Press.

Collier, Paul. 2009. *Wars, Guns, and Votes: Democracy in Dangerous Places.* New York: Harper.

Collier, Paul, Anke Hoeffler and Måns Söderbom. 2004. 'On the duration of civil war.' *Journal of Peace Research* 41(3): 253–73. doi.org/10.1177/0022343304043769.

Collins, Randall. 2008. *Violence: A Micro-Sociological Theory*. Princeton, NJ: Princeton University Press. doi.org/10.1515/9781400831753.

Colvin, Mark. 2000. *Crime and Coercion: An Integrated Theory of Chronic Criminality*. New York: Springer. doi.org/10.1057/9780312292775.

Colvin, Mark, Francis T. Cullen and Thomas Vander Ven. 2002. 'Coercion, social support, and crime: An emerging theoretical consensus.' *Criminology* 40(1): 19–42. doi.org/10.1111/j.1745-9125.2002.tb00948.x.

Commonwealth of Australia. 2014. *Vietnam Veterans Family Study*. 4 vols. Canberra: Department of Veterans' Affairs. Available at: www.dva.gov.au/documents-and-publications/vietnam-veterans-family-study.

Comstock, Nicole, L. Miriam Dickinson, Julie A. Marshall, Mah-J. Soobader, Mark S. Turbin, Michael Buchenau and Jill S. Litt. 2010. 'Neighborhood attachment and its correlates: Exploring neighborhood conditions, collective efficacy, and gardening.' *Journal of Environmental Psychology* 30(4): 435–42. doi.org/10.1016/j.jenvp.2010.05.001.

Cooney, Mark. 1997. 'The decline of elite homicide.' *Criminology* 35(3): 381–407. doi.org/10.1111/j.1745-9125.1997.tb01222.x.

Cooper, Alexia. 2012. *Homicide Trends in the United States, 1980–2008*. Washington, DC: US Department of Justice.

Cooper, Brittany. 2015. 'Intersectionality.' In Lisa Disch and Mary Hawkesworth (eds), *The Oxford Handbook of Feminist Theory*. Oxford, UK: Oxford University Press, pp. 385–406. doi.org/10.1093/oxfordhb/9780199328581.013.20.

Corballis, Michael C. 2014. *The Recursive Mind: The Origins of Human Language, Thought, and Civilization*. Princeton, NJ: Princeton University Press. doi.org/10.2307/j.ctt6wpzjd.

Costantini, Mauro, Iris Meco and Antonio Paradiso. 2018. 'Do inequality, unemployment and deterrence affect crime over the long run?' *Regional Studies* 52(4): 558–71. doi.org/10.1080/00343404.2017.1341626.

Couture, Joe, Ted Parker, Ruth Couture and Patti Laboucane. 2001. *A Cost–Benefit Analysis of Hollow Water's Community Holistic Circle Healing Process*. Ottawa: Aboriginal Corrections Policy Unit, Solicitor General of Canada.

Cramer, Christopher and Paul Richards. 2011. 'Violence and war in agrarian perspective.' *Journal of Agrarian Change* 11(3): 277–97. doi.org/10.1111/ j.1471-0366.2011.00312.x.

Crane, Jonathan. 1991. 'The epidemic theory of ghettos and neighborhood effects on dropping out and teenage childbearing.' *American Journal of Sociology* 96(5): 1226–59. doi.org/10.1086/229654.

Crary, David. 2014. 'Anti-gay laws, attitudes hold sway in many regions.' *Arizona Sun*, [Flagstaff, AZ], 17 January.

Crawford, Kate. 2021. *The Atlas of AI*. New Haven, CT: Yale University Press.

Crenshaw, Kimberlé W. 2017. *On Intersectionality: Essential Writings*. New York: The New Press.

Cressey, Donald R. and Charles A. Moore. 1980. *Corporation Codes of Ethical Conduct*. New York: Peat, Marwick & Mitchell Foundation.

Cullen, Francis T. 1994. 'Social support as an organizing concept for criminology.' *Justice Quarterly* 11(4): 527–59. doi.org/10.1080/07418829400092421.

Cullen, John B., K. Praveen Parboteeah and Martin Hoegl. 2004. 'Cross-national differences in managers' willingness to justify ethically suspect behaviors: A test of institutional anomie theory.' *Academy of Management Journal* 47(3): 411–21. doi.org/10.5465/20159590.

Cumming, Douglas, Robert Dannhauser and Sofia Johan. 2021. 'Reputational effects on non-compliance with financial market regulations.' In Benjamin van Rooij and D. Daniel Sokol (eds), *Cambridge Handbook of Compliance*. Cambridge, UK: Cambridge University Press, pp. 245–76. doi.org/10.1017/ 9781108759458.

Cunen, Celine, Nils L. Hjort and Havard M. Nygard. 2020. 'Statistical sightings of better angels: Analysing the distribution of battle-deaths in interstate conflict over time.' *Journal of Peace Research* 57(2): 221–34. doi.org/10.1177/ 0022343319896843.

Currie, Elliott. 1991. 'Crime in the market society.' *Dissent* (Spring): 254–59.

Dabla-Norris, Era, Kalpana Kochhar, Nujin Suphaphiphat, Franto Ricka and Evridiki Tsounta. 2015. *Causes and consequences of income inequality: A global perspective*. Staff Discussion Note, 15 June. Washington, DC: International Monetary Fund. doi.org/10.5089/9781513555188.006.

Dahl, Robert A. 1957. 'The concept of power.' *Behavioral Science* 2(3): 201–15. doi.org/10.1002/bs.3830020303.

Dahrendorf, Ralf. 1985. *Law and Order*. Boulder, CO: Westview Press.

Dancy, Geoff, Bridget Marchesi, Tricia Olsen, Leigh Payne, Andrew Reiter and Kathryn Sikkink. 2013. Stopping state agents of violence or promoting political compromise? The powerful role of transitional justice mechanisms. Paper presented at the 2013 American Political Science Association Conference Annual Meeting, Chicago, IL, 30 August.

Daniels, Cora. 2004. 'The man who changed medicine.' *FORTUNE Magazine*, 29 November. Available at: money.cnn.com/magazines/fortune/fortune_archive/2004/11/29/8192713/index.htm.

Davies, John Booth. 1997. *Drugspeak: The Analysis of Drug Discourse*. Reading, UK: Harwood Academic Publishers.

Davies, John B. and David W. Best. 1996. 'Demand characteristics and research into drug use.' *Psychology and Health* 11(2): 291–99. doi.org/10.1080/08870449608400258.

de Bono, Edward. 1985. *Conflicts: A Better Way to Resolve Them*. London: Harrap.

Deflem, Mathieu. 2018. 'Anomie, strain, and opportunity structure: Robert K. Merton's paradigm of deviant behavior.' In Ruth A. Triplett (ed.), *The Handbook of the History and Philosophy of Criminology*. Malden, MA: Wiley-Blackwell, pp. 140–55. doi.org/10.1002/9781119011385.ch8.

de Jong, Bart A., Kurt T. Dirks and Nicole Gillespie. 2016. 'Trust and team performance: A meta-analysis of main effects, moderators, and covariates.' *Journal of Applied Psychology* 101(8): 1134–50. doi.org/10.1037/apl0000110.

Dekeseredy, Walter S., Shahid Alvi and E. Andreas Tomaszewski. 2003. 'Perceived collective efficacy and women's victimization in public housing.' *Criminal Justice* 3(1): 5–27. doi.org/10.1177/1466802503003001453.

Dekker, Paul and Eric M. Uslaner (eds). 2003. *Social Capital and Participation in Everyday Life*. New York: Routledge. doi.org/10.4324/9780203451571.

Dekker, Sidney W.A. and Hugh Breakey. 2016. '"Just culture": Improving safety by achieving substantive, procedural and restorative justice.' *Safety Science* 85: 187–93. doi.org/10.1016/j.ssci.2016.01.018.

Dell, Melissa. 2015. 'Trafficking networks and the Mexican drug war.' *American Economic Review* 105(6): 1738–79. doi.org/10.1257/aer.20121637.

Denniss, Richard. 2017. *Curing Affluenza: How to Buy Less Stuff and Save the World*. Melbourne: Black Inc.

Denniss, Richard. 2020. 'Weal of fortune.' *The Monthly*, July: 11–12.

Denzin, Norman K. 1977. 'Notes on the criminogenic hypothesis: A case study of the American liquor industry.' *American Sociological Review* 42(6): 905–20. doi.org/10.2307/2094576.

Deutsch, Martin. 1967. *The Disadvantaged Child*. New York: Basic Books.

DiCristina Bruce. 2016. 'Durkheim's theory of anomie and crime: A clarification and elaboration.' *Australian and New Zealand Journal of Criminology* 49(3): 311–31. doi.org/10.1177/0004865815585391.

DiIulio, John J. 2009. 'More religion, less crime? Science, felonies, and the three faith factors.' *Annual Review of Law and Social Science* 5: 115–33. doi.org/10.1146/annurev.lawsocsci.093008.131603.

Dimmock, Stephen G., William C. Gerken and Nathaniel P. Graham. 2018. 'Is fraud contagious? Coworker influence on misconduct by financial advisors.' *Journal of Finance* 73(3): 1417–50. doi.org/10.1111/jofi.12613.

Dincer, Oguzhan C. and Burak Gunalp. 2008. *Corruption, income inequality, and poverty in the United States*. Nota di Lavoro No. 54.2008, June. Milan: Fondazione Eni Enrico Mattei. doi.org/10.2139/ssrn.1158446.

Dixon, Adam D. 2011. 'Variegated capitalism and the geography of finance: Towards a common agenda.' *Progress in Human Geography* 35(2): 193–210. doi.org/10.1177/0309132510372006.

Dixon-Fowler, Heather R., Daniel J. Slater, Jonathan L. Johnson, Alan E. Ellstrand and Andrea M. Romi. 2013. 'Beyond "does it pay to be green?" A meta-analysis of moderators of the CEP–CFP relationship.' *Journal of Business Ethics* 112(2): 353–66. doi.org/10.1007/s10551-012-1268-8.

Dlugonski, Deirdre, Bhibha M. Das and Tiesha Martin. 2015. 'Increasing collective efficacy for physical activity: Design and rationale of Moms UNITE for Health.' *Contemporary Clinical Trials* 45: 233–38. doi.org/10.1016/j.cct.2015.09.003.

Donohoo, Jenni. 2017. 'Collective teacher efficacy: The effect size research and six enabling conditions.' www.jennidonohoo.com/post/collective-teacher-efficacy-the-effect-size-research-and-six-enabling-conditions.

Doob, Anthony and Julian V. Roberts. 1983. *Sentencing: An Analysis of the Public's View of Sentencing*. Ottawa: Department of Justice, Canada.

Doob, Anthony and Julian V. Roberts. 1988. 'Public punitiveness and public knowledge of the facts: Some Canadian surveys.' In Nigel Walker and Mike Hough (eds), *Public Attitudes to Sentencing: Surveys from Five Countries*. Aldershot, UK: Gower, pp. 111–33.

Dorf, Michael C. and Charles F. Sabel. 1998. 'A constitution of democratic experimentalism.' *Columbia Law Review* 98(2): 267–473. doi.org/10.2307/1123411.

Downes, David. 1966. *The Delinquent Solution*. London: Routledge & Kegan Paul.

Doyle, Michael W. and Nicholas Sambanis. 2000. 'International peacebuilding: A theoretical and quantitative analysis.' *American Political Science Review* 94: 779–801. doi.org/10.2307/2586208.

Doyle, Michael W. and Nicholas Sambanis. 2006. *Making War and Building Peace: United Nations Peace Operations*. Princeton, NJ: Princeton University Press. doi.org/10.1515/9781400837694.

Drahos, Peter. 2004. 'Intellectual property and pharmaceutical markets: A nodal governance approach.' *Temple Law Review* 77(2): 401–24.

Drahos, Peter. 2021. *Survival Governance: Energy and Climate in the Chinese Century*. Oxford, UK: Oxford University Press. doi.org/10.1093/oso/9780197534755.001.0001.

Drahos, Peter with John Braithwaite. 2003. *Information Feudalism: Who Owns the Knowledge Economy?* London: Earthscan.

Dreher, Axel and Justina A.V. Fischer. 2011. 'Does government decentralization reduce domestic terror? An empirical test.' *Economics Letters* 111(3): 223–25. doi.org/10.1016/j.econlet.2010.11.048.

Dubow, Eric F., Paul Boxer, L. Rowell Huesmann, Khalil Shikaki, Simha Landau, Shira Dvir Gvirsman and Jeremy Ginges. 2010. 'Exposure to conflict and violence across contexts: Relations to adjustment among Palestinian children.' *Journal of Clinical Child and Adolescent Psychology* 39(1): 103–16. doi.org/10.1080/15374410903401153.

Duffield, Mark. 2001. *Global Governance and the New Wars*. London: Zed Books.

Dukes, Graham, John Braithwaite and James P. Moloney. 2014. *Pharmaceuticals, Corporate Crime and Public Health*. Cheltenham, UK: Edward Elgar Publishing. doi.org/10.4337/9781783471102.

Dularif, Muh, T. Sutrisno, Nurkholis and Erwin Saraswati. 2019. 'Is deterrence approach effective in combating tax evasion? A meta-analysis.' *Problems and Perspectives in Management* 17(2): 93–113. doi.org/10.21511/ppm.17(2).2019.07.

Dunford, Franklin W. 1990. 'System-initiated warrants for suspects of misdemeanor domestic assault: A pilot study.' *Justice Quarterly* 7(4): 631–53. doi.org/10.1080/07418829000090791.

Duriez, Stephanie A., Francis T. Cullen and Sarah M. Manchak. 2014. 'Is Project HOPE creating a false sense of hope? A case study in correctional popularity.' *Federal Probation* 78: 57–70.

Durkheim, Emile. 1933 [1893]. *The Division of Labor in Society*. New York: Macmillan.

Durkheim, Emile. 1952 [1897]. *Suicide: A Study in Sociology*. London: Routledge & Kegan Paul.

Durkheim, Emile. 1958. *Professional Ethics and Civic Morals*. Cornelia Brookfield, trans. New York: New Press.

Durkheim, Emile. 1965. *The Elementary Forms of Religious Life*. Joseph Ward, trans. New York: New Press.

Durlauf, Steven N. and Daniel S. Nagin. 2011a. 'Overview of "Imprisonment and crime: can both be reduced?"' *Criminology & Public Policy* 10(1): 9–12. doi.org/10.1111/j.1745-9133.2010.00681.x.

Durlauf, Steven N. and Daniel S. Nagin. 2011b. 'Imprisonment and crime: Can both be reduced?' *Criminology & Public Policy* 10(1): 13–54. doi.org/10.1111/j.1745-9133.2010.00680.x.

Dutton, Michael Robert. 1992. *Policing and Punishment in China: From Patriarchy to 'the People'*. Cambridge, UK: Cambridge University Press.

Duwe, Grant. 2013. 'Can Circles of Support and Accountability (COSA) work in the United States? Preliminary results from a randomized experiment in Minnesota.' *Sexual Abuse* 25(2): 143–65. doi.org/10.1177/1079063212453942.

Duwe, Grant. 2018. *Minnesota Circles of Support and Accountability (MnCoSA) at 50: Updated Results from a Randomized Controlled Trial*. Saint Paul: Minnesota Department of Corrections. Available at: mn.gov/doc/assets/2018%20MnCOSA%20Outcome%20Evaluation_tcm1089-326700.pdf.

Dyck, Alexander, Adair Morse and Luigi Zingales. 2010. 'Who blows the whistle on corporate fraud?' *The Journal of Finance* 65(6): 2213–53. doi.org/10.1111/j.1540-6261.2010.01614.x.

Dyreng, Scott D., Jeffrey L. Hoopes and Jaron H. Wilde. 2016. 'Public pressure and corporate tax behavior.' *Journal of Accounting Research* 54(1): 147–86. doi.org/10.1111/1475-679X.12101.

Ebrey, Patricia Buckley. 1991. *Confucianism and Family Rituals in Imperial China: A Social History of Writing about Rites.* Princeton, NJ: Princeton University Press. doi.org/10.1515/9781400862351.

Eck, John and Edward R. Maguire. 2000. 'Have changes in policing reduced violent crime? An assessment of the evidence.' In Alfred Blumstein and Joel Wallman (eds), *The Crime Drop in America.* New York: Cambridge University Press, pp. 207–65. doi.org/10.1017/CBO9780511616167.008.

Eck, John and David L. Weisburd. 2015. 'Crime places in crime theory.' *Crime and Place: Crime Prevention Studies* 4: 1–33.

Eckstein, Harry. 1975. 'Case study and theory in political science.' In Fred Greenstein and Nelson Polsby (eds), *Handbook of Political Science. Volume 7: Strategies of Enquiry.* Reading, MA: Addison-Wesley, pp. 79–132.

Edelman, Meredith. 2020. Judging the church: Legal systems and accountability for clerical sexual abuse of children. PhD dissertation, The Australian National University, Canberra.

Edmark, Karin. 2005. 'Unemployment and crime: Is there a connection?' *Scandinavian Journal of Economics* 107(2): 353–73. doi.org/10.1111/j.1467-9442.2005.00412.x.

Eells, Rachel Jean. 2011. Meta-analysis of the relationship between collective teacher efficacy and student achievement. PhD dissertation, Loyola University, Chicago.

Ehrensaft, Miriam K., Patricia Cohen, Jocelyn Brown, Elizabeth Smailes, Henian Chen and Jeffrey G. Johnson. 2003. 'Intergenerational transmission of partner violence: A 20-year prospective study.' *Journal of Consulting and Clinical Psychology* 71(4): 741–53. doi.org/10.1037/0022-006X.71.4.741.

Eisenberg, Melvin Aron. 1975. 'Legal models of management structure in the modern corporation: Officers, directors, and accountants.' *California Law Review* 63: 375–462. doi.org/10.2307/3479758.

Eisinger, Jesse. 2017. *The Chickenshit Club: Why the Justice Department Fails to Prosecute Executives.* New York: Simon & Schuster.

Eisler, Riane T. 1987. *The Chalice and the Blade: Our History, Our Future.* Cambridge, MA: Harper & Row.

Eisner, Manuel. 2001. 'Modernization, self-control and lethal violence: The long-term dynamics of European homicide rates in theoretical perspective.' *The British Journal of Criminology* 41(4): 618–38. doi.org/10.1093/bjc/41.4.618.

Eisner, Manuel. 2003. 'Long-term historical trends in violent crime.' *Crime and Justice* 30: 83–142. doi.org/10.1086/652229.

Eisner, Manuel. 2008. 'Modernity strikes back? The latest increase in interpersonal violence (1960–1990) in historical perspective.' *International Journal of Conflict and Violence* 2(2): 288–316.

Eisner, Manuel. 2014. 'From swords to words: Does macro-level change in self-control predict long-term variation in levels of homicide?' *Crime and Justice* 43: 65–134. doi.org/10.1086/677662.

Eisner, Manuel. 2017. 'Interpersonal violence on the British Isles, 1200–2016.' In Alison Liebling, Shadd Maruna and Lesley McAra (eds), *The Oxford Handbook of Criminology*. Oxford, UK: Oxford University Press, pp. 565–86. doi.org/10.1093/he/9780198719441.003.0026.

Eisner, Manuel. 2018. *Interactive London Medieval Murder Map*. [Online.] Cambridge, UK: Institute of Criminology, University of Cambridge. Available at: www.vrc.crim.cam.ac.uk/vrcresearch/london-medieval-murder-map.

Elbakidze, Levan and Yanhong Jin. 2012. 'Victim countries of transnational terrorism: An empirical characteristics analysis.' *Risk Analysis* 32(12): 2152–65. doi.org/10.1111/j.1539-6924.2012.01815.x.

Elgar, Frank J., Wendy Craig, William Boyce, Anthony Morgan and Rachel Vella-Zarb. 2009. 'Income inequality and school bullying: Multilevel study of adolescents in 37 countries.' *Journal of Adolescent Health* 45(4): 351–59. doi.org/10.1016/j.jadohealth.2009.04.004.

Elias, Norbert. 1969. *The Civilizing Process. Volume 1: The History of Manners.* Oxford, UK: Blackwell.

Elias, Norbert. 1982. *The Civilizing Process. Volume 2: State Formation and Civilization*. Oxford, UK: Basil Blackwell.

Elias, Norbert. 1996. *The Germans: Power Struggles and the Development of Habitus in the Nineteenth and Twentieth Centuries*. New York: Columbia University Press.

Elliott, Delbert S. 1962. 'Delinquency and perceived opportunity.' *Sociological Inquiry* 32(2): 216–22. doi.org/10.1111/j.1475-682X.1962.tb00542.x.

Elliott, Ian A. and Anthony R. Beech. 2013. 'A UK cost–benefit analysis of circles of support and accountability interventions.' *Sexual Abuse* 25(3): 211–29. doi.org/10.1177/1079063212443385.

Ellis, Christopher J. and John Fender. 2011. 'Information cascades and revolutionary regime transitions.' *The Economic Journal* 121(553): 763–92. doi.org/10.1111/j.1468-0297.2010.02401.x.

Ellison, Christopher G. 1991. 'Religious involvement and subjective well-being.' *Journal of Health and Social Behavior* 32(1): 80–99. doi.org/10.2307/2136801.

Ellsberg, Daniel. 2017. *The Doomsday Machine: Confessions of a Nuclear War Planner*. London: Bloomsbury Publishing.

Ember, Carol R. and Melvin Ember. 1994. 'War, socialization, and interpersonal violence: A cross-cultural study.' *Journal of Conflict Resolution* 38(4): 620–46. doi.org/10.1177/0022002794038004002.

Engel, Robin S., Nicholas Corsaro and M. Murat Ozer. 2017. 'The impact of police on criminal justice reform: Evidence from Cincinnati, Ohio.' *Criminology & Public Policy* 16(2): 375–402. doi.org/10.1111/1745-9133.12299.

Engels, Friedrich. 2010. *The Origin of the Family, Private Property and the State*. London: Penguin.

Erchak, Gerald M. 1994. 'Family violence.' In Carol R. Ember and Melvin Ember (eds), *Research Frontiers in Anthropology*. Englewood Cliffs, NJ: Prentice-Hall, pp. 3–18.

Erchak, Gerald M. and Richard Rosenfeld. 1994. 'Societal isolation, violent norms and gender relations: A re-examination and extension of Levinson's model of wife beating.' *Cross-Cultural Research* 28: 111–33. doi.org/10.1177/106939719402800202.

Esteban, Joan and Debraj Ray. 2011. 'A model of ethnic conflict.' *Journal of the European Economic Association* 9(3): 496–521. doi.org/10.1111/j.1542-4774.2010.01016.x.

European Economic Council (EEC). 1993. 'Council Regulation (EEC) No. 1836/93 (29 June 1993) Allowing Voluntary Participation by Companies in the Industrial Sector in a Community Eco-Management Audit Scheme.' *Official Journal of the European Community* L 168/1 (10.7.1993).

Evans, Peter B. 1995. *Embedded Autonomy: States and Industrial Transformation*. Princeton, NJ: Princeton University Press. doi.org/10.1515/9781400821723.

Evans, Peter B., Dietrich Rueschemeyer and Theda Skocpol (eds). 1985. *Bringing the State Back In*. New York: Cambridge University Press. doi.org/10.1017/CBO9780511628283.

Fagan, Abigail A., Emily M. Wright and Gillian M. Pinchevsky. 2014. 'The protective effects of neighborhood collective efficacy on adolescent substance abuse and violence following exposure to violence.' *Journal of Youth and Adolescence* 43(9): 1498–512. doi.org/10.1007/s10964-013-0049-8.

Fagan, Jeffrey and Deanna L. Wilkinson. 1998. 'Guns, youth violence, and social identity in inner cities.' *Crime and Justice* 24: 105–88. doi.org/10.1086/449279.

Fagan, Jeffrey, Deanna L. Wilkinson and Garth Davies. 2007. 'Social contagion of violence.' In Daniel J. Flannery, Alexander T. Vazsonyi and Irwin D. Waldman (eds), *The Cambridge Handbook of Violent Behavior and Aggression*. New York: Cambridge University Press, pp. 688–723. doi.org/10.1017/CBO9780511816840.037.

Fagan, Jeffrey, Frank Zimring and June Kim. 1998. 'Declining homicide in New York City: A tale of two trends.' *Journal of Criminal Law and Criminology* 88(4): 1277–317. doi.org/10.2307/1144257.

Fajnzylber, Pablo, Daniel Lederman and Norman Loayza. 1998. *Determinants of Crime Rates in Latin America and the World: An Empirical Assessment*. Washington, DC: World Bank Publications. doi.org/10.1596/0-8213-4240-1.

Fajnzylber, Pablo, Daniel Lederman and Norman Loayza. 2000. 'Crime and victimization: An economic perspective.' *Economía* 1(1): 219–302. doi.org/10.1353/eco.2000.0004.

Fakir, Adnan M.S., Azraf Uddin Ahmad, K.M. Masnun Hosain, Mostafa Rafid Hossain and Ridhim Sadman Gani. 2017. 'The comparative effect of corruption and Piketty's second fundamental law of capitalism on inequality.' *Economic Analysis and Policy* 55: 90–105. doi.org/10.1016/j.eap.2017.04.006.

Falk, Armin, Andreas Kuhn and Josef Zweimüller. 2011. 'Unemployment and right-wing extremist crime.' *The Scandinavian Journal of Economics* 113(2): 260–85. doi.org/10.1111/j.1467-9442.2011.01648.x.

Fanon, Frantz. 1965. *The Wretched of the Earth*. New York: Grove Press.

Farberman, Harvey A. 1975. 'A criminogenic market structure: The automobile industry.' *Sociological Quarterly* 16(4): 438–57. doi.org/10.1111/j.1533-8525.1975.tb00962.x.

Farrall, Stephen, Emily Gray and Phil Mike Jones. 2020. 'Politics, social and economic change, and crime: Exploring the impact of contextual effects on offending trajectories.' *Politics & Society* 48(3): 357–88. doi.org/10.1177/0032329220942395.

Farrall, Stephen and Susanne Karstedt. 2020. *Respectable Citizens—Shady Practices: The Economic Morality of the Middle Classes.* Oxford, UK: Oxford University Press. doi.org/10.1093/oso/9780199595037.001.0001.

Farrell, Graham, Nick Tilley and Andromachi Tseloni. 2014. 'Why the crime drop?' In Michael Tonry (ed.), *Crime and Justice. Volume 43: Why Crime Rates Fall and Why They Don't.* Chicago: University of Chicago Press, pp. 421–90. doi.org/10.1086/678081.

Farrington, David P. 2003. 'Developmental and life-course criminology: Key theoretical and empirical issues—The 2002 Sutherland Award address.' *Criminology* 41(2): 221–25. doi.org/10.1111/j.1745-9125.2003.tb00987.x.

Farrington, David P., Friedrich Lösel, Maria M. Ttofi and Nikos Theodorakis. 2012. *School Bullying, Depression and Offending Behaviour Later in Life: An Updated Systematic Review of Longitudinal Studies.* Stockholm: Swedish National Council for Crime Prevention.

Fattah, Ezzat A. and Vincent F. Sacco. 1989. *Crime and Victimization of the Elderly.* New York: Springer-Verlag. doi.org/10.1007/978-1-4613-8888-3.

FCPA Professor. 2020. 'Scrutiny alerts and updates.' *FCPA Professor*, 24 August. Available at: fcpaprofessor.com/scrutiny-alerts-updates-8/#more-29600.

Fearon, James D. and David D. Laitin. 2000. 'Violence and the social construction of ethnic identity.' *International Organization* 54(4): 845–77. doi.org/10.1162/002081800551398.

Fearon, James D. and David D. Laitin. 2003. 'Ethnicity, insurgency and civil war.' *American Political Science Review* 97(1): 75–90. doi.org/10.1017/S0003055403000534.

Feeley, Malcolm M. 1979. *The Process is the Punishment: Handling Cases in a Lower Criminal Court.* New York: Sage.

Ferguson, Niall. 2006. *The War of the World: Twentieth-Century Conflict and the Descent of the West.* New York: Penguin.

Files, Rebecca. 2012. 'SEC enforcement: Does forthright disclosure and cooperation really matter?' *Journal of Accounting and Economics* 53(1–2): 353–74. doi.org/10.1016/j.jacceco.2011.06.006.

Filiu, Jean-Pierre. 2015. *From Deep State to Islamic State: The Arab Counter-Revolution and its Jihadi Legacy*. New York: Oxford University Press.

Financial Crisis Inquiry Commission (FCIC). 2010. *The Official Transcript: First Public Hearing of the Financial Crisis Inquiry Commission, Wednesday, January 13, 2010*. Washington, DC. Available at: fcic-static.law.stanford.edu/cdn_media/fcic-testimony/2010-0113-Transcript.pdf.

Fisse, Brent. 1982. 'Reconstructing corporate criminal law: Deterrence, retribution, fault, and sanctions.' *South California Law Review* 56: 1141–246.

Fisse, Brent and John Braithwaite. 1983. *The Impact of Publicity on Corporate Offenders*. Albany: SUNY Press.

Fisse, Brent and John Braithwaite. 1993. *Corporations, Crime and Accountability*. Cambridge, UK: Cambridge University Press. doi.org/10.1017/CBO978 0511659133.

Fitzpatrick, Michael. 2006. 'The Cutter incident: How America's first polio vaccine led to a growing vaccine crisis.' *Journal of the Royal Society of Medicine* 99(3): 156. doi.org/10.1177/014107680609900320.

Flaherty, Martin S. 1996. 'The most dangerous branch.' *Yale Law Journal* 105: 1725–840. doi.org/10.2307/797234.

Fleming, Christopher M., Matthew Manning, Hien-Thuc Pham and Margarita Vorsina. 2020. 'Ethnic economic inequality and fatalities from terrorism.' *Journal of Interpersonal Violence* (15 December). doi.org/10.1177/0886260 520976226.

Florida, Richard. 2014. *The Rise of the Creative Class, Revisited*. Revised and expanded. New York: Basic Books.

Forbes. 2016. 'The richest self made women in the world 2016.' *Forbes*, 2 March. Available at: www.forbes.com/pictures/heik45id/zhou-qunfei/#6c1104ce3506.

Ford, Cristie L. 2008. 'New governance, compliance, and principles-based securities regulation.' *American Business Law Journal* 45(1): 1–60. doi.org/10.1111/j.1744-1714.2008.00050.x.

Ford, Cristie L. and David Hess. 2009. 'Can corporate monitorships improve corporate compliance?' *Journal of Corporations Law* 34(3): 680–711.

Ford, Cristie L. and David Hess. 2011. 'Corporate monitorships and new governance regulation: In theory, in practice, and in context.' *Law & Policy* 33(4): 509–41. doi.org/10.1111/j.1467-9930.2011.00347.x.

Forsyth, Miranda. 2018a. Cascades of war and sorcery related violence in Bougainville. MS submitted for publication.

Forsyth, Miranda. 2018b. Contagion and containment of sorcery accusations and related violence in Enga province, Papua New Guinea. MS submitted for publication.

Fortna, Virginia Page. 2003. 'Inside and out: Peacekeeping and the duration of peace after civil and interstate wars.' *International Studies Review* 5(4): 97–114. doi.org/10.1111/j.1079-1760.2003.00504010.x.

Fortna, Virginia Page. 2008. *Does Peacekeeping Work? Shaping Belligerents' Choices After Civil War.* Princeton, NJ: Princeton University Press. doi.org/10.1515/9781400837731.

Fortna, Virginia Page and Lise Morje Howard. 2008. 'Pitfalls and prospects in the peacekeeping literature.' *Annual Review of Political Science* 11: 283–301. doi.org/10.1146/annurev.polisci.9.041205.103022.

Foucault, Michel. 1977. *Discipline and Punish: The Birth of the Prison.* New York: Pantheon.

Fowler, James H. and Nicholas A. Christakis. 2010. 'Cooperative behavior cascades in human social networks.' *Proceedings of the National Academy of Sciences* 107(12): 5334–38. doi.org/10.1073/pnas.0913149107.

Freeman, Jody. 2003. 'Extending public law norms through privatization.' *Harvard Law Review* 116: 1285–352. doi.org/10.2307/1342728.

Freilich, Joshua D. and Graeme Newman. 2018. 'Regulating crime: The new criminology of crime control.' *The ANNALS of the American Academy of Political and Social Science* 679: 8–18. doi.org/10.1177/0002716218784853.

Frey, Bruno S. 2017. 'Policy consequences of pay-for-performance and crowding-out.' *Journal of Behavioral Economics for Policy* 1(1): 55–59.

Frey, Bruno S. and Benno Torgler. 2007. 'Tax morale and conditional cooperation.' *Journal of Comparative Economics* 35(1): 136–59. doi.org/10.1016/j.jce.2006.10.006.

Friedrichs, David O. (ed.). 1998. *State Crime. Volume I: Exposing, Sanctioning, and Preventing State Crime.* Aldershot, UK: Ashgate.

Friedrichs, David O. 2010. *Trusted Criminals: White Collar Crime in Contemporary Society.* 4th edn. Belmont, CA: Wadsworth.

Friesen, Lana. 2012. 'Certainty of punishment versus severity of punishment: An experimental investigation.' *Southern Economic Journal* 79(2): 399–421. doi.org/10.4284/0038-4038-2011.152.

Froestad, Jan and Clifford Shearing. 2012. *Security Governance, Policing, and Local Capacity.* Boca Raton, FL: CRC Press. doi.org/10.1201/b13772.

Fromm, Erich. 1942. *The Fear of Freedom.* London: Routledge & Kegan Paul.

Fukuyama, Francis. 1995. *Trust: The Social Virtues and the Creation of Prosperity.* London: Hamish Hamilton.

Fukuyama, Francis. 2014. *Political Order and Political Decay.* New York: Farrar, Straus & Giroux.

Galanter, Marc. 1997. 'Spiritual recovery movements and contemporary medical care.' *Psychiatry* 60(3): 211–23. doi.org/10.1080/00332747.1997.11024799.

Gale, Dennis E. 1996. *Understanding Urban Unrest: From Reverend King to Rodney King.* Thousand Oaks, CA: Sage Publications.

Gallagher, Thomas H., Amy D. Waterman, Alison G. Ebers, Victoria J. Fraser and Wendy Levinson. 2003. 'Patients' and physicians' attitudes regarding the disclosure of medical errors.' *The Journal of the American Medical Association* 289(8): 1001–7. doi.org/10.1001/jama.289.8.1001.

Gangl, Katharina, Eva Hofmann and Erich Kirchler. 2015. 'Tax authorities' interaction with taxpayers: A conception of compliance in social dilemmas by power and trust.' *New Ideas in Psychology* 37: 13–23. doi.org/10.1016/j.newideapsych.2014.12.001.

Garland, David. 1990. *Punishment and Modern Society: A Study in Social Theory.* Oxford, UK: Oxford University Press. doi.org/10.7208/chicago/9780226922508.001.0001.

Garland, David. 2001. *The Culture of Control.* Oxford, UK: Oxford University Press.

Garnaut, Ross. 2021. *Reset: Restoring Australia after the Pandemic Recession.* Melbourne: La Trobe University Press.

Garrett, Brandon L. 2007. 'Structural reform prosecution.' *Virginia Law Review* 93(4): 853–957.

Garrett, Brandon L. 2011. 'Globalized corporate prosecutions.' *Virginia Law Review* 97(8): 1775–869.

Garrett, Brandon L. 2014. *Too Big to Jail.* Boston, MA: Harvard University Press. doi.org/10.4159/9780674735712.

Garrett, Brandon L. 2015. 'The corporate criminal as scapegoat.' *Virginia Law Review* 101(7): 1789–853. doi.org/10.2139/ssrn.2557465.

Garrett, Brandon L. 2020. 'Declining corporate prosecutions.' *American Criminal Law Review* 57: 109–53.

Garrett, Brandon L., Nan Li and Shivaram Rajgopal. 2019. 'Do heads roll? An empirical analysis of CEO turnover and pay when the corporation is federally prosecuted.' *Journal of Law, Finance, and Accounting* 4(2): 137–81. doi.org/10.1561/108.00000036.

Gartner, Rosemary and Liam Kennedy. 2018. 'War and postwar violence.' *Crime and Justice* 47(1): 1–67. doi.org/10.1086/696649.

Gartner, Rosemary and Bill McCarthy. 1991. 'The social distribution of femicide in urban Canada, 1921–1988.' *Law & Society Review* 25(2): 287–311. doi.org/10.2307/3053800.

Gebhardt, Miriam. 2016. *Crimes Unspoken: The Rape of German Women at the End of the Second World War.* London: Polity.

Geis, Gilbert. 1967. 'White collar crime: The heavy electrical equipment antitrust case of 1961.' In Marshall B. Clinard and Richard Quinney (eds), *Criminal Behavior Systems: A Typology.* New York: Holt, Rinehart & Winston, pp. 139–51.

Geis, Gilbert and Colin Goff. 1990. Edwin Sutherland and the FBI: The evil of banality. Paper presented to Edwin Sutherland Conference on White-Collar Crime, Indiana University, Bloomington, May.

Geis, Gilbert and Colin Goff. 1992. 'Lifting the cover from undercover operations: J. Edgar Hoover and some of the other criminologists.' *Crime, Law and Social Change* 18(1–2): 91–104. doi.org/10.1007/BF00230626.

Geneva Call. 2020. *Annual Report 2019.* Geneva: Geneva Call. Available at: www.genevacall.org/wp-content/uploads/2020/06/WEB_GEC-RA-2019_V14.pdf.

Geneva Declaration Secretariat. 2011. *Global Burden of Armed Violence 2011: Lethal Encounters.* Cambridge, UK: Cambridge University Press. Available at: www.genevadeclaration.org/measurability/global-burden-of-armed-violence/global-burden-of-armed-violence-2011.html.

Gerlach, Christian. 2010. *Extremely Violent Societies: Mass Violence in the Twentieth-Century World*. Cambridge, UK: Cambridge University Press. doi.org/10.1017/CBO9780511781254.

Ghobarah, Hazem Adam, Paul Huth and Bruce Russett. 2003. 'Civil wars kill and maim people—Long after the shooting stops.' *American Political Science Review* 97(2): 189–202. doi.org/10.1017/S0003055403000613.

Gibson, Christopher, Molly Slothower and Lawrence W. Sherman. 2017. 'Sweet spots for hot spots? A cost-effectiveness comparison of two patrol strategies.' *Cambridge Journal of Evidence-Based Policing* 1(4): 225–43. doi.org/10.1007/s41887-017-0017-8.

Giddens, Anthony. 1979. *Central Problems in Social Theory*. Berkeley, CA: University of California Press. doi.org/10.1007/978-1-349-16161-4.

Giddens, Anthony. 1984. *The Constitution of Society: Outline of the Theory of Structuration*. Cambridge, UK: Polity Press.

Gilbert, Keon L., Sandra C. Quinn, Robert M. Goodman, James Butler and John Wallace. 2013. 'A meta-analysis of social capital and health: A case for needed research.' *Journal of Health Psychology* 18(11): 1385–99. doi.org/10.1177/1359105311435983.

Gilligan, Michael J. and Ernest J. Sergenti. 2008. 'Do UN interventions cause peace? Using matching to improve causal inference.' *Quarterly Journal of Political Science* 3(2): 89–122. doi.org/10.1561/100.00007051.

Giordano, Peggy C., Stephen A. Cernkovich and Jennifer L. Rudolph. 2002. 'Gender, crime and desistance: Toward a theory of cognitive transformation.' *American Journal of Sociology* 107(4): 990–1064. doi.org/10.1086/343191.

Giordano, Peggy C., Monica A. Longmore, Ryan D. Schroeder and Patrick M. Seffrin. 2008. 'A life-course perspective on spirituality and desistance from crime.' *Criminology* 46(1): 99–132. doi.org/10.1111/j.1745-9125.2008.00104.x.

Gladwell, Malcolm. 2000. *The Tipping Point: How Little Things Can Make a Big Difference*. London: Abacus.

Glaeser, Edward L., Bruce Sacerdote and Jose A. Scheinkman. 1996. 'Crime and social interactions.' *The Quarterly Journal of Economics* 111(2): 507–48. doi.org/10.2307/2946686.

Gleditsch, Kristian Skrede. 2002. *All Politics Is Local: The Diffusion of Conflict, Integration, and Democratization*. Ann Arbor: University of Michigan Press.

Gleditsch, Kristian Skrede. 2007. 'Transnational dimensions of civil war.' *Journal of Peace Research* 44(3): 293–309. doi.org/10.1177/0022343307076637.

Gobert, James and Maurice Punch. 2003. *Rethinking Corporate Crime.* Cambridge, UK: Cambridge University Press.

Goddard, Roger D., Linda Skrla and Serena J. Salloum. 2017. 'The role of collective efficacy in closing student achievement gaps: A mixed methods study of school leadership for excellence and equity.' *Journal of Education for Students Placed at Risk* 22(4): 220–36. doi.org/10.1080/10824669.2017.13 48900.

Godziszewski, Bartosz and Michal Kruszka. 2013. 'Stability of banking system in Poland and activity of the KNF—Polish Financial Supervision Authority.' *CESifo Forum* 14(1): 29–34.

Gold, Russell and Ben Casselman. 2010. 'Drilling process attracts scrutiny in rig explosion.' *Wall Street Journal*, 30 April 2010.

Goldstone, Jack A. 2008. *Using Quantitative and Qualitative Models to Forecast Instability.* Washington, DC: United States Institute of Peace.

Golub, Andrew and Bruce D. Johnson. 1996. 'The crack epidemic: Empirical findings support an hypothesized diffusion of innovation process.' *Socio-Economic Planning Sciences* 30(3): 221–31. doi.org/10.1016/0038-0121(96) 00005-5.

Goodin, Robert E. 2008. 'First talk, then vote.' In Robert E. Goodin (ed.), *Innovating Democracy: Democratic Theory and Practice after the Deliberative Turn.* New York: Oxford University Press, pp. 108–24. doi.org/10.1093/acprof:oso/9780199547944.003.0006.

Gottfredson, Michael R. and Travis Hirschi. 1990. *A General Theory of Crime.* Stanford, CA: Stanford University Press.

Gottschalk, Petter. 2020. *The Convenience of White-Collar Crime in Business.* Cham, Switzerland: Springer. doi.org/10.1007/978-3-030-37990-2.

Gould, Madelyn S. 1990. 'Suicide clusters and media exposure.' In Susan J. Blumenthal and David J. Kupfer (eds), *Suicide Over the Life Cycle: Risk Factors, Assessment, and Treatment of Suicidal Patients.* Washington, DC: American Psychiatric Association, pp. 517–32.

Grabosky, Peter N. 1989. *Wayward Governance: Illegality and its Control in the Public Sector.* Canberra: Australian Institute of Criminology.

Grabosky, Peter N. 1990a. 'Citizen co-production and corruption control.' *Corruption and Reform* 5(2): 125–51.

Grabosky, Peter N. 1990b. 'Professional advisers and white collar illegality: Towards explaining and excusing professional failure.' *University of New South Wales Law Journal* 13(1): 73–96.

Grabosky, Peter N. 1992. 'Law enforcement and the citizen: Non-governmental participants in crime prevention and control.' *Policing and Society: An International Journal of Research and Policy* 2(4): 249–71. doi.org/10.1080/10439463.1992.9964647.

Grabosky, Peter N. 1994a. 'Beyond the regulatory state.' *Australian and New Zealand Journal of Criminology* 27(2): 192–97. doi.org/10.1177/000486589402700207.

Grabosky, Peter N. 1994b. 'Green markets: Environmental regulation by the private sector.' *Law & Policy* 16: 419. doi.org/10.1111/j.1467-9930.1994.tb00132.x.

Grabosky, Peter N. 1995a. 'Counterproductive regulation.' *International Journal of the Sociology of Law* 23(4): 347–69. doi.org/10.1016/S0194-6595(05)80003-6.

Grabosky, Peter N. 1995b. 'Using non-governmental resources to foster regulatory compliance.' *Governance* 8(4): 527–50. doi.org/10.1111/j.1468-0491.1995.tb00226.x.

Grabosky, Peter N. 2017. 'Meta-regulation.' In Peter Drahos (ed.), *Regulatory Theory: Foundations and Applications*. Canberra: ANU Press, pp. 149–61. doi.org/10.22459/RT.02.2017.09.

Grabosky, Peter and John Braithwaite. 1986. *Of Manners Gentle: Enforcement Strategies of Australian Business Regulatory Agencies*. Oxford: Oxford University Press.

Gramsci, Antonio. 1971. *Selections from the Prison Notebooks of Antonio Gramsci*. Quintin Hoare and Geoffrey Nowell Smith, eds and trans. New York: International Publishers.

Granovetter, Mark S. 1973. 'The strength of weak ties.' *American Journal of Sociology* 78(6): 1360–80. doi.org/10.1086/225469.

Gray, Felicity. Forthcoming. 'A different kind of weapon: Ethical dilemmas and nonviolent civilian protection.' In Austin Choi-Fitzpatrick, Douglas Irvin-Erickson and Ernesto Verdeja (eds), *Wicked Problems: The Ethics of Action for Peace, Rights, and Justice*. Oxford: Oxford University Press.

Green, Duncan. 2016. *How Change Happens*. Oxford, UK: Oxford University Press. doi.org/10.1093/acprof:oso/9780198785392.001.0001.

Green, Penny. 1990. *The Enemy Without: Policing and Class Consciousness in the Miners' Strike*. Milton Keynes, UK: Open University Press.

Green, Penny and Tony Ward. 2004. *State Crime: Governments, Violence and Corruption*. London: Pluto Press.

Greenspan, Alan. 2008. 'I was wrong about the economy, sort of.' *The Guardian*, 24 October.

Gregor, A. James. 1981. 'Confucianism and the political thought of Sun Yat-Sen.' *Philosophy East and West* 31(1): 55–70. doi.org/10.2307/1399066.

Greif, Avner. 1989. 'Reputation and coalitions in medieval trade: Evidence on the Maghribi traders.' *Journal of Economic History* 49(4): 857–82. doi.org/10.1017/S0022050700009475.

Groß, Eva M., Andreas Hövermann and Steven F. Messner. 2018. 'Marketized mentality, competitive/egoistic school culture, and delinquent attitudes and behavior: An application of institutional anomie theory.' *Criminology* 56(2): 333–69. doi.org/10.1111/1745-9125.12173.

Groshkova, Teodora, David Best and William White. 2013. 'The assessment of recovery capital: Properties and psychometrics of a measure of addiction recovery strengths.' *Drug and Alcohol Review* 32(2): 187–94. doi.org/10.1111/j.1465-3362.2012.00489.x.

Gross, Edward. 1978. 'Organizations as criminal actors.' In Paul R. Wilson and John Braithwaite (eds), *Two Faces of Deviance: Crimes of the Powerless and Powerful*. Brisbane: University of Queensland Press, pp. 198–213.

Gruner, Richard. 1988. 'To let the punishment fit the organization: Sanctioning corporate offenders through corporate probation.' *American Journal of Criminal Law* 16: 1–106.

Guerra, Nancy G., L. Rowell Huesmann and Anja Spindler. 2003. 'Community violence exposure, social cognition, and aggression among urban elementary school children.' *Child Development* 74(5): 1561–76. doi.org/10.1111/1467-8624.00623.

Guevara, Ernesto. 2003 [1967]. 'Create two, three, many Vietnams [Message to the Tricontinental].' In David Deutschmann (ed.), *Che Guevara: A Reader*. Expanded 2nd edn. Minneapolis: Ocean Press, pp. 350–64.

Gully, Stanley M., Kara A. Incalcaterra, Aparna Joshi and J. Matthew Beaubien. 2002. 'A meta-analysis of team-efficacy, potency, and performance: Interdependence and level of analysis as moderators of observed relationships.' *Journal of Applied Psychology* 87(5): 819–32. doi.org/10.1037/0021-9010. 87.5.819.

Gunningham, Neil. 1995. 'Environment, self-regulation, and the chemical industry: Assessing responsible care.' *Law & Policy* 17(1): 57–109. doi.org/10.1111/j.1467-9930.1995.tb00139.x.

Gunningham, Neil. 1996. 'From adversarialism to partnership? ISO 14000 and regulation.' In Australian Centre for Environmental Law, *ISO 14000: Regulation, Trade and Environment. Proceedings of Conference, 2 July 1996, Hyatt Hotel, Canberra*. Canberra: The Australian National University.

Gunningham, Neil and Peter Grabosky. 1998. *Smart Regulation*. Oxford, UK: Oxford University Press.

Gunningham, Neil and Darren Sinclair. 2012. *Managing Mining Hazards: Regulation, Safety and Trust*. Sydney: The Federation Press.

Gupta, Sanjeev, Hamid Davoodi and Rosa Alonso-Terme. 2002. 'Does corruption affect income inequality and poverty?' *Economics of Governance* 3(1): 23–45. doi.org/10.1007/s101010100039.

Gurr, Ted R. 1970. *Why Men Rebel*. Princeton, NJ: Princeton University Press.

Gurr, Ted R. (ed.). 1980. *Handbook of Political Conflict: Theory and Research*. New York: The Free Press.

Gurr, Ted R. 1981. 'Historical trends in violent crime: A critical review of the evidence.' *Crime and Justice* 3: 295–353. doi.org/10.1086/449082.

Gurr, Ted R. 1993. *Minorities at Risk*. Washington, DC: United States Institute of Peace Press.

Gurr, Ted R. (ed.). 2000. *Peoples Versus States: Minorities at Risk in the New Century*. Washington, DC: United States Institute of Peace.

Gyimah-Brempong, Kwabena. 2002. 'Corruption, economic growth, and income inequality in Africa.' *Economics of Governance* 3(3): 183–209. doi.org/10.1007/s101010200045.

Haas, Nicole E., Maarten Van Craen, Wesley G. Skogan and Diego M. Fleitas. 2015. 'Explaining officer compliance: The importance of procedural justice and trust inside a police organization.' *Criminology and Criminal Justice* 15(4): 442–63. doi.org/10.1177/1748895814566288.

Haber, Stephen. 2013. *Crony Capitalism and Economic Growth in Latin America: Theory and Evidence.* Stanford, CA: Hoover Institution Press.

Habermas, Jürgen. 1985. *The Theory of Communicative Action. Volume 2: Lifeworld and System.* T. McCarthy, trans. Boston, MA: Beacon Press.

Haines, Fiona and Christine Parker. 2017. 'Moving towards ecological regulation: The role of criminalisation.' In Cameron Holley and Clifford Shearing (eds), *Criminology and the Anthropocene.* London: Routledge, pp. 81–108. doi.org/10.4324/9781315541938-4.

Hale, Henry E. 2013. 'Regime change cascades: What we have learned from the 1848 revolutions to the 2011 Arab uprisings.' *Annual Review of Political Science* 16: 331–53. doi.org/10.1146/annurev-polisci-032211-212204.

Hall, Lauren Jay, David Best, Clare Ogden-Webb, Jacqui Dixon and Rob Hislop. 2018. 'Building bridges to the community: The Kirkham Family Connectors (KFC) prison programme.' *The Howard Journal of Crime and Justice* 57(4): 518–35. doi.org/10.1111/hojo.12289.

Hall, Peter A. and David W. Soskice (eds). 2001. *Varieties of Capitalism: The Institutional Foundations of Comparative Advantage.* Oxford, UK: Oxford University Press.

Halpern, David. 2001. 'Moral values, social trust and inequality: Can values explain crime?' *The British Journal of Criminology* 41(2): 236–51. doi.org/10.1093/bjc/41.2.236.

Hamilton, Alexander, James Madison and John Jay. 1963. *The Federalist Papers.* New York: Mentor Books.

Hampson, Fen Osler. 1996. *Nurturing Peace: Why Peace Settlements Succeed or Fail.* Washington, DC: United States Institute of Peace.

Handler, Joel F. 1989. 'Community care for the frail elderly: A theory of empowerment.' *Ohio State Law Journal* 50(3): 541–60.

Haraway, Donna. 2015. 'Anthropocene, capitalocene, plantationocene, chthulucene: Making kin.' *Environmental Humanities* 6(1): 159–65. doi.org/10.1215/22011919-3615934.

Harcourt, Bernard E. 2001. *Illusion of Order: The False Promises of Broken Windows Policing.* Cambridge, MA: Harvard University Press.

Hardyns, Wim, Veerle Vyncke, Arne De Boeck, Lieven Pauwels and Sara Willems. 2016. 'Are collective efficacy, disorder and social support associated with one's quality of life? Evidence from the multilevel SWING study in Belgium.' *Applied Research in Quality of Life* 11(3): 739–56. doi.org/10.1007/s11482-015-9393-z.

Harff, Barbara. 2017. 'Genocide and political mass murder.' In Michael Stohl, Mark I. Lichbach and Peter Nils Grabosky (eds), *States and Peoples in Conflict: Transformations of Conflict Studies*. New York: Routledge, pp. 208–30. doi.org/10.4324/9781315623634-12.

Harriott, Anthony. 2011. 'The emergence and evolution of organized crime in Jamaica: New challenges to law enforcement and society.' *West Indian Law Journal* 36(2): 3–28.

Harris, Nathan. 2001. 'Shaming and shame: Regulating drink-driving.' In Eliza Ahmed, Nathan Harris, John Braithwaite and Valerie Braithwaite (eds), *Shame Management through Reintegration*. Cambridge, UK: Cambridge University Press, pp. 73–210.

Harris, Nathan. 2017. 'Shame in regulatory settings.' In Peter Drahos (ed.), *Regulatory Theory: Foundations and Applications*. Canberra: ANU Press, pp. 59–76. doi.org/10.22459/RT.02.2017.04.

Hattie, John. 2009. *Visible Learning: A Synthesis of Over 800 Meta-Analyses Relating to Achievement*. New York: Routledge. doi.org/10.4324/9780203887332.

Hattie, John. 2012. *Visible Learning for Teachers: Maximising Impact on Learning*. New York: Routledge. doi.org/10.4324/9780203181522.

Haug, Wolfgang Fritz. 1986. *Critique of Commodity Aesthetics: Appearance, Sexuality and Advertising in Capitalist Society*. Robert Bock, trans. Cambridge, UK: Polity Press.

Haugh, Todd. 2021. 'Criminalized compliance.' In Benjamin van Rooij and D. Daniel Sokol (eds), *Cambridge Handbook of Compliance*. Cambridge, UK: Cambridge University Press, pp. 133–42. doi.org/10.1017/9781108759458.

Hawken, Angela and Mark Kleiman. 2009. *Managing drug involved probationers with swift and certain sanctions: Evaluating Hawaii's HOPE*. Washington, DC: National Institute of Justice. Available at: www.ojp.gov/pdffiles1/nij/grants/229023.pdf.

Hazra, Devika and Zhen Cui. 2018. 'Macroeconomic determinants of crime: Evidence from India.' *Journal of Quantitative Economics* 16(1): 187–98. doi.org/10.1007/s40953-018-0127-6.

Hegre, Håvard, Tanja Ellingsen, Scott Gates and Nils Peter Gleditsch. 2001. 'Toward a democratic civil peace? Democracy, political change, and civil war, 1816–1992.' *American Political Science Review* 95(1): 33–48. doi.org/ 10.1017/S0003055401000119.

Hegre, Håvard and Håvard Mokleiv Nygård. 2015. 'Governance and conflict relapse.' *Journal of Conflict Resolution* 59(6): 984–1016. doi.org/10.1177/ 0022002713520591.

Heidemann, Gretchen, Julie A. Cederbaum, Sidney Martinez and Thomas P. LeBel. 2016. 'Wounded healers: How formerly incarcerated women help themselves by helping others.' *Punishment & Society* 18(1): 3–26. doi.org/ 10.1177/1462474515623101.

Heirigs, Mark H. and Matthew D. Moore. 2018. 'Gender inequality and homicide: A cross-national examination.' *International Journal of Comparative and Applied Criminal Justice* 42(4): 273–85. doi.org/10.1080/01924036.20 17.1322112.

Hendin, Herbert and Ann Pollinger Haas. 1991. 'Suicide and guilt as manifestations of PTSD in Vietnam combat veterans.' *The American Journal of Psychiatry* 148(5): 586–91. doi.org/10.1176/ajp.148.5.586.

Henne, Kathryn and Emily Troshynski. 2013. 'Mapping the margins of intersectionality: Criminological possibilities in a transnational world.' *Theoretical Criminology* 17(4): 455–473.

Herbert, Tania. 2007. *Commercial sexual exploitation of children in the Solomon Islands: A report focusing on the presence of the logging industry in a remote region.* Solomon Islands: Christian Care Centre, The Anglican Church of Melanesia.

Hertzler, Joyce O. 1934. 'On golden rules.' *The International Journal of Ethics* 44(4): 418–36. doi.org/10.1086/intejethi.44.4.2378256.

Hess, David and Cristie L. Ford. 2008. 'Corporate corruption and reform undertakings: A new approach to an old problem.' *Cornell International Law Journal* 41: 307–46.

Hess, G. Dale. 2020. *The impact of a regional nuclear conflict between India and Pakistan: Two views.* NAPSNet Special Reports, 23 September. Berkeley, CA: Nautilus Institute for Security and Sustainability. Available at: nautilus.org/ napsnet/napsnet-special-reports/the-impact-of-a-regional-nuclear-conflict-between-india-and-pakistan-two-views/.

Higgins, Polly, Damien Short and Nigel South. 2013. 'Protecting the planet: A proposal for a law of ecocide.' *Crime, Law and Social Change* 59(3): 251–66. doi.org/10.1007/s10611-013-9413-6.

Hilbert, Richard A. 1989. 'Durkheim and Merton on anomie: An unexplained contrast and its derivatives.' *Social Problems* 36(3): 242–50. doi.org/10.2307/800693.

Hindess, Barry. 1996. *Discourses of Power: From Hobbes to Foucault.* Oxford, UK: Blackwell.

Hinkle, Joshua C., David Weisburd, Cody W. Telep and Kevin Petersen. 2020. 'Problem-oriented policing for reducing crime and disorder: An updated systematic review and meta-analysis.' *Campbell Systematic Reviews* 16(2): e1089. doi.org/10.1002/cl2.1089.

Hipp, John R. and James C. Wo. 2015. 'Collective efficacy and crime.' *International Encyclopedia of the Social and Behavioral Sciences* 4: 169–73. doi.org/10.1016/B978-0-08-097086-8.45045-2.

Hipple, Natalie Kroovand, Jeff Gruenewald and Edmund F. McGarrell. 2014. 'Restorativeness, procedural justice, and defiance as predictors of reoffending of participants in family group conferences.' *Crime & Delinquency* 60(8): 1131–57. doi.org/10.1177/0011128711428556.

Hobbes, Thomas. 1651. *Leviathan.* Project Gutenberg. [Online.] Available at: www.gutenberg.org/ebooks/3207.

Hobsbawm, Eric. 1994. *The Age of Extremes: The Short Twentieth Century, 1914–1991.* London: Abacus.

Hodges, Christopher. 2015. *Law and Corporate Behaviour: Integrating Theories of Regulation, Enforcement, Compliance and Ethics.* London: Hart.

Hogg, Russell. 2013. 'Punishment and "the people": Rescuing populism from its critics.' In Kerry Carrington, Matthew Ball, Erin O'Brien and Juan Marcellus Tauri (eds), *Crime, Justice and Social Democracy: International Perspectives.* New York: Palgrave Macillan.

Holley, Cameron, Clifford Shearing, Cameron Harrington, Amanda Kennedy and Tariro Mutongwizo. 2018. 'Environmental security and the Anthropocene: Law, criminology, and international relations.' *Annual Review of Law and Social Science* 14: 185–203. doi.org/10.1146/annurev-lawsocsci-101317-030945.

Holmes, Stephen. 1995. *Passions and Constraint: On the Theory of Liberal Democracy.* Chicago: University of Chicago Press.

Homel, Jacqui. 2013. 'Does bullying others at school lead to adult aggression? The roles of drinking and university participation during the transition to adulthood.' *Australian Journal of Psychology* 65(2): 98–106. doi.org/10.1111/ajpy.12002.

Homel, Ross. 1988. *Policing and Punishing the Drinking Driver: A Study of General and Specific Deterrence.* New York: Springer-Verlag. doi.org/10.1007/978-1-4684-7077-2.

Homel, Ross, Brian Bumbarger, Kate Freiburg and Sara Branch. 2017. 'Sustaining crime prevention at scale: Transforming delivery system through prevention science.' In Brent Teasdale and Mindy Bradley (eds), *Preventing Crime and Violence.* New York: Springer, pp. 351–76. doi.org/10.1007/978-3-319-44124-5_29.

Hong, Seung-Hun. 2016. Dynamics of reciprocal regulation. PhD dissertation, The Australian National University, Canberra.

Honig, Maria, Samantha Petersen, Tom Herbstein, Saul Roux, Deon Nel and Clifford Shearing. 2015. 'A conceptual framework to enable the changes required for a one-planet future.' *Environmental Values* 24(5): 663–88. doi.org/10.3197/096327115X14384223590258.

Hood, Christopher, Oliver James, Colin Scott, George W. Jones and Tony Travers. 1999. *Regulation Inside Government: Waste Watchers, Quality Police, and Sleaze-Busters.* Oxford, UK: Oxford University Press.

Hopkins, Belinda. 2003. *Just Schools: A Whole School Approach to Restorative Justice.* London: Jessica Kingsley Publishers.

Houweling, Henk W. and Jan Geert Siccama. 1985. 'The epidemiology of war, 1816–1980.' *Journal of Conflict Resolution* 29(4): 641–63. doi.org/10.1177/0022002785029004007.

Houweling, Henk W. and Jan Geert Siccama. 1988. *Studies of War.* Dordrecht: Martinus Nijhoff Publishers.

Hövermann, Andreas and Steven F. Messner. 2019. 'Institutional imbalance, marketized mentality, and the justification of instrumental offenses: A cross-national application of institutional anomie theory.' *Justice Quarterly* 38(3): 406–32. doi.org/10.1080/07418825.2019.1590621.

Howley, Patrick. 2002. *Breaking Spears and Mending Hearts: Peacemakers and Restorative Justice in Bougainville.* Sydney: The Federation Press.

Hsieh, Ching-Chi and Meredith D. Pugh. 1993. 'Poverty, income inequality, and violent crime: A meta-analysis of recent aggregate data studies.' *Criminal Justice Review* 18(2): 182–202. doi.org/10.1177/073401689301800203.

Hudson, Margaret. 1986. 'Elder mistreatment: Current research.' In Karl A. Pillemer and Rosalie S. Wolf (eds), *Elder Abuse: Conflict in the Family*. Dover, MA: Auburn House, pp. 125–66.

Hudson, Valerie M., Bonnie Ballif-Spanville, Mary Caprioli and Chad F. Emmett. 2012. *Sex and World Peace*. New York: Columbia University Press.

Hudson, Valerie M., Mary Caprioli, Bonnie Ballif-Spanville, Rose McDermott and Chad F. Emmett. 2009. 'The heart of the matter: The security of women and the security of states.' *International Security* 33(3): 7–45. doi.org/10.1162/isec.2009.33.3.7.

Huesmann, L. Rowell, Eric F. Dubow, Paul Boxer, Simha F. Landau, Shira Dvir Gvirsman and Khalil Shikaki. 2017. 'Children's exposure to violent political conflict stimulates aggression at peers by increasing emotional distress, aggressive script rehearsal, and normative beliefs favoring aggression.' *Development and Psychopathology* 29(1): 39–50. doi.org/10.1017/S095457 9416001115.

Hughes, Lorine A., Lonnie M. Schaible and Benjamin R. Gibbs. 2015. 'Economic dominance, the "American Dream", and homicide: A cross-national test of institutional anomie theory.' *Sociological Inquiry* 85(1): 100–28. doi.org/10.1111/soin.12065.

Hultman, Lisa, Jacob Kathman and Megan Shannon. 2013. 'United Nations peacekeeping and civilian protection in civil war.' *American Journal of Political Science* 57(4): 875–91. doi.org/10.1111/ajps.12036.

Humphreys, Keith. 2017. 'Avoiding globalisation of the prescription opioid epidemic.' *The Lancet* 390(10093): 437–39. doi.org/10.1016/S0140-6736 (17)31918-9.

Humphreys, Keith, Janet C. Blodgett and Todd H. Wagner. 2014. 'Estimating the efficacy of Alcoholics Anonymous without self-selection bias: An instrumental variables re-analysis of randomized clinical trials.' *Alcoholism: Clinical and Experimental Research* 38(11): 2688–94. doi.org/10.1111/acer.12557.

Humphreys, Macartan and Jeremy M. Weinstein. 2008. 'Who fights? The determinants of participation in civil war.' *American Journal of Political Science* 52(2): 436–55. doi.org/10.1111/j.1540-5907.2008.00322.x.

Huntington, Samuel. 1991. *The Third Wave: Democratization in the Late Twentieth Century*. Oklahoma City: University of Oklahoma Press.

Huntington, Samuel. 2006. *Political Order in Changing Societies*. New Haven, CT: Yale University Press.

Hutchcroft, Paul David. 1998. *Booty Capitalism: The Politics of Banking in the Philippines*. Ithaca, NY: Cornell University Press. doi.org/10.7591/97815 01738630.

Inglehart, Ronald. 1997. *Modernization and Postmodernization: Cultural, Economic and Political Change in 43 Societies*. Princeton, NJ: Princeton University Press. doi.org/10.1515/9780691214429.

Institute of Medicine and National Research Council. 2013. *Contagion of Violence: Workshop Summary*. Washington, DC: The National Academies Press.

Intergovernmental Science-Policy Platform on Biodiversity and Ecosystem Services (IPBES). 2019. *Nature's dangerous decline 'unprecedented'; species extinction rates accelerating*. UN Report, 6 May. Paris: IPBES.

Intravia, Jonathan, Benjamin R. Gibbs, Kevin T. Wolff, Rocio Paez, Allison Bernheimer and Alex R. Piquero. 2018. 'The mediating role of street code attitudes on the self-control and crime relationship.' *Deviant Behavior* 39(10): 1305–21. doi.org/10.1080/01639625.2017.1410611.

Intravia, Jonathan, Eric A. Stewart, Patricia Y. Warren and Kevin T. Wolff. 2016. 'Neighborhood disorder and generalized trust: A multilevel mediation examination of social mechanisms.' *Journal of Criminal Justice* 46: 148–58. doi.org/10.1016/j.jcrimjus.2016.05.003.

Irwin, Will A. and Richard A. Liroff. 1974. *Economic Disincentives for Pollution Control: Legal, Political and Administrative Dimensions, Band 1*. Washington, DC: Office of Research and Development, US Environmental Protection Agency.

Jaccoud, Mylene. 1998. 'Restoring justice in native communities in Canada.' In Lode Walgrave (ed.), *Restorative Justice for Juveniles: Potentialities, Risks and Problems for Research*. Leuven, Belgium: Leuven University Press, pp. 285–99.

Jackson, Aubrey L. 2016. 'The combined effect of women's neighborhood resources and collective efficacy on IPV.' *Journal of Marriage and Family* 78(4): 890–907. doi.org/10.1111/jomf.12294.

Jacobs, James B., Coleen Friel and Robert Raddick. 2001. *Gotham Unbound: How New York City was Liberated from the Grip of Organized Crime*. New York: NYU Press.

Jakobsen, Tor G. and Indra De Soysa. 2009. 'Give me liberty, or give me death! State repression, ethnic grievance and civil war, 1981–2004.' *Civil Wars* 11(2): 137–57. doi.org/10.1080/13698240802631061.

Jang, Sung Joon and Aaron B. Franzen. 2013. 'Is being "spiritual" enough without being religious? A study of violent and property crimes among emerging adults.' *Criminology* 51(3): 595–627. doi.org/10.1111/1745-9125.12013.

Jaspan, Norman and Hillel Black. 1960. *The Thief in the White Collar.* Philadelphia: Lippincott.

Jawadi, Fredj, Sushanta K. Mallick, Abdoulkarim Idi Cheffou and Anish Augustine. 2021. 'Does higher unemployment lead to greater criminality? Revisiting the debate over the business cycle.' *Journal of Economic Behavior & Organization* 182: 448–71. doi.org/10.1016/j.jebo.2019.03.025.

Jeffery, W.J. 1970. 'The forty thieves.' *FBI Law Enforcement Bulletin* 39: 17–19.

Jenkins, Anne L. 1994. 'The role of managerial self-efficacy in corporate compliance with the law.' *Law and Human Behavior* 18(1): 71–88. doi.org/10.1007/BF01499145.

Jessop, Bob. 2014. 'Capitalist diversity and variety: Variegation, the world market, compossibility and ecological dominance.' *Capital & Class* 38(1): 45–58. doi.org/10.1177/0309816813513087.

Job, Jenny and Monica Reinhart. 2003. 'Trusting the Tax Office: Does Putnam's thesis relate to tax?' *Australian Journal of Social Issues* 38(3): 299–322. doi.org/10.1002/j.1839-4655.2003.tb01148.x.

Johannesen, Niels and Tim Stolper. 2017. *The deterrence effect of whistleblowing: An event study of leaked customer information from banks in tax havens.* Working Paper 2017-4. Munich: Max Planck Institute for Tax Law and Public Finance. doi.org/10.2139/ssrn.2972511.

Johnson, Byron R. and Sung Joon Jang. 2011. 'Crime and religion: Assessing the role of the faith factor.' In Richard Rosenfeld, Kenna Quinet and Crystal Garcia (eds), *Contemporary Issues in Criminological Theory and Research: The Role of Social Institutions.* Belmont, CA: Wadsworth, pp. 117–49.

Johnson, Ralph W. and Gardner M. Brown, Jr. 1976. *Cleaning Up Europe's Waters: Economics, Management, and Policies.* New York: Praeger.

Johnstone, Gerry. 2013. *Restorative Justice: Ideas, Values, Debates.* London: Routledge. doi.org/10.4324/9780203804841.

Johr, Barbara. 1992. 'Die Ereignisse in Zahlen [The events in numbers].' In Helke Sander and Barbara Johr (eds), *Befreier und Befreite: Krieg, Vergewaltigungen, Kinder* [*Liberators Take Liberties: War, Rape, Children*]. München: Antje Kunstmann, pp. 46–73.

Jugert, Philipp, Katharine H. Greenaway, Markus Barth, Ronja Büchner, Sarah Eisentraut and Immo Fritsch. 2016. 'Collective efficacy increases pro-environmental intentions through increasing self-efficacy.' *Journal of Environmental Psychology* 48: 12–23. doi.org/10.1016/j.jenvp.2016.08.003.

Jung, Dong I. and John J. Sosik. 2002. 'Transformational leadership in work groups: The role of empowerment, cohesiveness, and collective-efficacy on perceived group performance.' *Small Group Research* 33(3): 313–36. doi.org/10.1177/10496402033003002.

Kaiser, Marie, Philipp Kuwert, Elmar Braehler and Heide Glaesmer. 2018. 'Long-term effects on adult attachment in German occupation children born after World War II in comparison with a birth-cohort-matched representative sample of the German general population.' *Aging & Mental Health* 22(2): 197–207. doi.org/10.1080/13607863.2016.1247430.

Kalecki, Michael. 1943. 'Political aspects of full employment.' *Political Quarterly* 14: 1–5. doi.org/10.1111/j.1467-923X.1943.tb01016.x.

Kalyvas, Stathis. 2003. 'The ontology of "political violence": Action and identity in civil wars.' *Perspectives on Politics* 1(3): 475–94. doi.org/10.1017/S1537592703000355.

Kalyvas, Stathis. 2006. *The Logic of Violence in Civil War*. New York: Cambridge University Press. doi.org/10.1017/CBO9780511818462.

Kanno-Youngs, Zolan and David E. Sanger. 2021. 'U.S. accuses China of hacking Microsoft.' *The New York Times*, 19 July. Available at: www.nytimes.com/2021/07/19/us/politics/microsoft-hacking-china-biden.html.

Kaplan, Mark S., Nathalie Huguet, Bentson H. McFarland and Jason T. Newsom. 2007. 'Suicide among male veterans: A prospective population-based study.' *Journal of Epidemiology & Community Health* 61(7): 619–24. doi.org/10.1136/jech.2006.054346.

Kapuscinski, Cezary A., John Braithwaite and Bruce Chapman. 1998. 'Unemployment and crime: Toward resolving the paradox.' *Journal of Quantitative Criminology* 14(3): 215–43. doi.org/10.1023/A:1023033328731.

Karmen, Andrew. 2000. *New York Murder Mystery: The True Story Behind the Crime Crash of the 1990s*. New York: New York University Press.

Karpoff, Jonathan M. 2012. 'Does reputation work to discipline corporate misconduct?' In Timothy G. Pollock and Michael L. Barnett (eds), *The Oxford Handbook of Corporate Reputation*. Oxford, UK: Oxford University Press, pp. 361–82. doi.org/10.1093/oxfordhb/9780199596706.013.0018.

Karpoff, Jonathan M., D. Scott Lee and Gerald S. Martin. 2008a. 'The consequences to managers for financial misrepresentation.' *Journal of Financial Economics* 88: 193–215. doi.org/10.1016/j.jfineco.2007.06.003.

Karpoff, Jonathan M., D. Scott Lee and Gerald S. Martin. 2008b. 'The cost to firms of cooking the books.' *Journal of Financial and Quantitative Analysis* 43(3): 581–611. doi.org/10.1017/S0022109000004221.

Karstedt, Susanne. 2001. 'Comparing cultures, comparing crime: Challenges, prospects and problems for a global criminology.' *Crime, Law and Social Change* 36(3): 285–308. doi.org/10.1023/A:1012223323445.

Karstedt, Susanne. 2003. 'Legacies of a culture of inequality: The Janus face of crime in post-communist countries.' *Crime, Law and Social Change* 40(2): 295–320. doi.org/10.1023/A:1025767204705.

Karstedt, Susanne. 2006. 'Democracy, values, and violence: Paradoxes, tensions, and comparative advantages of liberal inclusion.' *The ANNALS of the American Academy of Political and Social Science* 605(1): 50–81. doi.org/10.1177/0002716206288248.

Karstedt, Susanne. 2011a. 'Exit: The state, globalisation, state failure and crime.' In David Nelken (ed.), *Comparative Criminal Justice and Globalization*. Dartmouth, UK: Ashgate, 107–22.

Karstedt, Susanne. 2011b. 'Our sense of justice: Values, justice and punishment.' In Stephan Parmentier, Lode Walgrave, Ivo Aertsen, Jeroen Maesschalck and Letizia Paoli (eds), *The Sparking Discipline of Criminology: John Braithwaite and the Construction of Critical Social Science and Social Justice*. Leuven, Belgium: Leuven University Press, pp. 33–58. doi.org/10.2307/j.ctt9qf1n0.6.

Karstedt, Susanne. 2012a. 'Contextualising mass atrocity crimes: The dynamics of "extremely violent societies".' *European Journal of Criminology* 9(5): 499–513. doi.org/10.1177/1477370812454646.

Karstedt, Susanne. 2012b. 'Organised crime, democracy and democratization: How vulnerable are democracies?' In Caroline Y. Robertson-von Trotha (ed.), *Organised Crime: Dark Sides of Globalization*. Baden-Baden, Germany: Nomos Publishing, pp. 95–112. doi.org/10.5771/9783845239057-95.

Karstedt, Susanne. 2014a. Global hotspots of violence: How to focus intervention and prevention. Presentation to 2014 Global Violence Reduction Conference, King's College, University of Cambridge, 17–19 September.

Karstedt, Susanne. 2014b. 'State crime: The European experience.' In Klára Kerezsi, Sonja Snacken, Sophie Body-Gendrot and René Lévy (eds), *The Routledge Handbook of European Criminology*. London: Routledge, pp. 125–53.

Karstedt, Susanne. 2015. 'Does democracy matter? Comparative perspectives on violence and democratic institutions.' *European Journal of Criminology* 12(4): 457–81. doi.org/10.1177/1477370815584499.

Karstedt, Susanne. 2017. 'Scaling criminology: From street violence to atrocity crimes.' In Peter Drahos (ed.), *Regulatory Theory: Foundations and Applications*. Canberra: ANU Press, pp. 465–82. doi.org/10.22459/RT.02.2017.27.

Karstedt, Susanne and Stephen Farrall. 2006. 'The moral economy of everyday crime: Markets, consumers and citizens.' *The British Journal of Criminology* 46(6): 1011–36. doi.org/10.1093/bjc/azl082.

Karstedt, Susanne, Hollie Nyseth Brehm and Laura C. Frizzell. 2021. 'Genocide, mass atrocity, and theories of crime: Unlocking criminology's potential.' *Annual Review of Criminology* 4: 75–97. doi.org/10.1146/annurev-criminol-061020-022050.

Karstedt-Henke, Susanne and Bernhard Crasmoller. 1991. 'Risks of being detected. Chances of getting away.' In Josine Junger-Tas, Leonieke Boendermaker and Peter H. van der Laan (eds), *The Future of the Juvenile Justice System*. Leuven, Belgium: Acco, pp. 33–62.

Kaskutas, Lee Ann. 2009. 'Alcoholics Anonymous effectiveness: Faith meets science.' *Journal of Addictive Diseases* 28(2): 145–57. doi.org/10.1080/10550880902772464.

Katz, Jack. 1988. *Seductions of Crime: Moral and Sensual Attractions of Doing Evil*. New York: Basic Books.

Katz, Sara and Moshe Stupel. 2015. 'Enhancing collective efficacy in mathematics through cooperative implementation of a multiple solution task in a higher education classroom: A qualitative action research.' *Education* 5(4): 98–110.

Kaufman, Joanne M., Cesar J. Rebellon, Sherod Thaxton and Robert Agnew. 2008. 'A general strain theory of racial differences in criminal offending.' *Australian and New Zealand Journal of Criminology* 41(3): 421–37. doi.org/10.1375/acri.41.3.421.

Kelly, John F. 2017. 'Is Alcoholics Anonymous religious, spiritual, neither? Findings from 25 years of mechanisms of behavior change research.' *Addiction* 112(6): 929–36. doi.org/10.1111/add.13590.

Kennedy, David M. 2009. *Deterrence and Crime Prevention: Reconsidering the Prospect of Sanction*. New York: Routledge.

Kennedy, David M. 2017. 'On "changing how police view arrest".' *Criminology & Public Policy* 16(2): 403–9. doi.org/10.1111/1745-9133.12305.

Kennedy, David M., Mark A.R. Kleiman and Anthony A. Braga. 2017. 'Beyond deterrence.' In Nick Tilley and Aiden Sidebottom (eds), *Handbook of Crime Prevention and Community Safety*. London: Routledge, pp. 157–82. doi.org/10.4324/9781315724393-8.

Kennedy, Jay P. 2020. 'From a trickle to a potential torrent: Crime and crime prevention as cascade phenomena.' *International Journal of Comparative and Applied Criminal Justice* 44(3): 189–99. doi.org/10.1080/01924036.2020.1737954.

Ketcham, Ralph (ed.). 1986. *The Anti-Federalist Papers and the Constitutional Convention Debates*. New York: Mentor Books.

Keynes, John Maynard. 2018 [1936]. *The General Theory of Employment, Interest, and Money*. New York: Springer. doi.org/10.1007/978-3-319-70344-2.

Khezri, Haidar. 2019. 'Kurds targeted in Turkish attack include thousands of female fighters who battled Islamic State.' *The Conversation*, 14 October. Available at: theconversation.com/kurds-targeted-in-turkish-attack-include-thousands-of-female-fighters-who-battled-islamic-state-125100.

Kiiwan, Kent A. 1995. 'The use and abuse of power: The Supreme Court and separation of powers.' *The ANNALS of the American Academy of Political and Social Science* 537(1): 76–84. doi.org/10.1177/0002716295537000007.

Kilcullen, David. 2011. *The Accidental Guerrilla: Fighting Small Wars in the Midst of a Big One*. Oxford, UK: Oxford University Press.

Kim, Sang-Weon and William Alex Pridemore. 2005. 'Social change, institutional anomie and serious property crime in transitional Russia.' *The British Journal of Criminology* 45(1): 81–97. doi.org/10.1093/bjc/azh082.

King, Neil, Jr, and Christopher Cooper. 2004. 'Army hired Cuba interrogators via same disputed system in Iraq.' *The Wall Street Journal*, 15 July. Available at: www.wsj.com/articles/SB108984291394664058.

Kinsey, Karyl A. 1986. 'Theories and models of tax cheating.' *Criminal Justice Abstracts* 2: 403–25.

Kirk, David S. 2009. 'Unraveling the contextual effects on student suspension and juvenile arrest: The independent and interdependent influences of school, neighborhood, and family social controls.' *Criminology* 47(2): 479–520. doi.org/10.1111/j.1745-9125.2009.00147.x.

Kirkpatrick, Grant. 2008. *The corporate governance lessons from the financial crisis.* Financial Market Trends Vol. 2009/1. Paris: OECD Publishing. doi.org/10.1787/fmt-v2009-art3-en.

Kis-Katos, Krisztina, Helge Liebert and Günther G. Schulze. 2014. 'On the heterogeneity of terror.' *European Economic Review* 68: 116–36. doi.org/10.1016/j.euroecorev.2014.02.009.

Kleiman, Mark. 2009. *When Brute Force Fails: How to Have Less Crime and Less Punishment.* Princeton, NJ: Princeton University Press. doi.org/10.1515/9781400831265

Klein, Steven. 2020. 'The power of money: Critical theory, capitalism, and the politics of debt.' *Constellations* 27(1): 19–35. doi.org/10.1111/1467-8675.12448.

Klusemann, Stefan. 2012. 'Massacres as process: A micro-sociological theory of internal patterns of mass atrocities.' *European Journal of Criminology* 9(5): 468–80. doi.org/10.1177/1477370812450825.

Knauft, Bruce M. 1987. 'Reconsidering violence in simple human societies: Homicide among the Gebusi of Papua New Guinea.' *Current Anthropology* 28(4): 457–500. doi.org/10.1086/203549.

Knauft, Bruce M. 2002. *Exchanging the Past: A Rainforest World Before and After.* Chicago: University of Chicago Press.

Knauft, Bruce M. 2013. *The Gebusi: Lives Transformed in a Rainforest World.* 3rd edn. New York: McGraw Hill.

Knauft, Bruce M. and Anne-Sylvie Malbrancke. 2017. *Homicide reduction and conflict management in the Nomad sub-district, Papua New Guinea.* Project Report. New York: The Harry Frank Guggenheim Foundation.

Knight, Tony. 1985. 'Schools and delinquency.' In Allan Borowski and James M. Murray (eds), *Juvenile Delinquency in Australia.* Melbourne: Methuen, pp. 257–76.

Kochel, Tammy Rinehart, George W. Burruss and David Weisburd. 2015. *St Louis County hot spots in residential areas (SCHIRA) final report: Assessing the effects of hot spots policing strategies on police legitimacy, crime, and collective efficacy.* Carbondale, IL: Southern Illinois University.

Kochel, Tammy Rinehart and David Weisburd. 2019. 'The impact of hot spots policing on collective efficacy: Findings from a randomized field trial.' *Justice Quarterly* 36(5): 900–28. doi.org/10.1080/07418825.2018.1465579.

Koht, Halvdan. 1972. 'The Nobel Peace Prize Presentation Speech by Halvdan Koht, member of the Nobel Committee, 10 December 1931.' In Frederick W. Haberman (ed.), Nobel Lectures: *Peace 1926–1950.* Amsterdam: Elsevier Publishing Company. Available at: www.nobelprize.org/prizes/peace/1931/ceremony-speech/.

Kohut, Heinz. 1972. 'Thoughts on narcissism and narcissistic rage.' *The Psychoanalytic Study of the Child* 27(1): 360–400. doi.org/10.1080/0079 7308.1972.11822721.

Kokko, Katja, Lea Pulkkinen, L. Rowell Huesmann, Eric F. Dubow and Paul Boxer. 2009. 'Intensity of aggression in childhood as a predictor of different forms of adult aggression: A two-country (Finland and United States) analysis.' *Journal of Research on Adolescents* 19(1): 9–34. doi.org/10.1111/j.1532-7795.2009.00579.x.

Ko Ko, Naing and John Braithwaite. 2019. 'Baptist policing in Burma: Swarming, vigilantism or community self-help?' *Policing and Society* 30(6): 688–703. doi.org/10.1080/10439463.2019.1585849.

Kornhauser, Ruth R. 1978. *Social Sources of Delinquency: An Appraisal of Analytic Models.* Chicago: University of Chicago Press.

Kosolapov, Nikolay. 2008. 'Threshold-point of the US–Russian conflict probability.' *International Trends* 6(3): 15–25.

Kraakman, Rainer H. 1984. 'Corporate liability strategies and the costs of legal controls.' *The Yale Law Journal* 93: 857–98. doi.org/10.2307/796101.

Krajicek, David J. 2017. 'FBI reports violent crime surge, but what does it mean?' *The Crime Report*, 25 September. New York: John Jay College of Criminal Justice. Available at: thecrimereport.org/2017/09/25/fbi-reports-violent-crime-surge-but-what-does-it-mean/.

Kramer, Ronald C., Raymond J. Michalowski and David Kauzlarich. 2002. 'The origins and development of the concept and theory of state-corporate crime.' *Crime & Delinquency* 48(2): 263–82. doi.org/10.1177/0011128702048002 005.

Krastev, Ivan and Stephen Holmes. 2019. *The Light that Failed: A Reckoning*. Colchester, UK: Allen Lane.

Krieger, Tim and Daniel Meirrieks. 2019. 'Income inequality, redistribution and domestic terrorism.' *World Development* 116: 125–36. doi.org/10.1016/j.worlddev.2018.12.008.

Krueger, Alan B. and Jitka Malečková. 2003. 'Education, poverty and terrorism: Is there a causal connection?' *Journal of Economic Perspectives* 17(4): 119–44. doi.org/10.1257/089533003772034925.

Krygier, Martin. 1996a. 'Is there constitutionalism after communism? Institutional optimism, cultural pessimism, and the rule of law.' *International Journal of Sociology* 26(4): 17–47. doi.org/10.1080/15579336.1996.11770146.

Krygier, Martin. 1996b. 'Virtuous circles: Antipodean reflections on power, institutions, and civil society.' *East European Politics and Societies* 11(1): 36–88. doi.org/10.1177/0888325497011001002.

Krygier, Martin. 2017. 'Tempering power.' In Maurice Adams, Anne Meuwese and Ernst Hirsch Ballin (eds), *Constitutionalism and the Rule of Law: Bridging Idealism and Realism*. Cambridge, UK: Cambridge University Press, pp. 34–59. doi.org/10.1017/9781316585221.002.

Krygier, Martin. 2019. 'What's the point of the rule of law?' *Buffalo Law Review* 67(3): 743–92.

Krygier, Martin and Adam Czarnota. 2006. 'After postcommunism: The next phase.' *Annual Review of Law and Social Science* 12: 199–229.

Kun, Ferenc, Imre Varga, Sabine Lennartz-Sassinek and Ian G. Main. 2014. 'Rupture cascades in a discrete element model of a porous sedimentary rock.' *Physics Review Letters* 112(6): 1–5. doi.org/10.1103/PhysRevLett.112.065501.

Kuran, Timur. 1998. 'Ethnic norms and their transformation through reputational cascades.' *The Journal of Legal Studies* 27(S2): 623–59. doi.org/10.1086/468038.

Kurrild-Klitgaard Krueger, Peter, Mogens K. Justesen and Robert Klemmensen. 2006. 'The political economy of freedom, democracy and transnational terrorism.' *Public Choice* 128(1–2): 289–315. doi.org/10.1007/s11127-006-9055-7.

Kuttippurath, Jayanarayanan and Prijitha J. Nair. 2017. 'The signs of Antarctic ozone hole recovery.' *Scientific Reports* 7(1): 1–8. doi.org/10.1038/s41598-017-00722-7.

Lacey, Nicola. 2008. *The Prisoners' Dilemma: Political Economy and Punishment in Contemporary Democracies*. Cambridge, UK: Cambridge University Press. doi.org/10.1017/CBO9780511819247.

Lackey, Jennifer H. 2016. A model of rural delinquency: Collective efficacy in rural schools. PhD dissertation, Bowling Green State University, Bowling Green, OH.

Laclau, Ernesto. 2005. *On Populist Reason*. London: Verso.

Laclau, Ernesto and Chantal Mouffe. 1985. *Hegemony and Socialist Strategy: Towards a Radical Democratic Politics*. London: Verso.

LaFree, Gary and Kriss A. Drass. 2002. 'Counting crime booms among nations: Evidence for homicide victimization rates, 1956 to 1998.' *Criminology* 40(4): 769–800. doi.org/10.1111/j.1745-9125.2002.tb00973.x.

LaFree, Gary, Michael A. Jensen, Patrick A. James and Aaron Safer-Lichtenstein. 2018. 'Correlates of violent political extremism in the United States.' *Criminology* 56(2): 233–68. doi.org/10.1111/1745-9125.12169.

Lajeunesse, Thérèse. 1993. *Community Holistic Circle Healing: Hollow Water First Nation*. Ottawa: Corrections Branch, Solicitor General Canada.

Lake, David A. and Donald Rothchild (eds). 1998. *The International Spread of Ethnic Conflict: Fear, Diffusion and Escalation*. Princeton, NJ: Princeton University Press. doi.org/10.1515/9780691219752.

Lampert, Nick. 1984. 'Law and order in the USSR: The case of economic and official crime.' *Soviet Studies* 36(3): 366–85. doi.org/10.1080/09668138408411539.

Landau, Simha F. 1997. 'Homicide in Israel: Its relation to subjective stress and support indicators on the macro level.' *Homicide Studies* 1(4): 377–400. doi.org/10.1177/1088767997001004005.

Landau, Simha F. 2003. 'Societal costs of political violence: The Israeli experience.' *Palestine–Israel Journal of Politics, Economics, and Culture* 10(1): 28–35.

Landau, Simha F., Shira Dvir Gvirsman, L. Rowell Huesmann, Eric F. Dubow, Paul Boxer, Jeremy Ginges and Khalil Shikaki. 2010. 'The effects of exposure to violence on aggressive behavior: The case of Arab and Jewish children in Israel.' In Karin Osterman (ed.), *Indirect and Direct Aggression*. Frankfurt am Main: Peter Lang, pp. 321–43.

Landau, Simha F. and Danny Pfeffermann. 1988. 'A time-series analysis of violent crime and its relation to prolonged states of warfare: The Israeli case.' *Criminology* 26(3): 489–504. doi.org/10.1111/j.1745-9125.1988.tb00852.x.

Landes, William. 1978. 'An economic study of US aircraft hijacking, 1961–1976.' *Journal of Law and Economics* 21(1): 1–32. doi.org/10.1086/466909.

Landis, Judson R. 1962. Social class differentials in self, value, and opportunity structure as related to delinquency potential. PhD dissertation, Ohio State University, Columbus.

Langton, Marcia. 1992. 'The Wentworth Lecture: Aborigines and policing—Aboriginal solutions from Northern Territory communities.' *Australian Aboriginal Studies* 2: 2–14.

Lansky, Melvin R. 1984. 'Violence, shame, and the family.' *International Journal of Family Psychiatry* 5(1): 21–40.

Lansky, Melvin R. 1987. 'Shame and domestic violence.' In Donald L. Nathanson (ed.), *The Many Faces of Shame*. New York: Guilford, pp. 335–62.

Lappi-Seppälä, Tapio and Martti Lehti. 2014. 'Cross-comparative perspectives on global homicide trends.' *Crime and Justice* 43(1): 135–230. doi.org/10.1086/677979.

Latimer, Jeff, Craig Dowden and Danielle Muise. 2001. *The Effectiveness of Restorative Justice Practices: A Meta-Analysis*. Ottawa: Research and Statistics Division, Department of Justice Canada.

Latour, Bruno. 1986. 'The powers of association.' In John Law (ed.), *Power, Action and Belief: A New Sociology of Knowledge?* London: Routledge & Kegan Paul, pp. 264–80.

Lattimore, Pamela K., Doris Layton MacKenzie, Gary Zajac, Debbie Dawes, Elaine Arsenault and Stephen Tueller. 2016. 'Outcome findings from the HOPE demonstration field experiment.' *Criminology and Public Policy* 15(4): 1103–41. doi.org/10.1111/1745-9133.12248.

Laub, John H. and Robert J. Sampson. 2003. *Shared Beginnings, Divergent Lives: Delinquent Boys to Age 70*. Cambridge, MA: Harvard University Press.

Laudet, Alexandre B. and William L. White. 2008. 'Recovery capital as prospective predictor of sustained recovery, life satisfaction and stress among former poly-substance users.' *Substance Use & Misuse* 43(1): 27–54. doi.org/10.1080/10826080701681473.

Leach, Colin Wayne and Atilla Cidam. 2015. 'When is shame linked to constructive approach orientation? A meta-analysis.' *Journal of Personality and Social Psychology* 109(6): 983–1002. doi.org/10.1037/pspa0000037.

Leamy, Mary, Victoria Bird, Clair Le Boutillier, Julie Williams and Mike Slade. 2011. 'Conceptual framework for personal recovery in mental health: Systematic review and narrative synthesis protocol.' *The British Journal of Psychiatry* 199(6): 445–52. doi.org/10.1192/bjp.bp.110.083733.

LeBel, Thomas P., Matt Richie and Shadd Maruna. 2015. 'Helping others as a response to reconcile a criminal past: The role of the wounded healer in prisoner reentry programs.' *Criminal Justice and Behavior* 42(1): 108–20. doi.org/10.1177/0093854814550029.

Lederman, Daniel, Norman Loayza and Ana Maria Menendez. 2002. 'Violent crime: Does social capital matter?' *Economic Development and Cultural Change* 50(3): 509–39. doi.org/10.1086/342422.

Lee, Mark H. 2020. *How to Grow a Robot.* Cambridge, MA: MIT Press. doi.org/10.7551/mitpress/12511.001.0001.

Lee, Matthew T., Maria E. Pagano, Byron R. Johnson, Stephen G. Post, George S. Leibowitz and Matthew Dudas. 2017. 'From defiance to reliance: Spiritual virtue as a pathway towards desistence, humility, and recovery among juvenile offenders.' *Spirituality in Clinical Practice* 4(3): 161–75. doi.org/10.1037/scp0000144.

Leithwood, Kenneth and Jingping Sun. 2012. 'The nature and effects of transformational school leadership: A meta-analytic review of unpublished research.' *Educational Administration Quarterly* 48(3): 387–423. doi.org/10.1177/0013161X11436268.

Lemmon, Gayle Tzemach. 2021. *The Daughters of Kobani: A Story of Rebellion, Courage, and Justice.* New York: Penguin.

Leonard, William N. and Marvin Glenn Weber. 1970. 'Automakers and dealers: A study of criminogenic market forces.' *Law & Society Review* 4(3): 407–24. doi.org/10.2307/3053094.

Leone, Andrew J., Edward Xuejun Li and Michelle Liu. 2021. 'On the SEC's 2010 enforcement cooperation program.' *Journal of Accounting and Economics* 71(1): 101355. doi.org/10.1016/j.jacceco.2020.101355.

Lessing, Benjamin. 2018. *Making Peace in Drug Wars: Crackdowns and Cartels in Latin America.* Cambridge, UK: Cambridge University Press. doi.org/10.1017/9781108185837.

Levi-Faur, David. 2014. 'The welfare state: A regulatory perspective.' *Public Administration* 92(3): 599–614. doi.org/10.1111/padm.12063.

Levine, Donald N. 1988. *The Flight from Ambiguity: Essays in Social and Cultural Theory*. Chicago: University of Chicago Press.

Levinson, David. 1989. *Family Violence in Cross-Cultural Perspective*. Thousand Oaks, CA: Sage Publications. doi.org/10.1007/978-1-4757-5360-8_18.

Lewis, Helen. 1971. *Shame and Guilt in Neurosis*. New York: International Universities Press.

Lewis, Michael. 2010. *The Big Short: Inside the Doomsday Machine*. New York: W.W. Norton.

Li, Chen, Huanhuan Zheng and Yunbo Liu. 2020. 'The hybrid regulatory regime in turbulent times: The role of the state in China's stock market crisis in 2015–2016.' *Regulation & Governance*: 1–17. doi.org/10.1111/rego.12340.

Li, Wei and Brooke Ackerly. 2021. '(Ren)ovating feminism: Confucian feminism in times of political transformation in China.' *Proceedings of MidWest Political Science Association Annual Conference*.

Lieberman, Jethro Koller. 1973. *How the Government Breaks the Law*. Baltimore, MD: Penguin.

Lifton, Robert Jay. 1986. *The Nazi Doctors: Medical Killing and the Psychology of Genocide*. New York: Basic Books.

Lilley, Robert J. 2007. *Taken by Force: Rape and American GIs in Europe during World War II*. New York: Palgrave Macmillan.

Lin, Ming-Jen. 2008. 'Does unemployment increase crime? Evidence from US data 1974–2000.' *Journal of Human Resources* 43(2): 413–36. doi.org/10.1353/jhr.2008.0022.

Linder, Wolf and André Bächtiger. 2005. 'What drives democratisation in Asia and Africa?' *European Journal of Political Research* 44(6): 861–80. doi.org/10.1111/j.1475-6765.2005.00250.x.

Linebarger, Paul Myron Anthony. 1937. *The Political Doctrines of Sun Yat-sen: An Exposition of the San Min Chu I. Volume 1*. Baltimore, MD: Johns Hopkins University Press.

Lipsey, Mark W. 2009. 'The primary factors that characterize effective interventions with juvenile offenders: A meta-analytic overview.' *Victims and Offenders* 4(2): 124–47. doi.org/10.1080/15564880802612573.

Lipsky, Michael. 2010. *Street-Level Bureaucracy: Dilemmas of the Individual in Public Service*. New York: Russell Sage Foundation.

Lipton, Douglas S., Robert Martinson and Judith Wilks. 1975. *The Effectiveness of Correctional Treatment: A Survey of Treatment Evaluation Studies*. New York: Praeger.

Liu, Jianhong and George B. Palermo. 2009. 'Restorative justice and Chinese traditional legal culture in the context of contemporary Chinese criminal justice.' *Asia Pacific Journal of Police & Criminal Justice* 7(1): 49–68.

Liu, Jianhong, Ruohui Zhao, Haiyan Xiong and Jinlin Gong. 2012. 'Chinese legal traditions: Punitiveness versus mercy.' *Asia Pacific Journal of Police & Criminal Justice* 9(1): 17–33.

Llewellyn, Jennifer J. 2012. 'Integrating peace, justice and development in a relational approach to peacebuilding.' *Ethics and Social Welfare* 6(3): 290–302. doi.org/10.1080/17496535.2012.704386.

Loader, Ian and Richard Sparks. 2013. *Public Criminology?* London: Routledge. doi.org/10.4324/9780203846049.

Locke, John. 1960. *Two Treatises of Government*. Cambridge, UK: Cambridge University Press.

Loftin, Colin. 1986. 'Assaultive violence as a contagious social process.' *Bulletin of the New York Academy of Medicine* 62(5): 550–55.

Lorde, Audre. 1984. 'The master's tools will never dismantle the master's house.' In *Sister Outsider: Essays and Speeches*. Berkeley, CA: Crossing Press, pp. 110–14.

Łoś, Maria (ed.). 1990. *The Second Economy in Marxist States*. New York: St Martin's Press. doi.org/10.1007/978-1-349-20422-9.

Lu, Hong. 1999. 'Bang jiao and reintegrative shaming in China's urban neighborhoods.' *International Journal of Comparative and Applied Criminal Justice* 23(1): 115–25.

Lukes, Steven. 1974. *Power: A Radical View*. London: Macmillan.

Lundahl, Brad W., Chelsea Kunz, Cynthia Brownell, Derrik Tollefson and Brian L. Burke. 2010. 'A meta-analysis of motivational interviewing: Twenty-five years of empirical studies.' *Research on Social Work Practice* 20(2): 137–60. doi.org/10.1177/1049731509347850.

Ma, Herbert Han-Pao. 1963. 'Chinese control yuan: An independent supervisory organ of the state.' *Washington University Law Quarterly* 1963(4): 401–26.

MacCoun, Robert J. and Peter Reuter. 2001. *Drug War Heresies: Learning from Other Vices, Times, and Places*. New York: Cambridge University Press. doi.org/10.1017/CBO9780511754272.

MacDonagh, Oliver. 1961. *A Pattern of Government Growth 1800–60: The Passenger Acts and their Enforcement*. London: MacGibbon & Kee.

Mahbubani, Kishore. 2020. *Has China Won? The Chinese Challenge to American Primacy*. New York: Hachette Book Group.

Maher, Amanda. 2016. 'What Skinner misses about Machiavelli's freedom: Inequality, corruption and institutional origins of civic virtue.' *The Journal of Politics* 78(4): 1003–15. doi.org/10.1086/686803.

Maimon, David, Christopher R. Browning and Jeanne Brooks-Gunn. 2010. 'Collective efficacy, family attachment, and urban adolescent suicide attempts.' *Journal of Health and Social Behavior* 51(3): 307–24. doi.org/10.1177/0022146510377878.

Makarios, Matthew D. and Travis C. Pratt. 2012. 'The effectiveness of policies and programs that attempt to reduce firearm violence: A meta-analysis.' *Crime & Delinquency* 58(2): 222–44. doi.org/10.1177/0011128708321321.

Makkai, Toni and John Braithwaite. 1993. 'Praise, pride and corporate compliance.' *International Journal of the Sociology of Law* 21: 73–91.

Makkai, Toni and John Braithwaite. 1994a. 'The dialectics of corporate deterrence.' *Journal of Research in Crime and Delinquency* 31(4): 347–73. doi.org/10.1177/0022427894031004001.

Makkai, Toni and John Braithwaite. 1994b. 'Reintegrative shaming and compliance with regulatory standards.' *Criminology* 32(3): 361–85. doi.org/10.1111/j.1745-9125.1994.tb01158.x.

Manchak, Sarah M. and Francis T. Cullen. 2015. 'Intervening effectively with juvenile offenders: Answers from meta-analysis.' In Julien Morizot and Lila Kazemian (eds), *The Development of Criminal and Antisocial Behavior*. New York: Springer, pp. 477–90. doi.org/10.1007/978-3-319-08720-7_30.

Manin, Bernard. 1994. 'Checks, balances and boundaries: The separation of powers in the constitutional debate of 1787.' In Biancamaria Fontana (ed.), *The Invention of the Modern Republic*. Cambridge, UK: Cambridge University Press, pp. 27–62. doi.org/10.1017/CBO9780511558443.003.

Mann, Michael. 1986. *The Sources of Social Power. Volume 1: A History of Power from the Beginning to AD 1760*. Cambridge, UK: Cambridge University Press.

Mann, Michael. 1993. *The Sources of Social Power. Volume II: The Rise of Classes and Nation-States, 1760–1914*. Cambridge, UK: Cambridge University Press.

Marc, Alexandre. 2016. *Conflict and Violence in the 21st Century: Current Trends as Observed in Empirical Research and Statistics*. Washington, DC: World Bank Group.

Marks, Monique. 2001. *Young Warriors*. Johannesburg: University of Witwatersrand Press.

Marmot, Michael and Sharon Friel. 2008. 'Global health equity: Evidence for action on the social determinants of health.' *Journal of Epidemiology & Community Health* 62(12): 1095–97. doi.org/10.1136/jech.2008.081695.

Marongiu, Pietro and Graeme Newman. 1987. *Vengeance: The Fight against Injustice*. Totowa, NJ: Rowman & Littlefield.

Maršanić, Vlatka Boričević, Branka Aukst Margetić, Iva Zečević and Miroslav Herceg. 2014. 'The prevalence and psychosocial correlates of suicide attempts among inpatient adolescent offspring of Croatian PTSD male war veterans.' *Child Psychiatry & Human Development* 45(5): 577–87. doi.org/10.1007/s10578-013-0426-2.

Marsavelski, Aleksandar and John Braithwaite. 2018. 'The best way to rob a bank.' *International Journal for Crime, Justice and Social Democracy* 7(1): 123–38. doi.org/10.5204/ijcjsd.v7i1.466.

Marsavelski, Aleksandar and John Braithwaite. 2020. 'Transitional justice cascades.' *Cornell International Law Journal* 53(2). Available at: papers.ssrn.com/sol3/papers.cfm?abstract_id=3380304.

Marsavelski, Aleksandar, Furtuna Sheremeti and John Braithwaite. 2018. 'Did nonviolent resistance fail in Kosovo?' *The British Journal of Criminology* 58(1): 218–36. doi.org/10.1093/bjc/azx002.

Marshall, Shelley. 2019. *Living Wage: Regulatory Solutions to Informal and Precarious Work in Global Supply Chains*. Oxford, UK: Oxford University Press. doi.org/10.1093/oso/9780198830351.001.0001.

Marti, José Luis and Philip Pettit. 2010. *A Political Philosophy in Public Life: Civic Republicanism in Zapatero's Spain*. Princeton, NJ: Princeton University Press. doi.org/10.1515/9781400835058.

Martin, Randy. 2000. 'Anomie, spirituality, and crime.' *Journal of Contemporary Criminal Justice* 16(1): 75–98. doi.org/10.1177/1043986200016001005.

Maruna, Shadd. 2001. *Making Good*. Washington, DC: American Psychological Association.

Marx, Karl. 1973. *Economic and Philosophic Manuscripts of 1844*. M. Milligan, trans. London: Lawrence & Wishart.

Masclet, David, Claude Montmarquette and Nathalie Viennot-Briot. 2019. 'Can whistleblower programs reduce tax evasion? Experimental evidence.' *Journal of Behavioral and Experimental Economics* 83: 101459. doi.org/10.1016/j.socec.2019.101459.

Masten, Ann S., Glenn I. Roisman, Jeffrey D. Long, Keith B. Burt, Jelena Obradović, Jennifer R. Riley, Kristen Boelcke-Stennes and Auke Tellegen. 2005. 'Developmental cascades: Linking academic achievement and externalizing and internalizing symptoms over 20 years.' *Developmental Psychology* 41(5): 733–46. doi.org/10.1037/0012-1649.41.5.733.

Matza, David. 1964. *Delinquency and Drift*. New York: Wiley.

Mawson, E., D. Best, M. Beckwith, G.A. Dingle and D.I. Lubman. 2015. 'Social identity, social networks and recovery capital in emerging adulthood: A pilot study.' *Substance Abuse Treatment, Prevention, and Policy* 10(45). doi.org/10.1186/s13011-015-0041-2.

Maxwell, Gabrielle and Allison Morris. 2002. 'The role of shame, guilt, and remorse in restorative justice processes for young people.' In Elmar G.M. Weitekamp and Hans-Jürgen Kerner (eds), *Restorative Justice: Theoretical Foundations*. Cullompton, UK: Willan, pp. 267–84.

Mazzolini, Gabriele, Laura Pagani and Alessandro Santoro. 2017. *The deterrence effect of real-world operational tax audits*. Working Paper No. 359. Milan: Department of Economics, Management, and Statistics, University of Milano-Bicocca. doi.org/10.2139/ssrn.2914374.

McCloy, John J. 1976. *The Great Oil Spill*. New York: Chelsea House.

McCold, Paul. 2008. 'Evaluation of a restorative milieu: Restorative practices in context.' In Holly Ventura (ed.), *Restorative Justice: From Theory to Practice. Sociology of Crime, Law and Deviance Series, Volume 11*. Bingley, UK: Emerald Group Publishing, pp. 99–138. doi.org/10.1016/S1521-6136(08)00405-3.

McCoy, Alfred W. 1972. *The Politics of Heroin in Southeast Asia*. New York: Harper Torchbooks.

McEvoy, Kieran and Peter Shirlow. 2009. 'Re-imagining DDR: Ex-combatants, leadership and moral agency in conflict transformation.' *Theoretical Criminology* 13(1): 31–59. doi.org/10.1177/1362480608100172.

McEwan, Desmond, Geralyn R. Ruissen, Mark A. Eys, Bruno D. Zumbo and Mark R. Beauchamp. 2017. 'The effectiveness of teamwork training on teamwork behaviors and team performance: A systematic review and meta-analysis of controlled interventions.' *PLoS One* 12(1): e0169604. doi.org/10.1371/journal.pone.0169604.

McLeigh, Jill D., James R. McDonell and Osnat Lavenda. 2018. 'Neighborhood poverty and child abuse and neglect: The mediating role of social cohesion.' *Children and Youth Services Review* 93: 154–60. doi.org/10.1016/j.childyouth.2018.07.018.

Meister, Robert. 1999. 'Forgiving and forgetting: Lincoln and the politics of national recovery.' In Carla Hesse and Robert Post (eds), *Human Rights in Political Transitions*. New York: Zone Press, pp. 135–75.

Melander, Erik. 2005. 'Gender equality and interstate armed conflict.' *International Studies Quarterly* 49(4): 695–714. doi.org/10.1111/j.1468-2478.2005.00384.x.

Mendoza, Juan P., Jacco L. Wielhouwer and Erich Kirchler. 2017. 'The backfiring effect of auditing on tax compliance.' *Journal of Economic Psychology* 62: 284–94. doi.org/10.1016/j.joep.2017.07.007.

Mennis, Jeremy and Philip Harris. 2011. 'Contagion and repeat offending among urban juvenile delinquents.' *Journal of Adolescence* 34(5): 951–63. doi.org/10.1016/j.adolescence.2010.12.001.

Merry, Sally Engle. 2006. *Human Rights and Gender Violence: Translating International Law into Local Justice*. Chicago: University of Chicago Press. doi.org/10.7208/chicago/9780226520759.001.0001.

Merton, Robert K. 1938. 'Social structure and anomie.' *American Sociological Review* 3(5): 672–82. doi.org/10.2307/2084686.

Merton, Robert K. 1968. *Social Theory and Social Structure*. Enlarged edn. New York: The Free Press.

Merton, Robert K. 1995. 'Opportunity structure: The emergence, diffusion, and differentiation of a sociological concept, 1930s–1950s.' In Freda Adler and William S. Laufer (eds), *The Legacy of Anomie Theory: Advances in Criminological Research. Volume 6*. New Brunswick, NJ: Transaction Publishers, pp. 3–78. doi.org/10.1201/9780429335945-2.

Merton, Robert K. 1997. 'On the evolving synthesis of differential association and anomie theory: A perspective from the sociology of science.' *Criminology* 35: 517–25. doi.org/10.1111/j.1745-9125.1997.tb01228.x.

Messerschmidt, James W. 2006. 'Review symposium: The forgotten victims of World War II—Masculinities and rape in Berlin, 1945.' *Violence Against Women* 12(7): 706–12. doi.org/10.1177/1077801206290691.

Messner, Steven F. and Richard Rosenfeld. 1997. 'Political restraint of the market and levels of criminal homicide: A cross-national application of institutional-anomie theory.' *Social Forces* 75(4): 1393–416. doi.org/10.1093/sf/75.4.1393.

Messner, Steven F. and Richard Rosenfeld. 2001. 'An institutional-anomie theory of crime.' In Raymond Paternoster and Ronet Bachman (eds), *Explaining Criminals and Crime*. Los Angeles: Roxbury, pp. 151–60.

Messner, Steven F. and Richard Rosenfeld. 2013. *Crime and the American Dream*. Belmont, CA: Wadsworth.

Messner, Steven F., Lening Zhang, Sheldon X. Zhang and Colin P. Gruner. 2017. 'Neighborhood crime control in a changing China: Tiao-Jie, Bang-Jiao, and neighborhood watches.' *Journal of Research in Crime and Delinquency* 54(4): 544–77. doi.org/10.1177/0022427816682059.

Michalowski, Raymond and Kevin Bitten. 2005. 'Transnational environmental crime.' In Philip Reichel (ed.), *Handbook of Transnational Crime and Justice*. Thousand Oaks, CA: Sage, pp. 139–59. doi.org/10.4135/9781412976183. n8.

Miguel, Edward, Sebastián M. Saiegh and Shanker Satyanath. 2008. *National cultures and soccer violence*. NBER Working Paper No. 13968. Cambridge, MA: National Bureau of Economic Research. doi.org/10.3386/w13968.

Mikler, John. 2009. *Greening the Car Industry: Varieties of Capitalism and Climate Change*. Cheltenham, UK: Edward Elgar Publishing. doi.org/10.4337/9781849802246.

Miller, Susan L. and M. Kristen Hefner. 2015. 'Procedural justice for victims and offenders? Exploring restorative justice processes in Australia and the US.' *Justice Quarterly* 32(1): 142–67. doi.org/10.1080/07418825.2012.760643.

Miller, William R. 2007. 'Bring addiction treatment out of the closet.' *Addiction* 102(6): 863. doi.org/10.1111/j.1360-0443.2007.01830.x.

Mills, Michael J., Owen B. Toon, Julia Lee-Taylor and Alan Robock. 2014. 'Multidecadal global cooling and unprecedented ozone loss following a regional nuclear conflict.' *Earth's Future* 2(4): 161–76. doi.org/10.1002/2013 EF000205.

Min, Jiayin. 1995. *The Chalice and the Blade in Chinese Culture: Gender Relations and Social Models*. Beijing: China Social Sciences Publication House.

Mitchell, Ronald. 1994a. *Intentional Oil Pollution at Sea: Environmental Policy and Treaty Compliance.* Cambridge, MA: MIT Press.

Mitchell, Ronald. 1994b. 'Regime design matters: Intentional oil pollution and treaty compliance.' *International Organization* 48(3): 425–58. doi.org/10.1017/S0020818300028253.

Mittal, Mamta, Lalit Mohan Goyal, Jasleen Kaur Sethi and D. Jude Hemanth. 2019. 'Monitoring the impact of economic crisis on crime in India using machine learning.' *Computational Economics* 53(4): 1467–85. doi.org/10.1007/s10614-018-9821-x.

Moffitt, Terrie E., Avshalom Caspi, Honalee Harrington and Barry J. Milne. 2002. 'Males on the life-course-persistent and adolescence-limited antisocial pathways: Follow-up at age 26 years.' *Development and Psychopathology* 14(1): 179–207. doi.org/10.1017/S0954579402001104.

Mohler, George. 2013. 'Modeling and estimation of multi-source clustering in crime and security data.' *The Annals of Applied Statistics* 7(3): 1525–39. doi.org/10.1214/13-AOAS647.

Mok, Louis W.Y. and Dennis S.W. Wong. 2013. 'Restorative justice and mediation: Diverged or converged?' *Asian Journal of Criminology* 8(4): 335–47. doi.org/10.1007/s11417-013-9170-6.

Montesquieu, Charles-Louis de Secondat, Baron de. 1977. *The Spirit of the Laws: A Compendium of the First English Edition, Edited, with an Introduction, Notes and Appendixes, by David Wallace Carrithers.* Thomas Nugent, trans. Berkeley, CA: University of California Press.

Moore, Barrington. 1966. *Social Origins of Dictatorship and Democracy.* Boston, MA: Beacon Press.

Moore, Sally Falk. 1978. *Law as Process: An Anthropological Approach.* London: Routledge & Kegan Paul.

Morenoff, Jeffrey D., Robert J. Sampson and Stephen W. Raudenbush. 2001. 'Neighborhood inequality, collective efficacy, and the spatial dynamics of urban violence.' *Criminology* 39(3): 517–58. doi.org/10.1111/j.1745-9125.2001.tb00932.x.

Morgan, Bronwen. 2003. 'The economization of politics: Meta-regulation as a form of nonjudicial legality.' *Social & Legal Studies* 12(4): 489–523. doi.org/10.1177/0964663903012004004.

Morgenson, Gretchen. 2010. 'Raters ignored proof of unsafe loans, panel is told.' *The New York Times*, 26 September. Available at: www.nytimes.com/2010/09/27/business/27ratings.html.

Morgenthau, Hans. 1973. *Politics among Nations*. 5th edn. New York: Alfred A. Knopf.

Morris, Ian. 2014. *War! What Is It Good For? Conflict and the Progress of Civilization from Primates to Robots*. New York: Farrar, Straus & Giroux.

Morris, Nancy A. and Gary LaFree. 2016. 'Country-level predictors of terrorism.' In Gary LaFree and Joshua D. Frelich (eds), *The Handbook of the Criminology of Terrorism*. New York: Wiley, pp. 93–117. doi.org/10.1002/9781118923986.ch6.

Morris, Norval and Gordon J. Hawkins. 1969. *The Honest Politician's Guide to Crime Control*. Chicago: University of Chicago Press.

Morrison, Brenda. 2007. *Restoring Safe School Communities: A Whole School Response to Bullying, Violence and Alienation*. Sydney: The Federation Press.

Mouffe, Chantal. 2005. *On the Political*. London: Routledge.

Mouffe, Chantal. 2013. *Agonistics: Thinking the World Politically*. London: Verso.

Mouffe, Chantal. 2018. *For a Left Populism*. London: Verso.

Mouzos, Jenny. 2001. *Indigenous and Non-Indigenous Homicides in Australia: A Comparative Analysis*. Canberra: Australian Institute of Criminology.

Muggah, Robert and Keith Krause. 2011. 'Closing the gap between peace operations and post-conflict insecurity: Towards a violence-reduction agenda.' In James Cockayne and Adam Lupel (eds), *Peace Operations and Organized Crime: Enemies or Allies?* London: Routledge, pp. 174–89.

Muir, Rick and Imogen Parker. 2014. *Many to Many: How the Relational State Will Transform Public Services*. London: Institute for Public Policy Research.

Muller, Christopher, Robert J. Sampson and Alix S. Winter. 2018. 'Environmental inequality: The social causes and consequences of lead exposure.' *Annual Review of Sociology* 44: 263–82. doi.org/10.1146/annurev-soc-073117-041222.

Nagin, Daniel S. 2013. 'Deterrence in the twenty-first century.' *Crime and Justice* 42(1): 199–263. doi.org/10.1086/670398.

Nagin, Daniel S., Francis T. Cullen and Cheryl L. Jonson. 2009. 'Imprisonment and reoffending.' *Crime and Justice* 38(1): 115–200. doi.org/10.1086/599202.

Nagin, Daniel S. and Robert J. Sampson. 2019. 'The real gold standard: Measuring counterfactual worlds that matter most to social science and policy.' *Annual Review of Criminology* 2: 123–45. doi.org/10.1146/annurev-criminol-011518-024838.

Nagin, Daniel S., Robert M. Solow and Cynthia Lum. 2015. 'Deterrence, criminal opportunities, and police.' *Criminology* 53(1): 74–100. doi.org/10.1111/1745-9125.12057.

Nagin, Daniel S. and Cody W. Telep. 2021. 'Procedural justice and legal compliance.' In Benjamin van Rooij and D. Daniel Sokol (eds), *Cambridge Handbook of Compliance*. Cambridge, UK: Cambridge University Press, pp. 385–403. doi.org/10.1017/9781108759458.027.

Nagin, Daniel S. and David Weisburd. 2013. 'Evidence and public policy: The example of evaluation research in policing.' *Criminology & Public Policy* 12(4): 651–79. doi.org/10.1111/1745-9133.12030.

Naji, Abu Bakr. 2004. *The Management of Savagery: The Most Critical Stage through Which the Umma Will Pass*. William F. McCants, trans. [Online publication.] Accessed at: azelin.files.wordpress.com/2010/08/abu-bakr-naji-the-management-of-savagery-the-most-critical-stage-through-which-the-umma-will-pass.pdf [page discontinued].

Narvey, Chelsey, Nicole Leeper Piquero and Alex R. Piquero. 2021. 'Countries where women have more positive interactions with economic decisions and legal rights have lower homicide rates: An exploratory study.' *Journal of Family Violence* 36: 63–73. doi.org/10.1007/s10896-020-00148-2.

National Security Archive. 2020a. 'False warnings of Soviet missile attacks put US forces on alert in 1979–1980.' In William Burr (ed.), *Briefing Book #699*, 16 March. Washington, DC: National Security Archive.

National Security Archive. 2020b. 'National security archive posts key records on strategic nuclear planning, presidential control, and new weapons.' In William Burr (ed.), *Briefing Book #705*, 22 May. Washington, DC: National Security Archive.

Native Counselling Services of Alberta. 2001. *A Cost–Benefit Analysis of Hollow Water's Community Holistic Circle Healing Process*. Ottawa: Public Safety, Canada.

Needleman, Martin L. and Carolyn Needleman. 1979. 'Organizational crime: Two models of criminogenesis.' *The Sociological Quarterly* 20(4): 517–28. doi.org/10.1111/j.1533-8525.1979.tb01232.x.

Negri, Antonio and Michael Hardt. 2000. *Empire*. Cambridge, MA: Harvard University Press.

Nepal, Mani, Alok K. Bohara and Kishore Gawande. 2011. 'More inequality, more killings: The Maoist insurgency in Nepal.' *American Journal of Political Science* 55(4): 886–906. doi.org/10.1111/j.1540-5907.2011.00529.x.

Neustadt, Richard E. and Ernest R. May. 1986. *Thinking in Time: Uses of History in Decision Making*. New York: Macmillan.

New York State Special Commission on Attica. 1972. *Attica: The Official Report of the New York State Special Commission on Attica*. New York: Praeger Publishers.

The New York Times. 2010. 'All Clayton trending reports 1st quarter 2006 – 2nd quarter 2007.' *The New York Times*, 26 September.

Nguyen, Tomson H. and Henry N. Pontell. 2010. 'Mortgage origination fraud and the global economic crisis: A criminological analysis.' *Criminology and Public Policy* 9(3): 591–612. doi.org/10.1111/j.1745-9133.2010.00653.x.

Nickson, Ray and Alice Neikirk. 2018. *Managing Transitional Justice: Expectations of International Criminal Trials*. New York: Palgrave Macmillan. doi.org/10.1007/978-3-319-77782-5.

Nilsson, Desirée. 2006. In the shadow of settlement: Multiple rebel groups and precarious peace. Doctoral dissertation, Faculty of Social Sciences, Department of Peace and Conflict Research, Uppsala University, Sweden. Available at: www.diva-portal.org/smash/record.jsf?pid=diva2%3A168691&dswid=-3789.

Nivette, Amy E. 2011. 'Cross-national predictors of crime: A meta-analysis.' *Homicide Studies* 15(2): 103–31. doi.org/10.1177/1088767911406397.

Nivette, Amy E., Manuel Eisner, Tina Malti and Denis Ribeaud. 2015. 'The social and developmental antecedents of legal cynicism.' *Journal of Research in Crime and Delinquency* 52(2): 270–98. doi.org/10.1177/0022427814557038.

Nordin, Martin and Daniel Almén. 2017. 'Long-term unemployment and violent crime.' *Empirical Economics* 52(1): 1–29. doi.org/10.1007/s00181-016-1068-6.

North, Douglass. 1990. *Institutional Change and Economic Performance*. Cambridge, UK: Cambridge University Press.

North, Douglass, John Wallis and Barry Weingast. 2009. *Violence and Social Orders: A Conceptual Framework for Interpreting Recorded Human History.* New York: Cambridge University Press. doi.org/10.1017/CBO9780511575839.

Nowak, Martin A. 2012. 'Evolving cooperation.' *Journal of Theoretical Biology* 299: 1–8. doi.org/10.1016/j.jtbi.2012.01.014.

Nunn, Nathan. 2008. 'The long-term effects of Africa's slave trades.' *The Quarterly Journal of Economics* 123(1): 139–76. doi.org/10.1162/qjec.2008.123.1.139.

Obaji, Philip. 2020. 'Mali coup leaders seized power days after returning from military training camp in Russia.' *The Daily Beast*, [New York], 21 August.

O'Brien, Justin. 2009. *Engineering a Financial Bloodbath: How Sub-Prime Securitization Destroyed the Legitimacy of Financial Capitalism.* London: Imperial College Press. doi.org/10.1142/p565.

Odgers, Candice L., Terrie E. Moffitt, Laura M. Tach, Robert J. Sampson, Alan Taylor, Charlotte L. Matthews and Avshalom Caspi. 2009. 'The protective effects of neighborhood collective efficacy on British children growing up in deprivation: A developmental analysis.' *Developmental Psychology* 45(4): 942–57. doi.org/10.1037/a0016162.

The Office of the Prosecutor (OTP). 2013. *Strategic Plan June 2012–2015.* 11 October. The Hague: International Criminal Court Office of the Prosecutor. Available at: www.icc-cpi.int/iccdocs/otp/OTP-Strategic-Plan-2013.pdf.

O'Keefe, Kate and Aruna Viswanatha. 2018. 'US warned Kushner about Wendi Deng Murdoch.' *Wall Street Journal*, 15 January.

Olsen, Tricia D., Leigh A. Payne and Andrew G. Reiter. 2010. *Transitional Justice in the Balance: Comparing Processes, Weighing Efficacy.* Washington, DC: United States Institute of Peace Press.

Open Society Institute. 2020. *Restorative Practices in Baltimore City Schools.* Baltimore, MD: Open Society Institute.

Organisation for Economic Co-operation and Development (OECD). 2019. 'General government spending.' *OECD Data.* [Online.] Paris: OECD. Available at: data.oecd.org/gga/general-government-spending.htm.

Orwell, George. 1949. *1984.* London: Secker & Warburg.

Osterloh, Margit and Buno S. Frey. 2013. 'Motivation governance.' In Anna Grandori (ed.), *Handbook of Economic Organization.* Cheltenham, UK: Edward Elgar Publishing.

Ostrom, Elinor. 1990. *Governing the Commons: The Evolution of Institutions of Collective Action.* New York: Cambridge University Press. doi.org/10.1017/CBO9780511807763.

O'Toole, Brian I., Mark Dadds, Sue Outram and Stanley V. Catts. 2018. 'The mental health of sons and daughters of Australian Vietnam veterans.' *International Journal of Epidemiology* 47(4): 1051–59. doi.org/10.1093/ije/dyy010.

Otterman, Michael, Richard Hil and Paul Wilson. 2010. *Erasing Iraq: The Human Costs of Carnage.* London: Pluto Press.

Page, Andrew, S. Morrell and R. Taylor. 2002. 'Suicide and political regime in New South Wales and Australia during the 20th century.' *Journal of Epidemiology & Community Health* 56(10): 766–72. doi.org/10.1136/jech.56.10.766.

Paik, Haejung and George Comstock. 1994. 'The effects of television violence on antisocial behavior: A meta-analysis.' *Communication Research* 21(4): 516–46. doi.org/10.1177/009365094021004004.

Pali, Brunilda and Emanuela Biffi. 2019. *Environmental Justice: Restoring the Future.* Leuven, Belgium: European Forum for Restorative Justice.

Papachristos, Andrew V. and David S. Kirk. 2015. 'Changing the street dynamic: Evaluating Chicago's group violence reduction strategy.' *Criminology & Public Policy* 14(3): 525–58. doi.org/10.1111/1745-9133.12139.

Papachristos, Andrew V., Christopher Wildeman and Elizabeth Roberto. 2015. 'Tragic, but not random: The social contagion of nonfatal gunshot injuries.' *Social Science & Medicine* 125: 139–50. doi.org/10.1016/j.socscimed.2014.01.056.

Pare, Paul-Philippe and Richard Felson. 2014. 'Income inequality, poverty and crime across nations.' *The British Journal of Sociology* 65(3): 434–58. doi.org/10.1111/1468-4446.12083.

Parker, Christine. 2002. *The Open Corporation: Effective Self-Regulation and Democracy.* Cambridge, UK: Cambridge University Press. doi.org/10.1017/CBO9780511550034.

Parker, Christine. 2004. 'Restorative justice in business regulation? The Australian Competition and Consumer Commission's use of enforceable undertakings.' *The Modern Law Review* 67: 209–46. doi.org/10.1111/j.1468-2230.2004.00484.x.

Parker, Christine. 2006. 'The "compliance" trap: The moral message in responsive regulatory enforcement.' *Law & Society Review* 40(3): 591–622. doi.org/10.1111/j.1540-5893.2006.00274.x.

Parker, Christine, Rachel Carey, Josephine De Costa and Gyorgy Scrinis. 2017. 'Can the hidden hand of the market be an effective and legitimate regulator? The case of animal welfare under a labeling for consumer choice policy approach.' *Regulation & Governance* 11(4): 368–87. doi.org/10.1111/rego.12147.

Parker, Christine and Sharon Gilad. 2011. 'Internal corporate compliance management systems: Structure, culture and agency.' In Christine Parker and Vibeke Lehmann Nielsen (eds), *Explaining Compliance: Business Responses to Regulation*. Cheltenham, UK: Edward Elgar Publishing, pp. 170–97.

Parsons, Christopher A., Johan Sulaeman and Sheridan Titman. 2018. 'The geography of financial misconduct.' *The Journal of Finance* 73(5): 2087–137. doi.org/10.1111/jofi.12704.

Parsons, Talcott. 1990. 'Prolegomena to a theory of social institutions.' *American Sociological Review* 55(3): 319–33. doi.org/10.2307/2095758.

Partnoy, Frank. 1997. 'Financial derivatives and the costs of regulatory arbitrage.' *Journal of Corporation Law* 22: 211–56.

Partnoy, Frank. 2000. 'Why markets crash and what law can do about it.' *University of Pittsburgh Law Review* 61: 741–817. doi.org/10.2139/ssrn.183473.

Partnoy, Frank. 2003. *Infectious Greed: How Deceit and Greed Corrupted the Financial Markets*. London: Profile Books.

Passas, Nikos. 1990. 'Anomie and corporate deviance.' *Contemporary Crises* 14(2): 157–78. doi.org/10.1007/BF00728269.

Passas, Nikos. 1997. 'The mirror of global evils: A review essay on the BCCI affair.' *Trends in Organized Crime* 2(3): 49. doi.org/10.1007/BF02901610.

Passas, Nikos and Robert Agnew (eds). 1997. *The Future of Anomie Theory*. Boston, MA: Northeastern University Press.

Paternoster, Raymond and Sally Simpson. 1996. 'Sanction threats and appeals to morality: Testing a rational choice model of corporate crime.' *Law & Society Review* 30(3): 549–83. doi.org/10.2307/3054128.

Patterson, Gerald R. 1982. *Coercive Family Process*. Eugene, OR: Castalia Publishing Company.

Patterson, Gerald R. 2008. 'A comparison of models for interstate wars and for individual violence.' *Perspectives on Psychological Science* 3(3): 203–23. doi. org/10.1111/j.1745-6924.2008.00075.x.

Patterson, Gerald R. and Lew Bank. 1989. 'Some amplifying mechanisms for pathologic processes in families.' In Megan R. Gunnar and Esther Thelen (eds), *Systems and Development: The Minnesota Symposia on Child Psychology*. Hillsdale, NJ: Lawrence Erlbaum Associates, pp. 167–209.

Paul Hastings. 2012. 'Lessons learned from Pfizer's settlement of FCPA claims.' *Client Alerts*. Los Angeles, CA: Paul Hastings LLC. Available at: www.paul hastings.com/insights/client-alerts/lessons-learned-from-pfizers-settlement-of-fcpa-claims.

Peake, Gordon and Miranda Forsyth. Forthcoming. 'Street level bureaucrats in a relational state: The case of Bougainville.' *Public Administration and Development*. doi.org/10.1002/pad.1911.

Pease, Ken. 1998. *Repeat victimisation: Taking stock*. Police Research Group Crime Detection and Prevention Series Paper 90. London: The Home Office.

Peck, Jamie. 2013. 'Disembedding Polanyi: Exploring Polanyian economic geographies.' *Environment and Planning A: Economy and Space* 45(7): 1536–44. doi.org/10.1068/a46253.

Peck, Jamie and Nik Theodore. 2007. 'Variegated capitalism.' *Progress in Human Geography* 31(6): 731–72. doi.org/10.1177/0309132507083505.

Pei, Wei. 2016. 'Harmony, law and criminal reconciliation in China: A historical perspective.' *Erasmus Law Review* 9(1):18–29. doi.org/10.5553/ELR.000065.

Pennell, Joan and Gale Burford. 2000. 'Family group decision making: Protecting children and women.' *Child Welfare* 79(2): 131–58.

Permanent Subcommittee on Investigations. 2011. *Wall Street and the Financial Crisis: Anatomy of a Financial Collapse—Majority and Minority Staff Report*. 13 April. Washington, DC: Committee on Homeland Security and Governmental Affairs, United States Senate. Available at: www.hsgac.senate. gov/imo/media/doc/PSI%20REPORT%20-%20Wall%20Street%20&%20 the%20Financial%20Crisis-Anatomy%20of%20a%20Financial%20Collapse %20(FINAL%205-10-11).pdf.

Perrin, Christian, Nicholas Blagden, Belinda Winder and Gayle Dillon. 2017. '"It's sort of reaffirmed to me that I'm not a monster, I'm not a terrible person": Sex offenders' movements toward desistance via peer-support roles in prison.' *Sexual Abuse: A Journal of Research and Treatment* 30(7): 759–80. doi.org/10.1177/1079063217697133.

Perry, William J. and Tom Z. Collina. 2020. *The Button: The New Nuclear Arms Race and Presidential Power from Truman to Trump*. Dallas, TX: BenBella Books.

Petrich, Damon M., Travis C. Pratt, Cheryl Lero Jonson and Francis Cullen. 2021. 'Custodial sanctions and reoffending: A meta analytic review.' *Crime and Justice* 50(1). doi.org/10.1086/715100.

Petrunik, Michael and Clifford D. Shearing. 1988. 'The "I", the "Me" and the "It": Moving beyond the Meadian conception of self.' *Canadian Journal of Sociology* 13(4): 435–50. doi.org/10.2307/3340815.

Pettit, Philip. 1997. *Republicanism: A Theory of Freedom and Government*. Oxford, UK: Oxford University Press.

Pettit, Philip. 2012. *On the People's Terms: A Republican Theory and Model of Democracy*. New York: Cambridge University Press. doi.org/10.1017/CBO9781139017428.

Pettit, Philip. 2014. *Just Freedom: A Moral Compass for a Complex World*. New York: W.W. Norton.

Phillips, Brian J. 2015. 'How does leadership decapitation affect violence? The case of drug trafficking organizations in Mexico.' *The Journal of Politics* 77(2): 324–36. doi.org/10.1086/680209.

Phillips, Keri. 2018. 'The legacy of the Global Financial Crisis.' *Rear Vision*, [ABC Radio National], 16 September. Available at: www.abc.net.au/radionational/programs/rearvision/the-legacy-of-the-global-financial-crisis/10195876.

Phillips, Linda Ree. 1983. 'Abuse and neglect of the frail elderly at home: An exploration of theoretical relationships.' *Journal of Advanced Nursing* 8(5): 379–92. doi.org/10.1111/j.1365-2648.1983.tb00461.x.

Piatkowska, Sylwia J., Steven F. Messner, Colin Gruner and Eric P. Baumer. 2020. 'The "new fiscal criminology": State-level changes in crime rates and the structure of tax systems.' *Justice Quarterly*. doi.org/10.1080/07418825.2020.1731572.

Piketty, Thomas. 2014. *Capital in the Twenty-First Century*. Cambridge, MA: Harvard University Press. doi.org/10.4159/9780674369542.

Pinker, Steven. 2011. *The Better Angels of Our Nature*. New York: Viking.

Pinotti, Paolo. 2015a. 'The causes and consequences of organised crime: Preliminary evidence across countries.' *The Economic Journal* 125(586): F158–74. doi.org/10.1111/ecoj.12238.

Pinotti, Paolo. 2015b. 'The economic costs of organised crime: Evidence from southern Italy.' *The Economic Journal* 125(586): F203–32. doi.org/10.1111/ecoj.12235.

Pinquart, Martin. 2017. 'Associations of parenting dimensions and styles with externalizing problems of children and adolescents: An updated meta-analysis.' *Developmental Psychology* 53(5): 873–932. doi.org/10.1037/dev0000295.

Piquero, Alex R. and Matthew Hickman. 1999. 'An empirical test of Tittle's control balance theory.' *Criminology* 37(2): 319–43. doi.org/10.1111/j.1745-9125.1999.tb00488.x.

Piquero, Alex and Nicole Leeper Piquero. 1998. 'On testing institutional anomie with varying specifications.' *Studies on Crime and Crime Prevention* 7: 61–84.

Plato. 1892. *Laws, II: The Dialogues of Plato*. Vol. 72, 3rd edn, Benjamin Jowett, trans. Oxford, UK: Clarendon Press.

Pleitgen, Fred and Catriona Davies. 2010. 'How Poland became only EU nation to avoid recession.' *CNN*, 29 June.

Pocock, John Greville Agard. 2016. *The Machiavellian Moment: Florentine Political Thought and the Atlantic Republican Tradition*. Princeton, NJ: Princeton University Press. doi.org/10.1515/9781400883516.

Polanyi, Karl. 1957 [1944]. *The Great Transformation*. Boston, MA: Beacon Press.

Policardo, Laura and Edgar J. Sánchez Carrera. 2018. 'Corruption causes inequality, or is it the other way around? An empirical investigation for a panel of countries.' *Economic Analysis and Policy* 59: 92–102. doi.org/10.1016/j.eap.2018.05.001.

Policardo, Laura, Edgar J. Sánchez Carrera and Wiston Adrian Risso. 2019. 'Causality between income inequality and corruption in OECD countries.' *World Development Perspectives* 14: 100–2. doi.org/10.1016/j.wdp.2019.02.013.

Polk, Kenneth. 1994. *When Men Kill: Scenarios of Masculine Violence*. Cambridge, UK: Cambridge University Press.

Polk, Kenneth and David Ranson. 1991. 'The role of gender in intimate homicide.' *Australian and New Zealand Journal of Criminology* 24(1): 15–24. doi.org/10.1177/000486589102400102.

Pontell, Henry N. 1978. 'Deterrence: Theory versus practice.' *Criminology* 16(1): 3–22. doi.org/10.1111/j.1745-9125.1978.tb01394.x.

Pontell, Henry N., William K. Black and Gilbert Geis. 2014. 'Too big to fail, too powerful to jail? On the absence of criminal prosecutions after the 2008 financial meltdown.' *Crime, Law, and Social Change* 61(1): 1–13. doi.org/10.1007/s10611-013-9476-4.

Pontell, Henry N. and Kitty Calavita. 1992. 'Bilking bankers and bad debts: White-collar crime and the savings and loan crisis.' In Kip Schlegel and David Weisburd (eds), *White-Collar Crime Reconsidered*. Boston, MA: Northeastern University Press, pp. 195–213.

Porter, Amanda. 2016. 'Decolonizing policing: Indigenous patrols, counter-policing and safety.' *Theoretical Criminology* 20(4): 548–65. doi.org/10.1177/1362480615625763.

Porter, Amanda. 2018. 'Non-state policing, legal pluralism and the mundane governance of crime.' *Sydney Law Review* 40: 445–67.

Power, Michael. 1997. *The Audit Society: Rituals of Verification.* Oxford, UK: Oxford University Press.

Pratt, John. 2007. *Penal Populism.* New York: Routledge. doi.org/10.4324/9780203963678.

Pratt, Travis C. and Francis T. Cullen. 2005. 'Assessing macro-level predictors and theories of crime: A meta-analysis.' *Crime and Justice* 32: 373–450. doi.org/10.1086/655357.

Pratt, Travis C., Francis T. Cullen, Christine S. Sellers, L. Thomas Winfree Jr, Tamara D. Madensen, Leah E. Daigle, Noelle E. Fearn and Jacinta M. Gau. 2010. 'The empirical status of social learning theory: A meta-analysis.' *Justice Quarterly* 27(6): 765–802. doi.org/10.1080/07418820903379610.

Pratt, Travis C. and Jillian J. Turanovic. 2018. 'Celerity and deterrence.' In Daniel S. Nagin, Francis T. Cullen and Cheryl Lero Jonson (eds), *Deterrence, Choice, and Crime: Contemporary Perspectives*. New York: Routledge, pp. 187–210.

Presser, Lois. 2013. *Why We Harm.* New Brunswick, NJ: Rutgers University Press.

Pridemore, William A. 2005. 'Social structure and homicide in post-Soviet Russia.' *Social Science Research* 34(4): 732–56. doi.org/10.1016/j.ssresearch.2004.12.005.

Pridemore, William A. 2011. 'Poverty matters: A reassessment of the inequality–homicide relationship in cross-national studies.' *The British Journal of Criminology* 51(5): 739–72. doi.org/10.1093/bjc/azr019.

Pridemore, William A., Mitchell B. Chamlin and John K. Cochran. 2007. 'An interrupted time-series analysis of Durkheim's social deregulation thesis: The case of the Russian Federation.' *Justice Quarterly* 24(2): 271–90. doi.org/10.1080/07418820701294813.

Pruitt, Sarah. 2017. 'The Nazis developed sarin gas during WWII, but Hitler was afraid to use it.' *History.com*, 12 April [updated 1 April 2019]. [Online.] Available at: www.history.com/news/the-nazis-developed-saringas-but-hitler-was-afraid-to-use-it.

Przeworski, Adam, Michael Alvarez, Jose Antonio Cheibub and Fernando Limongi. 2000. *Democracy and Development*. Cambridge, UK: Cambridge University Press. doi.org/10.1017/CBO9780511804946.

Psacharopoulos, George and Harry Anthony Patrinos. 2018. 'Returns to investment in education: A decennial review of the global literature.' *Education Economics* 26(5): 445–58. doi.org/10.1080/09645292.2018.1484426.

Putnam, Robert D. 1988. 'Diplomacy and domestic politics: The logic of two-level games.' *International Organization* 42(3): 427–60. doi.org/10.1017/S0020818300027697.

Putnam, Robert D. 1993. *Making Democracy Work: Civic Traditions in Modern Italy*. Princeton, NJ: Princeton University Press. doi.org/10.1515/9781400820740.

Putnam, Robert D. 1995. 'Tuning in, tuning out: The strange disappearance of social capital in America.' *PS: Political Science & Politics* 28(4): 664–84. doi.org/10.2307/420517.

Putnam, Robert D. 2000. *Bowling Alone: The Collapse and Renewal of American Community*. New York: Simon & Schuster.

Putnam, Robert D. and C. Randall Henning. 1989. 'The Bonn Summit of 1978: A case study in coordination.' In Richard N. Cooper, Barry Eichengreen, Gerald Holtham, Robert D. Putnam and C. Randall Henning, *Can Nations Agree? Issues in International Economic Cooperation*. Washington, DC: Brookings Institution Press, pp. 12–140.

Pyrooz, David C., Jillian J. Turanovic, Scott H. Decker and Jun Wu. 2016. 'Taking stock of the relationship between gang membership and offending: A meta-analysis.' *Criminal Justice and Behavior* 43(3): 365–97. doi.org/10.1177/0093854815605528.

Quetelet, Lambert Adolphe Jacques. 1842. *A Treatise on Man and the Development of His Faculties*. R. Knox, trans. Edinburgh: William & Robert Chambers.

Quiggin, John. 2019. *Economics in Two Lessons: Why Markets Work So Well, and Why They Can Fail So Badly.* Princeton, NJ: Princeton University Press. doi.org/10.1515/9780691186108.

Quiggin, John. 2020. 'Paying for what we used to own: The strange case of CSL.' *The Conversation*, 27 November.

Quinn, J. Michael, T. David Mason and Mehmet Gurses. 2007. 'Sustaining the peace: Determinants of civil war recurrence.' *International Interactions* 33(2): 167–93. doi.org/10.1080/03050620701277673.

Quinones, Sam. 2015. *Dreamland: The True Tale of America's Opiate Epidemic.* New York: Bloomsbury Publishing USA.

Raab, Selwyn. 1980. 'Ex-owner says mob took over chemicals firm.' *The New York Times*, 24 November.

Rains, Stephen A. 2013. 'The nature of psychological reactance revisited: A meta-analytic review.' *Human Communication Research* 39(1): 47–73. doi. org/10.1111/j.1468-2958.2012.01443.x.

Ramalingam, Ben. 2013. *Aid on the Edge of Chaos: Rethinking International Cooperation in a Complex World.* Oxford, UK: Oxford University Press.

Rauktis, Mary E., Sharon McCarthy, David Krackhardt and Helen Cahalane. 2010. 'Innovation in child welfare: The adoption and implementation of family group decision making in Pennsylvania.' *Children and Youth Services Review* 32(5): 732–39. doi.org/10.1016/j.childyouth.2010.01.010.

Reed, Stanley. 2020. 'BP reports a huge loss and vows to increase renewables investment.' *The New York Times*, 4 August.

Rees, Joseph. 2009. *Hostages of Each Other: The Transformation of Nuclear Safety Since Three Mile Island.* Chicago: University of Chicago Press.

Regan, Anthony. 2010. *Light Intervention: Lessons from Bougainville.* Washington, DC: United States Institute of Peace.

Regan, Patrick M. and Daniel Norton. 2005. 'Greed, grievance, and mobilization in civil wars.' *Journal of Conflict Resolution* 49(3): 319–36. doi. org/10.1177/0022002704273441.

Reiner, Robert. 2020. *Social Democratic Criminology.* London: Routledge. doi.org/ 10.4324/9781315296777.

Reinhart, Carmen M. and Kenneth S. Rogoff. 2009. *This Time is Different: Eight Centuries of Financial Folly.* Princeton, NJ: Princeton University Press. doi.org/ 10.1515/9781400831722.

Reisner, Jon Michael, Eunmo Koo, Elizabeth Clare Hunke and Manvendra Krishna Dubey. 2019. 'Reply to comment by Robock et al. on "Climate impact of a regional nuclear weapon exchange: An improved assessment based on detailed source calculations".' *Journal of Geophysical Research: Atmospheres* 124: 12959–62. doi.org/10.1029/2019JD031281.

Reiss, Albert J. and Albert L. Rhodes. 1961. 'The distribution of juvenile delinquency in the social class structure.' *American Sociological Review* 26(5): 720–32. doi.org/10.2307/2090201.

Reitzel-Jaffe, Deborah and David A. Wolfe. 2001. 'Predictors of relationship abuse among young men.' *Journal of Interpersonal Violence* 16(2): 99–115. doi.org/10.1177/088626001016002001.

Reno, William. 1995. *Corruption and State Politics in Sierra Leone.* New York: Cambridge University Press.

Reno, William. 1999. *Warlord Politics and African States.* Boulder, CO: Lynne Rienner Publishers.

Reyntjens, Filip. 2009. *The Great African War: Congo and Regional Geopolitics, 1996–2006.* Cambridge, UK: Cambridge University Press. doi.org/10.1017/CBO9780511596698.

Richani, Nazi. 2007. Systems of violence and their political economy in post-conflict situations. Latin American Studies Program, Political Science Department, Kean University, Union, NJ.

Richards, David A.J. 1993. *Conscience and the Constitution: History, Theory, and Law of the Reconstruction Amendments.* Princeton, NJ: Princeton University Press. doi.org/10.1515/9781400863563.

Ridzuan, Sulhi. 2019. 'Inequality and the environmental Kuznets curve.' *Journal of Cleaner Production* 228: 1472–81. doi.org/10.1016/j.jclepro.2019.04.284.

Riordan, Catherine. 2013. Post-conflict governments 1975–2004: Designing effective assistance. PhD dissertation, University College, Dublin.

Ríos, Viridiana. 2013. 'Why did Mexico become so violent? A self-reinforcing violent equilibrium caused by competition and enforcement.' *Trends in Organized Crime* 16(2): 138–55. doi.org/10.1007/s12117-012-9175-z.

Roberts, Andrea L., Stephen E. Gilman, Garrett Fitzmaurice, Michele R. Decker and Karestan C. Koenen. 2010. 'Witness of intimate partner violence in childhood and perpetration of intimate partner violence in adulthood.' *Epidemiology* 21(6): 809–18. doi.org/10.1097/EDE.0b013e3181f39f03.

Roberts, Geoffrey. 2013. *Victory at Stalingrad: The Battle That Changed History.* London: Routledge. doi.org/10.4324/9781315835785.

Robinson, Laurie O. 2011. 'Exploring certainty and severity: Perspectives from a federal perch.' *Criminology & Public Policy* 10(1): 85–92. doi.org/10.1111/j.1745-9133.2010.00689.x.

Rodrik, Dani. 2000. 'Institutions for high-quality growth: What they are and how to acquire them.' *Studies in Comparative International Development* 35(3): 3–31. doi.org/10.1007/BF02699764.

Rodrik, Dani. 2011. *The Globalization Paradox.* New York: Norton.

Rørbæk, Lasse Lykke and Allan Toft Knudsen. 2015. 'Maintaining ethnic dominance: Diversity, power, and violent repression.' *Conflict Management and Peace Science* (24 November): 1–20. doi.org/10.1177/0738894215612996.

Rorie, Melissa L. 2020. *The Handbook of White-Collar Crime.* New York: Wiley. doi.org/10.1002/9781118775004.

Rose, Richard. 1998. *Getting things done in an anti-modern society: Social capital networks in Russia.* Social Capital Initiative Working Paper No. 6. Washington, DC: The World Bank.

Rosefielde, Steven. 1996. 'Stalinism in post-communist perspective: New evidence on killings, forced labour and economic growth in the 1930s.' *Europe–Asia Studies* 48(6): 959–87. doi.org/10.1080/09668139608412393.

Rosenau, James N. 1990. *Turbulence in World Politics: A Theory of Change and Continuity.* Princeton, NJ: Princeton University Press. doi.org/10.1515/9780691188522.

Rosenfeld, Richard and Steven F. Messner. 1991. 'The social sources of homicide in different types of societies.' *Sociological Forum* 6(1): 51–70. doi.org/10.1007/BF01112727.

Rosenheck, Robert and Alan Fontana. 1998. 'Transgenerational effects of abusive violence on the children of Vietnam combat veterans.' *Journal of Traumatic Stress* 11(4): 731–42. doi.org/10.1023/A:1024445416821.

Roser, Max. 2015. 'War and peace after 1945.' *Our World in Data.* [Online resource.] Available at: ourworldindata.org/uploads/2016/02/ourworld indata_exampe-data-entry-with-annotations-%E2%80%93-war-and-peace-after-1945-2.pdf.

Rosoff, Stephen M., Henry N. Pontell and Robert Tillman. 2002. *Profit without Honor: White-Collar Crime and the Looting of America*. Upper Saddle River, NJ: Prentice Hall.

Ross, Jeffrey Ian (ed.). 2000. *Controlling State Crime: An introduction*. New Brunswick, NJ: Transaction Publishers.

Ross, Jeffrey Ian and Gregg Barak. 2000. *Varieties of State Crime and its Control*. Monsey, NY: Criminal Justice Press.

Ross, Marc Howard. 1985. 'Internal and external conflict and violence: Cross-cultural evidence and a new analysis.' *The Journal of Conflict Resolution* 29(4): 547–79. doi.org/10.1177/0022002785029004001.

Ross, Rupert. 1996. *Returning to the Teachings: Exploring Aboriginal Justice*. London: Penguin.

Rossner, Meredith. 2013. *Just Emotions: Rituals of Restorative Justice*. Oxford, UK: Oxford University Press. doi.org/10.1093/acprof:oso/9780199655045. 001.0001.

Roth, Randolph. 2012. *American Homicide*. Cambridge, MA: Harvard University Press. doi.org/10.2307/j.ctvjghvxh.

Rothe, Dawn L. and David O. Friedrichs. 2014. *Crimes of Globalization: New Directions in Critical Criminology*. London: Routledge. doi.org/10.4324/ 9780203727409.

Rothe, Dawn L. and David Kauzlarich (eds). 2014. *Towards a Victimology of State Crime*. London: Routledge. doi.org/10.4324/9780203083536.

Rubak, Sune, Annelli Sandbæk, Torsten Lauritzen and Bo Christensen. 2005. 'Motivational interviewing: A systematic review and meta-analysis.' *British Journal of General Practice* 5(513): 305–12.

Rubin, Michael. 2014. *Dancing with the Devil: The Perils of Engaging Rogue Regimes*. New York: Encounter.

Rudolph, Maximilian and Peter Starke. 2020. 'How does the welfare state reduce crime? The effect of program characteristics and decommodification across 18 OECD countries.' *Journal of Criminal Justice* 68: 101684. doi.org/ 10.1016/j.jcrimjus.2020.101684.

Sabel, Charles F. and William H. Simon. 2004. 'Destabilization rights: How public law litigation succeeds.' *Harvard Law Review* 117: 1016–101. doi.org/ 10.2307/4093364.

Saiya, Nilay. 2018. *Weapon of Peace: How Religious Liberty Combats Terrorism*. Cambridge, UK: Cambridge University Press. doi.org/10.1017/97811 08565127.

Salehyan, Idean and Kristian Skrede Gleditsch. 2006. 'Refugees and the spread of civil war.' *International Organization* 60(2): 335–66. doi.org/10.1017/ S0020818306060103.

Sambanis, Nicholas. 2001. 'Do ethnic and nonethnic civil wars have the same causes? A theoretical and empirical enquiry (Part I).' *Journal of Conflict Resolution* 45(3): 259–82. doi.org/10.1177/0022002701045003001.

Sambanis, Nicholas. 2004. 'Using case studies to expand economic models of civil war.' *Perspectives on Politics* 2(2): 259–79. doi.org/10.1017/ S1537592704040149.

Sambanis, Nicholas. 2008. 'Short- and long-term effects of United Nations peace operations.' *The World Bank Economic Review* 22(1): 9–32. doi.org/10.1093/ wber/lhm022.

Sampson, Robert J. 2012. *Great American City: Chicago and the Enduring Neighborhood Effect*. Chicago: University of Chicago Press. doi.org/10.7208/ chicago/9780226733883.001.0001.

Sampson, Robert J. 2019. 'Neighborhood effects and beyond: Explaining the paradoxes of inequality in the changing American metropolis.' *Urban Studies* 56(1): 3–32. doi.org/10.1177/0042098018795363.

Sampson, Robert J. and Dawn Jeglum Bartusch. 1998. 'Legal cynicism and (subcultural?) tolerance of deviance: The neighborhood context of racial differences.' *Law & Society Review* 32(4): 777–804. doi.org/10.2307/827739.

Sampson, Robert J. and John H. Laub. 1995. *Crime in the Making: Pathways and Turning Points through Life*. Cambridge, MA: Harvard University Press.

Sampson, Robert J., Stephen W. Raudenbush and Felton Earls. 1997. 'Neighborhoods and violent crime: A multilevel study of collective efficacy.' *Science* 277(5328): 918–24. doi.org/10.1126/science.277.5328.918.

Sand, Peter H. 1973. 'The socialist response: Environmental protection law in the German Democratic Republic.' *Ecology Law Quarterly* 3(3): 451–505.

Sander, Helke and Barbara Johr (eds). 2005. *Befreier und Befreite: Krieg, Vergewaltigungen, Kinder* [*Liberators Take Liberties: War, Rape, Children*]. München: Antje Kunstmann.

Sapsomboon, Somroutai and Supalak G. Khundee. 2007. 'Referendum law or penalty law?' *The Nation Thailand*, 6 July.

Sarfaty, Galit A. 2021. 'Global supply chain auditing.' In Benjamin van Rooij and D. Daniel Sokol (eds), *The Cambridge Handbook of Compliance*. Cambridge, UK: Cambridge University Press, pp. 977–88. doi.org/10.1017/9781108759458.

Savage, Joanne and Christina Yancey. 2008. 'The effects of media violence exposure on criminal aggression: A meta-analysis.' *Criminal Justice and Behavior* 35(6): 772–91. doi.org/10.1177/0093854808316487.

Savolainen, Jukka. 2000. 'Inequality, welfare state, and homicide: Further support for the institutional anomie theory.' *Criminology* 38(4): 1021–42. doi.org/10.1111/j.1745-9125.2000.tb01413.x.

Scalmer, Sean. 2011. *Gandhi in the West: The Mahatma and the Rise of Radical Protest*. Cambridge, UK: Cambridge University Press.

Schargrodsky, Ernesto and Lucia Freira. 2021. *Inequality and Crime in Latin America and the Caribbean: New Data for an Old Question*. New York: UNDP Working Paper for the 2021 Human Development Report.

Scheff, Thomas J. 1987. 'The shame–rage spiral: A case study of an interminable quarrel.' In Helen Block Lewis (ed.), *The Role of Shame in Symptom Formation*. Hillsdale, NJ: Lawrence Erlbaum, pp. 109–49.

Scheff, Thomas J. 1990. *Microsociology: Discourse, Emotion, and Social Structure*. Chicago: University of Chicago Press.

Scheff, Thomas J. 1994. *Bloody Revenge: Emotions, Nationalism, and War*. New York: Westview Press.

Scheff, Thomas J., Suzanne M. Retzinger and Michael T. Ryan. 1989. 'Crime, violence, and self-esteem: Review and proposals.' In Andrew Mecca, Neil J. Smelser and John Vasconcellos (eds), *The Social Importance of Self-Esteem*. Los Angeles, CA: University of California Press, pp. 165–99.

Schell-Busey, Natalie, Sally S. Simpson, Melissa Rorie and Mariel Alper. 2016. 'What works? A systematic review of corporate crime deterrence.' *Criminology & Public Policy* 15(2): 387–416. doi.org/10.1111/1745-9133.12195.

Scheuerman, Heather L. and Shelley Keith. 2022. 'Experiencing shame: Does gender affect the interpersonal dynamics of restorative justice.' *Feminist Criminology* 17(1): 116–38. doi.org/10 1177/15570851211034556.

Schiff, Mara F. 1999. 'The impact of restorative interventions on juvenile offenders.' In Lode Walgrave and Gordon Bazemore (eds), *Restorative Juvenile Justice*. Monsey, NY: Criminal Justice Press, pp. 327–56.

Schneider, Friedrich. 2002. *Size and Measurement of the Informal Economy in 110 Countries*. Canberra: Workshop of Centre for Tax System Integrity, The Australian National University.

Schneider, Friedrich. 2005. *The size of shadow economies of 145 countries all over the world: First results over the period 1999 to 2003*. IZA Discussion Papers No. 1431. Bonn: Institute for the Study of Labor. doi.org/10.2139/ssrn.636661.

Schneider, Friedrich and Andreas Buehn. 2018. 'Shadow economy: Estimation methods, problems, results and open questions.' *Open Economics* 1(1): 1–29. doi.org/10.1515/openec-2017-0001.

Schoepfer, Andrea and Alex R. Piquero. 2006. 'Self-control, moral beliefs, and criminal activity.' *Deviant Behavior* 27(1): 51–71. doi.org/10.1080/016396290968326.

Schoepfer, Andrea and Nicole Leeper Piquero. 2006. 'Exploring white-collar crime and the American dream: A partial test of institutional anomie theory.' *Journal of Criminal Justice* 34(3): 227–35. doi.org/10.1016/j.jcrimjus.2006.03.008.

Schoepfer, Andrea, Nicole Leeper Piquero and Lynn Langton. 2014. 'Low self-control versus the desire-for-control: An empirical test of white-collar crime and conventional crime.' *Deviant Behavior* 35(3): 197–214. doi.org/10.1080/01639625.2013.834758.

Scholz, John T. and Wayne B. Gray. 1990. 'OSHA enforcement and workplace injuries: A behavioral approach to risk assessment.' *Journal of Risk and Uncertainty* 3(3): 283–305. doi.org/10.1007/BF00116786.

Scorzafave, Luiz Guilherme and Milena Karla Soares. 2009. 'Income inequality and pecuniary crimes.' *Economics Letters* 104(1): 40–42. doi.org/10.1016/j.econlet.2009.03.021.

Scott, James C. 1998. *Seeing Like a State: How Certain Schemes to Improve the Human Condition Have Failed*. New Haven, CT: Yale University Press.

Scott, Rachel. 1974. *Muscle and Blood: The Massive, Hidden Agony of Industrial Slaughter in America*. New York: E.P. Dutton.

Sellin, Thorsten. 1926. 'Is murder increasing in Europe?' *The ANNALS of the American Academy of Political and Social Science* 125(1): 29–34. doi.org/10.1177/000271622612500104.

Sen, Amartya. 1999. *Development as Freedom*. New York: Alfred A. Knopf.

Sharkey, Patrick. 2018. *Uneasy Peace: The Great Crime Decline, the Renewal of City Life, and the Next War on Violence*. New York: Norton.

Sharkey, Patrick, Gerard Torrats-Espinosa and Delaram Takyar. 2017. 'Community and the crime decline: The causal effect of local nonprofits on violent crime.' *American Sociological Review* 82(6): 1214–40. doi.org/10.1177/0003122417736289.

Sharpston, M.J. 1970. 'The economics of corruption.' *New Society* 16(426): 944–46.

Shaw, Clifford R. and Henry D. McKay. 1942. *Juvenile Delinquency and Urban Areas*. Chicago: University of Chicago Press.

Shaw, George Bernard. n.d. 'George Bernard Shaw quotes: Caesar and Cleopatra.' *AZQuotes*. [Online.] Available at: www.azquotes.com/quote/934069#google_vignette.

Shaw, Martin, Danny Dorling and G. Davey Smith. 2002. 'Mortality and political climate: How suicide rates have risen during periods of Conservative government, 1901–2000.' *Journal of Epidemiology and Community Health* 56(10): 723–25. doi.org/10.1136/jech.56.10.723.

Shearing, Clifford and Richard V. Ericson. 1991. 'Culture as figurative action.' *The British Journal of Sociology* 42(4): 481–506. doi.org/10.2307/591444.

Shearing, Clifford and Philip C. Stenning (eds). 1987. *Private Policing*. Beverly Hills, CA: Sage.

Shearing, Clifford and Jennifer Wood. 2003. 'Nodal governance, democracy, and the new "denizens".' *Journal of Law and Society* 30(3): 400–19. doi.org/10.1111/1467-6478.00263.

Sheffrin, Steven M. and Robert K. Triest. 1992. 'Can brute deterrence backfire? Perceptions and attitudes in taxpayer compliance.' In Joel Slemrod (ed.), *Why People Pay Taxes: Tax Compliance and Enforcement*. Ann Arbor: University of Michigan Press, pp. 193–218.

Sherman, Lawrence W. 1978. *Scandal and Reform: Controlling Police Corruption*. Berkeley, CA: University of California Press. doi.org/10.1525/9780520319318.

Sherman, Lawrence W. 1992. *Policing Domestic Violence*. New York: The Free Press.

Sherman, Lawrence W. 1993. 'Defiance, deterrence and irrelevance: A theory of the criminal sanction.' *Journal of Research in Crime and Delinquency* 30(4): 445–73. doi.org/10.1177/0022427893030004006.

Sherman, Lawrence W. 1995. 'Hot spots of crime and criminal careers of places.' In John Eck and David L. Weisburd (eds), *Crime and Place. Volume 4.* Monsey, NY: Willow Tree Press.

Sherman, Lawrence W. 2011. 'Offender desistance policing (ODP): Less prison and more evidence of rehabilitating offenders.' In Thomas Bliesener, Andreas Beelmann and Mark Stemmler (eds), *Antisocial Behavior and Crime: Contributions of Developmental and Evaluation Research to Prevention and Intervention.* Cambridge, MA: Hogrefe Publishing, pp. 199–218.

Sherman, Lawrence W. 2014. 'Experiments in criminal sanctions: Labeling, defiance, and restorative justice.' In David P. Farrington and Joseph Murray (eds), *Labeling Theory: Empirical Tests.* New Brunswick, NJ: Transaction Publishers.

Sherman, Lawrence W., Patrick R. Gartin and Michael E. Buerger. 1989. 'Hot spots of predatory crime: Routine activities and the criminology of place.' *Criminology* 27(1): 27–55. doi.org/10.1111/j.1745-9125.1989.tb00862.x.

Sherman, Lawrence W. and Heather Strang. 1997. *Restorative justice and deterring crime.* RISE Working Paper No. 4. Canberra: Law Program, Research School of Social Sciences, The Australian National University.

Sherman, Lawrence W., Heather Strang, Geoffrey C. Barnes, John Braithwaite, Nova Inkpen and Min-Mee Teh. 1998. *Experiments in Restorative Policing: A Progress Report.* Canberra: The Australian National University.

Short, James F. 1964. 'Gang delinquency and anomie.' In Marshall B. Clinard (ed.), *Anomie and Deviant Behaviour.* New York: The Free Press, pp. 98–127.

Short, James F. and Fred L. Strodtbeck. 1965. *Group Process and Gang Delinquency.* Chicago: University of Chicago Press.

Shover, Neal, Glenn S. Coffey and Dick Hobbs. 2003. 'Crime on the line: Telemarketing and the changing nature of professional crime.' *The British Journal of Criminology* 43(3): 489–505. doi.org/10.1093/bjc/43.3.489.

Shover, Neal and Andrew Hochstetler. 2005. *Choosing White-Collar Crime.* New York: Cambridge University Press. doi.org/10.1017/CBO9780511803482.

Shur-Ofry, Michal and Ofer Malcai. 2021. 'Collective action and social contagion: Community gardens as a case study.' *Regulation & Governance* 15(1): 63–81. doi.org/10.1111/rego.12256.

Sikkink, Kathryn. 2011. *The Justice Cascade: How Human Rights Prosecutions Are Changing World Politics*. New York: Norton.

Simons, Ronald L., Leslie Gordon Simons, Callie Harbin Burt, Gene H. Brody and Carolyn Cutrona. 2005. 'Collective efficacy, authoritative parenting and delinquency: A longitudinal test of a model integrating community- and family-level processes.' *Criminology* 43(4): 989–1029. doi.org/10.1111/j.1745-9125.2005.00031.x.

Simpson, Sally S. 2002. *Corporate Crime, Law, and Social Control*. Cambridge, UK: Cambridge University Press. doi.org/10.1017/CBO9780511606281.

Simpson, Sally S., Carole Gibbs, Melissa Rorie, Lee Ann Slocum, Mark A. Cohen and Michael Vandenbergh. 2013. 'An empirical assessment of corporate environmental crime-control strategies.' *The Journal of Criminal Law and Criminology* 103: 231–78.

Skinner, Quentin. 2012. *Liberty Before Liberalism*. Cambridge, UK: Cambridge University Press.

Skocpol, Theda. 2013. *Diminished Democracy: From Membership to Management in American Civic Life. Volume 8*. Norman, OK: University of Oklahoma Press.

Skogan, Wesley G. 1990. *Disorder and Decline: Crime and the Spiral of Decay in American Cities*. Berkeley, CA: University of California Press.

Slothower, Molly, Peter Neyroud, Jamie Hobday, Lawrence Sherman, Barak Ariel, Eleanor Neyroud and Geoffrey Barnes. 2017. *The Turning Point Project 2-year outcomes*. Report to Chief Officers. Birmingham, UK: West Midlands Police.

Smith, Peter K. and Susanne Robinson. 2019. 'How does individualism-collectivism relate to bullying victimisation?' *International Journal of Bullying Prevention* 1(1): 3–13. doi.org/10.1007/s42380-018-0005-y.

Sobek, David, M. Rodwan Abouharb and Christopher G. Ingram. 2006. 'The human rights peace: How the respect for human rights at home leads to peace abroad.' *Journal of Politics* 68: 519–29. doi.org/10.1111/j.1468-2508.2006.00442.x.

Soltes, Eugene. 2020. 'Paper versus practice: A field investigation of integrity hotlines.' *Journal of Accounting Research* 58(2): 429–72. doi.org/10.1111/1475-679X.12302.

Soltes, Eugene. 2021. 'The professionalization of compliance.' In Benjamin van Rooij and D. Daniel Sokol (eds), *Cambridge Handbook of Compliance*. Cambridge, UK: Cambridge University Press, pp. 27–36. doi.org/10.1017/9781108759458.003.

Sørensen, Eva. 2006. 'Meta governance: The changing role of politicians in processes of democratic governance.' *American Review of Public Administration* 36(1): 98–114. doi.org/10.1177/0275074005282584.

Sørensen, Eva and Jacob Torfing (eds). 2016. *Theories of Democratic Network Governance*. New York: Springer.

Sorokin, Pitirim A. 1928. *Contemporary Sociological Theories*. New York: Harper.

Sorokin, Pitirim A. and Walter A. Lunden. 1959. *Power and Morality: Who Shall Guard the Guardians?* Boston, MA: Porter Sargent.

Spalding, Andrew Brady. 2015. 'Restorative justice for multinational corporations.' *Ohio State Law Journal* 76: 357–408. doi.org/10.2139/ssrn.2403930.

Sparrow, Malcolm K. 2000. *The Regulatory Craft*. Washington, DC: Brookings Institution Press.

Spas, Jayson, Susan Ramsey, Andrea L. Paiva and L.A.R. Stein. 2012. 'All might have won, but not all have the prize: Optimal treatment for substance abuse among adolescents with conduct problems.' *Substance Abuse: Research and Treatment* 6: 141–55. doi.org/10.4137/SART.S10389.

Spierenburg, Pieter. 2008. *A History of Murder: Personal Violence in Europe from the Middle Ages to the Present*. Cambridge, UK: Polity.

Spierenburg, Pieter. 2013. *Violence and Punishment: Civilizing the Body through Time*. Cambridge, UK: Polity.

Spruit, Anouk, Frans Schalkwijk, Eveline Van Vugt and Geert Jan Stams. 2016. 'The relation between self-conscious emotions and delinquency: A meta-analysis.' *Aggression and Violent Behavior* 28: 12–20. doi.org/10.1016/j.avb.2016.03.009.

Stack, Steven. 2005. 'Suicide in the media: A quantitative review of studies based on nonfictional stories.' *Suicide and Life-Threatening Behavior* 35(2): 121–33. doi.org/10.1521/suli.35.2.121.62877.

Stajkovic, Alexander D., Dongseop Lee and Anthony J. Nyberg. 2009. 'Collective efficacy, group potency, and group performance: Meta-analyses of their relationships, and test of a mediation model.' *Journal of Applied Psychology* 94(3): 814–28. doi.org/10.1037/a0015659.

Stamatel, Janet P. 2016. 'Democratic cultural values as predictors of cross-national homicide variation in Europe.' *Homicide Studies* 20(3): 239–56. doi.org/10.1177/1088767915611178.

Stamatel, Janet P. and Samuel H. Romans. 2018. 'The effects of wars on postwar homicide rates: A replication and extension of Archer and Gartner's classic study.' *Journal of Contemporary Criminal Justice* 34(3): 287–311. doi.org/10.1177/1043986218769989.

Stanard, Rebecca Powell. 1999. 'The effect of training in a strengths model of case management on client outcomes in a community mental health center.' *Community Mental Health Journal* 35(2): 169–79. doi.org/10.1023/A:1018724831815.

Steadman, Lyle. 1971. Neighbours and killers: Residence and dominance among the Hewa of New Guinea. PhD dissertation, The Australian National University, Canberra.

Stearns, Peter N. 1986. 'Old age family conflict: The perspective of the past.' In Karl A. Pillemer and Rosalie S. Wolf (eds), *Elder Abuse: Conflict in the Family*. Dover, MA: Auburn House, pp. 3–24.

Sterling, Robert, Corrine Slusher and Stephen Weinstein. 2008. 'Measuring recovery capital and determining its relationship to outcome in an alcohol dependent sample.' *The American Journal of Drug and Alcohol Abuse* 34(5): 603–10. doi.org/10.1080/00952990802308114.

Stockman, Farah. 2004. 'Army finds 49 abuse cases.' *The Boston Globe*, 23 July. Available at: archive.boston.com/news/nation/articles/2004/07/23/army_finds_49_abuse_cases/.

Stotland, Ezra. 1976. 'Self-esteem and violence by guards and state troopers at Attica.' *Correctional Psychologist* 3(1): 85–96. doi.org/10.1177/009385487600300107.

Stotland, Ezra and J. Martinez. 1976. 'Self-esteem and mass violence at Kent State.' *International Journal of Group Tensions* 6(3–4): 3–14.

Strang, Heather, Lawrence W. Sherman, Evan Mayo-Wilson, Daniel Woods and Ariel Barak. 2013. 'Restorative justice conferencing (RJC) using face-to-face meetings of offenders and victims: Effects on offender recidivism and victim satisfaction—A systematic review.' *Campbell Systematic Reviews* 9(1): 1–59. doi.org/10.4073/csr.2013.12.

Strauss-Kahn, Dominique. 2010. After the Global Financial Crisis: The road ahead for Europe. Address to the Warsaw School of Economics, Warsaw, Poland, 29 March. Available at: www.imf.org/en/News/Articles/2015/09/28/04/53/sp032910.

Stringham, Edward Peter and John Levendis. 2010. 'The relationship between economic freedom and homicide.' In James Gwartney, Joshua Hall and Robert Lawson (eds), *Economic Freedom of the World: 2010 Annual Report*. Vancouver: Fraser, pp. 203–17.

Stults, Brian J. and Eric P. Baumer. 2008. 'Assessing the relevance of anomie theory for explaining spatial variation in lethal criminal violence: An aggregate-level analysis of homicide within the United States.' *International Journal of Conflict and Violence* 2(2): 215–47.

Sunstein, Cass R. 1988. 'Beyond the republican revival.' *The Yale Law Journal* 97(8): 1539–90. doi.org/10.2307/796540.

Sunstein, Cass R. 1997. *Free Markets and Social Justice*. New York: Oxford University Press.

Sutherland, Edwin H. 1947. *Principles of Criminology*. Philadelphia: Lippincott.

Sutherland, Edwin H. 1983. *White Collar Crime: The Uncut Version*. New Haven, CT: Yale University Press.

Sutherland, Edwin H. and Donald R. Cressey. 1984. 'Differential association theory.' In Delos H. Kelly (ed.), *Deviant Behavior: A Text-Reader in the Sociology of Deviance*. 2nd edn. New York: St Martin's Press, pp. 93–99.

Suttles, Gerald D. 1968. *The Social Order of the Slum: Ethnicity and Territory in the Inner City*. Chicago: University of Chicago Press.

Swan, Kyle. 2016. 'Onion routing and tor.' *Georgetown Law Technology Review* 1(1): 110–18.

Swanson, David. 2021. 'At least 36% of US mass shooters have been trained by the US military.' *CounterPunch*, [Petrolia, CA], 24 March.

Sykes, Gresham M. and David Matza. 1957. 'Techniques of neutralization: A theory of delinquency.' *American Sociological Review* 22(6): 664–70. doi.org/10.2307/2089195.

Taft, Donald R. 1966. 'Influence of the general culture on crime.' *Federal Probation* 30: 15–23.

Takemae, Eiji. 2003. *The Allied Occupation of Japan*. London: Bloomsbury.

Tambiah, Stanley. 1996. *Leveling Crowds: Ethnonationalist Conflicts and Collective Violence in South Asia*. Berkeley, CA: University of California Press. doi.org/10.1525/9780520918191.

Tanaka, Yuri. 2018. *Hidden Horrors: Japanese War Crimes in World War II*. New York: Rowman & Littlefield. doi.org/10.4324/9780429040016.

Taylor, Frederick. 2005. *Dresden: Tuesday, 13 February 1945*. London: Bloomsbury.

Taylor, Ian. 1980. 'Inequality, crime and public policy.' *The British Journal of Criminology* 20(2): 183–85. doi.org/10.1093/oxfordjournals.bjc.a047162.

Taylor, Ian, Paul Walton and Jock Young. 1973. *The New Criminology: For a Theory of Social Deviance*. London: Routledge.

Taylor, John. 1950 [1814]. *An Inquiry into the Principles and Policy of the Government of the United States*. New Haven, CT: Yale University Press.

Taylor, Ralph B. 2001. *Breaking Away from Broken Windows*. Boulder, CO: Westview Press.

Teig, Ellen, Joy Amulya, Lisa Bardwell, Michael Buchenau, Julie A. Marshall and Jill S. Litt. 2009. 'Collective efficacy in Denver, Colorado: Strengthening neighborhoods and health through community gardens.' *Health and Place* 15(4): 1115–22. doi.org/10.1016/j.healthplace.2009.06.003.

Testa, Alexander, Joseph K. Young and Christopher Mullins. 2017. 'Does democracy enhance or reduce lethal violence? Examining the role of the rule of law.' *Homicide Studies* 21(3): 219–39. doi.org/10.1177/1088767917698181.

Thaker, Jagadish, Edward Maibach, Anthony Leiserowitz, Xiaoquan Zhao and Peter Howe. 2016. 'The role of collective efficacy in climate change adaptation in India.' *Weather, Climate, and Society* 8(1): 21–34. doi.org/10.1175/WCAS-D-14-00037.1.

Thomas, Shaun A., Drew C. Medaris and Cody R. Tuttle. 2018. 'Southern culture and aggravated assault: Exploring the generality of the southern culture of violence.' *Sociological Spectrum* 38(2): 103–16. doi.org/10.1080/02732173.2018.1430637.

Thompson, Edward Palmer. 1963. *The Making of the English Working Class*. London: Penguin.

Thornton, William H. and Songok Han Thornton. 2012. *Toward a Geopolitics of Hope*. New Delhi: Sage Publications. doi.org/10.4135/ 9788132114031.

Tian, Yu, Yulong Bian, Piguo Han, Fengqiang Gao and Peng Wang. 2017. 'Class collective efficacy and class size as moderators of the relationship between junior middle school students' externalizing behavior and academic engagement: A multilevel study.' *Frontiers in Psychology* 8: 1–9. doi.org/ 10.3389/fpsyg.2017.01219.

Tienhaara, Kyla. 2018. *Green Keynesianism and the Global Financial Crisis.* New York: Routledge.

Tilly, Charles. 1975. 'Reflections on the history of European statemaking.' In Charles Tilly (ed.), *The Formation of National States in Western Europe.* Princeton, NJ: Princeton University Press.

Tilly, Charles. 1985. 'War making and state making as organized crime.' In Peter Evans, Dietrich Rueschemeyer and Theda Skocpol (eds), *Bringing the State Back In.* Cambridge, UK: University of Cambridge Press, pp. 169–91. doi.org/ 10.1017/CBO9780511628283.008.

Tilly, Charles. 1992. *Coercion, Capital, and European States, AD 990–1990.* Oxford, UK: Blackwell.

Tittle, Charles R. 1995. *Control Balance: Toward a General Theory of Deviance.* Boulder, CO: Westview Press.

Tittle, Charles R., Wayne J. Villemez and Douglas A. Smith. 1982. 'One step forward, two steps back: More on the class/criminality controversy.' *American Sociological Review* 47(3): 435–38. doi.org/10.2307/2095002.

Toby, Jackson and Marcia Toby. 1957. *Low School Status as a Predisposing Factor in Subcultural Delinquency.* Washington, DC: US Office of Education & Rutgers University.

Toft, Monica Duffy. 2010. *Securing the Peace: The Durable Settlement of Civil Wars.* Princeton, NJ: Princeton University Press. doi.org/10.1515/9781400831999.

Tonry, Michael. 2018. 'An honest politician's guide to deterrence.' In Daniel S. Nagin, Francis T. Cullen and Cheryl Lero Jonson (eds), *Deterrence, Choice, and Crime. Volume 23: Contemporary Perspectives.* New York: Routledge.

Towers, Sherry, Andres Gomez-Lievano, Maryam Khan, Anuj Mubayi and Carlos Castillo-Chavez. 2015. 'Contagion in mass killings and school shootings.' *PLoS One* 10(7): e0117259. doi.org/10.1371/journal.pone.0117259.

Travis, Jeremy, Bruce Western and F. Stevens Redburn (eds). 2014. *The Growth of Incarceration in the United States: Exploring Causes and Consequences.* Washington, DC: National Academies Press.

Trevaskes, Susan. 2009. 'Restorative justice or McJustice with Chinese characteristics?' In Mary Farquhar (ed.), *21st Century China: Views from Australia*. Newcastle upon Tyne, UK: Cambridge Scholars Publishing, pp. 77–96.

Trevelyan, George M. 1973. *English Social History*. London: Penguin.

Trevelyan, George M. 1985. *A Shortened History of England*. Harmondsworth, UK: Penguin.

True, Jacqui. 2012. *The Political Economy of Violence against Women*. Oxford, UK: Oxford University Press. doi.org/10.1093/acprof:oso/9780199755929.001.0001.

Tsvetkova, Milena and Michael W. Macy. 2014. 'The social contagion of generosity.' *PLoS One* (9)2: e87275. doi.org/10.1371/journal.pone.0087275.

Tu, Patricia Buckley. 1998. 'Probing the "three bonds" and "five relationships" in Confucian humanism.' In Walter H. Slote and George A. De Vos (eds), *Confucianism and the Family*. New York: SUNY Press, pp. 121–36.

Tuliao, Kristine Velasquez and Chung-wen Chen. 2019. 'Economy and supervisors' ethical values: Exploring the mediating role of noneconomic institutions in a cross-national test of institutional anomie theory.' *Journal of Business Ethics* 156(3): 823–38. doi.org/10.1007/s10551-017-3620-5.

Tung, William L. 1964. *The Political Institutions of Modern China*. The Hague: Martinus Nijhoff Publishers. doi.org/10.1007/978-94-015-1011-0.

Tuttle, James. 2019. 'Murder in the shadows: Evidence for an institutional legitimacy theory of crime.' *International Journal of Comparative and Applied Criminal Justice* 43(1): 13–27. doi.org/10.1080/01924036.2017.1397037.

Tversky, Amos and Daniel Kahneman. 1981. 'The Framing of Decisions and the Psychology of Choice'. *Science* 211(4481): 453–58.

Tyler, Tom R. 1990. *Why People Obey the Law*. New Haven, CT: Yale University Press.

Tyler, Tom R. and Yuen J. Huo. 2002. *Trust in the Law: Encouraging Public Cooperation with the Police and Courts*. New York: Russell Sage Foundation.

Tyler, Tom R., Lawrence Sherman, Heather Strang, Geoffrey C. Barnes and Daniel Woods. 2007. 'Reintegrative shaming, procedural justice, and recidivism: The engagement of offenders' psychological mechanisms in the Canberra RISE drinking-and-driving experiment.' *Law & Society Review* 41(3): 553–86. doi.org/10.1111/j.1540-5893.2007.00314.x.

Umbreit, Mark and Robert Coates. 1992. *Victim–Offender Mediation: An Analysis of Programs in Four States of the US*. Minneapolis, MN: Citizens Council Mediation Services.

Underwood, Lynn G. and Jeanne A. Teresi. 2002. 'The daily spiritual experience scale: Development, theoretical description, reliability, exploratory factor analysis, and preliminary construct validity using health-related data.' *Annals of Behavioral Medicine* 24(1): 22–33. doi.org/10.1207/S15324796ABM2401_04.

Unger, Roberto. 1983. *The Critical Legal Studies Movement*. Cambridge, MA: Harvard University Press. doi.org/10.2307/1341032.

Unger, Roberto. 1987. *False Necessity: Anti-Necessitarian Social Theory in the Service of Radical Democracy*. Cambridge, UK: Cambridge University Press.

United Nations Office on Drugs and Crime (UNODC). 2013. *Global Study on Homicide 2013: Trends, Contexts, Data*. Vienna: UNODC.

United Nations Office on Drugs and Crime (UNODC). 2019. *Global Study on Homicide 2019: Homicide Trends, Patterns and Criminal Justice Response*. Vienna: UNODC.

Unnever, James D. and Shaun L. Gabbidon. 2011. *A Theory of African American Offending: Race, Racism, and Crime*. New York: Routledge. doi.org/10.4324/9780203828564.

Urbina, Dante A. 2020. 'The consequences of the grabbing hand: Five selected ways in which corruption affects the economy.' *Economia* 43(85): 1–23. doi.org/10.18800/economia.202001.004.

Uslaner, Eric M. 2008. *Corruption, Inequality, and the Rule of Law*. Cambridge, UK: Cambridge University Press. doi.org/10.1017/CBO9780511510410.

Utter, Glenn H. and James L. True. 2000. 'The evolving gun culture in America.' *The Journal of American Culture* 23(2): 67–79. doi.org/10.1111/j.1542-734X.2000.2302_67.x.

Vadlamannati, Krishna Chaitanya. 2011. 'Why Indian men rebel? Explaining armed rebellion in the northeastern states of India, 1970–2007.' *Journal of Peace Research* 48(5): 605–619. doi.org/10.1177/0022343311412409.

Vally, Hassan. 2017. 'What's most likely to kill you? Measuring how deadly our daily activities are.' *The Conversation*, 21 February.

van der Heijden, Jeroen. 2020. *Responsive Regulation in Practice: A Review of the International Academic Literature.* Wellington: Victoria University. doi. org/10.2139/ssrn.3651924.

van der Meer, Tom W.G. 2017. 'Political trust and the "crisis of democracy".' *Oxford Research Encyclopedias: Politics*, 25 January. [Online.] doi.org/10.1093/acrefore/9780190228637.013.77.

van der Walt, Johan. Forthcoming. How are multinational corporations operating in Australia responding to greater tax transparency? PhD thesis, The Australian National University, Canberra.

van Klinken, Gerry. 2007. *Communal Violence and Democratization in Indonesia: Small Town Wars.* London: Routledge. doi.org/10.4324/9780203965115.

VanNostrand, Marie and Gina Keebler. 2007. 'Our journey toward pretrial justice.' *Federal Probation* 71(2): 20–25.

Varghese, Peter. 2020. *What should Australia do to manage risk in its relationship with the PRC?* Policy Brief, June. Sydney: China Matters.

Vaughan, Diane. 1983. *The Challenger Launch Decision: Risky Technology, Culture, and Deviance at NASA.* Chicago: University of Chicago Press.

Ventry, Dennis J., Jr. 2014. 'Not just whistling Dixie: The case for tax whistle blowers in the States.' *Villanova Law Review* 59: 425–502.

Verwimp, Philip. 2005. 'An economic profile of peasant perpetrators of genocide: Micro-level evidence from Rwanda.' *Journal of Development Economics* 77(2): 297–323. doi.org/10.1016/j.jdeveco.2004.04.005.

Vile, Maurice John Crawley. 1963. *Constitutionalism and Separation of Powers.* Oxford, UK: Clarendon Press.

Vlassenroot, Koen and Timothy Raeymaekers. 2009. 'Kivu's intractable security conundrum.' *African Affairs* 108(432): 475–84. doi.org/10.1093/afraf/adp039.

von Einsiedel, Sebastian. 2017. *Civil war trends and the changing nature of armed conflict.* Occasional Paper 10. Tokyo: Center for Policy Research, United Nations University.

Wager, Nadia and Chris Wilson. 2017. 'Circles of support and accountability: Survivors as volunteers and the restorative potential.' In Estelle Zinsstag and Marie Keenan (eds), *Restorative Responses to Sexual Violence: Legal, Social and Therapeutic Dimensions.* London: Routledge, pp. 265–82. doi.org/10.4324/9781315630595-14.

Waldman, Don E. 1978. *Antitrust Action and Market Structure.* Lexington, KY: Lexington Books.

Walgrave, Lode. 2013. *Restorative Justice, Self-Interest and Responsible Citizenship.* Cullompton, UK: Willan Publishing. doi.org/10.4324/9781843925668.

Walker, R.B. 1980. 'Tobacco smoking in Australia, 1788–1914.' *Australian Historical Studies* 19(75): 267–85. doi.org/10.1080/10314618008595638.

Wallace, Alison. 1986. *Homicide: The Social Reality.* Sydney: New South Wales Bureau of Crime Statistics and Research.

Wallace, Lacey N. 2015. 'Responding to violence with guns: Mass shootings and gun acquisition.' *The Social Science Journal* 52(2): 156–67. doi.org/10.1016/j.soscij.2015.03.002.

Wallace, Rodrick and Deborah Wallace. 1990. 'Origins of public health collapse in New York City: The dynamics of planned shrinkage, contagious urban decay and social disintegration.' *Bulletin of the New York Academy of Medicine* 66(5): 391–434.

Walmsley, Roy. 2019. 'World prison population list.' *The World Prison Brief.* [Online database.] London: Institute for Crime & Justice Policy Research, Birkbeck, University of London. Available at: www.prisonstudies.org/.

Walter, Barbara F. 2002. *Committing to Peace: The Successful Settlement of Civil Wars.* Princeton, NJ: Princeton University Press.

Walter, Barbara F., Lise Morje Howard and V. Page Fortna. 2020. 'The extraordinary relationship between peacekeeping and peace.' *British Journal of Political Science*, First View: 1–18. doi.org/10.1017/S000712342000023X.

Wang, Jia J. and Don Weatherburn. 2019. 'Are police cautions a soft option? Reoffending among juveniles cautioned or referred to court.' *Australian and New Zealand Journal of Criminology* 52(3): 334–47. doi.org/10.1177/0004865818794235.

Wang, Jing, Liang Feng, Paul I. Palmer, Yi Liu, Shuangxi Fang, Hartmut Bösch, Christopher W. O'Dell, Xiaoping Tang, Dongxu Yang, Lixin Liu and Chao Zong Xia. 2020. 'Large Chinese land carbon sink estimated from atmospheric carbon dioxide data.' *Nature* 586(7831): 720–23. doi.org/10.1038/s41586-020-2849-9.

Ward, Michael D. and Kristian Skrede Gleditsch. 2002. 'Location, location, location: An MCMC approach to modeling the spatial context of war and peace.' *Political Analysis* 10(2): 244–60. doi.org/10.1093/pan/10.3.244.

Wardak, Ali. 2018. *Social Control and Deviance: A South Asian Community in Scotland.* London: Routledge. doi.org/10.4324/9781315196794.

Wardak, Ali and John Braithwaite. 2013. 'Crime and war in Afghanistan: Part II—A Jeffersonian alternative?' *The British Journal of Criminology* 53(2): 197–214. doi.org/10.1093/bjc/azs066.

Warner, Kate, Julia Davis, Caroline Spiranovic, Helen Cockburn and Arie Freiberg. 2017. 'Measuring jurors' views on sentencing: Results from the Second Australian Jury Sentencing Study.' *Punishment and Society* 19(2): 180–202. doi.org/10.1177/1462474516660697.

Weatherburn, Don and Sara Rahman. 2021. *The Vanishing Criminal: Causes of Decline in Australia's Crime Rate.* Melbourne: Melbourne University Press.

Weatherford, Jack M. 2010. *The Secret History of the Mongol Queens: How the Daughters of Genghis Khan Rescued His Empire.* New York: Crown.

Weber, Max. 2002 [1904]. *The Protestant Ethic and the Spirit of Capitalism and Other Writings.* London: Penguin.

Wechsberg, Joseph. 1966. *The Merchant Bankers.* Boston, MA: Little, Brown & Company.

Weisburd, David, Michael Davis and Charlotte Gill. 2015. 'Increasing collective efficacy and social capital at crime hot spots: New crime control tools for police.' *Policing: A Journal of Policy and Practice* 9(3): 265–74. doi.org/10.1093/police/pav019.

Weisburd, David, David P. Farrington and Charlotte Gill. 2017. 'What works in crime prevention and rehabilitation: An assessment of systematic reviews.' *Criminology and Public Policy* 16(2): 415–49. doi.org/10.1111/1745-9133.12298.

Weisburd, David, Elizabeth R. Groff and Sue-Ming Yang. 2012. *The Criminology of Place: Street Segments and Our Understanding of the Crime Problem.* New York: Oxford University Press. doi.org/10.1093/acprof:oso/9780195369083.001.0001.

Weisburd, David, Cody W. Telep, Joshua C. Hinkle and John E. Eck. 2010. 'Is problem-oriented policing effective in reducing crime and disorder? Findings from a Campbell systematic review.' *Criminology & Public Policy* 9(1): 139–72. doi.org/10.1111/j.1745-9133.2010.00617.x.

Weisburd, David, Cody W. Telep, Doron Teichman and Dave McClure. 2011. 'Displacement of crime and diffusion of crime control benefits in large-scale geographic areas.' *Campbell Systematic Reviews* 7(1): 1–38. doi.org/10.1002/CL2.78.

Weisburd, David, Stanton Wheeler, Elin Warning and Nancy Bode. 1991. *Crimes of the Middle Classes: White-Collar Offenders in the Federal Courts*. New Haven, CT: Yale University Press.

Weisburd, David, Clair White, Sean Wire and David B. Wilson. 2021. 'Enhancing informal social controls to reduce crime: Evidence from a study of crime hot spots.' *Prevention Science* 22: 509–22. doi.org/10.1007/s11121-020-01194-4.

Weiss, Linda. 2014. *America Inc.? Innovation and Enterprise in the National Security State*. Ithaca, NY: Cornell University Press.

Weld, Dean and Sean Patrick Roche. 2017. 'A matter of time: A partial test of institutional anomie theory using cross-national time use data.' *Journal of Quantitative Criminology* 33(2): 371–95. doi.org/10.1007/s10940-016-9305-x.

Wells, Audrey. 2001. *The Political Thought of Sun Yat-sen: Development and Impact*. Basingstoke, UK: Palgrave. doi.org/10.1057/9781403919755.

Westendorf, Jasmine-Kim. 2015. *Why Peace Processes Fail: Negotiating Insecurity after Civil War*. Boulder, CO: Lynne Rienner Publishers.

Wheeler, Stanton. 1990. White-collar crime: Some reflections on a socio-legal research program. Paper presented to Edwin Sutherland Conference on White-Collar Crime, Indiana University, Bloomington, IN, May.

White, Rob (ed.). 2017. *Transnational Environmental Crime*. London: Routledge. doi.org/10.4324/9781315084589.

White, Rob and Ronald C. Kramer. 2015. 'Critical criminology and the struggle against climate change ecocide.' *Critical Criminology* 23(4): 383–99. doi.org/10.1007/s10612-015-9292-5.

White, William L. 2014. 'Recovery is contagious: Redux.' *Selected Papers of William L. White*, [Blog], 25 January. Available at: www.williamwhitepapers.com/blog/2014/01/recovery-is-contagious-redux.html.

White, William L. 2015. 'Recovery of social networks ("I story" to "We story").' *Selected Papers of William L. White*, [Blog], 24 July. Available at: www.williamwhitepapers.com/blog/2015/07/recovery-of-social-networks-i-story-to-we-story.html.

White, William L. and William Cloud. 2008. 'Recovery capital: A primer for addictions professionals.' *Counselor* 9(5): 22–27.

White, William L. and Ernest Kurtz. 2008. 'Twelve defining moments in the history of Alcoholics Anonymous.' In Anne Kaskutas and Marc Galanter (eds), *Recent Developments in Alcoholism*. New York: Plenum Publishing Corporation, pp. 37–57. doi.org/10.1007/978-0-387-77725-2_3.

Whyte, William F. 1943. *Street Corner Society: The Social Structure of an Italian Slum*. Chicago: University of Chicago Press.

Whyte, William H. 1956. *The Organization Man*. New York: Simon & Schuster.

Widom, Cathy S. 1989. 'The cycle of violence.' *Science* 244(4901): 160–66. doi.org/10.1126/science.2704995.

Wilde, Jaron H. 2017. 'The deterrent effect of employee whistleblowing on firms' financial misreporting and tax aggressiveness.' *The Accounting Review* 92(5): 247–80. doi.org/10.2308/accr-51661.

Wilf-Miron, Rachel, Irene Lewenhoff, Z. Benyamini and A. Aviram. 2003. 'From aviation to medicine: Applying concepts of aviation safety to risk management in ambulatory care.' *Quality & Safety in Health Care* 12(1): 35–39. doi.org/10.1136/qhc.12.1.35.

Wilkinson, Steven I. 2004. *Votes and Violence: Electoral Competition and Ethnic Riots in India*. New York: Cambridge University Press. doi.org/10.1017/CBO9780511510458.

Williams, Katherine. 2016. 'Book review: Crimes Unspoken: The Rape of German Women at the End of the Second World War by Miriam Gebhardt.' *LSE Review of Books*, 9 May. Available at: blogs.lse.ac.uk/lsereviewofbooks/2017/05/09/book-review-crimes-unspoken-the-rape-of-german-women-at-the-end-of-the-second-world-war-by-miriam-gebhardt/.

Williams, Phil. 1998. 'Organizing transnational crime: Networks, markets and hierarchies.' *Transnational Organized Crime* 4(3): 57–87.

Wilson, David B., Ajima Olaghere and Catherine S. Kimbrell. 2017. *Effectiveness of Restorative Justice Programs, OJJDP-Funded Research in Brief*. Washington, DC: Office of Juvenile Justice and Delinquency Prevention, Department of Justice.

Wilson, Dominic and Raluca Dragusanu. 2008. *The expanding middle class: The exploding world middle class and falling global inequality*. Goldman Sachs Economic Research Global Economics Papers Issue 170. New York: Goldman Sachs.

Wilson, James Q. 1975. *Thinking about Crime*. New York: Vintage.

Wilson, James Q. and Richard Herrnstein. 1985. *Crime and Human Nature*. New York: Simon & Schuster.

Wilson, Robin J., Franca Cortoni and Andrew J. McWhinnie. 2009. 'Circles of support & accountability: A Canadian national replication of outcome findings.' *Sexual Abuse* 21(4): 412–30. doi.org/10.1177/1079063209347724.

Wilson, William J. 2012. *The Truly Disadvantaged: The Inner City, the Underclass, and Public Policy*. Chicago: University of Chicago Press. doi.org/10.7208/chicago/9780226924656.001.0001.

Wimmer, Andreas, Lars-Erik Cederman and Brian Min. 2009. 'Ethnic politics and armed conflict: A configurational analysis of a new global data set.' *American Sociological Review* 74(2): 316–37. doi.org/10.1177/000312240907400208.

Wintemute, Gary. 2000. 'Guns and gun violence.' In Alfred Blumstein and Joel Wallman (eds), *The Crime Drop in America*. New York: Cambridge University Press, pp. 45–96. doi.org/10.1017/CBO9780511616167.004.

Wollstonecraft, Mary. 1792. *A Vindication of the Rights of Woman with Strictures on Moral and Political Subjects*. London: Joseph Johnson.

Wong, Dennis S.W. 2014. 'Harmony comes first (以和爲貴): Challenges facing the development of restorative justice in Asia.' *Restorative Justice: An International Journal* 2(1): 1–8. doi.org/10.5235/20504721.2.1.1.

World Bank. 2016. 'Proportion of seats held by women in national parliaments (%).' *World Bank Data*. [Online database.] Washington, DC: The World Bank. Available at: data.worldbank.org/indicator/SG.GEN.PARL.ZS.

World Bank. 2017. *World Development Report 2017: Governance and the Law*. Washington, DC: The World Bank.

World Bank. 2020. *The Deliberate Depression: Lebanon Economic Monitor*. Washington, DC: The World Bank.

Wright, Emily M. and Marie Skubak Tillyer. 2020. 'Neighborhoods and intimate partner violence against women: The direct and interactive effects of social ties and collective efficacy.' *Journal of Interpersonal Violence* 35(19–20): 3913–38. doi.org/10.1177/0886260517712276.

Wright, John Paul and Francis T. Cullen. 2001. 'Parental efficacy and delinquent behaviour: Do control and support matter?' *Criminology* 39(3): 677–706. doi.org/10.1111/j.1745-9125.2001.tb00937.x.

Wylie, Christopher. 2019. *Mindf*ck: Inside Cambridge Analytica's Plot to Break the World.* London: Profile Books.

Yamagishi, Toshio. 2001. 'Trust as a form of social intelligence.' In Karen S. Cook (ed.), *Trust in Society.* Russell Sage Foundation Series on Trust Volume 2. New York: Russell Sage Foundation, pp. 121–47.

Yan, Bing and Bo Wen. 2019. 'Income inequality, corruption and subjective well-being.' *Applied Economics* 52(12): 1311–26. doi.org/10.1080/0003684 6.2019.1661953.

Yang, Zhixu and Ziqiang Xin. 2020. 'Income inequality and interpersonal trust in China.' *Asian Journal of Social Psychology* 23(3): 253–63. doi.org/10.1111/ ajsp.12399.

Yeung, Karen. 2004. *Securing Compliance.* Oxford, UK: Oxford University Press.

You, Jong-sung. 2014. 'Land reform, inequality, and corruption: A comparative historical study of Korea, Taiwan, and the Philippines.' *The Korean Journal of International Studies* 12(1): 191–224. doi.org/10.14731/ kjis.2014.06.12.1.191.

You, Jong-sung and Sanjeev Khagram. 2005. 'A comparative study of inequality and corruption.' *American Sociological Review* 70(1): 136–57. doi.org/ 10.1177/000312240507000107.

Zahn, Margaret A. 1980. 'Homicide in the twentieth century United States.' In James A. Inciardi and Charles E. Faupel (eds), *History and Crime.* Beverly Hills, CA: Sage Publications, pp. 111–32.

Zehr, Howard. 2000. Journey of belonging. Paper presented to Fourth International Conference on Restorative Justice, Tübingen, Germany, 1–4 October.

Zehr, Howard. 2015. *The Little Book of Restorative Justice.* New York: Skyhorse Publishing.

Zhang, Jun and Jamie Peck. 2016. 'Variegated capitalism, Chinese style: Regional models, multi-scalar constructions.' *Regional Studies* 50(1): 52–78. doi.org/ 10.1080/00343404.2013.856514.

Zhang, Lening, Steven F. Messner and Sheldon Zhang. 2017. 'Neighborhood social control and perceptions of crime and disorder in contemporary urban China.' *Criminology* 55(3): 631–63. doi.org/10.1111/1745-9125.12142.

Zhang, Yan. 2021a. China: Powerhouse and resistor of restorative justice reform. PhD dissertation, The Australian National University, Canberra.

Zhang, Yan. 2021b. 'Police discretion and restorative justice in China: Stories from the street level police.' *International Journal of Offender Therapy and Comparative Criminology* 65(4): 498–520. doi.org/10.1177/0306624X20944686.

Zhang, Yan and Yiwei Xia. 2021. 'Can restorative justice reduce incarceration? A story from China.' *Justice Quarterly* 38(7): 1471–91. doi.org/10.1080/074 18825.2021.1950814.

Zhao, Ruohui and Liqun Cao. 2010. 'Social change and anomie: A cross-national study.' *Social Forces* 88(3): 1209–29. doi.org/10.1353/sof.0.0312.

Ziegler, Charles E. 1990. *Environmental Policy in the USSR*. Amherst, MA: University of Massachusetts Press.

Zierler, David. 2011. *The Invention of Ecocide: Agent Orange, Vietnam, and the Scientists Who Changed the Way We Think about the Environment*. Athens, GA: University of Georgia Press.

Zimring, Franklin E. 1981. 'Kids, groups and crime: Some implications of a well-known secret.' *Journal of Criminal Law and Criminology* 72: 867–85. doi.org/10.2307/1143269.

Zimring, Franklin E. 2011. *The City That Became Safe: New York's Lessons for Urban Crime and its Control*. New York: Oxford University Press. doi.org/ 10.1093/acprof:oso/9780199844425.001.0001.

Zuboff, Shoshana. 2019. *The Age of Surveillance Capitalism: The Fight for a Human Future at the New Frontier of Power*. London: Profile Books.